Use R!

Use R!

This series of inexpensive and focused books on R will publish shorter books aimed at practitioners. Books can discuss the use of R in a particular subject area (e.g., epidemiology, econometrics, psychometrics) or as it relates to statistical topics (e.g., missing data, longitudinal data). In most cases, books will combine LaTeX and R so that the code for figures and tables can be put on a website. Authors should assume a background as supplied by Dalgaard's Introductory Statistics with R or other introductory books so that each book does not repeat basic material.

More information about this series at http://www.springer.com/series/6991

Chris Chapman · Elea McDonnell Feit

R for Marketing Research and Analytics

Second Edition

 Springer

Chris Chapman
Google
Seattle, WA, USA

Elea McDonnell Feit
Drexel University
Philadelphia, PA, USA

ISSN 2197-5736 ISSN 2197-5744 (electronic)
Use R!
ISBN 978-3-030-14315-2 ISBN 978-3-030-14316-9 (eBook)
https://doi.org/10.1007/978-3-030-14316-9

Library of Congress Control Number: 2019932720

This Springer imprint is published by the registered company Springer Nature Switzerland AG
The registered company address is: Gewerbestrasse 11, 6330 Cham, Switzerland

Preface

We are here to help you learn R for marketing research and analytics.

R is a great choice for marketing analysts. It offers unsurpassed capabilities for fitting statistical models. It is extensible and able to process data from many different systems, in a variety of forms, for both small and large data sets. The R ecosystem includes the widest available range of established and emerging statistical methods and visualization techniques. Yet its use in marketing lags other fields such as statistics, econometrics, psychology, and bioinformatics. With your help, we hope to change that!

This book is designed for two audiences: practicing marketing researchers and analysts who want to learn R and students or researchers from other fields who wish to review selected marketing topics in an R context.

What are the prerequisites? Simply that you are interested in R for marketing, are conceptually familiar with basic statistical models such as linear regression, and are willing to engage in hands-on learning. This book will be particularly helpful to analysts who have some degree of programming experience and wish to learn R. In Chap. 1, we describe additional reasons to use R (and a few reasons perhaps *not* to use R).

The *hands-on* part is important. We teach concepts gradually in a sequence across the first seven chapters and ask you to *type* our examples as you work; this book is *not* a cookbook-style reference. We spend some time (as little as possible) in Part I on the basics of the R language and then turn in Part II to applied, real-world marketing analytics problems. Part III presents a few advanced marketing topics. Every chapter shows the power of R, and we hope each one will teach you something new and interesting.

Specific features of this book are:

- It is organized around marketing research tasks. Instead of generic examples, we put methods into the context of marketing questions.
- We presume only basic statistics knowledge and use a minimum of mathematics. This book is designed to be approachable for practitioners and does not dwell on equations or mathematical details of statistical models (although we give references to those texts).
- This is a didactic book that explains statistical concepts and the R code. We want you to understand what we're doing and learn how to avoid common problems in both statistics and R. We intend the book to be *readable* and to fulfill a different need than references and cookbooks available elsewhere.
- The applied chapters demonstrate progressive model building. We do not present "the answer" but instead show how an analyst might realistically conduct analyses in successive steps where multiple models are compared for statistical strength and practical utility.
- The chapters include visualization as a part of core analyses. We don't regard visualization as a standalone topic; rather, we believe it is an integral part of data exploration and model building.
- You will learn more than just R. In addition to core models, we include topics such as structural models and transaction analysis that may be new and useful even for experienced analysts.
- The book reflects both traditional and Bayesian approaches. Core models are presented with traditional (frequentist) methods, while later sections introduce Bayesian methods for linear models and conjoint analysis.
- Most of the analyses use simulated data, which provides practice in the R language along with additional insight into the structure of marketing data. If you are inclined, you can change the data simulation and see how the statistical models are affected.
- Where appropriate, we call out more advanced material on programming or models so that you may either skip it or read it, as you find appropriate. These sections are indicated by * in their titles (such as *This is an advanced section**).

What do we *not* cover? For one, this book teaches *R* for marketing and does not teach marketing research in itself. We discuss many marketing topics but omit others that would repeat analytic methods. As noted above, we approach statistical models from a conceptual point of view and skip the mathematics. A few specialized topics have been omitted due to complexity and space; these include customer lifetime value models and econometric time series models. In the R language, we do not cover the "tidyverse" (Sect. 1.5) because it is an optional part of the language and would complicate the learning process. Overall, we believe the topics here represent a great sample of marketing research and analytics practice. If you learn to perform these, you'll be well equipped to apply R in many areas of marketing.

Why are we the right teachers? We've used R and its predecessor S for a combined 35 years since 1997, and it is our primary analytics platform. We perform marketing analyses of all kinds in R, ranging from simple data summaries to complex analyses involving thousands of lines of custom code and newly created models.

We've also taught R to many people. This book grew from courses the authors have presented at American Marketing Association (AMA) events including the Academy of Marketing Analytics at Emory University and several years of the Advanced Research Techniques Forum (ART Forum). As noted in our Acknowledgements below, we have taught R to students in many workshops at universities and firms. At last count, more than 40 universities used the first edition in their marketing analytics courses. All of these students' and instructors' experiences have helped to improve the book.

What's New in the Second Edition

This second edition focuses on making the book more useful for students, self-learners, and instructors. The code has proven to be very stable. Except for one line (updated at the book's Web site), all of the code and examples from the first edition still work more than four years later. We have added one chapter, and otherwise, the marketing topics and statistical models are the same as in the first edition. The primary changes in this edition are:

- New **exercises** appear at the end of each chapter. Several of these use real-world data, and there are example solutions at the book's Web site.
- A **new chapter** discusses analysis of behavior sequences (Chap. 14) using Markov chains. These methods are applicable to many sources of behavioral and other data comprising sequences of discrete events, such as application usage, purchases, and life events, as well as non-marketing data including physical processes and genomic sequences. We use a published Web server log file to demonstrate the methods applied to real data.
- Classroom **slides** are available for instructors and self-learners at the book's Web site. These include the slides themselves, the raw code that they discuss, and Rmarkdown and LaTeX files that generate the slides and may be edited for your own use.
- For our various data sets, we present **additional details** about how such data might be acquired. For example, when a data set represents consumer survey data, we describe how the data might be gathered and a brief description of typical survey items.
- A new appendix describes options for **reproducible research** in R and explains the basics of R Notebooks (Appendix B). R Notebooks are a simple yet powerful way to create documents in R with integrated code, graphics, and formatted text. They may be used to create documents as simple as homework exercises,

or as complex as final deliverable reports for clients, with output in HTML, PDF, or Microsoft Word formats.

* We have updated other **content** as needed. This includes additional explanations, code, and charts where warranted; up-to-date references; and correction of minor errors.

Acknowledgements

We thank many people who made this book possible. First are many participants in our workshops and classes over the years, including students at Drexel University, Boston University, Temple University, the Wharton School of the University of Pennsylvania, and the University of Washington; practitioners at Google and URBN, Inc.; and workshop attendees at the Advanced Research Techniques Forum (ART Forum), the Sawtooth Software Conference, and the Academy of Marketing Analytics at Emory University. They provided valuable feedback, and we hope their questions and experiences will benefit you.

In the marketing academic and practitioner community, we had valuable feedback from Ken Deal, Fred Feinberg, Shane Jensen, Jake Lee, Hui Lin, Dave Lyon, Bruce McCullough, Bernd Skiera, Hiroshi Torii, and Randy Zwitch. Many readers of the book's first edition sent notes, reviewed it online, and reported errata. We appreciated the supportive and helpful comments.

Chris's colleagues in the research community at Google provided extensive feedback on portions of the book. We thank the following current and former Googlers: Eric Bahna, Mario Callegaro, Marianna Dizik, Rohan Gifford, Tim Hesterberg, Shankar Kumar, Norman Lemke, Paul Litvak, Katrina Panovich, Joe Paxton, Marta Rey-Babarro, Kerry Rodden, Dan Russell, Angela Schörgendorfer, Jason Schwarz, Steven Scott, Rebecca Shapley, Bob Silverstein, Gill Ward, John Webb, Ercan Yildiz, and Yori Zwols for their encouragement and comments.

The staff and editors at Springer helped us smooth the process, especially Hannah Bracken and Jon Gurstelle for the first edition, and Lorraine Klimowich and Nicholas Philipson for the second edition. The UseR! series editors, Robert Gentleman, Kurt Hornik, and Giovanni Parmigiani, provided early feedback. They have nurtured a superb series of R texts, and we are honored to contribute to it.

Much of this book was written in public and university libraries, and we thank them for their hospitality alongside their literary resources. Portions of the book were written during pleasant days at the New York Public Library, Christoph Keller Jr. Library at the General Theological Seminary (New York), New Orleans Public Library, British Library (London), University of California San Diego Giesel Library, University of Washington Suzzallo and Allen Libraries, Sunnyvale Public Library (California), West Osceola Public Library (Florida), Howard County Library System (Maryland), Montgomery County Public Libraries (Maryland),

Kennett Library (Pennsylvania), Utica Public Library (Michigan), Clinton-Macomb Public Library (Michigan), San Juan Island Library (Washington), and in the dining hall of Holden, Washington (see Sect. 2.4.4). We give special thanks to the Tokyo Metropolitan Central Library, where the first words, code, and outline were written, along with much more in both the first and second editions.

Our families supported us in weekends and nights of editing, and they endured more discussion of R than is fair for any layperson. Thank you, Cristi, Maddie, Jeff, and Zoe.

Most importantly, we thank *you*, the reader. We're glad you've decided to investigate R, and we hope to repay your effort. Let's start!

Seattle, WA, USA/New York, NY, USA   Chris Chapman
Philadelphia, PA, USA   Elea McDonnell Feit
January 2019

Contents

Part I
Basics of R

Chapter 1
Welcome to R

1.1 What is R?

As a marketing analyst, you have no doubt heard of R. You may have tried R and become frustrated and confused, after which you returned to other tools that are "good enough." You may know that R uses a command line and dislike that. Or you may be convinced of R's advantages for experts but worry that you don't have time to learn or use it.

We are here to help! Our goal is to present *just the essentials*, in the *minimal necessary time*, with *hands-on learning* so you will come up to speed as quickly as possible to be productive in R. In addition, we'll cover a few advanced topics that demonstrate the power of R and might teach advanced users some new skills.

A key thing to realize is that *R is a programming language*. It is *not* a "statistics program" like SPSS, SAS, JMP, or Minitab, and doesn't wish to be one. The official R Project describes R as "a language and environment for statistical computing and graphics." Notice that "language" comes first, and that "statistical" is coequal with "graphics." R is a great programming language for doing statistics. The inventor of the underlying language, John Chambers received the 1998 Association for Computing Machinery (ACM) Software System Award for a system that "will forever alter the way people analyze, visualize, and manipulate data ..." [5].

R was based on Chambers's preceding S language (S as in "statistics") developed in the 1970s and 1980s at Bell Laboratories, home of the UNIX operating system and the C programming language. S gained traction among analysts and academics in the 1990s as implemented in a commercial software package, S-PLUS. Robert Gentleman and Ross Ihaka wished to make the S approach more widely available and offered R as an open source project starting in 1997.

Since then, the popularity of R has grown geometrically. The real magic of R is that its users are able to contribute developments that enhance R with everything from additional core functions to highly specialized methods. And many do contribute!

© Springer Nature Switzerland AG 2019

C. Chapman and E. M. Feit, *R For Marketing Research and Analytics*, Use R!,
https://doi.org/10.1007/978-3-030-14316-9_1

Today there are over 13,000 packages of add on functionality available for R (see http://cran.r-project.org/web/packages for the latest count).

If you have experience in programming, you will appreciate some of R's key features right away. If you're new to programming, this chapter describes why R is special and Chap. 2 introduces the fundamentals of programming in R.

1.2 Why R?

There are many reasons to learn and use R. It is the platform of choice for the largest number of statisticians who create new analytics methods, so emerging techniques are often available first in R. R is rapidly becoming the default educational platform in university statistics programs and is spreading to other disciplines such as economics and psychology.

For analysts, R offers the largest and most diverse set of analytic tools and statistical methods. It allows you to write analyses that can be reused and that extend the R system itself. It runs on most operating systems and interfaces well with data systems such as online data and SQL databases. R offers beautiful and powerful plotting functions that are able to produce graphics vastly more tailored and informative than typical spreadsheet charts. Putting all of those together, R can vastly improve an analyst's overall productivity. Elea knows an enterprising analyst who used R to automate the process of downloading data and producing a formatted monthly report. The automation saved him almost 40 h of work each month…which he didn't tell his manager for a few months!

Then there is the community. Many R users are enthusiasts who love to help others and are rewarded in turn by the simple joy of solving problems and the fact that they often learn something new. R is a dynamic system created by its users, and there is always something new to learn. Knowledge of R is a valuable skill in demand for analytics jobs at a growing number of top companies.

R code is also inspectable; you may choose to trust it, yet you are also free to verify. All of its core code and most packages that people contribute are open source. You can examine the code to see exactly how analyses work and what is happening under the hood.

Finally, R is free. It is a labor of love and professional pride for the R Core Development Team, which includes eminent statisticians and computer scientists. As with all masterpieces, the quality of their devotion is evident in the final work.

1.3   Why Not R?

What's not to love? No doubt you've observed that not everyone in the world uses R. Being R-less is unimaginable to us yet there are reasons why some analysts might not want to use it.

One reason not to use R is this: until you've mastered the basics of the language, many simple analyses are cumbersome to do in R. If you're new to R and want a table of means, cross-tabs, or a t-test, it may be frustrating to figure out how to get them. R is about power, flexibility, control, iterative analyses, and cutting-edge methods, not point-and-click deliverables.

Another reason is if you do not like programming. If you're new to programming, R is a great place to start. But if you've tried programming before and didn't enjoy it, R will be a challenge as well. Our job is to help you as much as we can, and we will try hard to teach R to you. However, not everyone enjoys programming. On the other hand, if you're an experienced coder R will seem simple (perhaps deceptively so), and we will help you avoid a few pitfalls.

Some companies and their information technology or legal departments are skeptical of R because it is open source. It is common for managers to ask, "If it's free, how can it be good?" There are many responses to that, including pointing out the hundreds of books on R, its citation in peer-reviewed articles, and the list of eminent contributors (in R, run the `contributors()` command and web search some of them). Or you might try the engineer's adage: "It can be good, fast, or cheap: pick 2." R is good and cheap, but not fast, insofar as it requires time and effort to master.

As for R being free, you should realize that contributors to R actually do derive benefit; it just happens to be non-monetary. They are compensated through respect and reputation, through the power their own work gains, and by the contributions back to the ecosystem from other users. This is a rational economic model even when the monetary price is zero.

A final concern about R is the unpredictability of its ecosystem. With packages contributed by thousands of authors, there are priceless contributions along with others that are mediocre or flawed. The downside of having access to the latest developments is that many will not stand the test of time. It is up to you to determine whether a method meets your needs, and you cannot always rely on curation or authorities to determine it for you (although you will rapidly learn which authors and which experts' recommendations to trust). If you trust your judgment, this situation is no different than with any software. *Caveat emptor*.

We hope to convince you that for many purposes, the benefits of R outweigh the difficulties.

1.4   When R?

There are a few common use cases for R:

- You want access to methods that are newer or more powerful than available elsewhere. Many R users start for exactly that reason; they see a method in a journal article, conference paper, or presentation, and discover that the method is available only in R.
- You need to run an analysis many, many times. This is how the first author (hereafter, Chris) started his R journey; for his dissertation, he needed to bootstrap existing methods in order to compare their typical results to those of a new machine learning model. R is perfect for model iteration.
- You need to apply an analysis to multiple data sets. Because everything is scripted, R is great for analyses that are repeated across datasets. It even has tools available for automated reporting.
- You need to develop a new analytic technique or wish to have perfect control and insight into an existing method. For many statistical procedures, R is easier to code than other programming languages.
- Your manager, professor, or coworker is encouraging you to use R. We've influenced students and colleagues in this way and are happy to report that a large number of them are enthusiastic R users today.

By showing you the power of R, we hope to convince you that your current tools are *not* perfectly satisfactory. Even more deviously, we hope to rewrite your expectations about what *is* satisfactory.

1.4.1   R Versus Python, Julia, and Others

If you are new to programming, you might wonder whether to learn R or Python ... or Julia, Matlab, Ruby, Go, Java, C++, Fortran, or others. Each language has a somewhat unique value.

For interactive analyses and data visualization, with access to the latest developments in statistics, R is unmatched. On the other hand, if you want your analytic work to go into *production* and integrate with a larger system (such as a product or a web site), Python is a great choice [176]. If high performance is essential to you, such as working with massive data sets or models with high mathematical complexity, Julia is an excellent option [210]. Go is also designed for massive scalability.

Another factor is whether you want to program more generally beyond analytics, such as writing apps. Python is an excellent general purpose language. Many find Python more approachable than C or C++, and it has broader support for statistics and analytics than Go, Java, or Ruby.

If you often do a lot of directly mathematical work—such as writing equations for models—then R is a fine choice, although you might be more comfortable with Julia, Matlab, or even venerable Fortran (whose name abbreviates *for*mula *trans*lation).

If you work with other programmers, you might want to choose a language they know, so they can help you. At the same time, most languages interact well with others. For example, it is easy to write analytic code in R and to access it from Python (and vice versa). Similarly, it is easy in R to include code from C, C++ [49], Fortran, and SQL (Appendix C.1.4), among others. Many programmers end up using several languages and find that transitioning among them is not difficult.

In short, for analyses with high flexibility and a straightforward programming environment, R is a great choice.

1.5   Which R? Base or Tidy?

As the R language has evolved, it has begun to show diversity of syntax and commands that is analogous to linguistic dialects. In recent years, a significant distinction has appeared: *base R* (the core language) versus the *tidyverse*. The tidyverse is a vast set of add-on capabilities that extend base R with many new operators and functions, inspired by a powerful philosophy of data organization (Wickham and Grolemund [200]). It provides simple and efficient ways to manipulate, aggregate, and slice data; to visualize data; and to perform a wide range of analytic tasks from summarization to data mining.

Despite the power of the tidyverse, in this book we instead focus on programming in base R. Why? For several reasons:

- Fluency in base R is essential for all R users, so you must learn it. It is the basis for all R commands, packages, language structures, and analyses. Base R will always work, even when a particular section of code using it is less compact than a tidyverse alternative.
- The tidyverse introduces functions that duplicate many capabilities and approaches of base R, such as different commands to summarize data. We believe it is easier to learn a single dialect of a language first rather than to learn two dialects simultaneously.
- There are significant syntactic differences in the tidyverse. In particular, the tidyverse often uses "pipe" operators that cause program flow to be read *left-to-right*, whereas base R operations read *right-to-left*, as do most programming languages. In earlier chapters where we teach programming, covering both styles would be overly complicated for new programmers. (Imagine trying to read English in variable direction from one sentence to the next. For example, read this in reverse: Context in confusing *is* it but, read to difficult not is sentence this.)

- Many of the analyses in later chapters would not benefit from the tidyverse; they use packages that depend only on base R. Thus, learning the tidyverse approach would have relatively little benefit as the book progresses.
- Whereas this book focuses on statistical approaches to marketing problems, at the time of writing the tidyverse is optimized more for data manipulation and visualization. Thus we view it as complementary but somewhat outside the focus of this book.

There is one situation in which we recommend that you start with the tidyverse instead of base R: if your interest is primarily in routine data manipulation and visualization with little or no focus on statistical methods. For example, if you expect to produce many reports and charts summarizing data, and are not especially interested in statistical modeling or programming, the tidyverse approach may be especially productive for you at the beginning. Then you can learn more about base R later.

For most users, we recommend to become fluent in base R. With that under your belt, we recommend then to learn the tidyverse approach from a text that focuses on it, such as the excellent text from Wickham and Grolemund [200].

1.6 Using This Book

This book is intended to be *didactic* and *hands-on*, meaning that we want to teach you about R and the models we use in plain English, and we expect you to engage with the code interactively in R. It is designed for you to type the commands as you read. (We also provide code files for download from the book's web site; see Sect. 1.6.3 below.)

1.6.1 About the Text

R commands for you to run are presented in code blocks like this:

```
> citation()

To cite R in publications use:

  R Core Team (2018). R: A language and environment for statistical
  computing. R Foundation for Statistical Computing, Vienna, Austria.
  URL https://www.R-project.org/.
...
```

We describe these code blocks and interacting with R in Chap. 2. The code generally follows the Google style guide for R (available at https://google.github.io/styleguide/Rguide.xml) except when we thought a deviation might make the code or text clearer. (As you learn R, you will wish to make your code readable; the Google guide is very useful for code formatting.)

When we refer to R commands, add-on packages, or data in the text outside of code blocks, we set the names in monospace type like this: `citation()`. We include parentheses on function (command) names to indicate that they are functions, such as the `summary()` function (Sect. 2.4.1), as opposed to an object such as the `Groceries` data set (Sect. 12.2.1).

When we introduce or define significant new concepts, we set them in italic, such as *vectors*. Italic is also used simply for *emphasis*.

We teach the R language progressively throughout the book, and much of our coverage of the language is blended into chapters that cover marketing topics and statistical models. In those cases, we present crucial language topics in *Language Brief* sections (such as Sect. 3.4.5). To learn as much as possible about the R language, you'll need to read the Language Brief sections even if you only skim the surrounding material on statistical models.

Some sections cover deeper details or more advanced topics, and may be skipped. We note those with an asterisk in the section title, such as *Learning More**.

1.6.2 About the Data

Most of the data sets that we analyze in this book are *simulated* data sets. They are created with R code to have a specific structure. This has several advantages:

- It allows us to illustrate analyses where there is no publicly available marketing data. This is valuable because few firms share their proprietary data for analyses such as segmentation.
- It allows the book to be more self-contained and less dependent on data downloads.
- It makes it possible to alter the data and rerun analyses to see how the results change.
- It lets us teach important R skills for handling data, generating random numbers, and looping in code.
- It demonstrates how one can write analysis code while waiting for real data. When the final data arrives, you can run your code on the new data.

There arc two exceptions to our usage of simulated data. First, many end-of-chapter exercises use an actual e-commerce data set (Sect. 3.8.1). Second, we use actual store transaction data in Chap. 12; such data is complex to create and appropriate data has been publishcd [23].

We recommend you work through data simulation sections where they appear; they are designed to teach R and to illustrate points that are typical of marketing data. However, when you need data quickly to continue with a chapter, it is available for download as noted in the next section and again in each chapter.

Whenever possible you should also try to perform the analyses here with your own data sets. We work with data in every chapter, but the best way to learn is to adapt the analyses to other data and work through the issues that arise. Because this is an educational text, not a cookbook, and because R can be slow going at first, we recommend to conduct such parallel analyses on tasks where you are not facing urgent deadlines.

At the beginning, it may seem overly simple to repeat analyses with your own data, but when you try to apply an advanced model to another data set, you'll be much better prepared if you've practiced with multiple data sets all along. The sooner you apply R to your own data, the sooner you will be productive in R.

1.6.3 Online Material

This book has a companion website: http://r-marketing.r-forge.r-project.org. The website exists primarily to host the R code and data sets for download, although we encourage you to use those sparingly; you'll learn more if you type the code and create the data sets by simulation as we describe.

On the website, you'll find:

- A welcome page for news and updates: http://r-marketing.r-forge.r-project.org
- Code files in .R (text) format: http://r-marketing.r-forge.r-project.org/code
- Slides for classroom usage, along with R Markdown files used to create the slides: http://r-marketing.r-forge.r-project.org/slides
- Copies of data sets that are used in the book: http://r-marketing.r-forge.r-project. org/data. These are generally downloaded directly into R using the read.csv() command (you'll see that command in Sect. 2.6.2, and will find code for an example download in Sect. 3.1)
- A ZIP file containing all of the data and code files: http://r-marketing.r-forge.r-project.org/data/chapman-feit-rintro.zip

Links to online data are provided in the form of shortened goo.gl links to save typing. More detail on the online materials and ways to access the data are described in Appendix E.

1.6.4 When Things Go Wrong

When you learn something as complex as R or new statistical models, you will encounter many large and small warnings and errors. Also, the R ecosystem is dynamic and things will change after this book is published. We don't wish to scare you with a list of concerns, but we do want you to feel reassured about small discrepancies and to know what to do when larger bugs arise. Here are a few things to know and to try if one of your results doesn't match this book:

- **With R**. The basic error correction process when working with R is to check everything very carefully, especially parentheses, brackets, and upper- or lowercase letters. If a command is lengthy, deconstruct it into pieces and build it up again (we show examples of this along the way).
- **With packages** (add-on libraries). Packages add functionality to R and are regularly updated. Sometimes they change how they work, or may not work at all for a while. Some are very stable while others change often. If you have trouble installing one, do a web search for the error message. If output or details are slightly different than we show, don't worry about it. The error `"There is no package called ..."` indicates that you need to install the package (Sect. 2.2). For other problems, see the remaining items here or check the package's help file (Sect. 2.4.2).
- **With R warnings and errors**. An R "warning" is often informational and does not necessarily require correction. We call these out as they occur with our code, although sometimes they come and go as packages are updated. If R gives you an "error," that means something went wrong and needs to be corrected. In that case, try the code again, or search online for the error message. Also check the errata page on the book's website (Sect. 1.6.3), where we post any necessary updates to the code.
- **With data**. Our data sets are simulated and are affected by random number sequences. If you generate data and it is slightly different, try it again from the beginning; or load the data from the book's website (Sect. 1.6.3).
- **With models**. There are three things that might cause statistical estimates to vary: slight differences in the data (see the preceding item), changes in a package that lead to slightly different estimates, and statistical models that employ random sampling. If you run a model and the results are very similar but slightly different, you can assume that one of these situations occurred. Just proceed.
- **With output**. Packages sometimes change the information they report. The output in this book was current at the time of writing, but you can expect some packages will report things slightly differently over time.
- **With names that can't be located**. Sometimes packages change the function names they use or the structure of results. If you get a code error when trying to extract something from a statistical model, check its help file (Sect. 2.4.2); it may be that something has changed names.
- **When things turn out differently than expected**. For various reasons, R or RStudio may give results or errors that differ from previous occasions. For example, a plot command might not work although it has worked in the past. If none of the preceding tips help, we suggest to exit R or RStudio altogether, restart it, and repeat your steps from the beginning of a section.

Our overall recommendation is this. If a difference is small—such as the difference between a mean of 2.08 and 2.076, or a p-value of 0.726 versus 0.758—don't worry too much about it; you can usually safely ignore these. If you find a large difference—such as a statistical estimate of 0.56 instead of 31.92—try the code block again in the book's code file (Sect. 1.6.3).

1.7 Key Points

At the end of each chapter we summarize crucial lessons. For this chapter, there is only one key point: if you're ready to learn R, let's get started with Chap. 2!

Chapter 2
An Overview of the R Language

2.1 Getting Started

In this chapter, we cover just enough of the R language to get you going. If you're new to programming, this chapter will get you started well enough to be productive and we'll call out ways to learn more at the end. R is a great place to learn to program because its environment is clean and much simpler than traditional programming languages such as Java or C++. If you're an experienced programmer in another language, you should skim this chapter to learn the essentials.

We recommend you work through this chapter *hands-on* and be patient; it will prepare you for marketing analytics applications in later chapters.

2.1.1 Initial Steps

If you haven't already installed R, please do so. We'll skip the installation details except to say that you'll want at least the basic version of R (known as "R base") from the Comprehensive R Archive Network (CRAN): http://cran.r-project.org. If you are using:

- **Windows or Mac OS X**: Get the *compiled binary* version from CRAN.
- **Linux**: Use your package installer to add R. This might be a GUI installer as in Ubuntu's Software Center or a terminal command such as `sudo apt-get install R`. (See CRAN for more options.)

In either case, you don't need the *source code* version for purposes of this book.

After installing R, we recommend also to install RStudio [172], an integrated environment for writing R code, viewing plots, and reading documentation. RStudio is available for Windows, Mac OS X, and Linux at http://www.rstudio.com. Most users will want the *desktop* version. RStudio is optional and this book does not assume

© Springer Nature Switzerland AG 2019

C. Chapman and E. M. Feit, *R For Marketing Research and Analytics*, Use R!,
https://doi.org/10.1007/978-3-030-14316-9_2

that you're using it, although many R users find it to be convenient. Some companies may have questions about RStudio's Affero General Public License (AGPL) terms; if relevant, ask your technology support group if they allow AGPL open source software.

There are other variants of R available, including options that will appeal to experienced programmers who use Emacs, Eclipse, or other development environments. For more information on various R environments, see Appendix A.

2.1.2   Starting R

Once R is installed, run it; or if you installed RStudio, launch that. The R command line starts by default and is known as the *R console*. When this book was written, the R console looked like Fig. 2.1 (where some details depend on the version and operating system).

The ">" symbol at the bottom of the R console shows that R is ready for input from you. For example, you could type:

```
> x <- c(2, 4, 6, 8)
```

```
R version 3.5.1 (2018-07-02) -- "Feather Spray"
Copyright (C) 2018 The R Foundation for Statistical Computing
Platform: x86_64-apple-darwin15.6.0 (64-bit)

R is free software and comes with ABSOLUTELY NO WARRANTY.
You are welcome to redistribute it under certain conditions.
Type 'license()' or 'licence()' for distribution details.

  Natural language support but running in an English locale

R is a collaborative project with many contributors.
Type 'contributors()' for more information and
'citation()' on how to cite R or R packages in publications.

Type 'demo()' for some demos, 'help()' for on-line help, or
'help.start()' for an HTML browser interface to help.
Type 'q()' to quit R.

[R.app GUI 1.70 (7543) x86_64-apple-darwin15.6.0]

>
```

Fig. 2.1   The R console

As we show commands with ">", you should try them for yourself. So, right now, you should type "x <- c(2, 4, 6, 8)" into the R console followed by the Enter key.

This is a simple *assignment* command using the assignment operator "<-" to create a named object x that comprises a vector of numbers, (2, 4, 6, 8). The assignment operator <- can be pronounced as "gets" and is the way to assign values to R variables ("objects").

In reading our code listings, a few notes might help those who are new to programming. We list commands to R proceeded by the ">" symbol just as you would see in R. Sometimes a command is longer than one line and in those cases it continues with a "+" symbol that you don't type (R adds it automatically). Everything else in the code listings is output from R.

In code listings, we abbreviate long output with ellipses ("...") and sometimes add comments, which are anything on a line after "#". When we refer to code outside a listing box, we set it in monospace font so you will know it's an R command or object. In short, anything after ">" or "+" is something for you to type.

For some commands, R responds by printing something in the console. For example, when you type the name of a variable into the console like this:

```
> x
```

R responds by printing out the value of x. In this case, we defined x above as a vector of numbers:

```
[1] 2 4 6 8
```

We'll explain more about these results and the preceding "[1]" below.

2.2 A Quick Tour of R's Capabilities

Before we dive into the details of programming, we'd like to start with a tour of a relatively powerful analysis in R. This is a partial preview of other parts of this book, so don't worry if you don't understand the commands. We explain them briefly here to give you a sense of how an R analysis might be conducted. In this and later chapters, we explain all of these steps and many more analyses.

To begin, we install some add-on packages that we'll need:

```
> install.packages(c("lavaan", "semPlot", "corrplot", "multcomp"))
```

Most analyses require one or more packages in addition to those that come with R. After you install a package once, you don't have to install it again unless there is an update.

Now we load a data set from this book's website and examine it:

```
> satData <- read.csv("http://goo.gl/UDv12g")
> satData$Segment <- factor(satData$Segment)
> head(satData)
  iProdSAT iSalesSAT Segment iProdREC iSalesREC
1        6         2       1        4         3
2        4         5       3        4         4
3        5         3       4        5         4
...
> summary(satData)
    iProdSAT         iSalesSAT        Segment        iProdREC         iSalesREC
 Min.   :1.00     Min.   :1.000    1: 54     Min.   :1.000     Min.   :1.000
 1st Qu.:3.00     1st Qu.:3.000    2:131     1st Qu.:3.000     1st Qu.:3.000
 ...                               ...
 Max.   :7.00     Max.   :7.000              Max.   :7.000     Max.   :7.000
```

This data set exemplifies observations from a simple sales and product satisfaction survey. Such data might be gathered from a satisfaction survey answered by customers after purchasing a product, such as high end electronics or an automobile. The data set has 500 (simulated) consumers' answers to a survey with four items asking about satisfaction with a product (iProdSAT), sales (iSalesSAT) experience, and likelihood to recommend the product and salesperson (iProdREC and iSalesREC respectively).

The four satisfaction items have been answered on a 7 point rating scale that ranges from extremely dissatisfied ("1") to extremely satisfied ("7"). Each respondent is also assigned to a numerically coded segment (Segment). In the second line of R code above, we set Segment to be a categorical factor variable (a nominal value, because we don't want to model segments in terms of the arbitrary mathematical values). The segment membership was assigned by a clustering algorithm applied to the consumers' responses, such as one of the methods we explore in Chap. 11.

Next we chart a correlation matrix for the satisfaction responses, omitting the categorical Segment variable in column 3:

```
> library(corrplot)
corrplot 0.84 loaded
> corrplot.mixed(cor(satData[, -3]))
```

The library() command here is one we'll see often; it loads an add-on library of additional functions for R. The resulting chart is shown in Fig. 2.2. The lower triangle in Fig. 2.2 shows the correlations between item pairs, while the upper triangle visualizes those with circle size and color. The satisfaction items are highly correlated with one another, as are the likelihood-to-recommend items.

Does product satisfaction differ by segment? We compute the mean satisfaction for each segment using the aggregate() function, which we will discuss in Sect. 3.4.5:

```
> aggregate(iProdSAT ~ Segment, satData, mean)
  Segment iProdSAT
1       1 3.462963
2       2 3.725191
3       3 4.103896
4       4 4.708075
```

Fig. 2.2 A plot visualizing correlation between satisfaction and likelihood to recommend variables in a simulated consumer data set, N = 500. All items are positively correlated with one another, and the two satisfaction items are especially strongly correlated with one another, as are the two recommendation items. Chapter 4 discusses correlation analysis in detail

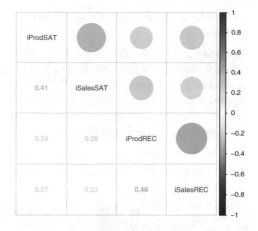

Fig. 2.3 Mean and confidence intervals for product satisfaction by segment. The X axis represents a Likert rating scale ranging 1–7 for product satisfaction. Chapter 5 discusses methods to compare groups

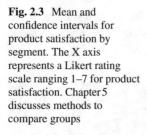
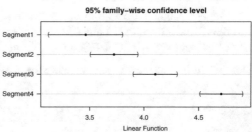

Segment 4 has the highest level of satisfaction, but are the differences statistically significant? We perform a oneway analysis of variance (ANOVA) and see that satisfaction differs significantly by segment:

```
> sat.anova <- aov(iProdSAT ~ -1 + Segment, satData)
> summary(sat.anova)
                 Df Sum Sq Mean Sq F value Pr(>F)
factor(Segment)   4   8628    2157    2161 <2e-16 ***
Residuals       496    495       1
---
Signif. codes:  0 '***' 0.001 '**' 0.01 '*' 0.05 '.' 0.1 ' ' 1
```

We plot the ANOVA model to visualize confidence intervals for mean product satisfaction by segment:

```
> library(multcomp)
Loading required package: mvtnorm
Loading required package: survival
...
> par(mar=c(4,8,4,2))
> plot(glht(sat.anova))
```

The resulting chart is shown in Fig. 2.3. It is easy to see that Segments 1, 2, and 3 differ modestly while Segment 4 is much more satisfied than the others. We will learn more about comparing groups and doing ANOVA analyses in Chap. 5.

R's open source platform has promoted a proliferation of powerful capabilities in advanced statistical methods. For example, many marketing analysts are interested in structural equation models, and R has multiple packages to fit structural equation models.

Let's fit a structural equation model to the satisfaction data. We define a model with latent variables—which we discuss in Chaps. 8 and 10—for satisfaction ("SAT") and likelihood-to-recommend ("REC"). We propose that the SAT latent variable is manifest in the two satisfaction items, while REC is manifest in the two likelihood-to-recommend items. As marketers, we expect and hope that the latent likelihood-to-recommend variable (REC) would be affected by the latent satisfaction (SAT).

This latent variable model is simpler to express in R than in English (note that the following is a single command, where the + at the beginning of lines is generated by R, not typed):

```
> satModel <- "SAT =~ iProdSAT + iSalesSAT
+              REC =~ iProdREC + iSalesREC
+              REC ~  SAT "
```

This model might be paraphrased as "Latent SATisfaction is observed as items iProdSAT and iSalesSAT. Latent likelihood to RECommend is observed as items iProdREC and iSalesREC. RECommendation varies with SATisfaction."

Next we fit that model to the data using the `lavaan` package:

```
> library(lavaan)
This is lavaan 0.6-3
lavaan is BETA software! Please report any bugs.
> sat.fit <- cfa (satModel, data=satData)
> summary(sat.fit, fit.m=TRUE)
lavaan 0.6-3 ended normally after 31 iterations
...
User model versus baseline model:
  Comparative Fit Index (CFI)                         0.995
...
```

The model converged and reported many statistics that we omit above, but we note that the model fits the data well with a Comparative Fit Index near 1.0 (see Chap. 10).

We visualize the structural model using the `semPlot` package:

```
> library(semPlot)
> semPaths(sat.fit, what="est",
+          residuals=FALSE, intercepts=FALSE, nCharNodes=9)
```

This produces the chart shown in Fig. 2.4. Each proposed latent variable is highly loaded on its manifest (observed) survey items. With an estimated coefficient of 0.76, customers' latent satisfaction is shown to have a strong association with their likelihood to recommend. See Chap. 10 for more on structural models and how to interpret and compare them.

That ends the tour. If this seems like an impressive set of capabilities, it is only the tip of the iceberg. Apart from loading packages, those analyses and visualizations required a total of only 15 lines of R code!

There is a price to pay for this power: you must learn about the structure of the R language. At first this may seem basic or even dull, but we promise that understanding the language will pay off. You will be able to apply the analyses we present in this book and understand how to modify the code to do new things.

Fig. 2.4 A structural model with path loadings for a model of product satisfaction and likelihood-to-recommend, using the `lavaan` and `semPlot` packages. Satisfaction has a strong relationship to likelihood-to-recommend (coefficient = 0.76) in the simulated consumer data. Chapter 10 discusses structural models

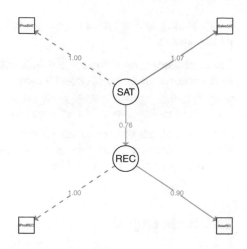

2.3 Basics of Working with R Commands

Like many programming languages, R is *case sensitive*. Thus, x and X are different. If you assigned x as in Sect. 2.1.2 above, try this:

```
> x
[1] 2 4 6 8
> X
Error: object 'X' not found
```

When working with the R console, you'll find it convenient to use the keyboard up and down arrow keys to navigate through previous commands that you've typed. If you make a small error, you can recall the command and edit it without having to type it all over. It's also possible to copy from and paste into the console when using other sources such as a help file.

Tip: although you could type directly into the R console, another option is to use a separate text editor such as the one built into R (select *File | New Script* from the R GUI menu in Windows, *File | New Document* in Mac OSX, or *File | New File | R Script* in RStudio).

With code in a separate file, you can easily edit or repeat commands. To run a command from a text file, you can copy and paste into the console, or use a keyboard shortcut to run it directly from R: use *CTRL+R* in standard R on Windows, *CTRL+Enter* in RStudio on Windows, or *Command+Enter* in standard R or RStudio on a Mac. (See Appendix A for other suggestions about R editors.) You do not have to highlight an entire line to run it; just type *CTRL+Enter* or *Command+Enter* anywhere on the line.

When you put code into a file, it is helpful to add comments. The "#" symbol signifies a *comment* in R, and everything on a line after it is ignored. For example:

```
> x <- c(2, 4, 6, 8)    # start a cheer
```

In this book, you don't need to type any of those comments; they just make the code more readable.

The command above defines x and ends with a comment. One might instead prefer to comment a whole line; R doesn't care:

```
> # start a cheer
> x <- c(2, 4, 6, 8)
```

Our code includes comments wherever we think it might help. As a politician might say about voting, we say *comment early and comment often*. It is much easier to document your code now than later.

2.4   Basic Objects

Like most programming languages, R differentiates between *data* and *functions* that perform actions. We'll spend a bit of time first looking at common data types in R, and then examine functions. We describe the three most important R data types: *vectors*, *lists*, and *data frames*. Later we introduce the process of writing *functions*. Sometimes we also use the term *object*; in R, "object" is a generic term that refers to data, functions, or anything else that the R system processes. (Experienced programmers: R is a *functional language*; although it is similar in some ways to procedural languages such as C++ and Visual Basic, in more important ways it is similar to Scheme and Lisp. For details, see the references in Sect. 2.10.)

2.4.1   Vectors

The simplest R object is a *vector*, a one-dimensional collection of data points of a similar kind (such as numbers or text). For instance, in the following code

```
> x <- c(2, 4, 6, 8)
```

…we tell R to create a vector of 4 numbers and name it x. The command c() indicates to R that you are entering the elements of a vector. Vectors commonly comprise numeric data, logical values, or character strings. Each of the following statements defines a vector with 4 items as members (and if you're not typing along in R, now is the time to start):

```
> xNum   <- c(1, 3.14159, 5, 7)
> xLog   <- c(TRUE, FALSE, TRUE, TRUE)
> xChar  <- c("foo", "bar", "boo", "far")
> xMix   <- c(1, TRUE, 3, "Hello, world!")
> xNum
[1] 1.00000 3.14159 5.00000 7.00000
```

The fourth element of xMix is the character string *Hello, world!*. The comma inside that string falls inside quotation marks and thus does not cause separation between elements as do the other commas. These four objects, xNum, xLog, xChar, and xMix, have different *types* of data. We'll say more about that in a moment.

Vectors may be added to one another with c():

```
> x2 <- c(x, x)
> x2
[1] 2 4 6 8 2 4 6 8
```

An overall view of an object can be obtained with the summary() function, whose results depend on the object type. For vectors of numerics, summary() gives range and central tendency statistics, whereas for vectors of characters it reports counts of the most frequent unique values—in this case, that each word occurs exactly once:

```
> summary(xNum)
   Min. 1st Qu.  Median    Mean 3rd Qu.    Max.
  1.000   2.606   4.071   4.035   5.500   7.000
> summary(xChar)
bar boo far foo
  1   1   1   1
```

Indexing denotes particular elements of a data structure. Vectors are indexed with square brackets, [and]. For instance, the second element of xNum is:

```
> xNum[2]
[1] 3.14159
```

We discuss indexing in depth below (Sect. 2.4.3).

At its core, R is a *mathematical* language that understands vectors, matrices, and other structures, as well as common mathematical functions and constants. When you need to write a statistical algorithm from scratch, many optimized mathematical functions are readily available. For example, R automatically applies operators across entire vectors:

```
> x2 + 1
[1] 3 5 7 9 3 5 7 9
> x2 * pi
[1]  6.283185 12.566371 18.849556 25.132741  6.283185 12.566371 18.849556 ...
> (x+cos(0.5)) * x2
[1]  5.755165 19.510330 41.265495 71.020660  5.755165 19.510330 41.265495 ...
```

The last example shows something to watch out for: when working with vectors, R *recycles* the elements to match a longer set. In the last command, x2 has 8 elements, while x has only 4. R will line them up and multiply x[1] * x2[1], x[2] * x2[2], and so forth. When it comes to x2[5], there is no matching element in x, so it goes back to x[1] and starts again. This can be a source of subtle and hard-to-find bugs. When in doubt, check the length() of vectors as one of the first steps in debugging:

```
> length(x)
[1] 4
> length(x2)
[1] 8
```

In order to keep things clear, matrix math uses different operators than vector math. For instance, %*% is used to multiply matrices instead of *. We do not cover math operations in detail here; see Sect. 2.4.6 below if you want to learn details about math operators in R.

When you create a vector, R automatically assigns a data *type* or *class* to all elements in the vector. Some common data types are logical (TRUE/FALSE), integer (0, 1, 2, ...), double (real numbers such as 1.1, 3.14159, etc.), and character ("a", "hello, world!", etc.).

When types are mixed in a vector, it holds values in the most general format. Thus, the vector "c(1, 2, 3.5)" is *coerced* to type `double` because the real number 3.5 is more general than an integer such as 1:

```
> c(1, 2, 3.5)
[1] 1.0 2.0 3.5
```

This may lead to surprises. When we defined the vector xMix above, it was coerced to a `character` type because only a character type can preserve the basic values of types as diverse as TRUE and "Hello, world!":

```
> xMix
[1] "1"              "TRUE"          "3"            "Hello, world!"
```

When operating on these, R tries to figure out what to do in a sensible way, but sometimes needs help. Consider the following operations:

```
> xNum[1]
[1] 1
> xMix[1]
[1] "1"
> xNum[1] + 1
[1] 2
> xMix[1] + 1
Error in xMix[1] + 1 : non-numeric argument to binary operator
```

When we attempt to add 1 to xNum and xMix, xNum[1]+1 succeeds while xMix[1]+1 returns an error that one of the arguments is not a number. We can explicitly force it to be numeric by *coercion* with the `as.numeric()` function:

```
> as.numeric(xMix[1])+1
[1] 2
```

It would be tedious to go though all of R's rules for coercing from one type to another, so we simply caution you always to check variable types when debugging because confusion about types is a frequent source of errors. The `str()` ("structure") function is a good way to see detailed information about an object:

```
> str(xNum)
 num [1:4] 1 3.14 5 7
> str(xChar)
 chr [1:4] "foo" "bar" "boo" "far"
> str(xMix)
 chr [1:4] "1" "TRUE" "3" "Hello, world!"
```

In these results, we see that xNum is a numeric vector (abbreviated "num") with elements that are indexed 1:4, while xChar and xMix are character vectors (abbreviated "chr").

2.4.2   Help! A Brief Detour

This is a good place to introduce help in R. R and its add-on packages form an enormous system and even advanced R users regularly consult the help files.

How to find help depends on your situation. If you know the name of a command or related command, use "?". For instance, now that you know the `as.numeric()` command, you may wonder whether there are similar commands for other types. Looking at help for a command you know is a good place to start:

```
> ?as.numeric
```

This calls up the R help system, as shown in Fig. 2.5.

R help files are arranged according to a specific structure that makes it easier for experienced R users to find information. Novice R users sometimes dislike help files because they can be very detailed, but once you grow accustomed to the structure, help files are a valuable reference.

Help files are organized into sections titled **Description**, **Usage**, **Arguments**, **Details**, **Value**, **References**, **See Also**, and **Examples**. We often find it helpful to go directly to the **Examples** section. These examples are designed to be pasted directly into the

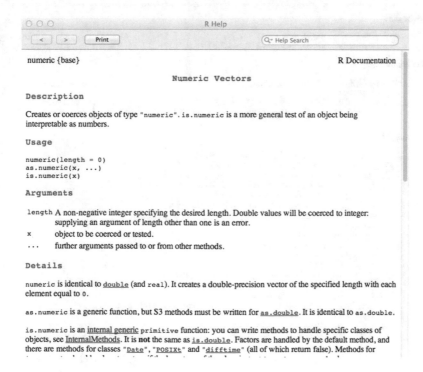

Fig. 2.5   R help for the `as.numeric()` command, using `?as.numeric`

R console to demonstrate a function. If there isn't an example that matches your use case, you can go back to the **Usage** and **Arguments** sections to understand more generally how to use a function. The **Value** section explains what type of object the function returns. If you find that the function you are looking at doesn't do quite what you want, it can be helpful to check out the **See Also** section, where you will find links to other related functions.

Now suppose you do *not* know the name of a specific command, but wish to find something related to a concept. The "??" command searches the Help system for a phrase. For example, the command ??anova finds many references to ANOVA models and utility functions, as shown in Fig. 2.6.

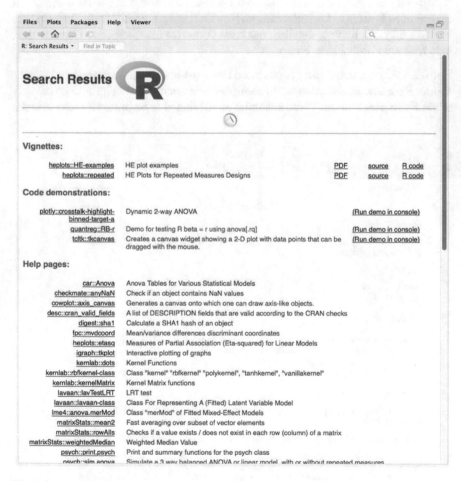

Fig. 2.6 Searching R help with ??anova, as shown in RStudio. The exact results depend on packages you have installed

The ? and ?? commands understand quotation marks. For instance, to get help on
the ? symbol itself, put it inside quotation marks (R standard is the double quote
character: "):

```
> ?"?"
```

Note that the help file for ? has the same subject headings as any other help file. It
doesn't tell you how to get help; it tells you how to use the ? function. This way of
thinking about help files may be foreign at first, but as you get to know the language
the consistency across the help files will make it easy for you to learn new functions
as the need arises.

There are other valuable resources besides the built-in help system. If you're are
looking for something related to a general area of investigation, such as regression
models or econometrics, and are not sure what exists, CRAN is very useful. CRAN
Task Views (http://cran.r-project.org/web/views/) provide annotated lists of packages of interest in high-level areas such as Bayesian statistics, machine learning, and
econometrics.

When working with an add-on package, you can check whether the authors have
provided a *vignette*, a PDF file that describes its usage. They are often linked from
a package's help file, but an especially convenient way to find them is with the
command `browseVignettes()`, which lists all vignettes for the packages you've
installed in a browser window.

If you run into a problem with something that seems it *ought* to work but doesn't,
try the official R-help mailing list (https://stat.ethz.ch/mailman/listinfo/r-help or the
R forums on StackOverflow (http://stackoverflow.com/tags/r/info). Both are fre-
quented by R contributors and experts who are happy to help if you provide a *complete
and reproducible* example of a problem.

Google web search understands "R" in many contexts, such as searching for
"R anova table".

Finally, there is a wealth of books covering specific R topics. At the end of each
chapter, we note books and sites that present more detail about the chapter's topics.

2.4.3 More on Vectors and Indexing

Now that you can find help when needed, let's look at vectors and indexing again.
Whereas `c()` defines arbitrary vectors, integer sequences are commonly defined
with the : operator. For example:

```
> xSeq <- 1:10
> xSeq
 [1]  1  2  3  4  5  6  7  8  9 10
```

When applying math to : sequences, be careful of operator precedence; ":" is
applied before many other math operators. Use parentheses when in doubt and
always double-check math on sequences:

```
> 1:5*2
[1]   2   4   6   8  10
> 1:(5*2)
[1]   1   2   3   4   5   6   7   8   9  10
```

Sequences are useful for indexing and you can use sequences inside [ ]:

```
> xNum
[1] 1.00000 3.14159 5.00000 7.00000
> xNum[2:4]
[1] 3.14159 5.00000 7.00000
> myStart <- 2
> xNum[myStart:sqrt(myStart+7)]
[1] 3.14159 5.00000
```

For complex sequences, use seq() ("sequence") and rep() ("replicate"). We won't cover all of their options, but here is a preview. Read this, try to predict what the commands do, and then run them:

```
> seq(from=-5, to=28, by=4)
> rep(c(1,2,3), each=3)
> rep(seq(from=-3, to=13, by=4), c(1, 2, 3, 2, 1))
```

With the last example, deconstruct it by looking first at the inner expression seq (from=-3, to=13, by=4). Each element of that vector will be replicated a certain number of times as specified in the second argument to rep(). More questions? Try ?rep.

Exclude items by using *negative indices*:

```
> xSeq
[1]   1   2   3   4   5   6   7   8   9  10
> xSeq[-5:-7]
[1]   1   2   3   4   8   9  10
```

In all of the R output, we've seen "[1]" at the start of the row. That indicates the vector position index of the first item printed on each row of output. Try these:

```
> 1:300
> 1001:1300
```

The result of an R vector operation is itself a vector. Try this:

```
> xNum[2:4]
> xSub <- xNum[2:4]
> xSub
```

The new object xSub is created by selecting the elements of xNum. This may seem obvious, yet it has profound implications because it means that the results of most operations in R are fully-formed, inspectable objects that can be passed on to other functions. Instead of just output, you get an object you can reuse, query, manipulate, update, save, or share.

Indexing also works with a vector of logical variables (TRUE/FALSE) that indicate which elements you want to select:

```
> xNum
[1] 1.00000 3.14159 5.00000 7.00000
> xNum[c(FALSE, TRUE, TRUE, TRUE)]
[1] 3.14159 5.00000 7.00000
```

This allows you to use logical expressions—which evaluate as a vector of logical values—to select subsets of data based on specific criteria. We discuss this more in later chapters and will use it frequently. Here is an example:

```
> xNum > 3
[1] FALSE   TRUE   TRUE   TRUE
> xNum[xNum > 3]
[1] 3.14159 5.00000 7.00000
```

When we index using the logical expression xNum > 3, R selects elements that correspond to TRUE values of that expression.

2.4.4   aaRgh! A Digression for New Programmers

At about this point when learning R, some students become incredulous. "I've got to type the name of a data set over and over?!" Yes. "I have to manually pick which rows or columns to include?!" Yes, sometimes, but you'll learn code approaches that are more general. "I can't just point and click on the data I want?!" No, you can't, at least not in this book or most R books. (Limited point and click and menus are available as add-ons in R—see Appendix A—but we strongly believe you'll be better suited by learning the power of the command line from the beginning.)

Thousands of analysts before you have felt the same way. What's different this time? They gave up but you won't! Seriously, R is not simple and yes, it demands a bit of effort. Our job is to help you through the difficulty so the effort pays off.

R reminds us of a mountain town, Holden, Washington. Holden is a remote village in the North Cascades; to get there requires a three hour ferry ride followed by an hour-long bus trip. Each bus up the mountain has a sign that declares, "The ride up is free. The trip down is costly." In other words, everyone is welcomed … but after one settles in, the place may become beloved and difficult to leave. Some people intend to make a short visit, yet end up staying for months or years.

R is similar to that mountain village: although it takes time and effort to arrive, after you settle in and know your way around, you might not want to leave. It has been many years since we have had a reason to use a statistics environment other than R.

2.4.5   Missing and Interesting Values

In statistics, missing values are important, and as a statistics environment, R understands them and includes a special constant for a missing value: NA. This is not a character object ("NA") but a constant in its own right. It is useful in several contexts. For instance, you might create a data object that will be filled in with values later:

```
> my.test.scores <- c(91, NA, NA)
```

Any math performed on a value of NA becomes NA:

```
> mean(my.test.scores)
[1] NA
> max(my.test.scores)
[1] NA
```

This may not be what you want, and you may tell R to ignore NA data rather than calculating on it. Many commands include an argument that instructs them to ignore missing values: na.rm=TRUE:

```
> mean(my.test.scores, na.rm=TRUE)
[1] 91
> max(my.test.scores, na.rm=TRUE)
[1] 91
```

A second approach is to remove NA values explicitly before calculating on them or assigning them elsewhere. This may be done most easily with the function na.omit():

```
> mean(na.omit(my.test.scores))
[1] 91
```

A third and more cumbersome alternative is to test for NA using the is.na() function, and then index data for the values that are *not* NA by adding the ! ("not") operator:

```
> is.na(my.test.scores)
[1] FALSE   TRUE   TRUE
> my.test.scores[!is.na(my.test.scores)]
[1] 91
```

One thing *never* to do in R is to use an actual numeric value such as -999 to indicate missing data. That will cause headaches at best and wrong answers at worst. Instead, as soon as you load such data into R, replace those values with NA using indices:

```
> my.test.scores <- c(91, -999, -999)
> mean(my.test.scores)
[1] -635.6667
> my.test.scores[my.test.scores < -900] <- NA
> mean(my.test.scores, na.rm=TRUE)
[1] 91
```

The third command tells R to select my.test.scores where the value is lower than -900 and replace those elements NA with.

R also handles infinity and undefined numbers, with constants Inf and NaN ("not a number"). For example, if we take the natural logarithm of positive and negative numbers:

```
> log(c(-1, 0, 1))
[1]   NaN  -Inf     0
Warning message:
In log(c(-1, 0, 1)) : NaNs produced
```

We get a warning because log() is undefined for negative numbers and log(-1) gives a value of NaN. Note also that $log(0) = -\infty$ (-Inf).

R tries to be helpful by watching out for such issues, warning you, and carrying on as best it can. You should watch for "Warning message" and clean up your data or math when it appears.

2.4.6 Using R for Mathematical Computation

As a programming environment for computational statistics, R has powerful capabilities for mathematics. In particular, it is highly optimized for vector and matrix operations, which include everything from indexing and iteration to complex operations such as matrix inversion and decomposition. This makes R an attractive alternative to software like Matlab for computation, simulation and optimization.

We do not cover such math in detail here for several reasons: it is tedious to read, many operations are obvious or easy to find, and advanced math is not necessarily used in day to day marketing analytics. Instead, we use math commands and operators with minor explanations as needed, trusting that you may use ? to learn more.

If you are interested in using R for mathematical computation, remember that ? understands quotation marks so you can read about operators using a help command such as ?"*". An entry point to matrix math is the matrix multiplication operator, %*%. If you need especially high performance, we have pointers on enhancing R's computation power in Appendix C.

2.4.7 Lists

Lists are collections of objects of any type. They are useful on their own, and are especially important to understand how R stores data sets, the topic of the following section.

Let's look at two of the objects we defined above, inspecting their structures with the str() command:

```
> str(xNum)
 num [1:4] 1 3.14 5 7
> str(xChar)
 chr [1:4] "foo" "bar" "boo" "far"
```

We see that these vectors are of type "numeric" and "character," respectively. All the elements in a vector must be the same type. We can combine these two vectors into a list using list():

```
> xList <- list(xNum, xChar)
> xList
[[1]]
[1] 1.00000 3.14159 5.00000 7.00000

[[2]]
[1] "foo" "bar" "boo" "far"
```

Using str(), we see that objects inside the list retain the types that they had as separate vectors:

```
> str(xList)
List of 2
 $ : num [1:4] 1 3.14 5 7
 $ : chr [1:4] "foo" "bar" "boo" "far"
```

Lists are indexed with double brackets ([[and]]) instead of the single brackets that vectors use, and thus xList comprises two objects that are indexed with [[1]] and [[2]]. We might index the objects and find summary information one at a time, such as:

```
> summary(xList[[1]])
   Min. 1st Qu.  Median    Mean 3rd Qu.    Max.
  1.000   2.606   4.071   4.035   5.500   7.000
```

It is often more convenient to run such a command on all members of the list at once. We can do that with the lapply() or "list *apply*" command.

With lapply() we must pay special attention to the argument order: lapply (OBJECT, FUNCTION). We use lapply() to produce a summary() for each member of the list:

```
> lapply(xList, summary)
[[1]]
   Min. 1st Qu.  Median    Mean 3rd Qu.    Max.
  1.000   2.606   4.071   4.035   5.500   7.000

[[2]]
bar boo far foo
  1   1   1   1
```

What this did was to separate xList into its separate list elements, [[1]] and [[2]]. Then it ran summary() on each one of those.

Using lapply() to iterate in this way saves a lot of work, especially with lists that may comprise dozens or hundreds of objects. It demonstrates that lists have two advantages: they keep data in one place regardless of constituent types, and they make it possible to apply operations automatically to diverse parts of that data.

Each element in a list may be assigned a name, which you can access with the names() function. You may set the names() when a list is created or at a later time. The following two list creation methods give the same result:

```
> xList <- list(xNum, xChar)                    # method 1: create, then name
> names(xList) <- c("itemnum", "itemchar")

> xList <- list(itemnum=xNum, itemchar=xChar) # method 2: create & name
> names(xList)
[1] "itemnum"  "itemchar"
```

A list may be indexed using its names rather than a numeric index. You can use $name or [["name"]] as you prefer:

```
> xList[[1]]                    # method 1: numeric
[1] 1.00000 3.14159 5.00000 7.00000
> xList$itemnum                 # method 2: $name reference
[1] 1.00000 3.14159 5.00000 7.00000
> xList[["itemnum"]]           # method 3: quoted name
[1] 1.00000 3.14159 5.00000 7.00000
```

List names are character strings and may include spaces and various special characters. Putting the name in quotes is useful when names include spaces.

This brings us to the most important object type in R: *data frames*.

2.5   Data Frames

Data frames are the workhorse objects in R, used to hold data sets and to provide data to statistical functions and models. A data frame's general structure will be familiar to any analyst: it is a rectangular object comprised of columns of varying data types (often referred to as "variables") and rows that each have a value (or missing value, NA) in each column ("observations").

You may construct a data frame with the data.frame() function, which takes as input a set of vectors of the same length:

```
> x.df <- data.frame(xNum, xLog, xChar)
    xNum   xLog xChar
1 1.00000  TRUE   foo
2 3.14159 FALSE   bar
3 5.00000  TRUE   boo
4 7.00000  TRUE   far
```

In this code, we use *dot notation* with a suffix .df that helps to clarify that x.df is a data frame. The .df is just part of the name as far as R is concerned—it doesn't enforce any special rules or type checking—and we use it only as a reminder.

In the resulting data frame we find three named columns that inherit their names from the contributing vectors. Each row is numbered sequentially starting from 1. Elements of a data frame may be indexed using [ROW, COLUMN] notation:

```
> x.df[2, 1]
[1] 3.14159

> x.df[1, 3]
[1] foo
Levels: bar boo far foo
```

The latter example shows us something new: by default, R converts character data in data frames to nominal *factors*. When xChar was added to the data frame, its values were added as the *levels* of a categorical (nominal) data type. Marketing analysts often work with categorical data such as gender, region, or different treatments in an experiment. In R, such values are stored internally as a vector of integers and a separate list of labels naming the categories. The latter are called levels and are accessed with the levels() function.

Converting character strings to factors is a good thing for data that you might use in a statistical model because it tells R to handle it appropriately in the model, but it's inconvenient when the data really is simple text such as an address or comments on a survey. You can prevent the conversion to factors by adding an option to data.frame() that sets stringsAsFactors=FALSE:

```
> x.df <- data.frame(xNum, xLog, xChar, stringsAsFactors=FALSE)
> x.df
    xNum   xLog xChar
1 1.00000  TRUE   foo
2 3.14159 FALSE   bar
3 5.00000  TRUE   boo
4 7.00000  TRUE   far
> x.df[1,3]
[1] "foo"
```

The value of x.df[1, 3] is now a character string and not a factor.
Indices can be left blank, which selects *all* of that dimension:

```
> x.df[2, ]  # all of row 2
    xNum   xLog xChar
2 3.14159 FALSE   bar

> x.df[ , 3]  # all of column 3
[1] "foo" "bar" "boo" "far"
```

Index data frames by using vectors or ranges for the elements you want. Use *negative indices* to omit elements:

```
> x.df[2:3, ]
    xNum   xLog xChar
2 3.14159 FALSE   bar
3 5.00000  TRUE   boo

> x.df[ , 1:2]    # two columns
    xNum   xLog
1 1.00000  TRUE
2 3.14159 FALSE
3 5.00000  TRUE
4 7.00000  TRUE

> x.df[-3, ]  # omit the third observation
    xNum   xLog xChar
1 1.00000  TRUE   foo
2 3.14159 FALSE   bar
4 7.00000  TRUE   far

> x.df[ , -2]  # omit the second column
    xNum xChar
1 1.00000   foo
2 3.14159   bar
3 5.00000   boo
4 7.00000   far
```

Indexing a data frame returns an object. The object will have whatever type suits that data: choosing a single element (row + column) yields a singular object (a vector of length one); choosing a column returns a vector; and choosing rows or multiple columns yields a new data frame. We can see this by using the str() inspector, which tells you more about the structure of the object:

```
> str(x.df[2, 1])
 num 3.14

> str(x.df[ , 2])
 logi [1:4] TRUE FALSE TRUE TRUE

> str(x.df[c(1, 3), ])     # use c() to get rows 1 and 3 only
'data.frame':    2 obs. of  3 variables:
 $ xNum : num  1 5
 $ xLog : logi  TRUE TRUE
 $ xChar: chr  "foo" "boo"
```

As with lists, data frames may be indexed by using the names of their columns:

```
> x.df$xNum
[1] 1.00000 3.14159 5.00000 7.00000
```

In short, data frames are the way to work with a data set in R. R users encounter data frames all the time, and learning to work with them is perhaps the single most important set of skills in R.

Let's create a new data set that is more representative of data in marketing research. We'll clean up our workspace and then create new data:

```
> rm(list=ls())              # caution, deletes all objects! See explanation below
> store.num <- factor(c(3, 14, 21, 32, 54))    # store id
> store.rev <- c(543, 654, 345, 678, 234)      # store revenue, $1000
> store.visits <- c(45, 78, 32, 56, 34)        # visits, 1000s
> store.manager <- c("Annie", "Bert", "Carla", "Dave", "Ella")
> (store.df <- data.frame(store.num, store.rev, store.visits,
+                          store.manager, stringsAsFactors=F))   # F = FALSE
   store.num store.rev store.visits store.manager
1          3       543           45         Annie
2         14       654           78          Bert
3         21       345           32         Carla
4         32       678           56          Dave
5         54       234           34          Ella
```

Notice that we specified that store number is a nominal *factor*, to tell R that it looks like a number but really isn't. We'll discuss that more in Sect. 3.1.1.

In the final command above, by putting parentheses around the whole expression, we tell R to assign the result of data.frame(store.num, store.rev, ...) to store.df and then evaluate the resulting object (store.df). This has the same effect as assigning the object and then typing its name again to see its contents. This trick sometimes saves typing.

We can now get a list of our store managers by selecting that column using the same $ notation that we used with lists:

```
> store.df$store.manager
[1] "Annie" "Bert"  "Carla" "Dave"  "Ella"
```

We can easily pass columns from the data frame to statistical functions using $ and a column name. For example, we can compute the average of store.rev from the store.df data frame using mean():

```
> mean(store.df$store.rev)
[1] 490.8
```

Similarly, we could use the cor() function, which computes the Pearson product-moment correlation coefficient (aka *Pearson's r*), to gauge the association between store visits and revenue in our data:

```
> cor(store.df$store.rev, store.df$store.visits)
[1] 0.8291032
```

We discuss correlation analysis in depth in Chap. 4.

You can obtain basic statistics for a data frame with summary():

```
> summary(store.df)
  store.num     store.rev       store.visits  store.manager
 3 :1       Min.   :234.0   Min.   :32    Length:5
 14:1       1st Qu.:345.0   1st Qu.:34    Class :character
 21:1       Median :543.0   Median :45    Mode  :character
 32:1       Mean   :490.8   Mean   :49
 54:1       3rd Qu.:654.0   3rd Qu.:56
            Max.   :678.0   Max.   :78
```

This shows us the frequency counts for the factor variable (store number), arithmetic summaries of the numeric variables, and the overall length of the text variable. Chapter 3 says much more about describing and summarizing data. (Note: the store.manager column might be summarized slightly differently, depending on the versions of packages loaded earlier in this chapter.)

2.6   Loading and Saving Data

There many ways to load and save data in R. In this section, we focus on the methods for storing data that are common in typical projects including how to save and read native R objects, how to save entire R sessions, and how to read and write CSV formats to move data in and out of other environments like Microsoft Excel.

Native ("binary") R objects are representations of objects in an R-specific format. If you need to save an object exclusively for R then this format will be useful to you. Use save() to write a binary object to disk and load() to read it.

Let's back up the store.df object to disk using save(OBJECT, FILE). Then we'll delete it from memory and use load(FILE) to restore it:

```
> save(store.df, file="store-df-backup.RData")
> rm(store.df)       # caution, only if save() gave no error
> mean(store.df$store.rev)     # error
Error in mean(store.df$store.rev) : object 'store.df' not found

> load("store-df-backup.RData")
> mean(store.df$store.rev)
[1] 490.8
```

save() can also take a group of objects as an argument; just replace the single object name with list=c() and fill in c() with a character vector. For instance:

```
> save(list=c("store.df","store.visits"), file="store-df-backup.RData")
```

When a file is loaded, its objects are placed into memory with the same names that they had when saved. *Important*: when a file is loaded, its objects silently overwrite any objects in memory with the same names! Consider the following:

```
> store.df <- 5
> store.df
[1]   5

> load("store-df-backup.RData")
> store.df
  store.num store.rev store.visits store.manager
1         3       543           45         Annie
2        14       654           78          Bert
```

In the example above, store.df is first assigned a new, simple value of 5 but this is overwritten by load() *with no warning*. When loading objects from files, we recommend to begin from a clean slate with no other objects in memory in order to reduce unexpected side effects.

Filenames may be specified with just the file name as above, in which case they are saved to the current R working directory, or as full paths in the format appropriate to your system. Note that Microsoft Windows uses \ to denote folders, which doesn't work in R (which expects Unix-style directory names using "/"). You must convert \ to either \\ or /, or else R will give an error.

Assuming the appropriate "R" folder exists, and replacing user to match your system, you could try:

```
# Works only on Windows:
> save(store.df, file="C:\\Documents and Settings\\user\\My Documents\\R\\
    store-df-backup.RData")

# Works on all systems (Mac OSX, Linux, and Windows):
> save(store.df, file="~/Documents/R/store-df-backup.RData")
```

The standard file suffix for native data files in R is .RData and we recommend to use that.

If specifying full paths seems cumbersome, you may change the R working directory. getwd() reports the working directory while setwd(PATH) sets it to a new location:

```
# example from author's Mac OS X system; yours will vary
> getwd()
[1] "/Users/chris"

> setwd("~/Documents/R")    # tilde is handled on UNIX-like systems
> getwd()
[1] "/Users/chris/Documents/R"
```

These commands do not create directories; you should do that in the operating system.

2.6.1 Image Files

The memory *image* of an entire session can be saved with the command save.image(FILE). If FILE is excluded, then it defaults to a file named ".RData". Standard R and R Studio both prompt you to save a memory image on closing, but you can also do it yourself by typing:

```
> save.image()     # saves file ".RData"
> save.image("mywork.RData")
```

It can be useful to save the contents of working memory if you wish to back up work in progress, although care is needed (Sect. 2.8). Do not let this substitute for creating reproducible scripts; a best practice is to create a script file as you work that can always reproduce an analysis up to the current point. By default, images save to the working directory as set above.

Workspace images are re-loaded with the general load() command, not with a special "image" version; an image is a collection of objects and no different than other files produced by save(). As we warned above, loading an image will silently overwrite current memory objects that have the same names as objects in the image, but does not remove other objects. In other words, loading an image does not *restore* memory to a snapshot of a previous state, but rather *adds* those contents to current memory.

```
> load("mywork.RData")
```

You can view files with the `list.files()` command, and delete them with `file.remove()` which accepts any number of file names. If you wish to clean up the files we made above (assuming you have not changed working directory):

```
> list.files()
[1] "mywork.RData"              "store-df-backup.RData"

> file.remove("mywork.RData", "store-df-backup.RData")
[1] TRUE TRUE
```

The status returned by `file.remove()` is a vector noting whether each file was removed (if so, then its status is TRUE) or not (FALSE, if it doesn't exist or is currently in use and cannot be removed).

2.6.2 CSV Files

Many analysts save data in *delimited* files such as comma-separated value (CSV) files and tab-separated value (TSV) files to move data between tools such as R, databases, and Microsoft Excel. We focus on CSV files; TSV and other delimited files are handled similarly.

First, let's create a CSV by writing `store.df` to a file. This works similarly to the `save()` command above, with syntax `write.csv(OBJECT, file="FILENAME")`. We strongly recommend to add the option `row.names=FALSE` to eliminate an extra, unnamed column containing labels for each row; those mostly get in the way when interchanging CSV files with other programs.

A handy way to test CSV files is to use the command *without* a file name, which sends the output to the console just as it would be written to a file:

```
> write.csv(store.df, row.names=FALSE)
"store.num","store.rev","store.visits","store.manager"
"3",543,45,"Annie"
"14",654,78,"Bert"
"21",345,32,"Carla"
"32",678,56,"Dave"
"54",234,34,"Ella"
```

R automatically includes a header row with variable names and puts quotation marks around character data.

Now let's write a real file and then read it using `read.csv(file=...)`:

```
> write.csv(store.df, file="store-df.csv", row.names=FALSE)
> read.csv("store-df.csv")                              # "file=" is optional
  store.num store.rev store.visits store.manager
```

1	3	543	45	Annie
2	14	654	78	Bert
3	21	345	32	Carla
4	32	678	56	Dave
5	54	234	34	Ella

By default, `read.csv()` prints the CSV contents to the R console formatted as a data frame. To *assign* the data to an object, use the assignment operator (`<-`). Let's read the CSV file and assign its data to a new object:,

```
> store.df2 <- read.csv("store-df.csv", stringsAsFactors=FALSE)
> store.df2$store.num <- factor(store.df2$store.num)
```

After reading the CSV file, we recreate `store.num` as a factor variable. One of the problems with CSV files is that they lose such distinctions because they are written out in plain text.

Now we check that the values are identical to the original data frame:

```
> store.df == store.df2
      store.num store.rev store.visits store.manager
[1,]       TRUE      TRUE         TRUE          TRUE
[2,]       TRUE      TRUE         TRUE          TRUE
[3,]       TRUE      TRUE         TRUE          TRUE
[4,]       TRUE      TRUE         TRUE          TRUE
[5,]       TRUE      TRUE         TRUE          TRUE
```

The operator `==` tells R to test whether the the two data frames are the same, element-by-element. Although `==` confirms equality, in general the function `all.equal(X, Y)` is more useful because it ignores tiny differences due to binary rounding error (there is an infinity of real numbers, which computers store as finite approximations). Also, the output of `all.equal()` is more compact:

```
> all.equal(store.df, store.df2)
[1] TRUE
```

R can handle many other file formats that we do not discuss in this book. These include *fixed format* files, *databases*, and *binary* files from other software such as Microsoft Excel, MATLAB, SAS, and SPSS. If you need to work with such data, we describe some of the options in Appendix C. A more general overview of options for data exchange is provided by the *R Data Import/Export* manual [157].

We'll clean up the unneeded object, "store.df2" (see Sect. 2.8 below):

```
> rm(store.df2)
```

2.7 Writing Your Own Functions*

The asterisk (*) in the title indicates that this is an optional section. We examine the basics of writing reusable functions, a fundamental programming skill. If you are new to programming, you might wish to skip this section for now and refer back to it when you encounter functions again in later chapters.

Many analyses in R are repetitive: compute statistics across slices of data such as different sales regions, produce analyses from new data sets such as successive calendar quarters, and so forth. R provides *functions* to let you write a set of commands once and reuse it with new data.

We can create a function in R quite easily. A common function we write is to compute the standard error of the mean for a vector of observed data. Such a function already exists in R, but is so simple that we sometimes write our own. In the infinite population version, the standard error is computed as the standard deviation of the data (sd()) divided by square root (sqrt()) of the sample size, which is the length of the vector holding the data. We can declare a function to do this in one line:

```
> se <- function(x) { sd(x) / sqrt(length(x)) }
```

The new function se() can then be used just like any other built-in function in R:

```
> se(store.df$store.visits)
[1] 8.42615
```

A function's results can also be assigned to other variables or used in additional functions. For example, we might compute the upper-bound 95% confidence interval as the mean + 1.96 standard error:

```
> mean(store.df$store.visits) + 1.96 * se(store.df$store.visits)
[1] 65.51525
```

This tells us that, if the present data are a good random sample from a larger set, we could expect the mean of other such samples to be 65.51 or less in 97.5% of the samples (97.5% because the 95% confidence interval is symmetric around 50%, extending from 2.5% to 97.5%). In other words, we can be highly confident from these data that the mean number of store visits is less than 65.52.

A schematic for a new function is: FUNCTIONNAME <- function(INPUTS) EXPR . In most cases, EXPR is a set of multiple lines that operate on the inputs. When there are multiple lines, they must be enclosed with braces { and }. By default, the return value of the function is the output of the last command in the function declaration.

As for the inputs to functions (such as x in se() above), there are a few things to know. First, you can name them with any legal variable name in R. They can accept any type of input. We use the term *argument* for inputs in this book (instead of *parameter*, which we reserve for statistical models). An argument has meaning only within its function; in programming jargon, it is *scoped* to the function. Thus, if you declare x as an argument, then x has a value inside that function as assigned when the function is called; outside the function it could have another value or not be declared. It is good practice in a function to use *only* variables that have been declared as arguments to the function; don't refer to *global* workspace variables whose existence is unpredictable.

If you've programmed in other languages, you may find it unusual that R does not specify types for function arguments. It allows an argument to be of any type and will try to use it as is, issuing warnings and errors as necessary. (Pay attention to them!) For example, if we try to compute the standard error of the character vector `store.df$store.manager`, we get a return value of NA along with a warning:

```
> se(store.df$store.manager)
[1] NA
Warning message:
In var(if (is.vector(x) || is.factor(x)) x else as.double(x), na.rm = na.rm)
  :
  NAs introduced by coercion
```

In Sect. 12.3.3 we introduce ways to identify object types when you need to determine them.

When writing a function, we recommend four conventions:

- Put *braces* around the body using { and }, even if it's just a one line function
- Create *temporary values* to hold results along the way inside the function
- *Comment* the function profusely
- Use the keyword `return()` to show the explicit value returned by the function.

Putting those recommendations together, the `se` function above might be rewritten as follows:

```
> se <- function(x) {
  # computes standard error of the mean
  tmp.sd <- sd(x)        # standard deviation
  tmp.N  <- length(x)    # sample size
  tmp.se <- tmp.sd / sqrt(tmp.N)    # std error of the mean
  return(tmp.se)
}
```

Perhaps this is overkill for such a simple function. However, when your functions get longer and you or your colleagues refer to them years later, you'll be glad that they are clean and well-documented.

A function is an object in memory just like data, and may be inspected, listed, and deleted in the same ways. In particular, one may inspect a function simply by typing its name (without the parentheses):

```
> se
function(x) {
  # computes standard error of the mean
  tmp.sd <- sd(x)        # standard deviation
  tmp.N  <- length(x)    # sample size
  tmp.se <- tmp.sd / sqrt(tmp.N)    # std error of the mean
  return(tmp.se)
}
```

This makes it possible to examine what a function is doing and works for many functions in R and add-on packages.

2.7.1 Language Structures*

This optional section is for experienced programmers and describes how the R language controls a sequence of commands in a script or function.

If you program in a language such as C or Java, the control structures in R will be familiar. Using TEST to indicate a Boolean value (or value coercible to Boolean) and EXPR for any language expression—which may include a block of expressions inside { and }—R provides:

```
if (TEST) EXPR [else EXPR.b]   # do EXPR if TEST is true, else EXPR.b

while (TEST) EXPR              # repeat EXPR while TEST is true

for (NAME in VECTOR) EXPR      # iterate EXPR for values of NAME from VECTOR

switch (INDEX, LIST)   # INDEXth statement or matching argument name from
     LIST

repeat EXPR            # repeats forever until 'break'; not recommended
```

Of these, we only use if() and for() in this book. We describe for() in more detail in Sect. 5.12, and cover if() in Sect. 5.1.3.

There is a caveat to these control structures. On the surface, R syntax appears similar to *imperative* programming languages (such as C, C++, and Java) but underneath it is a *functional* language whose approach more closely resembles Lisp, Clojure, or in particular, Scheme. To advance as an R programmer, you will wish to learn more about functional programming and the object models that underlie it. See Sect. 2.10 for pointers on advanced programming skills.

In addition to the standard if() statement, R provides a vectorized version: ifelse(TEST, YES, NO). ifelse() applies TEST to every element in a vector and returns the value of the expression YES for elements that pass the test as TRUE and the value of the expression NO for those that do not pass.

For example, here's how we can use ifelse() to test each number in a vector before applying a math function to it, and thus avoid a common error:

```
> x <- -2:2
> log(x)                      # warning, can't log() negative numbers
[1]       NaN        NaN     -Inf 0.0000000 0.6931472
Warning message:
In log(x) : NaNs produced

> ifelse(x > 0, x, NA)        # replace non-positive values with NA
[1] NA NA NA   1   2

> log(ifelse(x > 0, x, NA))   # no warning now
[1]        NA        NA       NA 0.0000000 0.6931472
```

2.7.2   Anonymous Functions*

Another useful feature is an *anonymous function* (also known as a *lambda expression*) which can substitute for a general expression and does not need to be declared separately as a named function. (We use the apply() function here, which is similar to lapply() that we saw above, but works on non-list data such as data frames; for full details, see Sect. 3.3.4.)

Suppose for some reason we want the median divided by 2 for columns of data. One solution is to take the `median()` of each column using the `apply()` function on the data's 2nd dimension (the columns), and then divide the result by 2:

```
> my.data <- matrix(runif(100), ncol=5)    # 100 random numbers in 5 columns
> apply(my.data, 2, median) / 2
[1] 0.2866528 0.2846884 0.2103075 0.2157465 0.2442849
```

The second command here applies the `median()` function to each column of data (because the `MARGIN` is given the value 2), and then divides the resulting vector by 2.

A second solution is a function with a name such as `halfmedian`, with `apply()`:

```
> halfmedian <- function (x) { median(x) / 2 }
> apply(my.data, 2, halfmedian)
[1] 0.2866528 0.2846884 0.2103075 0.2157465 0.2442849
```

This now applies our custom `halfmedian()` function to each column.

However, creating such a function adds clutter to the namespace. Unless you want to use such a function in multiple places, that is inefficient. A third way to solve the problem is to create an *anonymous function* that does the work in place with no function name:

```
> apply(my.data, 2, function(x) { median(x) / 2 } )
[1] 0.2866528 0.2846884 0.2103075 0.2157465 0.2442849
```

If you find yourself creating a short function that is only used once, consider whether an anonymous function might be simpler and clearer.

This example reveals a truth about R: there are often many ways to solve a problem, and the *best* way in general is the one that makes sense to you. As you learn more about R, your opinion of what is best will change and your code will become more elegant and efficient. R analysts are thus like economists in the famous joke: "if you ask five economists, you'll get six different opinions."

For further reference (without jokes), a formal outline of the R language is available in the *R Language Definition*, http://cran.r-project.org/doc/manuals/R-lang.pdf [158].

Because this book is about analytics, not programming, we don't cover the complete details of functions but just use them as necessary. To learn more about R's programming model, see the Learning More Sect. 2.10 and a longer example in Chap. 12.

2.8 Clean Up!

R keeps everything in memory by default, and when you exit (use the command `q()`, for *quit*) R offers to save the memory workspace to disk to be loaded next time. That is convenient but means that your workspace will become crowded unless you keep it clean. This can lead to subtle and irreproducible bugs in your analyses, when you believe an object has one value but in reality it has been kept around with some other, forgotten value.

We recommend a few steps to keep your workplace clean. Use the `ls()` (list objects) command periodically to see what you have in memory. If you don't recognize an object, use the `rm()` command to remove it. You can remove a single object by using its name, or a group of them with the `list=` argument plus a character vector of names, or a whole set following a pattern with `list=ls(pattern="STRING")` (tip: don't use "*" because it will match more than you expect):

```
> ls()
> rm(store.num)
> rm(list=c("store.rev", "store.visits"))
> rm(list=ls(pattern="store"))
```

It's better to start every session clean instead of saving a workspace. And as we've said, it's a good idea to *keep all important and reproducible code in a working script file*. This will make it easy to recreate an analysis and keep a workspace clean and reproducible.

To clean out memory and ensure you're starting from scratch at a given time, first you will wish to remove old data and other objects. In RStudio, you can do this by clicking the small "broom" icon in the environment window, or selecting *Session | Clear workspace* from the menu. Or, at the command line:

```
> rm(list=ls())    # deletes all visible objects in memory
```

A good second step is to restart the R interpreter. In RStudio, select *Session | Restart R* from the menu. This recovers memory and resets the workspace for subsequent analyses.

Alternatively, you may accomplish both steps by exiting without saving the workspace, and then restarting R or RStudio.

2.9   Key Points

Most of the present chapter is foundational to R, yet there are a few especially important points:

- For work that you want to preserve or edit, use a text editor and run commands from there (Sect. 2.3).
- Create vectors using `c()` for enumerated values, `seq()` for sequences, and `rep()` for repeated values (Sects. 2.4.1 and 2.4.3).
- Use the constant `NA` for missing values, not an arbitrary value such as −999 (Sect. 2.4.5).
- In R, data sets are most commonly `data.frame` objects created with a command such as `my.df <- data.frame(vector1, vector2, ...)` (Sect. 2.5) or by reading a data file.

- Vectors and data frames are most often indexed with specific numbers (x[1]), ranges (x[2:4]), negative indices (x[-3]) to omit data, and by boolean selection (x[x>3]) (Sects. 2.5 and 2.4.3).
- Data frames are indexed by [ROW, COLUMN], where a blank value means "all of that dimension" such as my.df[2,] for *row 2, all columns* (Sect. 2.5).
- You can also index a data frame with $ and a column name, such as my.df$id (Sect. 2.5).
- Read and write data in CSV format with read.csv() and write.csv() (Sect. 2.6.2).
- Functions are straightforward to write and extend R's capabilities. When you write a function, organize the code well and comment it profusely (Sect. 2.7).
- Clean up your workspace regularly to avoid clutter and bugs from obsolete variables (Sect. 2.8).

2.10 Learning More*

In this chapter, we have described enough of the R language to get you started for the applications in this book. Later chapters include additional instruction on the language as needed for their problems, often presented as separate *Language Brief* sections. If you wish to delve more deeply into the language itself, the following books can also help.

If you are new to statistics, programming, and R, Dalgaard's *An Introduction to R* [40] gives well-paced grounding in R and basic statistics commands. It is a great complement to this book for more practice with the R language.

For those who are experienced with statistics, *A Beginner's Guide to R* by Zuur *et al* [209] dives into R broadly at a more accelerated pace.

If you are an experienced programmer or want to learn the R language in detail, Matloff's *The Art of R Programming* [135] is a readable and enjoyable exposition of the language from a computer science perspective. John Chambers's *Software for Data Analysis* [29] is an advanced description of the R language model and its implementation. Wickham's *Advanced R* [197] focuses on functional programming in R and how to write more effective and reusable code.

Whereas this book focuses on teaching R at a conceptual level, it is also helpful to have more examples in a cookbook format. Albert and Rizzo approach that task from a largely regression-oriented perspective in *R by Example* [4]. A code-oriented collection that is lighter on statistics but deeper on programming is Teetor's *R Cookbook* [186]. Lander (2017) presents a mix of both approaches, language and statistics, applied to a variety of analytic problems in *R for Everyone* [124].

2.11 Exercises

2.11.1 Preliminary Note on Exercises

The exercises in each chapter are designed to reinforce the material. They are provided primarily for classroom usage but are also useful for self-study. On the book's website, we provide R files with example solutions at http://r-marketing.r-forge.r-project.org/exercises.

We strongly encourage you to complete exercises using a tool for *reproducible results*, so the code and R results will be shown together in a single document. If you are using RStudio, an easy solution is to use an *R Notebook*; see Appendix B for a brief overview of R Notebooks and other options. A simple R Notebook for classroom exercises is available at the book's website noted above.

For each answer, do not simply determine the answer and report it; instead write R code to find the answer. For example, suppose a question could be answered by copying two or more values from a summary command, and pasting them into the R console to compute their difference. Better programming practice is to write a command that finds the two values and then subtracts them with no additional requirement for you to copy or retype them. Why is that better? Although it may be more difficult to do once, it is more generalizable and reusable, if you needed to do the same procedure again. At this point, that is not so important, but as your analyses become complex, if will be important to eliminate manual steps that may lead to errors.

Before you begin, we would reemphasize a point noted in Sect. 2.7.2: there may be many ways to solve a problem in R. As the book progresses, we will demonstrate progressively better ways to solve some of the same problems. And R programmers may differ as to what constitutes "better." Some may prefer elegance while others prefer speed or ease of comprehension. At this point, we recommend that you *consider* whether a solution seems optimal, but don't worry too much about it. Getting a correct answer in any one of multiple possible ways is the most important outcome.

In various chapters the exercises build on one another sequentially; you may need to complete previous exercises in the chapter to answer later ones. Exercises preceded by an asterisk (*) correspond to one of the optional sections in a chapter.

2.11.2 Exercises

1. Create a text vector called Months with names of the 12 months of the year.
2. Create a numeric vector Summer, with Calendar month index positions for the summer months (inclusive, with 4 elements in all).
3. Use vector indexing to extract the text values of Months, indexed by Summer.

4. Multiply Summer by 3. What are the values of Months, when indexed by Summer multiplied by 3? Why do you get that answer?
5. What is the mean (average) summer month, as an integer value? Which value of Months corresponds to it? Why do you get that answer?
6. Use the floor() and ceiling() functions to return the upper and lower limits of Months for the average Summer month. (Hint: to find out how a function works, use R help if needed.)
7. Using the store.df data from Sect. 2.5, how many visits did Bert's store have?
8. It is easy to make mistakes in indexing. How can you confirm that the previous answer is actually from Bert's store? Show this with a command that produces no more than 1 row of console output.
9. *Write a function called PieArea that takes the length of a slice of pie and returns the area of the whole pie. (Assume that the pie is cut precisely, and the length of the slice is, in fact, the radius of the pie.) Note that [\]^ is the exponentiation operator in R.
10. *What is PieArea for slices with lengths 4.0, 4.5, 5.0, and 6.0?
11. *Rewrite the previous command as one line of code, without using the PieArea() function. Which of the two solutions do you prefer, and why?

Part II
Fundamentals of Data Analysis

Chapter 3
Describing Data

In this chapter, we tackle our first marketing analytics problem: summarizing and exploring a data set with descriptive statistics (mean, standard deviation, and so forth) and visualization methods. Such investigation is the simplest analysis one can do yet also the most crucial. It is important to describe and explore any data set before moving on to more complex analysis. This chapter will build your R skills and provide a set of tools for exploring your own data.

3.1 Simulating Data

We start by creating data to be analyzed in later parts of the chapter. Why simulate data and not work entirely with real datasets? There are several reasons. The process of creating data lets us practice and deepen R skills from Chap. 2. It makes the book less dependent on vagaries of finding and downloading online data sets. And it lets you manipulate the synthetic data, run analyses again, and examine how the results change.

Perhaps most importantly, data simulation highlights a strength of R: because it is easy to simulate data, R analysts often use simulated data to prove that their methods are working as expected. When we know what the data *should* say (because we created it), we can test our analyses to make sure they are working correctly before applying them to real data. If you have real data sets that you work with regularly, we encourage you to use those for the same analyses alongside our simulated data examples. (See Sect. 2.6 for more information on how to load data files.)

We encourage you to create data in this section step-by-step because we teach R along the way. However, if you are in a hurry to learn how to compute means, standard deviations and other summary statistics, you could quickly run the commands in this section to generate the simulated data. Alternatively, the following will load the data from the book's web site, and you can then go to Sect. 3.6:

```
> store.df <- read.csv("http://goo.gl/QPDdM1")
```

© Springer Nature Switzerland AG 2019   49
C. Chapman and E. M. Feit, *R For Marketing Research and Analytics*, Use R!,
https://doi.org/10.1007/978-3-030-14316-9_3

But if you're new to R, don't do that! Instead, work through the following section to create the data from scratch. If you accidentally ran the command above, you can use `rm(store.df)` to remove the data before proceeding.

3.1.1 Store Data: Setting the Structure

Our first data set represents observations of total sales by week for two products at a chain of stores. We begin by creating a data structure that will hold the data, a simulation of sales for the two products in 20 stores over two years, with price and promotion status. We remove most of the R output here to focus on the input commands. Type the following lines, but feel free to omit the comments (following "#"):

```
> k.stores <- 20      # 20 stores, using "k." for "constant"
> k.weeks <- 104      # 2 years of data each

# create a data frame of initially missing values to hold the data
> store.df <- data.frame(matrix(NA, ncol=10, nrow=k.stores*k.weeks))
> names(store.df) <- c("storeNum", "Year", "Week", "p1sales", "p2sales",
+                      "p1price", "p2price", "p1prom", "p2prom", "country")
```

We see the simplest summary of the data frame using `dim()`:

```
> dim(store.df)
[1] 2080   10
```

As expected, `store.df` has 2080 rows and 10 columns. We create two vectors that will represent the store number and country for each observation:

```
> store.num <- 101:(100+k.stores)
> (store.cty <- c(rep("US", 3), rep("DE", 5), rep("GB", 3), rep("BR", 2),
+               rep("JP", 4), rep("AU", 1), rep("CN", 2)))
 [1] "US" "US" "US" "DE" "DE" "DE" "DE" "DE" "GB" "GB" "GB" "BR" "BR" "JP" ...
> length(store.cty)   # make sure the country list is the right length
[1] 20
```

Now we replace the appropriate columns in the data frame with those values, using `rep()` to expand the vectors to match the number of stores and weeks:

```
> store.df$storeNum <- rep(store.num, each=k.weeks)
> store.df$country  <- rep(store.cty, each=k.weeks)
> rm(store.num, store.cty)   # clean up
```

Next we do the same for the `Week` and `Year` columns:

```
> (store.df$Week <- rep(1:52, times=k.stores*2))
   [1]  1  2  3  4  5  6  7  8  9 10 11 12 13 14 15 16 17 18 19 20 21 22 ...
> # try the inner parts of the next line to figure out how we use rep()
> (store.df$Year  <- rep(rep(1:2, each=k.weeks/2), times=k.stores))
   [1] 1 1 1 1 1 1 1 1 1 1 1 1 1 1 1 1 1 1 1 1 1 1 1 1 1 1 1 1 1 1 1 1 1 1 ...
```

We check the overall data structure with `str()`:

```
> str(store.df)
'data.frame':   2080 obs. of  10 variables:
 $ storeNum: int  101 101 101 101 101 101 101 101 101 101 ...
 $ Year    : int  1 1 1 1 1 1 1 1 1 1 ...
 $ Week    : int  1 2 3 4 5 6 7 8 9 10 ...
 $ p1sales : logi  NA NA NA NA NA NA ...
```

```
$ p2sales  : logi  NA NA NA NA NA NA ...
$ p1price  : logi  NA NA NA NA NA NA ...
$ p2price  : logi  NA NA NA NA NA NA ...
$ p1prom   : logi  NA NA NA NA NA NA ...
$ p2prom   : logi  NA NA NA NA NA NA ...
$ country  : chr   "US" "US" "US" "US" ...
```

The data frame has the right number of observations and variables, and proper column names.

R chose types for all of the variables in our data frame. For example, `store.df $country` is of type `chr` (character) because we assigned a vector of strings to it. However, country labels are actually discrete values and not just arbitrary text. So it is better to represent country explicitly as a categorical variable, known in R as a *factor*. Similarly, `storeNum` is a label, not a number as such. By converting those variables to factors, R knows to treat them as a categorical in subsequent analyses such as regression models. It is good practice to set variable types correctly as they are created; this will help you to avoid errors later.

We redefine `store.df$storeNum` and `store.df$country` as categorical using `factor()`:

```
> store.df$storeNum <- factor(store.df$storeNum)
> store.df$country  <- factor(store.df$country)
> str(store.df)
'data.frame':  2080 obs. of  10 variables:
 $ storeNum: Factor w/ 20 levels "101","102","103",..: 1 1 1 1 1 1 1 1 1 1 ...
... [rows omitted] ...
 $ country : Factor w/ 7 levels "AU","BR","CN",..: 7 7 7 7 7 7 7 7 7 7 ...
```

`storeNum` and `country` are now defined as factors with 20 and 7 levels, respectively.

It is a good idea to inspect data frames in the first and last rows because mistakes often surface there. You can use `head(x=DATA, n=NUMROWS)` and `tail()` commands to inspect the beginning and end of the data frame (we omit long output from the last two commands):

```
> head(store.df)    # defaults to 6 rows
  storeNum Year Week p1sales p2sales p1price p2price p1prom p2prom country
1      101    1    1      NA      NA      NA      NA     NA     NA      US
2      101    1    2      NA      NA      NA      NA     NA     NA      US
3      101    1    3      NA      NA      NA      NA     NA     NA      US
...
> head(store.df, 120)   # 120 rows is enough to check 2 stores; not shown
> tail(store.df, 120)   # make sure end looks OK too; not shown
```

All of the specific measures (sales, price, promotion) are shown as missing values (indicated by NA) because we haven't assigned other values to them yet, while the store numbers, year counters, week counters and country assignments look good. It's always useful to debug small steps like this as you go.

3.1.2 Store Data: Simulating Data Points

We complete `store.df` with random data for *store-by-week* observations of the sales, price, and promotional status of 2 products.

Before simulating random data, it is important to set the random number generation *seed* to make the process replicable. After setting a seed, when you draw random samples in the same sequence again, you get exactly the same (*pseudo*-)random numbers. Pseudorandom number generators (PRNGs) are a complex topic whose issues are out of scope here. If you are using PRNGs for something important you should review the literature; it has been said that whole shelves of journals could be thrown away due to poor usage of random numbers. (R has support for a wide array of pseudorandom sequences; see ?set.seed for details. A starting point to learn more abut PRNGs is Knuth [118].)

If you don't set a PRNG seed, R will select one for you, but you will get different random numbers each time you repeat the process. If you set the seed and execute commands in the order shown in this book, you will get the results that we show.

```
> set.seed(98250)    # a favorite US postal code
```

Now we can draw the random data. In each row of data—that is, one week of one year, for one store—we set the status of whether each product was promoted (value 1) by drawing from the *binomial distribution* that counts the number of "heads" in a collection of coin tosses (where the coin can have any proportion of heads, not just 50%).

To detail that process: we use the rbinom(n, size, p) (decoded as "*random binom*ial") function to draw from the binomial distribution. For every row of the store data, as noted by n=nrow(store.df), we draw from a distribution representing the number of heads in a single coin toss (size=1) with a coin that has probability p=0.1 for product 1 and p=0.15 for product 2. In other words, we randomly assigning 10% likelihood of promotion for product 1, and 15% likelihood for product 2.

```
> store.df$p1prom <- rbinom(n=nrow(store.df), size=1, p=0.1)   # 10% promoted
> store.df$p2prom <- rbinom(n=nrow(store.df), size=1, p=0.15)  # 15% promoted
> head(store.df)   # how does it look so far? (not shown)
```

Next we set a price for each product in each row of the data. We suppose that each product is sold at one of five distinct price points ranging from $2.19 to $3.19 overall. We randomly draw a price for each week by defining a vector with the five price points and using sample(x, size, replace) to draw from it as many times as we have rows of data (size=nrow(store.df)). The five prices are sampled many times, so we sample with replacement (replace=TRUE):

```
> store.df$p1price <- sample(x=c(2.19, 2.29, 2.49, 2.79, 2.99),
+                            size=nrow(store.df), replace=TRUE)
> store.df$p2price <- sample(x=c(2.29, 2.49, 2.59, 2.99, 3.19),
+                            size=nrow(store.df), replace=TRUE)
> head(store.df)   # now how does it look?
  storeNum Year Week p1sales p2sales p1price p2price p1prom p2prom country
1      101    1    1      NA      NA    2.29    2.29      0      0      US
2      101    1    2      NA      NA    2.49    2.49      0      0      US
3      101    1    3      NA      NA    2.99    2.99      1      0      US
...
```

Question: if *price* occurs at five discrete levels, does that make it a factor variable? That depends on the analytic question, but in general probably not. We often perform math on price, such as subtracting cost in order to find gross margin, multiplying by units to find total sales, and so forth. Thus, even though it may have only a few unique values, we want R to treat price as number, not a factor.

Our last step is to simulate the sales figures for each week. We calculate sales as a function of the relative prices of the two products along with the promotional status of each.

Item sales are in unit counts, so we use the Poisson distribution to generate count data: rpois(n, lambda), where n is the number of draws and lambda is the mean value of units per week. We draw a random Poisson count for each row (nrow(store.df), and set the mean sales (lambda) of Product 1 to be higher than that of Product 2:

```
# sales data, using poisson (counts) distribution, rpois()
# first, the default sales in the absence of promotion
> tmp.sales1 <- rpois(nrow(store.df), lambda=120)
> tmp.sales2 <- rpois(nrow(store.df), lambda=100)
```

Now we scale those counts up or down according to the relative prices. Price effects often follow a logarithmic function rather than a linear function, so we use log(price) here:

```
# scale sales according to the ratio of log(price)
> tmp.sales1 <- tmp.sales1 * log(store.df$p2price) / log(store.df$p1price)
> tmp.sales2 <- tmp.sales2 * log(store.df$p1price) / log(store.df$p2price)
```

We have assumed that sales vary as the *inverse* ratio of prices. That is, sales of Product 1 go up to the degree that the log(price) of Product 1 is lower than the log(price) of Product 2.

Finally, we assume that sales get a 30% or 40% lift when each product is promoted in store. We simply multiply the promotional status vector (which comprises all {0, 1} values) by 0.3 or 0.4 respectively, and then multiply the sales vector by that. We use the floor() function to drop fractional values and ensure integer counts for weekly unit sales, and put those values into the data frame:

```
# final sales get a 30% or 40% lift when promoted
> store.df$p1sales <- floor(tmp.sales1 * (1 + store.df$p1prom*0.3))
> store.df$p2sales <- floor(tmp.sales2 * (1 + store.df$p2prom*0.4))
```

Inspecting the data frame, we see that the data look plausible on the surface:

```
> head(store.df)
  storeNum Year Week p1sales p2sales p1price p2price p1prom p2prom country
1      101    1    1     127     106    2.29    2.29      0      0      US
2      101    1    2     137     105    2.49    2.49      0      0      US
3      101    1    3     156      97    2.99    2.99      1      0      US
...
```

A final command is useful to inspect data because it selects rows at random and thus may find problems buried inside a data frame away from the head or tail: some() from the car package [62]:

```
> install.packages("car")    # if needed
> library(car)
> some(store.df, 10)
   storeNum Year Week p1sales p2sales p1price p2price p1prom p2prom country
27      101    1   27     135      99    2.29    2.49      0      0      US
```

```
144          102     1    40     123      113     2.79    2.59       0         0      US
473          105     2     5     127       96     2.99    3.19       0         0      DE
...
```

Thanks to the power of R, we have created a simulated dataset with 20,800 values (2080 rows × 10 columns) using a total of 22 assignment commands. In the next section we explore the data that we created.

3.2 Functions to Summarize a Variable

Observations may comprise either *discrete* data that occurs at specific levels or *continuous* data with many possible values. We look at each type in turn.

3.2.1 Discrete Variables

A basic way to describe discrete data is with frequency counts. The `table()` function will count the observed prevalence of each value that occurs in a variable (i.e., a vector or a column in a data frame). In `store.df`, we may count how many times Product 1 was observed to be on sale at each price point:

```
> table(store.df$p1price)
2.19 2.29 2.49 2.79 2.99
 395  444  423  443  375
```

If your counts vary, that may be due to running commands in a different order or setting a different random number seed. The counts shown here assume that the commands have been run in the exact sequence shown in this chapter. There is no problem if your data is modestly different; just remember that it won't match the output here, or try Sect. 3.1.1 again.

One of the most useful features of R is that most functions produce an object that you can save and use for further commands. So, for example, if you want to save the table that was created by `table()`, you can just assign the same command to a named object:

```
> p1.table <- table(store.df$p1price)
> p1.table
2.19 2.29 2.49 2.79 2.99
 395  444  423  443  375
> str(p1.table)
 'table' int [1:5(1d)] 395 444 423 443 375
...
```

The `str()` command shows us that the object produced by `table()` is a special type called `table`. You will find many functions in R produce objects of special types. We can also easily pass `p1.table` to the `plot()` function to produce a quick plot.

```
> plot(p1.table)
```

Fig. 3.1 A simple bar plot produced by passing a table object to plot(). Default charts are sometimes unattractive, but there are many options to make them more attractive and useful

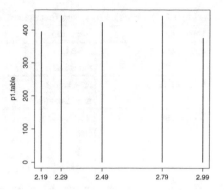

You can see from the resulting bar plot in Fig. 3.1 that the product was on sale at each price point roughly the same number of times. R chose a type of plot suitable for our table object, but it is fairly ugly and the labels could be clearer. Later in this chapter we show how to modify a plot to get better results.

An analyst might want to know how often each product was promoted at each price point. The table() command produces two-way *cross tabs* when a second variable is included:

```
> table(store.df$p1price, store.df$p1prom)

        0    1
  2.19 354   41
  2.29 398   46
  2.49 381   42
  2.79 396   47
  2.99 343   32
```

At each price level, Product 1 is observed to have been promoted approximately 10% of the time (as expected, given how we created the data in Sect. 3.1.1). In fact, we can compute the exact fraction of times product 1 is on promotion at each price point, if we assign the table to a variable and then divide the second column of the table by the the sum of the first and second columns:

```
> p1.table2 <- table(store.df$p1price, store.df$p1prom)
> p1.table2[, 2] / (p1.table2[, 1] + p1.table2[, 2])
      2.19       2.29       2.49       2.79       2.99
0.10379747 0.10360360 0.09929078 0.10609481 0.08533333
```

The second command takes the second column of table p1.table—the column with counts of how often the product is promoted—and divides by the total count to get the proportion of times the product was promoted at each price point. R automatically applies math operators + and / across the entire columns.

By combining operating results in this way, you can easily produce exactly the results you want along with code that can repeat the analysis on demand. This is very helpful to marketing analysts who produce weekly or monthly reports for sales, web traffic, and the like.

Table 3.1   Distribution functions that operate on a numeric vector

Describe	Function	Value
Extremes	`min(x)`	Minimum value
	`max(x)`	Maximum value
Central Tendency	`mean(x)`	Arithmetic mean
	`median(x)`	Median
Dispersion	`var(x)`	Variance around the mean
	`sd(x)`	Standard deviation (`sqrt(var(x))`)
	`IQR(x)`	Interquartile range, 75th - 25th %'ile
	`mad(x)`	Median absolute deviation (a robust variance estimator)
Points	`quantile(x, probs=c(...))`	Percentiles

3.2.2   Continuous Variables

Counts are useful when we have a small number of categories, but with continuous data it is more helpful to to summarize the data in terms of its distribution. The most common way to do that is with mathematical functions that describe the range of the data, its center, the degree to which it is concentrated or dispersed, and specific points that may be of interest (such as the 90th percentile). Table 3.1 lists some R functions to calculate statistics for numeric vector data, such as numeric columns in a data frame.

Following are examples of those common functions:

```
> min(store.df$p1sales)
[1] 73
> max(store.df$p2sales)
[1] 225
> mean(store.df$p1prom)
[1] 0.1
> median(store.df$p2sales)
[1] 96
> var(store.df$p1sales)
[1] 805.0044
> sd(store.df$p1sales)
[1] 28.3726
> IQR(store.df$p1sales)
[1] 37
> mad(store.df$p1sales)
[1] 26.6868
> quantile(store.df$p1sales, probs=c(0.25, 0.5, 0.75))
25% 50% 75%
113 129 150
```

In the case of `quantile()` we have asked for the 25th, 50th, and 75th percentiles using the argument `probs=c(0.25, 0.5, 0.75)`, which are also known as the *median* (50th percentile, same as the `median()` function) and the edges of the *interquartile range*, the 25th and 75th percentiles.

For skewed and asymmetric distributions that are common in marketing, such as unit sales or household income, the arithmetic mean() and standard deviation sd() may be misleading; in those cases, the median() and interquartile range (IQR(), the range of the middle 50% of data) are often more useful to summarize a distribution.

Change the probs= argument in quantile() to find other quantiles:

```
> quantile(store.df$p1sales, probs=c(0.05, 0.95))  # central 90% of data
 5%  95%
93  184
> quantile(store.df$p1sales, probs=0:10/10)
   0%    10%    20%    30%    40%    50%    60%    70%    80%    90%   100%
 73.0  100.0  109.0  117.0  122.6  129.0  136.0  145.0  156.0  171.0  263.0
```

The second example here shows that we may use sequences in many places in R; in this case, we find every 10th percentile by creating a simple sequence of 0:10 and dividing by 10 to yield the vector 0, 0.1, 0.2 ... 1.0. You could also do this using the sequence function (seq(from=0, to=1, by=0.1)), but 0:10/10 is shorter and more commonly used.

Suppose we wanted a summary of the sales for product 1 and product 2 based on their median and interquartile range. We might assemble these summary statistics into a data frame that is easier to read than the one-line-at-a-time output above. We create a data frame to hold our summary statistics and then populate it using functions from Table 3.1. We name the columns and rows, and fill in the cells with function values:

```
> mysummary.df <- data.frame(matrix(NA, nrow=2, ncol=2))
> names(mysummary.df) <- c("Median Sales", "IQR")
> rownames(mysummary.df) <- c("Product 1", "Product 2")
> mysummary.df["Product 1", "Median Sales"] <- median(store.df$p1sales)
> mysummary.df["Product 2", "Median Sales"] <- median(store.df$p2sales)
> mysummary.df["Product 1", "IQR"] <- IQR(store.df$p1sales)
> mysummary.df["Product 2", "IQR"] <- IQR(store.df$p2sales)
> mysummary.df
          Median Sales IQR
Product 1          129  37
Product 2           96  29
```

With this custom summary we can easily see that median sales are higher for product 1 (129 versus 96) and that the variation in sales of product 1 (the IQR across observations by week) is also higher. Once we have this code, we can easily run it the next time we have new sales data to produce a revised version of our table of summary statistics. Such code might be a good candidate for a custom function you can reuse (see Sects. 2.7 and 11.3.1). We'll see a shorter way to create this summary in Sect. 3.3.4.

3.3 Summarizing Data Frames

As useful as functions such as mean() and quantile() are, it is tedious to apply them one at a time to columns of a large data frame, as we did with the summary table above. R provides a variety of ways to summarize data frames without writing extensive code. We describe three approaches: the basic `summary()` command, the `describe()` command from the `psych` package, and the R approach to iterating over variables with `apply()`.

3.3.1 *summary()*

As we saw in Sect. 2.5, `summary()` is a good way to do a preliminary inspection of a data frame or other object. When you use `summary()` on a data frame, it reports a few descriptive statistics for every variable:

```
> summary(store.df)
    storeNum           Year            Week           p1sales          p2sales
 101    : 104   Min.   :1.0   Min.   : 1.00   Min.   : 73    Min.   : 51.0
 102    : 104   1st Qu.:1.0   1st Qu.:13.75   1st Qu.:113    1st Qu.: 84.0
 103    : 104   Median :1.5   Median :26.50   Median :129    Median : 96.0
 104    : 104   Mean   :1.5   Mean   :26.50   Mean   :133    Mean   :100.2
 105    : 104   3rd Qu.:2.0   3rd Qu.:39.25   3rd Qu.:150    3rd Qu.:113.0
 106    : 104   Max.   :2.0   Max.   :52.00   Max.   :263    Max.   :225.0
 (Other):1456
    p1price         p2price          p1prom           p2prom        country
 Min.   :2.190   Min.   :2.29   Min.   :0.0   Min.   :0.0000   AU:104
 1st Qu.:2.290   1st Qu.:2.49   1st Qu.:0.0   1st Qu.:0.0000   BR:208
 Median :2.490   Median :2.59   Median :0.0   Median :0.0000   CN:208
 Mean   :2.544   Mean   :2.70   Mean   :0.1   Mean   :0.1385   DE:520
 3rd Qu.:2.790   3rd Qu.:2.99   3rd Qu.:0.0   3rd Qu.:0.0000   GB:312
 Max.   :2.990   Max.   :3.19   Max.   :1.0   Max.   :1.0000   JP:416
                                                                US:312
```

`summary()` works similarly for single vectors, with a horizontal rather than vertical display:

```
> summary(store.df$Year)
   Min. 1st Qu.  Median    Mean 3rd Qu.    Max.
   1.0     1.0     1.5     1.5     2.0     2.0
```

The `digits=` argument is helpful if you wish to change the precision of the display:

```
> summary(store.df, digits=2)
    storeNum          Year           Week          p1sales         p2sales
 101    : 104   Min.   :1.0   Min.   : 1    Min.   : 73   Min.   : 51
 102    : 104   1st Qu.:1.0   1st Qu.:14    1st Qu.:113   1st Qu.: 84
 ...
    p1price        p2price         p1prom          p2prom        country
 Min.   :2.2   Min.   :2.3   Min.   :0.0   Min.   :0.00   AU:104
 1st Qu.:2.3   1st Qu.:2.5   1st Qu.:0.0   1st Qu.:0.00   BR:208
 ...
```

R generally uses *digits* to mean *significant digits* regardless of absolute magnitude or the decimal position. Thus, `digits=3` does not mean "three decimal places" but instead "three significant positions." Output conforming to `digits=` is not guaranteed; the format may be different in various cases such as reporting integer values and for factors.

Perhaps the most important use for `summary()` is this: *after importing data, use* `summary()` *to do a quick quality check.* Check the `min` and `max` for outliers or miskeyed data, and check to see that the `mean` and `median` are reasonable and similar to one another (if you expect them to be similar, of course). This simple inspection often turns up errors in the data!

3.3.2 *describe()*

Another useful command is describe() from the psych package [163]. To use describe(), install the psych package if you haven't done so already and make it available with library():

```
> install.packages("psych")
Installing package ...
> library(psych) # may warn about "masked" objects, is OK
```

describe() reports a variety of statistics for each variable in a data set, including *n*, the count of observations; *trimmed mean*, the mean after dropping a small proportion of extreme values; and statistics such as *skew* and *kurtosis* that are useful when interpreting data with regard to normal distributions.

```
> describe(store.df)
          vars    n   mean     sd median trimmed    mad   min    max range  skew
storeNum*    1 2080  10.50   5.77  10.50   10.50   7.41  1.00  20.00  19.0  0.00
Year         2 2080   1.50   0.50   1.50    1.50   0.74  1.00   2.00   1.0  0.00
Week         3 2080  26.50  15.01  26.50   26.50  19.27  1.00  52.00  51.0  0.00
p1sales      4 2080 133.05  28.37 129.00  131.08  26.69 73.00 263.00 190.0  0.74
...
country*    10 2080   4.55   1.72   4.50    4.62   2.22  1.00   7.00   6.0 -0.29
          kurtosis   se
storeNum*    -1.21 0.13
Year         -2.00 0.01
Week         -1.20 0.33
p1sales       0.66 0.62
...
country*     -0.81 0.04
```

By comparing the the trimmed mean to the overall mean, one might discover when outliers are skewing the mean with extreme values. describe() is especially recommended for summarizing survey data with discrete values such as 1–7 Likert scale items from surveys (items that use a scale with ordered values such as "Strongly disagree (1)" to "Strongly agree (7)" or similar).

Note that there is an * next to the labels for storeNum and country in the output above. This is a warning; storeNum and country are factors and these summary statistics may not make sense for them. describe() treats each store number as an integer and computes statistics based on those integers. This may be useful when your factors are in a meaningful order. When data include character strings or other non-numeric data, describe() gives an error, "non-numeric argument." These problems may be solved by selecting only the variables (columns) that are numeric with matrix indices. For example, if we wished to describe only columns 2 and 4–9, then we could use the following:

```
> describe(store.df[ , c(2, 4:9)])
        vars    n   mean     sd median trimmed    mad   min    max range skew
Year       1 2080   1.50   0.50   1.50    1.50   0.74  1.00   2.00   1.0 0.00
p1sales    2 2080 133.05  28.37 129.00  131.08  26.69 73.00 263.00 190.0 0.74
p2sales    3 2080 100.16  24.42  96.00   98.05  22.24 51.00 225.00 174.0 0.99
p1price    4 2080   2.54   0.29   2.49    2.53   0.44  2.19   2.99   0.8 0.28
p2price    5 2080   2.70   0.33   2.59    2.69   0.44  2.29   3.19   0.9 0.32
...
```

3.3.3 Recommended Approach to Inspecting Data

We can now recommend a general approach to inspecting a data set after compiling or importing it; replace "my.data" and "DATA" with the names of your objects:

1. Import your data with read.csv() or another appropriate function and check that the importation process gives no errors.
2. Convert it to a data frame if needed (my.data <- data.frame(DATA) and set column names (names(my.data) <- c(...)) if needed.
3. Examine dim() to check that the data frame has the expected number of rows and columns.
4. Use head(my.data) and tail(my.data) to check the first few and last few rows; make sure that header rows at the beginning and blank rows at the end were not included accidentally. Also check that no good rows were skipped at the beginning.
5. Use some() from the car package to examine a few sets of random rows.
6. Check the data frame structure with str() to ensure that variable types and values are appropriate. Change the type of variables—especially to factor types—as necessary.
7. Run summary() and look for unexpected values, especially min and max that are unexpected.
8. Load the psych library and examine basic descriptives with describe(). Reconfirm the observation counts by checking that n is the same for each variable, and check trimmed mean and skew (if relevant).

3.3.4 apply()*

An advanced and powerful tool in R is the apply() command. apply(x=DATA, MARGIN=MARGIN, FUN=FUNCTION) runs any function that you specify on each of the rows and/or columns of an object. If that sounds cryptic, well …it is. In R the term *margin* is a two-dimensional metaphor that denotes which "direction" you want to do something: either along the rows (MARGIN=1) or columns (MARGIN=2), or both simultaneously (MARGIN=c(1, 2)).

Here's an example: suppose we want to find the mean of every column of store.df, except for store.df$Store, which isn't a number and so doesn't have a mean. We can apply() the mean() function to the *column* margin of the data like this:

```
> apply(store.df[,2:9], MARGIN=2, FUN=mean)
      Year          Week       p1sales       p2sales      p1price      p2price
 1.5000000    26.5000000   133.0485577   100.1567308    2.5443750    2.6995192
    p1prom        p2prom
 0.1000000     0.1384615
```

As it happens, colMeans() does the same thing as the command above, but apply gives you the flexibility to apply any function you like. If we want the *row* means instead, we simply change the margin to 1:

```
> apply(store.df[,2:9], 1, mean)
 [1] 29.9475 31.2475 32.9975 29.2725 31.2600 31.7850 27.5225 30.7850 28.0725
[10] 31.5600 30.5975 32.5850 25.6350 29.3225 27.9225 30.5350 31.4475 ...
```

Although row means make little sense for this data set, they can be useful for other kinds of data.

Similarly, we might find the `sum()` or `sd()` for multiple columns with `margin=2`:

```
> apply(store.df[,2:9], 2, sum)
    Year     Week   p1sales   p2sales   p1price   p2price   p1prom   p2prom
  3120.0  55120.0  276741.0  208326.0    5292.3    5615.0    208.0    288.0
> apply(store.df[,2:9], 2, sd)
     Year      Week    p1sales     p2sales     p1price     p2price    ...
0.5001202 15.0119401 28.3725990 24.4241905  0.2948819   0.3292181    ...
```

What if we want to know something more complex? In our discussion of functions in Sect. 2.7, we noted the ability to define an ad hoc *anonymous function*. Imagine that we are checking data and wish to know the difference between the mean and median of each variable, perhaps to flag skew in the data. Anonymous function to the rescue! We can `apply` that calculation to multiple columns using an anonymous function:

```
> apply(store.df[,2:9], 2, function(x) { mean(x) - median(x) } )
     Year      Week    p1sales     p2sales     p1price     p2price     p1prom
   p2prom
0.0000000 0.0000000 4.0485577 4.1567308 0.0543750 0.1095192 0.1000000 0.1384615
```

This analysis shows that the mean of p1sales and the mean of p2sales are larger than the median by about four sales per week, which suggests there is a right-hand tail to the distribution. That is, there are some weeks with very high sales that pull the mean up. (Note that we only use this to illustrate an anonymous function; there are better, more specialized tests of skew, such as those in the `psych` package.)

Experienced programmers: your first instinct, based on experience with procedural programming languages, might be to solve the preceding problem with a `for()` loop that iterates the calculation across columns. That is possible in R but less efficient and less "R-like". Instead, try to think in terms of functions that are applied across data as we do here.

There are specialized versions of `apply()` that work similarly with lists and other object types besides data frames. If interested, check `?tapply` and `?lapply`.

All of these functions, including `apply()`, `summary()` and `describe()` return values that can be assigned to an object. For example, using `apply`, we can produce our customized summary data frame from Sect. 3.2.2 in 5 lines of code rather than 7:

```
> mysummary2.df <- data.frame(matrix(NA, nrow=2, ncol=2))
> names(mysummary2.df) <- c("Median Sales", "IQR")
> rownames(mysummary2.df) <- names(store.df)[4:5] # names from the data frame
> mysummary2.df[, "Median Sales"] <- apply(store.df[, 4:5], 2, median)
> mysummary2.df[, "IQR"]          <- apply(store.df[, 4:5], 2, IQR)
> mysummary2.df
        Median Sales IQR
p1sales          129  37
p2sales           96  29
```

If there were many products instead of just two, the code would still work if we changed the number of allocated rows, and `apply()` would run automatically across all of them.

Now that we know how to summarize data with statistics, it is time to visualize it.

3.4   Single Variable Visualization

We start by examining plots that are part of the base R system. We examine histograms, density plots, and box plots, and take an initial look at more complex graphics including maps. Later chapters build on these foundational plots and introduce more that are available in other packages. R has many options for graphics including dedicated plotting packages such as `ggplot2` and `lattice`, and specialized plots that are optimized for particular data such as correlation analysis.

3.4.1   Histograms

A fundamental plot for a single continuous variable is the *histogram*. Such a plot can be produced in R with the `hist()` function:

```
> hist(store.df$p1sales)
```

The result, which will appear in the graphical display of base R or RStudio, is shown in Fig. 3.2. It is not a bad start. We see that the weekly sales for product 1 range from a little less than 100 to a bit more than 250. Because axes should always be labeled, R tried to provide reasonable labels based on the variables we passed to `hist()`.

Fig. 3.2 A basic histogram using `hist()`

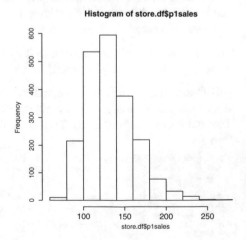

That plot was easy to make but the visual elements are less than pleasing, so we will improve it. For future charts, we will show either the basic chart or the final one, and will not demonstrate the successive steps to build one up. However, we go through the intermediate steps here so you can see the process of how to evolve a graphic in R.

As you work through these steps, there are four things you should understand about graphics in R:

- R graphics are produced through commands that often seem tedious and require trial and iteration.
- Always use a text editor when working on plot commands; they rapidly become too long to type, and you will often want to try slight variants and to copy and paste them for reuse.
- Despite the difficulties, R graphics can be very high quality, portable in format, and even beautiful.
- Once you have code for a useful graphic, you can reuse it with new data. It is often helpful to tinker with previous plotting code when building a new plot, rather than recreating it.

Our first improvement to Fig. 3.2 is to change the title and axis labels. We do that by adding arguments to the `hist()` command:

```
main="..."    : sets the main title
xlab="..."    : sets the X axis label
ylab="..."    : sets the Y axis label
```

We add the title and axis labels to our plot command:

```
> hist(store.df$p1sales,
+       main="Product 1 Weekly Sales Frequencies, All Stores",
+       xlab="Product 1 Sales (Units)",
+       ylab="Count" )
```

The result is shown in Fig. 3.3 and is improved but not perfect; it would be nice to have more granularity (more bars) in the histogram. While we're at it, let's add a bit of color. We adjust the graphic by asking for more bins (*breaks*) and color the histogram bars light blue. Here are the arguments involved:

```
breaks=NUM    : suggest NUM bars in the result
col="..."     : color the bars
```

When specifying colors, R knows many by name, including the most common ones in English ("red", "blue", "green", etc.) and less common (such as "coral" and "burly-wood"). Many of these can be modified by adding the prefix "light" or "dark" (thus "lightgray", "darkred", and so forth). For a list of built-in color names, run the `colors()` command.

We add `breaks=` and `col=` arguments to our code, with the result shown in Fig. 3.4:

Fig. 3.3 The same histogram, with improved labels

Fig. 3.4 The histogram after adding color and dividing the counts into a larger number of bins (breaks)

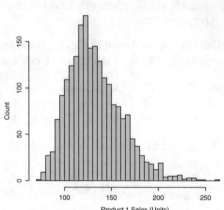

```
> hist(store.df$p1sales,
+      main="Product 1 Weekly Sales Frequencies, All Stores",
+      xlab="Product 1 Sales (Units)",
+      ylab="Count",
+      breaks=30,             # more columns
+      col="lightblue")       # color the bars
```

Comparing Fig. 3.4 with Fig. 3.3 we notice a new problem: the y-axis value for the height of the bars changes according to count. The count depends on the number of bins and on the sample size. We can make it absolute by using *relative frequencies* (technically, the *density* estimate) instead of counts for each point. This makes the Y axis comparable across different sized samples.

Figure 3.4 also has ugly and oddly centered numbering on the X axis. Instead of using hist()'s default *tick marks* (axis numbers), we remove the axis in order to replace it with one more to our liking. The arguments for relative frequency and removing the X axis are:

`freq=FALSE`   : use density instead of counts on Y axis
`xaxt="n"`   : X axis text is set to "none"

Now we need to create the replacement axis. This can be done with `axis (side=MARGIN, at=VECTOR)`. Note that `axis()` is a second command and not an argument to `hist()`; `hist()` creates the plot and then `axis()` modifies it.

Here is the amended code. First we call `hist()` to create a new plot without an X axis :

```
> hist(store.df$p1sales,
+       main="Product 1 Weekly Sales Frequencies, All Stores",
+       xlab="Product 1 Sales (Units)",
+       ylab="Relative frequency",
+       breaks=30,
+       col="lightblue",
+       freq=FALSE,              # freq=FALSE means plot density, not counts
+        xaxt="n")               # xaxt="n" means "x axis tick marks == no"
```

With `axis()`, we specify which axis to change using a argument: `side=1` alters the X axis while `side=2` alters the Y axis (the top and right axes are `side=3` and `side=4`, respectively). We have to tell it where to put the labels, and the argument `at=VECTOR` specifies the new tick marks for the axis. These are easily made with the `seq()` function to generate a sequence of numbers:

```
> axis(side=1, at=seq(60, 300, by=20))  # add "60", "80", ...
```

The updated histogram is shown in Fig. 3.5. It is looking good now!

Finally, we add a smoothed estimation line. To do this, we use the `density()` function to estimate density values for the `p1sales` vector, and add those to the chart with the `lines()` command. The `lines()` command adds elements to the current plot in the same way we saw above for the `axis` command.

Fig. 3.5 Histogram with relative frequencies (density estimates) and improved axis tick mark labels

Fig. 3.6 Final histogram
with density curve

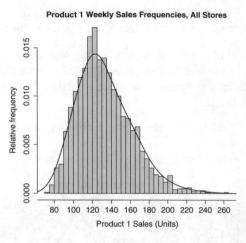

Figure 3.6 is now very informative. Even someone who is unfamiliar with the data can easily tell that this plot describes weekly sales for product 1 and that the typical sales range from about 80 to 200.

```
> lines(density(store.df$p1sales, bw=10),     # "bw= ..." adjusts the
      smoothing
+         type="l", col="darkred", lwd=2)      # lwd = line width
```

The process we have shown to produce this graphic is representative of how analysts use R for visualization. You start with a default plot, change some of the options, and use functions like axis() and density() to alter features of the plot with complete control. Although at first this will seem cumbersome compared to the drag-and-drop methods of other visualization tools, it really isn't much more time consuming if you use a code editor and become familiar with the plotting functions' examples and help files. It has the great advantage that once you've written the code, you can reuse it with different data.

Exercise: modify the code to create the same histogram for product 2. It requires only minor change to the code whereas with a drag-and-drop tool, you would start all over. If you produce a plot often, you could even write it as a custom function.

3.4.2   Boxplots

Boxplots are a compact way to represent a distribution. The R boxplot() command is straightforward; we add labels and use the option horizontal=TRUE to rotate the plot 90° to look better:

```
> boxplot(store.df$p2sales, xlab="Weekly sales", ylab="P2",
        main="Weekly sales of P2, All stores", horizontal=TRUE)
```

Fig. 3.7 A simple example
of boxplot ()

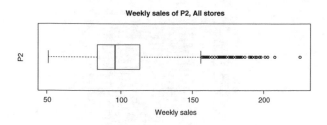

Figure 3.7 shows the resulting graphic. The boxplot presents the distribution more compactly than a histogram. The median is the center line while the 25th and 75th percentiles define the *box*. The outer lines are *whiskers* at the points of the most extreme values that are no more than 1.5 times the width of the box away from the box. Points beyond the whiskers are outliers drawn as individual circles. This is also known as a *Tukey boxplot* (after the statistician, Tukey) or as a *box-and-whiskers* plot.

Boxplots are even more useful when you compare distributions by some other factor. How do different stores compare on sales of product 2? The boxplot () command makes it easy to compare these by specifying a response *formula* using *tilde notation*, where the tilde ("~") separates the *response variable* (sometimes called a *dependent* variable) from the *explanatory variable* (sometimes rather misleadingly called an *independent variable*). In this case, our response variable is p2sales and we want to plot it with regards to the explanatory variable storeNum. This may be easiest to understand with the R code:

```
> boxplot(store.df$p2sales ~ store.df$storeNum, horizontal=TRUE,
+         ylab="Store", xlab="Weekly unit sales", las=1,
+         main="Weekly Sales of P2 by Store")
```

The first portion of the command may be read as "boxplot p2sales by Store." Formulas like this are pervasive in R and are used both for plotting and for estimating models. We discuss formulas in detail in Sect. 5.2.1 and Chap. 7.

We added one other argument to the plot: las=1. That forces the axes to have text in the horizontal direction, making the store numbers more readable. The result is Fig. 3.8, where stores are roughly similar in sales of product 2 (this is not a statistical test of difference, just a visualization).

We see in Fig. 3.8 that the stores are similar in unit sales of P2, but do P2 sales differ in relation to in-store *promotion*? In this case, our explanatory variable would be the promotion variable for P2, so we use boxplot () with the response formula again, replacing storeNum with the promotion variable p2prom.

This is a good time to introduce two shortcut commands that make life easier. Many commands for statistics and plotting understand the data=DATAFRAME argument, and will use variables from data without specifying the full name of the data frame. This makes it easy to repeat analyses on different data sets that include the same variables. All you have to do is change the argument for data=.

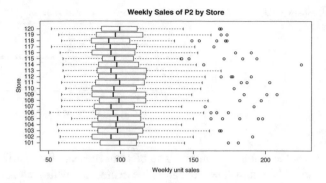

Fig. 3.8 `boxplot()` of sales by store

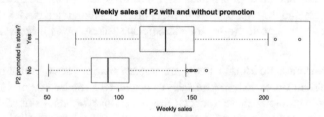

Fig. 3.9 Boxplot of product sales by promotion status

```
> boxplot(p2sales ~ p2prom, data=store.df, horizontal=TRUE, yaxt="n",
+         ylab="P2 promoted in store?", xlab="Weekly sales",
+         main="Weekly sales of P2 with and without promotion")
> axis(side=2, at=c(1,2), labels=c("No", "Yes"))
```

In this plot we also used `axis()` to replace the default Y axis with one that is more informative. The result is shown in Fig. 3.9. There is a clear visual difference in sales on the basis of in-store promotion!

While boxplots are a standard tool for visualizing the distribution of multiple continuous variables, they are sometimes criticized because they do not provide fairly limited information about the distribution. A newer alternative is to place multiple density plots (like the smoothed line in Fig. 3.6) on the same chart for easy comparison. The `beanplot` package allows you to do this with syntax very similar to `boxplot()`:

```
> beanplot(p2sales ~ p2prom, data=store.df, horizontal=TRUE, yaxt="n",
+          what=c(0,1,1,0), log="", side="second",
+          ylab="P2 promoted in store?", xlab="Weekly sales",
+          main="Weekly sales of P2 with and without promotion")
> axis(side=2, at=c(1,2), labels=c("No", "Yes"))
```

The only additional inputs required for `beanplot()` (versus `boxplot()`) are `what=c(1,1,1,0)`, which controls the features of the plot (see `?beanplot` for more details), `log=""`, which prevents `beanplot()` from using a log-scale axis and `side="second"`, which tells `beanplot` to compute a density plot. The output, shown in Fig. 3.10, replaces the box-and-whiskers with a density plot for each group. This format is more accessible especially in business settings where many may

Fig. 3.10 Beanplot of product sales by promotion status

be unfamiliar with boxplots. There are several variations of plots that improve on the boxplot, which you may find under names such as *violin, ridge, dot, strip,* and *bean* plots. There is not yet a standard nomenclature for this family of plots.

To wrap up: boxplots and their newer alternatives are powerful tools to visualize a distribution and make it easy to explore how an outcome variable is related to another factor. In Chaps. 4 and 5 we explore many more ways to examine data association and statistical tests of relationships.

3.4.3 QQ Plot to Check Normality*

This is an optional section on a graphical method to evaluate a distribution more formally. You may wish to skip to Sect. 3.4.4 on cumulative distributions or Sect. 3.4.5 that describes how to compute aggregate values in R.

Quantile-quantile (QQ) plots are a good way to check one's data against a distribution that you think it should come from. Some common statistics such as the correlation coefficient r (to be precise, the *Pearson product-moment correlation coefficient*) are interpreted under an assumption that data are normally distributed. A QQ plot can confirm that the distribution is, in fact, normal by plotting the *observed* quantiles of your data against the quantiles that would be *expected* for a normal distribution.

To do this, the qqnorm() command compares data versus a normal distribution; you can use qqline() to add a diagonal line for easier reading. We check p1sales to see whether it is normally distributed:

```
> qqnorm(store.df$p1sales)
> qqline(store.df$p1sales)
```

The QQ plot is shown in Fig. 3.11. The distribution of p1sales is far from the line at the ends, suggesting that the data is not normally distributed. The upward curving shape is typical of data with high positive skew.

What should you do in this case? If you are using models or statistical functions that assume normally distributed data, you might wish to transform your data. As we've already noted, a common pattern in marketing data is a logarithmic distribution. We examine whether p1sales is more approximately normal after a log() transform:

Fig. 3.11 QQ plot to check
distribution. The tails of the
distribution bow away from
the line that represents an
exact normal distribution,
showing that the distribution
of p1sales is skewed

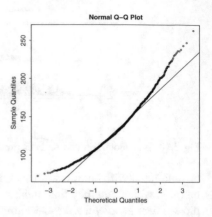

Fig. 3.12 QQ plot for the
data after log()
transformation. The sales
figures are now much better
aligned with the solid line
that represents an exact
normal distribution

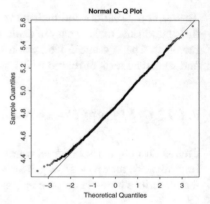

```
> qqnorm(log(store.df$p1sales))
> qqline(log(store.df$p1sales))
```

The QQ plot for log(p1sales) is shown in Fig. 3.12. The points are much closer
to the solid line, indicating that the distribution of log(store.df$p1sales) is
much approximately normal than the untransformed variable.

We recommend that you use qqnorm() (and the more general qqplot() command) regularly to test assumptions about your data's distribution. Web search will
reveal further examples of common patterns that appear in QQ plots and how to
interpret them.

3.4.4 Cumulative Distribution*

This is another optional section, but one that can be quite useful. If you wish to skip
ahead to cover just the fundamentals, you should continue with Sect. 3.4.5.

Another useful univariate plot involves the impressively named *empirical cumulative
distribution function* (ECDF). It is less complex than it sounds and is simply a plot

that shows the cumulative proportion of data values in your sample. This is an easy way to inspect a distribution and to read off percentile values.

Before that we should explain an important thing to know about the R `plot()` command: `plot()` can make only a few plot types on its own and otherwise must be given an *object* that includes more information such as *X* and *Y* values. Many R functions produce objects automatically that are suitable as input for `plot()`. A typical pattern looks like this:

```
> my.object <- FUNCTION(my.data)      # not real code
> plot(my.object)
```

...or combined into a single line as:

```
> plot(FUNCTION(my.data))             # not real code
```

We plot the ECDF of `p1sales` by combining a few steps. First, we use the `ecdf()` function to find the ECDF of the data. Then we wrap `plot()` around that, adding options such as titles. Next we put some nicer-looking labels on the Y axis that relabel the proportions as percentiles. The `paste()` function combines a number vector (0, 10, 20, ...) with the "%" symbol to make each label.

Suppose we also want to know where we should expect 90% of sales figures to occur, i.e., the 90th percentile for weekly sales of P1. We can use the function `abline()` to add vertical and horizontal lines at the 90th percentile. We do not have to tell R the exact value at which to draw a line for the 90th percentile; instead we use `quantile( , pr=0.9)` to find it:

```
> plot(ecdf(store.df$p1sales),
+       main="Cumulative distribution of P1 Weekly Sales",
+       ylab="Cumulative Proportion",
+       xlab=c("P1 weekly sales, all stores", "90% of weeks sold <= 171 units"
+       ),
+       yaxt="n")
> axis(side=2, at=seq(0, 1, by=0.1), las=1,
+       labels=paste(seq(0,100,by=10), "%", sep=""))
> abline(h=0.9, lty=3)       # "h=" for horizontal line; "lty=3" for dotted
> abline(v=quantile(store.df$p1sales, pr=0.9), lty=3)  # "v=" vertical line
```

The result is Fig. 3.13 we often use cumulative distribution plots both for data exploration and for presenting data to others. They are a good way to highlight data features such as discontinuities in the data, long tails, and specific points of interest.

3.4.5 Language Brief: `by()` and `aggregate()`

What should we do if we want to break out data by factors and summarize it, a process you might know as "cross-tabs" or "pivot tables"? For example, how can we compute the mean sales by store? We have voluminous data (every store by every week by each product) but many marketing purposes only need an aggregate figure such as a total or mean. We saw in Sect. 3.3.4 how to summarize data with various statistics

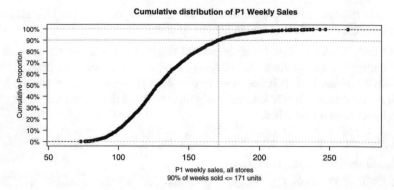

Fig. 3.13 Cumulative distribution plot with lines to emphasize the 90th percentile. The chart identifies that 90% of weekly sales are lower than or equal to 171 units. Other values are easy to read off the chart. For instance, roughly 10% of weeks sell less than 100 units, and fewer than than 5% sell more than 200 units

and plots, and to summarize across columns with the `apply()` function. Now we will see how to summarize by a factor within the data itself using the commands `by()` and `aggregate()`.

Let's look first at `by(data=DATA, INDICES=INDICES, FUN=FUNCTION)`. `by()` uses `INDICES` as grouping factors to divide `DATA` into subgroups. Then it applies the function `FUN` to each subgroup.

This is easier to understand in the context of an example. Suppose we wish to find the average sales of P1 by store. The `DATA` would be the weekly sales for each store, `store.df$p1sales`. We wish to split this by store, so the `INDICES` (actually, "index" in this case) would be `store.df$storeNum`. Finally, we get the average of each of those groups by using the `mean` function. Here is the complete command to break out mean sales of P1 by store:

```
> by(store.df$p1sales, store.df$storeNum, mean)
store.df$storeNum: 101
[1] 130.5385
-------------------------------------------------------------------
store.df$storeNum: 102
[1] 134.7404
. . .
```

To group it by more than one factor, use a `list()` of factors. For instance, we can obtain the mean of `p1sales` by store and by year:

```
> by(store.df$p1sales, list(store.df$storeNum, store.df$Year), mean)
: 101
: 1
[1] 127.7885
-------------------------------------------------------------------
: 102
: 1
[1] 129.7115
. . .
```

A limitation of `by()` is that the result is easy to read but not structured for reuse. How can we save the results as data to use for other purposes such as plotting?

The answer is `aggregate()` which operates almost identically to `by()` but returns a nicely formatted data frame. The following computes the total (`sum()`) sales of P1 by country:

```
> aggregate(store.df$p1sales, by=list(country=store.df$country), sum)
  country       x
1      AU 14544
2      BR 27836
3      CN 27381
4      DE 68876
5      GB 40986
6      JP 55381
7      US 41737
```

How does this work? Just as with `by()`, `aggregate(x=DATA, by=BY, FUN=FUNCTION)` applies a particular function (`FUN`) according to divisions of the data specified by a factor (`by`). We want to find the total sales by country, so we apply the `sum` function by `store.df$country`.

If we want to save the result as a new data frame, we simply assign it somewhere—as we do now because we will use it in Sect. 3.4.6 to make a map:

```
> p1sales.sum <- aggregate(store.df$p1sales,
+                          by=list(country=store.df$country), sum)

> p1sales.sum
  country       x
1      AU 14544
2      BR 27836
3      CN 27381
...
```

`aggregate()` gave us a nicely structured data frame with our summary. We will see further options for `aggregate()` in Sect. 5.2.1.

3.4.6 Maps

We often need to plot marketing data on a map. A common variety is a *choropleth* map, which uses graphics or color to indicate values of a variable such as income or sales. We consider how to do this for a world map using the `rworldmap` package [182].

Here is a routine example. Suppose that we want to chart the total sales by country. We use `aggregate()` as in Sect. 3.4.5 to find the total sales of P1 by country:

```
p1sales.sum <- aggregate(store.df$p1sales,
                         by=list(country=store.df$country), sum)
```

To make a map, we'll use the `rworldmap` package for plotting routines [182], plus the `RColorBrewer` package [148] to generate some better-looking colors.

```
> install.packages(c("rworldmap", "RColorBrewer"))  # if needed
> library(rworldmap)
> library(RColorBrewer)
```

First, we have to associate the aggregated data to specific map regions using the country codes. This can be done with the `joinCountryData2Map()` function, which matches country locations (`store.df$country`) for data points with the corresponding international standard names (*ISO* names) and returns a map object:

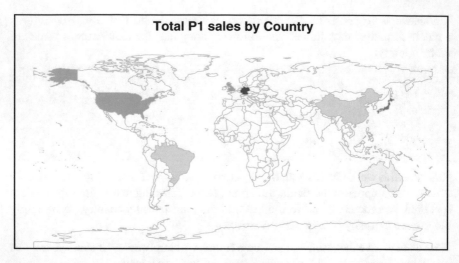

Fig. 3.14 World map for P1 sales by country, using `rworldmap`

```
> p1sales.map <- joinCountryData2Map(p1sales.sum, joinCode = "ISO2",
+                                     nameJoinColumn = "country")
```

Let's inspect that command more closely. The data object that we wish to map is the `p1sales.sum` aggregated data frame. We place that on a map according to the 2-letter country names (`joinCode="ISO2"`) which are present in the data object as the `"country"` column.

Next we draw the resulting map object using `mapCountryData()`, selecting colors from the `RColorBrewer` package "Greens" palette. We plot the column named `x` because that is the default name that the `aggregate()` function gives in the aggregated data fame:

```
> mapCountryData(p1sales.map, nameColumnToPlot="x",
+                mapTitle="Total P1 sales by Country",
+                colourPalette=brewer.pal(7, "Greens"),
+                catMethod="fixedWidth", addLegend=FALSE)
```

The result is shown in Fig. 3.14, known as a *choropleth* chart.

Although such maps are popular, they can be misleading. In *The Wall Street Journal Guide to Information Graphics*, Wong explains that choropleth charts are problematic because they confuse geographic area with scaled quantities ([205], p. 90). For instance, in Fig. 3.14, China is more prominent than Japan not because it has a higher value but because it is larger in size. We acknowledge the need for caution despite the popularity of such maps.

For more complex charts, there are options in `?rworldmap` for drawing regional maps, more granular areas, setting color palettes, using locations other than country codes, and so forth. For other mapping options, see the suggestions in Sect. 3.7 below.

3.5 Key Points

The following guidelines and pointers will help you to describe data accurately and quickly:

- Consider simulating data before collecting it, in order to test your assumptions and develop initial analysis code (Sect. 3.1).
- Always check your data for proper structure and data quality using `str()`, `head()`, `summary()`, and other basic inspection commands (Sect. 3.3.3).
- Describe discrete (categorical) data with `table()` (Sect. 3.2.1) and inspect continuous data with `describe()` from the `psych` package (Sect. 3.3.2).
- Histograms (Sect. 3.4.1), boxplots, and beanplots (Sect. 3.4.2) are good for initial data visualization.
- Use `by()` and `aggregate()` to break out your data by grouping variables (Sect. 3.4.5).
- Advanced visualization methods include cumulative distribution (Sect. 3.4.4), normality checks (Sect. 3.4.3), and mapping (Sect. 3.4.6).

3.6 Data Sources

Data such as `store.df` might be derived from a database at a firm's headquarters office, where weekly sales figures are gathered. The data often might come from an automated data system such as point-of-sale machines reporting to in-store databases and then up to headquarters databases, although at other times it might be gathered and entered manually. A common situation would be to have transaction data in a SQL database, which is then aggregated to total up sales by week and store number, with the results exported to a CSV file. Another common situation would be to gather the data in a spreadsheet program, where it might be aggregated with a function such as pivot tables, and then exported to CSV.

We can assume that such a database would contain hundred or thousands of items—as we see in actual store transaction data in Chap. 12—but for purposes here we have simplified it to two items.

As a side note, although we used a CSV file to store the data set online for those who don't simulate it (Sect. 3.1), CSV format is not required to get data into R. R can also read data from SQL databases directly, and can import directly from many spreadsheet programs as well as other sources. See Appendix C.1.1 for more about data formats.

3.7   Learning More*

Plotting. We demonstrate plotting in R throughout this book. R has multiple, often disjoint solutions for plotting and in this text we use plots as appropriate without going deeply into their details. The *base* plotting system comes standard in R and appears in commands such as hist() and plot().

Two popular and powerful packages that produce more complex graphics are lattice[173] and ggplot2[198]. The choice between lattice and ggplot2 is largely a matter of personal preference and style. We sometimes suspect that lattice appeals more to scientists and engineers while ggplot2 appeals to computer scientists and social scientists. Chang's *R Graphics Cookbook* [31] is a single volume overview of many kinds of plots available in R, focused on the ggplot2 package.

Wong's *The Wall Street Journal Guide to Information Graphics* [205] presents fundamentals of good style for effective graphics in any business context (not specific to R).

Maps. Producing maps in R is an especially complex topic. Maps require three essential components: *shape files* that define the borders of areas (such as country or city boundaries); *spatial translation* of one's data (for instance, a database to match Zip codes in your data to the relevant areas on a map); and *plotting software* to perform the actual plotting. R packages such as rworldmap usually provide access to all three of those elements.

As of this writing, the landscape of available packages and tools for mapping in R was changing rapidly. We use the rworldmap package here for its simplicity. For more complex tasks, the ggplot2 package [198] serves as the basis for a sophisticated mapping tool, the ggmap package [113].

3.8   Exercises

3.8.1   E-Commerce Data for Exercises

Starting in this chapter, many of our exercises use a real data set contributed to the authors by an e-commerce site. The data set comprises responses to intercept surveys asked when users visited the site, along with data about each user's site activity such as number of pages visited and whether a sale was completed. Identifying details for the site and customers have been removed but the observations otherwise are actual data.

We will load the data set first, and then explain a few of its observations. To load the data from CSV format, use the following command (or load ecommerce-data.csv from a local location if you have downloaded it, as noted in Sect. 1.6.3).

```
> ecomm.df <- read.csv("https://goo.gl/hzRyFd")
> summary(ecomm.df)
```

As a reminder, Sect. 2.11 discussed our general approach and recommendations for exercises.

3.8.2 Exercises

1. How many observations and variables are in the e-commerce data set?
2. Compute a frequency table for the country of origin for site visits. After the United States, which country had the most visitors?
3. Compute a two-way frequency table for the intent to purchase (intentWas PlanningToBuy), broken out by user profile.
4. What are the proportions of parents who intended to purchase? the proportions of teachers who did? For each one, omit observations for whom the intent is unknown (blank).
5. Among US states (recorded in the variable region), which state had the most visitors and how many?
6. Solve the previous problem for the state with the most visitors, using the which.max() function (or repeat the same answer, if you already used it).
7. Draw a histogram for the number of visits to the site (behavNumVisits). Adjust it for more detail in the lower values. Color the bars and add a density line.
8. Draw a horizontal boxplot for the number of site visits.
9. Which chart from the previous two exercises, a histogram or a boxplot, is more useful to you, and why?
10. Draw a boxplot for site visits broken out with a unique row for each profile type. (Note: if the chart margins make it unreadable, try the following command before plotting: par(mar=c(3, 12, 2, 2)). After plotting, you can use the command par(mar=c(5, 4, 4, 2) + 0.1) to reset the chart margins.)
11. *Write a function called MeanMedDiff that returns the absolute difference between the mean and the median of a vector.
12. *What is the mean-median difference for number of site visits?
13. *What is the mean-median difference for site visits, after excluding the person who had the most visits?
14. *Use the apply() function to find the mean-median difference for the 1/0 coded behavioral variables for onsite behaviors.
15. *Write the previous command using an anonymous function (see Sect. 2.7.2) instead of MeanMedDiff().
16. *Do you prefer the named function for mean-median difference (Mean MaxDiff()), or an anonymous function? Why? What is a situation for each in which it might be preferable?

Chapter 4
Relationships Between Continuous Variables

Experienced analysts understand that the most important insights in marketing analysis often come from understanding relationships between variables. While it is helpful to understand single variables, such as how many products are sold at a store, more valuable insight emerges when we understand relationships such as "Customers who live closer to our store visit more often than those who live farther away," or "Customers of our online shop buy as much in person at the retail shop as do customers who do not purchase online."

Identifying these kinds of relationships helps marketers to understand how to reach customers more effectively. For example, if people who live closer to a store visit more frequently and buy more, then an obvious strategy would be to send advertisements to people who live in the area.

In this chapter we focus on understanding the relationships between pairs of variables in multivariate data, and examine how to visualize the relationships and compute statistics that describe their associations (correlation coefficients). These are the most important ways to assess relationships between continuous variables. While it might seem appealing to go straight into building regression models (see Chap. 7), we caution against that. The first step in any analysis is to explore the data and its basic properties. This chapter continues the data exploration and visualization process that we reviewed for single variables in Chap. 3. It often saves time and heartache to begin by examining the relationships among pairs of variables before building more complex models.

4.1 Retailer Data

We simulate a data set that describes customers of a multi-channel retailer and their transactions for one year. This data includes a subset of customers for whom we have survey data on product satisfaction.

© Springer Nature Switzerland AG 2019

C. Chapman and E. M. Feit, *R For Marketing Research and Analytics*, Use R!,
https://doi.org/10.1007/978-3-030-14316-9_4

As in Chap. 3, we present the code that generates this data as a way to teach more about R syntax. However, if you prefer to jump right into the analysis, you could quickly run all the commands in Sect. 4.1.1 and then continue with Sect. 4.2 where we begin plotting the data.

Alternatively, the following will load the data from this book's website:

```
> cust.df <- read.csv("http://goo.gl/PmPkaG")
```

However, you will learn more about R if you work through the simulation code instead of downloading the data.

4.1.1 Simulating the Data

In this section, we create a data set for 1000 customers of a retailer that sells products in stores and online. This data is typical of what one might sample from a company's customer relationship management (CRM) system. We begin by setting a random number seed to make the process repeatable (as described in Sect. 3.1.2) and creating a data frame to store the data:

```
> set.seed(21821)
> ncust <- 1000
> cust.df <- data.frame(cust.id=as.factor(c(1:ncust)))
```

We declare a variable `ncust` for the number of customers in the synthetic data set and use that variable wherever we need to refer to the number of customers. This is a good practice, as it allows you to change `ncust` in just one place in your code and then re-run the code to generate a new data set with a different number of customers.

Next we create a number of variables describing the customers, add those variables to the `cust.df` data frame, and inspect them with `summary()`:

```
> cust.df$age <- rnorm(n=ncust, mean=35, sd=5)
> cust.df$credit.score <- rnorm(n=ncust, mean=3*cust.df$age+620, sd=50)
> cust.df$email <- factor(sample(c("yes", "no"), size=ncust, replace=TRUE,
+                         prob=c(0.8, 0.2)))
> cust.df$distance.to.store <- exp(rnorm(n=ncust, mean=2, sd=1.2))

> summary(cust.df)
    cust.id            age          credit.score      email      distance.to.store
 1      :   1   Min.   :19.34   Min.   :543.0   no :186   Min.   :   0.2136
 2      :   1   1st Qu.:31.43   1st Qu.:691.7   yes:814   1st Qu.:   3.3383
 3      :   1   Median :35.10   Median :725.5             Median :   7.1317
 4      :   1   Mean   :34.92   Mean   :725.5             Mean   :  14.6553
 5      :   1   3rd Qu.:38.20   3rd Qu.:757.2             3rd Qu.:  16.6589
 6      :   1   Max.   :51.86   Max.   :880.8             Max.   : 267.0864
 (Other):994
```

We add new variables to `cust.df` data frame using simple assignment (`<-`) to a name with $ notation. Columns in data frames can be easily created or replaced in this way, as long as the vector has the appropriate length (or is recycled to fit the length).

The customers' ages (`age`) are drawn from a normal distribution with mean 35 and standard deviation 5 using `rnorm(n, mean, sd)`. Credit scores (`credit.`

score) are also simulated with a normal distribution, but in that case we specify that the mean of the distribution is related to the customer's age, with older customers having higher credit scores on average. We create a variable (email) indicating whether the customer has an email on file, using the sample function that was covered in Chap. 3.

Our final variable for the basic CRM data is distance.to.store, which we assume follows the exponential of the normal distribution. That gives distances that are all positive, with many distances that are relatively close to the nearest store and fewer that are far from a store. To see the distribution for yourself, try hist(cust.df$distance.to.store). Formally, we say that distance.to.store follows a *lognormal* distribution. (This is sufficiently common that there is a built in function called rlnorm(n, meanlog, sdlog) that does the same thing as taking the exponential of rnorm().)

4.1.2 Simulating Online and In-store Sales Data

Our next step is to create data for the online store: one year totals for each customer for online visits and transactions, plus total spending. We simulate the number of visits with a *negative binomial* distribution, a discrete distribution often used to model counts of events over time. Like the lognormal distribution, the negative binomial distribution generates positive values and has a long right-hand tail, meaning that in our data most customers make relatively few visits and a few customers make many visits. Data from the negative binomial distribution can be generated using rnbinom():

```
> cust.df$online.visits <- rnbinom(ncust, size=0.3,
+                          mu = 15 + ifelse(cust.df$email=="yes", 15, 0)
+                          - 0.7 * (cust.df$age-median(cust.df$age)))
```

We model the mean (mu) of the negative binomial with a baseline value of 15. The size argument sets the degree of dispersion (variation) for the samples. We add an average 15 online visits for customers who have an email on file, using ifelse() to generate a vector of 0 or 15 as appropriate. Finally, we add or subtract visits from the target mean based on the customer's age relative to the sample median; customers who are younger are simulated to make more online visits. To see exactly how this works, try cutting and pasting pieces of the code above into the R console.

For each online visit that a customer makes, we assume there is a 30% chance of placing an order and use rbinom() to create the variable online.trans. We assume that amounts spent in those orders (the variable online.spend) are lognormally distributed:

```
> cust.df$online.trans <- rbinom(ncust, size=cust.df$online.visits, prob=0.3)
> cust.df$online.spend <- exp(rnorm(ncust, mean=3, sd=0.1)) *
+                          cust.df$online.trans
```

The random value for amount spent per transaction—sampled with exp(rnorm())
is multiplied by the variable for number of transactions to get the total amount spent.

Next we generate in-store sales data similarly, except that we don't generate a count
of store visits; few customers visit a physical store without making a purchase and
even if customers did visit without buying, the company probably couldn't track the
visit. We assume that transactions follow a negative binomial distribution, with lower
average numbers of visits for customers who live farther away. We model in-store
spending as a lognormally distributed variable simply multiplied by the number of
transactions:

```
> cust.df$store.trans <- rnbinom(ncust, size=5,
+                                mu=3 / sqrt(cust.df$distance.to.store))
> cust.df$store.spend <- exp(rnorm(ncust, mean=3.5, sd=0.4)) *
+                            cust.df$store.trans
```

As always, we check the data along the way:

```
> summary(cust.df)
     cust.id         age          credit.score     email      distance.to.store
 1      :  1   Min.   :19.34   Min.   :543.0   no :186   Min.   :  0.2136
 2      :  1   1st Qu.:31.43   1st Qu.:691.7   yes:814   1st Qu.:  3.3383
 ...
  online.spend       store.trans      store.spend
 Min.   :  0.00   Min.   : 0.000   Min.   :  0.00
 1st Qu.:  0.00   1st Qu.: 0.000   1st Qu.:  0.00
 Median : 37.03   Median : 1.000   Median : 30.05
 ...
```

4.1.3 Simulating Satisfaction Survey Responses

It is common to for retailers to survey their customers and record responses in the
CRM system. Our last simulation step is to create survey data for a subset of the
customers.

To simulate survey responses, we assume that each customer has an unobserved
overall satisfaction with the brand. We generate this overall satisfaction from a normal
distribution:

```
> sat.overall <- rnorm(ncust, mean=3.1, sd=0.7)
> summary(sat.overall)
   Min. 1st Qu.  Median    Mean 3rd Qu.    Max.
  0.617   2.632   3.087   3.100   3.569   5.293
```

We assume that overall satisfaction is a psychological construct that is not directly
observable. Instead, the survey collects information on two items: satisfaction with
service, and satisfaction with the selection of products. We assume that customers'
responses to the survey items are based on unobserved levels of satisfaction *overall*
(sometimes called the "halo" in survey response) plus the specific levels of satisfaction with the service and product selection.

To create such a score from a halo variable, we add sat.overall (the halo)
to a random value specific to the item, drawn using rnorm(). Because survey

responses are typically given on a discrete, ordinal scale (i.e., "very unsatisfied", "unsatisfied", etc.), we convert our continuous random values to discrete integers using the `floor()` function.

```
> sat.service <- floor(sat.overall + rnorm(ncust, mean=0.5, sd=0.4))
> sat.selection <- floor(sat.overall + rnorm(ncust, mean=-0.2, sd=0.6))
> summary(cbind(sat.service, sat.selection))
  sat.service      sat.selection
 Min.   :0.000    Min.   :-1.000
 1st Qu.:3.000    1st Qu.: 2.000
 ...
 Max.   :6.000    Max.   : 5.000
```

Note that we use `cbind()` to temporarily combine our two vectors of data into a matrix, so that we can get a combined summary with a single line of code. The summary shows that our data now ranges from −1 to 6. However, a typical satisfaction item might be given on a 5-point scale. To fit that, we replace values that are greater than 5 with 5, and values that are less than 1 with 1. This enforces the *floor* and *ceiling* effects often noted in survey response literature.

We set the ceiling by indexing with a vector that tests whether each element of `sat.service` is greater than 5): `sat.service[sat.service > 5]`. This might be read as "sat.service, where sat.service is greater than 5." For the elements that are selected—which means that the expression evaluates as TRUE—we replace the current values with the ceiling value of 5. We do the same for the floor effects (< 1, replacing with 1) and likewise for the ceiling and floor of `sat.selection`. While this sounds quite complicated, the code is simple:

```
> sat.service[sat.service > 5] <- 5
> sat.service[sat.service < 1] <- 1
> sat.selection[sat.selection > 5] <- 5
> sat.selection[sat.selection < 1] <- 1
> summary(cbind(sat.service, sat.selection))
  sat.service      sat.selection
 Min.   :1.000    Min.   :1.000
 ...
 Max.   :5.000    Max.   :5.000
```

Using this type of syntax to replace values in a vector or matrix is common in R, and we recommend that you try out some variations (being careful not to overwrite the `cust.df` data, of course).

4.1.4 Simulating Non-response Data

Because some customers do not respond to surveys, we eliminate the simulated answers for a subset of respondents who are modeled as not answering. We do this by creating a variable of TRUE and FALSE values called `no.response` and then assigning a value of NA for the survey response for customers whose `no.response` is TRUE. As we have discussed, NA is R's built-in constant for missing data.

We model non-response as a function of age, with higher likelihood of not responding to the survey for older customers:

```
> no.response <- as.logical(rbinom(ncust, size=1, prob=cust.df$age/100))
> sat.service[no.response] <- NA
> sat.selection[no.response] <- NA
> summary(cbind(sat.service, sat.selection))
  sat.service      sat.selection
 Min.   :1.00    Min.   :1.000
 1st Qu.:3.00    1st Qu.:2.000
 Median :3.00    Median :2.000
 Mean   :3.07    Mean   :2.401
 3rd Qu.:4.00    3rd Qu.:3.000
 Max.   :5.00    Max.   :5.000
 NA's   :341     NA's   :341
```

summary() recognizes the 341 customers with NA values and excludes them from the statistics.

Finally, we add the survey responses to cust.df and clean up the workspace:

```
> cust.df$sat.service <- sat.service
> cust.df$sat.selection <- sat.selection
> summary(cust.df)
     cust.id          age           credit.score     email       distance.to.store
 1      :  1   Min.   :19.34   Min.   :543.0   no :186   Min.   :   0.2136
 2      :  1   1st Qu.:31.43   1st Qu.:691.7   yes:814   1st Qu.:   3.3383
 ...
   store.spend      sat.service     sat.selection
 Min.   :  0.00   Min.   :1.000   Min.   :1.000
 ...
 Max.   :705.66   Max.   :5.000   Max.   :5.000
                  NA's   :341     NA's   :341

> rm(ncust, sat.overall, sat.service, sat.selection, no.response)
```

The data set is now complete and ready for analysis.

4.2 Exploring Associations Between Variables with Scatterplots

Our analysis begins by checking the data with str() to review its structure:

```
> str(cust.df)
'data.frame':   1000 obs. of  12 variables:
 $ cust.id          : Factor w/ 1000 levels "1","2","3","4",..: 1 2 3 ...
 $ age              : num  22.9 28 35.9 30.5 38.7 ...
 $ credit.score     : num  631 749 733 830 734 ...
 $ email            : Factor w/ 2 levels "no","yes": 2 2 2 2 1 2 2 2 1 1 ...
 $ distance.to.store: num  2.58 48.18 1.29 5.25 25.04 ...
 $ online.visits    : num  20 121 39 1 35 1 1 48 0 14 ...
 $ online.trans     : int  3 39 14 0 11 1 1 13 0 6 ...
 $ online.spend     : num  58.4 756.9 250.3 0 204.7 ...
 $ store.trans      : num  4 0 0 2 0 2 0 2 4 0 3 ...
 $ store.spend      : num  140.3 0 0 95.9 0 ...
 $ sat.service      : num  3 3 NA 4 1 NA 3 2 4 3 ...
 $ sat.selection    : num  3 3 NA 2 1 NA 3 3 2 2 ...
```

As we noted above, in this data frame each row represents a different customer. For each, there is a flag indicating whether the customer has an email address on file (email), along with the customer's age, credit.score, and distance to the nearest physical store (distance.to.store).

Additional variables report one-year total visits to the online site (online.visits) as well as online and in-store transaction counts (online.trans and store.trans) plus one-year total spending online and in store (online.spend and store.spend). Finally, the data contains survey ratings of satisfaction with the service and product selection at the retail stores (sat.service and sat.selection. Some of the survey values are NA for customers without survey responses. All values are numeric, except that cust.df$cust.id and cust.df$email are factors (categorical). We'll say more shortly about why the details of the data structure are so important.

4.2.1 Creating a Basic Scatterplot with `plot()`

We begin by exploring the relationship between each customer's age and credit score using plot(x, y), where x is the x-coordinate vector for the points and y is the y-coordinate vector:

```
> plot(x=cust.df$age, y=cust.df$credit.score)
```

The code above produces the graphic shown in the left panel of Fig. 4.1, a fairly typical scatterplot. There is a large mass of customers in the center of the plot with age around 35 and credit score around 725, and fewer customers at the margins. There are not many younger customers with very high credit scores, nor older customers with very low scores, which suggests an association between age and credit score.

The default settings in plot() produce a quick plot that is useful when you are exploring the data for yourself; plot() adjusts the x- and y-axes to accommodate the range of the data and labels the axes using variable names. But if we present the plot to others, we ought to provide more informative labels for the axes and chart title:

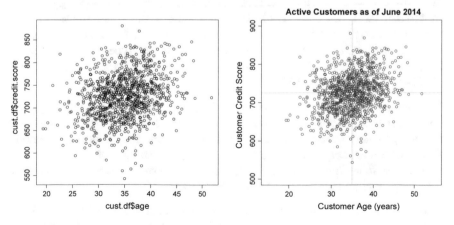

Fig. 4.1 Basic scatterplot of customer age versus credit score using default settings in plot() function (left), and a properly labeled version of the same plot (right)

```
> plot(cust.df$age, cust.df$credit.score,
+      col="blue",
+      xlim=c(15, 55), ylim=c(500, 900),
+      main="Active Customers as of June 2014",
+      xlab="Customer Age (years)", ylab="Customer Credit Score ")
> abline(h=mean(cust.df$credit.score), col="dark blue", lty="dotted")
> abline(v=mean(cust.df$age), col="dark blue", lty="dotted")
```

We do not specifically name x= and y= here because, when names of arguments are omitted, a function such as plot() assumes that they line up in order as listed in a function's definition (and shown in help). We use the argument col to color the points blue. xlim and ylim set a range for each axis. main, xlab and ylab provide a descriptive title and axis labels for the chart. The result on the right side of Fig. 4.1 is labeled well enough that someone viewing the chart can easily understand what it depicts.

After creating the plot, we use abline() to add lines to the plot, to indicate the average age and average credit score in the data. We add a horizontal line at mean(cust.df$credit.score) using abline(h=), and a vertical line at the mean age with abline(v=).

Often, plots are built-up using a series of commands like this. The first step is to use plot() to set up the basic graphics; then add features with other graphics commands. Some of the most useful functions are points() to add specific points, abline() to add a line by slope and intercept, lines() to add a set of lines by coordinates, and legend() to add a legend (see Sect. 4.2.3). Each of these adds elements to a plot that has already been created using plot().

Before we move on, we should make an important note about how the plot() command works in R. When you type plot() into the console, R looks at what type of data you are trying to plot and, based on the data type, R will choose a specific lower-level plotting function, known as a *method*, that is appropriate to the data you are trying to plot. When we call plot() with vectors of x and y coordinates, R uses the plot.default() function. However, there are many other plotting functions for different data types. For example, if you plot the cust.df data frame by typing plot(cust.df) into the console, R will use plot.data.frame() instead of plot.default(). This produces one of several plot types depending on the number of dimensions in the data frame; in this case, it produces a scatterplot matrix, which we review in Sect. 4.4.2.

While this may seem like an obtuse detail of the language, it is important to general R users for two reasons. First, help files for generic functions like plot() and summary() may be rather *un*helpful because they describe the generic methods; often you need to navigate to the help file for the specific method that you are using. For instance, to learn more about the plotting function we are using in this chapter, you should type ?plot.default into the console.

Second, when plot() produces something unexpected, it may be because R has selected a different method than you expect. If so, check the data types of the variables you're sending to plot() because R uses those to select a plot method. Despite this complexity, generic functions are convenient because you only have to remember one function name such as `plot()` instead of many. When you need to figure out more, you can check the methods available for `plot()`, depending on the packages you are using, by typing `methods(plot)`.

We next turn to an important marketing question: in our data, do customers who buy more online buy less in stores? We start by plotting online sales against in-store sales:

```
> plot(cust.df$store.spend, cust.df$online.spend,
+      main="Customers as of June 2014",
+      xlab="Prior 12 months in-store sales ($)",
+      ylab="Prior 12 months online sales ($)",
+      cex=0.7)
```

The resulting plot in Fig. 4.2 is typical of the skewed distributions that are common in behavioral data such as sales or transaction counts; most customers purchase rarely so the data is dense near zero. The resulting plot has a lot of points along the axes; we use the `cex` option, which scales down the plotted points to 0.7 of their default size so that we can see the points a bit more clearly. The plot shows that there are a large number of customers who didn't buy anything on one of the two channels (the points along the axes), along with a smaller number of customers who purchase fairly large amounts on one of the channels.

Because of the skewed data, Fig. 4.2 does not yet give a good answer to our question about the relationship between online and in-store sales. We investigate further with a histogram of just the in-store sales (see Sect. 3.4 for `hist()`):

```
> hist(cust.df$store.spend,
+      breaks=(0:ceiling(max(cust.df$store.spend)/10))*10,
+      main="Customers as of June 2014",
+      xlab="Prior 12 months in-store sales ($)",
+      ylab="Count of customers")
```

Fig. 4.2 Scatterplot of online sales versus in-store sales for the customers in our data set

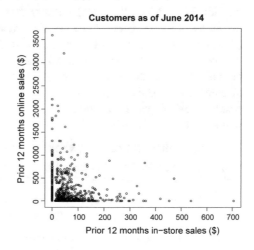

Fig. 4.3 A histogram of
prior 12 months online sales
reveals more clearly a large
number of customers who
purchase nothing along with
a left-skewed distribution of
sales among those who
purchase something

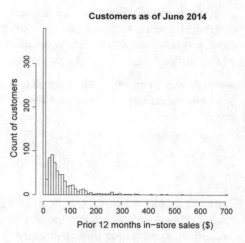

The histogram in Fig. 4.3 shows clearly that a large number of customers bought nothing in the online store (about 400 out of 1000). The distribution of sales among those
who do buy has a mode around $20 and a long right-hand tail with a few customers
whose 12 month spending was high. Such distributions are typical of spending and
transaction counts in customer data. Data with a highly-skewed distribution like this
should be transformed before plotting, as we will discuss in Sect. 4.2.3.

4.2.2   Color-Coding Points on a Scatterplot

Another question is whether the propensity to buy online versus in store is related
to our email efforts (as reflected by whether or not a customer has an email address
on file). We can add the email dimension to the plot in Fig. 4.2 by coloring in
the points for customers whose email address is known to us. To do this, we use
plot() arguments that allow us to draw different colors (col=) and symbols for
the points (pch=). Each argument takes a vector that specifies the option—the color
or symbol—that you want for each individual point. Thus, if we provide a vector
of colors of the same length as the vectors of x and y values, col= will use the
corresponding colors for each point. Constructing such vectors can be tricky, so we
will build them up slowly.

To begin, we first declare vectors for the color and point types that we want to use:

```
> my.col <- c("black", "green3")
> my.pch <- c(1, 19) # R's symbols for solid and open circles (see ?points)
```

We use green3 as a slightly darker shade of green. It is often helpful to review all
the color names in colors() to find such options.

With these defined, we can select the appropriate color and plotting symbol for each
customer simply by using cust.df$email to index them. How does this work?

The factor `email` is converted to a numeric value under the hood (1 for `no` and 2 for `yes`) and then that value is used to select colors.

Let's see how that works (using just the `head()` of the data for brevity). First we see that `email` is a factor, which we could coerce to numeric values:

```
> head(cust.df$email)
[1] yes yes yes yes no  yes
Levels: no yes
> as.numeric(head(cust.df$email))
[1] 2 2 2 2 1 2
```

If we use those numbers to index `my.col` then we get the matching color for each value of `email`:

```
> my.col[as.numeric(head(cust.df$email))]
[1] "green3" "green3" "green3" "green3" "black"  "green3"
```

However, it's tedious (although error-resistant) to write `as.numeric()` all the time, and R understands what we want just by indexing with the factor directly:

```
> my.col[head(cust.df$email)]
[1] "green3" "green3" "green3" "green3" "black"  "green3"
```

Now that we have a vector of colors, we can pass it as the `col` option in `plot()` to get a plot where customers with emails on file are plotted in green and customers without email addresses on file are plotted in black. We use a similar strategy for setting the point styles using the `pch` option, such that customers without email addresses have open circles instead of solid. The complete code is:

```
> plot(cust.df$store.spend, cust.df$online.spend,
+       cex=0.7,
+       col=my.col[cust.df$email], pch=my.pch[cust.df$email],
+       main="Customers as of June 2014",
+       xlab="Prior 12 months in-store sales ($)",
+       ylab="Prior 12 months online sales ($)" )
```

The resulting plot appears in the left panel of Fig. 4.4.

When we created Fig. 4.1 earlier, we used an option `col="blue"` and it turned all of the points blue. This is because if the vector you pass for `col` is shorter than the length of `x` and `y`, then R recycles the values. Thus, if your `col` vector has one element, all the points will be that single color. Similarly, if you were to pass the vector `c("black", "green3")`, then `plot` would simply make alternating points black or green, which might not be what you want. Usually what you'll want is to create a vector that exactly matches the length of your data by starting with a shorter vector as we did here, and then indexing it with `[]` such that you extract a value for each one of your data points. That can be difficult to get right in practice, so we encourage you to experiment with these examples until you understand how it works.

4.2.3 Adding a Legend to a Plot

Given that we've colored some points in our chart, it would be helpful to add a legend that explains the colors. We can do this using `legend()`.

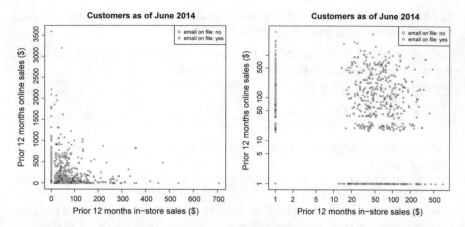

Fig. 4.4 Scatterplots of online sales versus in-store sales by customer. On the left, we see a typical extremely skewed plot using raw sales values; data is grouped along the x and y axes because many customers purchase nothing. On the right, plotting the log() of sales separates zero and non-zero values more clearly, and reveals the association among those who purchase in the two channels (see Sect. 4.2.4)

```
> legend(x="topright", legend=paste("email on file:", levels(cust.df$email)),
+        col=my.col, pch=my.pch)
```

The legend() function can be frustrating, but the idea is relatively simple. The first input to legend() is x=LOCATION, which sets the location of the legend on the plot. Then you specify the legend argument, which is a vector of labels that you want to include in the legend. In the present case, we use paste() to create the labels "email on file: no" and "email on file: yes" by adding the constant string "email on file:" to the factor levels of email. Next, you define the markers to associate with those labels in the legend. Because we defined these with my.col and my.pch, we reuse those here.

Although the code to create the legend is compact, it is a hassle to track the details of labels, colors, and symbols. Our recommendation is to define the argument values in a reusable way as we have done here using definition vectors such as my.col and my.pch. An alternative would be to invest in learning a specialized graphics package such as lattice or ggplot2. Those packages handle legends in more sophisticated ways that we do not explore in depth here (see Sect. 3.7).

4.2.4 Plotting on a Log Scale

With raw values as plotted in the left panel of Fig. 4.4, it is still difficult to see whether there is a different relationship between in-store and online purchases for those with and without emails on file, because of the heavy skew in sales figures. A common solution for such scatterplots with skewed data is to plot the data on a *logarithmic* scale. This is easy to do with the `log=` argument of `plot()`: set `log="x"` to plot the x-axis on the log scale, `log="y"` for the y-axis, or `log="xy"` for both axes.

For `cust.df`, because both online and in-store sales are skewed, we use a log scale for both axes:

```
> plot(cust.df$store.spend + 1, cust.df$online.spend + 1,
+       log="xy", cex=0.7,
+       col=my.col[cust.df$email], pch=my.pch[cust.df$email],
+       main="Customers as of June 2014",
+       xlab="Log of prior 12 months in-store sales ($)",
+       ylab="Log of prior 12 months online sales ($)" )
> legend(x="topright", legend=paste("email on file:", levels(cust.df$email)),
+        col=my.col, pch=my.pch)
```

In this code, we plot ...*spend* + 1 to avoid problems due to the fact that `log(0)` is infinite (in the negative direction). In the right hand side of Fig. 4.4, the axes are now logarithmic; for instance, the distance from 1–10 is the same as 10–100.

On the right-hand panel of Fig. 4.4, it is easy to see a large number of customers with no sales (the points at x=1 or y=1, which correspond to zero sales because we added 1). It now appears that there is little or no association between online and in-store sales; the scatterplot among customers who purchase in both channels shows no pattern. Thus, there is no evidence here to suggest that online sales have cannabalized in-store sales (a formal test of that would be complex, but the present data do not argue for such an effect in any obvious way).

We also see in Fig. 4.4 that customers with no email address on file show slightly lower online sales than those with addresses; there are somewhat more black circles in the lower half of the plot than the upper half. If we have been sending email promotions to customers, then this suggests that the promotions might be working. An experiment to confirm that hypothesis could be an appropriate next step.

Did it take work to produce the final plot on the right side of Fig. 4.4? Yes, but the result shows how a well-crafted scatterplot can present a lot of information about relationships in data. Looking at the right-hand panel of Fig. 4.4, we have a much better understanding of how online and offline sales are related to each other, and whether each relates to having customers' email status.

4.3 Combining Plots in a Single Graphics Object

Sometimes we want to visualize several relationships at once. For instance, suppose we wish to examine whether customers who live closer to stores spend more in store, and whether those who live further away spend more online. Those involve different spending variables and thus need separate plots. If we plot several such things individually, we end up with many individual charts. Luckily, R can produce a single graphic that consists of multiple plots. You do this by telling R that you want multiple plots in a single graphical object with the `par(mfrow=...)` command; then simply plot each one with `plot()` as usual.

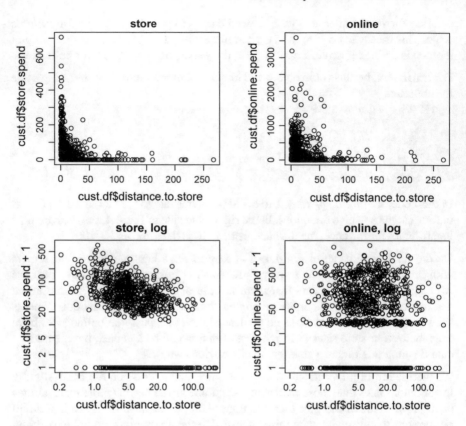

Fig. 4.5 A single graphic object consisting of multiple plots shows that distance to store is related to in-store spending, but seems to be unrelated to online spending. The relationships are easier to see when spending and distance are plotted on a log scale using log="xy" in the two lower panels

It is easiest to see how this works with an example:

```
> par(mfrow=c(2, 2))
> plot(cust.df$distance.to.store, cust.df$store.spend, main="store")
> plot(cust.df$distance.to.store, cust.df$online.spend, main="online")
> plot(cust.df$distance.to.store, cust.df$store.spend+1, log="xy",
+      main="store, log")
> plot(cust.df$distance.to.store, cust.df$online.spend+1, log="xy",
+      main="online, log")
```

Instead of four separate plots from the individual plot() commands, this code produces a single graphic with four panels as shown in Fig. 4.5. The first line sets the graphical parameter mfrow to c(2, 2), which instructs R to create a single graphic comprising a two by two arrangement of plots, which begins on the first row and moves from left to right.

Although the plots in Fig. 4.5 are not completely labelled, we see in the lower left panel that there may be a negative relationship between customers' distances to the nearest store and *in-store* spending. Customers who live further from their nearest store spend less in store. However, on the lower right, we don't see an obvious relationship between distance and *online* spending.

After using `par(mfrow=)`, you can return to a single plot layout with `par(mfrow=c(1,1))`.

4.4 Scatterplot Matrices

4.4.1 *pairs()*

In our customer data, we have a number of variables that might be associated with each other; `age`, `distance.to.store`, and `email` all might be related to online and offline transactions and to spending. When you have several variables such as these, it is good practice to examine scatterplots between all pairs of variables before moving on to more complex analyses.

To do this, R provides the convenient function `pairs(formula, data)`, which makes a separate scatterplot for every combination of variables:

```
> pairs(formula = ~ age + credit.score + email +
+                   distance.to.store + online.visits + online.trans +
+                   online.spend + store.trans + store.spend,
+        data=cust.df)
```

The first input to `pairs` is a formula listing the variables to include from a data frame. Formulas are used in many R functions and we describe more about them in Chaps. 5 and 7. For now it is sufficient to know that in `pairs()`, the formula is composed with a ~ followed by the variables to include, separated by +. If you want to transform a variable, include the math in the formula. For example, to plot the `log()` of `online.spend`, you would include `log(online.spend)` in the formula.

The second input is `data=cust.df`, which tells `pairs` that we want to use the `cust.df` data frame as the source of data for the plot.

The resulting plot is shown in Fig. 4.6 and is called a *scatterplot matrix*. Each position in this matrix shows a scatterplot between two variables as noted in the diagonal for each row and column. For example, the plot in the second row and third column is a scatterplot of `cust.df$age` on the y-axis versus `cust.df$distance.to.store` on the x-axis.

We can see relationships between variables quickly in a scatterplot matrix. In the fifth row and sixth column we see a strong linear association between `online.visits` and `online.trans`; customers who visit the website more frequently make more online transactions. Looking quickly over the plot, we also see that customers with a higher number of online transactions have higher total online spending (not a surprise), and similarly, customers with more in-store transactions also spend more in-store. This simple command produced a lot of information to consider.

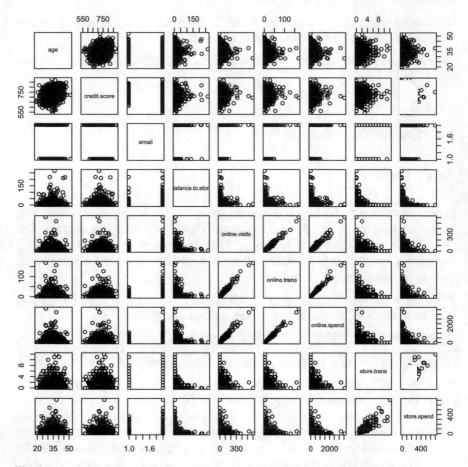

Fig. 4.6 A scatterplot matrix for the customer data set produced using pairs()

In addition to using the formula notation above, it is also possible to pass a data frame directly to pairs and when you do that, pairs() creates a scatterplot matrix including all the columns in your data frame. In the code below, we select columns 2–10 from cust.df and pass the resulting data frame to pairs, which gives us the same plot as shown in Fig. 4.6:

```
> pairs(cust.df[ , c(2:10)])    # chart not printed; same as above
```

While this results in compact code, we recommend instead to use the formula version as shown above; it is robust to future changes in cust.df that might re-order the columns. Over time, it becomes a habit to think about how your R code might be re-used in the future.

4.4.2 *scatterplotMatrix()*

Scatterplot matrices are so useful for data exploration that several add-on packages offer additional versions them. We want to point out two other scatterplot matrix functions that we find valuable. The `scatterplotMatrix()` function in the `car` package (abbreviating "*c*ompanion to *a*pplied *r*egression" [62]) adds a number of features over `pairs()`, including adding smoothed lines on scatterplots and univariate density plots on the diagonal. The syntax for `scatterplotMatrix()` is similar to `pairs()`:

```
> library(car)     # install if needed
> scatterplotMatrix(formula = ~ age + credit.score + email +
+                     distance.to.store + online.visits + online.trans +
+                     online.spend + store.trans + store.spend,
+                   data=cust.df)
```

In Fig. 4.7, we have density plots on the diagonal that show us the distribution of each variable, where it is easy to see that all of the numeric variables except `age`

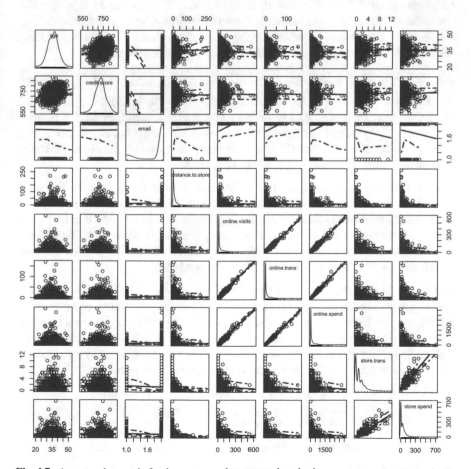

Fig. 4.7 A scatterplot matrix for the customer data set produced using `scatterplotMatrix()`

and `credit.score` are highly left skewed. The solid lines show linear fit lines (see Chap. 7), while the dotted lines show smoothed fit lines with confidence intervals. The smoothed lines on the bivariate scatterplots suggest the extent to which associations are linear. For instance, the smoothed line on the plot of `age` versus `distance.to.store` is nearly flat and shows that there is no linear association between those variables.

A limitation of Figs. 4.6 and 4.7 concerns the display of the `email` variable. `email` is a binary factor with values `yes` and `no`, and a scatterplot is not ideal to visualize a discrete variable. You will wish to keep those limitations in mind when interpreting the plots.

4.5 Correlation Coefficients

Although scatterplots provide a lot of visual information, when there are more than a few variables, it can be helpful to assess the relationship between each pair with a single number. One measure of the relationship between two variables is the *covariance*, which can be computed for any two variables using the `cov` function:

```
> cov(cust.df$age, cust.df$credit.score)
[1] 63.23443
```

If values x_i and y_i tend to go in the same direction—to be both higher or both lower than their respective means—across observations, then they have a positive covariance. If $cov(x, y)$ is zero, then there is no (linear) association between x_i and y_i. Negative covariance means that the variables go in opposite directions relative to their means: when x_i is lower, y_i tends to be higher.

However, it difficult to interpret the magnitude of covariance because the scale depends on the variables involved. Covariance will be different if the variables are measured in cents versus dollars or in inches versus centimeters. So, it is helpful to scale the covariance by the standard deviation for each variable, which results in a standardized, rescaled *correlation coefficient* known as the *Pearson product-moment correlation coefficient*, often abbreviated as the symbol r.

Pearson's r is a continuous metric that falls in the range $[-1, +1]$. It is $+1$ in the case of a perfect positive linear association between the two variables, and -1 for perfect negative linear association. If there is little or no linear association, r will be near 0. On a scatterplot, data with $r = 1$ or $r = -1$ would have all points along a straight line (up or down, respectively). This makes r an easily interpreted metric to assess whether two variables have a close linear association or not.

In R, we compute correlation coefficient r with the `cor()` function:

```
> cor(cust.df$age, cust.df$credit.score)
[1] 0.2545045
```

r is identical to rescaling the covariance by the joint standard deviations (but more convenient):

```
> cov(cust.df$age, cust.df$credit.score) /
+ (sd(cust.df$age)*sd(cust.df$credit.score))
[1] 0.2545045
```

What value of *r* signifies an *important* correlation between two variables in marketing? In engineering and physical sciences, physical measurements may demonstrate extremely high correlations; for instance, *r* between the lengths and weights of pieces of steel rod might be 0.9, 0.95, or even 0.999, depending on the uniformity of the rods and the precision of measurement. However, in social sciences such as marketing, we are concerned with human behavior, which is less consistent and more difficult to measure. This results in lower correlations, but they are still important.

We often use *Cohen's Rules of Thumb*, which come out of the psychology tradition [34]. Cohen proposed that for correlations between variables describing people, $r = 0.1$ should be considered a *small* or *weak* association, $r = 0.3$ might be considered to be *medium* in strength, and $r = 0.5$ or higher could be considered to be *large* or *strong*. Cohen's interpretation of a *large* effect was that such an association would be easily noticed by casual observers. A *small* effect would require careful measurement to detect yet might be important to our understanding and to statistical models.

Importantly, interpretation of *r* according to Cohen's rules of thumb depends on the assumption that the variables are *normally distributed* (also known as *Gaussian*) or are approximately so. If the variables are not normal, but instead follow a logarithmic or other distribution that is skewed or strongly non-normal in shape, then these thresholds do not apply. In those cases, it can be helpful to transform your variables to normal distributions before interpreting, as we discuss in Sect. 4.5.3 below.

4.5.1 Correlation Tests

In the code above, cor(age, credit.score) shows $r = 0.25$, a medium-sized effect by Cohen's standard. Is this also statistically significant? We can use the function cor.test() to find out:

```
> cor.test(cust.df$age, cust.df$credit.score)
    Pearson's product-moment correlation

data:  cust.df$age and cust.df$credit.score t = 8.3138, df = 998,
p-value = 3.008e-16 alternative\index{P-value} hypothesis:
true correlation is not equal to 0 95 percent confidence
interval\index{Confidence interval}:
 0.1955974 0.3115816
sample estimates:
      cor
0.2545045
```

This tells us that $r = 0.25$ and the 95% confidence interval is $r = 0.196 - 0.312$. Because the confidence interval for *r* does not include 0 (and thus has p-value of $p < 0.05$), the association is statistically significant. Such a correlation, showing a medium-sized effect and statistical significance, probably should not be ignored in subsequent analyses (for more about that problem, known as *collinearity*, see Sect. 9.1).

4.5.2   Correlation Matrices

For more than two variables, you can compute the correlations between all pairs
x, y at once as a *correlation matrix*. Such a matrix shows $r = 1.0$ on the diagonal
because $cor(x, x) = 1$. It is also symmetric; $cor(x, y) = cor(y, x)$. We compute a
correlation matrix by passing multiple variables to `cor()`:

```
> cor(cust.df[, c(2, 3, 5:12)])
                          age credit.score distance.to.store online.visits
age                1.000000000   0.254504457        0.00198741   -0.06138107
credit.score       0.254504457   1.000000000       -0.02326418   -0.01081827
distance.to.store  0.001987410  -0.023264183        1.00000000   -0.01460036
online.visits     -0.061381070  -0.010818272       -0.01460036    1.00000000
online.trans      -0.063019935  -0.005018400       -0.01955166    0.98732805
online.spend      -0.060685729  -0.006079881       -0.02040533    0.98240684
store.trans        0.024229708   0.040424158       -0.27673229   -0.03666932
store.spend        0.003841953   0.042298123       -0.24149487   -0.05068554
sat.service                 NA            NA                NA            NA
sat.selection               NA            NA                NA            NA
                  online.trans online.spend store.trans  store.spend
age               -0.06301994  -0.060685729  0.02422971  0.003841953
credit.score      -0.00501840  -0.006079881  0.04042416  0.042298123
...
```

In the second column of the first row, we see that `cor(age, credit.store)` =
`0.254` as above. We can easily scan to find other large correlations; for instance, the
correlation between `store.trans, distance.to.store` = -0.277, showing
that people who live further from a store tend to have fewer in-store transactions.
`cor()` did not compute correlations for `sat.selection` and `sat.service`
because they have some NA values. The argument `use="complete.obs"` would
instruct R to use only cases without NA values; try it for practice.

Rather than requiring one to scan a matrix of numbers, the `corrplot` package
charts correlation matrices nicely with `corrplot()` and `corrplot.mixed()`:

```
> library(corrplot)     # for correlation plot, install if needed
> library(gplots)       # color interpolation, install if needed
> corrplot.mixed(corr=cor(cust.df[ , c(2, 3, 5:12)], use="complete.obs"),
+                upper="ellipse", tl.pos="lt",
+                upper.col = colorpanel(50, "red", "gray60", "blue4"))
```

The resulting graphic is shown in Fig. 4.8. We will explain the code and features
of the plot. The main argument to `corrplot.mixed` is a correlation matrix and
we use `cor(..., use="complete.obs")` to provide this, excluding the NA
values.

In Fig. 4.8, numeric values of r are shown in the lower triangle of the matrix. The upper
triangle displays ellipses (because we used the argument `upper="ellipse"`).
These ellipses are tighter, progressively closer to being lines, for larger values of
r, and are rounder, more like circles for r near zero. They are also shaded blue for
positive direction, and red for negative (and show corresponding positive or negative
slope).

This makes it easy to find the larger correlations in the data: `age` is positively
correlated with `credit.score`; `distance.to.store` is negatively correlated
with `store.trans` and `store.spend`; `online.visits`, `online.trans`,
and `online.spend` are all strongly correlated with one another, as are `store`.

Fig. 4.8 A correlation plot produced using `corrplot.mixed()` from the `corrplot` package is an easy way to visualize all of the correlations in the data. Correlations close to zero are plotted as circular and gray (using the color scheme we specified), while magnitudes away from zero produce ellipses that are increasingly tighter and blue for positive correlation and red for negative

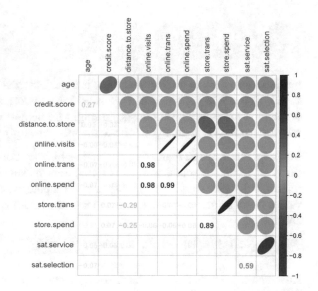

trans and `store.spend`. In the survey items, `sat.service` is positively correlated with `sat.selection`.

`corrplot.mixed()` has numerous options that let you customize a chart. For this plot, we use the options `upper="ellipse"` to visualize the correlations as ellipses and `tl.pos="lt"` to place the variable name labels on the left and top of the matrix. The correlations in this case are mostly small in magnitude, which produces a very light chart with the default colors. We use `colorpanel()` from the `gplots` package to generate a set of colors anchored at 3 points ("red", "gray60", and "blue4") and tell `corrplot.mixed()` to use that set of colors instead of its default. You could try other colors and see how the plot is affected; the `colors()` command will list all the names of colors that R understands.

While it is impossible to draw strong conclusions based on associations such as Fig. 4.8, finding large correlations should inform subsequent analysis or suggest hypotheses.

4.5.3 Transforming Variables Before Computing Correlations

Correlation coefficient r measures the *linear* association between two variables. If the relationship between two variables is not linear, it would be misleading to interpret r. For example, if we create a random variable that ranges from -10 to 10—using `runif()` to sample random uniform values—and then compute the correlation between that variable and its square, we get a correlation close to zero:

```
> set.seed(49931)
> x <- runif(1000, min=-10, max=10)
> cor(x, x^2)
[1] -0.003674254
```

r is near zero despite the fact that there is a perfect *nonlinear* relationship between x and x^2. So, it is important that we consider transformations before assessing the correlation between two variables. (It might be helpful to plot x and x^2 by typing plot(x, x^2), so that you can see the relationship.)

Many relationships in marketing data are nonlinear. For example, as we see in the cust.df data, the number of trips a customer makes to a store may be *inversely* related to distance from the store. When we compute the correlation between the raw values of distance.to.store and store.spend, we get a modest negative correlation:

```
> cor(cust.df$distance.to.store, cust.df$store.spend)
[1] -0.2414949
```

However, if we transform distance.to.store to its *inverse* ($1/distance$), we find a much stronger association:

```
> cor(1/cust.df$distance.to.store, cust.df$store.spend)
[1] 0.4329997
```

In fact, the inverse square root of distance shows an even greater association:

```
> cor(1/sqrt(cust.df$distance.to.store), cust.df$store.spend)
[1] 0.4843334
```

How do we interpret this? Because of the inverse *square root* relationship, someone who lives 1 mile from the nearest store will spend quite a bit more than someone who lives 5 miles away, yet someone who lives 20 miles away will only buy a little bit more than someone who lives 30 miles away.

These transformations are important when creating scatterplots between variables as well. For example, examine the scatterplots in Fig. 4.9 for raw distance.to. fRcstore versus store.spend, as compared to the inverse square root of distance.to.store versus store.spend. We create those two charts as follows:

```
> plot(cust.df$distance.to.store, cust.df$store.spend)
> plot(1/sqrt(cust.df$distance.to.store), cust.df$store.spend)
```

The association between distance and spending is much clearer with the transformed data as shown in the right-hand panel of Fig. 4.9.

To review, it is important to consider transforming variables to approximate normality before computing correlations or creating scatterplots; the appropriate transformation may help you to see associations more clearly. As we noted in Sect. 4.5, interpretation of r with rules of thumb requires data to be approximately normal.

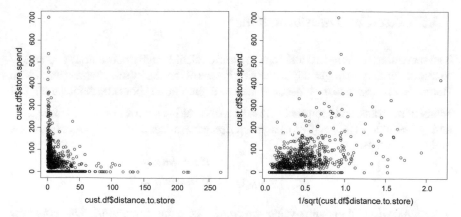

Fig. 4.9 A transformation of `distance.to.store` to its inverse square root makes the association with `store.trans` more apparent in the right-hand chart, as compared to the original values on the left

4.5.4 Typical Marketing Data Transformations

Considering all the possible transforms may seem impossible, but because marketing data often concerns the same kinds of data in different data sets—counts, sales, revenue, and so forth—there are a few common transformations that often apply. For example, as we discussed when simulating the data for Chap. 3, unit sales are often related to the logarithm of price.

In Table 4.1, we list common transformations that are often helpful with different types of marketing variables.

For most purposes, these standard transformations are appropriate and theoretically sound. However, when these transformations don't work or you want to determine the very best transformation, there is a general-purpose transformation function that can be used instead, and we describe that next.

Table 4.1 Common transformations of variables in marketing

Variable	Common transform
Unit sales, revenue, household income, price	$log(x)$
Distance	$1/x$, $1/x^2$, $log(x)$
Market or preference share based on a utility value (Sect. 9.2.1)	$\frac{e^x}{1+e^x}$
Right-tailed distributions (generally)	$\sqrt{x}$ or $log(x)$ (watch out for $log(x \leq 0)$)
Left-tailed distributions (generally)	x^2

4.5.5 Box-Cox Transformations*

The remaining sections in the chapter are optional, although important. If you're new to this material, you might skip to the Key Points at the end of this chapter (Sect. 4.7). Remember to return to these sections later and learn more about correlation analysis!

Many of the transformations in Table 4.1 involve taking a power of x: x^2, $1/x = x^{-1}$, and $\sqrt{x} = x^{-0.5}$. The *Box-Cox transformation* generalizes this use of power functions and is defined as:

$$y_i^{(lambda)} \begin{cases} = \frac{y_i^{lambda}-1}{lambda} & \text{if } lambda \neq 0 \\ = log(y_i) & \text{if } lambda = 0 \end{cases} \tag{4.1}$$

where *lambda* can take any value and *log* is the natural logarithm. One could try different values of *lambda* to see which transformation makes the distribution best fit the normal distribution. (We will see in Chap. 7 that it is also common to use transformed data that makes a linear regression have normally distributed residuals.) Because transformed data is more approximately normal, it is more suitable to assess the strength of association using the rules of thumb for r (Sect. 4.5).

Instead of trying values of *lambda* by hand, there is an automatic way to find the optimal value: use the `powerTransform(object=DATA)` function. We find the best Box-Cox transformation for `distance.to.store` using `powerTransform()` as follows:

```
> library(car)
> powerTransform(cust.df$distance.to.store)
Estimated transformation parameters
cust.df$distance.to.store
            -0.003696395
```

This tells us that that the value of *lambda* to make distance as similar as possible to a normal distribution is -0.003696. We extract that value of `lambda` using using the `coef()` function and create the transformed variable using `bcPower(U=DATA, lambda)`:

```
> lambda <- coef(powerTransform(1/cust.df$distance.to.store))
> bcPower(cust.df$distance.to.store, lambda)
   [1]   0.950421270   3.902743543   0.251429693   1.664085284   3.239908993
   [6]   2.931485684   2.243992143   1.940984081   2.565290889   1.896458754
  [11]   1.898262423   0.411047042   4.101597125   1.359172873   3.8973383223
...
```

To see how this changes `cust.df$distance.to.store`, we plot two histograms comparing the transformed and untransformed variables:

```
> par(mfrow=c(1,2))
> hist(cust.df$distance.to.store,
+       xlab="Distance to Nearest Store", ylab="Count of Customers",
+       main="Original Distribution")
> hist(bcPower(cust.df$distance.to.store, lambda),
+       xlab="Box-Cox Transform of Distance", ylab="Count of Customers",
+       main="Transformed Distribution")
```

The resulting graphs in Fig. 4.10 shows the highly skewed original distribution on the left and the transformed distribution on the right, which is much approximately normally distributed.

Fig. 4.10 A Box-Cox transformation of `distance.to.store` makes the distribution closer to Normal

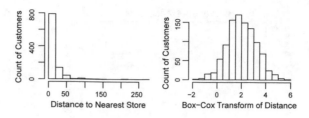

If you attempt to transform a variable that is already close to normally distributed, `powerTransform()` will report a value of `lambda` that is close to 1. For example, if we find the Box-Cox transform for `age`, we get `lambda` very close to 1, suggesting that a transformation is not required:

```
> powerTransform(cust.df$age)
Estimated transformation parameters
cust.df$age
1.036142
```

Finally, we can compute correlations for the transformed variable. These correlations will often be larger in magnitude than correlations among raw, untransformed data points. We check *r* between distance and in-store spending, transforming both of them first:

```
> l.dist  <- coef(powerTransform(cust.df$distance.to.store))
> l.spend <- coef(powerTransform(cust.df$store.spend+1))
>
> cor(bcPower(cust.df$distance.to.store, l.dist),
+     bcPower(cust.df$store.spend+1, l.spend))
[1] -0.4683126
```

The relationship between distance to the store and spending can be interpreted as strong and negative.

In practice, you could consider Box-Cox transformations on all variables with skewed distributions before computing correlations or creating scatterplots. This will increase the chances that you will find and interpret important associations between variables.

4.6 Exploring Associations in Survey Responses

Many marketing data sets include variables where customers provide ratings on a discrete scale, such as a 5- or 7-point rating scale. These are *ordinal* (ranked) variables and it can be a bit tricky to assess associations among them. For instance, in the `cust.df` data, we have response on a 5-point scale for two satisfaction items, satisfaction with the retailer's service and with the retailer's product selection.

What is the problem? Consider a simple `plot()` of the two 5-point items:

```
> plot(cust.df$sat.service, cust.df$sat.selection,
+      xlab="Customer Satisfaction with Service",
+      ylab="Customer Satisfaction with Selection",
+      main="Customers as of June 2014")
```

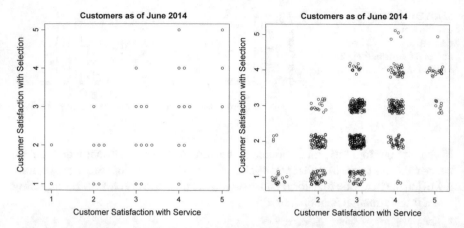

Fig. 4.11 A scatter plot of responses on a survey scale (left) is not very informative. Using jitter (right) makes the plot more informative and reveals the number of observations for each pair of response values

The resulting plot shown in the left-hand panel of Fig. 4.11 is not very informative. Because `cust.df$sat.service` and `cust.df$sat.selection` only take integer values from 1 to 5, the points for customers who gave the same responses are drawn on top of each other. The main thing we learn from this plot is that customers reported most of the possible pairs of values, except that ratings rarely showed a difference between the two items of 3 or more points (there were no pairs for (1, 4), (1, 5), (5, 2), or a few other combinations).

This poses a problem both for visualization and, as it turns out, for assessing the strength of association. We'll see next how to improve the visualization.

4.6.1 *jitter()*

One way to make a plot of ordinal values more informative is to *jitter* each variable, adding a small amount of random noise to each response. This moves the points away from each other and reveals how many responses occur at each combination of (*x*, *y*) values.

R provides the function `jitter()` to do this:

```
> plot(jitter(cust.df$sat.service), jitter(cust.df$sat.selection),
+       xlab="Customer Satisfaction with Service",
+       ylab="Customer Satisfaction with Selection",
+       main="Customers as of June 2014")
```

The result is shown in the right-hand panel of Fig. 4.11, where it is easier to see that the ratings (3, 2) and (3, 3) were the most common responses. It is now clear that there is a positive relationship between the two satisfaction variables. People who are more satisfied with selection tend to be more satisfied with service.

4.6.2 *polychoric()**

The constrained observations from ratings scales affect assessment of correlation with metrics such as Pearson's *r* because the number of available scale points constrains the potential range and specificity of *r*. An alternative to the simple computation of *r* is a *polychoric* correlation coefficient, which is designed specifically for ordinal responses.

The concept of a polychoric correlation is that respondents have continuous values in mind when they answer on a rating scale. However, because the scales are limited to a small number of points, respondents must select discrete values and choose points on the scale that are closest to the unobserved latent continuous values. The polychoric estimate attempts to recover the correlations between the hypothetical latent (unobserved) continuous variables.

We examine whether the sat.service survey item is associated with sat. selection. Because we have responses for only some customers, we set an index vector resp to identify the customers with responses to examine. Then we look at the *r* correlation coefficient from cor():

```
> resp <- !is.na(cust.df$sat.service)
> cor(cust.df$sat.service[resp], cust.df$sat.selection[resp])
[1] 0.5878558
```

To compute the polychoric correlation coefficient, we use polychoric() from the psych package:

```
> library(psych)
> polychoric(cbind(cust.df$sat.service[resp],
+                   cust.df$sat.selection[resp]))
Call: polychoric(x = cbind(cust.df$sat.service[resp], cust.df$sat.selection[
     resp]))
Polychoric correlations
     C1   C2
R1 1.00
R2 0.62 1.00

 with tau of
       1      2     3    4
[1,] -1.83 -0.72 0.54 1.7
[2,] -0.99  0.12 1.26 2.4
# warning omitted (caused by simulated data's lack of error)
```

This is somewhat more complex information than the simple output of cor(). At the top of the output, polychoric() reports the polychoric correlation matrix. The values range [−1, 1] and are interpreted in the same way as Pearson's *r*. (In fact, they are the values of Pearson's *r* between the estimated latent continuous variables.) In our satisfaction data, we can see that the polychoric correlation is quite high at *rho* = 0.62. Like cor(), polychoric() can produce a correlation matrix for multiple variables.

The second output section under "with a tau of" describes how the estimated latent scores are mapped to the discrete item values. For each variable (in our case just two), there are 4 *cut points*: if a customer's latent satisfaction is below the first cut point, the survey response is the first value on the scale (i.e., 1). For latent scores between the 1th and 2th cut points, the survey response is the second value (2), and so forth. Reviewing the cut points can be informative about how the scale is performing and whether it has adequate discrimination of responses versus the estimated latent scores.

4.7   Key Points

Following are some of the important points to consider when analyzing relationships between variables.

Visualization

- `plot(x, y)` creates scatterplots where x is a vector of x-values to be plotted and y is a vector of the same length with y-values (Sect. 4.2.1.)
- When preparing a plot for others, the plot should be labeled carefully using arguments such as `xlab`, `ylab` and `main`, so that the reader can easily understand the graphic (Sect. 4.2.1.)
- You can color-code a plot by passing a vector of color names or color numbers as the `col` parameter in `plot()` (Sect. 4.2.2).
- Use the `legend()` command to add a legend so that readers will know what your color coding means (Sect. 4.2.3).
- The `cex=` argument is helpful to adjust point sizes on a scatterplot (Sect. 4.2.1)
- A scatterplot matrix is a good way to visualize associations among several variables at once; options include `pairs()` (Sect. 4.4.1) and `scatterplotMatrix()` from the `cars` package (Sect. 4.4.2).
- Many functions such as `plot()` call a *generic function* that determines what to do based on the type of data. When a plotting function does something unexpected, checking data types with `str()` will often reveal the problem (Sect. 4.2.1).
- When variables are highly skewed, it is often helpful to draw the axes on a logarithmic scale using the by setting the `log` argument of the `plot()` function to `log="x"`, `log="y"`, or `log="xy"` (Sect. 4.2.4). Alternatively, the variables might be transformed to a more interpretable distribution (Sect. 4.5.3).

Statistics

- `cor(x, y)` computes the Pearson correlation coefficient r between variables x and y. This measures the strength of the linear relationship between the variables (Sect. 4.5).
- `cor()` will produce a correlation matrix when it is passed several or many variables. A handy way to visualize these is with the `corrplot` package (Sect. 4.5.2).
- `cor.test()` assesses statistical significance and reports the confidence interval for r (Sect. 4.5.1).
- For many kinds of marketing data, the magnitude of r may be interpreted by Cohen's rules of thumb ($r=0.1$ is a weak association, $r=0.3$ is medium, and $r=0.5$ is strong), although this assumes that the data are approximately normal in distribution (Sect. 4.5).

- When the relationship between two variables is nonlinear, r does not give an accurate assessment of the association. Computing r between transformed variables may make associations more apparent (Sect. 4.5.3.)
- There are common distributions that often occur in marketing, such as unit sales being related to $log(price)$. Before modeling associations, plot histograms of your variables and assess potential transformations of them (Sect. 4.5.4).
- An automated way to select an optimal transformation is to use a Box-Cox transform (Sect. 4.5.5).
- The function `polychor()` from the `psych` package is useful to compute correlations between survey responses on ordinal ratings scales (Sect. 4.6.2).

4.8 Data Sources

The data set in this chapter is typical of a customer table that might be compiled from several sources. Store purchase data could be gathered from a point of sale (POS) transaction system, where the consumer is identified via a loyalty card, telephone number, or similar identification. Online data might be gathered from an e-commerce site, with identification by email address. Satisfaction data could be collected in a survey platform, and recruited through an email broadcast to customers. Commonly, there would be a unified table such as "accounts" that holds all of the identifiers for a customer—email address, an internal account number, phone number, name, and so forth—so the data may be cross-referenced. As an aside, when combining such data, take care not to include personal identifiers in the final data sets unless it is necessary; use internal account numbers instead (or, ideally, disguised or encrypted versions of them).

In a typical system, these data would be in different locations: a POS system for the stores, a web database for online sales, and a survey platform such as Qualtrics for the survey data. An analyst would then *join* the data on the basis of the common user identifiers in the "accounts" table to compile a unified data set. The details of how to perform such data operations are outside our scope, except to note that they might be performed in R using the `merge()` function, or performed separately with SQL `SELECT ... JOIN` commands (see Appendix C.1.4). We assume here that the in-store, online, and survey data have already been combined into a single data set.

4.9 Learning More*

Plotting. As we mentioned at the end of Chap. 3, plotting in R is a complete topic and the subject of several books. We've demonstrated fundamental plotting methods that work for many analyses. Those who do a great deal of plotting or need to produce high-quality graphics for presentation might consider learning `ggplot2` [198] or `lattice` [173].

Correlation analysis. The analysis of variable associations is important for several reasons: it often reveals interesting patterns, it is relatively straightforward to interpret, and it is the simplest case of multivariate analysis. Despite the apparent simplicity there are numerous issues to consider, some of which we have considered here. A classic text for learning about correlation analysis in depth and how to perform it well while avoiding pitfalls, is Cohen, Cohen, and West (2003), *Applied Multiple Regression/Correlation Analysis for the Behavioral Sciences* [36], although it is not specific to R.

Analyzing survey scale responses. Much of the data in that we analyze in marketing involves customers' responses to survey ratings scales, and in Sect. 4.6.2 we mentioned some of the challenges with such ordinal response data. Although `polychor()` is a useful tool when analyzing survey data, there are other advanced options. For example, the `bayesm` package [167] provides the function `rscaleUsage()`, which estimates differences in how each customer uses a scale (see also the material on scale usage in Rossi et al. [168]). Using `bayesm` requires knowledge of Bayesian methods, which we introduce in Chap. 5.

4.10   Exercises

The following exercises use the e-commerce data set as described in Sect. 3.8.1.

1. The e-commerce data set (Sect. 3.8.1) includes the number of visits a user made to the site (`behavNumVisits`). Plot this using a histogram, and then again by plotting a table of frequencies. Which plot is a better starting place for visualization, and why?
2. Adjust the table plot from the previous exercise to improve it. Use logarithmic values for the numbers of visits instead of raw counts, and add a chart title and axis labels.
3. The default Y axis on the previous plot is somewhat misleading. Why? Remove the default Y axis, and replace it with better labels. (Note: for logarithmic values, labels that begin with digits 1, 2, and 5—such as 1, 2, 5, 10, 20, 50, etc.—may be useful.) Make the Y axis readable for all labels.
4. The variable `behavPageViews` is a factor variable, but we might like to do computations on the number of views. Create a new variable `pageViewInt` that is an integer estimate of the number of page views for each row, and add it to `ecomm.df`. Be conservative with the estimates; for example, when the data say "10+" views, code only as many as are indicated with confidence.
5. Plot a histogram of the newly added integer estimate of page views (`pageViewInt`).

Site visits and page views. For the next several exercises, we consider whether frequent visitors are likely to view more pages on the site. It is plausible to think that frequent visitors might view more pages in a session because they are more engaged users, or that frequent visitors would view fewer pages because they are more familiar with the site. We will see what the data suggest.

6. For a first exploration, make a scatterplot for the integer estimate of page views vs. the number of site visits. Should number of visits be on a log scale? Why or why not?
7. There are only a few values of X and Y in the previous plot. Adjust the plot to visualize more clearly the frequencies occurring at each point on the plot.
8. What is the Pearson's r correlation coefficient between number of visits and the integer estimate of page views? What is the correlation if you use log of visits instead?
9. Is the correlation from the previous exercise statistically significant?
10. Is Pearson's r a good estimate for the relationship of these two variables? Why or why not?
11. *What is the polychoric correlation coefficient between number of visits and integer page views? Is it a better estimate than Pearson's r in this case?
12. Overall, what do you conclude about the relationship between the number of times a user has visited the site and the number of page views in a given session?

Salaries data. For the remaining exercises, we use the `Salaries` data from the `car` package.

13. How do you load the `Salaries` data from the car package? (Hint: review the `data()` function.) Within R itself, how can you find out more detail about the `Salaries` data set?
14. Using the `Salaries` data, create scatterplot matrix plots using two different plotting functions. Which do you prefer and why?
15. Which are the numeric variables in the `Salaries` data set? Create a correlation plot for them, with correlation coefficients in one area of the plot. Which two variables are most closely related?

Chapter 5
Comparing Groups: Tables and Visualizations

Marketing analysts often investigate differences between groups of people. Do men or women subscribe to our service at a higher rate? Which demographic segment can best afford our product? Does the product appeal more to homeowners or renters? The answers help us to understand the market, to target customers effectively, and to evaluate the outcome of marketing activities such as promotions.

Such questions are not confined to differences among people; similar questions are asked of many other kinds of groups. One might be interested to group data by geography: does Region A perform better than Region B? Or time period: did same-store sales increase after a promotion such as a mailer or a sale? In all such cases, we are comparing one group of data to another to identify an effect.

In this chapter, we examine the kinds of comparisons that often arise in marketing, with data that illustrates a consumer segmentation project. We review R procedures to find descriptive summaries by groups, and then visualize the data in several ways.

5.1 Simulating Consumer Segment Data

We begin by creating a data set that exemplifies a consumer segmentation project. For this example, we are offering a subscription-based service (such as cable television or membership in a warehouse club) and have collected data from N = 300 respondents on *age, gender, income, number of children*, whether they *own or rent* their homes, and whether they currently *subscribe* to the offered service or not. We use this data in several later chapters as well.

In this data, each respondent has been assigned to one of four consumer segments: "Suburb mix," "Urban hip," "Travelers," or "Moving up." (In this chapter we do not address *how* such segments might be created; we just presume to know them. We look at how to cluster respondents in Chap. 11.)

© Springer Nature Switzerland AG 2019
C. Chapman and E. M. Feit, *R For Marketing Research and Analytics*, Use R!,
https://doi.org/10.1007/978-3-030-14316-9_5

Segmentation data is moderately complex and we separate our code into three parts:

1. Definition of the data structure: the demographic variables (age, gender, and so forth) plus the segment names and sizes.
2. Parameters for the distributions of demographic variables, such as the mean and variance of each.
3. Code that iterates over the segments and variables to draw random values according to those definitions and parameters.

By organizing the code this way, it becomes easy to change some aspect of the simulation to draw data again. For instance, if we wanted to add a segment or change the mean of one of the demographic variables, only minor change to the code would be required. We also use this structure to teach new R commands that appear in the third step to generate the data.

If you wish to load the data directly, it is available from the book's web site:

```
> seg.df <- read.csv("http://goo.gl/qw303p")
> summary(seg.df)
      age            gender         income             kids          ownHome
 Min.   :19.26   Female:157   Min.   : -5183   Min.   :0.00   ownNo :159
 1st Qu.:33.01   Male  :143   1st Qu.: 39656   1st Qu.:0.00   ownYes:141
 ...
```

However, we recommend that you at least read the data generation sections. We teach important R language skills—looping and if() statements—in Sects. 5.1.2 and 5.1.3.

5.1.1 Segment Data Definition

Our first step is to define general characteristics of the dataset: the variable names, data types, segment names, and sample size for each segment:

```
> segVars <- c("age", "gender", "income", "kids", "ownHome", "subscribe")
> segVarType <- c("norm", "binom", "norm", "pois", "binom", "binom")
> segNames <- c("Suburb mix", "Urban hip", "Travelers", "Moving up")
> segSize <- c(100, 50, 80, 70)
```

The first variable segVars specifies and names the variables to create. segVar Type defines what kind of data will be present in each of those variables: normal data (continuous), binomial (yes/no), or Poisson (counts). Next we name the four segments with the variable segNames and specify the number of observations to generate in each segment (segSize). For instance, looking at the first entry in segNames and segSize, the code says that we will create N = 100 observations (as specified by segSize[1]) for the "Suburb mix" segment (named by segNames[1]).

Although those variables are enough to determine the *structure* of the data set—the number of rows (observations) and columns (demographic variables and segment assignment)—they do not yet describe the *values* of the data. The second step is to define those values. We do this by specifying distributional parameters such as the mean for each variable within each segment.

There are four segments and six demographic variables, so we create a 4 × 6 matrix to hold the *mean* of each. The first row holds the mean values of each of the six variables for the first segment; the second row holds the mean values for the second segment, and so forth. We do this as follows:

```
> segMeans <- matrix( c(
+    40, .5, 55000, 2, .5, .1,
+    24, .7, 21000, 1, .2, .2,
+    58, .5, 64000, 0, .7, .05,
+    36, .3, 52000, 2, .3, .2  ), ncol=length(segVars), byrow=TRUE)
```

How does this work? It specifies, for example, that the first variable (which we defined above as `age`) will have a mean of 40 for the first segment, 24 for the second segment, and so forth. When we draw the random data later in this section, our routine will look up values in this matrix and sample data from distributions with those parameters.

In the case of binomial and Poisson variables, we only need to specify the mean. In these data `gender`, `ownHome`, and `subscribe` will be simulated as binomial (yes/no) variables, which requires specifying the probability for each draw. `kids` is represented as a Poisson (count) variable, whose distribution is specified by its mean. (Note that we use these distributions for simplicity and do not mean to imply that they are necessarily the *best* distributions to fit real observations of these variables. For example, real observations of income are better represented with a skewed distribution.)

However, for normal variables—in this case, `age` and `income` the first and third variables—we additionally need to specify the *variance* of the distribution, the degree of dispersion around the mean. So we create a second 4 × 6 matrix that defines the standard deviation for the variables that require it:

```
> # standard deviations for each segment (NA = not applicable for variable)
> segSDs <- matrix( c(
+    5, NA, 12000, NA, NA, NA,
+    2, NA,  5000, NA, NA, NA,
+    8, NA, 21000, NA, NA, NA,
+    4, NA, 10000, NA, NA, NA  ), ncol=length(segVars), byrow=TRUE)
```

Putting those two matrices together, we have fully defined the distributions of the segments. For instance, look at the third line of each matrix, which corresponds to the "Travelers" segment. The matrices specify that the mean `age` of that segment will be 58 years (looking at the first matrix) and that it will have a standard deviation of 8 years (second matrix). Also it will be approximately 50% male (looking at the second column), with an average income of $64000 and $21000 standard deviation. By storing values in *look-up tables* this way, we can easily change the definitions for future purposes without digging through detailed code. Such separation between data definition and procedural code is a good programming practice.

With these data definitions in place, we we are ready to generate data. This uses `for()` loops and `if()` blocks, so we review those before continuing with the simulation process in Sect. 5.1.4.

5.1.2 Language Brief: `for()` Loops

Our dataset involves six random variables for age, gender, and so forth, and four segments. So, we need to draw random numbers from $6 \times 4 = 24$ different distributions. Luckily, the structure of each of those random number draws is very similar, and we can use `for()` loops to *iterate* over the variables and the segments.

The `for()` command iterates over a vector of values such as `1:10`, assigning successive values to an *index* variable and running a statement block on each iteration. Here is a simple example:

```
> for (i in 1:10) { print(i) }
[1]  1
[1]  2
[1]  3
...
[1]  10
```

The value of `i` takes on the values from 1 to 10, and the loop executes 10 times in all, running the `print()` command for each successive value of `i`.

If you've programmed before, this will be quite familiar—but there are a couple of twists. The index variable in R `for()` loops can take on any scalar value, not just integers, and it can operate on any vector including those that are defined elsewhere or are unordered. Consider the following where we define a vector of real numbers, `i.seq`, and iterate over its values:

```
> (i.seq <- rep(sqrt(seq(from=2.1, to=6.2, by=1.7)), 3))
[1] 1.449138 1.949359 2.345208 1.449138 1.949359 2.345208 1.449138 1.949359 ...
> for (i in i.seq ) { print(i) }
[1] 1.449138
[1] 1.949359
...
[1] 2.345208
```

An index vector may comprise character elements instead of numeric:

```
> for (i in c("Hello ","world, ","welcome to R!")) { cat(i) }
Hello world, welcome to R!
```

We use the `cat()` command for output here instead of `print()` because of its greater flexibility.

The brackets ("`{`" and "`}`") enclose the statements that you want to loop over and are only strictly required when a loop executes a block of more than one statement. However, we recommend for clarity to use brackets with all loops and control structures as we've done here.

By tradition the most common index variable is named "`i`" (and inner loops commonly use "`j`") but you may use any legal variable name. It is a nice practice to give your index variable a descriptive-but-short name like `seg` for segments or `cust` for customers.

There is one thing to *avoid* with `for()` loops in R: indexing on `1:length(some Variable)`. Suppose for the example above, we wanted not the *value* of each element in `i.seq` but its *position* (1, 2, 3, etc.). It would seem natural to write something like this:

```
> for (i in 1:length(i.seq)) { cat("Entry", i, "=", i.seq[i], "\n") }
Entry 1 = 1.449138
Entry 2 = 1.949359
...
```

Don't! This works in many cases but R has a better solution: `seq_along`
`(someVariable)`, which gives a vector of 1, 2, 3, etc. of the same length as
`someVariable`. Write the following instead:

```
> for (i in seq_along(i.seq)) { cat("Entry", i, "=", i.seq[i], "\n") }
Entry 1 = 1.449138
Entry 2 = 1.949359
...
```

Why? Because `seq_along()` protects against common errors when the index
vector has zero length or is inadvertently reversed. To see what happens when `for()`
has a zero-length vector, look at the following buggy code:

```
> i.seq <- NULL
> # maybe we have a bunch of other code, and then ...
> for (i in 1:length(i.seq)) { print (i) }        # bad
[1] 1
[1] 0
```

What happened? If `i.seq` is NULL, why does it appear to have length 2? The answer
is that it doesn't. We told R to do this: start a `for()` loop with the value of 1, and
then continue until you reach an index value that matches the length of the vector
`i.seq`, which happens to be 0. R complied precisely and iterated over the vector
`1:0`. That is, it started with 1 on the first iteration, and then 0 on the second iteration,
which then matched the length of `i.seq`.

The proper way to write this is to use `seq_along()`:

```
> i.seq <- NULL
> for (i in seq_along(i.seq)) { print (i) }        # better
```

This time the index vector has zero length, so nothing is printed. Whenever you find
yourself or a colleague writing "`for (i in 1:length ...)`," stop right there
and fix it. One day this will save you from a hard-to-find bug ...and every day you'll
be writing better R!

Many R and functional language programmers prefer to avoid `for()` loops and
instead use `apply()` functions and the like (Sect. 3.3.4), which automatically work
across vector or list objects. We suggest a mixed approach: do whichever makes
more sense to you. For many R newcomers, the logic of a `for()` loop is obvious
and easier to write reliably than an equivalent such as a list apply (`lapply()`). As
you gain experience in R and become comfortable with functions, we recommend
to reduce the reliance on `for()`.

5.1.3   Language Brief: *if()* Blocks

Like most programming languages, R provides `if()` statements to handle conditional code execution. The formal syntax is `if (statement1) statement2`
`else statement3` but we suggest the following code template:

```
# dummy code, not executed
if (condition1) {
  statements
} else if (condition2) {
  statements
} else {
  statements
}
```

A *condition* is the part that evaluates to be TRUE or FALSE, and it goes inside parentheses. For example, we might write if (segment==1) { ... } to do something when the value of segment is 1. (Advanced note: An if() condition may in fact be any R statement and will be coerced to a logical value but you should take care to make sure it resolves to be a *single*, *logical* TRUE or FALSE value.)

The else if() blocks and final else block in the template are optional and are evaluated only when the preceding if() statement evaluates as FALSE. The else if() blocks are just sequenced if() statements and may be chained indefinitely. In case you're wondering, there is no requirement for an else block to handle cases that if() does not match; there is an implicit "else do nothing and just continue."

We strongly encourage to use brackets ("{" and "}") around all conditional statement blocks as we've done in the template above. This makes code more readable, avoids syntactical ambiguities, and helps prevent bugs when lines are added or deleted in code. Note that when brackets are followed by an else block, the closing bracket ("}") generally *must* be on the same line as else.

There is a common error with if() statements: accidentally or mistakenly using a logical *vector* instead of a single logical value for the condition. Consider:

```
> x <- 1:5
> if (x > 1) {
+   print ("hi")
+ } else {
+   print ("bye")
+ }
[1] "bye"
Warning message:
In if (x > 1) { :
  the condition has length > 1 and only the first element will be used
```

R warns us that the condition is not a single value. It then evaluates x[1] > 1 as FALSE, so it skips to the else statement and evaluates that. This is probably not what the programmer intended with this code. There are two possibilities that are likely responsible for this code problem. First, the programmer might have forgotten that x is a vector instead of a single value. The warning about "length > 1" tells us to examine our code for that problem.

A second possibility is that the programmer wanted to evaluate *all* of the values of x and act on each one of them. However, the if() statement is about program flow—in R jargon, it is not vectorized—and thus it evaluates only a single condition per if(). To perform conditional evaluation on every element of a vector, use ifelse(test, yes, no) instead:

```
> ifelse(x > 1, "hi", "bye")
[1] "bye" "hi"  "hi"  "hi"  "hi"
```

In this case, the condition `x > 1` is evaluated for each element of `x`. That is, it tests whether `x[1] > 1` and then `x[2] > 1` and so forth. When a test evaluates as `TRUE`, the function returns the first ("yes") value; for others it returns the second ("no") value. The "yes" and "no" values may be functions as needed. For instance, in a silly case:

```
> fn.hi  <- function() { "hi" }
> fn.bye <- function() { "bye" }
> ifelse(x > 1, fn.hi(), fn.bye() )
[1] "bye" "hi"  "hi"  "hi"  "hi"
```

Experienced programmers: applying functions conditionally along a vector in this way is one way to avoid `for()` loops in R as we mentioned in Sect. 5.1.2.

5.1.4 Final Segment Data Generation

Armed with `for()` and `if()` and the data definitions above, we are ready to generate the segment data. The logic we follow is to use nested `for()` loops, one for the segments and another within that for the set of variables. (As mentioned in Sects. 5.1.2 and 5.1.3, one could do this without `for()` loops in keeping with the functional programming paradigm of R. However, we use `for()` loops here for clarity and simplicity, and recommend that you code similarly; write whatever code is clearest and easiest to maintain.)

To outline how this will work, consider the following *pseudocode* (sentences organized like code):

```
Set up data frame "seg.df" and pseudorandom number sequence
For each SEGMENT i in "segNames" {
  Set up a temporary data frame "this.seg" for this SEGMENT's data
  For each VARIABLE j in "segVars" {
    Use nested if() on "segVarType[j]" to determine data type for VARIABLE
    Use segMeans[i, j] and segSDs[i, j] to
    ... Draw random data for VARIABLE (within SEGMENT) with
    ... "segSize[i]" observations
  }
  Add this SEGMENT's data ("this.seg") to the overall data ("seg.df")
}
```

Pseudocode is a good way to outline and debug code conceptually before you actually write it. In this case, you can compare the pseudocode to the actual R code to see how we accomplish each step. Translating the outline into R, we write:

```
> seg.df <- NULL
> set.seed(02554)

> # iterate over segments and create data for each
> for (i in seq_along(segNames)) {
+   cat(i, segNames[i], "\n")
+
+   # empty matrix to hold this particular segment's data
+   this.seg <- data.frame(matrix(NA, nrow=segSize[i], ncol=length(segVars)))
+
+   # within segment, iterate over variables and draw appropriate random data
+   for (j in seq_along(segVars)) {     # and iterate over each variable
+     if (segVarType[j] == "norm") {    # draw random normals
+       this.seg[,j] <- rnorm(segSize[i], mean=segMeans[i,j], sd=segSDs[i,j])
+     } else if (segVarType[j] == "pois") {     # draw counts
```

```
+        this.seg[, j] <- rpois(segSize[i], lambda=segMeans[i, j])
+      } else if (segVarType[j] == "binom") {    # draw binomials
+        this.seg[, j] <- rbinom(segSize[i], size=1, prob=segMeans[i, j])
+      } else {
+        stop("Bad segment data type: ", segVarType[j])
+      }
+    }
+    # add this segment to the total dataset
+    seg.df <- rbind(seg.df, this.seg)
+ }
```

The core commands occur inside the `if()` statements: according to the data type we want ("norm"[al], "pois"[son], or "binom"[ial]), use the appropriate pseudorandom function to draw data (the function `rnorm(n, mean, sd)`, `rpois(n, lambda)`, or `rbinom(n, size, prob)`, respectively). We draw all of the values for a given variable within a given segment with a single command (drawing all the observations at once, with length specified by `segSize[i]`).

There are a few things to note about this code. As in Sect. 5.1.2 we use `seq_along()` to set up the `for()` loops. To see that the code is working and to show progress, we use `cat("some output message", counter, "\n")` inside the loop (`\n` ends a line so the next iteration will be on a new line of output). That results in the following output as the code runs:

```
1 Suburb mix
2 Urban hip
3 Travelers
4 Moving up
```

Inside the first loop (the `i` loop), we predefine `this.seg` as a data frame with the desired number of rows and columns, but full of missing values (NA). Why? Whenever R grows an object in memory—such as adding a row—it makes a copy of the object. This uses twice the memory and slows things down; by preallocating, we avoid that. In small data sets like this one, it hardly matters, but with larger data sets, it can make a huge difference in speed. Also, R can easily draw random values for all respondents in a segment at once and this makes it easier to do so. Finally, it adds a bit of error checking: if a result doesn't fit into the data frame where it *should* fit, we will get a warning or error.

By filling temporary and placeholder objects with missing values (NA) instead of 0 or blank values, we add another layer of error-checking: if we `describe()` the object and discover missing values where we expect data, we know there is a code error.

We finish the `if()` blocks in our code with a `stop()` command that executes in the case that a proposed data type doesn't match what we expect. There are three `if()` tests for the expected data types, and a final `else` block in case none of the `if`s matches. This protects us in the case that we mistype a data type or if we try to use a distribution that hasn't been defined in the random draw code, such as a gamma distribution. This `stop()` condition would cause the code to exit immediately and print an error string.

Notice that we are doing a lot of thinking ahead about how our code might change and potentially break in the future to ensure that we would get a warning when something goes wrong. Our code also has another advantage that you may not notice right away: we call each random data function such as `rnorm` in exactly one place. If we discover that there was something wrong with that call—say we wanted to change one of the parameters of the call—we only need to make the correction in one place. This sort of planning is a hallmark of good programming in R or any other language. While it might seem overly complex at first, many of these ideas will become habitual as you write more programs.

To finish up the data set, we perform a few housekeeping tasks: we name the columns, add segment membership, and convert each binomial variable to a labeled factor:

```
# make the data frame names match what we defined
names(seg.df) <- segVars
# add segment membership for each row
seg.df$Segment   <- factor(rep(segNames, times=segSize))
# convert the binomial variables to nicely labeled factors
seg.df$ownHome   <- factor(seg.df$ownHome, labels=c("ownNo", "ownYes"))
seg.df$gender    <- factor(seg.df$gender, labels=c("Female", "Male"))
seg.df$subscribe <- factor(seg.df$subscribe, labels=c("subNo", "subYes"))
```

We may now inspect the data. As always, we recommend a data inspection plan as noted in Sect. 3.5, although we only show one of those steps here:

```
> summary(seg.df)
      age          gender         income            kids          ownHome
 Min.   :19.26   Female:157   Min.   : -5183   Min.   :0.00   ownNo :159
 1st Qu.:33.01   Male  :143   1st Qu.: 39656   1st Qu.:0.00   ownYes:141
 Median :39.49                Median : 52014   Median :1.00
 Mean   :41.20                Mean   : 50937   Mean   :1.27
 ...
```

The data frame is now suitable for exploration. And we have reusable code: we could create data with more observations, different segment sizes, or segments with different distributions or means by simply adjusting the matrices that define the segments and running the code again.

As a final step we save the data frame as a backup and to use again in later chapters (Sects. 11.2 and 12.4). Change the destination if you have created a folder for this book or prefer a different location:

```
> save(seg.df, file="~/segdf-Rintro-Ch5.RData")
```

5.2 Finding Descriptives by Group

For our consumer segmentation data, we are interested in how measures such as household income and gender vary for the different segments. With this insight, a firm might develop tailored offerings for the segments or engage in different ways to reach them.

An ad hoc way to do this is with data frame indexing: find the rows that match some criterion, and then take the mean (or some other statistic) for the matching observations on a variable of interest. For example, to find the mean income for the "Moving up" segment:

```
> mean(seg.df$income[seg.df$Segment == "Moving up"])
[1] 53090.97
```

This says "from the income observations, take all cases where the Segment column is 'Moving up' and calculate their mean." We could further narrow the cases to "Moving up" respondents who also do not subscribe using Boolean logic:

```
> mean(seg.df$income[seg.df$Segment == "Moving up" &
+                    seg.df$subscribe=="subNo"])
[1] 53633.73
```

This quickly becomes tedious when you wish to find values for multiple groups.

As we saw briefly in Sect. 3.4.5, a more general way to do this is with `by(data, INDICES, FUN)`. The result of `by()` is to divide `data` into groups for each of the unique values in `INDICES` and then apply the `FUN` function to each group:

```
> by(seg.df$income, seg.df$Segment, mean)
seg.df$Segment: Moving up
[1] 53090.97
---------------------------------------------------------------
seg.df$Segment: Suburb mix
[1] 55033.82
...
```

With `by()`, keep in mind that `data` is the first argument and the splitting factors `INDICES` come second. You can break out the results by multiple factors if you supply factors in a `list()`. For example, we can break out by segment and subscription status:

```
> by(seg.df$income, list(seg.df$Segment, seg.df$subscribe), mean)
: Moving up
: subNo
[1] 53633.73
---------------------------------------------------------------
: Suburb mix
: subNo
[1] 54942.69
...
: Urban hip
: subYes
[1] 20081.19
```

Our favorite command for computing a function to each group is `aggregate()` as we introduced in Sect. 3.4.5. `aggregate()` works almost identically to `by` in its *list* form (we'll see another form of `aggregate()` momentarily), except that it takes a list for even a single factor:

```
> aggregate(seg.df$income, list(seg.df$Segment), mean)
     Group.1        x
1  Moving up 53090.97
2 Suburb mix 55033.82
3  Travelers 62213.94
4  Urban hip 21681.93
```

A first advantage of `aggregate()` is this: the result is a data frame. As we saw in Sect. 3.4.5, you can save the results of `aggregate()` to an object, which you can then index, subject to further computation, write to a file, or manipulate in other ways.

Here's an example: suppose we wish to add a "segment mean" column to our data set, a new observation for each respondent that contains the mean income for their respective segment so we can compare respondents' incomes to those typical for their segments. We can do this by first aggregating the mean incomes into a table, and then indexing that by segment to look up the appropriate value for each row of our data:

```
> seg.income.mean <- aggregate(seg.df$income, list(seg.df$Segment), mean)
> seg.df$segIncome <- seg.income.mean[seg.df$Segment, 2]
```

When we check the data, we see that each row has an observation that matches its segment mean (some() does a random sample of rows, so your output may vary):

```
> library(car)
> some(seg.df)
        age gender   income kids ownHome subscribe    Segment segIncome
58  34.46528   Male 60971.76    2   ownNo      subNo Suburb mix  55033.82
79  42.31337   Male 49674.79    0  ownYes      subNo Suburb mix  55033.82
124 22.30333 Female 24541.24    1   ownNo      subNo  Urban hip  21681.93
136 23.08861   Male 33909.50    3   ownNo      subNo  Urban hip  21681.93
158 43.35230   Male 51787.88    0   ownNo      subNo  Travelers  62213.94
...
```

It is worth thinking about how this works. In the following command:

```
> seg.df$segIncome <- seg.income.mean[seg.df$Segment, 2]
```

... we see this index for the rows: seg.df$Segment. If we evaluate that on its own, we see that it is a vector with one entry for each row of seg.df:

```
> seg.df$Segment
  [1] Suburb mix Suburb mix Suburb mix Suburb mix Suburb mix Suburb mix
      Suburb mix
...
[295] Moving up  Moving up  Moving up  Moving up  Moving up  Moving up
Levels: Moving up Suburb mix Travelers Urban hip
```

Now let's see what happens when we index seg.income.mean with that vector:

```
> seg.income.mean[seg.df$Segment, ]
         Group.1        x
2     Suburb mix 55033.82
2.1   Suburb mix 55033.82
...
1.68   Moving up 53090.97
1.69   Moving up 53090.97
```

The result is a a data frame in which each row of seg.income.mean occurs many times in the order requested.

Finally, selecting the second column of that gives us the value to add for each row of seg.df:

```
> seg.income.mean[seg.df$Segment, 2]
  [1] 55033.82 55033.82 55033.82 55033.82 55033.82 55033.82 55033.82 55033.82
...
[297] 53090.97 53090.97 53090.97 53090.97
```

We generally do not like adding derived columns to primary data because we like to separate data from subsequent computation, but we did so here for illustration. We now remove that column by setting its value to NULL:

```
> seg.df$segIncome <- NULL
```

This use of aggregate() exemplifies the power of R to extract and manipulate data with simple and concise commands. You may recall that we said this was the *first* advantage of aggregate(). The second advantage is even more important and we describe it next.

5.2.1 Language Brief: Basic Formula Syntax

R provides a standard way to describe relationships among variables through *formula* specification. A formula uses the tilde ($\sim$) operator to separate *response variables* on the left from *explanatory variables* on the right. The basic form is:

$$y \sim x \qquad\qquad \text{(Simple formula)}$$

This is used in many contexts in R, where the meaning of *response* and *explanatory* depend on the situation. For example, in linear regression, the simple formula above would model *y* as a linear function of *x*. In the case of the `aggregate()` command, the effect is to aggregate *y* according to the levels of *x*.

Let's see that in practice. Instead of `aggregate(seg.df$income, list (seg.df$Segment), mean)` we can write:

```
> aggregate(income ~ Segment, data=seg.df, mean)
     Segment    income
1  Moving up 53090.97
...
```

The general form is `aggregate(formula, data, FUN)`. In our example, we tell R to "take `income` by `Segment` within the data set `seg.df`, and apply `mean` to each group."

The formula "$y \sim x$" might be pronounced in various contexts as "*y* in response to *x*," "*y* is modeled by *x*," "*y* varies with *x*," and so forth. R programmers often become so accustomed to this syntax that they just say "*y* tilde *x*." This syntax may seem like nothing special at first, but formulas are used in many different contexts throughout R. We will encounter many uses for formulas later in this book, and discuss additional forms of them in Sect. 7.5.1.

5.2.2 Descriptives for Two-Way Groups

A common task in marketing is cross-tabulating, separating customers into groups according to two (or more) factors. Formula syntax makes it easy to compute a cross tab just by specifying multiple explanatory variables:

$$y \sim x1 + x2 + \cdots \qquad\qquad \text{(Multiple variable formula)}$$

Using this format with `aggregate()`, we write:

```
> aggregate(income ~ Segment + ownHome, data=seg.df, mean)
     Segment ownHome    income
1  Moving up  ownNo 54497.68
2 Suburb mix  ownNo 54932.83
...
7  Travelers ownYes 61889.12
8  Urban hip ownYes 23059.27
```

We now have a separate group for each combination of Segment and ownHome and can begin to see how income is related to both the Segment and the ownHome variables.

A formula can be extended to include as many grouping variables as needed:

```
> aggregate(income ~ Segment + ownHome + subscribe, data=seg.df, mean)
     Segment ownHome subscribe   income
1   Moving up   ownNo    subNo 55402.89
...
8   Urban hip  ownYes    subNo 23993.93
9   Moving up   ownNo   subYes 50675.70
...
16  Urban hip  ownYes   subYes 19320.64
```

As we saw for one-way aggregate, the result can be assigned to a data frame object and indexed:

```
> agg.data <- aggregate(income ~ Segment + ownHome, data=seg.df, mean)
> agg.data[2, ]
     Segment ownHome   income
2 Suburb mix   ownNo 54932.83
> agg.data[2, 3]
[1] 54932.83
```

The aggregate command allows us to compute functions of continuous variables, such as the mean of income or age) for any combination of factors (Segment, ownHomeand so forth). This is such a common task in marketing research that there used to be entire companies who specialized in producing cross tabs. As we've just seen, these are not difficult to compute in R.

We might also want to know the *frequency* with which different combinations of Segment and ownHome occur. We can compute frequencies using table(factor1, factor2, ...) to obtain one-way or multi-way counts:

```
> with(seg.df, table(Segment, ownHome))
            ownHome
Segment      ownNo ownYes
  Moving up     47     23
  Suburb mix    52     48
  Travelers     20     60
  Urban hip     40     10
```

There are 10 observed customers in the "Urban hip" segment who own their own homes, and 60 in the "Travelers" segment.

Suppose we want a breakdown of the number of kids in each household (kids) by Segment:

```
> with(seg.df, table(kids, Segment))
    Segment
kids Moving up Suburb mix Travelers Urban hip
   0        13         11        80        17
   1        17         36         0        17
   2        18         22         0        11
   3        13         19         0         4
...
```

This tells us that we have 17 "Urban hip" respondents with 0 kids, 22 "Suburb mix" respondents with 2 kids, and so forth. It represents purely the count of incidence for each crossing point between the two factors, kids and Segment. In this case we are treating kids as a factor and not a number.

However, `kids` is actually a count variable; if a respondent reported 3 kids, that is a count of 3 and we could add together the counts to get the total number of children reported in each segment. `xtabs(formula, data)` provides a handy way to do this. It works with counts to find their total:

```
> xtabs(kids ~ Segment, data=seg.df)
Segment
 Moving up Suburb mix   Travelers   Urban hip
       134         192           0          55
```

Now we know that our "Urban hip" respondents reported a total of 55 kids, while the "Travelers" reported none. You might think of other ways this could be done in R as well. One alternative is `aggregate( ..., sum)`:

```
> aggregate(kids ~ Segment, data=seg.df, sum)
      Segment kids
1   Moving up  134
2  Suburb mix  192
3   Travelers    0
4   Urban hip   55
```

Another option is to multiply the frequency table by marginal number of kids and add it up:

```
> seg.tab <- with(seg.df, table(kids, Segment))
> apply(seg.tab*0:7, 2, sum)
 Moving up Suburb mix   Travelers   Urban hip
       134         192           0          55
```

`apply( , 2, sum)` is better expressed using `colSums()`:

```
> seg.tab <- with(seg.df, table(kids, Segment))
> colSums(seg.tab*0:7)
 Moving up Suburb mix   Travelers   Urban hip
       134         192           0          55
```

We have belabored this in order to show that R typically has many ways to arrive at the same result. This may seem overly complex yet it is a good thing. One reason is that there are multiple options to match your style and situation. Each method produces results in a different format, and one format might work better in some situation than another. For instance, we've argued that the format from `aggregate()` is often more useful than `by()`. Another reason is that you can do the same thing in two different ways and compare the answers, thus testing your analyses and uncovering potential errors.

5.2.3 Visualization by Group: Frequencies and Proportions

Suppose we plot the proportion of subscribers for each segment to understand better which segments use the subscription service. Apart from making four separate plots, it isn't obvious how to do this with the tools we have learned so far. We could use `table()` along with `barplot()` (from Sect. 3.2.1) to get a plot showing the number of subscribers and non subscribers overall, but breaking this out by `segment` would require lots of work to separate the data and label the plots correctly.

Fig. 5.1 Conditional histogram for proportion of subscribers within each segment, using `lattice`

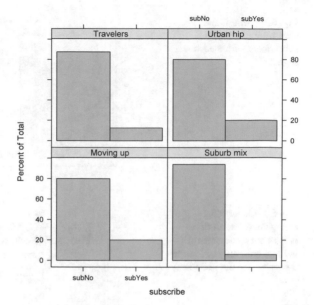

Happily, the `lattice` package provides a useful solution: `histogram(formula, data, type)` is similar to `hist()` but understands formula notation including *conditioning* on a factor, which means to separate the plot into multiple panes based on that factor. Conditioning is indicated with the symbol "|". This is easiest to understand in an example:

```
> library(lattice)
> histogram(~subscribe | Segment, data=seg.df)
```

You will notice that there is no response variable before the tilde (~) in this formula, only the explanatory variable (`subscribe`) after it. `histogram()` automatically assumes that we want to plot the proportion of people at each level of `subscribe`. We condition the plot on `Segment`, telling `histogram` to produce a separate histogram for each segment. The result is shown in Fig. 5.1.

In Fig. 5.1, we see that the "Suburban mix" segment is least likely to subscribe to our service. While this data doesn't tell us why that might be, it does suggest that the company might investigate and perhaps either improve the product to make it more appealing to this group or else stop marketing to them.

The default in `histogram()` is to plot *proportions* within each group so that the values are relative to the group size. If we wanted actual *counts* instead, we could include the argument `type="count"`. We do that, adding options for color and changing the `layout` to 4 columns and 1 row:

```
> histogram(~subscribe | Segment, data=seg.df, type="count",
+           layout=c(4,1), col=c("burlywood", "darkolivegreen"))
```

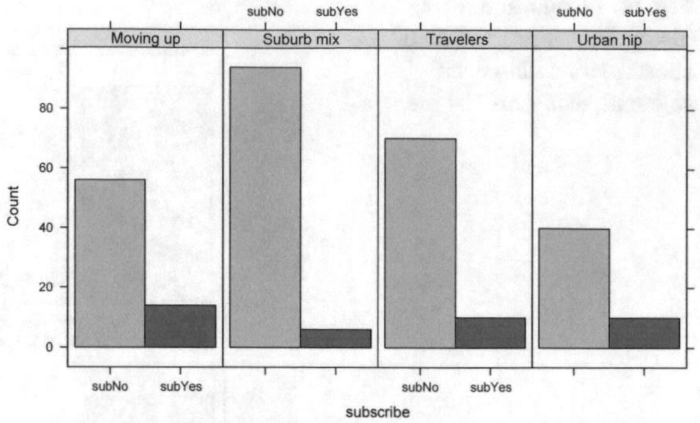

Fig. 5.2 Conditional
histogram for *count* of
subscribers within each
segment

Fig. 5.3 Conditional
histogram for subscribers,
broken out by segment (in
the four columns) and home
ownership (in the two rows)

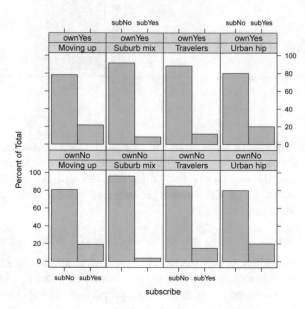

This produces Fig. 5.2. By plotting the counts, we can see which segments are larger, but it is difficult and potentially misleading to compare the count of subscribers across groups of different sizes.

You can condition on more than one factor; just include it in the conditioning part of the formula with "+". For example, what is the proportion of subscribers within each segment, by home ownership? We add ownHome to the formula in histogram():

```
> histogram(~subscribe | Segment + ownHome, data=seg.df)
```

The result is Fig. 5.3. In this plot, the top and bottom rows of Fig. 5.3 are similar, and we conclude that differences in subscription rate according to home ownership within segment are small. An implication is that the company should continue to market to both homeowners and non-homeowners.

Fig. 5.4 Proportion of subscribers by segment using prop.table and barchart

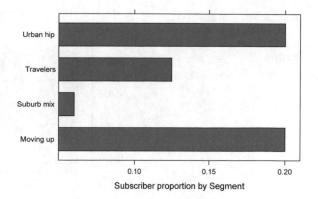

Finally, we could plot just "yes" proportions instead of both "yes" and "no" bars. There are several ways to do this; we'll do so by introducing the prop.table (table, margin) command. If you wrap prop.table(..., margin= ...) around a regular table() command, it will give you the proportions for each cell with respect to the entire table (by default), or just the rows (margin=1), or the columns (margin=2).

We would like to know the proportion of subscribers within each segment, which are the columns in table(...$subscribe, $Segment), so we use prop. table(..., margin=2) as follows:

```
> prop.table(table(seg.df$subscribe, seg.df$Segment), margin=2)
          Moving up Suburb mix Travelers Urban hip
    subNo     0.800      0.940     0.875     0.800
    subYes    0.200      0.060     0.125     0.200
```

To plot just the "yes" values, we use barchart() and select only the second row of the prop.table() result:

```
> barchart(prop.table(table(seg.df$subscribe, seg.df$Segment), margin=2)[2, ],
+          xlab="Subscriber proportion by Segment", col="darkolivegreen")
```

The result is Fig. 5.4, which strongly communicates that the Suburb mix segment has an apparent low subscription rate. Note that this visual impression is amplified by the fact that barchart() started the X axis at 0.05, not at 0, which is rather misleading. In practice, you might adjust that using the xlim=c(low, high) argument to barchart(); we leave that as an exercise. We will see more examples of barcharts in the next section.

5.2.4 Visualization by Group: Continuous Data

In the previous section we saw how to plot counts and proportions. What about continuous data? How would we plot income by segment in our data? A simple

Fig. 5.5 Average income by
segment using
`prop.table` and
`barchart`

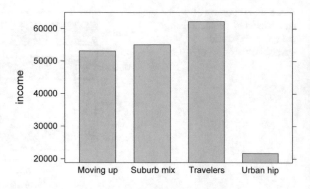

Fig. 5.6 Average income by
segment and home
ownership, using
`aggregate` and
`barchart`

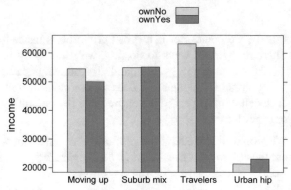

way is to use `aggregate()` to find the mean income, and then use `barchart()`
from the `lattice` package to plot the computed values:

```
> seg.mean <- aggregate(income ~ Segment, data=seg.df, mean)
> library(lattice)
> barchart(income~Segment, data=seg.mean, col="grey")
```

The result is Fig. 5.5.

How do we split this out further by home ownership? First we have to aggregate
the data to include both factors in the formula. Then we tell `barchart()` to use
`ownHome` as a grouping variable by adding the argument `groups=factor`. Doing
that, and also adding a `simpleTheme` option to improve the chart colors, we have:

```
> seg.income.agg <- aggregate(income ~ Segment + ownHome, data=seg.df, mean)
> barchart(income ~ Segment, data=seg.income.agg,
+             groups=ownHome, auto.key=TRUE,
+             par.settings = simpleTheme(col=terrain.colors(2)) )
```

This produces a passable graphic as shown in Fig. 5.6 although it still looks as if it
came from a spreadsheet program. We can do better in R.

A more informative plot for comparing values of continuous data, like `income` for
different groups is a *box-and-whiskers* plot, which we first encountered in Sect. 3.4.2.
A boxplot is better than a barchart because it shows more about the *distributions* of
values.

Fig. 5.7 Box-and-whiskers
plot for income by segment
using `boxplot`

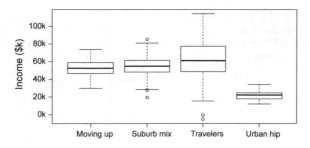

Fig. 5.8 Box-and-whiskers
plot for income by segment
using `bwplot`

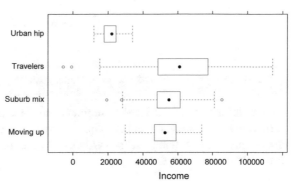

`boxplot()` works with formula syntax to plot a box-and-whiskers plot by factor.
Adding improved labels for the Y axis (see Sect. 3.4), we write:

```
> boxplot(income ~ Segment, data=seg.df, yaxt="n", ylab="Income ($k)")
> ax.seq <- seq(from=0, to=120000, by=20000)
> axis(side=2, at=ax.seq, labels=paste(ax.seq/1000, "k", sep=""), las=1)
```

We can now see in Fig. 5.7 that the income for "Travelers" is higher and also has
a greater range, with a few "Travelers" reporting very low incomes. The range of
income for "Urban hip" is much lower and tighter. Although box-and-whisker plots
are not common in business reporting, they encode a lot more information than the
averages shown in Fig. 5.4. Box-and-whisker plots, or their more modern cousins (see
Sect. 3.4.2), should be more common business communications, since they provide
more information than a barplot of averages.

An even better option for box-and-whiskers plots is the `bwplot()` command from
the `lattice` package, which produces better looking charts and allows multi-factor
conditioning. One point of caution is that `bwplot()` uses the model formula in a
direction opposite than you might expect; you write `Segment` *s* ~ income. We
plot a horizontal box-and-whiskers for income by segment as follows:

```
> bwplot(Segment ~ income, data=seg.df, horizontal=TRUE, xlab = "Income")
```

The `lattice` box-and-whiskers is shown in Fig. 5.8.

We can break out home ownership as a conditioning variable using " | `ownHome`"
in the formula:

Fig. 5.9 Box-and-whiskers plot for income by segment and home ownership using `bwplot`

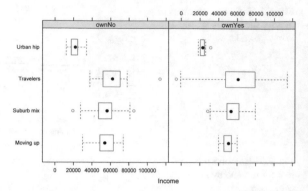

```
> bwplot(Segment ~ income | ownHome, data=seg.df, horizontal=TRUE,
+        xlab="Income")
```

The conditioned plot for income by segment and home ownership is shown in Fig. 5.9. In this chart we discover—among other things—that in our simulated data the Travelers segment has a much wider distribution of income among those who own their homes than those who don't.

5.3 Key Points

This was a crucial chapter for doing everyday analytics with R. Following are some of the lessons.

In R code in general:

- When writing `for()` loops, use `seq_along()` instead of `1:length()` (Sect. 5.1.2)
- For `if()` and `for()` blocks, always use brackets ("{" and "}") for improved readability and reliability (Sect. 5.1.3)
- When creating a data object from scratch, pre-populate it with missing data (`NA`) and then fill it in, for speed and reliability (Sect. 5.1.1)

When describing and visualizing data for groups:

- The `by()` command can split up data and automatically apply functions such as `mean()` and `summary()` (Sect. 5.2)
- `aggregate()` is even more powerful: it understands formula models and produces a reusable, indexable object with its results (Sects. 5.2 and 5.2.1)
- Frequency of occurrence can be found with `table()`. For count data, especially when using formulas, `xtabs()` is useful (Sect. 5.2.2)
- Charts of proportions and occurrence by a factor are well suited to the `lattice` package `histogram()` command (Sect. 5.2.2)

- Plots for continuous data by factor may use `barchart()`, or even better, box-and-whiskers plots with `boxplot()` (Sect. 5.2.4) or bean plots (Sect. 3.4.2). The `lattice` package extends boxplots to multiple factors using formula specification in the `bwplot()` command (Sect. 5.2.4).

5.4   Data Sources

Segmentation data is commonly obtained from three sources: account profile information (such as gender and age), survey data (such as home ownership and household income), and account behavior (such as subscribing to a service). These might be collected in a unified data set—for example, when survey items are asked during account sign up—or combined from separate waves of data collection, such as surveys emailed to customers. We assume here that the data have already been gathered and compiled (see Sect. 4.8).

Finally, in addition to the descriptive data, there are segment assignments, such as the "Urban hip" and "Travelers" segments. These might be assigned through a clustering or classification method (Chap. 11), expert assignment, or a *typing tool*—perhaps a simple script that implements segment membership logic. In the present data, we assume that those segment assignments have been made.

5.5   Learning More*

The topics in this chapter are foundational both for programming skills in R and for applied statistics. To gain skill in aspects of R programming that we introduce in this chapter, we recommend Matloff's *The Art of R Programming* [135]. We presented charts in this chapter using the `lattice` package, which is described in detail in an eponymous book: Sarkar's *Lattice* [173].

In Chap. 6 we continue our investigation with methods that formalize group comparisons and estimate the statistical strength of differences between groups.

5.6   Exercises

The following exercises use the e-commerce data set as described in Sect. 3.8.1.

1. Using the integer approximation of page views (see Exercises in Sect. 4.10), describe page views for parents, teachers, and health professionals. Use a `by()` or `aggregate()` function as appropriate.
2. Repeat the previous task, this time using a `for()` loop to iterate over the groups.

3. Comparing the previous two approaches—grouping versus a for() loop—
   which do you prefer, and why? What is a time when the other approach might be
   preferable?
4. What are the proportions of men and women among the various visitor profiles
   (teacher, parent, relative, etc.)? For this question, don't count observations where
   the gender is not specified as male or female.
5. Considering parents, teachers, and health professionals, which group has made
   the most purchases recently? Answer with both descriptives and a visualization.
6. In answering the previous question, you might use either counts or proportions.
   Do they give you the same answer? If not, show an example. What is a business
   question for which counts would be preferable? What is a question for which
   proportions would be preferable?
7. When we split the profiles into men and women, and consider completed purchases on the site (variable behavAnySale) which combination of profile and
   gender made the highest number of purchases? Which had the highest rate of
   purchase, relative to total number of observations?

Chapter 6
Comparing Groups: Statistical Tests

In Chap. 5 we saw how to break out data by groups and inspect it with tables and charts. In this chapter we continue our discussion and address the question, "It looks different, but is it really different?" This involves our first inferential statistical procedures: chi-square, t-tests, and analysis of variance (ANOVA). In the final section, we introduce a Bayesian approach to compare groups.

6.1 Data for Comparing Groups

In this chapter, we continue with the data from Chap. 5. If you saved it at that time, you could load it again with a command such as:

```
> load("~/segdf-Rintro-Ch5.RData")      # modify directory as needed
> summary(seg.df)
       age              gender         income              kids          ownHome
 Min.   :19.26    Female:157    Min.    : -5183    Min.   :0.00     ownNo  :159
 1st Qu.:33.01    Male  :143    1st Qu.:  39656    1st Qu.:0.00     ownYes :141
 ...
```

Alternatively, you could create the data following the procedure in Sect. 5.1. Or download it from this book's web site:

```
> seg.df <- read.csv("http://goo.gl/qw303p")
> summary(seg.df)
       age              gender         income              kids          ownHome
 Min.   :19.26    Female:157    Min.    : -5183    Min.   :0.00     ownNo  :159
 1st Qu.:33.01    Male  :143    1st Qu.:  39656    1st Qu.:0.00     ownYes :141
 ...
```

6.2 Testing Group Frequencies: `chisq.test()`

Much of the work we do in marketing analytics and marketing research involves summarizing the differences between groups using group averages and cross tabs as we described in Sect. 5.2. However, a good analyst is able to use *statistical tests* to

© Springer Nature Switzerland AG 2019
C. Chapman and E. M. Feit, *R For Marketing Research and Analytics*, Use R!,
https://doi.org/10.1007/978-3-030-14316-9_6

determine whether differences are real or might instead be due to minor variation
("noise") in the data. In the rest of the book, we largely focus on statistical tests that
help to identify real differences.

One of the simplest statistical tests is the *chi-square* test, which is used with frequency
counts such as those produced by `table`. A chi-square test determines whether the
frequencies in cells are significantly different from what one would expect on the
basis of their total counts.

In our segment data, we might ask whether there are equal numbers of respondents in each segment, given a marginal count of N = 300 observations. In R,
we use the `chisq.test()` command. One thing to remember is that in general
`chisq.test()` operates on a *table* (such as produced by `table()`). To see how
this works, let's look at the process using simple data before we tackle the question
for our segments. Experimenting with simple data is always a good idea when trying
a new command.

For the first example, we create a table where the data comprises 95 observations of
the numbers 1 to 4 and where the counts of each are almost, but not quite identical.
We then test this with `chisq.test()`:

```
> tmp.tab <- table(rep(c(1:4), times=c(25,25,25,20)))
> tmp.tab
 1  2  3  4
25 25 25 20

> chisq.test(tmp.tab)
   Chi-squared test for given probabilities

data:   tmp.tab
X-squared = 0.78947, df = 3, p-value = 0.852
```

In this code, we generate 95 observations of 1:4, compile those into a table, and
then test that table for chi-square independence. The test evaluates the likelihood of
seeing such a result under the *null hypothesis* that the data were randomly sampled
from a large population where the values 1:4 are *equally distributed*, given a marginal
count of N = 95 observations. The *p-value* of 0.852 tells us that there is an estimated
85% chance of seeing a data set with differences similar to or greater than those in
our table, if the null hypothesis is true. We conclude that under the assumptions of
the chi-square test, our table does not suggest real differences in frequency between
the four cells. Put another way, this data shows no evidence that the groups in the
population are of unequal size, under the assumption of random sampling.

Compare that to the following, which differs from the code above by a single
character—we change the number of observations of "4" from `20` to `10`:

```
> tmp.tab <- table(rep(c(1:4), times=c(25,25,25,10)))
> tmp.tab
 1  2  3  4
25 25 25 10

> chisq.test(tmp.tab)

   Chi-squared test for given probabilities
```

```
data:   tmp.tab
X-squared = 7.9412, df = 3, p-value = 0.04724
```

In this case, we could conclude from the *p*-value of 0.047 that we we can reject the null hypothesis of no difference between the cells with "95% confidence." In other words, the data in this sample suggests that the distribution of the values 1:4 is likely to be unequal in the larger population, assuming the data are a random sample. In general, a *p*-value less than 0.10 or 0.05 suggests that there is a difference between groups.

As an aside, there are disagreements among statisticians about the meaning of null hypotheses and the value of traditional significance testing. We do not advocate classical significance testing in particular, but report the methods here because they are widely used in marketing to gauge the strength of evidence in a data set. We believe the classical methods are imperfect but nevertheless useful and important to know. For review and discussion of the controversies and alternatives, see [35, 101, 119]. In Sect. 6.6 we introduce Bayesian methods that do not rely on this kind of null hypothesis.

In the results above, if we had a smaller sample we would not get the same result for the significance test even if the relative proportion of customers in each group was the same. Significance tests are sensitive to both the observed difference and the sample size. To see this, we can create data with the same proportions but one fifth as many observations by dividing `tmp.tab` by 5.

```
> tmp.tab <- tmp.tab/5
> tmp.tab
1 2 3 4
5 5 5 2

> chisq.test(tmp.tab)
  Chi-squared test for given probabilities

data:   tmp.tab
X-squared = 1.5882, df = 3, p-value = 0.6621

Warning message:
In chisq.test(tmp.tab) : Chi-squared approximation may be incorrect
```

This shows a non-significant result—no evidence of a real difference in group sizes—even though the proportion of people in the "4" group is the same as in the larger sample above where the result was significant. This highlights one of the cautions about statistical significance testing: it is dependent on sample size as well as on the real effect. By the way, the warning occurs when doing `chisq.test()` where some cells have very few observations; that poses questions about sample size that we set aside for now.

Returning to our simulated segment data, which has a N = 300 observations, we ask whether the segment sizes are significantly different from one another (assuming that our 300 customers are a random sample of a larger population). We use the same procedure as above, combining `chisq.test()` and `table()` into one command:

```
> chisq.test(table(seg.df$Segment))
  Chi-squared test for given probabilities

data:    table(seg.df$Segment)
X-squared = 17.333, df = 3, p-value = 0.0006035
```

The answer to our question is "yes, there are differences in segment size." That is, with $p = 0.0006$, our sample does not support the hypothesis that there are identical numbers of customers in each segment.

Is subscription status independent from home ownership, as we hypothesized when we plotted the data in Sect. 5.2? That is, in our simulated data, are respondents just as likely to subscribe or not, without regard to home ownership status (and conversely, are they just as likely to own a home or not, independent of subscription status)? We construct a two-way table and test it:

```
> table(seg.df$subscribe, seg.df$ownHome)

          ownNo ownYes
  subNo    137    123
  subYes    22     18

> chisq.test(table(seg.df$subscribe, seg.df$ownHome))
  Pearson's Chi-squared test with Yates' continuity correction

data:    table(seg.df$subscribe, seg.df$ownHome)
X-squared = 0.0104, df = 1, p-value = 0.9187
```

The null hypothesis in this case is that the factors are unrelated, i.e., that the counts in the cells are as one might expect from the marginal proportions. Based on the high p-value, we cannot reject the null hypothesis of no difference, and conclude that the factors are unrelated and that home ownership is independent of subscription status in our data. Although people in general have a low subscription rate—and thus there are many more non-subscribers than subscribers in both groups—there is no *relationship* between subscription rate and home ownership.

You should be aware of one aspect of chisq.test() for 2×2 tables: chisq. test() defaults to using *Yates' correction*, which adjusts the chi-square statistic in light of the fact that the assumption of continuous data is imperfect when data comes from a lumpy binomial distribution. If you want the results to match traditional values such as calculation by hand or spreadsheet, turn that off with correct=FALSE:

```
> chisq.test(table(seg.df$subscribe, seg.df$ownHome), correct=FALSE)
  Pearson's Chi-squared test

data:    table(seg.df$subscribe, seg.df$ownHome)
X-squared = 0.074113,
df = 1, p-value = 0.7854
```

The test statistics and p-values change slightly across these commands, but the conclusion is the same: the factors are independent (or, more precisely and in the logic of significance testing, there is little evidence that they are *not* independent).

6.3 Testing Observed Proportions: **binom.test()**

When we are dealing with observations that have only two values, we can consider them to be a binomial (two-valued) variable. We illustrate this by taking a brief break from marketing data. On the day of Superbowl XLVIII in 2014, played in the New York City area, Chris took a walk in Manhattan and observed 12 groups of Seattle fans and 8 groups of Denver fans.

Suppose we assume the observations are a random sample of a binomial value (either Seattle or Denver fandom). Is the observed value of 60% Seattle fans significantly different from equal representation (which would be 50% each)? We use binom.test(successes, trials, probability) to test the likelihood of randomly observing 12 cases out of 20 in one direction, if the true likelihood is 50%:

```
> binom.test(12, 20, p=0.5)
  Exact binomial test

data:  12 and 20
number of successes = 12, number of trials = 20, p-value = 0.5034
alternative hypothesis: true probability of success is not equal to 0.5
95 percent confidence interval:
 0.3605426 0.8088099
sample estimates:
probability of success
                  0.6
```

Based on our data, the 95% confidence interval is 36–81%, which includes the null hypothesis value of 50%. Thus, we conclude that observing 60% Seattle fans in a sample of 20 does not conclusively demonstrate that there are more Seattle fans in the larger group of fans roaming New York. We could also interpret the p-value ($p = 0.5034$) as being non-significant, i.e., as failing to support the idea that the results are different from the null hypothesis.

6.3.1 About Confidence Intervals

We have mentioned *confidence intervals* several times, and should take a moment to discuss them because they are widely misunderstood. Our definition of a 95% confidence interval is this: it captures the values that we would expect to see 95% of the time if we repeatedly estimated a statistic using *random samples* of the *same sample size*. When that confidence interval excludes the null hypothesis—such as a hypothesis of 0.5 probability in a binomial test, or a mean difference of 0 when testing a difference between groups—the result is said to be *statistically significant*.

There are many misunderstandings of confidence intervals and statistical significance. Confidence intervals (CIs) do *not* express "how confident we are in the answer" because they do not reflect the degree of confidence in the assumptions. For example, true random sampling is rare, so the presumption of random sampling is usually not completely justified; but that additional uncertainty is not reflected in a CI. CIs are often misunderstood to imply that "the true value lies in the CI range," when in fact it is the other way around; *if* the true value were what we obtained, then we would expect estimates to fall within the CI range 95% of the time in additional samples. Finally, statistical significance does not imply practical *importance* or the meaningfulness of a result; a tiny difference can be statistically significant with a large sample even when it is not actionable or interpretable as a business matter.

In practice, we suggest that before interpreting a result, make sure it is statistically significant for some level of confidence interval (95%, or possibly 80, 90 or 99% depending on how sensitive the matter is). If it is not significant, then your evidence for the result is weak, and you should not interpret it. In that case, ignore the result or collect more data. You might also report it as "non-significant," but only if your audience is sophisticated enough to understand what that means. If the result *is* significant, then proceed with your interpretation and reporting, taking care with how you describe "confidence." Interpret results in light of their importance, not their statistical significance (once it has been established). We recommend to report— and when appropriate, to chart—confidence intervals whenever feasible rather than reporting single point estimates. By reporting CIs, one presents a more complete and accurate description to stakeholders.

Note that this discussion applies to the interpretation of significance in classical statistics (which covers most of this book, and is what practitioners mostly use). We briefly review the Bayesian alternative to confidence intervals (known as *credible intervals*) in Sect. 6.6.2. In general, the cautions expressed above do not directly apply to Bayesian models (there are different considerations), yet the practical recommendations about interpretation and reporting are the same.

There is a general function in R to determine the confidence intervals for a statistical model: `confint()`, which we use in the next section.

6.3.2 More About `binom.test()` and Binomial Distributions

Now that we understand confidence intervals, let's look at `binom.test()` again. What if we had observed 120 out of 200 groups as being Seattle fans, the same proportion as before but in a larger sample?

```
> binom.test(120, 200, p=0.5)
... number of successes = 120, number of trials = 200, p-value =
0.005685 ...
95 percent confidence interval:
 0.5285357 0.6684537
```

With 120/200 cases, the confidence interval no longer includes 50%. If we had observed this, it would be evidence for a preponderance of Seattle fans. Correspondingly, the *p*-value is less than 0.05, indicating a statistically significant difference.

With R, we can ask much more about the distribution. For example, what are the odds that we would observe 8–12 Seattle fans out of 20, if the true rate is 50%? We use the density estimate for a binomial distribution across the range of interest and sum the point probabilities:

```
> sum(dbinom(8:12, 20, 0.5))
[1] 0.736824
```

If we observe 20 fans, and the true split is 50%, there is a 73.7% chance that we would observe between 8 and 12 fans (and thus a $1 - p$ or 27.3% chance of observing fewer than 8 or more than 12).

An "exact" binomial test (the classical method) may be overly conservative in its estimation of confidence intervals [2]. One alternative method is to use binom.confint(, method="agresti-coull"), available in the binom package [45] (you may need to install that package):

```
> library(binom)
> binom.confint(12, 20, method="ac")   # same as "agresti-coull"
          method   x   n mean      lower      upper
1 agresti-coull 12 20   0.6 0.3860304 0.7817446
```

With the Agresti-Coull method, the confidence interval is slightly smaller but still includes 50%. The binom package also computes several other variants on binomial tests, including a Bayesian version.

Finally, Chris also observed that among the 20 groups, 0 had a mixture of Seattle and Denver fans (as inferred from their team clothing). Based on that observation, what should we conclude is the *most likely* proportion of groups that comprise mixed fans? We use the Agresti-Coull method because exact tests have no confidence interval for 0% or 100% observations:

```
> binom.confint(0, 20, method="ac")
          method x   n mean       lower      upper
1 agresti-coull 0 20    0 -0.0286844 0.1898096
```

The negative lower bound may be ignored as an artifact, and we conclude that although Chris observed 0 cases, the occurrence of mixed fandom groups is likely to be somewhere between 0 and 19%.

6.4 Testing Group Means: t.test()

A t-test compares the mean of one sample against the mean of another sample (or against a specific value such as 0). The important point is that it compares the *mean* for exactly *two* sets of data. For instance, in the segment data we might ask whether household income is different among those who own a home and those who do not.

Before applying any statistical test or model, it is important to examine the data and check for skew, discontinuities, and outliers. Many statistical tests assume that the data follows a normal distribution or some other smooth continuous distribution; skewness or outliers violate those assumptions and might lead to an inaccurate test.

One way to check for non-normal distributions is to plot the data with a boxplot or histogram. We have already plotted income above (Figs. 5.7, 5.8, 5.9) and thus skip that step. Additionally, we can check histograms for income overall as well as by home ownership:

```
> hist(seg.df$income)   # not shown
> with(seg.df, hist(income[ownHome=="ownYes"]))   # not shown
> with(seg.df, hist(income[ownHome=="ownNo"]))    # not shown
```

We omit those figures for brevity. Overall, in these histograms and in the boxplots above, income is approximately normally distributed (as it should be, given the data generation procedure, Sect. 5.1).

Now we are ready to test whether home ownership overall is related to differences in income, across *all* segments, using t.test(formula, data). We write the formula using income as the response variable to be modeled on the basis of ownHome as the explanatory variable:

```
> t.test(income ~ ownHome, data=seg.df)

  Welch Two Sample t-test

data:  income by ownHome
t = -3.2731, df = 285.25, p-value = 0.001195
alternative hypothesis: true difference in means is not equal to 0
95 percent confidence interval:
 -12080.155   -3007.193
sample estimates:
 mean in group ownNo mean in group ownYes
           47391.01             54934.68
```

There are several important pieces of information in the output of t.test(). First we see that the *t statistic* is −3.2, with a *p*-value of 0.0012. This means that the null hypothesis of *no difference* in income by home ownership is rejected. The data suggest that people who own their homes have higher income.

Next we see that the 95% confidence interval for the difference is −3007 to −12080. If these are representative data of a larger population, we can have 95% confidence that the group difference is between those values. Finally, we see the sample means for our data: mean income is $47391 for the rent (ownNo) condition, and $54935 for the ownership condition.

What about the difference within the Travelers segment? In Fig. 5.9, we saw that household income appeared to have a wider distribution among members of the Travelers segment who own homes than those who do not. Does that also reflect a difference in the mean income for the two groups? We use the filter data=subset(data, condition) to select just Travelers and repeat the test:

```
> t.test(income ~ ownHome, data=subset(seg.df, Segment=="Travelers"))

  Welch Two Sample t-test

data:  income by ownHome
t = 0.26561, df = 53.833, p-value = 0.7916
alternative hypothesis: true difference in means is not equal to 0
95 percent confidence interval:
 -8508.993 11107.604
sample estimates:
 mean in group ownNo mean in group ownYes
           63188.42             61889.12
```

The confidence interval of -8508 to 11107 includes 0, and thus we conclude—as evidenced in the *p*-value of 0.79—that there is not a significant difference in mean income among those Travelers in our data who own homes and who don't.

We might be puzzled: we saw in the first t-test that there *is* a significant difference in income based on home ownership, but in the second test that there's *no* significant difference within Travelers. Any difference must lie largely outside the Travelers group.

How can we locate where the difference lies? A t-test across all segments will not work because there are four segments and a t-test only compares two groups. We could test income within each segment, one at a time, but this is not a good idea because multiple tests increase the likelihood of finding a spurious difference (a "Type I error"). To track down the difference, we need a more robust procedure that handles multiple groups; we turn to that next.

6.5 Testing Multiple Group Means: Analysis of Variance (ANOVA)

An *analysis of variance* (ANOVA) compares the means of multiple groups. Technically, it does this by comparing the degree to which groups differ as measured by variance in their means (from one another), relative to the variance of observations around each mean (within each group). Hence the importance of *variance* in the name. More casually, you can think of it as testing for difference among multiple means, assuming that the groups have similar variance.

An ANOVA can handle single factors (known as *one-way* ANOVA), two factors (*two-way*), and higher orders including interactions among factors. A complete discussion of ANOVA would take more space than we have here, yet we use it to address our question from the previous section: which factors are related to differences in mean income in the segment data? Specifically, is income related to home ownership, or to segment membership, or both?

The basic R commands for ANOVA are `aov(formula, data)` to set up the model, followed by `anova(model)` to display a standard ANOVA summary. We look at income by home ownership first, and assign the `aov()` model to an object so we can use it with `anova()`. `aov()` uses the standard formula interface to model `income` as a response to `ownHome`:

```
> seg.aov.own <- aov(income ~ ownHome, data=seg.df)
> anova(seg.aov.own)
Analysis of Variance Table

Response: income
             Df      Sum Sq    Mean Sq F value    Pr(>F)
ownHome       1  4.2527e+09 4252661211  10.832  0.001118 **
Residuals   298  1.1700e+11  392611030
---
Signif. codes:  0 '***' 0.001 '**' 0.01 '*' 0.05 '.' 0.1 ' ' 1
```

The value of `Pr(>F)` for `ownHome` is the *p*-value and reflects that there is significant variation in `income` between those who do and do not own their own homes. (This is a slightly different test but the same conclusion that we obtained from the t-test in Sect. 6.4).

What about income by segment? We model that and save the `aov` object:

```
> seg.aov.seg <- aov(income ~ Segment, data=seg.df)
> anova(seg.aov.seg)
Analysis of Variance Table

Response: income
             Df      Sum Sq    Mean Sq F value     Pr(>F)
Segment       3  5.4970e+10 1.8323e+10  81.828  < 2.2e-16 ***
Residuals   296  6.6281e+10 2.2392e+08
...
```

The value of `Pr(>F)` is very close to zero, confirming that income varies significantly by segment. (If you're wondering, $2.2e-16$ means 2.2×10^{-16} and is the smallest non-zero number that R will typically report in Mac OS X. It is the value of the R constant `.Machine$double.eps` that expresses the tolerance of floating point differences.)

If income varies by *both* home ownership and segment, does that mean that a more complete model should include both? We can add both factors into the ANOVA model to test this:

```
> anova(aov(income ~ Segment + ownHome, data=seg.df))
Analysis of Variance Table

Response: income
             Df      Sum Sq    Mean Sq F value Pr(>F)
Segment       3  5.4970e+10 1.8323e+10 81.6381 <2e-16 ***
ownHome       1  6.9918e+07 6.9918e+07  0.3115 0.5772
Residuals   295  6.6211e+10 2.2444e+08
...
```

The results indicate that when we try to explain differences in income by both `Segment` and `ownHome`, segment is a significant predictor ($p \ll 0.01$) but home ownership is *not* a significant predictor. Yet the previous results said that it *was* significant. What's the difference? What is happening is that segment and home ownership are not independent, and the effect is captured sufficiently by segment membership alone. Home ownership accounts for little more over and above what is explained by `Segment`.

Could it be that home ownership is related to income in some segments but not in others? This would be represented in our model by an *interaction* effect. In a model formula, "+" indicates that variables should be modeled for main effects only. We can instead write ":" for an interaction or "*" for both main effect and interaction. We test main effects and interaction of home ownership and segment:

```
> anova(aov(income ~ Segment * ownHome, data=seg.df))
Analysis of Variance Table

Response: income
                  Df     Sum Sq    Mean Sq F value  Pr(>F)
Segment            3 5.4970e+10 1.8323e+10 81.1305  <2e-16 ***
ownHome            1 6.9918e+07 6.9918e+07  0.3096  0.5784
Segment:ownHome    3 2.6329e+08 8.7762e+07  0.3886  0.7613
Residuals        292 6.5948e+10 2.2585e+08
...
```

Again, segment is a significant predictor, while home ownership and the interaction of segment with home ownership are not significant. In other words, segment membership is again the best predictor on its own. We discuss interaction effects further in Chap. 7.

6.5.1   Model Comparison in ANOVA*

Another capability of the `anova()` command is to compare two or more models, using the syntax `anova(model1, model2, ...)` We can compare the `aov()` model with segment alone versus the model with both segment and income:

```
> anova(aov(income ~ Segment, data=seg.df),
+        aov(income ~ Segment + ownHome, data=seg.df))
Analysis of Variance Table

Model 1: income ~ Segment
Model 2: income ~ Segment + ownHome
  Res.Df        RSS Df Sum of Sq      F Pr(>F)
1    296 6.6281e+10
2    295 6.6211e+10  1  69918004 0.3115 0.5772
```

This tells us that Model 2—which includes both segment and home ownership—is not significantly different in overall fit from Model 1. If it were better, the null hypothesis of no difference would be rejected, as shown by a *p*-value ("Pr(>F)") less than 0.05.

It is essential to note that model comparison as performed by the `anova()` command *only* makes sense in the case of nested models. In this context, a model *A* is *nested* within another model *B* when one or more parameters of *B* can be fixed or removed to yield model *A*. In the present case, income ~ Segment is nested within income ~ Segment + ownHome because we can remove ownHome and arrive at the former model. Because they are nested, the two models may be compared by `anova()` or other functions that perform likelihood comparisons.

The model income ~ Segment is *not* nested within income ~ subscribe + ownHome because no amount of removing or fixing parameters in the latter model will produce the former. Thus, those two models could not be compared by anova() in a meaningful way. If you try to compare them, R may produce some output but it is not generally interpretable.

The question of how to compare non-nested models is one we do not tackle in depth in this book, although it recurs in our discussion of structural models in Chap. 10. If you wish to learn more about the issues and methods for general model comparison, a good place to start is to review the literature on the Akaike information criterion (AIC) and Bayesian information criterion (BIC). We review BIC briefly in Sect. 11.3.5.

6.5.2 Visualizing Group Confidence Intervals

A good way to visualize the results of an ANOVA is to plot confidence intervals for the group means. This will reveal more about whether the differences are substantial in magnitude or not. We use the multcomp (multiple comparison) package and its glht(model) (general linear hypothesis) command [100]. You may need to install the "multcomp" package on your system.

Let's take a look at what glht() does. We assign an aov() to an object and inspect it with glht():

```
> library(multcomp)
> seg.aov <- aov(income ~ Segment, data=seg.df)
> glht(seg.aov)

     General Linear Hypotheses

Linear Hypotheses:
                          Estimate
(Intercept) == 0             53091
SegmentSuburb mix == 0        1943
SegmentTravelers == 0         9123
SegmentUrban hip == 0       -31409
```

There is a problem: the default aov() model has an intercept term (corresponding to the Moving up segment) and all other segments are relative to that. This may be difficult for decision makers or clients to understand, so we find it preferable to remove the intercept by adding "-1" to the model formula:

```
> seg.aov <- aov(income ~ -1 + Segment, data=seg.df)
> glht(seg.aov)

     General Linear Hypotheses

Linear Hypotheses:
                          Estimate
SegmentMoving up == 0        53091
SegmentSuburb mix == 0       55034
SegmentTravelers == 0        62214
SegmentUrban hip == 0        21682
```

With the intercept removed, glht() gives us the mean value for each segment. We plot that, using the, par(mar=...) command to add some extra margins for large axis labels:

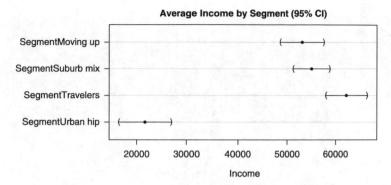

Fig. 6.1 Confidence intervals for income by segment, from an analysis of variance model with `aov()` and `glht()`

```
> par(mar=c(6,10,2,2))    # adjusts margins to preserve axis labels
> plot(glht(seg.aov),
+      xlab="Income", main="Average Income by Segment (95% CI)")
```

The result is Fig. 6.1. The dot shows the mean for each segment, and bars reflect the confidence interval. In Fig. 6.1 we see confidence intervals for the mean income of each segment. It is clear that the average income of Urban hip segment members is substantially lower than the other three groups.

6.5.3   Variable Selection in ANOVA: Stepwise Modeling*

Building models iteratively by adding and removing variables—as an exploratory procedure—can be done automatically with the `step(model)` command. This performs *stepwise* model selection by testing models one at time while changing the variables in the model to see whether the change improves the model. There are options for both *backward* (starting with a larger set of variables and progressively cutting them) and *forward* (adding variables) procedures. The `step()` command uses the Akaike information criterion (AIC) to compare models on the basis of overall fit balanced with model complexity [3].

We perform a backward stepping procedure here (the default direction) by specifying a complete main effect model using the formula shorthand "response ~." The "." is shorthand for "all other variables (except the response variable)." By default this models all main effects without interactions. Higher order effects in this case may be added with superscript notation, such as ".^2" for two-way interactions, but it is usually good to avoid such indiscriminate interaction modeling.

For our `aov()` model for income, the command to run the stepwise procedure for main effects and save the resulting best model is:

```
> seg.aov.step <- step(aov(income ~ ., data=seg.df))
Start:  AIC=5779.17
income ~ age + gender + kids + ownHome + subscribe + Segment

              Df  Sum of Sq         RSS      AIC
- age          1  4.7669e+06  6.5661e+10  5777.2
- ownHome      1  1.0337e+08  6.5759e+10  5777.6
- kids         1  1.3408e+08  6.5790e+10  5777.8
- subscribe    1  1.5970e+08  6.5816e+10  5777.9
- gender       1  2.6894e+08  6.5925e+10  5778.4
<none>                        6.5656e+10  5779.2
- Segment      3  1.9303e+10  8.4959e+10  5850.5

Step:  AIC=5777.19
income ~ gender + kids + ownHome + subscribe + Segment
... [several steps] ...
Step:  AIC=5772.02
income ~ Segment

            Df Sum of Sq         RSS      AIC
<none>                     6.6281e+10  5772.0
- Segment    3  5.497e+10  1.2125e+11  5947.2
```

We see that step() started by modeling income with all six other variables, went
through several steps of removing variables, and concluded with the "best" model
as income ~ Segment.

We examine the result of step(), which was saved in a model object, using the
standard anova() command:

```
> anova(seg.aov.step)
Analysis of Variance Table

Response: income
            Df       Sum Sq     Mean Sq F value     Pr(>F)
Segment      3  5.4970e+10  1.8323e+10  81.828  < 2.2e-16 ***
Residuals  296  6.6281e+10  2.2392e+08
---
Signif. codes:  0 '***' 0.001 '**' 0.01 '*' 0.05 '.' 0.1 ' ' 1
```

Stepwise procedures must be used with caution. They should not be used to determine a final model, and they may encourage inadvertent or deliberate p-hacking (e.g.,
exploring data to find a relationship, and subsequently claiming that relationship to be
a theory-based hypothesis). When using stepwise procedures, consider strong replication processes, such as those suggested for classification models (Sect. 11.4). In
more general cases—where there may be dozens, hundreds, or thousands of available
variables—variable selection is better informed by procedures such as a lasso [188]
or random forest [21] procedure. We examine random forest models in Sect. 11.4.2.

6.6 Bayesian ANOVA: Getting Started*

This is an advanced section that is primarily recommended for readers who have
some familiarity with the principles of Bayesian analysis and seek an introduction to
Bayesian models in R. We do *not* provide a comprehensive overview of the methods,

and assume that the reader is generally familiar with Bayesian concepts such as a *prior*, *posterior*, and *posterior sampling*.

For other readers, we attempt to give enough context to make the concepts approachable. Although this may be insufficient for a real project, it introduces how such models work and demonstrates the steps involved. We refer you to Sect. 6.8 for additional references.

6.6.1 Why Bayes?

We suggest analysts consider Bayesian analyses instead of traditional ("frequentist") statistical models when possible. Bayesian analysis is often a more direct way to tackle the questions we usually want to know: "Is this hypothesis likely to be true?", "How much confidence should I have?", and "What are the most likely values?" A Bayesian analysis does not take refuge in the double and triple negatives of traditional models ("we failed to reject the null hypothesis that there is no difference between the models"). Instead, it answers, "Given these data, how likely is the difference?"

Despite the advantages, there are reasons Bayesian analyses are not more common: there are fewer Bayesian teachers, texts, and practitioners; many Bayesian texts are dense with formulas; and the field is rapidly developing and some contentious issues have not been settled. Perhaps most importantly, available software packages are designed to make traditional models easy to run and that ease has not yet been brought to many areas of Bayesian practice. For an analyst, it may be easier and more productive to use traditional models in day-to-day work. Happily, Bayesian and traditional methods often lead to the same business conclusions (although not always).

R is on the forefront of making Bayesian methods more widely available. This is made possible by the many contributors to R, and by the R language itself which is well suited for the iterated analyses that Bayesian methods require. In this section, we demonstrate a starting point for a Bayesian version of ANOVA.

6.6.2 Basics of Bayesian ANOVA*

There are many options in R for Bayesian analyses (see the Bayesian task view on CRAN: http://cran.r-project.org/web/views/). The MCMCpack package is a robust, fast, and powerful Bayesian kit. However, we opt here to use the BayesFactor package for its simplicity. In particular, BayesFactor has sensible defaults for weakly informative prior probabilities [142, 170] and makes model comparison easy. You will need to install the BayesFactor package for the following code.

We use the lmBF(formula, data) command to specify our ANOVA model as a linear model for income modeled by the Segment factor:

```
> set.seed(96761)
> library(BayesFactor)  # install if needed
> seg.bf1 <- lmBF(income ~ Segment, data=seg.df)
```

We set a pseudorandom number seed because this function will take *draws* from the *posterior distribution*. What does that mean? Briefly, a common way to estimate a Bayesian model is to do repeated assessments of how well a proposed model fits the data.

To understand this we must consider the concept of a *parameter*. We have not used the term yet, but a statistical model estimates one or more parameters that define the presumed distribution. For example, a t-test compares the mean of two groups, and the parameter it estimates is the difference between the means. An ANOVA model can also be used to estimate the mean. It was confidence in the estimation of that parameter that we plotted in Sect. 6.5.2.

Common Bayesian models operate by selecting initially random values for model parameters (such as the mean for a segment). The process then retains the parameter according to the likelihood that it fits the data and prior expectation (an estimated starting point, if we have one), and iterates that process thousands or even millions of times. The retained estimates are the *draws* from the posterior distribution for the parameters, while the final estimated distribution of them is the *posterior distribution*. The end result is a large sample of possible parameters and their likelihoods, or in other words, an outline of the most likely parameters for a given model. Again, see Sect. 6.8 for more.

After fitting the model for income ~ Segment, we might inspect it directly. However, instead of starting to interpret a model, it is preferable to have a sense that it is an *adequate* model. So we first compare it to the alternative we considered in Sect. 6.5.1, which modeled income ~ Segment + ownHome. We would then interpret the Segment-only model if it fits the data better (or fits just as well but is simpler).

Model comparison in BayesFactor is performed by using the "/" operator to find the ratio of the models' Bayes Factors. We have the first model seg.bf1 from above, and now fit the second model with two factors that we wish to compare:

```
> seg.bf2 <- lmBF(income ~ Segment + ownHome, data=seg
  .df)
0
|----|----|----|----|----|----|----|----|----|----|
*****************************************************|
> seg.bf1 / seg.bf2
Bayes factor analysis
--------------
[1] Segment : 6.579729 +/- 1.62%

Against denominator:
  income ~ Segment + ownHome
```

This tells us that the ratio of Bayes Factors for model 1 (~ Segment) versus model 2 (~ Segment + ownHome) is 6.58. This means that model 1 is the preferable model by a factor of 6.58.

To find the model parameters and their credible ranges, we use the `posterior (model, index, draws)` command to draw 10000 samples of the possible parameters from model 1:

```
> seg.bf.chain <- posterior(seg.bf1, 1, iterations = 10000)
0
                                   %
|----|----|----|----|----|----|----|----|----|----|
**************************************************|
```

The draws are known as a *chain* because they are estimated by a Markov chain process; we skip those details (see [73]).

Before we examine the estimates, we should inspect whether the draws *converged* to stable values such that the estimates are reliable. In BayesFactor, we simply call `plot()` on the chain object. We select columns 1:6 from the draws because there are six parameters we care about: the population mean and variance (*mu* and *sigma*) and the estimates of means for the four segments:

```
> plot(seg.bf.chain[ , 1:6])    # check console: may need <Return> to see all
```

The charts for the first three parameters are shown in Fig. 6.2; we omit the other three charts because they are nearly identical. We interpret the charts as follows. On the left, we see the estimated parameter values (y axis) plotted against the draw sequence (x axis). These form a fat but straight line, sometimes called a "fuzzy caterpillar", which means the estimates varied around a stable central point; thus they converged.

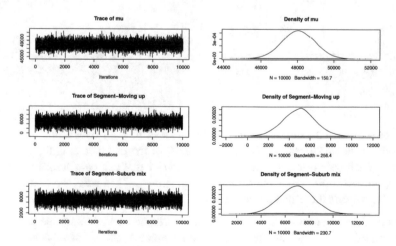

Fig. 6.2 Trace plot for draws from the posterior distribution of a Bayesian ANOVA for income by segment, for the first three parameters. The left hand charts show trace convergence; right hand charts show the posterior distributions for the parameters

(If they had not converged, the plot would show erratic variations up or down, or would spread out increasingly rather than being straight.)

On the right, we see a density plot of the values. The density shape is approximately normal, which matches the assumption of the regression model. Thus, the charts confirm that the model was stable and converged (note that these don't mean the model is *useful*, only that it achieved a stable estimate).

6.6.3   Inspecting the Posterior Draws*

We now examine the parameters as expressed in our posterior draw chain. A simple summary() of the chain shows us the estimates:

```
> summary(seg.bf.chain)

Iterations = 1:10000
Thinning interval - 1
Number of chains = 1
Sample size per chain = 10000

1. Empirical mean and standard deviation for each variable,
   plus standard error of the mean:

                      Mean          SD  Naive SE Time-series SE
mu                 4.806e+04 8.969e+02 8.969e+00      8.804e+00
Segment-Moving up  4.951e+03 1.548e+03 1.548e+01      1.548e+01
Segment-Suburb mix 6.927e+03 1.373e+03 1.373e+01      1.373e+01
Segment-Travelers  1.398e+04 1.487e+03 1.487e+01      1.518e+01
Segment-Urban hip -2.586e+04 1.777e+03 1.777e+01      1.956e+01
sig2               2.259e+08 1.856e+07 1.856e+05      1.856e+05
g_Segment          2.138e+00 3.359e+00 3.359e-02      3.359e-02

2. Quantiles for each variable:

                       2.5%        25%        50%        75%      97.5%
mu                 4.631e+04  4.745e+04  4.805e+04  4.868e+04  4.982e+04
Segment-Moving up  1.925e+03  3.916e+03  4.968e+03  5.961e+03  8.054e+03
Segment-Suburb mix 4.243e+03  5.996e+03  6.934e+03  7.857e+03  9.608e+03
Segment-Travelers  1.104e+04  1.297e+04  1.399e+04  1.499e+04  1.690e+04
Segment-Urban hip -2.934e+04 -2.703e+04 -2.586e+04 -2.466e+04 -2.239e+04
sig2               1.923e+08  2.128e+08  2.249e+08  2.378e+08  2.647e+08
g_Segment          3.765e-01  7.949e-01  1.298e+00  2.284e+00  8.738e+00
```

The first section of the summary ("1. Empirical mean and ...") gives arithmetic central tendency estimates for the 10000 draws of each of the parameters in the chain: the mean of each parameter, the standard deviation of that estimate across the 10000 draws, and so forth. The second result ("Quantiles ...") is what we prefer to use instead; it reports the actual observed quantiles for each of the parameters.

Note that the model estimates an overall mu that is the best guess for the population mean regardless of segment effects, and then estimates each segment as a deviation from that. However, for many purposes, it is more useful to have direct estimates for the mean of each segment rather than its deviation. To estimate the direct values for each segment, we add the population value (mu) to the deviations for each segment. However, we cannot simply do that with the *aggregate* numbers here by adding the mu row to each of the other rows. Why not? Because the best estimates of segment totals are found *within* each draw; we need to compute segment values at that level and then summarize those estimates. Luckily that is easy to do in R.

To see how, let's examine the chain object:

```
> head(seg.bf.chain)
...
          mu Segment-Moving up Segment-Suburb mix Segment-Travelers  ...
[1,] 48055.75         4964.3105           6909.032          13983.21 ...
[2,] 47706.52         6478.1497           7816.873          12160.32 ...
[3,] 48362.90         5228.0718           6654.030          12565.87 ...
[4,] 49417.43         5300.9543           7249.228          12218.89 ...
...
```

We see rows (10000 in all) for the draws, and columns for the estimates for each segment. By indexing the chain, we confirm that it is arranged as a matrix:

```
> seg.bf.chain[1:4, 1:5]
          mu Segment-Moving up Segment-Suburb mix Segment-Travelers  ...
[1,] 48055.75          4964.310           6909.032          13983.21 ...
[2,] 47706.52          6478.150           7816.873          12160.32 ...
[3,] 48362.90          5228.072           6654.030          12565.87 ...
[4,] 49417.43          5300.954           7249.228          12218.89 ...
```

This means that simple vector math will work to find within-draw estimates for each row. We do this by adding column 1, the population estimate, to each of the other columns 2–5. We test this first on rows 1 : 4 only:

```
> seg.bf.chain[1:4, 2:5] + seg.bf.chain[1:4, 1]
     Segment-Moving up Segment-Suburb mix Segment-Travelers Segment-Urban hip
[1,]          53020.06           54964.78          62038.95          22199.20
[2,]          54184.67           55523.40          59866.84          21251.18
[3,]          53590.97           55016.93          60928.77          23914.93
[4,]          54718.38           56666.66          61636.32          24648.35
```

It works, so now we compute that total for all rows and assign the result to a new object. Then we get quantiles from that object as the overall best estimates of segment income:

```
> seg.bf.chain.total <- seg.bf.chain[, 2:5] + seg.bf.chain[, 1]
> seg.bf.ci <- t(apply(seg.bf.chain.total, 2,
+                 quantile, pr=c(0.025, 0.5, 0.975)))
> seg.bf.ci
                        2.5%      50%     97.5%
Segment-Moving up   49582.08 53020.98 56522.05
Segment-Suburb mix  52039.66 54988.99 57867.29
Segment-Travelers   58799.46 62048.33 65355.62
Segment-Urban hip   17992.85 22216.26 26450.56
```

In the apply() command, we applied the quantile() function to the columns with the probabilities that we wanted for a 95% credible interval. Then we transposed the result with t() to be more readable (treating the segments as "cases").

Those values are the best estimates of the 95% credible range for the estimate of *average income* as modeled by segment, under the assumptions of our model.

6.6.4 Plotting the Bayesian Credible Intervals*

We can plot the credible intervals from the previous section using the capability of the `ggplot2` package to plot error bars. Install the "ggplot2" package if needed. The `ggplot2` commands work best with data frames, so we coerce our credible interval object `seg.bf.ci` to a data frame and add a column for segment names:

```
> library(ggplot2)
> seg.bf.df <- data.frame(seg.bf.ci)
> seg.bf.df$Segment <- rownames(seg.bf.df)
```

Now we construct the chart in three steps. We add elements corresponding to the values of segment quartiles in the summary data frame:

```
> p <- ggplot(seg.bf.df, aes(x=Segment, y=X50., ymax=X97.5., ymin=X2.5.))
```

We add points for the *y* values (the estimated median in this case), and add the 2.5% and 97.5% quartiles as "error bars" (which are automatically associated with the names `ymax` and `ymin` as we set above):

```
> p <- p + geom_point(size=4) + geom_errorbar(width=0.2) + ylab("Income")
```

Finally we draw that plot object while adding a title and flipping the plot coordinates so the segments are nicely on the left:

```
> p + ggtitle("95% CI for Mean Income by Segment") + coord_flip()
```

The result is Fig. 6.3, a chart that is easy to explain yet comes from a powerful underlying Bayesian model.

You might notice that the Bayesian results in Fig. 6.3 are not all that different from the classical results in Fig. 6.1. This is to be expected because they come from the same data. In fact, if the model is exactly correct and the population is infinite, then as the sample size approaches infinity, the Bayesian and classical confidence intervals will be the same.

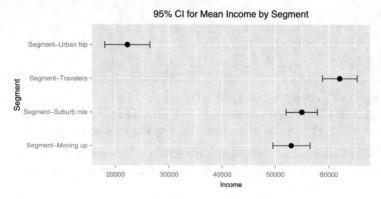

Fig. 6.3 Using `ggplot2` to plot the credible intervals for income by segment from the Bayesian posterior draws

In that case, why one would want to use the Bayesian approach? One answer will come in Chaps. 7 and 13 when we introduce *hierarchical* methods that are more flexibly modeled in a Bayesian framework. Another answer is that data are never infinite, and in our opinion Bayesian models more directly address confidence in models for the data you actually have.

As you can see from R provides powerful capability for Bayesian analysis. R's open-source structure has made it easier for the software to keep pace with a rapidly evolving field. If you run into limitations with existing packages, you can use R's programming language to accomplish tasks (as we did here to compute posterior draws for total segment income).

6.7 Key Points

This chapter introduced formal statistical tests in R. Following are some of the important lessons. To perform statistical tests on differences by group:

- `chisq.test()` (Sect. 6.2) and `binom.test()` (Sect. 6.3) find confidence intervals and perform hypothesis tests on tables and proportion data, respectively. The `binom` package offers options such as Agresti-Coull and Bayesian versions of binomial tests that may be more informative and robust than standard exact binomial tests (Sect. 6.3).
- A `t.test()` is a common way to test for differences between the means of two groups (or between one group and a fixed value) (Sect. 6.4).
- Analysis of variance (ANOVA) is a more general way to test for differences in mean among several groups that are identified by one or more factors. The basic model is fit with `aov()` and common summary statistics are reported with `anova()` (Sect. 6.5).
- The `anova()` command is also useful to compare two or more ANOVA or other linear models, provided that they are nested models (Sect. 6.5.1).
- Stepwise model selection with `step()` is one way to evaluate a list of variables to select a well-fitting model, although we recommend that it be used with caution as other procedures may be more appropriate (Sect. 6.5.3).

We reviewed a few advanced topics for statistical models and data visualization:

- Plotting a `glht()` object from the `multcomp` package is a good way to visualize confidence intervals for ANOVA models (Sect. 6.5.2).
- A relatively straightforward starting point for Bayesian ANOVA and other linear models is the `BayesFactor` package (Sect. 6.6).
- Bayesian models should be evaluated for the stability and distribution of their estimated parameters using trace and density plots (Sect. 6.6).
- Credible intervals (and other types of intervals) may be plotted with the `ggplot2` option to add `geom_errorbar()` lines for groups (Sect. 6.6.4).

6.8 Learning More*

For categorical data analysis, which we briefly sampled with our discussion of chi-square and binomial tests, the best starting place—although not specific to R—is Agresti's *An Introduction to Categorical Data Analysis* [1].

T-tests and ANOVA are nothing more than flavors of general linear models, which we cover in more depth in Chap. 7. In the R domain, there are many books on linear models. A readable text that focuses on understanding basic models and getting them right is Fox and Weisberg's *An R Companion to Applied Regression* [62].

Readings on Bayesian data analysis vary tremendously in mathematical prerequisites and authors' styles. McElreath's Statistical Rethinking is an excellent exposition of Bayesian models in R, designed to teach both intuition and practical, computational usage of the models with basic college mathematics [136]. Kruschke's *Doing Bayesian Data Analysis* [120] is an undergraduate textbook that uses R and builds intuition from the ground up with high school level mathematics. It is a lengthy and thorough exposition of Bayesian thinking. A standard text that moves faster with more mathematics is Gelman et al. *Bayesian Data Analysis* [73]. For advanced marketing applications, especially hierarchical linear models and stated choice models, a standard text is Rossi, Allenby, and McCulloch's *Bayesian Statistics and Marketing* [168].

We presented charts in this chapter using the `ggplot2` package, which is described in detail in an eponymous book: Wickham's *ggplot2* [198].

6.9 Exercises

The following exercises use the e-commerce data set as described in Sect. 3.8.1.

1. Among Teachers and Parents who visited the site, which group was more likely to know the product of interest in advance (variable productKnewWhatWanted)? Answer with both descriptive statistics and visualization.
2. In the previous exercise, should you limit observations to just those with product knowledge of "Yes" or "No"? Why or why not? How does it change the result?
3. Is the difference in prior product knowledge (variable `productKnewWhat Wanted`) statistically significantly different for teachers versus parents? (*Hint*: make a table of counts, and then select only the rows and columns needed for testing.)
4. Using the integer approximation of page views (see Exercises in Sect. 4.10), describe page views for parents, teachers, and health professionals. Use a `by()` or `aggregate()` function as appropriate.
5. What is the proportion of teachers who had prior product knowledge, and what is the proportion for parents?

6. Suppose we believe that the parent proportion in the previous exercise is the true value for both parents and teachers. How do we compare the observed proportion for teachers to that? Is is statistically significantly different? What is the 95% confidence interval for the observations among teachers?

7. Using the integer approximation of page views (see Exercises in Sect. 4.10), compare the mean number of page views for Parents and Teachers. Which is higher? Is the difference statistically significant? What is the confidence interval for the difference?

8. Compare estimated page views (variable `pageViewInt`) for all profile groups. Are the groups statistically significantly different? Answer and visualize the differences.

9. Repeat the previous exercise, and limit the data to just Parents and Teachers. Explain and visualize. Is the answer different than in the previous exercise? Why?

10. *Repeat the previous comparison for page views among just Teachers and Parents, using a Bayesian Analysis of Variance. Report the statistics and visualize it. Is the answer the same or different as obtained from classical ANOVA?

11. *Write a function of your own to compute proportions from a table of frequency counts. Compare your code to that in `prop.table()`. (Don't forget that you can see the code for most functions by typing the name of the function into the command line.)

Chapter 7
Identifying Drivers of Outcomes: Linear Models

In this chapter we investigate linear models, which are often used in marketing to explore the relationship between an outcome of interest and other variables. A common application in survey analysis is to model satisfaction with a product in relation to specific elements of the product and its delivery; this is called "satisfaction drivers analysis." Linear models are also used to understand how price and advertising are related to sales, and this is called "marketing mix modeling." There are many other situations in which it is helpful to model an outcome, known formally as a *response* or *dependent* variable, as a function of predictor variables (also known as *explanatory* or *independent* variables). Once a relationship is estimated, one can use the model to make predictions or forecasts of the likely outcome for other values of the predictors.

In this chapter, we illustrate linear modeling with a satisfaction drivers analysis using survey data for customers who have visited an amusement park. In the survey, respondents report their levels of satisfaction with different aspects of their experience, and their overall satisfaction. Marketers frequently use this type of data to figure out what aspects of the experience *drive* overall satisfaction, asking questions such as, "Are people who are more satisfied with the rides also more satisfied with their experience overall?" If the answer to this question is "no," then the company will know to invest in improving other aspects of the experience.

An important thing to understand is that *driver* does *not* imply causation. A linear model only assumes an association among variables. Consider a survey of automobile purchasers that finds a positive association between satisfaction and price paid. If a brand manager wants customers to be more satisfied, does this imply that she should raise prices? Probably not. It is more likely that price is associated with higher quality, which then leads to higher satisfaction. Results should be interpreted cautiously and considered in the context of domain knowledge.

Linear models are a core tool in statistics, and R provides an excellent set of functions for estimating them. As in other chapters, we review the basics and demonstrate how to conduct linear modeling in R, yet the chapter does not review everything that

© Springer Nature Switzerland AG 2019
C. Chapman and E. M. Feit, *R For Marketing Research and Analytics*, Use R!,
https://doi.org/10.1007/978-3-030-14316-9_7

one would wish to know in practice. We encourage readers who are unfamiliar with linear modeling to supplement this chapter with a review of linear modeling in a statistics or marketing research textbook, where it might appear under a name such as *regression analysis*, *linear regression*, or *least-squares fitting*.

7.1   Amusement Park Data

In this section, we simulate data for a hypothetical survey of visitors to an amusement park. This data set comprises a few objective measures: whether the respondent visited on a weekend (which will be the variable `weekend` in the data frame), the number of children brought (`num.child`), and distance traveled to the park (`distance`). There are also subjective measures of satisfaction: expressed satisfaction overall (`overall`) and satisfaction with the rides, games, waiting time, and cleanliness (`rides`, `games`, `wait`, and `clean`, respectively).

Unlike earlier chapters, in this one we recommend that you *skip* the simulation section and download the data. There is no new R syntax, and this will allow you to review the models without knowing the outcome in advance. To download and check:

```
> sat.df <- read.csv("http://goo.gl/HKnl74")
> str(sat.df)
'data.frame':    500 obs. of  8 variables:
 $ weekend  : Factor w/ 2 levels "no","yes": 2 2 1 2 1 1 2 1 1 2 ...
 $ num.child: int  0 2 1 0 4 5 1 0 0 3 ...
 $ distance : num  114.6 27 63.3 25.9 54.7 ...
...
```

If you have the data, skip to Sect. 7.2 for now, and return later to review the simulation code.

7.1.1   Simulating the Amusement Park Data

To start the data simulation, we set the random number seed to make the process repeatable and declare a variable for the number of observations:

```
> set.seed(08226)
> nresp <- 500    # number of survey respondents
```

Our hypothetical survey includes four questions about a customer's satisfaction with different dimensions of a visit to the amusement park: satisfaction with rides (`rides`), games (`games`), waiting times (`wait`), and cleanliness (`clean`), along with a rating of overall satisfaction (`overall`). In such surveys, respondents often answer similarly on all satisfaction questions; this is known as the *halo effect*.

We simulate a satisfaction halo with a random variable for each customer, `halo`, that does not appear in the final data but is used to influence the other ratings:

```
> halo <- rnorm(n=nresp, mean=0, sd=5)
```

We generate responses for the satisfaction ratings by adding each respondent's halo to the value of another random variable that is specific to the survey item (satisfaction with rides, cleanliness, and so forth).

We add a constant just to adjust the range slightly, and convert the continuous values to integers using `floor()`. This gives us a final value for each satisfaction item on a 100-point scale. Although scales rating 1–5, 1–7, or 1–11 may be more common in practice, such discrete scales introduce complications that we discuss in Sect. 7.8; those would detract from our presentation here. So we assume that the data comes from a 100-point scale. Such near-continuous values might be obtained by measuring where respondents mark levels of satisfaction along a line on paper or by touching a screen.

Creating the `nresp` responses can be done in just one line per variable:

```
> rides <- floor(halo + rnorm(n=nresp, mean=80, sd=3)+1)
> games <- floor(halo + rnorm(n=nresp, mean=70, sd=7)+5)
> wait <- floor(halo + rnorm(n=nresp, mean=65, sd=10)+9)
> clean <- floor(halo + rnorm(n=nresp, mean=85, sd=2)+1)
```

By adding `halo` to the response for each question, we create positive correlation between the responses. The constants +1, +5, and +9 are arbitrary to adjust the ranges just for appearance. You can verify the correlation between variables that share the halo by using `cor()`:

```
> cor(rides, games)
[1] 0.4551851
```

Satisfaction surveys often include other questions related to the customer experience. For the amusement park data, we include whether the visit was on a weekend, how far the customer traveled to the park in miles, and the number of children in the party. We generate this data using two functions: `rlnorm(n, meanlog, sdlog)` to sample a log-normal distribution for `distance`, and `sample(x, size, replace)` to sample discrete distributions for `weekend` and number of children (`num.child`):

```
> distance <- rlnorm(n=nresp, meanlog=3, sdlog=1)
> num.child <- sample(x=0:5, size=nresp, replace=TRUE,
+                     prob=c(0.3, 0.15, 0.25, 0.15, 0.1, 0.05))
> weekend <- as.factor(sample(x=c("yes", "no"), size=nresp, replace=TRUE,
+                     prob=c(0.5,0.5)))
```

We create the overall satisfaction rating as a function of ratings for the various aspects of the visit (satisfaction with rides, cleanliness, and so forth), distance traveled, and the number of children:

```
> overall <- floor(halo + 0.5*rides + 0.1*games + 0.3*wait + 0.2*clean +
+                 0.03*distance + 5*(num.child==0) + 0.3*wait*(num.child>0) +
+                 rnorm(n=nresp, mean=0, sd=7) - 51)
```

Although this is a lengthy formula, it is relatively simple with five parts:

1. It includes `halo` to capture the latent satisfaction (also included in `rides` and the other ratings)

2. It adds the satisfaction variables (`rides`, `games`, `wait`, and `clean`) with a weight for each one
3. It includes weighted contributions for other influences such as `distance`
4. There is random normal variation using `rnorm()`
5. It uses `floor()` to produce an integer, with a constant -51 that adjusts the total to be 100 points or less

When a variable like `overall` is a linear combination of other variables plus random noise, we say that it follows a *linear model*. Although these ratings are not a model of real amusement parks, the structure exemplifies the kind of linear model one might propose. With real data, one would wish to discover the contributions from the various elements, which are the weights associated with the various predictors. In the next section, we examine how to fit such a linear model.

Before proceeding, we combine the data points into a data frame and remove unneeded objects from the workspace:

```
> sat.df <- data.frame(weekend, num.child, distance, rides, games, wait,
+ clean, overall)
> rm(nresp, weekend, distance, num.child, halo, rides, games, wait, clean,
+     overall)
```

7.2   Fitting Linear Models with `lm()`

Every modeling effort should begin with an inspection of the data, so we start with a `summary()` of the data:

```
> summary(sat.df)
 weekend       num.child           distance                rides            games
 no :259    Min.   :0.000    Min.    :  0.5267    Min.    : 72.00    Min.    : 57.00
 yes:241    1st Qu.:0.000    1st Qu.: 10.3181    1st Qu.: 82.00    1st Qu.: 73.00
 ...
            Max.   :5.000    Max.    :239.1921    Max.    :100.00    Max.    :100.00
         wait                clean               overall
 Min.   : 40.0    Min.    : 74.0    Min.    :  6.00
 1st Qu.: 62.0    1st Qu.: 84.0    1st Qu.: 40.00
 ...
 Max.   :100.0    Max.    :100.0    Max.    :100.00
```

The data comprise eight variables from a survey of satisfaction with a recent visit to an amusement park. The first three variables describe features of the visit: `weekend` is a factor with two levels, `no` and `yes`; `num.child` is the number of children in the party, 0–5; and `distance` is the distance traveled to the park. The remaining five variables are satisfaction ratings for the customers' experience of the rides, games, wait times, cleanliness, and overall experience of the park, on a 100 point scale.

7.2.1 Preliminary Data Inspection

Before modeling, there are two important things to check: that each individual variable has a reasonable distribution, and that joint relationships among the variables are appropriate for modeling.

We do an initial check of the variable distributions and relationships in `sat.df` using `scatterplotMatrix()` as described in Sect. 4.4.2:

```
> library(car)
> scatterplotMatrix(sat.df)
```

The result is Fig. 7.1, where we see in the diagonal elements that each of the satisfaction rating density plots is close to normally distributed, but `distance` has a highly skewed distribution. For most purposes it is a good idea to transform such a variable to a more normal distribution. As we discussed in Sect. 4.5.4, a common transformation for such data is a logarithmic transform; we take the `log()` of `distance` and add that to the data frame:

```
> sat.df$logdist <- log(sat.df$distance)
```

We could then run `scatterplotMatrix(sat.df)` again (or run `hist(sat.df$logdist)`) to confirm that the new variable `logdist` is more normally distributed.

To check the relationships among variables, we examine the bivariate scatterplots shown in Fig. 7.1. They show few concerns apart from the need to transform `distance`. For example, the pairwise scatterplots of our continuous measures are generally elliptical in shape, which is a good indication that they are appropriate to use in a linear model. One question, however, concerns the fact that the variables in the lower right of Fig. 7.1 are positively correlated.

Why is this a concern? A common issue with marketing data and especially satisfaction surveys is that variables may be highly correlated with one another. Although we as marketers care about individual elements of customers' experiences such as their amusement park experience with rides and games, when completing a survey, the respondents might not give independent ratings to each of those items. They may instead form an overall *halo* rating and rate individual elements of the experience in light of that overall feeling.

When variables are strongly related in this way, it is difficult to assess their individual effects with statistical models. As we will see in Sect. 9.1, the effect can be so severe that the relationships become uninterpretable without taking some action to handle the high correlations.

Given the positive associations shown in Fig. 7.1, we investigate the correlation structure further using `cor()` and `corrplot()` as demonstrated in Sect. 4.5.2:

```
> corrplot.mixed(cor(sat.df[ , c(2, 4:9)]), upper="ellipse")
```

We selected columns `c(2, 4:9)` to exclude the categorical variable `weekend` and the raw variable `distance` that we transformed as `logdist`. The result is the

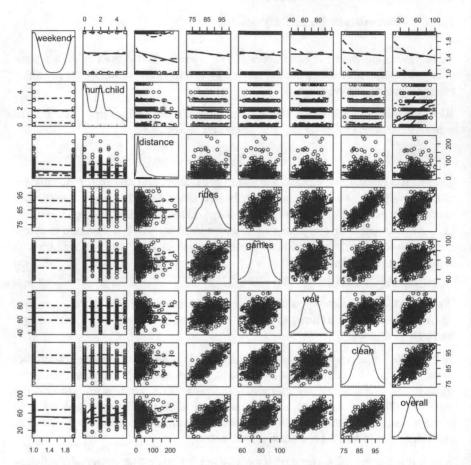

Fig. 7.1 An inspection of data using `scatterplotMatrix()` before we perform further modeling. This reveals that `distance` has a highly skewed distribution and should be transformed before modeling. Several variables, such as `rides` and `clean`, are obviously correlated and should be examined further for the strength of association

correlation plot shown in Fig. 7.2. We see that the satisfaction items are moderately to strongly associated with one another. However, none of the items appear to be nearly identical, as would be indicated by correlations exceeding $r > 0.8$ for several of them, or $r > 0.9$ for particular pairs. Thus, on an initial inspection, it appears to be acceptable to proceed with modeling the relationships among these variables.

In Chap. 9 we discuss how to assess this question in more detail and what to do when high correlations pose a more significant problem. In Chap. 8 we discuss strategies to find underlying dimensions that appear in highly correlated data.

Fig. 7.2 A correlation plot
for the amusement park data.
Inspection of the item
associations is always
recommended before linear
modeling, in order to check
for extremely high
correlations between items
(such as $r > 0.9$). In the
present data, `rides` and
`clean` are highly related
($r = 0.79$) but not so
strongly that remediation is
strictly required

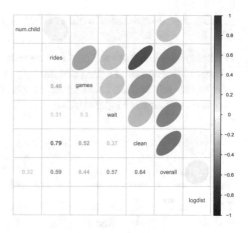

7.2.2 Recap: Bivariate Association

The goal of a satisfaction drivers analysis is to discover relationships between customers' satisfaction with features of the of the service (or product) and their overall
experience. For example, to what extent is satisfaction with the park's rides related
to overall experience? Is the relationship strong or weak? One way to assess this is
to plot those two variables against each other as we did in Chap. 4:

```
> plot(overall~rides, data=sat.df,
+       xlab="Satisfaction with Rides", ylab="Overall Satisfaction")
```

This creates a plot similar to the one in Fig. 7.3, except that it does not include the
blue line (but we'll get to that soon). The points on the plot show that there is a
tendency for people with higher satisfaction with rides to also have higher overall
satisfaction.

Fig. 7.3 Scatterplot
comparing satisfaction with
rides to overall satisfaction
among recent visitors to an
amusement park

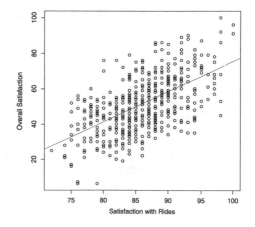

7.2.3   Linear Model with a Single Predictor

A linear model estimates a best fit line through the cloud of points. The function to
estimate a linear model is lm(formula, data), where data is a data frame containing the data and formula is a R formula, as we saw in Sect. 6.5 for anova().
To estimate a linear model relating overall satisfaction to satisfaction with rides, we
write:

```
> lm(overall ~ rides, data=sat.df)
...
Coefficients:
(Intercept)           rides
    -94.962           1.703
```

The formula above can be read as "overall varies with rides." When we
call lm(), R finds a line that best fits the relationship of sat.df$rides and
sat.df$overall. In the output, R repeats the model for reference and reports
two Coefficients, which are the intercept and the slope of the fitted line. Those
can be used to determine the best estimate for any respondent's report of overall
based on knowing his or her value for rides. For example, from this model we
would expect that a customer who gives a rating of 95 for satisfaction with rides
would give an overall rating of:

```
> -94.962 + 1.703*95
[1] 66.823
```

Using coefficients manually is not very efficient. This brings us to our next topic,
lm; objects.

7.2.4   lm Objects

Like most other R functions, lm() returns an object that we can save and use for
other purposes. Typically, we assign the result of lm() to an object that is used in
subsequent lines of code. For example, we can assign the result of lm() to a new
object m1:

```
> m1 <- lm(overall ~ rides, data=sat.df)
```

We can then reuse the model by accessing m1. If we redraw the scatterplot for
overall ~ rides, we can add the linear fit line using abline(m1):

```
> plot(overall ~ rides, data=sat.df,
+        xlab="Satisfaction with Rides", ylab="Overall Satisfaction")
> abline(m1, col='blue')
```

The result is shown in Fig. 7.3. abline() recognizes that it is dealing with an lm
object and uses the slope and the intercept from m1 to draw the line.

We can also inspect the m1 object:

```
> str(m1)
List of 12
 $ coefficients : Named num [1:2]  -95 1.7
  ..- attr(*, "names")= chr [1:2] "(Intercept)" "rides"
 $ residuals    : Named num [1:500]  -6.22 11.78 11.18 -17.93 19.89 ...
 ...
```

This shows us that the m1 object is a list with 12 specific members that contain everything lm() knows about the model. (To refresh yourself on list objects, see Chap. 2.) The first element of this list is $coefficients, which you can inspect:

```
> m1$coefficients
(Intercept)        rides
 -94.962246     1.703285
```

You don't have to use the full name m1$coefficients. In many places in R, it works to abbreviate long names, such as m1$coef.

As with other types of R objects, there is a summary() function for lm objects that summarizes features of the fitted model, reporting much more than the short output we saw from lm() above:

```
> summary(m1)
...
Residuals:
    Min     1Q  Median      3Q     Max
-33.597 -10.048   0.425   8.694  34.699

Coefficients:
            Estimate Std. Error t value Pr(>|t|)
(Intercept) -94.9622     9.0790  -10.46   <2e-16 ***
rides         1.7033     0.1055   16.14   <2e-16 ***
---
Signif. codes:  0 '***' 0.001 '**' 0.01 '*' 0.05 '.' 0.1 ' ' 1

Residual standard error: 12.88 on 498 degrees of freedom
Multiple R-squared:  0.3434,    Adjusted R-squared:  0.3421
F-statistic: 260.4 on 1 and 498 DF,  p-value: < 2.2e-16
```

This summarizes the principal information to review for a linear model. More advanced models are reported similarly, so it is useful to become familiar with this format. In addition to listing the model that was estimated, we get information about coefficients, residuals, and the overall fit.

The most important section is labeled Coefficients and shows the model coefficients in the Estimate column. The coefficient for rides is 1.70, so each additional rating point for rides is estimated to result in an increase of 1.7 points of overall rating. (In case you're wondering, the coefficient for the (Intercept) shows where the linear model line crosses the y-axis, but this is usually not interpretable in a satisfaction drivers analysis—for instance, there is no such thing as a possible negative rating on our scale—so it is generally ignored by marketing analysts.)

The Std. Error column indicates uncertainty in the coefficient estimate. The "t value", p-value ("Pr(>|t|)"), and significance codes indicate a *Wald test*, which assesses whether the coefficient is significantly different than zero. A traditional estimate of a 95% confidence interval for the coefficient estimate is that it will fall within

$\pm 1.96 \times std.error$. In this case, $1.7033 \pm 1.96 \times 0.1055 = (1.495, 1.910)$. So we are confident—assuming the model is appropriate and the data are representative— that the coefficient for `ride` is 1.495–1.910.

Although you could compute the confidence intervals by hand, the `confint()` function will compute them for you:

```
> confint(m1)
                    2.5 %       97.5 %
(Intercept)  -112.800120   -77.124371
rides           1.495915     1.910656
```

This confirms our computation by hand, that the best estimate for the relationship `overall ~ rides` is 1.496–1.911 (with slight differences due to rounding). It is a best practice to report the range of an estimate, not just the single best point.

The `Residuals` section in the `summary(m1)` output tells us how closely the data follow the best fit line. A *residual* is the difference between the model-predicted value of a point and its actual value. In Fig. 7.3, this is the vertical distance between a plotted point (actual value) and the blue line (predicted value).

In the summary of m1, we see that the residuals are quite wide, ranging from -33.597 to 34.699, which means our predictions can be quite a bit off for any given data point (more than 30 points on the rating scale). The quartiles of the residuals suggest that they are fairly symmetric around 0. As we discuss in Sect. 7.2.5, that is a good sign that the model is unbiased (although perhaps imprecise).

In the last section of the output, `summary(m1)` provides measures of how well the model fits the data. The first is the *residual standard error*, an estimate of the standard error of the residuals. Like the residuals, this is a measure of how close the data points are to the best estimate line. (You can directly check this by examining the standard deviation of the residuals using `sd(m1$residuals)`, which will be similar.)

The second line reports the estimate of *R-squared*, a measure of how much variation in the dependent variable is captured by the model. In this case, the R-squared is 0.3434, indicating that about a third of the variation in overall satisfaction is explained by variation in satisfaction with rides. When a model includes only a single predictor, R-squared is equal to the square of the correlation coefficient r between the predictor and the outcome:

```
> cor(sat.df$overall, sat.df$rides)^2
[1] 0.3433799
```

Finally, the line labeled `F-statistic:` provides a statistical test of whether the model predicts the data better than simply taking the average of the outcome variable and using that as the single prediction for all the observations. In essence, this test tells whether our model is better than a model that predicts overall satisfaction using no predictors. (For reasons we will not describe in detail, this is the same test reported by the `anova()` function that we saw in Chap. 5; you could find the same value with `anova(m1)`. Check a statistics textbook for a description of the *F-test* in more detail.) In the present case, the `F-statistic` shows a p-value $<< .05$, so we reject the null hypothesis that a model without predictors performs as well as model m1.

7.2.5 Checking Model Fit

Because it is easy to fit linear models, too many analysts fit models and report results without considering whether the models are *reasonable*. However, there are a variety of ways to assess model fit and adequacy that are easy to perform in R. While we can't possibly cover this material comprehensively, we would like to give you a few pointers that will help you assess model adequacy.

There are several assumptions when a linear model is fitted to data. The first is that the relationship between the predictors and the outcomes is *linear*. If the relationship is not linear, then the model will make systematic errors. For example, if we generate data where y is a function of the square of x and then fit a linear model y ~ x, this will draw a straight line through a cloud of points that is curved.

```
> x <- rnorm(500)
> y <- x^2 + rnorm(500)
> toy.model <- lm(y~x)
```

If you inspect the model by typing summary(toy.model), you will see that the fitted coefficient for x is -0.01159 and the Wald significance test indicates that the coefficient is not significantly different from zero. Without model checking, a sloppy analyst might conclude that x is not related to y. However, if we plot x versus y and then draw our fitted line on the plot, we can see more clearly what is going on.

```
> plot(y~x)
> abline(toy.model)
```

The resulting plot is shown on the left side of Fig. 7.4. The plot shows that our fitted linear model (illustrated with a blue line) completely misses the curvature in the relationship between x and y.

Another assumption of a linear model is that prediction errors—the parts of the data that do not exactly fit the model—are normally distributed and look like random

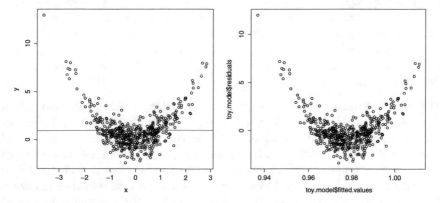

Fig. 7.4 Fitting a linear model when the true relationship is non-linear (as shown on the left) results in unusual residual patterns (shown on the right)

noise with no pattern. One way to examine this is to plot the model's *fitted values* (the predictions) versus the *residuals* (the prediction errors).

```
> plot(toy.model$fitted.values, toy.model$residuals)
```

This results in the plot on the right side of Fig. 7.4 and you can see from the plot that there is a clear pattern in the residuals: our model under-predicts the value of y near zero and over-predicts far from zero. When you come across this problem in real data, the solution is usually to transform x; you can use the methods described in Sect. 4.5.4 to find a transformation that is suitable. If you begin by inspecting scatterplots as we recommend in Sect. 7.2.1, you will be unlikely to commit such a simple error. Still, it is good to know that later checks can help prevent errors as well.

We can look at this same diagnostic plot for our satisfaction drivers data. R suggests four specific plots to assess the fit of linear model objects and you can look at all four simply by using plot() with any lm object. To see all four plots at once, we par(mfrow=c(2,2)) first:

```
> par(mfrow=c(2,2))
> plot(m1)
```

In Fig. 7.5, the first plot (in the upper left corner) shows the fitted values versus residuals for m1, just as we produced manually for our toy y ~ x model. In Fig. 7.5 there is no obvious pattern between the fitted values for overall satisfaction and the residuals; this is consistent with the idea that the residuals are due to random error, and supports the notion that the model is adequate.

The second plot in the lower left of Fig. 7.5 is similar to the first, except that instead of plotting the *raw* residual value, it plots the *square root* of the standardized residual. Again, there should be no clear pattern; if there were it might indicate a non-linear relationship. Observations with high residuals are flagged as potential outliers, and R labels them with row numbers in case we wish to inspect them in the data frame.

A common pattern in residual plots is a *cone* or *funnel*, where the range of errors gets progressively larger for larger fitted values. This is called *heteroskedasticity* and is a violation of linear model assumptions. A linear model tries to maximize fit to the line; when values in one part of the range have a much larger spread than those in another area, they have undue influence on the estimation of the line. Sometimes a transformation of the predictor or outcome variable will resolve heteroskedasticity (see Sect. 4.5.3).

The third result of plot() for lm objects is a *Normal QQ plot*, as in the upper right of Fig. 7.5. A QQ plot helps you see whether the residuals follow a normal distribution, another key assumption (see Sect. 3.4.3). It compares the values that residuals would be *expected* to take if they are normally distributed, versus their actual values. When the model is appropriate, these points are similar and fall close to a diagonal line; when the relationship between the variables is non-linear or otherwise does not match the assumption, the points deviate from the diagonal line. In the present case, the QQ plot suggests that the data fits the assumption of the model.

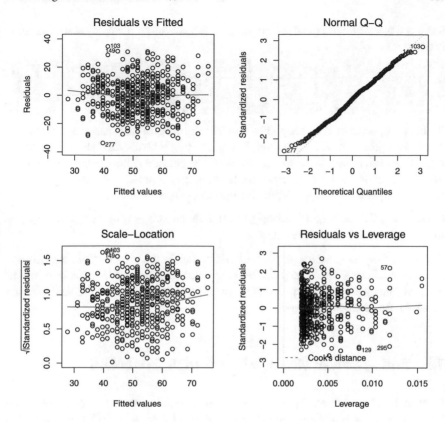

Fig. 7.5 Diagnostic plots for the model relating overall satisfaction to satisfaction with rides

The final plot in the lower right panel of Fig. 7.5 again helps to identify potential *outliers*, observations that may come from a different distribution than the others. Outliers are a problem because, if they are far from other points, they unduly influence the fitted line. We do not want one or a very few observations to have a large effect on the coefficients. The lower right plot in Fig. 7.5 plots the *leverage* of each point, a measure of how much influence the point has on the model coefficients. When a point has a high residual and high leverage, it indicates that the point has both a different pattern (residual) and undue influence (leverage). One measure of the leverage of a data point is *Cook's distance*, an estimate of how much predicted (y) values would change if the model were re-estimated with that point eliminated from the data. If you have observations with high Cook's distance, this chart would show dotted lines for the distances; in the present case, there are none.

Still, in the lower right of Fig. 7.5, three points are automatically labeled with row numbers because they are potentially problematic outliers based on high standardized residual distance and leverage on the model. We do not recommend routinely removing outliers, yet we do recommend to inspect them and determine whether there is a problem with the data. We inspect the identified points by selecting those rows:

```
> sat.df[c(57, 129, 295),]
    weekend num.child distance rides games wait clean overall  logdist
57      yes         2 63.29248    98    87   89   100     100 4.147767
129     yes         0 11.89550    76    77   51    77       6 2.476161
295      no         0 11.74474    98    83   63    92      45 2.463406
```

In this case, none of the data points is obviously invalid (for instance, with values below 1 or greater than 100), although row 129 might be checked for input correctness; an overall rating of 6 on the survey would be unusual although perhaps accurate. We generally do not omit outliers except when they represent obvious errors in the data. In the present case, we would keep all of the observations.

Overall, Fig. 7.5 looks good and suggests that the model relating overall satisfaction to satisfaction with rides is reasonable.

But we've only examined a single variable so far. In the next section, we consider multiple predictors. For brevity, in following sections we omit the checks of model adequacy that were shown in this section, but we encourage you to check and interpret plot() for the models.

7.3   Fitting Linear Models with Multiple Predictors

Now that we've covered the basics of linear models using just one predictor, we turn to the problem of assessing multiple drivers of satisfaction. Our goal is to sort through all of the features of the park—rides, games, wait times, and cleanliness—to determine which ones are most closely related to overall satisfaction.

To estimate our first multiple variable model, we call lm with a formula describing the model:

```
> m2 <- lm(overall ~ rides + games + wait + clean, data=sat.df)
> summary(m2)
...
Residuals:
    Min      1Q  Median      3Q     Max
-29.944  -6.841   1.072   7.167  28.618

Coefficients:
              Estimate Std. Error t value Pr(>|t|)
(Intercept) -131.40919    8.33377 -15.768  < 2e-16 ***
rides          0.52908    0.14207   3.724 0.000219 ***
games          0.15334    0.06908   2.220 0.026903 *
wait           0.55333    0.04781  11.573  < 2e-16 ***
clean          0.98421    0.15987   6.156 1.54e-09 ***
---
Signif. codes:  0 '***' 0.001 '**' 0.01 '*' 0.05 '.' 0.1 ' ' 1

Residual standard error: 10.59 on 495 degrees of freedom
Multiple R-squared:  0.5586,    Adjusted R-squared:  0.5551
F-statistic: 156.6 on 4 and 495 DF,  p-value: < 2.2e-16
```

Looking first at the model fit statistics at the bottom of the output, we see that our prediction was improved by including all the satisfaction items in the model. The R-squared increased to 0.5586, meaning that about half the variation in overall ratings is explained by the ratings for specific features. The residual standard error is now 10.59, meaning that the predictions are more accurate. Our residuals also appear to be symmetric. As noted above, we recommend also to inspect the model using plot() to confirm that there are no patterns in the residuals indicative of non-linearity or outliers, although we omit that step here.

Next we examine the model coefficients. Each coefficient represents the strength of the relationship between satisfaction with that feature and overall satisfaction, conditional on the values of the other predictors. All four features are identified as being statistically significant (p-value, shown as Pr(>|t|), < 0.05). Rather than just comparing the numbers in the output, it can be helpful to visualize the coefficients. We use the coefplot package [125] to do this, calling coefplot() for our model, and adding intercept=FALSE to plot just the individual item coefficients:

```
> library(coefplot)    # install if necessary
> coefplot(m2, intercept=FALSE, outerCI=1.96, lwdOuter=1.5,
+          ylab="Rating of Feature",
+          xlab="Association with Overall Satisfaction")
```

We use coefplot() arguments to set the outer confidence interval to a width of 1.96 standard errors (using outerCI=1.96, which corresponds to a 95% confidence interval) and to increase the size of the plotted lines slightly with lwdOuter=1.5.

The result is shown in Fig. 7.6 where we see that satisfaction with cleanliness is estimated to be the most important feature associated with overall satisfaction, followed

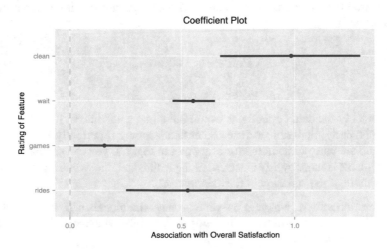

Fig. 7.6 A coefficient plot produced with coefplot() for an initial multivariate lm() model of satisfaction in the amusement park data. In the model, satisfaction with cleanliness is most strongly associated with overall satisfaction, and rides and wait times are also associated

by satisfaction with the rides and wait times. Satisfaction with games is estimated to
be relatively less important.

A plot of coefficients is often a key output from a satisfaction drivers analysis. Sorting
the plot so that the coefficients are in order based on their estimated coefficient may
make it easier to quickly identify the features that are most closely related to overall
satisfaction if you have a large number of predictors.

7.3.1 Comparing Models

Now that we have two model objects, m1 and m2 we might ask which one is better.
One way to evaluate models is to compare their R-squared values.

```
> summary(m1)$r.squared
[1] 0.3433799
> summary(m2)$r.squared
[1] 0.558621
```

Based on the R-squared values we can say that m2 explains more of the variation in
satisfaction than m1. However, a model with more predictors usually has a higher
R^2, so we could instead compare *adjusted* R-squared values, which control for the
number of predictors in the model.

```
> summary(m1)$adj.r.squared
[1] 0.3420614
> summary(m2)$adj.r.squared
[1] 0.5550543
```

The adjusted R-squared still suggests that the m2 explains more of the variation in
overall satisfaction, even accounting for the fact that m2 uses more predictors.

To compare the predictions of the models visually, we plot the fitted versus actual
values for each:

```
> plot(sat.df$overall, fitted(m1), col='red',
+       xlim=c(0,100), ylim=c(0,100),
+       xlab="Actual Overall Satisfaction", ylab="Fitted Overall Satisfaction")
> points(sat.df$overall, fitted(m2), col='blue')
> legend("topleft", legend=c("model 1", "model 2"),
+         col=c("red", "blue"), pch=1)
```

If the model fit the data perfectly, it would fall along a 45° line in this plot, but, of
course, it is nearly impossible to fit customer satisfaction data perfectly. By comparing
the red and the blue points in the resulting plot in Fig. 7.7, you can see that the blue
cloud of points is more tightly clustered along a diagonal line, which shows that m2
explains more of the variation in the data than m1.

For a more formal test, which is possible because the models here are nested (see
Sect. 6.5.1), we can use anova() function to determine whether m2 explains more
of the variation than m1:

Fig. 7.7 Comparison of
fitted versus actual values for
linear models m1 and m2

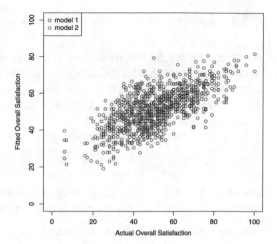

```
> anova(m1, m2)
Analysis of Variance Table

Model 1: overall ~ rides
Model 2: overall ~ rides + games + wait + clean
  Res.Df    RSS Df Sum of Sq       F     Pr(>F)
1    498  82612
2    495  55532  3     27080  80.463 < 2.2e-16 ***
---
Signif. codes:  0 '***' 0.001 '**' 0.01 '*' 0.05 '.' 0.1 ' ' 1
```

The low p-value indicates that the additional predictors in m2 significantly improve
the fit of the model. If these two models were the only ones under consideration, we
would interpret m2 instead of m1.

We should also point out that the coefficient for rides changed from m1 to m2.
The value in m1 was $1.70 \times rides$, while in m2 it is $0.529 \times rides$. Why is this
happening? The reason is because rides is not independent of all the other variables;
Fig. 7.1 shows that customers who are more satisfied with the rides tend to be more
satisfied with the wait times and games. When those variables are added as predictors
in model m2, they now perform some of the work in predicting the overall rating,
and the contribution of rides is a smaller share of the total model.

Neither coefficient for rides is more correct in itself because a coefficient is not
right or wrong but part of a larger model. Which model is preferable? Because model
m2 has better overall fit, we would interpret its coefficient for rides, but only in
the context of the total model. In the sections below, we see that as the structure of
a model changes, the coefficients generally change as well (unless the variables are
entirely uncorrelated, which only happens in designed experiments).

7.3.2 Using a Model to Make Predictions

As we saw for the single variable case, we could use the model coefficients to predict the `overall` outcome for different combinations of the explanatory variables. For example, if we wanted to predict the overall rating for a customer who rated the four separate aspects as 100 points each, we could multiply those ratings by the coefficients and add the intercept:

```
> coef(m2)["(Intercept)"] + coef(m2)["rides"]*100 + coef(m2)["games"]*100 +
+       coef(m2)["wait"]*100 + coef(m2)["clean"]*100
(Intercept)
   90.58612
```

The best estimate is 90.586 using model m2. Because `coef(m2)` is a named vector, we access the individual coefficients here using their names.

The prediction equation above is clunky to type, and there are more efficient ways to compute model predictions. One way is to use matrix operations to multiply coefficients by a vector of predictor values:

```
> coef(m2)%*%c(1, 100, 100, 100, 100)
          [,1]
[1,] 90.58612
```

We could also use `predict(object, newdata)` where `newdata` is a data frame with the same column names as the data that was used to estimate the model. For example, if we want to find the predictions for the first 10 customers in our data set we would pass the first 10 rows of `sat.df` to `predict`:

```
> predict(m2, sat.df[1:10,])
       1        2        3        4        5        6        7 ...
46.60864 54.26012 51.17289 50.30434 52.94625 27.87214 36.27435 ...
```

This predicts satisfaction for the first 10 customers. The predictions for observations used to estimate the model are also stored in the model object (in this case, the m2 object), and can be accessed with `fitted()`:

```
> fitted(m2)[1:10]
       1        2        3        4        5        6        7 ...
46.60864 54.26012 51.17289 50.30434 52.94625 27.87214 36.27435 ...
```

7.3.3 Standardizing the Predictors

Thus far, we have interpreted raw coefficients in order to evaluate the contributions of ratings on the shared 100 point scale. However, if the variables have different *scales*, such as a survey where `rides` is rated on a 1–10 scale while cleanliness is rated 1–5 scale, then their coefficient values would not be directly comparable. In the present data, this occurs with the `distance` and `logdist` variables, which are not on a 100 point scale.

When you wish to compare coefficients, it can be helpful to *standardize* data on a common scale before fitting a model (and *after* transforming any variables to a more normal scale). The most common standardization converts values to zero-centered *units of standard deviation*. This subtracts a variable's `mean` from each observation and then divides by the standard deviation (`sd()`). This could be done using math, such as:

```
> (sat.df$rides - mean(sat.df$rides)) / sd(sat.df$rides)
[1]  0.21124774  0.21124774 -0.15486620  0.39430471 -0.33792317  ...
```

This process is so common that R includes the `scale()` function to perform it:

```
> scale(sat.df$rides)
             [,1]
[1,]   0.21124774
[2,]   0.21124774
[3,]  -0.15486620
...
```

In the remainder of the chapter, we do not want to worry about the scale of our variables, only their relative contributions, so we create a scaled version of `sat.df` called `sat.std`:

```
> sat.std <- sat.df[ , -3]   # sat but remove distance
> sat.std[ , 3:8] <- scale(sat.std[ , 3:8])
> head(sat.std)
  weekend num.child      rides        games         wait        clean     overall
1     yes         0  0.2112477  -0.69750817  -0.918784090   0.21544189  -0.2681587
2     yes         2  0.2112477  -0.08198737   0.566719693  -0.17555973   0.8654385
3      no         1 -0.1548662   0.16422095   0.009655775   0.01994108   0.6135280
...
```

In this code, we first copied `sat.df` to the new data frame `sat.std`, dropping the untransformed values of `distance` with `[ , -3]` because we use `logdist` instead. Then we standardized each of the numeric columns. We do not standardize `weekend` because it is a factor variable rather than numeric. We leave `num.child` as is for now because we have not yet analyzed it.

Note that we do not alter the original data frame `sat.df` when standardizing it. Instead, we copy it to a new data frame and alter the new one. This process makes it easier to recover from errors; if anything goes wrong with `sat.std` we can just run these few commands again to recreate it.

The question of standardizing values depends primarily on how you want to use a model's coefficients. If you want to interpret coefficients in terms of the original scales, then you would not standardize data first. However, in driver analysis we are usually more concerned with the relative contribution of different predictors and wish to compare them, and standardization assists with this. Additionally, we often transform variables before analysis such that they are no longer on the original scale.

After standardizing, you should check the results. A standardized variable should have a mean of 0 and values within a few units of the mean. Checking the `summary()`:

```
> summary(sat.std)
 weekend       num.child            rides                  games
 no :259    Min.    :0.000    Min.    :-2.53461    Min.    :-2.66717
 yes:241    1st Qu.:0.000    1st Qu.:-0.70404    1st Qu.:-0.69751
            Median :2.000    Median : 0.02819    Median :-0.08199
            Mean   :1.738    Mean   : 0.00000    Mean   : 0.00000
            3rd Qu.:3.000    3rd Qu.: 0.76042    3rd Qu.: 0.77974
            Max.   :5.000    Max.   : 2.59099    Max.   : 2.62630
...
```

We see that `sat.std` matches expectation.

There is a technical point we should mention when standardizing variables. If the outcome and predictors are all standardized, their means will be zero and thus the intercept will be zero. However, that does *not* imply that the intercept could be removed from the model. The model is estimated to minimize error in the overall fit, which includes error for the intercept. This implies that the intercept should remain in a model after standardization if it would be there otherwise (as it usually should be; see Sect. 7.5.1).

7.4   Using Factors as Predictors

While m2 above was reasonable, we can continue to improve it. It is typical to try many models before arriving at a final one.

For the next step, we wonder whether satisfaction is different for customers who come on the weekend, travel farther, or have more children. We add these predictors to the model using standardized data:

```
> m3 <- lm(overall ~ rides + games + wait + clean +
+                    weekend + logdist + num.child, data = sat.std)
> summary(m3)
...
Coefficients:
               Estimate Std. Error  t value Pr(>|t|)
(Intercept)    -0.37271    0.04653   -8.009 8.41e-15 ***
rides           0.21288    0.04197    5.073 5.57e-07 ***
games           0.07066    0.03026    2.335   0.0199 *
wait            0.38138    0.02777   13.734  < 2e-16 ***
clean           0.29690    0.04415    6.725 4.89e-11 ***
weekendyes     -0.04589    0.05141   -0.893   0.3725
logdist         0.06470    0.02572    2.516   0.0122 *
num.child       0.22717    0.01711   13.274  < 2e-16 ***
...
Multiple R-squared:  0.6786,    Adjusted R-squared:  0.674
F-statistic: 148.4 on 7 and 492 DF,  p-value: < 2.2e-16
```

The model summary shows a substantial improvement in fit (R-squared of 0.6786) and the coefficients for `logdist` and `num.child` are significantly greater than zero, suggesting that people who travel further and have more children have higher overall satisfaction ratings.

Notice that the coefficient for `weekend` is labeled `weekendyes`, which seems a bit unusual. Recall that `weekend` is a factor variable, but a factor doesn't fit naturally in our linear model; you can't multiply yes by a number. R handles this by converting the data to a numeric value where 1 is assigned to the value of yes and 0 to no. It labels the output so that we know which direction the coefficient applies to. So, we can interpret the coefficient as meaning that on average those who come on the weekend rate their overall satisfaction -0.046 standard units (standard deviations) lower than those who come on a weekday. A convenient feature of R is that it does this automatically for factor variables, which are common in marketing.

In fact, we used a linear model with a factor as a predictor in Chap. 5, when we compared groups using ANOVA. An ANOVA model is a linear model with a factor as a predictor, and the command we learned in Chap. 5, aov(), internally calls lm() to fit the model. aov(overall ~ weekend, data=sat.std) and lm(overall ~ weekend, data=sat.std) fit the same model, although the result is reported differently because of tradition.

If they are the same, which should one use? We generally prefer to use lm because it is a more flexible method and allows us to include both numeric and factor predictors in the same model. (For those of you who were wondering, this explains why we used the linear modeling function lmBF to fit a Bayesian ANOVA model in Chap. 5.)

When your data includes factors, you must be careful about the data type. For example, num.child is a numeric variable, ranging 0–5, but it doesn't necessarily make sense to treat it as a number, as we did in m3. In doing so, we implicitly assume that satisfaction goes up or down linearly as a function of the number of children, and that the effect is the same for each additional child. (Anyone who has taken a group of children to an amusement park might guess that this is an unreasonable assumption.)

We correct this by converting num.child to a factor and re-estimating the model:

```
> sat.std$num.child.factor <- factor(sat.std$num.child)
> m4 <- lm(overall ~ rides + games + wait + clean +
+                    weekend + logdist + num.child.factor, data=sat.std)
> summary(m4)
...
Coefficients:
                  Estimate Std. Error t value Pr(>|t|)
(Intercept)       -0.69100    0.04488 -15.396  < 2e-16 ***
rides              0.22313    0.03541   6.301 6.61e-10 ***
...
num.child.factor1  1.01610    0.07130  14.250  < 2e-16 ***
num.child.factor2  1.03732    0.05640  18.393  < 2e-16 ***
num.child.factor3  0.98000    0.07022  13.955  < 2e-16 ***
num.child.factor4  0.93154    0.08032  11.598  < 2e-16 ***
num.child.factor5  1.00193    0.10369   9.663  < 2e-16 ***
...
Multiple R-squared:  0.7751,    Adjusted R-squared:   0.77
F-statistic: 152.9 on 11 and 488 DF,  p-value: < 2.2e-16
```

We now see that there are 5 fitted coefficients for num.child.factor: one for parties with 1 child, one for parties with 2 children, etc. There is not a coefficient for num.child.factor0, because it is the baseline level to which the other coefficients are added when they apply. We interpret each coefficient as the difference between that level of the factor and the baseline level. So, parties with 1 child rate their overall satisfaction on average 1.016 standard deviations higher than parties without children.

Internally, R has created a new variable num.child.factor1 that is equal to 1 for those cases where num.child.factor represents one child (a factor level of "1"), and is 0 otherwise. Similarly, num.child.factor2 is 1 for cases with two children, and 0 otherwise, and so forth. The coefficient for num.child.factor2 is 1.037, meaning that people with two children rate their overall satisfaction on average a full standard deviation higher than those with no children.

A striking thing about m4 is that the increase in overall satisfaction is about the same regardless of how many children there are in the party—about 1 standard deviation higher for any number of children. This suggests that we don't actually need to estimate a different increase for each number of children. In fact, if the increase is the same for 1 child as for 5 children, attempting to fit a model that scales increasingly per child would result in a less accurate estimate.

Instead, we declare a new variable called has.child that is TRUE when the party has children in it and FALSE when the party does not have children. We then estimate the model using that new factor variable. We also drop weekend from the model because it doesn't seem to be a significant predictor:

```
> sat.std$has.child <- factor(sat.std$num.child > 0)
> m5 <- lm(overall ~ rides + games + wait + clean + logdist + has.child,
+                   data=sat.std)
> summary(m5)
...
Coefficients:
               Estimate Std. Error t value Pr(>|t|)
(Intercept)    -0.70195    0.03906 -17.969  < 2e-16 ***
rides           0.22272    0.03512   6.342 5.12e-10 ***
...
has.childTRUE   1.00565    0.04683  21.472  < 2e-16 ***
...
Multiple R-squared:  0.7741,    Adjusted R-squared:  0.7713
F-statistic: 281.5 on 6 and 493 DF,  p-value: < 2.2e-16
```

Is this still a good model? The change in R-squared between model m4 and m5 is negligible, suggesting that our simplification did not deteriorate the model fit.

Model m5 estimates overall satisfaction to be about 1 standard deviation higher for parties with children. However, one might now wonder how children influence other aspects of the ratings. For instance, is the relationship between satisfaction and waiting times different for parties with and without children? One might guess from experience that wait time would be more important to parties with children. To explore this question, we need to incorporate *interactions* into the model.

7.5   Interaction Terms

We can include an interaction of two terms by using the : operator between variables in a formula. For instance, to estimate overall as a function of rides plus the interaction of wait and has.child, we could write the formula as overall ~

`rides + wait:no.child`. There are other ways in R to write interaction terms (see Sect. 7.5.1) but for our first model we will specify them explicitly in this way.

We create a new model with interactions between the satisfaction ratings and two variables that describe the visit: `no.child` and `weekend`:

```
> m6 <- lm(overall ~ rides + games + wait + clean +
+                    weekend + logdist + has.child +
+                    rides:has.child + games:has.child + wait:has.child +
+                    clean:has.child + rides:weekend + games:weekend +
+                    wait:weekend + clean:weekend, data=sat.std)
> summary(m6)
...
Coefficients:
                       Estimate Std. Error t value Pr(>|t|)
...
rides:has.childTRUE    0.057837   0.073070   0.792  0.42902
games:has.childTRUE   -0.064043   0.052797  -1.213  0.22572
wait:has.childTRUE     0.350649   0.047241   7.423 5.21e-13 ***
clean:has.childTRUE   -0.001854   0.079710  -0.023  0.98146
rides:weekendyes       0.061784   0.067750   0.912  0.36225
games:weekendyes       0.018511   0.049036   0.377  0.70597
wait:weekendyes        0.035168   0.044463   0.791  0.42936
clean:weekendyes      -0.027305   0.071005  -0.385  0.70074
...
```

The model object m6 now includes eight interaction terms between ratings for features of the park and `no.child` and `weekend`. Only one of these interactions is significant: the `wait:no.child` interaction. This suggests we could drop the non-significant interactions to create a new model m7:

```
> m7 <- lm(overall ~ rides + games + wait + clean + logdist + has.child +
+                    wait:has.child, data=sat.std)
> summary(m7)
...
Coefficients:
                    Estimate Std. Error t value Pr(>|t|)
(Intercept)         -0.69316    0.03684 -18.814  < 2e-16 ***
rides                0.21264    0.03313   6.419 3.24e-10 ***
games                0.04870    0.02394   2.034   0.0425 *
wait                 0.15095    0.03688   4.093 4.98e-05 ***
clean                0.30244    0.03485   8.678  < 2e-16 ***
logdist              0.02919    0.02027   1.440   0.1504
has.childTRUE        0.99830    0.04416  22.606  < 2e-16 ***
wait:has.childTRUE   0.34688    0.04380   7.920 1.59e-14 ***
...
Multiple R-squared:  0.7996,    Adjusted R-squared:  0.7968
F-statistic: 280.5 on 7 and 492 DF,  p-value: < 2.2e-16
```

In these results, we see that attending the park with children is a predictor of higher satisfaction, and waiting time is more important predictor among those with children (`wait:has.childTRUE`) than those without children. We don't know the reason for this, but perhaps children go on more rides and their parents are therefore more influenced by wait times.

One might further tune the model by considering whether `logdist` is still needed; we'll leave that to the reader and assume that model m7 is the final model.

What do we do with these results as marketers? We identify several possible marketing interventions. If we want to increase satisfaction overall, we could perhaps do so by trying to increase the number of visitors with children. Alternatively, if we want to

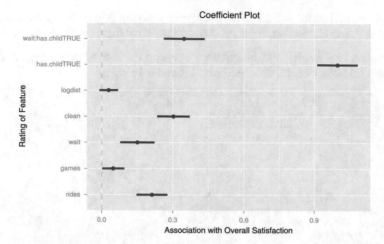

Fig. 7.8 Satisfaction drivers for visitors to an amusement park (simulated). The model reveals that the variable most strongly (and positively) associated with satisfaction is visiting the park with children. Satisfaction with waiting time is a stronger predictor of overall satisfaction among visitors with children than those without, as shown in the `wait:has.childTRUE` interaction. Of the individual park features, satisfaction with cleanliness is most associated with overall satisfaction

appeal to visitors without children, we might engage in further research to understand why their ratings are lower. If we are allocating budget to personnel, the importance of cleanliness suggests continuing to allocate resources there (as opposed, say, to games). We might also want to learn more about the association between children and waiting time, and whether there are things we could do to make waiting less frequent or more enjoyable.

There are many more such questions one could pose from results like these; a crucial step in analysis is to think carefully about the implications and where one might be able to make a product or market intervention. When considering actions to take, it is especially important to remember that the model assesses association, not causation. Possible changes in outcome should be viewed as hypotheses suggested by the model, to be confirmed separately.

To share these results with others, it is helpful to create a new satisfaction drivers plot using `coefplot()`:

```
> library(coefplot)   # install if needed
> coefplot(m7, intercept=FALSE, outerCI=1.96, lwdOuter=1.5,
+          ylab="Rating of Feature",
+          xlab="Association with Overall Satisfaction")
```

The result is Fig. 7.8 summarizing the relative contribution of each element on overall satisfaction.

When including interaction terms in a model, there are two important points. First, it is especially important to consider standardizing the predictors when modeling interactions in order to have an interpretable and comparable scale for coefficients.

Second, one should always include main effects (such as x + y) when including an interaction effect (x:y). If you don't estimate the main effects, you won't know whether a purported interaction is in fact due to an interaction, or is instead due to one of the individual variables' unestimated main effects.

7.5.1   Language Brief: Advanced Formula Syntax*

This section is optional for those who wish to construct more complex formulas with interaction effects. As in the examples above, we generally write formulas using only + (for main effects) and : (specific interactions), but the following may help create more compact formulas when you have many variables or interactions.

As we've seen, you can include an interaction between x and z by including x:z in the formula. If you want to include two variables along with their interaction, you can use x*z, which is the equivalent to writing x + z + x:z.

To include *all* of the predictors in your data frame in the model, use a ., writing write y ~ . You can also *omit* any variable using –x. Thus, y ~ . – x means "include all the variables except x."

The intercept can be removed from a model by including –1 in the formula. This is ill-advised in general linear models with continuous predictors, because it forces the line to go through the origin $(0, 0)$, which alters the other coefficients. However, it can be helpful in some kinds of models, such as those with purely categorical predictors.

Table 7.1 summarizes the common options for formula syntax and their interpretation in terms of a linear equation (where β is a model coefficient with β_0 for the intercept, β_1 for the first predictor, and so forth; ε is the error term).

Table 7.1 Syntax for including interactions in model formulas

R Formula syntax	Linear model	Description
y ~ x	$y_i = \beta_0 + \beta_1 x_i + \varepsilon_i$	y is a linear function of x
y ~ x - 1	$y_i = \beta_1 x_i + \beta_2 z_i + \varepsilon_i$	Omit the intercept
y ~ x + z	$y_i = \beta_0 + \beta_1 x_i + \beta_2 z_i + \varepsilon_i$	y is a linear combination of x and z
y ~ x:z	$y_i = \beta_0 + \beta_1 x_i z_i + \varepsilon_i$	Include the interaction between x and z
y ~ x*z	$y_i = \beta_0 + \beta_1 x_i + \beta_2 z_i + \beta_3 x_i z_i + \varepsilon_i$	Include x, z and the interaction between them
y ~ (u + v + w)^3	$y_i = \beta_0 + \beta_1 u_i + \beta_2 v_i + \beta_3 w_i + \beta_4 u_i v_i + \beta_5 u_i w_i + \beta_6 v_i w_i + \beta_7 u_i v_i w_i + \varepsilon_i$	Include u, v, and w, and all interactions among them up to three-way (u:v:w)
y ~ (u+v+w)^3 - u:v	$y_i = \beta_0 + \beta_1 u_i + \beta_2 v_i + \beta_3 w_i + \beta_5 u_i w_i + \beta_6 v_i w_i + \beta_7 u_i v_i w_i + \varepsilon_i$	Include these variables and all interactions up to three-way, but remove the u:v interaction

7.5.2   Caution! Overfitting

Now that we've seen the complete process of creating a model, from initial data inspection to the potential implications, we have a caution about linear models. As you become more comfortable with linear models, you may want to put more and more predictors into your equation. Be careful about that.

A typical satisfaction drivers survey might include dozens of different features. As you add predictors to a model, estimates of the coefficients become less precise due to both the number of effects and associations among the variables. This shows up in the lm() output as larger standard errors of the coefficients, indicating lower confidence in the estimates. This is one reason we like to plot confidence intervals for coefficients, as in Fig. 7.8.

Despite the potentially low confidence in estimates, as you add variables to a model, the value of R^2 will become higher and higher. On a first impression, that might seem as if the model is getting better and better. However, if the estimates of the coefficients are imprecise, then the utility of the model will be poor; it could lead to making the wrong inferences about relationships in your data.

This process of adding too many variables and ending up with a less precise or inappropriate model is called *overfitting*. One way to avoid it is to keep a close eye on the standard errors for the coefficients; small standard errors are an indicator that there is sufficient data to estimate the model. Another approach is to select a subset of the data to *hold out* and not use to estimate the model. After fitting the model, use predict() on the hold out data and see how well it performs. Overfitted models will perform poorly when predicting outcomes for holdout data. Stepwise model selection is a traditional approach to select variables while attempting to avoid overfitting; the step() function we saw in Sect. 6.5.3 works for lm objects the same as for aov models.

We recommend to keep models as parsimonious as possible. Although it is tempting to create large, impressive, omnibus models, it is usually more valuable in marketing practice to identify a few interventions with clear and confident interpretations.

7.5.3   Recommended Procedure for Linear Model Fitting

We followed a lengthy process to arrive at the final model m7, and it is helpful to recount the general steps we recommend in creating such a linear model.

1. Inspect the data to make sure it is clean and has the structure you expect, following the outline in Sect. 3.3.3.
2. Check the distributions of the variables to make sure they are not highly skewed (Sect. 7.2.1). If one is skewed, consider transforming it (Sect. 4.5.4).

3. Examine the bivariate scatterplots and correlation matrix (Sect. 7.2.1) to see whether there are any extremely correlated variables (such as $r > 0.9$, or several with $r > 0.8$). If so, omit some variables or consider transforming them if needed; see Sect. 9.1 for further discussion.
4. If you wish to estimate coefficients on a consistent scale, standardize the data with scale() (Sect. 7.3.3).
5. After fitting a model, check the residual quantiles in the output. The residuals show how well the model accounts for the individual observations (Sect. 7.2.4).
6. Check the standard model plots using plot(), which will help you judge whether a linear model is appropriate or whether there is nonlinearity, and will identify potential outliers in the data (Sect. 7.2.4).
7. Try several models and compare them for overall interpretability and model fit by inspecting the residuals' spread and overall R^2 (Sect. 7.3.1). If the models are nested, you could also use anova() for comparison (Sect. 6.5.1).
8. Report the confidence intervals of the estimates with your interpretation and recommendations (Sect. 7.3).

7.5.4 Bayesian Linear Models with MCMCregress()*

In this section, we review how the satisfaction analysis could be performed with Bayesian methods. This is an optional section; if you're not familiar with Bayesian methods, you could skip this section or review the basics in Sect. 6.6.

Like lm() above, Bayesian inference for a linear model attempts to estimate the most likely coefficients relating the outcome to the explanatory variables. However, the Bayesian method does this by sampling the posterior distribution of model coefficients (Sect. 6.6.2), using a procedure known as Markov-chain Monte Carlo (MCMC).

The package MCMCpack includes MCMCregress(), which estimates Bayesin linear models; it makes a Bayesian estimation of the model as easy as calling lm(). We call MCMCregress() to estimate the model m7 from above, supplying an identical formula and data frame as we used earlier with lm() (Sect. 7.5):

```
> library(MCMCpack)
...
> m7.bayes <- MCMCregress(overall ~ rides + games + wait + clean + logdist +
+                                    has.child + wait:has.child, data=sat.std)
> summary(m7.bayes)
Iterations = 1001:11000
Thinning interval = 1
Number of chains = 1
Sample size per chain = 10000

1. Empirical mean and standard deviation for each variable,
   plus standard error of the mean:

                 Mean       SD   Naive SE Time-series SE
(Intercept)  -0.69331  0.03702  0.0003702      0.0003702
rides         0.21262  0.03351  0.0003351      0.0003301
```

```
games             0.04885 0.02400 0.0002400       0.0002400
wait              0.15096 0.03683 0.0003683       0.0003683
clean             0.30205 0.03515 0.0003515       0.0003515
logdist           0.02891 0.02029 0.0002029       0.0002029
has.childTRUE     0.99837 0.04441 0.0004441       0.0004441
wait:has.childTRUE 0.34733 0.04358 0.0004358      0.0004358
sigma2            0.20374 0.01306 0.0001306       0.0001306

2. Quantiles for each variable:

                      2.5%        25%        50%        75%      97.5%
(Intercept)       -0.764177  -0.71841  -0.69345  -0.66861  -0.62004
rides              0.145773   0.19015   0.21290   0.23499   0.27833
games              0.001507   0.03285   0.04876   0.06453   0.09668
wait               0.079481   0.12629   0.15060   0.17602   0.22353
clean              0.233243   0.27832   0.30218   0.32581   0.37076
logdist           -0.010923   0.01539   0.02885   0.04262   0.06869
has.childTRUE      0.910071   0.96896   0.99857   1.02800   1.08498
wait:has.childTRUE 0.261291   0.31780   0.34720   0.37724   0.43211
sigma2             0.179781   0.19454   0.20311   0.21213   0.23094
```

What does this tell us? The important thing to understand is that MCMCregress()
has drawn 10000 samples from the estimated distribution of possible coefficients for
model m7. It then describes those 10000 sets of estimates in two ways: using central
tendency statistics (mean and standard deviation, in the output section labeled "1."),
and again using distribution quantiles (in output section "2.").

We can compare the values to those from lm() in Sect. 7.5 above. There, we
saw that rides had an estimated coefficient of 0.2126; here the mean of the
Bayesian estimates is 0.2126 and the median is 0.2129. Similarly, lm() estimated
wait:has.child as 0.9983; the mean Bayesian estimate is 0.9984 and the median
is 0.9986. The coefficients estimated by the classical and Bayesian models are nearly
identical.

Despite the similar model coefficients, there are two notable differences between this
output and the output from lm(). First, it includes 2. Quantiles ... because
the Bayesian posterior distribution may be asymmetric; the distribution of estimates
could be skewed.

Second, the Bayesian output does not include statistical tests or p-values; null hypothesis tests are not emphasized in the Bayesian paradigm. Instead, to determine whether
a parameter is likely to be non-zero (or to compare it to any other value), check the
2.5 and 97.5 %'iles and directly interpret the credible interval. For instance, in the
quantiles above, the 2.5–97.5%'iles for logdist range (-0.01092, 0.06869) and
we conclude that the coefficient for logdist is not credibly different from 0 at a
level of 95% confidence. However, all of the other coefficients are different from
zero.

Note that MCMCregress() is similar to lmBF() in the BayesFactor package that we used in Sect. 6.6. Both functions produce draws from the posterior of
a linear model, which you can then summarize using the summary(). We used
MCMCregress() here because lmBF() does not estimate interaction coefficients
(at the time of writing). It is common in R that different packages do similar things,
yet may be better or worse for a specific problem.

If the Bayesian estimates are so similar to those from `lm()`, what is the advantage? The results here are similar for two reasons. First, we have plenty of data and a well-behaved model. Second, classical methods such as `lm()` are eminently suited to estimation of linear models. In Chap. 9 we examine hierarchical Bayesian models, in which more advantages of the Bayesian approach emerge; we later continue that investigation with choice models in Chap. 13.

We also believe, as noted in Sect. 6.6.1, that inferences such as hypothesis testing are clearer and more interpretable in the Bayesian approach. In fitting models, it is not always the case that classical and Bayesian estimates are so similar, and when they differ, we are more inclined to trust the Bayesian estimates.

7.6 Key Points

There are many applications for linear models in marketing: satisfaction drivers analysis, advertising response modeling, customer churn modeling, and so forth. Although these use different kinds of data, they are all implemented in similar ways in R. The following points are some of the important considerations for such analyses. We also summarized the basic process of linear modeling in Sect. 7.5.3.

- Linear models relate continuous scale *outcome* variables to *predictors* by finding a straight line that best fits the points. A basic linear model function in R is `lm(formula, data)`. `lm()` produces an object that can be used with `plot()`, `summary()`, `predict()`, and other functions to inspect the model fit and estimates of the coefficients.
- Before modeling, it is important to check the data quality and the distribution of values on each variable. For distributions, approximately normal distributions are generally preferred, and data such as counts and revenue often need to be transformed. Also check that variables do not have excessive correlation (Sect. 7.2.1).
- To interpret coefficients on a standardized scale, such that they are comparable to one another, you will either need predictors that are on identical scales or that have been standardized to be on a uniform scale. The most common standardization is conversion to units of standard deviation, performed by `scale()` (Sect. 7.3.3).
- A linear model assumes that the relationship between predictors and an outcome is linear and that errors in fit are symmetric with similar variability across their range (a property known as *homoskedasticity*). Results may be misleading when these assumptions do not match the data. `plot()` of a model can help you assess whether these assumptions are reasonable for your data (Sect. 7.2.5.)
- The `summary()` function for `lm` objects provides output that analysts review most frequently, reporting model coefficients along with their standard errors and p-values for hypothesis tests assessing whether the coefficients differ from zero (Sect. 7.2.4)

- Factor variables may be included in a model simply by adding the name of the factor to the model formula. R automatically converts the factor into dummy-coded 0/1 values for each level. You must check the direction shown in the output to ensure you interpret these correctly (Sect. 7.4).
- An interaction is a predictor that is the product of two other predictors, and thus assesses the degree to which the predictors reinforce (or cancel) one another. You can model an interaction between x and y by including x:y in a model formula (Sect. 7.5).
- Model building is the process of adding and removing predictors from a model to find a set of predictors that fits the data well. We can compare the fit of different models using the R-squared value or, if models are nested (see Sect. 6.5) by using the more formal ANOVA test (`anova()`) (Sect. 7.3.1).
- You can fit a Bayesian version of a linear model using `MCMCregress()` from the `MCMCpack` package. The usage is nearly identical to `lm()`. The resulting coefficient estimates are assessed as expressing the most likely values (known as credible intervals) under the assumption that the model is appropriate (Sect. 7.5.4).
- We recommend to interpret coefficients in terms of their estimated ranges, such as confidence intervals in the case of `lm()` (Sect. 7.2.4) or credible intervals from Bayesian estimates (Sect. 7.5.4). A plot of the coefficient ranges for `lm` objects can be created with the `coefplot` package (Sect. 7.3).

7.7 Data Sources

This kind of data we considered in this chapter usually comes from a consumer survey written in a survey platform such as Qualtrics or SurveyMonkey and hosted online. A respondent sample might be obtained by asking customers exiting the park to answer the survey on a tablet, by sending bulk mail to an existing list of known customers (from a customer database) or to an email list otherwise collected online (such as visitors who "sign up for our newsletter"), or by surveying an online *panel* of respondents managed by a third party research supplier.

There are several important considerations for data quality with surveys. One set of issues concerns sample quality; the respondents may be biased due to list composition (for example, surveying only customers who are willing to stop on their way out of the park), channel bias (if you send the survey by email, you don't reach people who do not use email), non-response bias (different groups may respond at different rates), and other factors. Another set of issues relates to the reliability and construct validity of the items you pose (see Sects. 8.3 and 10.2).

It is also important to consider the overall survey experience, and the clarity and usability of its individual items. If your respondents do not understand the questions in the way you intended, the results can be difficult to interpret. A common example is a question about a customer's likelihood to recommend a product, as used to compute the popular "Net Promoter Score." If customers say they would not recommend a

product, is that because they don't like the product or because they would not discuss
the product with friends? For more on survey design issues, see Callegaro, Manfreda,
and Vehovar (2015) and Callegaro et al, eds. (2014) [27, 28].

7.8   Learning More*

In this chapter we've given an overview of linear modeling in R and its application
to satisfaction drivers analysis. The same modeling approach could be applied to
many other marketing applications, such as advertising response (or *marketing mix*)
modeling [20], customer retention (or *churn*) modeling, and pricing analysis.

We covered traditional linear models in this chapter, which relate continuous or near-
continuous outcomes to predictors. Other models apply in cases where the variables
are different in structure, such as binary outcomes or counts. However, the process
of estimating those is similar to the steps here. Such models include poisson and
binomial regression model for outcomes that are counts, hazard regression for event
occurrence (also known as timing regression or survival modeling), and logistic
regression for binary outcomes (see Sect. 9.2). R covers all of these models with the
generalized linear model (GLM) framework, an elegant way of representing many
families of models, and such models can be estimated with the `glm()` function.
To learn more about generalized models, consult an introduction to GLM such as
Dobson and Barnett (2018) [43].

In our synthetic satisfaction drivers data, hypothetical customers rated satisfaction
on a 100-point scale, making it reasonable for us to analyze the data as if the ratings
were continuous. However, many survey studies collect ratings on a 5- or 7- point
scale, which may be questionable to fit with a linear model. Although many analysts
use `lm()` for outcomes on 5- or 7-point scales, an alternative is a *cut-point model*,
such as an ordered logit or probit model. Such a model will fit the data better and
won't make nonsensical predictions like a rating of 6.32 on a 5-point scale (as `lm()`
might). These models can be fit with the `polr()` function from the MASS package
[192].

A more sophisticated model for ordinal ratings data is a Bayesian scale-usage heterogeneity model, as described by Rossi, Allenby and McCullough (2005) [168].
This models that different customers (and cultures) may use scales in different ways;
some customers may give systematically higher or lower scores than others due to
differences in interpreting the rating scale. When this is modeled, it is possible to
find a better estimate of the underlying satisfaction levels. A Bayesian estimation
procedure for such models is implemented in the `bayesm` package [167].

In this chapter, we used models in which an effect has uniform influence. For example,
we assumed that the effect of satisfaction with cleanliness is a single influence that
is the same for every respondent (or, more precisely, whose *average* influence is
the same, apart from random individual variation). You might instead consider a

model in which the effect varies for different people, with both a group-level and an individual-level effect, known as a *hierarchical* model. We examine ways to estimate individual-level effects using hierarchical models in Chap. 9.

Finally, many data sets have variables that are highly correlated (known as *collinearity*), and this can affect the stability and trustworthiness of linear modeling. In Sect. 9.1 we introduce additional ways to check for collinearity and strategies to mitigate it. One approach is to reduce the number of dimensions under consideration by extracting underlying patterns from the correlated variables; we review such *principal component* and *factor analytic* procedures in Chap. 8.

7.9   Exercises

7.9.1   Simulated Hotel Satisfaction and Account Data

For these and some later exercises, we use a simulated dataset for a hotel. The data combine customers' responses to a satisfaction survey with basic account information from their hotel stays. These are the sort of data that you might acquire from an email survey is sent to users, where an disguised identifier links the surveys responses to account data. Another common source of similar data is an online system where a pop-up survey asks satisfaction questions, and the answers can be related to the user's account (the real data set referenced in Sect. 3.8.1 is an example).

To access the hotel data set, load the data from CSV format online as follows, or load from a local location as file `hotelsat-data.csv` if you have already downloaded it (see Sect. 1.6.3).

```
> hotel.df <- read.csv("https://goo.gl/oaWKgt")
> summary(hotel.df)
```

These data include 18 items asking about satisfaction with various aspects of the hotel (cleanliness, dining experience, staff, satisfaction with elite status perks, and so forth), each on a 7 point rating scale. (In reality, we would rarely recommend asking 18 separate satisfaction items! However, we will use all of them for some investigations in later chapters.) In addition to the survey responses, the data include each respondent's corresponding number of nights stayed at the hotel, the distance traveled, reason for visiting, their elite membership level, and the average amounts spent per night on the room, dining, and WiFi.

7.9.2   Exercises

1. Visualize the distributions of the variables in the hotelsatisfaction data. Are there variables that might be understood better if they are transformed? Which

variables and what transforms would you apply? (Suggestion: for efficiency, it may help to divide the data set into smaller sets of similar variables.)

2. What are the patterns of correlations in the data? Briefly summarize any patterns you observe, in 2–4 sentences.

3. Consider just the three items for cleanliness (satCleanRoom, satClean Bath, and satCleanCommon). What are the correlation coefficients among those items? Is there a better measure than Pearson's r for those coefficients, and why? Does it make a difference in these data? (Consider the notes in Sect. 4.5.)

4. Management wants to know whether satisfaction with elite membership perks (satPerks) predicts overall satisfaction (satOverall). Assume that sat Perks is a predictor and we want to know how satOverall is associated with changes in it. How do you interpret the relationship?

5. We might wish to control the previous satPerks model for other influences, such as satisfaction with the Front Staff (satFrontStaff) and with the city location (satCity). How do you change the previous model to do this? Model and interpret the result. Is the answer different than in the model with only Perks? Why or why not?

6. Suppose we have a business strategy to maximize satisfaction with elite recognition (satRecognition) among our Gold and Platinum elite members. To do so, we might invest more in the front staff, room cleanliness, the points that we award elite members, or the membership perks given to them. Which of those strategies might we want to consider first, according to these data, if we wish to increase Gold and Platinum member satisfaction with elite recognition?

7. What are some problems with using the present data to answer that strategic question? What data would you need to give a better answer?

8. Considering the results in the previous question, would you recommend to invest more in room cleanliness? Why or why not?

9. Now we are examining ways to improve revenue in the restaurant. Management wants to understand the relationship of average food spend per night with elite status (eliteStatus) and satisfaction with food price (satDiningPrice). Model this and interpret it.

10. How does satisfaction relate to spending in our restaurant? On one side, we might expect dining satisfaction to be higher when food costs less, because customers are often happy about lower prices. However, we might also expect the exact opposite relationship, where satisfied diners spend more. Which relationship is better supported by these data?

11. Plot the predicted food spend per night in dollars, as a function of nights stayed. (Suggestion: fit a linear model with one predictor.) In our data, no one stayed 40 nights. But if someone had, what would be a good guess as to their average food spend per night?

12. Is the association between nights spent and spending on food different among Platinum elite members? Visualize the difference. What does this suggest for a restaurant strategy? Is this consistent with findings in the previous models (Exercises 9–11 above)?

13. Fit the elite recognition model (Exercise 6 above) using Bayesian regression. Which variables are most associated with members' satisfaction with recognition?

14. How do those Bayesian coefficient estimates compare to the classical linear model estimates in Exercise 6? Visualize the relationship among the coefficients from each. What is the correlation coefficient?

15. Which model do you prefer, classical or Bayesian? Why?

Part III
Advanced Marketing Applications

Chapter 8
Reducing Data Complexity

Marketing data sets often have many variables—many *dimensions*—and it is advantageous to reduce these to smaller sets of variables to consider. For instance, we might have many items on a consumer survey that reflect a smaller number of underlying concepts such as *customer satisfaction* with a service, *category leadership* for a brand, or *luxury* for a product. If we can reduce the data to its underlying dimensions, we can more clearly identify the underlying relationships among concepts.

In this chapter we consider three common methods to reduce data complexity by reducing the number of dimensions in the data. *Principal component analysis* (PCA) attempts to find uncorrelated linear dimensions that capture maximal variance in the data. *Exploratory factor analysis* (EFA) also attempts to capture variance with a small number of dimensions while seeking to make the dimensions interpretable in terms of the original variables. *Multidimensional scaling* (MDS) maps similarities among observations in terms of a low-dimension space such as a two-dimensional plot. MDS can work with metric data and with non-metric data such as categorical or ordinal data.

In marketing, PCA is often associated with *perceptual maps*, which are visualizations of respondents' associations among brands or products. In this chapter we demonstrate perceptual maps for brands using principal component analysis. We then look at ways to draw similar perceptual inferences from factor analysis and multidimensional scaling.

8.1 Consumer Brand Rating Data

We investigate dimensionality using a simulated data set that is typical of consumer *brand perception* surveys. This data reflects consumer ratings of *brands* with regard to *perceptual adjectives* as expressed on survey items with the following form:

© Springer Nature Switzerland AG 2019

C. Chapman and E. M. Feit, *R For Marketing Research and Analytics*, Use R!,
https://doi.org/10.1007/978-3-030-14316-9_8

On a scale from 1 to 10—where 1 is *least* and 10 is *most*—how *[ADJECTIVE]* is *[BRAND A]*?

In this data, an observation is one respondent's rating of a brand on one of the adjectives. Two such items might be:

1. How *trendy* is *Intelligentsia Coffee*?
2. How much of a *category leader* is *Blue Bottle Coffee*?

Such ratings are collected for all the combinations of adjectives and brands of interest.

The data here comprise simulated ratings of 10 brands ("a" to "j") on 9 adjectives ("performance," "leader," "latest," "fun," and so forth), for N = 100 simulated respondents. The data set is provided on this book's web site. We start by loading and checking the data:

```
> brand.ratings <- read.csv("http://goo.gl/IQl8nc")
> head(brand.ratings)
  perform leader latest fun serious bargain value trendy rebuy brand
1       2      4      8   8       2       9     7      4     6     a
2       1      1      4   7       1       1     1      2     2     a
...
> tail(brand.ratings)
...
999      1      1      7   5       1       1     2      5     1     j
1000     7      4      7   8       4       1     2      5     1     j
```

Each of the 100 simulated respondents has observations data on each of the 10 brands, so there are 1000 total rows. We inspect the summary() and str() to check the data quality and structure:

```
> summary(brand.ratings)
    perform             leader            latest              fun
 Min.   : 1.000    Min.   : 1.000    Min.   : 1.000    Min.   : 1.000
 1st Qu.: 1.000    1st Qu.: 2.000    1st Qu.: 4.000    1st Qu.: 4.000
 Median : 4.000    Median : 4.000    Median : 7.000    Median : 6.000
...
> str(brand.ratings)
'data.frame':   1000 obs. of  10 variables:
...
 $ rebuy  : int  6 2 6 1 1 2 1 1 1 1 ...
 $ brand  : Factor w/ 10 levels "a","b","c","d",..: 1 1 1 1 1 1 1 1 1 1 ...
```

We see in summary() that the ranges of the ratings for each adjective are 1–10. In str(), we see that the ratings were read as numeric while the brand labels were properly interpreted as factors. In short, the data appear to be clean and formatted appropriately.

There are nine perceptual adjectives in this data set. Table 8.1 lists the adjectives and the kind of survey text that they might reflect.

8.1.1 Rescaling the Data

It is often good practice to rescale raw data. This makes data more comparable across individuals and samples. A common procedure is to *center* each variable by subtracting its mean from every observation, and then *rescaling* those centered values

Table 8.1 Adjectives in the `brand.rating` data and examples of survey text that might be used to collect rating data

Perceptual adjective (column name)	Example survey text
Perform	*Brand* has strong performance
Leader	*Brand* is a leader in the field
Latest	*Brand* has the latest products
Fun	*Brand* is fun
Serious	*Brand* is serious
Bargain	*Brand* products are a bargain
Value	*Brand* products are a good value
Trendy	*Brand* is trendy
Rebuy	I would buy from *Brand* again

as units of standard deviation. This is commonly called *standardizing, normalizing,* or *Z scoring* the data (Sect. 7.3.3).

In R, data could be standardized in this way with a mathematical expression using `mean()` and `sd()`:

```
> x <- 1:1000
> x.sc <- (x - mean(x)) / sd(x)
> summary(x.sc)
   Min. 1st Qu.  Median    Mean 3rd Qu.    Max.
-1.7290 -0.8647  0.0000  0.0000  0.8647  1.7290
```

As we saw in Sect. 7.3.3, a simpler way is to use `scale()` to rescale all variables at once. We never want to alter raw data, so we assign the raw values first to a new data frame `brand.sc` and alter that:

```
> brand.sc <- brand.ratings
> brand.sc[, 1:9] <- data.frame(scale(brand.ratings[, 1:9]))
> summary(brand.sc)
    perform              leader               latest               fun
 Min.   :-1.0888    Min.   :-1.3100    Min.   :-1.6878    Min.   :-1.84677
 1st Qu.:-1.0888    1st Qu.:-0.9266    1st Qu.:-0.7131    1st Qu.:-0.75358
 Median :-0.1523    Median :-0.1599    Median : 0.2615    Median :-0.02478
 Mean   : 0.0000    Mean   : 0.0000    Mean   : 0.0000    Mean   : 0.00000
 3rd Qu.: 0.7842    3rd Qu.: 0.6069    3rd Qu.: 0.9113    3rd Qu.: 0.70402
 Max.   : 1.7206    Max.   : 2.1404    Max.   : 1.2362    Max.   : 1.43281
 ...
```

We add `data.frame()` around `scale()` to clean up the resulting object for simplicity, removing information about the scaling process. We name the new data frame with extension ".sc" to remind ourselves that observations have been scaled. We operate on columns 1–9 because the 10th column is a factor variable for brand. We see that the mean of each adjective is correctly 0.00 across all brands because the data is rescaled. Observations on the adjectives have a spread (difference between `min` and `max`) of roughly 3 standard deviation units. This means the distributions are *platykurtic*, flatter than a standard normal distribution, because we would expect a range of more than 4 standard deviation units for a sample of this size. (Platykurtosis is a common property of survey data, due to floor and ceiling effects.)

Fig. 8.1 Correlation plot for the simulated consumer brand ratings. This visualization of the basic data appears to show three general clusters that comprise *fun/latest/trendy*, *rebuy/bargain/value*, and *perform/leader/serious* respectively

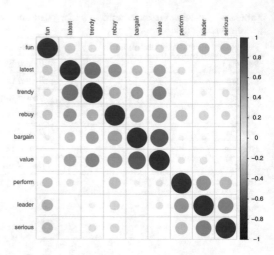

We use `corrplot()` for initial inspection of bivariate relationships among the variables:

```
> library(corrplot)
> corrplot(cor(brand.sc[, 1:9]), order="hclust")
```

As before, we plot columns 1–9 because the 10th column is the non-numeric brand label. In `corrplot()`, the argument `order="hclust"` reorders the rows and columns according to variables' similarity in a hierarchical cluster solution (see Sect. 11.3.2 for more on hierarchical clustering). The result is shown in Fig. 8.1, where we see that the ratings seem to group into three clusters of similar variables, a hypothesis we examine in detail in this chapter.

8.1.2 Aggregate Mean Ratings by Brand

Perhaps the simplest business question in these data is: "What is the average (mean) position of the brand on each adjective?" We can use `aggregate()` (see Sects. 3.4.5 and 5.2.1) to find the mean of each variable by brand:

```
> brand.mean <- aggregate(. ~ brand, data=brand.sc, mean)
> brand.mean
  brand     perform      leader     latest          fun      serious     bargain
1     a -0.88591874  -0.5279035  0.4109732   0.6566458  -0.91894067  0.21409609
2     b  0.93087022   1.0707584  0.7261069  -0.9722147   1.18314061  0.04161938
...
```

Before proceeding, we perform a bit of housekeeping on the new `brand.mean` object. We name the rows with the brand labels that `aggregate()` put into the `brand` column, and then we remove that column as redundant:

```
> rownames(brand.mean) <- brand.mean[, 1]  # use brand for the row names
> brand.mean <- brand.mean[, -1]           # remove brand name column
```

Fig. 8.2 A heatmap for the mean of each adjective by brand. Brands *f* and *g* are similar—with high ratings for *rebuy* and *value* but low ratings for *latest* and *fun*. Other groups of similar brands are *b/c*, *i/h/d*, and *a/j*

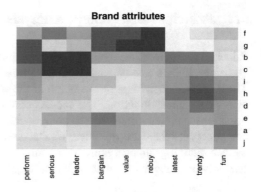

Brand attributes

The resulting matrix is now nicely formatted with brands by row and adjective means in the columns:

```
> brand.mean
       perform      leader     latest         fun     serious      bargain
a  -0.88591874  -0.5279035  0.4109732   0.6566458  -0.91894067   0.21409609
b   0.93087022   1.0707584  0.7261069  -0.9722147   1.18314061   0.04161938
...
```

A *heatmap* is a useful way to examine such results because it colors data points by the intensities of their values. We use `heatmap.2()` from the `gplots` package [193] with colors from the `RColorBrewer` package [148] (install those if you need them):

```
> library(gplots)
> library(RColorBrewer)
> heatmap.2(as.matrix(brand.mean),
+           col=brewer.pal(9, "GnBu"), trace="none", key=FALSE, dend="none",
+           main="\n\n\n\n\nBrand attributes")
```

`heatmap.2()` is a complex function. In the code above, we coerce `brand.mean` to be a matrix as `heatmap.2()` expects. We color the map using greens and blues from `RColorBrewer`'s "GnBu" palette and turn off a few options that otherwise clutter the heatmap (`trace`, `key`, and `dendrogram`). We improve title alignment by adding blank lines with \n before the title text.

The resulting heatmap is shown in Fig. 8.2. In this chart's green-to-blue (`"GnBu"`) palette a green color indicates a low value and dark blue indicates a high value; lighter colors are for values in the middle of the range. The brands are clearly perceived differently with some brands rated high on performance and leadership (brands *b* and *c*) and others rated high for value and intention to rebuy (brands *f* and *g*). By default, `heatmap.2()` sorts the columns and rows in order to emphasize similarities and patterns in the data, which is why the rows and columns in Fig. 8.2 are ordered in an unexpected way. It does this using a form of hierarchical clustering (see Sect. 11.3.2).

Looking at Figs. 8.1 and 8.2 we could guess at the groupings and relationships of adjectives and brands. For example, there is similarity in the color pattern across columns for the *bargain/value/rebuy*; a brand that is high on one tends to be high on another. But it is better to formalize such insight, and the remainder of this chapter discusses how to do so.

8.2   Principal Component Analysis and Perceptual Maps

Principal Component Analysis (PCA) recomputes a set of variables in terms of linear
equations, known as *components*, that capture linear relationships in the data [108].
The first component captures as much of the variance as possible from all variables
as a single linear function. The second component captures as much variance as
possible that remains after the first component. This continues until there are as many
components as there are variables. We can use this process to reduce data complexity
by then retaining and analyzing only a subset of those components—such as the first
one or two components—that explain a large proportion of the variation in the data.

8.2.1   PCA Example

We explore PCA first with a simple data set to see and develop intuition about what
is happening. We create highly correlated data by copying a random vector `xvar`
to a new vector `yvar` while replacing half of the data points. Then we repeat that
procedure to create `zvar` from `yvar`:

```
> set.seed(98286)
> xvar <- sample(1:10, 100, replace=TRUE)
> yvar <- xvar
> yvar[sample(1:length(yvar), 50)] <- sample(1:10, 50, replace=TRUE)
> zvar <- yvar
> zvar[sample(1:length(zvar), 50)] <- sample(1:10, 50, replace=TRUE)
> my.vars <- cbind(xvar, yvar, zvar)
```

`yvar` will be correlated with `xvar` because 50 of the observations are identical
while 50 are newly sampled random values. Similarly, `zvar` keeps 50 values from
`yvar` (and thus also inherits some from `xvar`, but fewer). We compile those three
vectors into a matrix.

We check one of the three possible bivariate plots along with the correlation matrix.
If we simply plotted the raw data, there would be many overlapping values because
the responses are discrete (integers 1–10). To separate and visualize multiple points
with the same values, we `jitter()` them (Sect. 4.6.1):

```
> plot(yvar ~ xvar, data=jitter(my.vars))
> cor(my.vars)
          xvar      yvar      zvar
xvar 1.0000000 0.5969717 0.2496469
yvar 0.5969717 1.0000000 0.5231468
zvar 0.2496469 0.5231468 1.0000000
```

The bivariate plot in Fig. 8.3 shows a clear linear trend for `yvar` versus `xvar` on
the diagonal. In the correlation matrix, `xvar` correlates highly with `yvar` and less
so with `zvar`, as expected, and `yvar` has strong correlation with `zvar` (using the
rules of thumb from Sect. 4.5).

Using intuition, what would we expect the components to be from this data? First,
there is shared variance across all three variables because they are positively correlated. So we expect to see one component that picks up that association of all three

Fig. 8.3 Scatterplot of correlated data with discrete values, using `jitter()` to separate the values slightly for greater visual impact of overlapping points

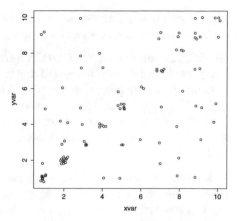

variables. After that, we expect to see a component that shows that `xvar` and `zvar` are more differentiated from one another than either is from `yvar`. That implies that `yvar` has a unique position in the data set as the only variable to correlate highly with both of the others, so we expect one of the components to reflect this uniqueness of `yvar`.

Let's check the intuition. We use `prcomp()` to perform PCA:

```
> my.pca <- prcomp(my.vars)
> summary(my.pca)
Importance of components:
                          PC1    PC2    PC3
Standard deviation      3.9992 2.4381 1.6269
Proportion of Variance  0.6505 0.2418 0.1077
Cumulative Proportion   0.6505 0.8923 1.0000
```

There are 3 components because we have 3 variables. The first component accounts for 65% of the explainable linear variance, while the second accounts for 24%, leaving 11% for the third component. How are those components related to the variables? We check the rotation matrix, which is helpfully printed by default for a PCA object:

```
> my.pca
Standard deviations:
[1] 3.999154 2.438079 1.626894

Rotation:
             PC1          PC2         PC3
xvar  -0.6156755   0.63704774   0.4638037
yvar  -0.6532994  -0.08354009  -0.7524766
zvar  -0.4406173  -0.76628404   0.4676165
```

Interpreting PCA rotation loadings is difficult because of the multivariate nature— factor analysis is a better procedure for interpretation, as we will see later in this chapter—but we examine the loadings here for illustration and comparison to our expectations. In component 1 (PC1) we see loading on all 3 variables as expected from their overall shared variance (the negative direction is not important; the key is that they are all in the same direction).

In component 2, we see that `xvar` and `zvar` are differentiated from one another as expected, with loadings in opposite directions. Finally, in component 3, we see resid-

ual variance that differentiates `yvar` from the other two variables and is consistent
with our intuition about `yvar` being unique.

In addition to the loading matrix, PCA has computed scores for each of the principal
components that express the underlying data in terms of its loadings on those components. Those are present in the PCA object as the `$x` matrix, where the columns
(`[ , 1]`, `[ , 2]`, and so forth) may be used to obtain the values of the components for each observation. We can use a small number of those columns in place of
the original data to obtain a set of observations that captures much of the variation
in the data.

A less obvious feature of PCA, but implicit in the definition, is that extracted PCA
components are *uncorrelated* with one another, because otherwise there would be
more linear variance that could have been captured. We see this in the `scores`
returned for observations in a PCA model, where the off-diagonal correlations are
effectively zero (approximately 10^{-15} as shown in R's scientific notation):

```
> cor(my.pca$x)    # components have zero correlation
              PC1              PC2              PC3
PC1  1.000000e+00    4.808932e-16    1.768720e-15
PC2  4.808932e-16    1.000000e+00   -1.174441e-15
PC3  1.768720e-15   -1.174441e-15    1.000000e+00
```

8.2.2   Visualizing PCA

A good way to examine the results of PCA is to map the first few components, which
allows us to visualize the data in a lower-dimensional space. A common visualization
is a *biplot*, a two-dimensional plot of data points with respect to the first two PCA
components, overlaid with a projection of the variables on the components. We use
`biplot()` to generate this:

```
> biplot(my.pca)
```

The result is Fig. 8.4, where every data point is plotted (and labeled by row number)
according to its values on the first two components. Such plots are especially helpful
when there are a smaller number of points (as we will see below for brands) or when
there are clusters (as we see in Chap. 11).

In Fig. 8.4, there are arrows that show the best fit of each of the variables on the
principal components—a projection of the variables onto the 2-dimensional space
of the first two PCA components, which explain a large part of the variation in the
data. These are useful to inspect because the *direction* and *angle* of the arrows reflect
the relationship of the variables; a closer angle indicates higher positive association,
while the relative direction indicates positive or negative association of the variables.

In the present case, we see in the variable projections (arrows) that `yvar` is closely
aligned with the first component (X axis). In the relationships among the variables
themselves, we see that `xvar` and `zvar` are more associated with `yvar`, relative to

Fig. 8.4 A `biplot()` of a principal component analysis solution for the simple, constructed example, showing data points plotted on the first two components

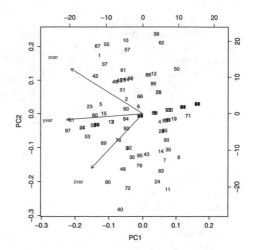

the principal components, than either is with the other. Thus, this visually matches our interpretation of the correlation matrix and loadings above.

By plotting against principal components, a biplot benefits from the fact that components are uncorrelated; this helps to disperse data on the chart because the x- and y-axes are independent. When there are several components that account for substantial variance, it is also useful to plot components beyond the first and second. This can be done with the `choices` argument to `biplot()`.

8.2.3 PCA for Brand Ratings

Let's look at the principal components for the brand rating data (refer to Sect. 8.1 above if you need to load the data). We find the components with `prcomp()`, selecting just the rating columns 1–9:

```
> brand.pc <- prcomp(brand.sc[, 1:9])
> summary(brand.pc)
Importance of components:
                          PC1    PC2    PC3    PC4     PC5     PC6     PC7
Standard deviation     1.726 1.4479 1.0389 0.8528 0.79846 0.73133 0.62458 ...
Proportion of Variance 0.331 0.2329 0.1199 0.0808 0.07084 0.05943 0.04334 ...
Cumulative Proportion  0.331 0.5640 0.6839 0.7647 0.83554 0.89497 0.93831 ...
```

The default `plot()` for a PCA is a *scree plot*, which shows the successive proportion of additional variance that each component adds. We plot this as a line chart using `type="l"` (lower case "L" for *line*):

```
> plot(brand.pc, type="l")
```

The result is Fig. 8.5. A scree plot is often interpreted as indicating where additional components are not worth the complexity; this occurs where the line has an *elbow*, a kink in the angle of bending, a somewhat subjective determination. In Fig. 8.5,

Fig. 8.5 A scree plot() of a PCA solution shows the successive variance accounted by each component. For the brand rating data, the proportion largely levels out after the 3rd component

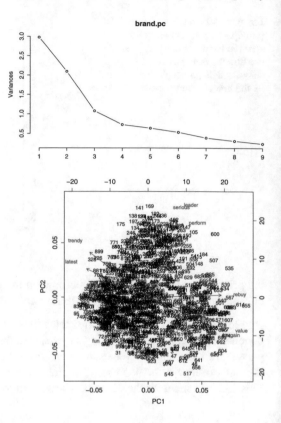

Fig. 8.6 A biplot of an initial attempt at principal component analysis for consumer brand ratings. Although we see adjective groupings on the variable loading arrows in red, and gain some insight into the areas where ratings cluster (as dense areas of observation points), the chart would be more useful if the data were first aggregated by brand

the elbow occurs at either component 3 or 4, depending on interpretation; and this suggests that the first 2 or 3 components explain most of the variation in the observed brand ratings.

A biplot() of the first two principal components—which biplot() selects by default for a PCA object—reveals how the rating adjectives are associated:

```
> biplot(brand.pc)
```

We see the result in Fig. 8.6, where adjectives map in four regions: category leadership ("serious," "leader," and "perform" in the upper right), value ("rebuy," "value," and "bargain"), trendiness ("trendy" and "latest"), and finally "fun" on its own.

But there is a problem: the plot of individual respondents' ratings is too dense and it does not tell us about the brand positions! A better solution is to perform PCA using *aggregated* ratings by brand. First we remind ourselves of the data that compiled the mean rating of each adjective by brand as we found above using aggregate() (see Sect. 8.1). Then we extract the principal components:

```
> brand.mean
     perform       leader      latest         fun     serious      bargain
a -0.88591874  -0.5279035  0.4109732   0.6566458 -0.91894067   0.21409609
b  0.93087022   1.0707584  0.7261069  -0.9722147  1.18314061   0.04161938
```

```
...
> brand.mu.pc <- prcomp(brand.mean, scale=TRUE)
> summary(brand.mu.pc)
Importance of components:
                          PC1    PC2    PC3     PC4     PC5     PC6     PC7
Standard deviation      2.1345 1.7349 0.7690 0.61498 0.50983 0.36662 0.21506
Proportion of Variance  0.5062 0.3345 0.0657 0.04202 0.02888 0.01493 0.00514
Cumulative Proportion   0.5062 0.8407 0.9064 0.94842 0.97730 0.99223 0.99737
...
```

In the call to `prcomp()`, we added `scale=TRUE` in order to rescale the data; even though the raw data was already rescaled, the aggregated means have a somewhat different scale than the standardized data itself. The results show that the first two components account for 84% of the explainable variance in the mean ratings, so we focus on interpreting results with regards to them.

8.2.4 Perceptual Map of the Brands

A biplot of the PCA solution for the mean ratings gives an interpretable *perceptual map*, showing where the brands are placed with respect to the first two principal components. We use `biplot()` on the PCA solution for the mean rating by brand:

```
> biplot(brand.mu.pc, main="Brand positioning", cex=c(1.5, 1))
```

We plot the brand labels with a 50% larger font using the *c*haracter *e*xpansion argument `cex=c(1.5, 1)`. The result is Fig. 8.7.

Before interpreting the new map, we first check that using mean data did not greatly alter the structure. Figure 8.7 shows a different spatial rotation of the adjectives, compared to Fig. 8.6, but the spatial position is arbitrary and the new map has the same overall grouping of adjectives and relational structure (for instance, seeing as in Fig. 8.6 that "serious" and "leader" are closely related while "fun" is rather distant from other adjectives). Thus the variable positions on the components are consistent with PCA on the full set of observations, and we go ahead to interpret the graphic.

What does the map tell us? First we interpret the adjective clusters and relationships and see four areas with well-differentiated sets of adjectives and brands that are positioned in proximity. Brands *f* and *g* are high on "value," for instance, while *a* and *j* are relatively high on "fun," which is opposite in direction from leadership adjectives ("leader" and "serious").

With such a map, one might form questions and then refer to the underlying data to answer them. For instance, suppose that you are the brand manager for brand *e*. What does the map tell you? For one thing, your brand is in the center and thus appears not to be well-differentiated on any of the dimensions. That could be good or bad, depending on your strategic goals. If your goal is to be a safe brand that appeals to many consumers, then a relatively undifferentiated position like *e* could be desirable. On the other hand, if you wish your brand to have a strong, differentiated perception, this finding would be unwanted (but important to know).

Fig. 8.7 A perceptual map
of consumer brands with
`biplot()` for aggregate
mean rating by brand. This
shows components almost
identical to those in Fig. 8.6
(although spatially rotated)
but the mean brand positions
are clear

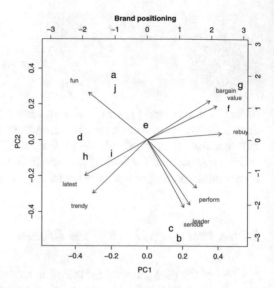

What should you do about the position of your brand *e*? Again, it depends on the
strategic goals. If you wish to increase differentiation, one possibility would be to
take action to shift your brand in some direction on the map. Suppose you wanted to
move in the direction of brand *c*. You could look at the specific differences from *c*
in the data:

```
> brand.mean["c", ] - brand.mean["e", ]
    perform    leader     latest      fun   serious    bargain       value ...
c 1.214314 0.9699315 -0.5587936 -1.140567 1.180621 -1.158594 -0.8588416 ...
```

This shows you that *e* is relatively stronger than *c* on "value" and "fun", which
suggests dialing down messaging or other attributes that reinforce those (assuming,
of course, that you truly want to move in the direction of *c*). Similarly, *c* is stronger
on "perform" and "serious," so those could be aspects of the product or message for
e to strengthen.

Another option would be *not* to follow another brand but to aim for differentiated
space where no brand is positioned. In Fig. 8.7, there is a large gap between the group
b and *c* on the bottom of the chart, versus *f* and *g* on the upper right. This area might
be described as the "value leader" area or similar.

How do we find out how to position there? Let's assume that the gap reflects approximately the average of those four brands (see Sect. 8.2.5 for some of the risks with
this assumption). We can find that average using `colMeans()` on the brands' rows,
and then take the difference of *e* from that average:

```
> colMeans(brand.mean[c("b", "c", "f", "g"), ]) - brand.mean["e", ]
    perform    leader     latest       fun   serious    bargain       value
e 1.174513 0.3910396 -0.9372789 -0.9337707 0.5732131 -0.2502787 0.07921355
...
```

This suggests that brand *e* could target the gap by increasing its emphasis on performance while reducing emphasis on "latest" and "fun."

To summarize, when you wish to compare several brands across many dimensions, it can be helpful to focus on just the first two or three principal components that explain variation in the data. You can select how many components to focus on using a scree plot, which shows how much variation in the data is explained by each principal component. A perceptual map plots the brands on the first two principal components, revealing how the observations related to the underlying dimensions (the components).

PCA may be performed using survey ratings of the brands (as we have done here) or with objective data such as price and physical measurements, or with a combination of the two. In any case, when you are confronted with multidimensional data on brands or products, PCA visualization is a useful tool for understanding how they differ from one another in the market.

8.2.5 Cautions with Perceptual Maps

There are three important caveats in interpreting perceptual maps. First, you must choose the level and type of aggregation carefully. We demonstrated the maps using mean rating by brand, but depending on the data and question at hand, it might be more suitable to use median (for ordinal data) or even modal response (for categorical data). You should check that the dimensions are similar for the full data and aggregated data before interpreting aggregate maps. You can do this by examining the variable positions and relationships in biplots of both aggregated data (such as means) and raw data (or a random subset of it), as we did above.

Second, the relationships are strictly relative to the product category and the brands and adjectives that are tested. In a different product category, or with different brands, adjectives such as "fun" and "leader" could have a very different relationship. Sometimes simply adding or dropping a brand can change the resulting map significantly because the positions are relative. In other words, if a new brand enters the market (or one's analysis), the other positions may change substantially. One must also be confident that all of the key perceptions (adjectives, in this example) have been assessed. One way to assess sensitivity here is to run PCA and biplot on a few different samples from your data, such as 80% of your observations, and perhaps dropping an adjective each time. If the maps are similar across those samples, you may feel more confident in their stability. And one should update perceptual maps frequently ; the map may change substantially if one or two competitors start emphasizing a new dimesion on which competitors were previously undifferentiated.

Third, it is frequently misunderstood that the positions of brands in such a map depend on their relative positioning in terms of the principal components, which are constructed composites of all dimensions. This means that *the strength of a brand on a single adjective cannot be read directly from the chart*. For instance, in Fig. 8.7, it might appear that brands b and c are weaker than d, h, and i on "latest" but are similar to one another. In fact, *b* is the single strongest brand on "latest" while *c* is weak on that adjective. Overall, *b* and *c* are quite similar to one another in terms of their scores on the two components that aggregate all of the variables (adjectives), but they are not necessarily similar on any single variable. Another way to look at this is that when we use PCA to focus on the first one or two dimensions in the data, we are looking at the largest-magnitude similarities, which may obscure smaller differences that do not show up strongly in the first one or two dimensions.

This last point is a common area of confusion with analysts and stakeholders who want to read adjective positions directly from a biplot. We recommend to explain that positions are not absolute but are *relative*. We often explain positions with language such as, "compared to its position on other attributes, brand X is *relatively* differentiated by perceptions of strength (or weakness) on such-and-such attribute."

Despite these caveats, perceptual maps can be a valuable tool. We use them primarily to form hypotheses and to provide material to inform strategic analyses of brand and product positioning. If they are used in that way—rather than as absolute assessments of position—they can contribute to engaging discussions about position and potential strategy.

Although we illustrated PCA with brand position, the same kind of analysis could be performed for product ratings, position of consumer segments, ratings of political candidates, evaluations of advertisements, or any other area where you have metric data on multiple dimensions that is aggregated for a modest number of discrete entities of interest.

In Chap. 9 we will see the usefulness of PCA for pre-processing highly correlated data prior to linear modeling. By extracting components, one can derive a reduced set of variables that captures as much of the variance as desired, yet where each of the measures is independent of the others.

8.3 Exploratory Factor Analysis

Exploratory factor analysis (EFA) is a family of techniques to assess the relationship of *constructs* (concepts) in surveys and psychological assessments. Factors are regarded as *latent variables* that cannot be observed directly, but are imperfectly assessed through their relationship to other variables.

In psychometrics, canonical examples of factors occur in psychological and educational testing. For example, "intelligence," "knowledge of mathematics," and "anxiety" are all abstract concepts (constructs) that are not directly observable in themselves. Instead, they are observed empirically through multiple behaviors, each one of which is an imperfect indicator of the underlying latent variable. These observed values are known as *manifest variables* and include indicators such as test scores, survey responses, and other empirical behaviors. Exploratory factor analysis attempts to find the degree to which latent, composite *factors* account for the observed variance of those manifest variables.

In marketing, we often observe a large number of variables that we believe should be related to a smaller set of underlying constructs. For example, we cannot directly observe *customer satisfaction* but we might observe responses on a survey that asks about different aspects of a customer's experience, jointly representing different facets of the underlying construct *satisfaction*. Similarly, we cannot directly observe *purchase intent*, *price sensitivity*, or *category involvement* but we can observe multiple behaviors that are related to them.

In this section, we use EFA to examine respondents' attitudes about brands, using the brand rating data from above (Sect. 8.1) and to uncover the latent dimensions in the data. Then we assess the brands in terms of those estimated latent factors.

8.3.1 Basic EFA Concepts

The result of EFA is similar to PCA: a matrix of factors (similar to PCA components) and their relationship to the original variables (*loadings* of the factors on the variables). Unlike PCA, EFA attempts to find solutions that are maximally *interpretable* in terms of the manifest variables. In general, it attempts to find solutions in which a small number of loadings for each factor are very high, while other loadings for that factor are low. When this is possible, that factor can be interpreted in terms of that small set of variables.

To accomplish this, EFA uses *rotations* that start with an uncorrelated (*orthogonal*) mathematical solution and then mathematically alter the solution to explain identical variance but with different loadings on the original variables. There are many such rotations available, and they typically share the goals of maximizing the loadings on a few variables while making factors as distinct as possible from one another.

Instead of reviewing that mathematically (see [145]), let's consider a loose analogy. One might think about EFA in terms of a pizza topped with large items such as tomato slices and mushrooms that will be cut into a certain number of slices. The pizza could be rotated and cut in an infinite number of ways that are all mathematically equivalent insofar as they divide up the same underlying structure.

However, some rotations are more useful than others because they fall in-between the large items rather than dividing them. When this occurs, one might have a "tomato slice," a"mushroom slice," a "half-and-half tomato and mushroom slice," and so forth. By rotating and cutting differently, one makes the underlying substance more interpretable relative to one's goals (such as having differentiated pizza slices). No rotation is inherently better or worse, but some are more useful than others. Similarly, the manifest variables in EFA can be sliced in many ways according to one's goals for interpreting the latent factors. We will see how this works in Sect. 8.3.3.

Because EFA produces results that are interpretable in terms of the original variables, an analyst may be able to interpret and act on the results in ways that would be difficult with PCA. For instance, EFA can be used to refine a survey by keeping items with high loading on factors of interest while cutting items that do not load highly. EFA is also useful to investigate whether a survey's items actually go together in a way that is consistent with expectations.

For example, if we have a 10-item survey that is supposed to assess the single construct *customer satisfaction*, it is important to know whether those items in fact go together in a way that can be interpreted as a single factor, or whether they instead reflect multiple dimensions that we might not have considered. Before interpreting multiple items as assessing a single concept, one might wish to test that it is appropriate to do so. In this chapter, we use EFA to investigate such structure. In Chap. 10, we will see how to test whether one's data are in fact consistent with an asserted structure.

EFA serves as a data reduction technique in three broad senses:

1. In the technical sense of dimensional reduction, we can use *factor scores* instead of a larger set of items. For instance, if we are assessing satisfaction, we could use a single satisfaction score instead of several separate items. (In Sect. 9.1.2 we review how this is also useful when observations are correlated.)
2. We can reduce uncertainty. If we believe *satisfaction* is imperfectly manifest in several measures, the combination of those will have less noise than the set of individual items.
3. We might also reduce data collection by focusing on items that are known to have high contribution to factors of interest. If we discover that some items are not important for a factor of interest, we can discard them from data collection efforts.

In this chapter we use the brand rating data to ask the following questions: How many latent factors are there? How do the survey items map to the factors? How are the brands positioned on the factors? What are the respondents' factor scores?

8.3.2 Finding an EFA Solution

The first step in exploratory factor analysis is to determine the number of factors to estimate. There are various ways to do this, and two traditional methods are to use a scree plot (Sect. 8.2.3), and to retain factors where the *eigenvalue* (a metric for proportion of variance explained) is greater than 1.0. An eigenvalue of 1.0 corresponds to the amount of variance that might be attributed to a single independent variable; a factor that captures less variance than such an item may be considered relatively uninteresting.

As we saw in Sect. 8.2.3, a scree plot of the brand rating data suggests 2 or 3 components. The nFactors package [160] (install if necessary) formalizes this analysis
with nScree():

```
> library(nFactors)
> nScree(brand.sc[, 1:9])
  noc naf nparallel nkaiser
1   3   2         3       3
```

nScree() applies several methods to estimate the number of factors from scree
tests, and in the present case three of the four methods suggest that the data set has
3 factors. We can examine the eigenvalues using eigen() on a correlation matrix:

```
> eigen(cor(brand.sc[, 1:9]))
$values
[1] 2.9792956 2.0965517 1.0792549 0.7272110 0.6375459 0.5348432 0.3901044
...
```

The first three eigenvalues are greater than 1.0, although barely so for the 3th value.
This again suggests 3—or possibly 2—factors.

The final choice of a model depends on whether it is useful. For EFA, a best practice
is to check a few factor solutions, including the ones suggested by the scree and
eigenvalue results. Thus, we test a 3-factor solution and a 2-factor solution to see
which one is more useful.

An EFA model is estimated with factanal(x, factors=K), where K is the
number of factors to fit. For a 2-factor solution, we write:

```
> factanal(brand.sc[, 1:9], factors=2)
...
Loadings:
        Factor1 Factor2
perform          0.600
leader           0.818
latest  -0.451
fun     -0.137  -0.382
serious          0.686
bargain  0.803
value    0.873   0.117
trendy  -0.534
rebuy    0.569   0.303
...
```

We have removed all of the information except for the loadings because those are
the most important to interpret (see "Learning More" in this chapter for material that
explains much more about EFA and the output of such procedures). Some of the
factor loadings are near zero, and are not shown; this makes EFA potentially easier
to interpret than PCA.

In the 2-factor solution, factor 1 loads strongly on "bargain" and "value," and therefore
might be interpreted as a "value" factor while factor 2 loads on "leader" and "serious"
and thus might be regarded as a "category leader" factor.

This is not a bad interpretation, but let's compare it to a 3-factor solution:

```
> factanal(brand.sc[, 1:9], factors=3)
...
Loadings:
        Factor1 Factor2 Factor3
perform          0.607
leader           0.810   0.106
```

```
latest    -0.163                    0.981
fun                      -0.398     0.205
serious                   0.682
bargain    0.826                   -0.122
value      0.867                   -0.198
trendy    -0.356                    0.586
rebuy      0.499     0.296         -0.298
```

The 3-factor solution retains the "value" and "leader" factors and adds a clear "latest" factor that loads strongly on "latest" and "trendy." This adds a clearly interpretable concept to our understanding of the data. It also aligns with the bulk of suggestions from the scree and eigen tests, and fits well with the perceptual maps we saw in Sect. 8.2.4, where those adjectives were in a differentiated space. So we regard the 3-factor model as superior to the 2-factor model because the factors are more interpretable.

8.3.3   EFA Rotations

As we described earlier, a factor analysis solution can be rotated to have new loadings that account for the same proportion of variance. Although a full consideration of rotations is out of scope for this book, there is one issue worth considering in any EFA: do you wish to allow the factors to be *correlated* with one another or not?

You might think that one should let the data decide. However, the question of whether to allow correlated factors is less a question about the *data* than it is about your *concept* of the underlying latent factors. Do you think the factors should be conceptually independent, or does it make more sense to consider them to be related? An EFA rotation can be obtained under either assumption.

The default in `factanal()` is to find factors that have zero correlation (using a *varimax* rotation). In case you're wondering how this differs from PCA, it differs mathematically because EFA finds latent variables that may be observed with error (see [145]) whereas PCA simply recomputes transformations of the observed data. In other words, EFA focuses on the underlying latent dimensions, whereas PCA focuses on transforming the dimensionality of the data.

Returning to our present data, we might judge that *value* and *leader* are reasonably expected to be related; in many categories, the leader can command a price premium, and thus we might expect those two latent constructs to be negatively correlated rather than independent of one another. This suggests that we could allow correlated factors in our solution. This is known as an *oblique* rotation ("oblique" because the dimensional axes are not perpendicular but are skewed by the correlation between factors).

A common oblique rotation is the "oblimin" rotation from the `GPArotation` package [11] (install if necessary). We add that to our 3-factor model with `rotation="oblimin"`:

```
> library(GPArotation)
> (brand.fa.ob <- factanal(brand.sc[, 1:9], factors=3, rotation="oblimin"))
...
Loadings:
        Factor1 Factor2 Factor3
perform          0.601
leader           0.816
latest                   1.009
fun             -0.381   0.229
serious          0.689
bargain  0.859
value    0.880
trendy  -0.267   0.128   0.538
rebuy    0.448   0.255  -0.226

...
Factor Correlations:
        Factor1 Factor2 Factor3
Factor1  1.0000  -0.388  0.0368
Factor2 -0.3884   1.000 -0.1091
Factor3  0.0368  -0.109  1.0000
...
```

When we compare this oblimin result to the default varimax rotation above, there are two main differences. First, the loadings are slightly different for the relationships of the factors to the adjectives. However, the loadings are similar enough in this case that there is no substantial change in how we would interpret the factors. There are still factors for "value," "leader," and "latest."

Second, the result includes a factor correlation matrix showing the relationships between the estimated latent factors. Factor 1 (value) is negatively correlated with Factor 2 (leader), $r = -0.39$, and is essentially uncorrelated with Factor 3 (latest), $r = 0.037$.

The negative correlation between factors 1 and 2 is consistent with our theory that brands that are leaders are less likely to be value brands, and thus we think this is a more interpretable result. However, in other cases a correlated rotation may or may not be a better solution than an orthogonal one; that is largely an issue to be decided on the basis of domain knowledge and interpretive utility rather than statistics.

In the output above, the item-to-factor loadings are displayed. In the returned model object, those are present as the $loadings element. We can the visualize item-factor relationships with a heatmap of $loadings:

```
> library(gplots)
> library(RColorBrewer)
> heatmap.2(brand.fa.ob$loadings,
+           col=brewer.pal(9, "Greens"), trace="none", key=FALSE, dend="none",
+           Colv=FALSE, cexCol = 1.2,
+           main="\n\n\n\n\nFactor loadings for brand adjectives")
```

The result is Fig. 8.8, which shows a distinct separation of items into 3 factors, which are roughly interpretable as *value*, *leader*, and *latest*. Note that the item rebuy, which reflects stated intention to repurchase, loads on both Factor1 (*value*) and Factor2 (*leader*). This suggests that in our simulated data, consumers say they would rebuy a brand for either reason, because it is a good value or because it is a leader.

Another useful graphic for factor analysis models is a *path diagram*, which shows latent variables and the individual items that load on them.

Fig. 8.8 A heatmap of
item-factor loadings

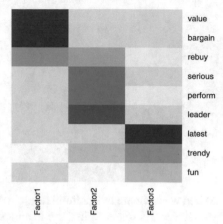

The semPlot package (install if needed) will draw a visual representation of a
factor analysis model. We use the procedure semPaths() to draw the paths. It is
a complex command and we add several arguments as explained below:

```
> library(semPlot)
> semPaths(brand.fa.ob, what="est", residuals=FALSE,
+         cut=0.3, posCol=c("white", "darkgreen"), negCol=c("white", "red"),
+         edge.label.cex=0.75, nCharNodes=7)
```

First we will explain the semPaths() call. We plotted the brand.fa.ob model
as fit above. To draw the loading estimates, we requested what="est". We omit
the residual estimates for manifest variables (an advanced topic we don't cover
in this book) using residuals=FALSE. Then we cut loadings with absolute
magnitude < 0.3 by adding cut=0.3 and the options posCol=c("white",
"darkgreen") and negCol=c("white", "red"). The posCol argument
says that positive *loadings* < 0.3 should be colored white (and thus not appear in
the output), while *loadings* > 0.3 should be darkgreen. The negCol argument
similarly excludes or colors red the *loadings* < 0. We adjust the loadings' text
size with edge.label.cex, and create room to spell out full variable names with
nCharNodes.

The result is shown in Fig. 8.9. Luckily, interpreting the path diagram is easier than
the code to create it! Latent variables are shown at the top and are traditionally
drawn with circles; these correspond to the three factors. Manifest variables appear
in squares at the bottom; these are the observed variables that load on the factors. The
strength of loading is shown on the path from each factor to its manifest variables,
with positive loading in green and negative loading in red (and with a negative sign).

We will see many more examples of path diagrams when we explore confirmatory
factor analysis and structural equation models in Chap. 10.

Overall, the result of the EFA for this data set is that instead of using 9 distinct
variables, we might instead represent the data with 3 underlying latent factors. We

Fig. 8.9 A path diagram for
the factor analysis solution,
which clearly displays the
three factors and their item
loadings ($|loadings| < 0.3$
are excluded). The graphic is
generated with
semPaths() from the
semPlot package

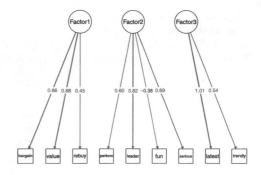

have seen that each factor maps to 2–4 of the manifest variables. However, this only
tells us about the relationships of the rating variables among themselves in our data;
in the next section, we use the estimated factor scores to learn about the *brands*.

8.3.4 Using Factor Scores for Brands

In addition to estimating the factor structure, EFA will also estimate latent factor
scores for each observation. In the present case, this gives us the best estimates of
each respondent's latent ratings for the "value,""leader," and "latest" factors. We can
then use the factor scores to determine brands' positions on the factors. Interpreting
factors eliminates the separate dimensions associated with the manifest variables,
allowing us to concentrate on a smaller, more reliable set of dimensions that map to
theoretical constructs instead of individual items.

Factor scores are requested from factanal() by adding the scores=... argument. We request *Bartlett* scores (see ?factanal), and extract them from the
factanal() object using $scores, storing them as a separate data frame:

```
> brand.fa.ob <- factanal(brand.sc[, 1:9], factors=3, rotation="oblimin",
+                       scores="Bartlett")
> brand.scores <- data.frame(brand.fa.ob$scores)   # get the factor scores
> brand.scores$brand <- brand.sc$brand             # get the matching brands
> head(brand.scores)
      Factor1      Factor2      Factor3 brand
1   1.6521364  -0.6886749   0.5256104     a
2  -1.4005333  -1.6681901  -0.6764121     a
...
```

The result is an estimated score for each respondent on each factor and brand. If we
wish to investigate individual-level correlates of the factors, such as their relationship
to demographics or purchase behavior, we could use these estimates of factor scores.
This can be very helpful in analyses such as regression and segmentation because
it reduces the model complexity (number of dimensions) and uses more reliable
estimates (factor scores that reflect several manifest variables). Instead of nine items,
we have three factors.

Fig. 8.10 A heatmap of the latent factor scores for consumer brand ratings, by brand

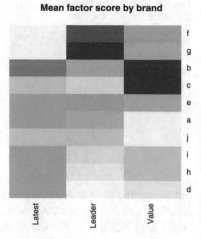

Mean factor score by brand

To find the overall position for a brand, we `aggregate()` the individual scores by brand as usual:

```
> brand.fa.mean <- aggregate(. ~ brand, data=brand.scores, mean)
```

We clean this up by assigning names for the rows (brands) and columns (factors):

```
> rownames(brand.fa.mean) <- brand.fa.mean[, 1]          # brand names
> brand.fa.mean <- brand.fa.mean[, -1]
> names(brand.fa.mean) <- c("Leader", "Value", "Latest")  # factor names
> brand.fa.mean
       Leader        Value        Latest
a   0.23158792  -1.06993703   0.39326652
b   0.09686823   1.51913070   0.72391174
...
```

Finally, a heatmap graphs the scores by brand:

```
> heatmap.2(as.matrix(brand.fa.mean),
+           col=brewer.pal(9, "GnBu"), trace="none", key=FALSE, dend="none",
+           cexCol=1.2, main="\n\n\n\n\nMean factor score by brand")
```

The result is Fig. 8.10. When we compare this to the chart of brand by adjective in Fig. 8.2, we see that the chart of factor scores is significantly simpler than the full adjective matrix. The brand similarities are evident again in the factor scores, for instance that *f* and *g* are similar, as are *b* and *c*, and so forth.

We conclude that EFA is a valuable way to examine the underlying structure and relationship of variables. When items are related to underlying constructs, EFA reduces data complexity by aggregating variables to create simpler, more interpretable latent variables.

In this exposition, we have only explored a small number of the possibilities for factor analysis; to learn more, see Sect. 8.7. You will also want to review Chap. 10, which considers the closely related topic of *confirmatory factor analysis* (CFA). CFA does not attempt to *find* a factor structure as EFA does, but rather *assesses* how well a proposed structure fits one's data.

8.4 Multidimensional Scaling

Multidimensional scaling (MDS) is a family of procedures that can also be used to find lower-dimensional representations of data. Instead of extracting underlying components or latent factors, MDS works instead with *distances* (also known as *similarities*). MDS attempts to find a lower-dimensional map that best preserves all the observed similarities between items.

If you have similarity data already, such as direct ratings of whether one product is like another, you can apply MDS directly to the data. If you have other kinds of data, such as the brand rating data we've considered in this chapter, then you must compute the distances between points before applying MDS. If you have *metric* data—where you consider the units of measurement to have interval or ratio properties—then you might simply calculate euclidian distances with the default dist() command, as we do for the mean ratings computed above:

```
> brand.dist <- dist(brand.mean)
```

A procedure to find an MDS solution for a distance matrix from metric data is cmdscale():

```
> (brand.mds <- cmdscale(brand.dist))
           [,1]        [,2]
a  -7.570113e-01  1.4619032
b   5.586301e-01 -2.1698618
...
```

The result of cmdscale() is a list of X and Y dimensions indicating 2-dimensional estimated plot coordinates for entities (in this case, brands). We see the plot locations for brands *a* and *b* in the output above. Given those coordinates, we can simply plot() the values and label them:

```
> plot(brand.mds, type="n")
> text(brand.mds, rownames(brand.mds), cex=2)
```

In this code, plot(..., type="n") tells R not to plot symbols. Instead, we add the brand labels to the plot with text(x, labels). The result is Fig. 8.11. The brand positions are grouped nearly identically to what we saw in the perceptual map in Fig. 8.7.

8.4.1 Non-metric MDS

For *non-metric* data such as rankings or categorical variables, you would use a different method to compute distance and an MDS algorithm that does not assume metric distances.

For purposes of illustration, let's convert the mean ratings to rankings instead of raw values; this will be non-metric, ordinal data. We apply rank() to the columns using lapply() and code each resulting column as an ordinal factor variable using ordered():

Fig. 8.11 A metric
multidimensional scaling
chart for mean brand rating,
using `cmdscale()`. The
brand positions are quite
similar to those seen in the
`biplot()` in Fig. 8.7

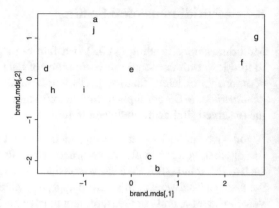

```
> brand.rank <- data.frame(lapply(brand.mean, function(x) ordered(rank(x))))
> str(brand.rank)
'data.frame':   10 obs. of  9 variables:
$ perform: Ord.factor w/ 10 levels "1"<"2"<"3"<"4"<..:  1 10 8 2 4 5 9 6 7 3
$ leader : Ord.factor w/ 10 levels "1"<"2"<"3"<"4"<..:  3 9 10 2 7 8 6 5 4 1
...
```

To find distances between the ranks, we use an alternative to `dist()`, `daisy()`
from the `cluster` package (see Sect. 11.3.2), which can handle non-metric data
such as rank ordering. In `daisy()`, we compute distance with the `gower` metric,
which handles mixed numeric, ordinal, and nominal data:

```
> library(cluster)
> brand.dist.r <- daisy(brand.rank, metric="gower")
```

Now that we have a distance matrix we apply the non-metric MDS function
`isoMDS()` to scale the data. Then we plot the result:

```
> brand.mds.r <- isoMDS(brand.dist.r)
initial   value 9.063777
...
converged
> plot(brand.mds.r$points, type="n")
> text(brand.mds.r$points, levels(brand.sc$brand), cex=2)
```

The `plot()` and `text()` commands are slightly different than those we saw above
for `cmdscale()`, because `isoMDS()` returns coordinates in the `$points` matrix
within its object.

The resulting chart is shown in Fig. 8.12. Compared to Fig. 8.11, we see that brand
positions in the non-metric solution are more diffuse. The X axis is arbitrarily
reversed, which is not important. Still, the nearest neighbors of brands are largely
consistent with the exception of brands *h* and *i*, which are separated quite a bit more
than in the metric solution. (This occurs because the rank-order procedure loses some
of the information that is present in the original metric data solution, resulting in a
slightly different map.)

We generally recommend principal component analysis as a more informative procedure than multidimensional scaling for typical metric or near-metric (e.g., survey

Fig. 8.12 A non-metric multidimensional scaling chart for mean brand ratings expressed as ordinal ranks, obtained using `daisy()` to find distances and `isoMDS()` for non-metric scaling. The brand groupings are similar to but more diffuse than those in Fig. 8.11

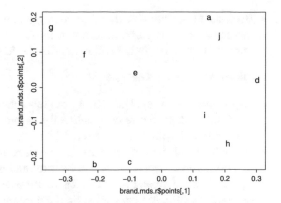

Likert scale) data. However, PCA will not work with non-metric data. In those cases, multidimensional scaling is a valuable alternative.

MDS may be of particular interest when handling text data such as consumers' feedback, comments, and online product reviews, where text frequencies can be converted to distance scores. For example, if you are interested in similarities between brands in online reviews, you could count how many times various pairs of brands occur together in consumers' postings. The co-occurrence matrix of counts—brand A mentioned with brand B, with brand C, and so forth—could be used as a measure of similarity between the two brands and serve as the distance metric in MDS (see [147]).

8.5 Key Points

Investigation of one's data complexity has several benefits. It allows inspection of the underlying dimensional relationships among variables, investigation of how observations such as brands or people vary on those dimensions, and estimation of a smaller number of more reliable dimensional scores. The following key points will assist you to investigate the underlying dimensions of your data.

Principal Component Analysis

- Principal component analysis (PCA) finds *linear functions* that explain maximal variance in observed data. A key concept is that such components are *orthogonal* (uncorrelated). The basic R command is `prcomp()` (Sect. 8.2.1).
- A common use for PCA is a *biplot* of aggregate scores for brands or people to visualize relationships. When this is done for attitudinal data such as brand ratings it is called a *perceptual map*. This is created by aggregating the statistic of interest by entity and charting with `biplot()` (Sect. 8.2.2).

- Because PCA components often load on many variables, the results must be inspected cautiously and in terms of relative position. It is particularly difficult to read the status of individual items from a PCA biplot (Sect. 8.2.5).

Exploratory Factor Analysis

- Exploratory factor analysis (EFA) models *latent variables* (factors) that are not observed directly but appear indirectly as observed *manifest variables*. A key procedure is factanal() (Sect. 8.3.1).
- A fundamental decision in EFA is the *number of factors* to extract. Common criteria involve inspection of a *scree* plot and extraction of factors such that all *eigenvalues* are greater than 1.0. There are useful tools to determine the number of factors in nFactors, but the final determination depends on one's theory and the utility of results (Sect. 8.3.2).
- EFA uses *rotation* to adjust an initial solution to one that is mathematically equivalent but more interpretable according to one's aims. Another key decision in EFA is whether one believes the underlying latent variables should be uncorrelated (calling for an *orthogonal* rotation such as varimax) or correlated (calling for an *oblique* rotation such as oblimin) (Sect. 8.3.3).
- After performing EFA, you can extract *factor scores* that are the best estimates for each observation (respondent) on each factor. These are present as $scores in factanal() objects if you request them with the scores argument (Sect. 8.3.4).

Multidimensional Scaling

- Multidimensional scaling (MDS) is similar to principal component analysis but is able to work with both *metric* and *non-metric* data. MDS requires a distance score obtained from dist() for metric data or a procedure such as daisy() for non-metric data. MDS scaling is then performed by cmdscale() for metric data or isoMDS() (or other options) for non-metric data (Sect. 8.4).

8.6 Data Sources

Data on brand perception is generally collected through an online survey administered to a respondent panel. In some cases, a survey might instead be administered on paper or through a digital intercept format, such as a pop-up survey on a web site or on a mobile device. For general considerations with online surveys, see Sect. 7.7. In this chapter, we consider methods both to analyze the data and to ensure that items relate to one another as intended (see also Chap. 10).

8.7 Learning More*

Principal component analysis. There is a large literature describing many procedures, options, and applications for each of the analyses in this chapter. With perceptual mapping, a valuable resource is Gower et al. [79] which describes common problems and best practices for perceptual maps. Jolliffe (2002) provides a comprehensive text on the mathematics and applications of principal component analysis [108].

Factor analysis.The literature on factor analysis is particularly voluminous although it often references statistics packages other than R. A good conceptual overview of exploratory factor analysis with procedural notes (but not R specific) is Fabrigar and Wegener (2011), *Exploratory Factor Analysis* [55]. A modestly more technical volume that covers exploratory and confirmatory models together, with a social science (psychology) point of view, is Thompson (2004), *Exploratory and Confirmatory Factor Analysis* [187]. For examination of the mathematical bases and procedures of factor analysis, a standard text is Mulaik (2009), *Foundations of Factor Analysis* [145].

The `psych` package [163] presents many additional tools and methods for factor analysis, especially in the context of traditional psychometric instruments such as surveys in general and tests of aptitude or personality. The `fa()` function in `psych` offers an alternative to the standard `factanal()` procedure with more options and more complete assessment of exploratory factor analysis models.

A companion to *exploratory* factor analysis is *confirmatory* factor analysis, which we discuss in Chap. 10. Whereas EFA infers factor structure from a data set, CFA tests a proposed model to see whether it corresponds well to observed data. A common use of EFA is to select items that load highly on underlying dimensions of interest. CFA allows you to confirm that the relationships between items and factors are maintained in new data sets.

Multidimensional scaling. There are many uses and options for multidimensional scaling beyond those considered in this chapter. A readable introduction to the methods and applications is Borg, Groenen, and Mair (2018), *Applied Multidimensional Scaling* [16]. The statistical foundations and methods are detailed in Borg and Groenen (2005), *Modern Multidimensional Scaling* [15].

8.8 Exercises

8.8.1 PRST Brand Data

For these exercises (and the exercises in Chap. 10), we use a simulated data set for four fictitious consumer electronic device brands: Papa, Romeo, Sierra, and Tango (abbreviated PRST). The brands have been rated by consumers on nine adjectives, each using a 7-point rating scale. The adjectives are "Adaptable," "Best Value," "Cutting Edge," "Delightful," "Exciting," "Friendly," "Generous," "Helpful," and "Intuitive." You will examine the relationships among the adjectives and the brands, considering both the statistical analyses and possible brand strategy.

First we load the data from the web site, or from a local file (change the directory as needed for your system0:

```
> prst1 <- read.csv("https://goo.gl/z5P8ce")   # web site
# prst1 <- read.csv("chapter8-brands1.csv")    # or a local file
> summary(prst1)
    Adaptable           BestValue          CuttingEdge          Delightful
 Min.   :1.000      Min.   :1.000      Min.   :1.00       Min.   :1.000
 1st Qu.:4.000      1st Qu.:3.000      1st Qu.:3.00       1st Qu.:3.000
 Median :4.000      Median :4.000      Median :4.00       Median :4.000
 Mean   :4.255      Mean   :3.849      Mean   :4.07       Mean   :3.983
 ...
```

8.8.2 Exercises

Basic Concepts

1. Summarize the PRST data. Should the data be rescaled?
2. Rescale the PRST data with a "Z score" procedure and examine the rescaled data. Does this confirm your decision in the previous exercise about whether to rescale the data?
3. Plot a correlation matrix for the adjective ratings. How many factors does it suggest?
4. Aggregate the mean of each adjective rating by brand. Plot a heatmap for the mean ratings by brand.

Principal Components Analysis

5. Extract the principal components in the PRST data. How many components are needed to explain the majority of variance in the PRST data? Visualize that.
6. Using principal components for the mean adjective ratings, plot the brands against the first two components. How do you interpret that? Now plot against the second and third components (hint: see ?biplot.princomp). Does this change your interpretation? What does this tell you about interpreting PCA results?
7. *(Thought exercise without code.)* Suppose you are the brand manager for Sierra, and you wish to change your position versus the market leader, Tango. What are some strategies suggested by the PCA positions?

Exploratory Factor Analysis

8. Consider an exploratory factor analysis (EFA) for the PRST adjective ratings. How many factors should we extract?

9. Find an EFA solution for the PRST data with an appropriate number of factors and rotation. What factor rotation did you select and why?
10. Draw a heatmap of the EFA factor loadings. Also draw a path diagram for the EFA solution.
11. Find the mean factor scores for each brand and plot a heatmap of them.
12. *(Thought exercise without code.)* Compare the factor score heatmap for PRST brands to the PCA interpretations in Exercise 6 above. Does the heatmap suggest different directions for the brand strategy for Sierra versus Tango?

Multidimensional Scaling

13. Plot a multidimensional scaling (MDS) map for the PRST brands using the mean adjective ratings. Which brands are most similar and most different?
14. *(Thought exercise without code.)* How does the MDS map relate to the PCA and EFA positions in the exercises above? What does it suggest for the strategy you considered in Exercise 6 above?

Chapter 9
Additional Linear Modeling Topics

As we noted in Chap. 7, the range of applications and methods in linear modeling and regression is vast. In this chapter, we discuss four additional topics in linear modeling that often arise in marketing:

- Handling highly correlated observations, which pose a problem known as *collinearity*, as mentioned in Sect. 7.2.1. In Sect. 9.1 we examine the problem in detail, along with ways to detect and remediate collinearity in a data set.
- Fitting models for yes/no, or *binary* outcomes, such as purchasing a product. In Sect. 9.2 we introduce *logistic regression* models to model binary outcomes and their influences.
- Finding a model for the preferences and responses of *individuals*, not only for the sample as a whole. In marketing, we often wish to understand individual consumers and the diversity of behavior and product interest among people. In Sect. 9.3 we consider *hierarchical linear models* (HLM) for consumer preference in ratings-based conjoint analysis data.
- In marketing, hierarchical models of individual preference are most often estimated using Bayesian methods. In Sect. 9.4 we continue the discussion of HLM by introducing *hierarchical Bayesian* (HB) methods, and we apply HB for ratings-based conjoint analysis.

Except for the two HLM sections, these topics are not especially closely related to one another; unlike other chapters in this book, they may be read independently within this chapter. Still, each section builds on models presented earlier in the book and will extend your knowledge of issues and applications for linear modeling. More importantly, each is a foundational part of a compete toolbox for marketing analysis.

© Springer Nature Switzerland AG 2019
C. Chapman and E. M. Feit, *R For Marketing Research and Analytics*, Use R!,
https://doi.org/10.1007/978-3-030-14316-9_9

9.1 Handling Highly Correlated Variables

We have mentioned several times (as in Sect. 7.2.1) that highly correlated explanatory variables cause problems with linear models. In this section, we examine why that is the case and strategies to address the problem.

We consider a question that might arise with the retail sales data in Chap. 4, which simulated summaries of 12 month online and in-store transactions by customer (see Sect. 4.1). The question is this: which variables are most predictive of online spending? If we wished to increase online spending by customers, which factors might we consider?

9.1.1 An Initial Linear Model of Online Spend

Either create the simulated retail sales data (Sect. 4.1) or load it from the book's website:

```
> cust.df <- read.csv("http://goo.gl/PmPkaG")
> summary(cust.df)
     cust.id              age          credit.score       email      distance.to.store
 Min.   :   1.0   Min.   :19.34   Min.   :543.0   no :186   Min.   :  0.2136
 1st Qu.: 250.8   1st Qu.:31.43   1st Qu.:691.7   yes:814   1st Qu.:  3.3383
 ...
```

Now we use `lm()` to model spend as a function of all other variables (`online.spend ~.`). We omit customers with zero online spend; having exactly zero spend is probably related to different factors than positive spend, and we are interested here in the associations for those who spend anything. We also index `[ , -1]` to omit the customer ID column:

```
> spend.m1 <- lm(online.spend ~ .,
+                data=subset(cust.df[ , -1], online.spend > 0))
> summary(spend.m1)
                Estimate Std. Error t value Pr(>|t|)
(Intercept)     6.718948  33.537665   0.200   0.8413
...
online.visits  -0.072269   0.204061  -0.354   0.7234
online.trans   20.610744   0.667450  30.880   <2e-16 ***
store.trans     0.135018   3.211943   0.042   0.9665
store.spend     0.001796   0.078732   0.023   0.9818
sat.service     5.638769   3.016181   1.870   0.0623 .
...
Multiple R-squared:  0.9831,    Adjusted R-squared:  0.9827
```

We have omitted much of the summary to show a few key points. First, online spend is closely related the number of online transactions (coefficient = 20.6) but not the number of online visits. That is puzzling. Second, the model accounts for almost all the available variance, $R^2 = 0.98$. These results should cause concern. Because online transactions are dependent on visits, shouldn't those two variables show a similar pattern? How could we be so lucky as to fit a model that nearly perfectly predicts online spending (insofar as it is assessed by R^2)? And notice that the standard error on `store.trans` is quite large, showing that its estimate is very uncertain.

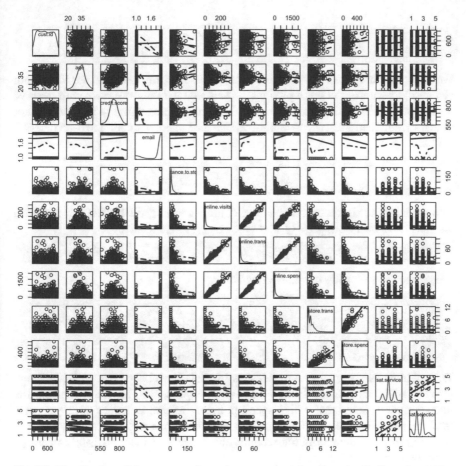

Fig. 9.1 Visualization of the customer data using `scatterplotMatrix()`. Several variables have extreme skew and other pairs are nearly perfectly correlated; both situations pose problems for linear modeling

If we turn to data visualization using `scatterplotMatrix()` (Sect. 7.2.1), we see some problems:

```
> library(car)
> scatterplotMatrix(cust.df)
```

The result in Fig. 9.1 shows variables with extreme skew and pairs of variables that are very highly correlated.

Our first step to remediate the situation is to transform the data using a Box-Cox transformation. Building on the transformation routines we saw in Sect. 4.5.5, we write a short function that uses `BoxCox.lambda()` from the `forecast` package to select the transformation *lambda* automatically [103]. At the same time, we standardize the data with `scale()` (Sect. 7.3.3):

```
> autoTransform <- function(x) {
+     library(forecast)
+     return(scale(BoxCox(x, BoxCox.lambda(x))))
+ }
```

We select the complete cases from our data frame, dropping the customer ID column
([, -1]) because it is not a predictor. Then we take only the rows with positive
online spend. We create a vector to index all the columns except email (which is not
numeric), and then lapply() the autoTransform() function to each numeric
column:

```
> cust.df.bc <- cust.df[complete.cases(cust.df), -1]
> cust.df.bc <- subset(cust.df.bc, online.spend > 0)
> numcols <- which (colnames(cust.df.bc) != "email")
> cust.df.bc[ , numcols] <- lapply(cust.df.bc[ , numcols], autoTransform )
```

The result is a data frame with standardized, more normally distributed values, which
we can check with summary() and scatterplotMatrix():

```
> summary(cust.df.bc)                  # output not shown
> scatterplotMatrix(cust.df.bc)        # output not shown
```

We refit the model using the transformed data:

```
> spend.m2 <- lm(online.spend ~ ., data=cust.df.bc)
> summary(spend.m2)
...
online.visits      -0.0003913   0.0126165   -0.031     0.975
online.trans        0.9960378   0.0126687   78.622    <2e-16 ***
..
Multiple R-squared:   0.9925,      Adjusted R-squared:   0.9923
```

The coefficients are smaller now because the data have been standardized. Transforming and standardizing the data, although a good idea, have not changed the
unbelievable estimate that online spend is highly related to transactions yet unrelated to visits. Indeed, the full model is no better than one that simply predicts
spending from the number of transactions alone (see Sect. 6.5.1 on using anova()
to compare models):

```
> spend.m3 <- lm(online.spend ~ online.trans, data=cust.df.bc)
> anova(spend.m3, spend.m2)
...
  Res.Df     RSS Df Sum of Sq        F  Pr(>F)
1    416  3.1539
2    407  3.1139  9  0.040001  0.5809  0.8129
```

The small difference between the model fits is reflected in the high p-value ($p =
0.8129$), and thus the null hypothesis of no difference between the models cannot be
rejected.

The problem here is *collinearity*: because visits and transactions are so highly related,
and also because a linear model assumes that effects are additive, an effect attributed
to one variable (such as transactions) is not available in the model to be attributed
jointly to another that is highly correlated (visits). This will cause the standard errors
of the predictors to increase, which means that the coefficient estimates will be
highly uncertain or *unstable*. As a practical consequence, this may cause coefficient
estimates to differ dramatically from sample to sample due to minor variations in the
data even when underlying relationships are the same.

9.1.2 Remediating Collinearity

The degree of collinearity in data can be assessed as the *variance inflation factor* (VIF). This estimates how much the standard error (variance) of a coefficient in a linear model is increased because of shared variance with other variables, compared to the situation if the variables were uncorrelated or simple single predictor regression were performed.

We assess VIF in the `spend.m2` model using `vif()` from the `car` package:

```
> library(car)
> vif(spend.m2)
            age     credit.score           email distance.to.store
       1.094949         1.112784        1.046874          1.297978
  online.visits     online.trans     store.trans       store.spend
       8.675817         8.747756      125.931383        123.435407
...
```

A common rule of thumb is that $VIF > 5.0$ indicates the need to mitigate collinearity. In `spend.m2`, the VIF indicates that collinearity should be addressed for the `online...` and `store...` variables.

There are three general strategies for mitigating collinearity:

- Omit variables that are highly correlated.
- Eliminate correlation by extracting principal components or factors for sets of highly-correlated predictors (see Chap. 8).
- Use a method that is robust to collinearity, i.e., something other than traditional linear modeling. There are too many options to consider this possibility exhaustively, but one method to consider would be a random forest approach, which only uses a subset of variables at a time (see Sect. 11.4.2).

Another option for the present data would be to construct a new measure of interest that combines the collinear variables (such as spend per transaction). For purposes here, we explore the first two options above and create models `spend.m4` and `spend.m5`.

We omit highly correlated variables for model `spend.m4` by excluding `online. trans` and `store. trans`, using – in the formula:

```
> spend.m4 <- lm(online.spend ~ . -online.trans -store.trans,
+                data=cust.df.bc)
> vif(spend.m4)
...
    online.visits      store.spend      sat.service     sat.selection
         1.026148         1.215208         1.507866          1.509001
> summary(spend.m4)
...
                  Estimate Std. Error t value Pr(>|t|)
(Intercept)     -0.0923395  0.0435047  -2.123   0.0344 *
age             -0.0333779  0.0178813  -1.867   0.0627 .
credit.score    -0.0084524  0.0180637  -0.468   0.6401
emailyes         0.1099655  0.0476011   2.310   0.0214 *
distance.to.store 0.0001702 0.0189271   0.009   0.9928
online.visits    0.9295374  0.0174184  53.365   <2e-16 ***
store.spend      0.0092463  0.0189552   0.488   0.6260
...
Multiple R-squared:  0.8791,    Adjusted R-squared:  0.8767
```

The VIF is now acceptable and we see that online visits are now the best predictor of online spend once we've left out online transactions. We can see that email status and age are also slightly related to online spend.

Another approach is to use the principal components of the correlated data. As you will recall from Chap. 8, principal components are uncorrelated (orthogonal). Thus, PCA provides a way to extract composite variables that are guaranteed to be free of collinearity with other variables that are included in the same PCA.

We use PCA to extract the first component for the online variables, and then do this again for the store variables, and add those two initial components to the data frame:

```
> pc.online <- prcomp(cust.df.bc[ , c("online.visits", "online.trans")])
> cust.df.bc$online <- pc.online$x[ , 1]
> pc.store <- prcomp(cust.df.bc[ , c("store.trans", "store.spend")])
> cust.df.bc$store <- pc.store$x[ , 1]
```

Then we fit a new model:

```
> spend.m5 <- lm(online.spend ~ email + age + credit.score +
+                               distance.to.store + sat.service +
+                               sat.selection + online + store,
+ data=cust.df.bc)
> summary(spend.m5)
...
                Estimate Std. Error  t value Pr(>|t|)
...
(Intercept)   -3.928e-02  2.410e-02   -1.630   0.1039
emailyes       4.678e-02  2.638e-02    1.773   0.0769 .
age           -1.695e-02  9.882e-03   -1.715   0.0871 .
...
online        -7.019e-01  6.933e-03 -101.247   <2e-16 ***
...
Multiple R-squared:  0.9631,     Adjusted R-squared:  0.9623

> vif(spend.m5)
          email                age    credit.score distance.to.store
       1.039458           1.081430        1.103206          1.224019
    sat.service      sat.selection          online             store
       1.508487           1.509001        1.032362          1.228073
```

VIF poses no problem in this model, and we see that online spend is still associated primarily with online activity (as captured in the first component of the PCA model, online) and perhaps slightly with email status and age. One caution when interpreting results that use principal components as explanatory variables is that the components have arbitrary numerical direction; the negative coefficient for online here does not imply that online activity results in lower sales.

Although this result—that online sales relate primarily to online activity—may at first appear to be uninteresting, it is better to have an obvious result than an incorrect result. This result might prompt us to collect other data, such as attitudes about our website or online shopping, to build a more complete understanding of factors associated with online spending.

9.2 Linear Models for Binary Outcomes: Logistic Regression

Marketers often observe yes/no outcomes: did a customer purchase a product? Did she take a test drive? Did she sign up for a credit card, or renew her subscription, or respond to a promotion? All of these kinds of outcomes are *binary* because they have only two possible observed states: *yes* or *no*.

At first it is tempting to fit such a model with a typical linear regression model as we saw in Chap. 7, predicting the outcome (1 = yes, 0 = no) as a linear combination of the features. That is not incorrect to do, but a more flexible and useful way to fit such outcomes is with a *logistic* model (also called a *logit* model for reasons we'll discuss below).

9.2.1 Basics of the Logistic Regression Model

The core feature of a logistic model is this: it relates the *probability* of an outcome to an *exponential function* of a predictor variable. We'll illustrate that and show the formula in a moment, but before examining that, let's consider why those are desirable properties and are improvements on a basic linear model.

By modeling the *probability* of an outcome, a logistic model accomplishes two things. First, it more directly models what we're interested in, which is a probability or proportion, such as the likelihood of a given customer to purchase a product, or the expected proportion of a segment who will respond to a promotion. Second, it limits the model to the appropriate range for a proportion, which is [0, 1]. A basic linear model as generated with lm() does not have such a limit and could estimate a nonsensical probability such as 1.05 or −0.04.

We ask indulgence to consider the formula here because it is instrumental in understanding how the model works. The equation for the logistic function is:

$$logistic : p(y) = \frac{e^{v_x}}{e^{v_x} + 1} \tag{9.1}$$

In this equation, the outcome of interest is y, and we compute its likelihood $p(y)$ as a function of v_x. We typically estimate v_x as a function of the features (x) of a product, such as price. v_x can take any real value, so we are able to treat it as a continuous function in a linear model. In that case, v_x is composed from one or more coefficients of the model and indicates the importance of the corresponding features of the product.

This formula gives a value between [0, 1]. The likelihood of y is less than 50% when v_x is negative, is 50% when $v_x = 0$, and is above 50% when v_x is positive. We compute this first by hand, and then switch to the equivalent, built-in `plogis()` function:

```
> exp(0) / (exp(0) + 1)   # computing logistic by hand; could use plogis()
[1] 0.5
> plogis(-Inf)            # infinitely low = likelihood 0
[1] 0
> plogis(2)               # moderate probability = 88% chance of outcome
[1] 0.8807971
> plogis(-0.2)            # weak likelihood
[1] 0.450166
```

Such a model is known as a *logit* model, which determines the value of v_x from the logarithm of the relative probability of occurrence of y:

$$logit : v_x = log\left(\frac{p(y)}{1 - p(y)}\right) \tag{9.2}$$

Again, R includes a built-in function `qlogis()` for the logit function:

```
> log(0.88 / (1-0.88))    # moderate high likelihood
[1] 1.99243
> qlogis(0.88)            # equivalent to hand computation
[1] 1.99243
```

In practice, the expressions *logit model* and *logistic regression* are used interchangeably.

9.2.2 Data for Logistic Regression of Season Passes

We considered an amusement park example in Chap. 7. Suppose that we now have data on the the sales of season tickets to the park. The data consist of a table of season ticket *pass sales* (with values of *yes* or *no*), on the basis of two factors: the *channel* used to extend the offer (email, postal mail, or in-person at the park) and whether it was *promoted* in a bundle offering the season ticket with another feature such as free parking, or not. The marketing question is this: are customers more likely to purchase the season pass when it is offered in the bundle (with free parking), or not?

In this section, we see how to simulate such data, and how to create a full data frame from tabulated data. If you wish to load the data from the website instead of working through the data creation, you can retrieve it with:

```
> pass.df <- read.csv("http://goo.gl/J8MH6A")
> pass.df$Promo <- factor(pass.df$Promo, levels=c("NoBundle", "Bundle"))
> summary(pass.df)
  Channel           Promo             Pass
 Email: 633    NoBundle:1482    NoPass :1567
 Mail :1328    Bundle  :1674    YesPass:1589
 Park :1195
```

Note that the second command above is required for reasons we describe in Sect. 9.2.5. Be sure to run it after loading the CSV and check that the `summary()` matches the above.

We encourage you to read the rest of this simulation section and the R language lessons it contains. But if you loaded the data and prefer to skip ahead to analysis, you could continue with Sect. 9.2.6.

9.2.3 Sales Table Data

Suppose that we have been given sales data as shown in Table 9.1.

Table 9.1 Counts of sales of season tickets broken out by promotion status (bundled or not bundled with a promotion), and channel by which a customer was reached (mail, at the park, by email)

| | Bought season pass (count): | | | Did not buy season pass (count): | |
	Bundle	NoBundle		Bundle	NoBundle
Mail	242	359	Mail	449	278
Park	639	284	Park	223	49
Email	38	27	Email	83	485

There are several ways to analyze tabular data as shown in Table 9.1, including chi-square analysis (Sect. 6.2), but a versatile approach when the data set is not too large is to convert it to long form and recreate a data frame of individual observations. This lets us use a full range of approaches such as linear modeling with minimal hassle.

To convert the data into such format, we first recreate the cross-tab data table in R. We begin this by reading the values from Table 9.1 one column at a time, putting them into a vector:

```
> pass.tab <- c(242, 639, 38, 359, 284, 27, 449, 223, 83, 278, 49, 485)
```

Next we add *dimensions* to the vector, which reformats it as a $3 \times 2 \times 2$ array, and set it to be an object of class "table":

```
> dim(pass.tab) <- c(3, 2, 2)
> class(pass.tab) <- "table"
```

We add the marginal labels to the table by setting its dimnames attribute:

```
> dimnames(pass.tab) <- list(Channel=c("Mail", "Park", "Email"),
+                            Promo=c("Bundle", "NoBundle"),
+                            Pass=c("YesPass", "NoPass") )
```

We describe more about class, table, and dimnames in optional Sect. 9.2.4 below. For now, we inspect the resulting table and confirm that it matches Table 9.1:

```
> pass.tab
, , Pass = YesPass
        Promo
Channel Bundle NoBundle
  Mail     242      359
  Park     639      284
  Email     38       27
...
```

We now have the data in R and are ready to create a full data frame from the table. Before that, we take a brief detour into the R language to understand the commands we just used.

9.2.4   Language Brief: Classes and Attributes of Objects*

In this optional section, we explore how the R language understands data types. If
you just want to continue with the logistic regression model, you could skip ahead
to Sect. 9.2.5.

Every object in R has an associated `class`, which functions use to determine how
to handle the object. For example, a vector of real numbers has a class of `numeric`,
while a data frame is a `data.frame`. The class of an object may be inspected
directly by `class()`:

```
> class(c(1, pi, exp(1)))
[1] "numeric"
> class(data.frame(1:10))
[1] "data.frame"
```

When we examine `str()`, the first thing listed is the class of the object and its raw
values:

```
> str(pass.tab)
 table [1:3, 1:2, 1:2] 242 639 38 359 284 27 449 223 83 278 ...
 - attr(*, "dimnames")=List of 3
  ..$ Channel: chr [1:3] "Mail" "Park" "Email"
  ..$ Promo  : chr [1:2] "Bundle" "NoBundle"
  ..$ Pass   : chr [1:2] "YesPass" "NoPass"
```

This code shows that `pass.tab` is an object of class `table` that comprises values
`242 639 ...`.

The `is.*()` set of functions tests whether an object is of some class (abbreviated
here with `*`). For example:

```
> is.table(pass.tab)
[1] TRUE
> is.character(pass.tab)
[1] FALSE
```

Class membership is non-exclusive. For example, tables are composed of counts,
and counts are numeric:

```
> is.numeric(pass.tab)
[1] TRUE
```

The `as.*()` functions attempt to treat (convert, or *coerce*) objects as other classes:

```
> as.numeric(pass.tab)
 [1] 242 639  38 359 284  27 449 223  83 278  49 485
> as.character(pass.tab)
 [1] "242" "639" "38"  "359" "284" "27"  "449" "223" "83"  "278" "49"  "485"
```

This shows how we could extract the vector of counts from our park table, and how
we might reformat them as character strings for printing, chart labeling, and similar
purposes.

In addition to `class`, objects can have other *attributes*. An attribute is a property
of an object other than its data, and typically tells R something important about the
object. Common attributes that we have used throughout the book are `names` for the
names of columns, `dim` for the dimensions of a matrix or data frame, and `class` to
specify the type of object. Each of these can be queried for an object:

```
> names(pass.tab)
NULL
> dim(pass.tab)
[1] 3 2 2
> class(pass.tab)
[1] "table"
```

In this case, the names for pass.tab are NULL because it is not a data frame or other object for which names are useful. However, we see that it has dim and class attributes. A table also has names for its rows and columns, which are known as dimnames:

```
> dimnames(pass.tab)
$Channel
[1] "Mail"    "Park"    "Email"
$Promo
[1] "Bundle"    "NoBundle"
...
```

Thus, Channel, the first dimension of the table, has elements "Mail", "Park", and "Email".

You can see all the attributes of an object with attributes():

```
> attributes(pass.tab)
$dim
[1] 3 2 2
$class
[1] "table"
...
```

Attributes may be changed using the assignment operator (<-). We often use this feature to set names of data frames, using names(DATA) <- c("name1", "name2", ...). In the code above, we converted pass.tab from a simple vector to a table by assigning class(pass.tab) <- "table" and setting its dim attribute. As you might imagine, this must be done very carefully! Setting an inappropriate class or dimension of an object will render it useless (but you can usually just change it back to make things work again).

We'll see another use for classes in Sect. 12.3.3, where we use objects' classes to determine how to handle multiple data types inside a function. To learn more about the R class and attribute system, review the R language reference [158] and Wickham's *Advanced R* [197].

9.2.5 Finalizing the Data

We have the data in a table pass.tab, which is suitable for analysis as is. However, because most data sets come in the form of an extended data frame with one observation per respondent, we expand it from a table to a complete data frame so the analysis will match typical data structures.

We use expand.dft() from the vcdExtra package [66] to expand the table to a data frame:

```
> library(vcdExtra)    # install if needed
> pass.df <- expand.dft(pass.tab)
> str(pass.df)
'data.frame':   3156 obs. of  3 variables:
 $ Channel: Factor w/ 3 levels "Email","Mail",..: 2 2 2 2 2 2 2 2 2 2 ...
 $ Promo  : Factor w/ 2 levels "Bundle","NoBundle": 1 1 1 1 1 1 1 1 1 1 ...
 $ Pass   : Factor w/ 2 levels "NoPass","YesPass": 2 2 2 2 2 2 2 2 2 2 ...
```

We now have a data frame with 3156 observations for whether a customer purchases a Pass, by Channel, with and without promotion (Promo).

We can use table() on this data to create cross-tabs other than those in Table 9.1. For example, to see purchases of a pass (Pass) by promotion bundle (Promo):

```
> table(pass.df$Pass, pass.df$Promo)
          Bundle NoBundle
  NoPass     755      812
  YesPass    919      670
```

Statistical modeling is a detail-oriented process, and before building a model from the data, there is one minor detail to attend to: the factors in pass.df are alphabetized— which is how R handles factor names by default—but that is counterintuitive. We might think that NoBundle should have a lower implicit value (such as "bundle − 0") than Bundle (which might be "bundle = 1"). However, in the table we just saw, NoBundle appears in the second column because it has a higher value thanks to alphabetic ordering.

In a regression model, that would mean that a positive effect of Bundle would have a *negative* value (think about it). Rather than having to remember such convoluted logic ("we see a negative effect for *no bundle*, which really means a *positive* effect for bundle after we reverse the signs ..."), it is easier just to set the order straight by reassigning that variable with the factor levels in the order we want:

```
> pass.df$Promo <- factor(pass.df$Promo, levels=c("NoBundle", "Bundle"))
> table(pass.df$Pass, pass.df$Promo)
          NoBundle Bundle
  NoPass       812    755
  YesPass      670    919
```

With the data ordered sensibly (*Bundle > NoBundle, YesPass > NoPass*), we proceed with modeling.

9.2.6 Fitting a Logistic Regression Model

A logistic regression model in R is fit as a *generalized linear model* (GLM) using a process similar to linear regression that we saw in Chap. 7 with lm(), but with the difference that a GLM can handle dependent variables that are not normally distributed. Thus, generalized linear models can be used to model data counts (such as number of purchases) or time intervals (such as time spent on a website) or binary variables (e.g., did/didn't purchase). The common feature of all GLM models is that they relate normally distributed predictors to a non-normal outcome using a function known as a *link*. This means that they are able to fit models for many different distributions using a single, consistent framework.

In the present case, we model a binary outcome, and the appropriate distribution is a *binomial* distribution (see Sect. 6.3). There are multiple functions and packages that can estimate a GLM in R, but the most common is the `glm(...)` function. `glm()` takes an argument `family=` that specifies the distribution for the outcome variable. For a binary outcome, set `family= binomial`. The default link function for a binomial model is the logit function that we saw in Sect. 9.2.1, so we do not have to specify that. (But, as an example, if we wished to use a probit link function instead, we could specify `family= binomial(link= "probit")`, and similarly for other link functions.)

Our marketing question was, "does the promotion bundle have an effect on season pass sales?" and we model this initially with a logistic regression of `Pass` on `Promo`, using `glm(..., family=binomial)` and syntax otherwise identical to `lm()`:

```
> pass.m1 <- glm(Pass ~ Promo, data=pass.df, family=binomial)
```

The initial model appears to confirm that the bundle is effective:

```
> summary(pass.m1)
...
Coefficients:
            Estimate Std. Error z value Pr(>|z|)
(Intercept) -0.19222    0.05219  -3.683 0.000231 ***
PromoBundle  0.38879    0.07167   5.425 5.81e-08 ***
...
```

There is a positive coefficient for the bundle condition, and the effect is statistically significant.

What does a coefficient of 0.3888 mean? We can use it to calculate the association of pass sales to the promotion bundle factor, by examining the ratio of success (using `plogis()`) to non-success ($1 - success$). A manual way to do this is to use `plogis()` directly:

```
> plogis(0.3888) / (1-plogis(0.3888))    # ratio of outcome % to alternative %
[1] 1.475209
```

This shows that the effect of `Bundle` is an estimated *odds ratio* of 1.475, meaning that customers are 1.475 times more likely to purchase the pass when it is offered in the bundle. Another way to think about this is that the bundle increases the purchase likelihood by 47.5%. An easier and equivalent way to calculate this is to exponentiate the coefficient:

```
> exp(0.3888)                              # identical
[1] 1.475209
```

We can find the odds ratios from the model by extracting the coefficients with `coef()` and using `exp()`:

```
> exp(coef(pass.m1))
(Intercept) PromoBundle
  0.8251232   1.4751962
```

We can obtain a confidence interval for the odds ratio using `exp(confint(model))`:

```
> exp(confint(pass.m1))
                 2.5 %    97.5 %
(Intercept) 0.744749 0.9138654
PromoBundle 1.282055 1.6979776
```

The odds ratio for the promotion bundle is estimated to be 1.28–1.70, a significant positive effect. This demonstrates that the promotion is highly effective, right? Not necessarily, because the effects are estimated *under the assumption that the model is the one we want to interpret.* But is the model Pass ~ Promo really the one we should interpret?

9.2.7 Reconsidering the Model

If we explore the data further, we notice something interesting. Consider a table of season pass purchases by channel:

```
> table(pass.df$Pass, pass.df$Channel)
          Email Mail Park
  NoPass    568  727  272
  YesPass    65  601  923
```

The channel that was most successful in selling season tickets was at the park, regardless of whether the promotion was offered.

A good way to visualize tables is with *mosaic* plots, which lay out "tiles" whose areas correspond to counts in a table. The vcd package [140] provides several ways to create mosaic plots (including the rather obvious mosaic() function). We use a so-called *doubledecker* plot here as it makes the relationships particularly clear in the present data:

```
> library(vcd)       # install if needed
> doubledecker(table(pass.df))
```

The result is shown in Fig. 9.2, where we see that the three channels have somewhat different effects. Sales of season passes are very successful at the park, and very unsuccessful by email. This implies that our model Pass ~ Promo may be inadequate and needs to account for the effect of Channel.

We model a main effect of channel by adding + Channel to the model formula:

```
> pass.m2 <- glm(Pass ~ Promo + Channel, data=pass.df, family=binomial)
> summary(pass.m2)
...
              Estimate Std. Error  z value Pr(>|z|)
(Intercept)   -2.07860    0.13167  -15.787  < 2e-16 ***
PromoBundle   -0.56022    0.09031   -6.203 5.54e-10 ***
ChannelMail    2.17617    0.14651   14.854  < 2e-16 ***
ChannelPark    3.72176    0.15964   23.313  < 2e-16 ***
...
```

The resulting model now estimates a strong *negative* contribution of the promotion bundle. We compute the odds ratios and their confidence intervals:

```
> exp(coef(pass.m2))
(Intercept) PromoBundle ChannelMail ChannelPark
  0.1251054   0.5710846   8.8125066  41.3371206
> exp(confint(pass.m2))
                  2.5 %      97.5 %
(Intercept)  0.09577568   0.1606189
PromoBundle  0.47793969   0.6810148
ChannelMail  6.65770550  11.8328173
ChannelPark 30.42959274  56.9295369
```

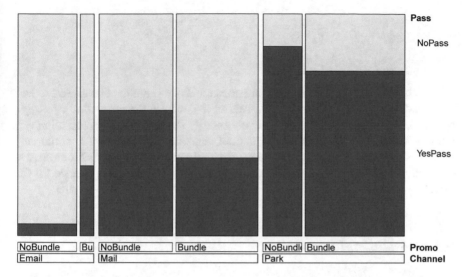

Fig. 9.2 A mosaic plot created with doubledecker() [140] for sales of season passes by channel and promotion in simulated amusement park data. Season passes ("YesPass," plotted as dark areas) are sold most frequently at the park and least frequently by email. The promotion bundle ("Bundle," the second column within each channel) is associated with higher sales through the email channel, but lower sales in regular mail and at the park, thus showing an interaction effect

In this model, promotion is associated with a 32–53% lower likelihood (reflecting the values 1.0–0.681 to 1.0–0.477) of purchasing a season pass. On the other hand, offers in person at the park are associated with season ticket sales 30–56x higher in this model.

But is this the appropriate model? Should we also consider an interaction effect, where Promo might have a different effect by Channel? Our data exploration suggests a possible interaction effect, especially because of the dramatically different pattern for the influence of Bundle in the Email channel in Fig. 9.2.

We add an interaction term using the : operator, as noted in Sect. 7.5:

```
> pass.m3 <- glm(Pass ~ Promo + Channel + Promo:Channel,
+                 data=pass.df, family=binomial)
> summary(pass.m3)
...
                          Estimate Std. Error  z value Pr(>|z|)
(Intercept)                -2.8883     0.1977  -14.608  < 2e-16 ***
PromoBundle                 2.1071     0.2783    7.571 3.71e-14 ***
ChannelMail                 3.1440     0.2133   14.743  < 2e-16 ***
ChannelPark                 4.6455     0.2510   18.504  < 2e-16 ***
PromoBundle:ChannelMail    -2.9808     0.3003   -9.925  < 2e-16 ***
PromoBundle:ChannelPark    -2.8115     0.3278   -8.577  < 2e-16 ***
...
```

The interaction of promotion with channel is statistically significant, and is strongly negative for the mail and in-park channels, as opposed to the baseline (omitted) email channel in these simulated data.

In the odds ratios, we see that the promotion is only 2–11% as effective through the mail and in-park channels as it is in email (the omitted reference level):

```
> exp(confint(pass.m3))
Waiting for profiling to be done...
                                 2.5 %          97.5 %
...
PromoBundle:ChannelMail   0.02795867      0.09102369
PromoBundle:ChannelPark   0.03135437      0.11360965
```

We now have a much better answer to our question. Is the promotion bundle effective? It depends on channel. There is good reason to continue the promotion campaign by email, but its success there does not necessarily imply the bundle promotion will work at the park or through a regular mail campaign. In case you're wondering how the statistical model is advantageous to simply interpreting Fig. 9.2, one answer is that the model estimates confidence intervals and statistical significance for the effect.

9.2.8   Additional Discussion

Before moving to the topic of hierarchical models, we have a few observations for the current section:

- Although we performed logistic regression here with categorical predictors (factor variables) due to the structure of the amusement park sales data, we could also use continuous predictors in glm(). Just add those to the right hand side of the model formula as we did with lm() in Chap. 7.
- We saw that the estimated effect of promotion in these data was positive when we estimated one model, yet negative when we estimated another, and this shows that it is crucial to explore data thoroughly before modeling or interpreting a model. For most marketing data, no model is ever definitive. However, though careful data exploration and consideration of multiple models, we may increase our confidence in our models and the inferences drawn from them.
- The data here are an example of *Simpson's paradox*, which is when the estimate of an aggregate effect is misleading and markedly different than the effect seen in underlying categories. A famous example occurred in graduate admissions at the University of California at Berkeley, where an apparent bias in admissions was due instead to the fact that different departments had different overall admissions rates and numbers of applicants [12]. In R, the Berkeley data are available as the table UCBAdmissions in the standard datasets package.

Logistic regression is a powerful method and one that is a particularly good fit for many marketing problems that have binary outcomes. To learn more, see Sect. 9.8. For modeling product choice among sets of alternatives, we cover choice models in Chap. 13.

9.3 Hierarchical Models

In Chap. 7 we saw how to estimate a linear model for data for a sample of respondents. What if we want to estimate the coefficients in the model for *each* respondent? As marketers, it can be very useful to determine individual-level effects such as which customers are more interested in a product or service, who among them wants which features, and who is most or least price sensitive. We can use such information to see the diversity of preference or for purposes such as customer targeting or segmentation (see Chap. 11).

To estimate both a population-level effect and an individual-level effect, we can use a *hierarchical* linear model (HLM). The model is hierarchical because individual responses are governed by a lower-level linear model and coefficients for each individual follow a distribution across the population (the upper-level model). There are various algorithms to fit such models, but the general approach is that the algorithm fits the overall model to all the data, and then attempts to determine best fit for each individual within that overall estimate (and repeats as necessary).

In general, a data set for HLM at an individual level needs multiple observations per individual. Such observations may come from responses over time (as in transactions or a customer relationship management system) or from multiple responses at one time (as in a survey with repeated measures). We consider the case of conjoint analysis, where a respondent rates multiple items on a survey at one time.

How is this different from simply adding the individual, store, or other grouping variable as a factor variable in the model? The key difference is that a factor variable would add a single term that adjusts the model up or down according to the individual. In HLM, however, we can estimate *every* coefficient—or any that we wish—for each individual.

There are other uses for hierarchical models besides customer-level estimation. For example, one might wish to estimate differences by a factor such as geographic region, store, salesperson, product, or promotion campaign. Each of these might provide many responses that could be grouped and allow estimation of a group-level effect within an overall hierarchy. We can't cover every application of HLM here— hierarchical models are the subject of entire books (e.g., Gelman and Hill [72])—yet we hope this discussion will help you to understand when and how they may be useful, and how to begin with them in R.

9.3.1 Some HLM Concepts

A few words of jargon are required. Hierarchical models distinguish two types of effects. One type is *fixed* effects, which are effects that are the same for every respondent. In a standard linear model (Chap. 7) all effects are fixed effects. For instance, in Sect. 9.1.2, we saw that online spend was highly associated with online transactions and slightly associated with age. Both of those estimates are fixed effects that predict the same pattern of association for everyone in the sample.

An HLM also estimates *random* effects, which are additional adjustments to the model coefficients estimated for each individual (or group). These are known as "random" because they are estimated as random variables that follow a distribution around the fixed estimates. However, for the estimate of each individual, they are *best* estimates according to the model, not random guesses in that sense.

Such models are also known as *multilevel* models, where individuals and the full sample are at different levels. They are a subset of models known as *mixed effect* models, where *mixed* reflects the fact that the total effect for each respondent has (at least) two effects that are combined: the overall fixed effect plus the individual-level random effect.

A final variation on mixed effects models is a *nested* model, where a factor of interest might occur only within subgroups of the total sample. For example, if we consider sales in response to different promotions that each occur at different stores, we might model both the effect of store (as a random effect, such that there are different sales intercepts for different stores) and the effect of promotion within store as a nested effect. We do not examine a nested model here, yet they may be also be fit using the lme4 package used below.

9.3.2   Ratings-Based Conjoint Analysis for the Amusement Park

For a hierarchical model, we return to the fictional amusement park from Sect. 7.1. The park is now considering designs for a new roller coaster and hopes to find out which roller coaster features appeal to its customers. They are considering coasters with various possible levels of maximum *speed* (40, 50, 60 or 70 mph), *height* (200, 300, or 400 feet), *construction* type (wood or steel), and *theme* (dragon or eagle). The stakeholders wish to know which combination of features would be most popular according to customers' stated preference.

One way to examine this is a survey that asks customers to rate different roller coasters (illustrated with photographs or videos for more realism). For example:

> On a 10 point scale, where 10 is the best and 1 is the worst, how would you rate a roller coaster that is made of **wood**, is **400 feet** high, has a maximum speed of **50 mph**, with a **dragon theme**?

Customers' ratings could be analyzed with a linear model where the ratings are predicted from the different features of the roller coasters. This would tell us the contribution of each feature to the total rating.

Additionally, we wish to understand these preferences at an individual level, such that we can see the distribution of preference or identify individuals for potential marketing actions. To do this, we use a hierarchical linear model (HLM) that estimates both the overall fixed effect and the individual level random effect.

In the following section we simulate consumers' ratings for such a survey. The code is brief and illustrative of the data, but if you wish to skip the simulation, you can load the data from the book's website:

```
> conjoint.df <- read.csv("http://goo.gl/G8knGV")
> conjoint.df$speed   <- factor(conjoint.df$speed)
> conjoint.df$height <- factor(conjoint.df$height)
> summary(conjoint.df)
    resp.id          rating          speed        height        const
 Min.   :  1.00   Min.   : 1.000   40: 800   200:1400   Steel :1400
 1st Qu.: 50.75   1st Qu.: 3.000   50:1200   300:1200   Wood  :1800
 ...
```

Given this data, you may skip to Sect. 9.3.4.

9.3.3 Simulating Ratings-Based Conjoint Data

In this section we simulate responses for a hypothetical conjoint analysis survey with 200 respondents who each rate the same set of 16 roller coaster profiles. If you have worked through the data simulation in previous chapters, this code should be relatively simple in structure, although a few functions are new.

We set the structure: 200 respondents who rate 16 designs, each with 4 roller coaster attributes:

```
> set.seed(12814)
> resp.id <- 1:200 # respondent ids
> nques <- 16      # number of conjoint ratings per respondent
> speed <- sample(as.factor(c("40", "50", "60", "70")), size=nques,
+                          replace=TRUE)
> height <- sample(as.factor(c("200", "300", "400")), size=nques, replace=
+     TRUE)
> const <- sample(as.factor(c("Wood", "Steel")), size= nques, replace=TRUE)
> theme <- sample(as.factor(c("Dragon", "Eagle")), size=nques, replace=TRUE)
```

In this example we assume that all respondents rate the same set of designs. Depending on your study's goal, you might instead want to have a different, random set for each respondent. A single set of designs is convenient for printed surveys, while an online study could easily have a different set for every respondent; we will see an example in Chap. 13.

Next we create a model matrix for the combinations of features to rate. We draw multivariate random normal values for respondents' preferences using mvrnorm() from the MASS package [192]:

```
> profiles.df <- data.frame(speed, height, const, theme)
> profiles.model <- model.matrix(~ speed + height + const + theme,
+                          data=profiles.df)
> library(MASS)      # a standard library in R
> weights <- mvrnorm(length(resp.id),
+                mu=c(-3, 0.5, 1, 3, 2, 1, 0, -0.5),
+                Sigma=diag(c(0.2, 0.1, 0.1, 0.1, 0.2, 0.3, 1, 1)))
```

model.matrix() converts the list of design attributes (profiles.df) into coded variables; it is similarly used by functions such as lm() to convert factors into variables for regression equations. You can compare `profiles.model` to `profiles.df` to see how this works. We use `mvrnorm()` to draw unique preference `weights` for each respondent. Estimating those later is the key feature that distinguishes a hierarchical model from a standard linear model.

Given the designs to be rated and individuals' preferences, we compile the simulated individual ratings. For each respondent, we multiply the preference weights by the design matrix to get the total preference (utility) for each design, adding some random noise with `rnorm()`. We convert the utility to a 10-point rating scale using `cut()` (see Sect. 12.4.1), and add the respondent's result to the overall data frame:

```
> conjoint.df <- NULL    # make sure there's no data yet
> for (i in seq_along(resp.id)) {
+    # create one respondent's ratings of the 16 items, plus error
+    utility <- profiles.model %*% weights[i, ] + rnorm(16)   # preference
+    rating <- as.numeric(cut(utility, 10))      # put on a 10-point scale
+    conjoint.resp <- cbind(resp.id=rep(i, nques), rating, profiles.df)
+    conjoint.df <- rbind(conjoint.df, conjoint.resp)
+ }
```

Building a data frame using `rbind()` repeatedly instead of preallocating a whole matrix is not efficient, but it is easy to understand and it is fast enough for this data set. For large data sets, it would be better to preallocate the data frame for the size needed and fill in the rows. With a bit of matrix manipulation, one might instead create the whole data frame at once; but a simple, readable method like the one here may be more effective overall if it's easier and more reliable to code.

9.3.4   An Initial Linear Model

We begin as always with a quick `summary` of our conjoint data to check it (create or load the data as described in Sect. 9.3.2 if needed):

```
> summary(conjoint.df)
      resp.id           rating          speed        height          const
 Min.   :  1.00   Min.   : 1.000   40: 800   200:1400   Steel:1400
 1st Qu.: 50.75   1st Qu.: 3.000   50:1200   300:1200   Wood :1800
 ...
```

Ratings of the designs range from 1 (strongly disprefer) to 10 (strong prefer). We also see the counts of the features that were shown in various combinations: `speed`, `height`, `const` and `theme`.

Our goal is to determine how the four features relate to the ratings. At an aggregate level, we might use `by()` to find the average rating for levels of each attribute. For example, the averages by `height` are:

```
> by(conjoint.df$rating, conjoint.df$height, mean)
conjoint.df$height: 200
[1] 3.657857
------------------------------------------------------------
conjoint.df$height: 300
[1] 7.254167
------------------------------------------------------------
conjoint.df$height: 400
[1] 5.05
```

The average rating for designs with 300 foot height is 7.25 points on the 10-point scale, compared to 3.66 and 5.05 for heights of 200 and 400 feet. So, respondents prefer the middle of our height range.

We could examine each individual feature in that way, but a more comprehensive linear model considers all of the effects in combination. To start, we'll estimate a regular linear model without a hierarchical component using `lm()` (Chap. 7):

```
> ride.lm <- lm(rating ~ speed + height + const + theme, data=conjoint.df)
> summary(ride.lm)
...
Coefficients:
             Estimate Std. Error t value Pr(>|t|)
(Intercept)   3.07307    0.08102  37.932  < 2e-16 ***
speed50       0.82077    0.10922   7.515 7.35e-14 ***
speed60       1.57443    0.12774  12.326  < 2e-16 ***
speed70       4.48697    0.15087  29.740  < 2e-16 ***
height300     2.94551    0.09077  32.452  < 2e-16 ***
height400     1.44738    0.12759  11.344  < 2e-16 ***
constWood    -0.11826    0.11191  -1.057    0.291
themeEagle   -0.75454    0.11186  -6.745 1.81e-11 ***
...
```

In this abbreviated output, the coefficients indicate the association with preference (the `rating`). The highest rated roller coaster on average would have a top speed of 70 mph, a height of 300 ft, steel construction, and the dragon theme (steel and dragon because wood and eagle have negative values). We estimate an overall rating for this most-desired coaster; it would be the intercept + speed70 + height300 (steel and dragon are included in the intercept), or $3.07 + 4.49 + 2.94 = 10.46$ points on our 10-point rating scale.

But wait! That's not possible; our scale is capped at 10 points. This shows that simply interpreting the "average" result can be misleading. The coefficients are estimated on the basis of designs that mostly combine both desirable and undesirable attributes, and are not as reliable at the extremes of preference. Additionally, it could happen that few people prefer that exact combination even though the individual features are each best on average.

Consider that the coefficient for `constWood` is near zero. Are people indifferent between wood and steel coasters, or do they have strong preferences that cancel out when averaged? If people are strongly but almost equally divided, that's important for us to know as marketers; it might suggest that we construct different rides that appeal to two different groups. On the other hand, if they are truly indifferent, we could choose between steel and wood on the basis of cost and other factors.

To understand our respondents better, we turn next to a hierarchical model that will estimate both the overall average preference level and individual preferences within the group.

9.3.5 Initial Hierarchical Linear Model with `lme4`

The linear model `ride.lm` has only fixed effects that are estimated at the sample level. In a hierarchical linear model, we add one or more individual-level effects to those.

The simplest HLM allows individuals to vary only in terms of the constant intercept. For example, we might expect that individuals vary in their usage of a rating scale such that some will rate our roller coaster designs higher or lower than the average respondent. This would be an individual-level random effect for the intercept term. To estimate an HLM with fixed effects plus a per-respondent intercept, we change the `lm()` model from above in three ways. First, instead of `lm()`, we use a hierarchical estimation function, `lmer()` from the `lme4` package [8].

Second, in the formula for `lmer()`, we specify the term(s) for which to estimate random effects. For the intercept, that is signified as simply "1". Third, we specify the grouping variable, for which a random effect will be estimated for each unique group. In our conjoint data, the group in the set of responses for a single respondent, which is identified in the data frame by respondent number, `resp.id`. With `lme4`, we specify the random effect and grouping variable with syntax using a vertical bar ("|") as `+ (predictors | group)`, or in this case for the intercept only, `+ (1 | resp.id)`.

We estimate this model using `lme4`, where the only difference from the call to `lm()` above is the addition of a term for random intercept by respondent:

```
> library(lme4)
> ride.hlm1 <- lmer(rating ~ speed + height + const + theme + (1 | resp.id),
+                   data=conjoint.df)
> summary(ride.hlm1)
...
Scaled residuals:
    Min      1Q  Median      3Q     Max
-3.3970 -0.6963  0.0006  0.6700  3.3689

Random effects:
 Groups   Name        Variance Std.Dev.
 resp.id  (Intercept) 0.3352   0.5789
 Residual             3.5358   1.8804
Number of obs: 3200, groups:  resp.id, 200

Fixed effects:
            Estimate Std. Error t value
(Intercept)  3.07307    0.08759  35.08
speed50      0.82077    0.10439   7.86
speed60      1.57443    0.12209  12.90
speed70      4.48697    0.14421  31.11
height300    2.94551    0.08676  33.953
height400    1.44738    0.12195  11.87
constWood   -0.11826    0.10696  -1.11
themeEagle  -0.75454    0.10692  -7.06
...
```

In this output, we see that the fixed effects are identical to those estimated by `lm()` above. But now we have also estimated a unique intercept term adjustment for each respondent. The output section labeled "Random effects" shows 3200 total observations (survey questions) grouped into 200 respondents for which a random effect was estimated (such as the effect for (`Intercept`)).

`fixef()` is an easy way to extract just the fixed (population level) effects:

```
> fixef(ride.hlm1)
(Intercept)     speed50     speed60     speed70    height300    height400 ...
  3.0730724   0.8207718   1.5744257   4.4869715    2.9455084    1.4473848 ...
```

The 200 respondent-level random effect estimates for intercept, which `summary` (`ride.hlm1`) does not display because there could be many of them, are accessed with `ranef()` (and we additionally use `head()` to shorten the output):

```
> head(ranef(ride.hlm1)$resp.id)
   (Intercept)
1  -0.65085634
2  -0.04821158
3  -0.31186866
...
```

The complete effect for each respondent comprises the overall fixed effects that apply to everyone, plus the individually-varying random effects (in this case, just the intercept). Those are accessed using `coef()`:

```
> head(coef(ride.hlm1)$resp.id)
   (Intercept)     speed50   speed60   speed70  height300  height400   constWood ...
1     2.422216  0.8207718  1.574426  4.486971   2.945508   1.447385  -0.1182553 ...
2     3.024861  0.8207718  1.574426  4.486971   2.945508   1.447385  -0.1182553 ...
3     2.761204  0.8207718  1.574426  4.486971   2.945508   1.447385  -0.1182553 ...
...
```

It is possible to estimate random effects for multiple grouping factors (hierarchical levels), so these effects must be extracted using the name of the grouping variable, which is `$resp.id`.

In `coef(ride.hlm1)$resp.id`, each respondent has the overall sample-level value of the effect on all coefficients except for intercept, and the final intercept coefficient is the same as the fixed effect plus the random effect. For example, for respondent 1, the intercept is 3.07 (`fixef`) −0.65 (`ranef`) = 2.42 (`coef`).

9.3.6   Complete Hierarchical Linear Model

The most common hierarchical model in marketing practice is to estimate a random effect parameter for every coefficient of interest for every respondent. This is easy to do with the `lme4` syntax; simply add all the variables of interest to the predictors in the random effects specification (`predictors | group`).

For the conjoint data, we write the random effects part of the formula as (`speed + height + const + theme | resp.id`). Before estimating that model, we should note that this is a much more complex model than the intercept model above. Whereas the random intercept-only HLM estimated 8 fixed parameters and 200 random effects, the full model will estimate 8 fixed effects plus 8 ∗ 200 random effects. And it will do this for a total data frame of 3200 observations.

This fact has two implications. First, the estimation can be rather slow, taking several minutes for the present model at the time of writing. Second, there are so many parameters that even 3200 observations is not a lot, and one can expect some difficulty finding a stable *converged* model.

With those facts in mind, we estimate the full model as follows (this will take some time, perhaps several minutes):

```
> ride.hlm2 <- lmer(rating ~ speed + height + const + theme +
+                         (speed + height + const + theme | resp.id),
+                   data=conjoint.df,
+                   control=lmerControl(optCtrl=list(maxfun=100000)))
```

Compared to model `ride.hlm1` above, this model has two changes. First, we added all four roller coaster factors to be estimated for random effects. This will give us individual estimates of preference for every feature, for each respondent. Second, we added a `control` argument to `lmer()`, which increases the `maxfun` number of iterations to attempt convergence from 10,000 iterations (the default) to 100,000. This allows the model to converge better, although it may issue warnings in some cases that depend on the package versions. (If so, ignore the warnings for now. Our discussion here is for illustration, not for an important business decision. For a model of importance, we recommend to run to convergence when possible.)

When you run into warnings, we suggest five potential remedies. First, increase the `control maxfun` argument by a factor of 2, 5, or 10 to see if convergence results (and repeat that if necessary). Second, check whether the $\max|\text{grad}|$ (maximum absolute value of the gradient in the optimization function; cf. [8]) is small, such as $max < 0.001$; if so, you may be okay. Alternatively, if $max >> .01$, such as $max = 0.10$, increase the iterations. Third, do a web search for the warnings you receive and consider the suggestions offered on R discussion forums. Fourth, consider using a different optimization function (see `lme4` documentation [8]). Fifth, consider collecting more data, or evaluate your data for internal consistency. Again, we skip these steps now primarily for convenience.

Fixed effects are extracted with `fixef()`:

```
> fixef(ride.hlm2)
(Intercept)      speed50       speed60       speed70     height300     height400 ...
  3.0730724    0.8207718     1.5744257     4.4869715     2.9455084     1.4473848 ...
```

This part of the `ride.hlm2` model is identical to the model estimated for `ride.hlm1` above, so the coefficients are identical.

The random effects now include an estimate for each parameter for each respondent. Again, because we grouped by `resp.id` and could have had multiple grouping factors, we request the `$resp.id` portion of the random effects using `ranef()`:

```
> head(ranef(ride.hlm2)$resp.id)
   (Intercept)       speed50        speed60       speed70     height300        height400
1  -1.1199669   -0.20604116   -0.12507852    0.10294441    0.10742922    -5.078259e-05
2  -1.0104411    0.24975639   -0.08224947    0.16263447    0.05610835     1.073264e+00
3  -1.0352138   -0.21870807    0.31082408   -0.29288315    0.34166414    -1.136045e-01
4   ...
```

Notice that the random intercepts are no longer identical to those estimated in model `ride.hlm1`, because we added seven explanatory variables and the predicted outcome rating points are distributed differently across the predictors.

We obtain the total coefficients for each respondent with `coef()`:

```
> head(coef(ride.hlm2)$resp.id)
  (Intercept)    speed50   speed60   speed70 height300 height400   constWood
1    1.953106 0.6147306 1.449347 4.589916  3.052938 1.4473340   0.1060565
2    2.062631 1.0705282 1.492176 4.649606  3.001617 2.5206483   1.4178031
3    2.037859 0.6020637 1.885250 4.194088  3.287173 1.3337803   0.4858069
...
```

Notice that the coefficients for `constWood` vary widely across respondents. Respondent 2 has a strong preference for wood over steel (1.42), while respondent 1 is almost indifferent (0.11). Histograms of the coefficients for each respondent can illustrate these large differences between customers, as we will illustrate in Sect. 9.4.3.

As a final sanity check to confirm that the model matches expectations, we choose a respondent (ID 196) and see that the coefficients are indeed the sum of the fixed and random effects:

```
> fixef(ride.hlm2) + ranef(ride.hlm2)$resp.id[196, ]
    (Intercept)    speed50   speed60   speed70 height300 height400 constWood ...
196    2.143066 0.7534546 1.271102 4.594398  2.949586 1.212745 2.580267 ...
> coef(ride.hlm2)$resp.id[196, ]
    (Intercept)    speed50   speed60   speed70 height300 height400 constWood ...
196    2.143066 0.7534546 1.271102 4.594398  2.949586 1.212745 2.580267 ...
```

In this code, the random effect and coefficient values for respondent 196 are retrieved by indexing that row within the corresponding `$resp.id` matrix.

9.3.7 Conclusion for Classical HLM

This concludes our discussion of classical hierarchical models; in the next section, we consider the Bayesian approach to HLM, which uses the same general conceptual model but a different estimation method.

In this section, we hope to have convinced you that, when you have multiple observations for an individual or other grouping factor of interest, you should consider a hierarchical model that estimates both sample-level and individual- or group-level effects. These models are relatively straightforward to estimate using the `lme4` package.

Besides *customer*-level models, which are most common in marketing, other factors for which one might wish to estimate a hierarchical model include *store*, *country*, *geographic region*, *advertising campaign*, *advertising creative*, *channel*, *bundle*, and *brand*.

If this section has inspired you to consider adding hierarchical modeling to your toolbox, see "Learning More" (Sect. 9.8) for pointers to other resources.

9.4 Bayesian Hierarchical Linear Models*

This is an optional section that you may skip if you are not interested in the Bayesian approach to estimate hierarchical models.

Hierarchical models may be fit with classical estimation procedures (such as the `lme4` package we saw above) yet they are particularly well-suited to Bayesian estimation. The method we use here is known as a *hierarchical Bayes* approach; *hierarchical* because it models individuals in relationship to an overarching distribution, and *Bayes* because it uses Bayesian estimation techniques to fit the models (see Sects. 6.6.1 and 6.6.2 for an introduction).

In this section, we apply a hierarchical Bayes (HB) method to estimate the hierarchical linear model for ratings-based (metric) conjoint analysis, using the same data set that we analyzed with classical hierarchical models in Sect. 9.3 above. Before continuing this section you should:

- Review the concepts of Bayesian linear models and MCMC estimation in Sect. 7.5.4
- Review the concepts of hierarchical linear models in Sects. 9.3 and 9.3.1
- Review the description of the amusement park conjoint analysis data in Sect. 9.3.2

Download the simulated amusement park conjoint analysis data as follows, or see Sect. 9.3.2:

```
> conjoint.df <- read.csv("http://goo.gl/G8knGV")
> conjoint.df$speed  <- factor(conjoint.df$speed)
> conjoint.df$height <- factor(conjoint.df$height)
> summary(conjoint.df)
    resp.id          rating          speed       height         const
 Min.   :  1.00   Min.   :1.000   40: 800   200:1400   Steel :1400
 1st Qu.: 50.75   1st Qu.:3.000   50:1200   300:1200   Wood  :1800
...
```

9.4.1   Initial Linear Model with `MCMCregress()`*

We start by estimating a non-hierarchical model using Bayesian methods, which allows us to check that our basic estimation procedures are working before we attempt a complex model. We model respondents' ratings of roller coaster designs as a function of roller coaster features using `MCMCregress()` to fit a simple linear model as we did in Sect. 7.5.4:

```
> library(MCMCpack)
> set.seed(97439)
> ride.mc1 <- MCMCregress(rating ~ speed + height + const + theme,
+                          data=conjoint.df)
> summary(ride.mc1)
...
                Mean      SD   Naive SE  Time-series SE
(Intercept)   3.0729  0.08112  0.0008112       0.0008112
speed50       0.8208  0.11061  0.0011061       0.0011126
speed60       1.5754  0.12889  0.0012889       0.0012889
speed70       4.4873  0.15002  0.0015002       0.0015002
height300     2.9444  0.09122  0.0009122       0.0009337
height400     1.4461  0.12934  0.0012934       0.0013367
constWood    -0.1187  0.11310  0.0011310       0.0011310
themeEagle   -0.7533  0.11308  0.0011308       0.0011308
sigma2        3.8705  0.09737  0.0009737       0.0009737
...
```

The overall effects are nearly identical to those estimated by the classical linear models in Sect. 9.3.5, which is it should be. We changed the estimation routine by using `MCMCregress`, but we did not change the model. With sufficient data, Bayesian and frequentist estiamtes will be nearly identical for the same model. Now that we've confirmed that our esimation algorithm is working, we are ready to add the hierarchical component to the model.

9.4.2   Hierarchical Linear Model with `MCMChregress()`*

We estimate a hierarchical model using `MCMChregress(fixed, random, group, data, r, R)`. Note the **h** for *hierarchical* buried in that function name. This is a slightly different syntax than `lme4` uses (as we reviewed in Sect. 9.3.5), as it separates the fixed and random effect specifications. The key arguments we use here are:

`fixed`   : formula for fixed effects at the higher level that are the same for all respondents

`random`   : formula for random effects that are estimated for each respondent

`group`   : name of the column with identifiers that group observations for the random effects

`data`   : the data frame with observations

`r, R`   : pooling arguments. We'll just set them for now; see below for detail

For `fixed` effects we specify the primary model to estimate: `rating ~ speed + height + const + theme`. For `random` effects, the most common models in marketing estimate all parameters of the model for every respondent, so we specify `random = ~ speed + height + const + theme`. Because we are estimating by individual, `group` is the respondent identifier, `"resp.id"`.

Estimation of this model may take several minutes to run. Here is the final code:

```
> set.seed(97439)
> ride.mc2 <- MCMChregress(fixed = rating ~ speed + height + const + theme,
+                          random = ~ speed + height + const + theme,
+                          group="resp.id", data=conjoint.df, r=8, R=diag(8))

Running the Gibbs sampler. It may be long, keep cool :)   ...
```

While the model runs, let's examine the two arguments `r` and `R`. A hierarchical model assumes that each respondent has a set of preferences (coefficients) drawn from a larger distribution that defines the range of possible preferences. The model is slow because it makes *thousands* of estimates of both the individuals' coefficients and the higher-order distributions that best describe those individuals.

Of course there are only a few observations for each respondent, and a model for a single person can not be estimated very well with such limited data. To improve estimation, the MCMC model *pools* information across respondents, allowing estimates to be more or less similar to one another based on the data. If several respondents dislike a feature, it's more likely (but not certain) that another randomly selected respondent will also dislike it; this expected similarity is used to improve estimates given sparse data.

That degree of pooling across respondents is adjusted by the final two arguments r and R. For most analyses, you can set r equal to the number of parameters in your model and R equal to a diagonal matrix with values along the diagonal equal to the number of parameters in your model, and the algorithm will determine the optimal level of pooling from the data. This can be done with the simple function diag(K), where K is the same number as r. However, if you plan to run hierarchical Bayesian models regularly, you will wish to learn more about pooling; check the references in Sect. 9.8.

By now, MCMChregress() from above should have finished, and we can review its result:

```
> str(ride.mc2)
List of 2
 $ mcmc   : mcmc [1:1000, 1:1674] 3.04 2.87 2.9 3.06 2.98 ...
 ..- attr(*, "dimnames")=List of 2
 .. ..$ : NULL
 .. ..$ : chr [1:1674] "beta.(Intercept)" "beta.speed50" "beta.speed60" "
   beta.speed70" ...
 ..- attr(*, "mcpar")= num [1:3] 1001 10991 10
 $ Y.pred: num [1:3200] 4.94 2.69 5.73 6.24 4.67 ...
```

The output of MCMChregress is a list with two items. The first item in this list is an mcmc object containing the draws from the posterior distribution of the parameters. A notable thing is that ride.mc2$mcmc contains 1674 columns. Why so many? The model estimates a set of 8 coefficients—the preferences for each attribute of our roller coasters—for every one of the 200 respondents. That's 1600 parameters plus a few more that describe the overall population distribution. For each of those parameters, it drew 1000 estimates from the posterior distribution for every respondent (see Sect. 6.6.2).

Let's look at the first 8 columns, estimated coefficients for the overall, population-level preferences:

```
> summary(ride.mc2$mcmc[ ,1:8])
...
                    Mean      SD Naive SE Time-series SE
beta.(Intercept)  3.0739  0.1694 0.005356       0.005457
beta.speed50      0.8168  0.1398 0.004422       0.004422
beta.speed60      1.5691  0.1618 0.005117       0.005569
beta.speed70      4.4849  0.1862 0.005889       0.005889
beta.height300    2.9474  0.1235 0.003904       0.003681
beta.height400    1.4578  0.1796 0.005680       0.005680
beta.constWood   -0.1128  0.1952 0.006172       0.005615
beta.themeEagle  -0.7542  0.1857 0.005871       0.005871
...
```

These estimates are nearly identical to the result of non-hierarchical MCMCregress in model ride.mc1 above. speed70 is still preferred and worth 4.5 points on our rating scale, preference for wood construction is near zero, and so forth.

Let's look at an example respondent; we pull and summarize the posterior draws for the parameters that are associated with respondent 196. We do this by finding columns that are named with "196" (the resp.id that we want). We accomplish that by indexing the columns with the results of the grepl() function that identifies elements of a character vector (in this case, column names) containing a particular string:

```
> summary(ride.mc2$mcmc[ , grepl(".196", colnames(ride.mc2$mcmc), fixed=TRUE)
   ])
...
                        Mean      SD Naive SE Time-series SE
b.(Intercept).196   -1.03806  0.6780  0.02144        0.02144
b.speed50.196        0.44049  0.5434  0.01718        0.01718
b.speed60.196        0.10442  0.6335  0.02003        0.02003
b.speed70.196        0.03807  0.7167  0.02266        0.02357
b.height300.196     -0.35414  0.5441  0.01721        0.01797
b.height400.196     -0.55132  0.7357  0.02327        0.02327
b.constWood.196      2.57915  0.8370  0.02647        0.02647
b.themeEagle.196    -1.41955  0.8220  0.02599        0.02599
...
```

Respondent 196 strongly prefers wood coasters; her ratings for them are 2.5 points higher on our 10 point scale than those for steel construction (the default level). On the other hand, she dislikes the eagle-themed design, rating it -1.4 points lower on average than the dragon theme. These preferences are rather different than the population averages above.

How could we use this information? The ideal roller coaster for respondent 196, according to her responses, would be a dragon-themed wood coaster with a top speed of 50mph and a height of 200 feet (the default level not shown). Although individual customization is impractical for roller coasters, a plausible marketing use would be to segment respondents' preferences to determine a mix of coasters (see Chap. 11). For instance, we might ask which new coaster would maximize preference over and above the coasters the park already has; in other words, we could investigate a product line extension. More immediately, if we have respondents' contact information, we could tailor marketing communications to this and similar respondents and tell them about wooden coasters at the park.

The MCMC output also informs our confidence of estimates. One could use the standard error of the mean estimate, but we recommend instead to use the values from the Quantiles section of the output. Let's look at the population estimates again, but focus on the quantiles::

```
> summary(ride.mc2$mcmc[ ,1:8])
...
2. Quantiles for each variable:

                     2.5%      25%      50%      75%    97.5%
beta.(Intercept)   2.7389   2.9594   3.0764  3.18818   3.4099
beta.speed50       0.5421   0.7251   0.8114  0.91274   1.0801
beta.speed60       1.2604   1.4636   1.5725  1.68365   1.8804
beta.speed70       4.1213   4.3599   4.4834  4.60792   4.8599
beta.height300     2.7114   2.8642   2.9501  3.03263   3.1779
beta.height400     1.0898   1.3429   1.4589  1.58500   1.8017
beta.constWood    -0.5219  -0.2464  -0.1105  0.01628   0.2698
beta.themeEagle   -1.0999  -0.8745  -0.7571 -0.63284  -0.3609
```

This tells us that the fixed effect estimate for speed70 had a value between 4.12–4.86 in 95% of the draws from the posterior distribution. Thus, we can use these values to express the credible interval for the parameters we report. An advantage of Bayesian statistics is that confidence in estimates can be stated directly, without resorting to discussion of null hypotheses.

*9.4.3   Inspecting Distribution of Preference**

We wondered above whether respondents were just indifferent to wooden versus steel coasters, or had significant differences. To investigate this in the estimated model, we need to do a bit of work. First, we extract out all the coefficients labeled b.constWood, which are the individual-level estimates for preference for wood construction. There are 200 columns for these coefficients, one for each customer in our data set.

Those values each represent a *difference* for the individual relative to the overall population, so we add the values to the baseline population estimate, beta.constWood. Because we have 1000 sets of estimates from the MCMC draws, we compute the total (individual plus population mean) for each of the 1000 draws from the posterior distribution, and summarize those totals. (Do *not* summarize first and then add.)

Although this process may sound complex, it is accomplished in a single, albeit cryptic, command:

```
> ride.constWood <- summary(ride.mc2$mcmc[ , grepl("b.constWood",
+                                        colnames(ride.mc2$mcmc))]
+                      + ride.mc2$mcmc[ , "beta.constWood"])
```

Deconstructing this code, it finds the columns in mcmc draws with "b.constWood" in their names; those are the individual differences in preference. It adds the population value, beta.constWood, to obtain the total preference for each respondent. Then it summarizes the result. (You might try parts of this code in the R console to see how this works.)

The result is that ride.constWood contains estimates from the posterior distribution for individual-level preference of wood over steel coasters. We plot these to see the distribution of individuals' preferences for wood coasters:

```
> hist(ride.constWood$statistics[,1],
+       main="Preference for Wood vs. Steel",
+       xlab="Rating points", ylab="Count of Respondents", xlim=c(-4,4))
```

We compare that to the distribution of preference for 60mph speed (versus baseline 40mph):

```
> ride.speed60 <- summary(ride.mc2$mcmc[,grepl("b.speed60",
+                                        colnames(ride.mc2$mcmc))]
+                      + ride.mc2$mcmc[,"beta.speed60"])
> hist(ride.speed60$statistics[,1],
+       main="Preference for 60mph vs. 40mph",
+       xlab="Rating points", ylab="Count of Respondents", xlim=c(-4,4))
```

The resulting charts are shown in Fig. 9.3. In the first, we see a wide range across individuals in preference of wood versus steel construction; some respondents have negative preference for wood, and thus prefer steel, while others prefer wood. The magnitude is very strong for some, corresponding to a difference in rating of up to 4 points. By comparison, in the second chart, preference for 60mph coasters over 40 mph is less diverse; all respondents prefer the faster speed.

This degree of variation among respondents is known as *heterogeneity*, and in addition to estimating the parameters (coefficients) for the population (beta.

<predictor name> as we saw above), MCMC hregress() also estimates their variance and covariance across the population of respondents. The results are named VCV. <predictor name>. <predictor name> in the output, where "VCV" abbreviates *variance covariance*. When the two predictor names are the same, this gives the variance estimate for a single parameter; when they are different, it is the covariance of two parameters.

For example, we can find the population mean and variance of the wood and 60mph parameters:

```
> summary(ride.mc2$mcmc[,c("beta.constWood", "VCV.constWood.constWood",
+ "beta.speed60","VCV.speed60.speed60")])
...
                          Mean      SD  Naive SE  Time-series SE
beta.constWood         -0.1128  0.1952  0.006172         0.005615
VCV.constWood.constWood  2.3458  0.3749  0.011855         0.014056
beta.speed60            1.5691  0.1618  0.005117         0.005569
VCV.speed60.speed60     0.5782  0.1351  0.004273         0.004939
...
```

The estimated variance for constWood is quite large at 2.34, demonstrating that there is large heterogeneity between respondents in preference for wooden roller coasters. On the other hand, the variance of the estimates for speed60 is much smaller at 0.58. This reflects the difference in distributions that we saw in the histograms in Fig. 9.3.

You might wish to predict respondents' interest in one or more fully-specified roller coaster designs, as opposed to interest in individual features. Such assessment is typical in conjoint analysis to predict product interest and is often known as *market simulation*. However, there is not yet an appropriate predict() function for MCMC models as there is for lm(). To obtain estimates of overall preference for a design, there are two choices. One option is to calculate the net level of interest by adding the columns of the MCMC draws that match your design (plus the baseline population estimates), and then summarize the level of interest for each respondent. Another option is to use a market simulation routine that compares preference between choices, such as the relative preference for your design versus some other

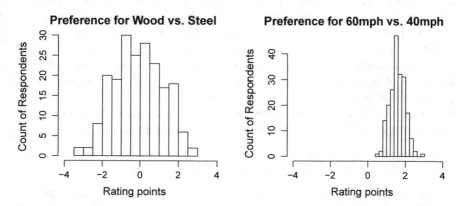

Fig. 9.3 Histograms of individual respondent preferences in a ratings-based conjoint analysis model

design; an example is available in Chapman et al. [33]. We discuss preference share estimation further in Chap. 13.

One other thing we should mention with regard to this model—as is illustrated in our data simulation and Fig. 9.3 as well as in the model's assumptions—is that individuals' estimates (random coefficients) are assumed to follow a multivariate normal distribution. This means that the model assumes most people's preferences are in the middle of the distribution, with fewer respondents who have strong preferences. If you have reason to suspect that there are separate groups with divergent and strong preferences, you might consider a mixture or latent class model, which is outside the scope of this chapter (see [168], Chap. 5).

We hope this introduction to hierarchical Bayesian models has demonstrated their value in understanding individual customers. Hierarchical modeling has become widespread in marketing because it allows us both to obtain model estimates at an individual level and to understand the diversity across customers. We'll have more to say about such models for conjoint analysis, in the form of choice-based con-joint analysis, in Chap. 13. These models are also common in customer-relationship management (CRM) applications, where the goal is to estimate a likely response or outcome of some sort for individual customers. We suggest to consider a Bayesian approach anytime that you are interested to fit a linear model.

9.5   A Quick Comparison of the Effects*

This is an optional section for those who completed both of the previous sections. In those sections we modeled the same data set using classical methods (Sect. 9.3) and Bayesian methods (Sect. 9.4). We saw that the estimates of the fixed effects are nearly identical in the two models (Sect. 9.4.1). What about the random, individual-level effects? How similar are they?

Before examining those effects, let's try to apply a bit of intuition to the problem. First, we might consider that the fixed effects, even with 3200 total observations are not exactly identical between the two methods. Second, we should expect that the individual-level effects, with only 16 observations per respondent would have much more variance (because variance is inversely proportional to the square root of the number of observations). When we consider that we are estimating 8 random effects per respondent given only 16 observations, we should expect a lot of uncertainty in the estimates. Third, we should understand that neither model can be regarded as *true*, but only expected to be (one hopes) an unbiased estimate.

To compare the models here, you need to fit both the `ride.hlm2` and `ride.mc2` models as we did above (Sects. 9.3.6 and 9.4.2, respectively).

We've seen that the mean fixed effect estimates are quite similar. We can check that visually by plotting the eight parameters of each against those from the other model.

Fig. 9.4 Fixed effects from the two hierarchical linear models, classical and Bayesian. The Bayesian method estimates (y-axis; estimated using `MCMCpack`) are nearly identical to the classical method estimates (x-axis; estimated using `lme4`) for these simulated data

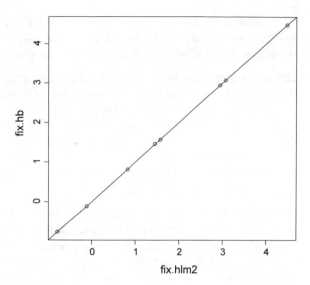

First we get the fixed effects from each, then we plot them against one another and add a 45° line to see how closely they align.

```
> fix.hlm <- fixef(ride.hlm2)
> fix.hb  <- colMeans(ride.mc2$mcmc[ , 1:8])
> plot(fix.hlm, fix.hb)
> abline(0,1)
```

Figure 9.4 shows that the fixed effects are nearly identical in the two models. Note that we use the abbreviation "HLM" to refer to the model estimated by `lme4` in order to distinguish it from "HB" for the Bayesian model, although both models are hierarchical linear models yet estimated with different methods.

The random effects have to be compared within respondent. We'll do this for just one respondent, ID 196 who we considered above. First, let's just consider the mean estimates of each random effect. We extract those using `ranef()` for the `lme4` model (Sect. 9.3.6) and `colMeans()` to take the mean effect estimated in the draws of the MCMC model (Sect. 9.4.2):

```
> ranef(ride.hlm2)$resp.id[196, ]
     (Intercept)      speed50        speed60      speed70     height300   height400
196   -0.9300065   -0.0673172   -0.3033236   0.1074266  0.004077387
-0.2346401
       constWood  themeEagle
196     2.698522   -1.438104
> colMeans(ride.mc2$mcmc[ , grepl (".196", colnames(ride.mc2$mcmc),
+                          fixed=TRUE)]) b.(Intercept).196
    b.speed50.196        b.speed60.196        b.speed70.196
       -1.03806213          0.44049447          0.10441996           0.03807113
    b.height300.196      b.height400.196      b.constWood.196   b.themeEagle.196
       -0.35414215         -0.55131679          2.57914806         -1.41954714
```

There are some overall similarities in the two sets of estimates for respondent 196, such as the strong negative effect for the eagle theme, relative to the same fixed effect, and strong positive for a wooden roller coasts. However, there are small to modest differences in some of the mean estimates. The MCMC process should prompt you to recall that Bayesian methods estimate not only a point estimate (the mean effect estimate reported above), but also a posterior *distribution* that reflects uncertainty.

One might compare estimates in various ways; in this case, we compare them visually. We'll do this by overlaying distribution curves for the two sets of estimates. In the case of the HB estimates, we have 1000 MCMC draws for each parameter, so we plot the `density()` estimate of those draws. For the HLM estimates, we construct a similar density estimate in the following way: we obtain the mean effect from `ranef()` and the standard deviation of the estimation from the "`postVar`" (variance) attribute of the `ranef()` random effect estimates for one respondent, and use those parameters to draw random points from that distribution.

Doing this process one time—plotting the density of the MCMC draws and then adding a distribution plot for the mean and standard deviation of the HLM estimate— would give us a comparison of one set of parameters such as the preference for one speed or design. We iterate that to compare multiple parameters. We do that for parameters 2–5, the first four non-intercept parameters, as follows:

```
> par(mfrow=c(2,2))           # make a 2x2 plot surface
> plot.xlim <- c(-3, 3)       # define limits for the x-axis
> for (i in 2:5) {            # first four parameters only, for convenience
+   # plot the MCMC density for random effect i
+   mcmc.col <- which(grepl(".196", colnames (ride.mc2$mcmc), fixed=TRUE))[i]
+   plot(density(ride.mc2$mcmc[ , mcmc.col]), xlab="",
+       ylim=c(0, 1.4), xlim=plot.xlim,
+     main=paste("HB & lmer density:",
+               colnames(ride.mc2$mcmc)[mcmc.col] ))
+   # add the HLM density for random effect i
+   hlm2.est <- ranef(ride.hlm2)$resp.id[196, i] # mean estimate
+   hlm2.sd <- sqrt(attr(ranef(ride.hlm2, condVar=TRUE)$resp.id,
+                   "postVar")[ , , 196][i, i])
+   seq.pts <- seq(from=plot.xlim[1], to=plot.xlim[2], length.out=1000) # range
+   # .. find density at x-axis points using dnorm() and add that to the plot
+   points(seq.pts, dnorm(seq.pts, mean=hlm2.est, sd=hlm2.sd),
+         col="red", pch=20, cex=0.05)
+   legend("topright", legend=c("red = lmer", "black = HB"),
+           text.col=c("red", "black"))
+ }
```

This code is lengthy but should not be difficult for you to deconstruct by this point. The two significant new elements here are that it uses `attr(..., "postVar")` to obtain the variance of the random effect estimate for the HLM model, and uses `dnorm()` to obtain a density estimate for 1000 points that match the HLM parameter distribution estimate, which it adds to the plot with `points()`.

The resulting chart in Fig. 9.5 shows that the density estimates from the two methods are largely overlapping. It is also congruent with our intuition above, as the results are different but not enormously so, and there is no reason to suspect either method is highly discrepant because the distributions are generally similar in range and central tendency, with just slightly higher variance in the MCMC estimates. Of course this is a comparison of only four parameters for a single respondent.

We could compare similarly across all 200 respondents, either graphically or statistically, but will leave that as an exercise for the reader. If we did so, what would

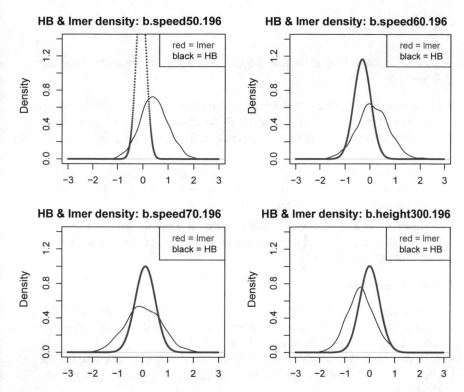

Fig. 9.5 A comparison of the estimates for four of the model parameters for respondent ID 196 in the MCMC and `lmer` results. The estimates for each respondent have substantial uncertainty but the distributions are generally similar and largely overlapping

we expect to see? Given that the fixed effects are nearly identical, we would expect that deviations between the models in the random effects would be close to zero and symmetric around zero. If you want to try this on your own, we can give you a preview: the median difference between the models' mean estimates of the random effects, across all 200 individuals, for the 8 parameters, ranges from -0.015–0.020, with a median of 0.003.

Given that the models are similar but not identical, you might wonder which is better, the classical or the Bayesian? The models themselves do not answer that; you would need to consider your assumptions, the degree to which you believe each model is appropriate (see Sect. 6.6.1), and if possible, which works better for your situation in regards to other metrics such as external validity. As we have noted, the models tend to show increasingly similar estimates with larger samples, while the Bayesian methods may yield more intuitive or useful estimates with small numbers of observations.

9.6 Key Points

We covered a lot of material in this chapter. Following are some important lessons.
Collinearity

- Collinearity occurs when two or more variables are highly associated. Including them in a linear model can result in confusing, nonsensical, or misleading results, because the model cannot differentiate the contribution from each of them (Sect. 9.1).

- The *variance inflation factor* (VIF) provides a measure of shared variance among variables in a model. A rule of thumb is that collinearity should be addressed for a variable when $VIF > 5$ (Sect. 9.1.2).

- Common approaches to fixing collinearity include omitting highly-correlated variables, and using principal components or factor scores (see Chap. 8) instead of individual items (Sect. 9.1.2).

Logistic Regression

- *Logistic regression* relates a binary outcome such as purchase to predictors that may include continuous and factor variables, by modeling the variables' association with the probability of the outcome (Sect. 9.2.1).
- A logistic regression model, also known as a *logit model*, is a member of the *generalized* linear models family, and is fit using `glm( , family=binomial)` (Sect. 9.2.6).
- Coefficients in a logit model can be interpreted in terms of *odds ratios*, the degree to which they are associated with the increased or decreased likelihood of an outcome. This is done simply by exponentiating the coefficients with `exp()` (Sect. 9.2.6).
- A statistically significant result does not always mean that the model is appropriate. It is important to explore data thoroughly and to construct models on the basis of careful consideration (Sect. 9.2.7).

Hierarchical Linear Models

- In common marketing discussion, a *hierarchical model* estimates both group level effects and individual differences in effects. Such models are popular in marketing because they provide insight into differences among customers (*heterogeneity*) and distribution of preference. Hierarchical linear models (HLM) are exemplified when we estimate the importance of effects for individuals as well as for an overall population (Sect. 9.3).
- Effects that are associated with all observations are known as *fixed* effects, and those that differ across various grouping levels are known as *random* effects (Sect. 9.3.1).
- These models are also known as *mixed effect* models, because the total effect for each person is composed of the effect for the overall population (the fixed effect) plus the per-individual (random) effect. We estimated an HLM using `lmer()` from the `lme4` package (Sect. 9.3.5).

- The difference between estimating hierarchical effects, as opposed to including the grouping variable as a factor in a standard linear model, is that a hierarchical model estimates *every* specified effect for each individual or group, not only a single adjustment term.
- The formula for a mixed effect model includes a grouping term, + (... | group). Common models have a different *intercept* by group using (1 | group) or different intercepts and slopes for predictors within each group using (predictor | group) (Sects. 9.3.5, 9.3.6). To estimate an individual-level model, the grouping term is typically the respondent identifier.
- Hierarchical models can be used to group observations at other levels than the individual level. For example, we might wish to group by store, advertising campaign, salesperson, or some other factor, if we want to estimate effects that are specific to such a grouping (Sect. 9.3.7).
- A common marketing application of HLM is conjoint analysis, to estimate both overall preference and individual differences in preference. In this chapter, we demonstrated ratings-based, or metric conjoint analysis (Sect. 9.3.2).

Bayesian Methods for Hierarchical Linear Models

- Hierarchical models in marketing are often estimated with Bayesian methods that are able to pool information and produce best estimates of both group and individual effects using potentially sparse data (Sect. 9.4.2).
- A Bayesian hierarchical linear model can be estimated using MCMChregress() in the MCMCpack package (Sect. 9.4.2).
- Model coefficients from a hierarchical model are inspected using summaries of the many estimates that are collected in an mcmc object (Sects. 9.4.2, 9.4.3).

9.7 Data Sources

In this final section, we offer some advice for where you might find similar data within your own organization.

In Sect. 9.1, we reanalyzed the data from Chap. 4, which describes customers online and offline transactions. In Sect. 9.2, we analyze data describing what promotional offers have been made to customes and whether they have redeemed those offers. This type of data is typically pulled from the customer relationship management (CRM) system or "customer 360" database, which is a central repository for all data describing interactions between the company and its customers. The CRM system draws this data from other systems such as the point-of-sale (cash register) system, the online retail system, the digital analytics platform, the email automation, records of direct mail, etc. If your company doesn't have a central CRM system, then you may need to pull this data together by contacting the owners of individual systems and then using tools like merge() in R. This is tedious and time-consuming work, so be thankful if your company has invested in a central database for customer analytics!

The direct ratings of product profiles analyze in Sects. 9.3 and 9.4, are nearly always collected by surveying customers. They are typically collected online, using a general web survey platform such as Qualtrics, Google Forms, or SurveyMonkey. Depending on the goals of the study, this survey can be emailed to existing customers or sent through a survey research panel that specializes in finding broader samples of consumers (including non-customers). In-person surveys are often executed by having a researcher intercept respondents in a public place and hand each resopndent a tablet to complete the survey online. Collecting this data is a very easy project for a first-time analyst; students can easily collect conjoint data as part of a term project.

An alternative to metric conjoint is choice-based conjoint where respondents chose from set of product profiles. We introduce choice-based conjoint in Chap. 13. Choice surveys require a more complex design and are often collected using or a more specialized platform, such as Sawtooth Software or Conjoint.ly.

One consideration in collecting conjoint data is to ensure that respondents understand the product options and are able to rate their preferences reliably. Commonly, we would educate respondents about the product features within the survey, or would collect data during an in-person, study where the product concepts are presented using images or prototypes and discussed by a group of consumers. This latter option is similar to a focus group with an additional data collection exercise. That format has the advantage of simultaneously collecting qualitative data that help us to understand the quantitatively-measured preferences. Some drawbacks are that in-person samples are expensive, potentially less representative, and subject to group-influence effects. We also caution against providing cusotmers with too much information about product options (i.e. more than they would typically get when shopping.) Elea once participated in a study where the engineer who developed a new feature presented it to respondents. After this appealing "sales pitch," nearly all the respondents indicated unreasonably strong preferences for this feature.

9.8   Learning More*

The topics in this chapter are drawn from the vast range of topics related to linear modeling, and the best general recommendation is to learn about those topics broadly, as in Harrell (2015) on strategies and issues for effective regression modeling [92] and Dobson and Barnett (2018) on general linear models [43]. The following notes provide further guidance on specific topics.

Collinearity. The best way to learn more about collinearity and how to detect and address it is to become more fluent in linear modeling in general. Good texts for learning broadly about regression modeling are Harrell [92], and Fox and Weisberg [62].

Logistic regression. Logistic regression models are especially common in health sciences (modeling improvement after treatment, for instance), and much of that literature is approachable for marketers with modest translation. Hosmer et al. [99] is a standard text on such models and demonstrates the importance of model building and assessment. Binary outcomes are also often the subject of models in the machine learning community. We consider machine learning models in the context of classification in Chap. 11. A general text on those methods is Kuhn and Johnson [123].

Hierarchical models. The best overall didactic text on hierarchical models is Gelman and Hill [72], which provides outstanding conceptual explanation and a breadth of models with detailed code in R. The one, comparatively minor limitation of Gelman and Hill is that its level of detail and discussion can make it difficult to determine what to do when confronted with an immediate modeling need.

Support for hierarchical models (also known as *mixed effects* models) is an evolving area in R. Besides the lme4 package that we used, another common package is nlme, which has a somewhat dated companion book, Pinheiro and Bates [153]. A more up-to-date and didactic text is Galecki and Burzykowski [69].

Bayesian hierarchical models. We have provided only an introduction to hierarchical Bayes models and their importance, and have not covered the implementation issues and problems that may arise. To learn more about such models, there are technical introductions at varying levels of mathematical sophistication from Kruschke [120], Gelman et al. [73], and Rossi, Allenby and McCullough [168]. Gelman and Hill [72] discusses hierarchical models from both Bayesian and non-Bayesian perspectives, with examples in R.

Many Bayesian texts, including several of those noted above, discuss the implementation of MCMC samplers (as in MCMCpack). There is a caveat: they show how to write an MCMC sampler in detail, such as the internal workings of MCMChregress(). That is a valuable and reusable skill but a very technical one. For some readers, it may be similar to having an automotive engineer teach you how to drive a sedan; it is highly informative but occasionally overwhelming.

MCMCpack includes functions for several other families of Bayesian models. A general framework that handles both mixed effects and multiple response data, using the MCMC approach, is available in the MCMCglmm package [86]. If you want to do hierarchical logistic regression in a Bayesian framework, you could consider MCMCglmm.

9.9 Exercises

9.9.1 Online Visits and Sales Data for Exercises

For exercises regarding collinearity and logistic regression, we will use a simulated data set that represents customer transactions together with satisfaction data, for web

Table 9.2   Variables in the `chaper9-sales` data set

Variable	Description	Variable	Description
`acctAge`	Tenure of the customer, in months	`visitsMonth`	Visits to the web site, in the most recent month
`spendToDate`	Customer's total lifetime spending	`spendMonth`	Spending, most recent month
`satSite`	1–10 satisfaction rating with the web site	`satQuality`	Rating for satisfaction with product quality
`satPrice`	Rating for satisfaction with prices	`satOverall`	Overall satisfaction rating
`region`	US geographic region	`coupon`	Whether coupon was sent to them for a particular promoted product
`purchase`	Whether they purchased the promoted product (with or without coupon)		

site visits and purchases. The variables are described in Table 9.2. We load the data locally or from the online site:

```
>  # sales.data.raw <- read.csv("chapter9-sales.csv") # local
>  sales.data.raw <- read.csv("https://goo.gl/4Akgkt") # online
>  summary(sales.data.raw)
      acctAge          visitsMonth        spendToDate         spendMonth      ...
  Min.   : 1.00     Min.   : 1.000     Min.   :   6.0      Min.   :   4.0    ...
  1st Qu.: 8.00     1st Qu.: 6.000     1st Qu.:  28.0      1st Qu.:   9.0    ...
  Median :13.00     Median : 7.000     Median :  45.0      Median :  17.0    ...
```

9.9.2   Exercises for Collinearity and Logistic Regression

Collinearity

1. In the sales data, predict the recent month's spending (`spendMonth`) on the basis of the other variables using a linear model. Are there any concerns with the model? If so, fix them and try the prediction again.
2. How does the prediction of the recent month's sales change when the variables are optimally transformed? Which model—transformed or not—is more interpretable?
3. Fit the linear model again, using a principal component extraction for satisfaction. What is the primary difference in the estimates from the previous models?

4. *(Thought exercise without code.)* When the model is fit with `region` as a predictor, it may show the West region with a large—possibly even the largest—effect. Yet it is not statistically significant whereas smaller effects are. Why could that be?

Logistic Regression

5. Using logistic regression, what is the relationship between the coupon being sent to some customers and whether the purchased the promoted product?
6. How does that model change if region, satisfaction, and total spending are added as predictors?
7. Is there an interaction between the coupon and satisfaction, in their relationship to purchase of the promoted product?
8. What is the best estimate for how much a coupon is related to increased purchase, as an odds ratio? Explain the meaning of this odds ratio using non-technical language.
9. What is the change in purchase likelihood, in relation to a change of 1 unit of satisfaction? (Hint: what is a unit of satisfaction in the model?) Approximately how many points would "1 unit" be, on the survey's 1–10 rating scale?
10. *(Thought exercise without code.)* Considering the product strategy, what questions are suggested by the apparent relationship between satisfaction and purchase? What possible explanations are there, or what else would you wish to know?

9.9.3 Handbag Conjoint Analysis Data for Exercises

In the remaining exercises, we consider a metric (ratings-based) conjoint exercise for handbags, using a new data set. Each of 300 simulated respondents rated the likelihood to purchase each of 15 handbags, which varied according to Color (black, navy blue, and gray), Leather finish (matte or shiny patent), Zipper color (gold or silver), and Price ($15, $17, $19, or $20). We load the data:

```
> # conjoint.df <- read.csv("chapter9-bag.csv") # local
> conjoint.df <- read.csv("https://goo.gl/gEKSQt") # online
> summary(conjoint.df)
    resp.id            rating           price           color       ...
 Min.   :  1.00   Min.   : 2.000   Min.   :15.00   black : 900   ...
 1st Qu.: 75.75   1st Qu.: 4.000   1st Qu.:15.00   gray  :1500   ...
```

9.9.4 Exercises for Metric Conjoint and Hierarchical Linear Models

11. Using the handbag data, estimate the likelihood to purchase as a function of the handbags' attributes, using a simple linear model.

12. Now fit the ratings conjoint model as a classical hierarchical model, fitting individual level estimates for each attribute's utility.
13. What is the estimated rating for a black bag with matte finish and a gold zipper, priced at $15? (Careful!)
14. Which respondents are most and least interested in a navy handbag?
15. Fit the hierarchical model again, using a Bayesian MCMC approach. How do the upper level estimates compare with those from the classical model?

Chapter 10
Confirmatory Factor Analysis and Structural Equation Modeling

In this chapter, we discuss structural equation models in R. We show how R can be used for both covariance-based and partial least squares modeling, and present basic guidelines for model assessment. We also demonstrate the power of R to simulate data and use such simulation to inform our expectations.

Structural models are helpful when your modeling needs meet any of these conditions: you need to evaluate interconnections of multiple data points that do not map neatly to the division between predictors and an outcome variable (as would be the case in linear modeling); you wish to include unobserved latent variables such as attitudes and estimate their relationships to one another or to observed data; or you wish to estimate the overall fit between observed data and a proposed model with latent variables or complex connections. From this point of view, structural models are closely related to both linear modeling because they estimate associations and model fit, and to factor analysis because they use latent variables.

The uses for structural models in marketing follow from those needs. For example, the models can be used to determine whether concepts on a survey match assumptions, for instance to assess whether items are in fact related to an underlying construct as one hopes; this is an extension of factor analysis (see Chap. 8). With regards to latent variables, the models can be used to estimate the association between outcomes such as purchase behavior and underlying attitudes that influence those, such as satisfaction and brand perception. An even more complex model would be one where several latent variables are simultaneously associated with one another in multiple ways. For example, brand perception, purchase intent, willingness to pay, and satisfaction all relate to one another as latent constructs, and also relate in multiple ways to observed consumer behaviors such as purchases.

We assume in this chapter that the reader is familiar with structural models and primarily wishes to learn the R approach to them. The topic is too complex for a single chapter although we attempt to present an overview that is understandable for any analyst. Section 10.1 provides a conceptual introduction for readers new to the area; experienced analysts may wish to skip to Sect. 10.1.1.

© Springer Nature Switzerland AG 2019
C. Chapman and E. M. Feit, *R For Marketing Research and Analytics*, Use R!,
https://doi.org/10.1007/978-3-030-14316-9_10

10.1   The Motivation for Structural Models

The real world rarely divides into nicely controlled experiments and marketers are often interested to test complex models. Consider a consumer's likelihood to purchase a new product. The likelihood will be influenced by many factors such as prior product experience, perception of brand and features, price sensitivity, promotional effects, and so forth.

Imagine that we are brand managers interested in the impact of *brand perception* on *likelihood to purchase*. One approach to assess this might be to collect survey data on stated likelihood to purchase the product and attitudes about the brand. In schematic terms, we might model this as a linear relationship (Chap. 7): *purchase ~ perception*. Yet whether we find an effect or not, our model is open to the challenge that there are many other possible variables that we didn't assess. Perhaps an effect we thought we found was due to prior experience and not to brand; or perhaps we didn't find an effect because we failed to account for a promotional campaign that influences the relationship.

Even imperfect assessment of those additional influences can improve our understanding. In a statistical model, any unbiased—even if incomplete—capture of variance will improve other parts of the model. For instance, we might only care about the relationship between *brand perception* on *likelihood to purchase*; yet if our model also includes *promotion* and *prior brand experience*, it will capture some of the variance due to those factors and give us a better, more realistic estimate for the relationship between brand and purchase. Including those influences will make us and our stakeholders more confident.

A common way to test complex models of this kind in marketing is *structural equation modeling* (SEM). It is impossible to model every possible influence in a market, and we don't recommend trying. Yet with SEM, it is feasible to do several things that improve our models: to include multiple influences, to posit unobserved concepts that underlie the observed indicators (i.e., constructs such as *brand preference*, *likelihood to purchase*, and *satisfaction*), to specify how those concepts influence one another, to assess the model's overall congruence to the data, and to determine whether the model fits the data better than alternative models.

As we will show, this is done by creating a graphical *path diagram* of influences and then estimating the strength of relationship for each path in the model. Such paths often concern two kinds of variables: *manifest* variables that are observed, i.e., that have data points, and *latent* variables that are conceived to underlie the observed data. For example, in the first model we examine, *product involvement* is conceived as a latent factor that underlies several other latent factors such as *image involvement*, and those factors in turn are observed as manifest variables on survey items. The set of relationships among the latent variables is called the *structural model*, while the linkage between those elements and the observed, manifest variables is the *measurement model*.

Structural models pose many potential pitfalls and have a great deal of specialized jargon. We attempt to use a minimum of technical jargon in this chapter, yet we urge you not to use this chapter as your only guide to such models. Despite that warning, we believe that the chapter demonstrates the power and importance of such models and will prepare you to learn more about them.

Structural equation models (SEM) are similar to linear regression models (Chap. 7) but differ in three regards. First, as noted above, SEM assesses the relationships among many variables, with models that may be more complex than simply predictors and outcomes. Second, whereas linear regression only models existing, observed variables, SEM allows modeling of latent variables that represent underlying constructs that are conceived as manifested imperfectly, perhaps through multiple indicators, in the observed data. Third, SEM allows relationships to have multiple "downstream" effects. For example, experience with a product (a stated variable on a survey) might related to brand perception (a latent construct expressed in several survey items) which then relates to willingness to pay (a latent construct) which relates observed behavior to purchase or not at a particular price point (perhaps in transaction data or as a stated choice on a survey item).

Finally, we close this introduction with a warning: with this potential for such connections among latent variables, it is tempting to interpret structural models as being about *causation* and many analysts, stakeholders, and even authors of academic papers do this. We believe that it is possible to use these models as part of causal reasoning but to do so requires attention to issues and models that are well outside the scope of this book. In general, however, we recommend that you consciously avoid all discussion of causation, and instead talk about *relationships* or *association among the latent variables*.

10.1.1   Structural Models in This Chapter

In examining R's capabilities to specify, test, and visualize structural equation models (SEM), we present two examples: a confirmatory factor analysis (CFA) model that evaluates an assessment scale for product involvement, and a more general SEM that models the likelihood to repurchase a product, as related to quality, value, price, and customer satisfaction of a prior purchase. In each case, we demonstrate how to simulate data for test purposes, how to specify and fit the proposed model, and how to assess the proposed model.

We also show two different SEM approaches: the most common but more demanding *covariance based* (CB-SEM) approach, and the more flexible *partial least squares* (PLS-SEM) approach. We start with CB-SEM because it is virtually synonymous with "SEM" in the literature, especially outside marketing. Nevertheless, PLS-SEM is often able to fit models in situations where CB-SEM fails and has become popular for marketing applications in the past decade, so we demonstrate it as well.

Several R packages are able to fit SEMs. In this chapter, we demonstrate CB-SEM using the `lavaan` package [166] (where *lavaan* abbreviates "*la*tent *va*riable *an*alysis") because of its simplicity for model specification and its rich set of available tools for data simulation, model comparison, and visualization. Then we demonstrate PLS-SEM with the `semPLS` package.

10.2   Scale Assessment: Confirmatory Factor Analysis (CFA)

We start by considering a survey scale that assesses *product involvement*, using the survey items shown in Table 10.1 [32]. This survey scale reflects a theoretical model in which product involvement is a hierarchical construct comprising three factors: *general* involvement with a product category, involvement with the *choices and features* of the product, and involvement with the category in terms of personal *image*.

On the survey, three subscales reflect those factors and could lead to higher or lower scores depending on how consumers view a product. For instance, as marketers we would expect digital cameras to engage consumers in terms of their technical features and thus to score high on *feature involvement*. By contrast, clothing is a key component of personal image, and could be expected to score high on *image involvement*. Either category might be high or low on *general involvement* according to the interests of a specific respondent. To consider other categories, a generic good such as paper might show low consumer involvement on all three factors, while automobiles might be relatively high on all three. This model was proposed as an alternative to a single factor model of product involvement, where involvement is simply high or low overall with no differentiation between factors such as feature or image involvement.

The three factor model here was named *PIES* as an abbreviation of the "*P*roduct *I*nvolvement and *E*nthusiasm *S*cale" [32]. It could be used in many marketing situations. For instance, if we assess that our product category is high on feature involvement, we might develop communication and positioning strategies that emphasize technical specifications. It may also be used to inform targeting: if we determine that a given demographic group views our category as important to their personal image, then we might target them with campaigns that highlight our product in terms of personal image.

The PIES structural model proposes four latent (unobserved) constructs that underlie product involvement: a *general* involvement factor (here abbreviated as "Gnr"), a *choice/feature* factor (hereafter "Feature" or "Ftr"), an *image* ("Img") factor, and a higher-order *PIE* factor (product involvement and engagement) that is conceived as the underlying level of interest underlying the other three factors. This hierarchical factor model is shown in Fig. 10.1. The relationships among these are linear

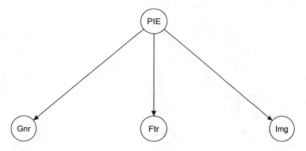

Fig. 10.1 PIES latent construct (factor) model, showing three factors of product involvement (General involvement = Gnr, Feature = Ftr, and Image = Img). These three latent factors relate to a higher-order, overall latent construct for involvement, PIE. None of these latent constructs is directly observed; for the observational model, see Fig. 10.2

relationships of unobserved, latent variables that match a particular theory about product involvement (and whose relationship we will specify and test below).

The three involvement factors and the higher-order PIE factor are modeled as *latent variables* that are not directly observed but are instead conceived to influence the survey items that *manifest* them. On the survey, each factor is represented by a subscale comprising several items, as shown in Table 10.1.

Table 10.1 The hierarchical product involvement (PIES) scale, showing the subscales (factors) and items. The survey would be given for a specific product category, filling in the blanks with a descriptive phrase such as "digital cameras" or "diet soda." From [32]

Item	Text	Reversed?
General scale		
i1	_____ are not very important to me	Yes
i2	I never think about _____	Yes
i3	I am very interested in _____	
Feature scale		
i4	In choosing a _____ I would look for some specific features or options	
i5	If I chose a new _____ I would investigate the available choices in depth	
i6	Some _____ are clearly better than others	
i7	If I were choosing a _____, I would wish to learn about the available options in detail	
Image scale		
i8	When people see someone's _____, they form an opinion of that person	
i9	A _____ expresses a lot about the person who owns it	
i10	You can learn a lot about a person by seeing the person's _____	
i11	It is important to choose a _____ that matches one's image	

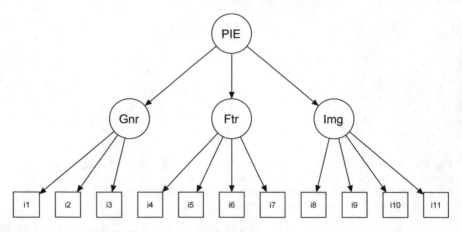

Fig. 10.2 The complete PIES model with latent factors and manifest scale items

In the hierarchical model, the overall PIE factor does not directly influence any items on the scale. Rather, it influences the other three factors as a higher order latent variable. The complete structural model, showing the hierarchical relation of the latent constructs and the manifest scale items that are observed for each construct, is shown in Fig. 10.2.

An analyst's question with PIES—and the question for the PIES authors in the cited paper—might be this: *is the PIES scheme a good model for some set of survey responses for the items in Table* 10.1? If we confirm that PIES is a good model, we will be much more confident in using this survey data to draw inferences about product involvement than if we had not assess the model. We show how SEM in R can address that question.

To do this, we use a particular application of SEM known as confirmatory factor analysis (CFA). In CFA, one specifies the factor structure and asks, "How well does the proposed model agree with the structure of the data?" We also address a closely related question, "Is that model better than some other specified model?"

10.2.1 Simulating PIES CFA Data

To demonstrate CFA, we create a simulated data set with known factor structure that corresponds to the PIES model in Table 10.1. We use this data to demonstrate how to assess a CFA model (which ordinarily would be done with data collected from respondents). Then we evaluate alternative models and discuss the importance of model comparison in CFA.

If you prefer to download the data for the CFA example:

```
> piesSimData <- read.csv("http://goo.gl/yT0XwJ")
> summary(piesSimData)
      i1                 i2                 i3                 i4                 i5
Min.    :1.000    Min.    :1.000    Min.    :1.00     Min.    :1.000    Min.    :1.000
1st Qu.:4.000    1st Qu.:3.000    1st Qu.:3.00     1st Qu.:3.000    1st Qu.:3.000
Median :4.000    Median :4.000    Median :4.00     Median :4.000    Median :4.000
Mean    :4.339    Mean    :4.104    Mean    :4.11     Mean    :4.039    Mean    :3.999
...
```

Once you have the data, you may proceed to Sect. 10.2.2. Otherwise, continue here; data generation for CFA turns out to be rather easy.

We use the `lavaan` package for core SEM (and CFA) functionality including data simulation and model fitting [166], and extend its capabilities for model comparison and visualization using two other packages, `semTools` [112] and `semPlot` [53]. Our first step is to install those packages and make them available in R:

```
> install.packages(c("lavaan", "semTools", "semPlot"))
> library(lavaan)
> library(semTools)
> library(semPlot)
```

In `lavaan`, a structural model may be specified using syntax that is rather similar to R's linear model formulas (Sect. 7.3). We specify two models here: (1) a *structural* model that we fit to the data and whose structure we wish to assess, and (2) a *data* model that we use only to generate simulated data for test purposes. The structural model is specified according to the model as shown in Fig. 10.2, written as a simple string that `lavaan` will parse:

```
> piesModel <- " General =~ i1 + i2 + i3
+                Feature =~ i4 + i5 + i6 + i7
+                Image   =~ i8 + i9 + i10 + i11
+                PIES =~ General + Feature + Image "
```

In SEM code we read the "=~" symbol as "is manifested by," which means that it is estimated to be a single variable that is a composite of the three items (with some degree of unreliability or error in each). Each line in this formula defines a new latent variable—General, Feature, and so forth—that does not appear in the data set but which `lavaan` will estimate for us based on the observed items i1, i2, etc. We can then use these latent variable in other parts of the formula to express additional relationships. For instance, in this code the latent variable PIES relates in turn to the other latent variables General, Feature, and Image. Such relationships of latent variables are a key differentiator between SEM and regular linear modeling.

The piesModel formulas say that PIES is manifested by three factors: General, Feature, and Image. Each of those is manifested by 3 or 4 of the items i1 through i11 as defined in Table 10.1.[1]

Next we simulate data similar to what might come from a PIES survey of consumers. (Of course if you only test a model against real data, then these data generation steps

---

[1] If you are experienced with other SEM software, you may wonder about details such as the need to fix a path for each factor and to specify error terms. Those are automatically handled by `lavaan` with defaults that are appropriate for many situations (for instance, having uncorrelated errors and fixing the first manifest variable path to 1.0).

are not required.) We define our data simulation model using the same SEM syntax, but add *factor loading coefficients* for the items and subfactors in order to specify the structural relationships. We use factor loadings that approximate those reported by the PIES authors [32]:

```
> piesDataModel <- " General =~ 0.9*i1 + 0.7*i2 + 0.5*i3
+                    Feature =~ 0.3*i3 + 0.7*i4 + 0.9*i5 + 0.5*i6  + 0.9*i7
+                    Image   =~ 0.2*i3 + 0.8*i8 + 0.9*i9 + 0.8*i10 + 0.7*i11
+                    PIES =~ 0.7*General + 0.8*Feature + 0.8*Image"
```

We generate a data set with that factor structure by setting a random number seed and using simulateData(MODEL, sample.nobs), where sample.nobs is the number of observations, or N. We choose N = 3600 to approximate data reported in the PIES paper:

```
> set.seed(10001)    # another island Zip code
> piesSimData.norm <- simulateData(piesDataModel, sample.nobs=3600)
> print(head(piesSimData.norm), digits=2)
    i1    i2    i3     i4     i5     i6     i7     i8     i9    i10     i11
1 -0.16  2.07  1.14  -1.746 -1.68  -1.79  -1.46  -0.032  1.82  0.610  -0.032
2 -0.38  2.27  0.79   0.922  0.23   0.35   0.51   0.963 -1.11 -0.037   0.792
3 -0.65 -3.00  0.25  -0.077 -0.35   0.12  -1.63  -0.766 -0.22 -1.220   0.462
...
```

Each row here represents a set of hypothetical survey responses from one respondent. Note that the generated data is continuous (drawn from a normal distribution with decimal values), so it is not yet appropriate for PIES; as survey responses, PIES items are 1–7 Likert-type scores [32].

In order to convert the continuous data to discrete survey data, we use the function cut(DATA, breaks=K) that divides continuous data into K groups, expressed as K factor levels (see Sect. 12.4.1 for more on cut()). We could do this separately for each of the 11 columns of data, but it is more instructive to do it in a way that is generalizable. That involves a few conceptual steps.

We use cut() to convert a vector of continuous numeric data into seven factors, using labels=FALSE to keep the result as integers instead of labeled, nominal values. Then we enclose that in an anonymous function that can be used repeatedly by apply(). We apply() that anonymous recoding function to each of the columns of our data set using the *list* version of apply(lapply()), and assemble the resulting set of discrete numeric vectors into a new data.frame. That comes together in amazingly compact R code (you should spend time deconstructing and tinkering with it to see how this works):

```
> piesSimData <- data.frame(lapply(piesSimData.norm,
+                           function(x) { cut(x, breaks=7, labels=FALSE) } ))
```

We now perform our usual data quality checks:

```
> library(car)
> some(piesSimData)
     i1 i2 i3 i4 i5 i6 i7 i8 i9 i10 i11
11    3  3  4  2  2  5  3  2  4   3   4
709   3  3  3  5  4  3  3  3  4   4   4
1392  4  3  3  3  4  4  3  4  4   5   4
...
> library(psych)
> describe(piesSimData)
```

```
      vars    n mean    sd median  trimmed   mad min max range   skew kurtosis    se
i1       1 3600 4.34  1.00      4     4.32  1.48   1   7     6  -0.07    -0.01 0.02
i2       2 3600 4.10  1.05      4     4.09  1.48   1   7     6  -0.01    -0.07 0.02
i3       3 3600 4.11  1.02      4     4.10  1.48   1   7     6  -0.01    -0.13 0.02
...
```

The data set now comprises discrete values from 1–7, averaging about 4, with good distribution properties (no skew, sd around 1, and so forth). We visualize the relationships among the items using `scatterplotMatrix()` from the `car` package [62], selecting a subset of the items—two items from each factor—to make inspection easier:

```
> library(car)
> library(RColorBrewer)
> scatterplotMatrix(piesSimData[, c(1, 2, 4, 5, 8, 9)],
+                     col=brewer.pal(3, "Paired"), ellipse=TRUE )
```

The result is shown in Fig. 10.3. In looking at the scatter plots, we see the situation as expected: items are discrete (as shown in the density plots on the diagonal), and items have higher correlation within a subscale (as in the off-diagonal plots for `i1` vs. `i2`) than they do across scales (such as `i1` vs. `i4`).

Because this data reflects a factor model, we may also do a quick inspection of the apparent factor structure. Although we use CFA to do a strong test of factor structure, it is useful to perform a brief check using the `factanal()` command to perform an exploratory factor analysis (EFA, see Sect. 8.3):

```
> factanal(piesSimData, factors=3)
...
Loadings:
     Factor1 Factor2 Factor3
i1    0.138   0.119   0.675
i2                    0.614
i3    0.277   0.362   0.476
i4    0.151   0.608
i5    0.126   0.715   0.102
i6            0.519
i7    0.133   0.678   0.154
i8    0.665   0.137   0.128
i9    0.706   0.138   0.130
i10   0.655   0.117   0.145
i11   0.632   0.126
...
```

We see three plausible factors comprising items i8–i11, i4–i7, and i1–i3 respectively, as we would expect (the factor order is irrelevant). As a reminder, the EFA model does *not* test or confirm the PIES model; that is what CFA does. Instead, EFA reassures us that the data look reasonable before proceeding.

To recap, the simulated data—created using just 4 commands in R—have the kind of structure that might be expected from a consumer survey using the items in Table 10.1. We now proceed to the CFA.

10.2.2 Estimating the PIES CFA Model

CFA assessment begins by defining the model that we wish to evaluate. In this case, we model the three PIES factors (latent variables), `General`, `Feature`, and `Image`

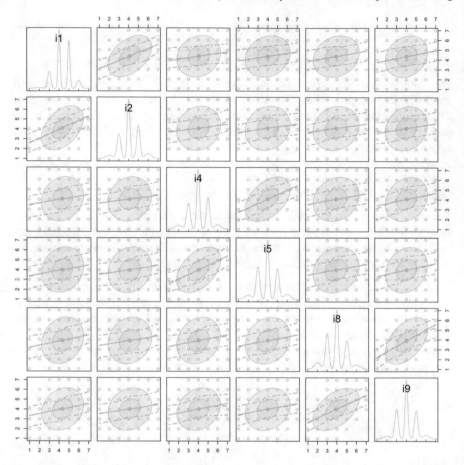

Fig. 10.3 Scatterplot matrix for selected items in the simulated PIES data. Individual items have discrete values that approximate a normal distribution (in the density plots on the diagonal). Items are all positively correlated. Items within a proposed factor, such as i1 and i2, show stronger association than those in differing factors

as manifest in items i1–i11. We then model the overall PIES latent variable as the composite of the other three factors (see Sect. 10.2.1 for an explanation of the formula syntax here):

```
> library(lavaan)
> piesModel <- " General =~ i1 + i2 + i3
+                 Feature =~ i4 + i5 + i6  + i7
+                 Image   =~ i8 + i9 + i10 + i11
+                 PIES =~ General + Feature + Image "
```

We fit this model to data using cfa(MODEL, data=DATA) and inspect the result with summary(FIT, fit.measures=TRUE). The output of summary(FIT) is lengthy in this case so we abbreviate it:

```
> pies.fit <- cfa(piesModel, data=piesSimData)
> summary(pies.fit, fit.measures=TRUE)
lavaan 0.6-3 ended normally after 41 iterations
```

```
...
  Number  of  observations                                        3600
...
  Comparative  Fit  Index  (CFI)                                  0.975
  Tucker-Lewis  Index  (TLI)                                      0.966
...
Root  Mean  Square  Error  of  Approximation:

  RMSEA                                                           0.041
  90  Percent  Confidence  Interval                      0.036    0.045
  P-value  RMSEA  <=  0.05                                        1.000

Standardized  Root  Mean  Square  Residual:

  SRMR                                                            0.030

Parameter  Estimates:
...
Latent  Variables:
                        Estimate   Std.Err   z-value   P(>|z|)
  General  =~
    i1                   1.000
    i2                   0.948      0.042     22.415    0.000
    i3                   1.305      0.052     25.268    0.000
  Feature  =~
    i4                   1.000
    i5                   1.168      0.037     31.168    0.000
    i6                   0.822      0.033     25.211    0.000
    i7                   1.119      0.036     31.022    0.000
  Image  =~
    i8                   1.000
    i9                   0.963      0.028     34.657    0.000
    i10                  0.908      0.027     33.146    0.000
    i11                  0.850      0.027     31.786    0.000
  PIES  =~
    General              1.000
    Feature              0.875      0.057     15.355    0.000
    Image                0.932      0.060     15.628    0.000
...
```

The CFA output establishes that the three-factor hierarchical model fits the data well. In the upper portion of the summary, we see that fit indices are strong (e.g., CFI $=0.975$) and residuals are low (e.g., RMSEA $=0.041$). The lower part of the summary shows that model parameters for the paths of latent variables to items, and for the upper-level PIES factor to the three subfactors, are all significant ("P $(> | z |)$" $= 0$), are similar to one another in magnitude (ranging 0.822–1.305), and are not far from 1.0 (a good thing because the items are intended to be used in simple additive subscales).

If these were real data, the CFA would establish both that the PIES hierarchical model fits well and—because the factor-item loadings are around 1.0—that it is reasonable to add up the items as a simple sum to form subscale scores, as is common for such surveys (instead of computing weighted factor scores).

The final model with fitted parameter estimates is plotted with the semPaths() command from the semPlot package. We use the argument edge.label.cex to scale the parameter font to be smaller and more readable. Many R packages use "cex" (character *expansion*) to rescale the font for some element of the plot (in this case, *edge labels*, i.e., parameter estimates). Setting cex >1.0 enlarges a font; cex $<$ 1.0 shrinks it. If you're looking for a way to rescale a font, try searching for "cex" in a plot routine's help file. The model is drawn as follows:

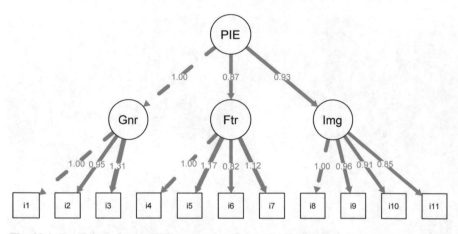

Fig. 10.4 Coefficients for the PIES structural model, using simulated consumer survey responses

```
> library(semPlot)
> semPaths(pies.fit, what="est", fade=FALSE, residuals=FALSE,
+          edge.label.cex=0.75)
```

The result is Fig. 10.4. This figure expresses some of the crucial information from the longer CFA text output above, in a more readable way. The graphical version makes it easy to see the relationships between the latent and manifest variables and to browse the coefficient values.

10.2.3   Assessing the PIES CFA Model

The PIES model fits the data extremely well. If this were real data, we'd be done, right?

No! A common error with SEM is to propose a model, fit the data, and then assert on the basis of fit indices that the model is "good." The problem is that some other, and perhaps more reasonable, model might be just as good or even better. Thus, there is an important second stage: establish that the proposed model fits *better* than a reasonable alternative model.

We test the PIES hierarchical model ("PIES 3+1") against two alternatives. The first is a single factor alternative where one underlying involvement factor manifests in all items (as in Fig. 10.5), which we call "PIES 1." PIES 1 is a simpler model that proposes product involvement to be a single latent factor; if it fits the data as well as PIES 3+1 then we could reject the more complex model and use this simple one instead. It is a good alternative to the hierarchical model both because it is simpler and because it focuses on the top level of the hierarchy, assessing whether it is advantageous to add the complications of the subfactors in PIES 3+1.

The second alternative we consider is an uncorrelated three-factor model, where three independent factors are manifest in the three respective sets of items (shown in

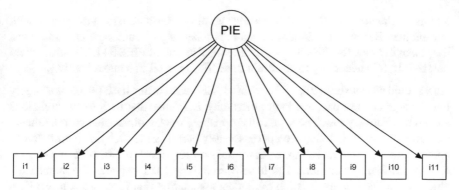

Fig. 10.5 A one-factor alternative model, PIES 1, in which a single latent factor of product involve-ment is manifest in all of the items, with no subfactors. We use this to test a simpler model than PIES 3+1 and determine whether it fits the data just as well

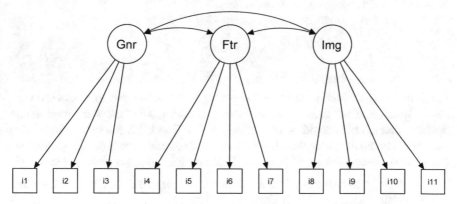

Fig. 10.6 A three-factor alternative, PIES 3. To differentiate this from the PIES 3+1 model, the latent factor correlations here are constrained to show weak association among the factors. This allows us to test a model where the factors express largely separate constructs as opposed to closely related ones

Fig. 10.6), or "PIES 3." This omits the top level, overall factor from the hierarchy and focuses on the three subfactors, asking whether they are better conceived as being separate instead of relating to a hierarchical model. If the PIES 3 model fit as well as PIES 3+1, we could reject the complication of the hierarchical model and consider using the subscales as independent, largely unrelated assessment measures.

We specify and fit a one-factor model for PIES 1 using `lavaan` as follows:

```
> piesModelNH1 <- " PIES =~ i1 + i2 + i3 + i4 + i5 + i6  +
+                          i7 + i8 + i9 + i10 + i11 "
> pies.fit.NH1 <- cfa(piesModelNH1, data=piesSimData)
```

This may issue warnings due to poor fit. Because we are interested in the comparison rather than the one-factor model in itself, we will ignore those.

There is a complication in asserting the PIES 3 model. We can see in Fig. 10.6 that the number of paths and manifest variables in PIES 3 is the same as in the baseline

3+1 hierarchical model (Fig. 10.2) because we allow the factors to be associated with one another. Because it estimates the same number of paths among all the variables, the global fit index for PIES 3 would be identical to that of PIES 3+1. To differentiate the models, it is necessary to constrain the PIES 3 model in some other way.

How should we constrain PIES 3? Because PIES 3 asserts that the 3 factors are largely independent and not part of a larger hierarchy, it implies that their intercorrelations should be relatively low. Thus, we could constrain the latent variable correlations to a small value such that they are not reasonably part of a hierarchy. A correlation of zero is unreasonable as it implies absolutely no relationship.[2] Instead of zero, we fix the non-hierarchical model to have correlation of 0.1 between the latent variables; this reflects an expectation of modest association that is too weak to justify a hierarchical model.

In lavaan we add the fixed relationships to the PIES 3 model syntax as additional lines and fit the model to the simulated data:

```
> piesModelNH3  <-  "  General  =~  i1  +  i2  +  i3
+                     Feature  =~  i4  +  i5  +  i6   +  i7
+                     Image    =~  i8  +  i9  +  i10  +  i11
+                     General  ~~  0.1*Feature
+                     General  ~~  0.1*Image
+                     Feature  ~~  0.1*Image  "
> pies.fit.NH3  <-  cfa(piesModelNH3,  data=piesSimData)
```

In this model specification, the "~~" operator specifies a correlation between variables. By using a fixed value 0.1, we specify that the value of the correlation should not be estimated but should be constrained to 0.1. The PIES 3 model requires that correlation be small among the latent factors, so we set the three possible correlations (General~Feature, General~Image, and Feature~Image) to our chosen value of 0.1.

The semTools package provides a command to compare CB-SEM (and therefore CFA) models: compareFit(MODEL1, MODEL2, ...). This reports individual fit measures for each model along with pairwise model comparisons. Our PIES models are *nested*, meaning that one might start with the hierarchical model and then fix some of the paths coefficient to derive the three-factor model (specifically, constraining the factor correlations to 0.1), and again could fix some paths to derive the single factor model (specifically, setting the factor correlations to 1.0 so that they are identical and thus a single factor).

Here is the comparison of all three models:

```
> library(semTools)
> summary(compareFit(pies.fit.NH1, pies.fit.NH3, pies.fit))
################### Nested Model Comparison #########################
                                   chi df       p delta.cfi
pies.fit - pies.fit.NH3         222.43  3   <.001    0.0222
pies.fit.NH3 - pies.fit.NH1    2774.50  0   <.001    0.2812

#################### Fit Indices Summaries #########################
```

---

[2] Always be wary of models that assert or test independence; a well-known phenomenon in human research is that within a given domain, "everything correlates with everything else." Paul Meehl referred to this as the "crud" factor in research, and showed that it leads to research that finds "significant" associations everywhere [137].

```
                 chisq df pvalue    cfi    tli         aic          bic rmsea  srmr
pies.fit.NH1 3284.581 44   .000†   .672   .589  108812.709   108948.860  .143  .102
pies.fit.NH3  510.078 44   .000†   .953   .941  106038.205   106174.356  .054  .078
pies.fit      287.649 41   .000†  .975†  .966†  105821.776†  105976.494†  .041†  .030†
```

To interpret the comparisons, we start by inspecting the second half of the report, the "Fit Indices Summaries." For the non-hierarchical three-factor model PIES 3 (pies.fit.NH3), the fit was strong (e.g., CFI = 0.953, RMSEA = 0.054). If that were the only model that we tested, we would have concluded that it was an excellent fit. Yet when we compare the PIES 3+1 model, pies.fit, the fit indices are stronger (CFI = 0.975, RMSEA = 0.041). The stronger fit indices are indicated by the dagger symbol ("†").

Is PIES 3+1 stronger than PIES 3? We turn to the upper portion of the report to examine the model comparison. The first line of output ("pies.fit - pies.fit.NH3") reports the Chi-square test of the difference between the two models: $Chisq = 222.43$, $df = 3$. This is a strong and statistically significant difference, $p < .001$. We also see in the results that the one-factor model PIES 1 was a poor fit (CFI = 0.672 in the fit index summary) and much worse in comparison to PIES 3+1 than even the non-hierarchical PIES 3 model. (In Sect. 11.3.5 we will also see how to interpret the bic values for model comparison.)

What does this tell us? For our data—which of course were simulated to fit the 3+1 model—the three-factor hierarchical model was an excellent fit in itself and was better than two reasonable alternative models. If this were the case in real data (as claimed in [32]), it would establish a strong argument for the model.

What does this mean for us as marketers? It means that, if we saw such results in a product category of interest to us, we would not assume that product involvement is a unitary, single factor. Instead, we would wish to use the somewhat more informative and differentiated hierarchical model that assess overall product interest alongside measures of feature and image involvement. Additionally, because the overall model fits the data well, it tells us that the 3+1 model is a good representation of associations in the data (relative to plausible alternatives). This enhances our confidence that the survey items really do assess what we intend.

We note two important lessons. First, the simulated data is useful to examine the likelihood of being able to support a model. Simulated data showed us that the non-hierarchical PIES 3 model could fit the data well—if interpreted on its own—even when the PIES 3+1 model was "true" given the data simulation process. Such tests with simulated data inform us about the *power* needed for model comparison.

Second, we see that simply establishing strong fit for a model is not enough; we also need to establish superiority over alternative models. If we only tested the non-hierarchical three-factor PIES 3 model, we might have concluded that it was an excellent model. Yet when we compare it to the PIES 3+1 hierarchical model, we find the latter is a better fit to the data. We will encounter this again when we consider more general SEM models.

For marketers, there is another implication: when we devise a survey scale, we should test the assumed factor model to ensure that it meets our expectation. Imagine that we write a survey that asks about product preferences in four areas: performance, price, appearance, and quality. If each area has a few survey items and we add them together—as is common with surveys—then we are implicitly asserting a four factor model for our survey. Before we use those added-up scores, we should check our assumption about factors. Does our model match the data as we *believe* it should? If not, we might draw very misleading conclusions from the data. Test the model! R and `lavaan` make it easy to do this in just a few lines of code.

10.3   General Models: Structural Equation Models

We now consider a more general form of structural models, where latent constructs may influence one another in more complex ways. We consider an example from Iacobucci [104] concerning customer satisfaction ratings and their effect on stated intention to repurchase HP printers. The data consisted of responses to 15 satisfaction

Table 10.2 A 15-item survey of purchase satisfaction, perceived value, and repurchase intent. Item (variable) names are listed in the first column. Each division (Quality, Cost, Value, etc.) represents a latent factor manifest in the three following items. From Iacobucci [104]

Item	Text
Quality	
q1	The quality of the HP printer I bought is excellent
q2	HP printers are known to be highly reliable
q3	I'm sure my HP printer will last a long time
Cost	
c1	The HP printer was reasonably priced
c2	HP sets fair prices for its products
c3	The 88HP printers are no more expensive than others
Value	
v1	I feel like I got good value for this purchase
v2	The quality of the printer is worth its cost
v3	I could tell my boss this purchase was good value
CSat	
cs1	I am very satisfied with my newly purchase HP printer
cs2	My printer is better than I expected it would be
cs3	I have no regrets about having bought this printer
Repeat	
r1	I would buy another HP if I had to buy another printer
r2	I would buy other HP products
r3	I would tell my friends and coworkers to buy HPs

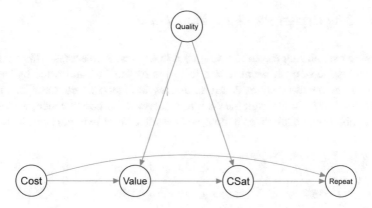

Fig. 10.7 A model of repeat purchase intent. In this model, the cost of a product is associated with both perception of value and intent to repurchase, while perception of quality relates to both perceived value and satisfaction, which is then associated with repurchase. From Iacobucci [104]

items, where there were 3 items each for factors of Quality, Cost (fair pricing), Value, Customer Satisfaction (CSat), and Repeat purchase intention.

The survey items, the variable names we use for them, and the higher-order latent factors (Quality, Cost, and so forth) are shown in Table 10.2.

The proposed structural model for the associations among the latent variables is shown in Fig. 10.7. For brevity, we omit consideration of the measurement model and the individual items for each factor.

As marketers, if we had collected consumer data from a survey such as this, we would have two goals. First, as we did with CFA above, we would wish to ascertain whether our proposed model of influence—for example, that perception of cost is associated with both perception of value and intent to repurchase, as shown in Fig. 10.7—is an adequate model for the data we have collected. Second, if the model fits the data well, we would answer questions about the relationships: how much does perception of quality relate to satisfaction? Is quality more important than perceived value? What is the largest determinant of stated intent to purchase again? And so forth.

To explore how to do this, we follow the same process as with CFA above. Specifically, we use a covariance-based SEM with four steps:

1. Define the structural model to be tested
2. Create simulated data that we use for illustration and debugging
3. Fit the model to the data
4. Compare the model to a simpler, alternative model

As always, simulating the data in step 2 is illustrative here; you would use your own data instead, although we believe additional simulation is useful.

10.3.1   The Repeat Purchase Model in R

We begin by specifying the structural model that we wish to assess. This consists of a left-hand name of each latent factor, followed by the "is manifested by" symbol, "=~" with the latent variables that it influences and its observed manifest variables (in this case, the 15 items from the customer survey). For convenience, we write the latent variables with capitalized names, and manifest items in lower case. In lavaan this is:

```
> satModel <- " Quality =~ CSat + Value + q1 + q2 + q3  + 0*Cost
+                Cost    =~ Value + Repeat + c1 + c2 + c3
+                Value   =~ CSat + v1 + v2 + v3
+                CSat    =~ Repeat + cs1 + cs2 + cs3
+                Repeat  =~ r1 + r2 + r3 "
```

We read the first line as saying, "Quality influences CSat and Value, and is manifested as items q1, q2, and q3." Notice that we specify a fixed loading of zero between *Cost* and *Quality*. That reflects Iacobucci's report that those factors had near zero relationship (specifically, correlation of −0.03, [104], p. 676). Also, we are not interested in their relationship in this model and constraining the relationship may prevent spurious model effects.[3] Continuing with the model, we read "Cost influences Value and Repeat purchase intention, and is manifested on items c1, c2, and c3," and similarly for the other lines.

Next we obtain simulated data to use. If you prefer to load the data instead of simulating it:

```
> satSimData <- read.csv("http://goo.gl/MhghRq")
> summary(satSimData)
      q1                q2               q3               c1               c2
 Min.   :1.00     Min.   :1.000    Min.   :1.000    Min.   :1.00     Min.   :1.000
 1st Qu.:3.00     1st Qu.:3.000    1st Qu.:3.000    1st Qu.:3.00     1st Qu.:3.000
 Median :4.00     Median :3.000    Median :4.000    Median :4.00     Median :4.000
 Mean   :3.95     Mean   :3.535    Mean   :3.805    Mean   :4.34     Mean   :4.185
 ...
```

Once you have the data, you may proceed to Sect. 10.3.2. Otherwise, continue with the following; once again, data simulation is surprisingly straightforward.

Using the loadings reported by Iacobucci ([104], p. 677), we write the data model as:

```
> satDataModel <- " Quality =~   0.59*CSat + 0.56*Value +
+                                 0.9*q1 + 0.9*q2 + 0.9*q3 + 0*Cost
+                   Cost    =~  -0.5*Value + -0.29*Repeat +
+                                 0.9*c1 + 0.9*c2 + 0.9*c3
+                   Value   =~   0.06*CSat + 0.9*v1 + 0.9*v2 + 0.9*v3
+                   CSat    =~   0.48*Repeat + 0.9*cs1 + 0.9*cs2 + 0.9*cs3
+                   Repeat  =~   0.9*r1 + 0.9*r2 + 0.9*r3 "
```

Then we simulate the data for N = 200 respondents, and convert to Likert type scaled values using the same approach as in Sect. 10.2.1:

---

[3]In general, fixing parameters is not recommended; the whole point of SEM is to estimate parameters. However, in some cases, especially with smaller samples as we consider here, it may help to focus a model on the influences under consideration if one constrains factors. It is possible with lavaan to constrain to any value, not just 0.

```
> set.seed(33706)    # continuing the island tour
> satData.norm <- simulateData(satDataModel, sample.nobs=200)
> satSimData <- data.frame(lapply(satData.norm,
+                                  function(x) { as.numeric(cut(x, breaks=7)) } ))
```

We omit here the data quality checks (see Sect. 10.2.1), but it is a good idea for you
to inspect those.

10.3.2   Assessing the Repeat Purchase Model

To fit the model, we use sem(MODEL, DATA) and add an argument, std.lv=
TRUE, to standardize the latent variables because we are interested to compare relative influence strength (the alternative is to treat them in terms of the unit scales of
the observed items, which might be of interest for CFA). In the abbreviated output,
we see a strong model fit (CFI $= 0.998$ and low residuals):

```
> sat.fit <- sem(satModel, data= satSimData, std.lv=TRUE)
> summary(sat.fit, fit.measures=TRUE)
lavaan 0.6-3 ended normally after 24 iterations
...
  Number of observations                             200

  Estimator                                           ML
  Minimum Function Test Statistic                 85.454
  Degrees of freedom                                  84
  P-value (Chi-square)                             0.435
...
User model versus baseline model:
  Comparative Fit Index (CFI)                      0.998
...
Root Mean Square Error of Approximation:
  RMSEA                                            0.009
  90 Percent Confidence Interval         0.000     0.040
  P-value RMSEA <= 0.05                             0.993

Standardized Root Mean Square Residual:
  SRMR                                             0.052
...
```

We plot the resulting structural coefficients for the proposed model with arguments for structural=TRUE to suppress the loadings for the manifest items
and nCharNodes=7 to put the full factor names in the latent variable circles:

```
> semPaths(sat.fit, what="est", fade=FALSE, residuals=FALSE,
+          layout="tree", structural=TRUE, nCharNodes=7, edge.label.cex=1)
```

The result is Fig. 10.8. Not surprisingly, the simulated data show effects close to what
we specified (but not exactly the same, which demonstrates that model recovery is
not perfect).

As we have already seen, a great fit in CB-SEM is not enough! We still need to
compare our proposed model to one or more plausible alternative models, in order
to demonstrate that our proposal is superior to other reasonable models.

How do we define an alternative model? It depends on your goal and theory. In
some cases, you might wish to compare to a simpler model, in order to show that
relationships are more complex or to fit a more precise model. In other cases, you
could compare to an existing model from the literature or previous research. In still

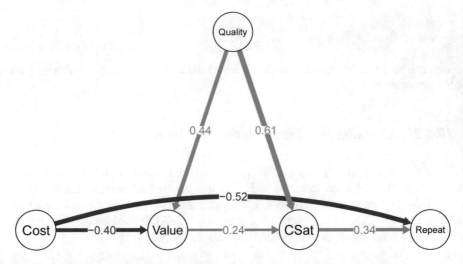

Fig. 10.8 Coefficient estimates for the repeat purchase model, using simulated data

others, you might show that a proposed complex model is too complex, and that a simpler model is more effective. As a general principle, we prefer to show that a model is better than a simpler model with fewer paths, and just as good as (i.e., not significantly worse than) a more complex model with a larger number of paths.

In the present case, our full model proposes that Quality and Cost do not have a simple relationship with single variables but are associated with multiple other variables. For instance, Cost influences not only perception of Value but also the likelihood of Repeat purchase. An alternative is a simpler, more obvious model, where each is associated with only a single other variable, such as Cost affecting Value but not directly influencing Repeat. To support our more complex model, we wish to show that the simpler model is inadequate. Thus, we define an alternative model where each latent variable only influences one other variable, giving us a model with 2 fewer paths as shown in Fig. 10.9. The alternative model specification in lavaan is:

```
> satAltModel <- " Quality =~ CSat   + q1 + q2 + q3 + 0*Cost
+                  Cost    =~ Value  + c1 + c2 + c3
+                  Value   =~ CSat   + v1 + v2 + v3
+                  CSat    =~ Repeat + cs1 + cs2 + cs3
+                  Repeat  =~ r1 + r2 + r3 "
```

We fit the alternative model to the simulated data with sem() and compare that fit to the proposed model with compareFit():

```
> satAlt.fit <- sem(satAltModel, data=satSimData, std.lv=TRUE)
> summary(compareFit(sat.fit, satAlt.fit, nested=TRUE))
#################### Nested Model Comparison ########################
                   chi df      p delta.cfi
sat.fit - satAlt.fit 37.51  2  <.001    0.0495

#################### Fit Indices Summaries ########################
            chisq df pvalue  cfi  tli      aic       bic rmsea srmr
sat.fit    85.454 84  .435† .998† .997† 9174.942† 9293.681† .009† .052†
satAlt.fit 122.962 86  .006  .949  .937 9208.449 9320.592  .046  .095
```

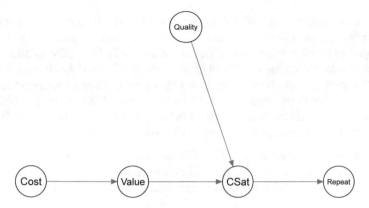

Fig. 10.9 An alternative structural model for repeat purchase influence, omitting the direct associations of cost with repeat purchase and of perceived quality with value

Once again we see that—taken on its own—the alternative model appears to be a good fit to the data (e.g., CFI=0.95, RMSEA=0.046) yet the proposed model is significantly better, showing Chi-square $(df = 2) = 37.51$ for the model difference, $p < .001$, and stronger fit indices with lower residuals.

If these were results from real data, we could draw a few conclusions. First, the model shows good fit to the observed (in this case, simulated) data, so we are able to interpret the results. Second, it is better than a simpler alternative model, which argues that our model is not an arbitrarily good fit but is preferable to a plausible alternative. Most importantly, we would use the coefficient estimates in the model to answer our substantive questions about the associations of the latent factors with the outcomes of interest to us as marketers. However, we omit this step here because we've done this several times for other models and it does not further advance our knowledge of R; see Iacobucci (2009) for conclusions in this case [104].

10.4 The Partial Least Squares (PLS) Alternative

The first two models we have considered in this chapter exemplify *covariance-based* structural equation modeling (CB-SEM). Such models attempt to account for as much of the total covariance in the data as possible, among all observed and latent variables. CB-SEM requires that a data set complies with relatively strict assumptions about data distributions (continuous data, normally distributed residuals), the number of indicators per factor (generally three or more), reliability of indicators, and sample size (some authorities recommend several hundred, although it is possible that samples of N=100 or even N=50 may be adequate when measures are very reliable; see Iacobucci [105]). When such assumptions are met, CB-SEM is a powerful tool that tests a model rigorously, assesses overall strength of the model, and allows for model comparison.

When data do not comply with the assumptions of CB-SEM or come from a modest sample size with potentially less reliable indicators, an alternative is *partial least squares* structural equation modeling (PLS-SEM). PLS-SEM is often able to yield estimates of path coefficients in models where CB-SEM would fail. However, PLS-SEM does not allow one to say much about model fit or comparative strength; there is no accepted measure of global "goodness of fit" that is comparable across models. Thus, we recommend CB-SEM when possible; but when CB-SEM fails, PLS-SEM may still give useful estimates of model influences.

In this section, we demonstrate PLS-SEM for the repeat purchase model that we examined above. We will see that PLS-SEM can estimate parameters with a sample where CB-SEM fails, but with greater uncertainty about the model's results.

10.4.1   PLS-SEM for Repeat Purchase

We conduct PLS with the `semPLS` package; install that for the following examples. We continue with the example from Iacobucci [104] of the influence of customer satisfaction and perceived value on intended repeat purchase of a computer printer. You may review that model—and find steps to create simulated data that we use here—in Sect. 10.3 above.

Let's see why PLS-SEM can be useful. Our simulated dataset (`satSimData`) has $N = 200$ observations, which was modeled successfully with CB-SEM. What if the sample were smaller? Let's take $N = 50$ rows and try to fit the CB-SEM model to those:

```
> set.seed(90704)
> satSimData2 <- satSimData[sample(nrow(satSimData), 50), ]
> describe(satSimData2)
      vars  n mean   sd median trimmed  mad min max range  skew kurtosis   se
q1       1 50 3.80 1.39      4    3.75 1.48   1   7     6  0.26    -0.23 0.20
...

> sat.fit2 <- sem(satModel, data= satSimData2, std.lv=TRUE)
Warning messages:
1: In lav_model_vcov(lavmodel = lavmodel, lavsamplestats = lavsamplestats,  :
   lavaan WARNING: could not compute standard errors!
...
```

Model estimation with `lavaan` fails because we do not have enough data.[4] If you inspect the model object, you will see extreme and nonsensical values:

```
> summary(sat.fit2, fit.measures=TRUE)
lavaan 0.6-3 ended normally after 9279 iterations
...
  Comparative Fit Index (CFI)                           0.727
...
Latent Variables:
                   Estimate   Std.Err  z-value  P(>|z|)
...
  Cost =~
    Value            -0.003        NA
    Repeat           -0.011        NA
    c1                0.014        NA
    c2               57.951        NA
```

---

[4]The small sample exacerbates another reason for estimation difficulty: our data is highly collinear due to the factor structure imposed when we simulated it to match the report by Iacobucci [104].

```
...
Variances:
                    Estimate    Std.Err   z-value   P(>|z|)
   .q1                 1.540         NA
...
    .c1                1.515         NA
    .c2            -3356.511         NA
...
```

It is unreasonable to think that one survey item about cost (c1) has nearly zero relationship while another (c2) is thousands of times more strongly related (57.29/0.014), or that one has thousands of times as much variance as another. This indicates model instability as the message from lavaan warned us.

We will try PLS-SEM instead. The first step is to define a *measurement* model that links underlying latent variables to their observed manifest variables such as survey items, and then to define a *structural* model that links latent variables to one another. In lavaan these were combined into a single step (cf. Sect. 10.3.1) but with the semPLS package they are separate.

Whereas lavaan uses a formula syntax to define relationships among variables, semPLS uses a matrix format. In this format, each row represents one "arrow" in a model. The first column of the row represents the *from* variable while the second column represents the *to* variable. Thus, an arrow from *Quality* to the manifest variable *q1* would be represented as a matrix line ("Quality", "q1").

The matrix definition is not as difficult as it may sound; we need only list the *from* and *to* entries in a simple format. Referring to the model in Sect. 10.3.1, we define the measurement model (latent to observed variables) model as:

```
> satPLSmm <- matrix(c(
+    "Quality",  "q1",
+    "Quality",  "q2",
+    "Quality",  "q3",
+    "Cost",     "c1",
+    "Cost",     "c2",
+    "Cost",     "c3",
+    "Value",    "v1",
+    "Value",    "v2",
+    "Value",    "v3",
+    "CSat",     "cs1",
+    "CSat",     "cs2",
+    "CSat",     "cs3",
+    "Repeat",   "r1",
+    "Repeat",   "r2",
+    "Repeat",   "r3" ), ncol=2, byrow=TRUE)
```

The structural model presents the latent variable relationships using the same kind of matrix format. Referring to the model shown in Fig. 10.7 we write:

```
> satPLSsm <- matrix(c(
+    "Quality",  "CSat",
+    "Quality",  "Value",
+    "Cost",     "Value",
+    "Cost",     "Repeat",
+    "Value",    "CSat",
+    "CSat",     "Repeat" ), ncol=2, byrow=TRUE)
```

We now fit the PLS model using the simulated 50-respondent data set. We use plsm(data, strucmod, measuremod) from semPLS to create a PLS model using the structural and measurement model matrices that we defined. Then we use sempls(model, data) to estimate the model parameters:

```
> library(semPLS)

> satPLS.mod <- plsm(data=satSimData2, strucmod=satPLSsm, measuremod=satPLSmm)
> satPLS.fit <- sempls(model=satPLS.mod, data=satSimData2)
All 50 observations are valid.
Converged after 14 iterations.
Tolerance: 1e-07
Scheme: centroid
```

We can now inspect the results. To begin, we examine the fit between the latent variables and the manifest observations (items), i.e., the estimated factor structure, using plsLoadings(MODEL). We see that the items have positive and moderate to high loadings, and are similar in magnitude within each latent variable:

```
> plsLoadings(satPLS.fit)
   Cost Quality Value CSat Repeat
c1  0.39      .      .    .      .
c2  0.82      .      .    .      .
c3  0.78      .      .    .      .
q1     .    0.54      .    .      .
...
```

Each of latent variables has a moderate to strong loading with its manifest variables, so we are reassured that the model reflects those relationships. If a latent variable failed to load significantly—for example, with factor loadings below 0.3 for any manifest variable, or below 0.5 for all of its manifest variables—then we would be concerned about the model, sample size, or reliability of the measures and would conduct further investigation (or, at a minimum, replicate the results, as in Sect. 10.4.3 below).

We now use pathCoeff(MODEL) to examine the structural coefficients between latent variables, which is what we most care about:

```
> pathCoeff(satPLS.fit)
         Cost Quality  Value   CSat Repeat
Cost        .       . -0.196      . -0.393
Quality     .       .  0.323  0.400      .
Value       .       .      .  0.062      .
CSat        .       .      .      .  0.231
Repeat      .       .      .      .      .
```

We see that cost has a negative influence on perceived value and likelihood to repeat purchase, while customer satisfaction has a positive influence on repeat purchase.

10.4.2   Visualizing the Fitted PLS Model*

This section is optional because it detours into modest additional requirements and file handling.

As we have seen, it is convenient to plot the results of structural models and interpret coefficients and models visually. For the PLS model, we can plot the structural coefficients using pathDiagram(MODEL, FILE, full=FALSE, ...) but this does not immediately create a plot within R. Instead, it outputs a .dot file that is then processed by the freely available Graphviz software package to produce a corresponding image as a PDF file [71]. Graphviz is available at http://www.graphviz.org.

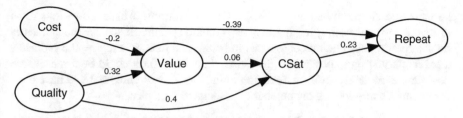

Fig. 10.10 PLS estimate for the repeat purchase model (with N=50)

Once Graphviz is installed, a PDF output file with the paths and coefficients for a fitted PLS model objected may be created with `pathDiagram`:

```
>    pathDiagram(satPLS.fit, file = "satPLSstruc", full = FALSE, digits = 2,
+        edge.labels = "values", output.type = "graphics", graphics.fmt = "pdf")
```

The result is shown in Fig. 10.10. Comparing the values to those obtained from the full sample with CB-SEM (Fig. 10.8) we see that the coefficients are identical in direction (positive or negative) and similar in relative magnitude.

Because PLS models do not assess global model fit, there is not a general way to compare CB-SEM and PLS-SEM results apart from interpreting the models and their implications, so it is not advisable to compare the coefficients directly between Figs. 10.8 and 10.10.

10.4.3 Assessing the PLS-SEM Model

Unlike CB-SEM, PLS-SEM models do not have a summary metric that allows global model assessment and comparison [90]. Instead, at a minimum we recommend three steps:

- Examine the model's coefficients for intelligibility, as we did in Sect. 10.4.1
- Examine the overall R^2 for the model, and determine (largely subjectively) whether sufficient variance is explained to be useful
- Bootstrap the model to examine coefficient stability

It is easy to find R^2 for each of the latent variables using the `rSquared(MODEL)` function:

```
> rSquared(satPLS.fit)
          R-squared
Cost            .
Quality         .
Value         0.18
CSat          0.18
Repeat        0.26
```

A problem with R^2 is that there is no general standard for whether the values are adequate. R^2 is a measure of overall variance explained within each part of the model, but its interpretation is dependent on what you might expect for a given type of data (in other words, it depends on your experience with models in a domain) and it can be increased simply by adding variables (i.e., overfitting). There are various rules of thumb for interpreting R^2, but they are domain specific. If we use the standards for interpreting correlation coefficients in behavioral data, where $r = 0.3$ indicates a moderately strong correlation (Sect. 4.5), then $R^2 > 0.09$ could be a reasonable goal for a moderately strong association in the model, assuming that you have been parsimonious in selecting the number of associated variables.

We recommend a more general approach that does not rely on R^2 and instead uses a bootstrap process to assess coefficient stability. In semPLS, this may be done with the bootsempls() command. We fit the PLS model object to 500 resampled sets of observations:

```
> set.seed(04635)
> satPLS.boot <- bootsempls(satPLS.fit, nboot=500, start="ones")
Resample: 500 Done.
Warning message:
In bootsempls(satPLS.fit, nboot = 500, start = "ones") :
  There were 445 apparent convergence failures;
  these are discarded from the 500 bootstrap replications returned.
> summary(satPLS.boot, type = "bca", level = 0.9)
Call: bootsempls(object = satPLS.fit, nboot = 500, start = "ones")

Lower and upper limits are for the 90 percent bca confidence interval

          Estimate     Bias Std.Error     Lower     Upper
lam_1_1     0.3920  0.00340    0.2337  -0.15589   0.63826
lam_1_2     0.8232 -0.00815    0.0936   0.53064   0.89002
...
beta_1_3   -0.1964 -0.06409    0.1206  -0.33148   0.18705
beta_2_3    0.3231 -0.00695    0.1489   0.09514   0.54770
beta_2_4    0.3996  0.05201    0.1064  -0.10458   0.51023
beta_3_4    0.0623 -0.00157    0.1614  -0.28754   0.29319
beta_1_5   -0.3935 -0.00866    0.1400  -0.53876  -0.00396
beta_4_5    0.2312 -0.00520    0.1533  -0.14174   0.42047
```

In examining the results, we see two indications of problems: a warning that approximately 90% of the PLS iterations failed to converge, and several model coefficients (such as the beta values that reflect the structural model) whose upper and lower bounds include 0, and for which we therefore do not have even *directional* confidence.

We can see the problems visually using a parallel plot. This plots all bootstraps estimates of the structural coefficients so we can see the spread in estimates; we use reflinesAt=0 to add a reference line at 0 in order to see direction, and include varnames to label the Y axis with friendly names:

```
> parallelplot(satPLS.boot, reflinesAt = 0, alpha=0.8,
+     varnames=attr(satPLS.boot$t, "path")[16:21],
+     main="Path coefficients in 500 PLS bootstrap iterations (N=50)")
```

The resulting plot is shown in Fig. 10.11, where the grey lines represent individual bootstrap estimates and the red lines show median (solid line) and outer 95% observed intervals (dotted lines). The estimates fluctuate widely for most of the coefficients. We read this by looking at the spread of estimates along each of the horizontal grid lines representing one model coefficient. For example, the influence of Cost on Repeat purchase is generally estimated to be strongly negative, but several of the estimates hold the relationship to be strongly positive. Additionally, 2 of the 6 coefficient ranges straddle the zero line and thus are not "significantly" different from zero.

Path coefficients in 500 PLS bootstrap iterations (N=50)

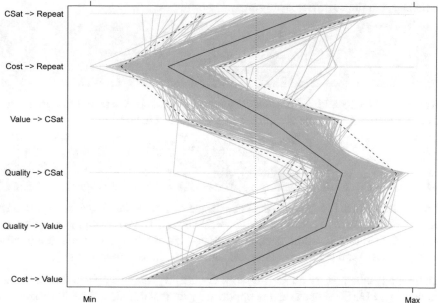

Fig. 10.11 Bootstrapped coefficients for the PLS model, showing divergent estimates for N = 50 observations. Each line plots the six estimated coefficients for one complete bootstrap iteration. The model is unstable with the small sample and 445 of 500 bootstrap iterations failed to converge, so these results come from the other 55 iterations

The convergence problems and bootstrap ranges demonstrate that estimates in our PLS model with N = 50 are unstable. However, whether they are useful in a given situation is a judgment call. Depending on the question at hand and the risks involved, an analyst might conclude that the estimates are not adequately reliable—or alternatively might conclude that, although the instability is not ideal, the estimates are still useful because they are more informative than nothing.

10.4.4   PLS-SEM with the Larger Sample

Is PLS-SEM more stable with the larger sample? We can examine that quickly for the full dataset from Sect. 10.3.1 with no need to respecify the model. The analysis is identical, except for using the full data (satSimData) in the modeling commands:

```
> satPLS.modF <- plsm(data=satSimData, strucmod=satPLSsm, measuremod=satPLSmm)
> satPLS.fitF <- sempls(model=satPLS.mod, data=satSimData)
All 200 observations are valid.
Converged after 7 iterations.
Tolerance: 1e-07
Scheme: centroid
```

We see that the path coefficients for the N = 200 data are similar to the N = 50 estimates, but the coefficients are somewhat different:

```
> pathCoeff(satPLS.fitF)
         Cost Quality Value  CSat Repeat
Cost        .       . -0.27     .  -0.32
Quality     .       .  0.30  0.34      .
Value       .       .     .  0.22      .
CSat        .       .     .     .   0.29
Repeat      .       .     .     .      .
```

As before, we check PLS-SEM stability with a bootstrap. We repeat the procedure from Sect. 10.4.3, this time with the model for the full dataset:

```
> set.seed(04635)
> satPLS.bootF <- bootsempls(satPLS.fitF, nboot=500, start="ones")
Resample: 500 Done.
> parallelplot(satPLS.bootF, reflinesAt = 0, alpha=0.8,
+     varnames=attr(satPLS.bootF$t, "path")[16:21],
+     main="Path coefficients in 500 PLS bootstrap iterations (N=200)")
```

The bootstrap with full N = 200 data converged on all 500 iterations (as opposed to almost 90% failures to converge with N = 50 above). The parallel plot of estimates in Fig. 10.12 shows bootstrap coefficient values that are grouped much more tightly (the gray lines) and confidence intervals that do not cross zero (red lines).

These are results that we could use more confidently than we obtained for N = 50. Either way, PLS-SEM opens up the opportunity for that decision. With the bootstrap

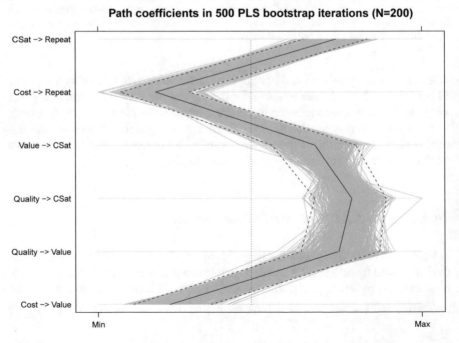

Fig. 10.12 Bootstrapped coefficients for the PLS model with a larger sample, showing tighter estimates with N = 200 observations

we were able to find instability with the smaller sample but stability for the larger. With such capability we can make an informed choice about whether to use imperfect results.

10.5   Key Points

We have seen two examples of complex models in marketing applications: to examine whether a survey instrument has good factor structure, and to estimate the relationship in survey data between customer satisfaction and intent to repurchase a product. Additionally, we saw how such models may be estimated in both covariance and partial least squares approaches.

The following suggestions will help you to succeed at this kind of modeling:

- Learn about structural models and their assumptions; do not fit them blindly. If you become discouraged by mathematical treatments, keep looking; the concepts can be challenging but there are excellent and readable expositions such as Kline [116].
- A structural equation model (SEM) relates observed manifest variables—such as data points or survey responses—to underlying latent variables. It estimates the strength of associations in a proposed model, as well as the degree to which the model fits the observed data.
- SEM may be used to check the factor structure of survey items and their relationships to proposed latent variables; this is known as confirmatory factor analysis (CFA). A good practice in survey research is to assess those relationships; do not simply assume that survey items relate to one another or to latent constructs as expected (Sect. 10.2).
- SEM can also be used to test more complex models than CFA, in which latent variables affect one another and are related to multiple sets of manifest variables.
- Two general approached to SEM are the covariance-based approach (CB-SEM), which attempts to model the relationships among the variables at once and thus is a strong test of the model, and the partial least squares approach (PLS-SEM), which fits parts of the data sequentially and has less stringent requirements.
- After you specify a CB-SEM model, simulate a data set using `simulateData()` from `lavaan` with reasonable guesses as to variable loadings. Use the simulated data to determine whether your model is likely to converge for the sample size you expect.
- Plot your specified model graphically and inspect it carefully to check that it is the model you intended to estimate.
- Whenever possible, specify one or two alternative models and check those in addition to your model. Before accepting a CB-SEM model, use `compareFit()` to demonstrate that your model fits the data better than alternatives.
- If you have data of varying quality, nominal categories, small sample, or problems converging a CB-SEM model, consider partial least squares SEM (PLS-SEM).

- For PLS-SEM, use a bootstrap procedure (such as `bootsempls()` in the `semPLS` package) to examine the stability of coefficients.

10.6 Learning More*

Structural models are a complex topic, and this chapter is intended primarily to demonstrate R's capability for experienced SEM users while inspiring others to learn more. To use SEM well, you will need substantial background in addition to this overview. For CB-SEM, an excellent text is Kline's *Principles and Practice of Structural Equation Modeling* [116]. Kline presents a social science perspective that is similar to many marketing applications, especially for application to survey data.

A guide to SEM models in R using the `lavaan` package is Beaujean [9]. The combination of Kline's *Principles* [116] for general concepts along with Beaujean's guide to implementation in R would provide a thorough grounding in SEM with R.

As you learn more about structural models, you will encounter SEM traditions that reflect a diversity of statistical foundations and applications. One difference involves model specification. The *Lisrel* tradition—named after one of the first SEM software programs [110, 111]—is exemplified in Iacobucci's article [104] and presents models in terms of matrix algebra and Greek lettering. This is a very precise way to specify models but is difficult for non-specialists. An alternative is the *Mplus* tradition—also named after a software program—which uses simpler equation style specifications. We generally recommend marketers to start with the latter kind of model specification, as we did in the present chapter.

PLS-SEM is popular for marketing applications but, unlike the case with CB-SEM, to date there have been few sources to learn about it. A paper from Hair et al. describes how to do PLS-SEM appropriately [90]. At the time of writing, other general references on PLS-SEM included a textbook [91] and a paper presenting an overview of marketing applications [96].

In R, there are several packages available for SEM. In this chapter we used the `lavaan` package [166] for CB-SEM and the `semPLS` package [141] for PLS-SEM. One of the earliest and widely used packages for SEM is the `sem` package [63], which has many examples available online for various models and situations (e.g., [61]). The OpenMx Project provides a powerful system for SEM in the `OpenMx` package [14].

10.7 Exercises

10.7.1 Brand Data for Confirmatory Factor Analysis Exercises

For the CFA exercises, we will use a second simulated sample for "PRST" ratings (see Sect. 8.8). The structure is identical to the data set in those exercises, but it is a new sample and omits product brand. First we load the data from a local or online location:

```
> prst2 <- read.csv("https://goo.gl/BTxyFB") # online
# prst2 <- read.csv("chapter10-cfa.csv")  # local alternative
> summary(prst2)
   Adaptable        BestValue        CuttingEdge       Delightful
 Min.   :1.00    Min.   :1.00    Min.   :1.000    Min.   :1.000   ...
 1st Qu.:3.00    1st Qu.:3.00    1st Qu.:3.000    1st Qu.:3.000   ...
 Median :4.00    Median :4.00    Median :4.000    Median :4.000   ...
 Mean   :4.13    Mean   :3.73    Mean   :3.812    Mean   :4.277   ...
```

10.7.2 Exercises for Confirmatory Factor Analysis

1. Plot a correlation matrix for the adjectives in the new data set, prst2. Is it similar in structure to the results of exploratory factor analysis in Sect. 8.8?
2. Using the EFA model from the Sect. 8.8 exercises as a guide, define a lavaan model for a 3-factor solution. Fit that model to the prst2 data for confirmatory factor analysis, and interpret the fit. (Note: in the lavaan model, consider setting the highest-loaded item loading to 1.0 for each factor's latent variable; this can help anchor the model. Also note that Adaptable may need to load on two factors.)
3. Plot the 3-factor model.
4. Now find an alternative 2-factor EFA model for the prst1 *exploratory* data. Define that as a CFA model for lavaan and fit it to the new prst2 confirmatory data. You will need to define a model that you think is a reasonable 2-factor model.
5. Compare the 2-factor model fit to the 3-factor model fit. Which model is preferable?

10.7.3 Purchase Intention Data for Structural Equation Model Exercises

For these exercises, we use a new simulated data set to model likelihood to purchase a new product. Respondents have rated the new product on three of the same adjectives used in the PRST exercises above: Ease of Use, Cutting Edge, and Best Value. Additionally, there are ratings for satisfaction with the previous model of the product, likelihood to purchase the new product, and satisfaction with the new product's cost. This gives a total of six manifest items. In the exercises, you will define structural models using those items along with latent variables, and assess fit with the data. First, load the data:

```
> intent.df <- read.csv("https://goo.gl/6U5aYr")   # online
# intent.df <- read.csv("chapter10-sem.csv")   # local alternative
> summary(intent.df)
   iCuttingEdge        iEaseOfUse         iBestValue       iPreviousModelRating
 Min.    : 1.000    Min.    : 1.000    Min.    : 1.000    Min.    : 1.000     ...
 1st Qu.: 5.000    1st Qu.: 4.750    1st Qu.: 4.000    1st Qu.: 4.000     ...
 Median : 6.000    Median : 6.000    Median : 6.000    Median : 5.000     ...
 Mean    : 6.072    Mean    : 5.643    Mean    : 5.645    Mean    : 5.355     ...
```

In this data set, all column names begin with the letter "i," such as "iCuttingEdge." This is to help distinguish the survey *items* (manifest variables) from latent variables that you will define for the SEM models.

10.7.4 Exercises for Structural Equation Models and PLS SEM

Structural Equation Models

6. Define an SEM model for the product ratings in `intent.df` using `lavaan` syntax. The model has three latent variables: *ProductRating*, *PurchaseInterest*, and *PurchaseIntent*. The core idea is that *ProductRating* points to *PurchaseInterest*, and that points further to *PurchaseIntent*. *ProductRating* is manifest as the items `iCuttingEdge`, `iEaseOfUse`, and `iBestValue`. *PurchaseInterest* combines *ProductRating* with the manifest item `iPreviousModelRating`. *PurchaseIntent* combines *PurchaseInterest* with item `iCost` and the manifest rating item `iPurchaseIntent`. Your question is this: what are the most important items related to the latent variable for purchase intent? Define this model and fit it to the intent data.

7. Now define a simpler model and compare it. For the simpler model, define *ProductRating* as manifest in `iBestValue` and `iEaseOfUse`. *PurchaseIntent* should combine *ProductRating* with `iCost` and `iPurchaseIntent`. There will be no *PurchaseInterest* latent variable. Fit this model, and visualize and interpret the result. What are the drivers of purchase intent here? Is this model preferable to the previous model? (Note: the question of whether it is better depends on interpretation, not an assessment of fit; the models use different variables, so most fit indices are not directly comparable.)

8. *(Stretch exercise.)* Define a few other plausible models. Does one of them fit the data better? Should you therefore conclude that it is the right model? What would be your next steps, if you wanted to assert that?

Partial Least Squares SEM

For these exercises, use the `intent.df` data as in the SEM exercises above.

9. Sample $N = 30$ observations from the purchase intent data, and fit the shorter SEM model from Exercise 7 to those data using regular, covariance-based SEM (i.e., `sem()`). (Note: results may vary by the random sample you take.) What do you observe? How do the estimates compare to the full sample results above?
10. Use Partial Least Squares SEM to estimate the model. How do the results of PLS-SEM compare to the covariance-based SEM estimates for drivers of purchase intent?
11. Using the $N = 30$ sample, bootstrap the PLS-SEM estimates for 200 runs. How large are the ranges for the parameter estimates? What does that tell you about the stability of results from this sample?
12. Take a larger sample for $N = 200$ and repeat the PLS-SEM bootstrap. How stable are the estimates with the larger sample? How do the estimated ranges of values compare to those from the $N = 30$ sample?
13. *(Stretch exercise that requires you to explore some new R graphing commands.)* A PLS-SEM bootstrap object collects all of the bootstrapped estimates for the model parameters. Compare the $N = 30$ versus $N = 200$ bootstraps with a graph for the best estimate and 95% observed intervals. Where do the estimates mostly agree or substantially disagree? (Hint: there are many ways to visualize the results. One approach is to compile the estimates for both sets and use `stat_summary()` from the `ggplot2` package.)

Chapter 11
Segmentation: Clustering and Classification

In this chapter, we tackle a canonical marketing research problem: finding, assessing, and predicting customer segments. In previous chapters we've seen how to assess relationships in the data (Chap. 4), compare groups (Chap. 5), and assess complex multivariate models (Chap. 10). In a real segmentation project, one would use those methods to ensure that data has appropriate multivariate structure, and then begin segmentation analysis.

Segmentation is not a well-defined process and analysts vary in their definitions of segmentation as well as their approaches and philosophy. The model in this chapter demonstrates our approach using basic models in R. As always, this should be supplemented by readings that we suggest at the end of the chapter.

We start with a warning: we have definite opinions about segmentation and what we believe are common misunderstandings and poor practices. We hope you'll be convinced by our views—but even if not, the methods here will be useful to you.

11.1 Segmentation Philosophy

The general goal of market segmentation is to find groups of customers that differ in important ways associated with product interest, market participation, or response to marketing efforts. By understanding the differences among groups, a marketer can make better strategic choices about opportunities, product definition, and positioning, and can engage in more effective promotion.

© Springer Nature Switzerland AG 2019   299
C. Chapman and E. M. Feit, *R For Marketing Research and Analytics*, Use R!,
https://doi.org/10.1007/978-3-030-14316-9_11

11.1.1   The Difficulty of Segmentation

The definition of segmentation above is a textbook description and does not reflect what is most difficult in a segmentation project: finding actionable business outcomes. It is not particularly difficult to find *groups* within consumer data; indeed, in this chapter we see several ways to do this, all of which "succeed" according to one statistical criterion or another. Rather, the difficulty is to ensure that the outcome is *meaningful* for a particular business need.

It is outside the range of this book to address the question of business need in general. However, we suggest that you ask a few questions along the following lines. If you were to find segments, what would you do about them? Would anyone in your organization use them? Why and how? Are the differences found large enough to be meaningful for your business? Among various solutions you might find, are there organizational efforts or politics that would make one solution more or less influential than another?

There is no magic bullet to find the "right" answer. In computer science the *no free lunch theorem* says that "for both static and time-dependent optimization problems, the average performance of any pair of algorithms across all possible problems is identical [204]." For segmentation this means that there is no all-purpose method or algorithm that is a priori preferable to others. This does not mean that the choice of a method is irrelevant or arbitrary; rather, one cannot necessarily determine in advance which approach will work best for a novel problem. As a form of optimization, segmentation is likely to require an iterative approach that successively tests and improves its answer to a business need.

Segmentation is like slicing a pie, and any pie might be sliced in an infinite number of ways. Your task as an analyst is to consider the infinity of possible data that might be gathered, the infinity of possible groupings of that data, and the infinity of possible business questions that might be addressed. Your goal is to find a solution within those infinities that represents real differences in the data and that informs and influences real business decisions.

Statistical methods are only part of the answer. It often happens that a "stronger" statistical solution poses complexity that makes it impossible to implement in a business context while a slightly "weaker" solution illuminates the data with a clear story and fits the business context so well that it can have broad influence.

To maximize chances of finding such a model, we recommend that an analyst expects—and prepares management to understand—two things. First, a segmentation project is not a matter of "running a segmentation study" or "doing segmentation analysis on the data." Rather, it is likely to take multiple rounds of data collection and analysis to determine the important data that should be collected in the first place, to refine and test the solutions, and to conduct rounds of interpretation with business stakeholders to ensure that the results are actionable.

11.1.2 Segmentation as Clustering and Classification

In this chapter, we demonstrate several methods in R that will get you started with segmentation analysis. We explore two distinct yet related areas of statistics: *clustering* or *cluster analysis* and *classification*. These are the primary branches of what is sometimes called *statistical learning*, i.e., learning from data through statistical model fitting.

A key distinction in statistical learning is whether the method is *supervised* or *unsupervised*. In *supervised learning*, a model is presented with observations whose outcome status (dependent variable) is known, with a goal to predict that outcome from the independent variables. For example, we might use data from previous direct marketing campaigns—with a known outcome of whether each target responded or not, plus other predictor variables—to fit a model that predicts likelihood of response in a new campaign. We refer to this process as *classification*.

In *unsupervised learning* we do not know the outcome groupings but are attempting to discover them from structure in the data. For instance, we might explore a direct marketing campaign and ask, "Are there groups that differ in how and when they respond to offers? If so, what are the characteristics of those groups?" We use the term *clustering* for this approach.

Clustering and classification are both useful in segmentation projects. Stakeholders often view segmentation as discovering groups in the data in order to derive new insight about customers. This obviously suggests clustering approaches because the possible customer groups are unknown. Still, classification approaches are also useful in such projects for at least two reasons: there may be outcome variables of interest that are known (such as observed in-market response) that one wishes to predict from segment membership, and if you use clustering to discover groups you will probably want to predict (i.e., classify) future responses into those groups. Thus, we view clustering and classification as complementary approaches.

A topic we do not address is how to determine what data to use for clustering, the observed *basis variables* that go into the model. That is primarily a choice based on business need, strategy, and data availability. Still, you can use the methods here to evaluate different sets of such variables. If you have a large number of measures available and need to determine which ones are most important, the *variable importance* assessment method we review in Sect. 11.4.3 might assist. Aside from that, we assume in this chapter that the basis variables have been determined (and we use the customer relationship data from Chap. 5).

There are hundreds of books, thousands of articles, and scores of R packages for clustering and classification methods, all of which propose hundreds of approaches with—as we noted above—no single "best" method. This chapter cannot cover clustering or classification in a comprehensive way, but we can give an introduction that will get you started, teach you the basics, accelerate your learning, and help you avoid some traps. As you will see, in most cases the process of fitting such models in R is extremely similar from model to model.

11.2 Segmentation Data

We use the segmentation data (object `seg.df`) from Chap. 5. If you saved that data
in Sect. 5.1.4, you can reload it:

```
> load("~/segdf-Rintro-Ch5.RData")
> seg.raw <- seg.df
> seg.df  <- seg.raw[ , -7]   # remove the known segment assignments
```

Otherwise, you could download the data set from the book website:

```
> seg.raw <- read.csv("http://goo.gl/qw303p")
> seg.df  <- seg.raw[ , -7]      # remove the known segment assignments
```

As you may recall from Chap. 5, this is a simulated data with four identified segments
of customers for a subscription product, and contains a few variables that are similar
to data from typical consumer surveys. Each observation has the simulated respondent's age, gender, household income, number of kids, home ownership, subscription
status, and assigned segment membership. In Chap. 5, we saw how to simulate this
data and how to examine group differences within it. Other data sources that are
often used for segmentation are customer relationship management (CRM) records,
attitudinal surveys, product purchase and usage, and most generally, any data set
with observations about customers.

The original data `seg.raw` contains "known" segment assignments that have been
provided for the data from some other source (as might occur from some human
coding process). Because our task here is to discover segments, we create a copy
`seg.df` that omits those assignments (omitting column 7), so we don't accidentally
include the known values when exploring applying segmentation methods. (Later,
in the classification section, we will use the correct assignments because they are
needed to train the classification models.)

We check the data after loading:

```
> summary(seg.df)
      age             gender        income          kids          ownHome   ...
 Min.   :19.26   Female:157   Min.   : -5183   Min.   :0.00   ownNo :159 ...
 1st Qu.:33.01   Male  :143   1st Qu.: 39656   1st Qu.:0.00   ownYes:141 ...
```

We use the subscription segment data in this chapter for two purposes: to examine
clustering methods that find intrinsic groupings (unsupervised learning), and to show
how classification methods learn to predict group membership from known cases
(supervised learning).

11.3 Clustering

We examine four clustering procedures that are illustrative of the hundreds of available methods. You'll see that the general procedure for finding and evaluating clusters
in R is similar across the methods.

To begin, we review two *distance-based* clustering methods, hclust() and kmeans(). Distance-based methods attempt to find groups that minimize the distance between members within the group, while maximizing the distance of members from other groups. hclust() does this by modeling the data in a tree structure, while kmeans() uses group centroids (central points).

Then we examine *model-based* clustering methods, Mclust() and poLCA(). Model-based methods view the data as a mixture of groups sampled from different distributions, but whose original distribution and group membership has been "lost" (i.e., is unknown). These methods attempt to model the data such that the observed variance can be best represented by a small number of groups with specific distribution characteristics such as different means and standard deviations. Mclust() models the data as a mixture of Gaussian (normal) variables, while poLCA() uses a latent class model with categorical (nominal) variables.

11.3.1 The Steps of Clustering

Clustering analysis requires two stages: finding a proposed cluster solution and evaluating that solution for one's business needs. For each method we go through the following steps:

- Transform the data if needed for a particular clustering method; for instance, some methods require all numeric data (e.g., kmeans(), Mclust()) or all categorical data (e.g., poLCA()).
- Compute a distance matrix if needed; some methods require a precomputed matrix of similarity in order to group observations (e.g., hclust()).
- Apply the clustering method and save its result to an object. For some methods this requires specifying the number (K) of groups desired (e.g., kmeans(), poLCA()).
- For some methods, further parse the object to obtain a solution with K groups (e.g., hclust()).
- Examine the solution in the model object with regards to the underlying data, and consider whether it answers a business question.

As we've already argued, the most difficult part of that process is the last step: establishing whether a proposed statistical solution answers a business need. Ultimately, a cluster solution is largely just a vector of purported group assignments for each observation, such as "1, 1, 4, 3, 2, 3, 2, 2, 4, 1, 4 ...." It is up to you to figure out whether that tells a meaningful story for your data.

A Quick Check Function

We recommend that you think hard about how you would know whether the solution—assignments of observations to groups—that is proposed by a clustering method is useful for your business problem. Just because some grouping is proposed by an algorithm does not mean that it will help your business. One way we often approach this is to write a simple function that summarizes the data and allows quick inspection of the high-level differences between groups.

A segment inspection function may be complex depending on the business need and might even include plotting as well as data summarization. For purposes here we use a simple function that reports the mean by group. We use mean here instead of a more robust metric such as median because we have several binary variables and mean() easily shows the mixture proportion for them (i.e., 1.5 means a 50% mix of 1 and 2). A very simple function is:

```
> seg.summ <- function(data, groups) {
+   aggregate(data, list(groups), function(x) mean(as.numeric(x)))
+ }
```

This function first splits the data by reported group (aggregate(..., list (groups), ...)). An anonymous function (function(x) ...) then converts all of a group's data to numeric (as.numeric(x)) and computes its mean(). Here's an example using the known segments from seg.raw:

```
> seg.summ(seg.df, seg.raw$Segment)
     Group.1      age gender    income      kids  ownHome subscribe
1   Moving up 36.33114    1.30 53090.97 1.914286 1.328571     1.200
2  Suburb mix 39.92815    1.52 55033.82 1.920000 1.480000     1.060
3   Travelers 57.87088    1.50 62213.94 0.000000 1.750000     1.125
4   Urban hip 23.88459    1.60 21681.93 1.100000 1.200000     1.200
```

This simple function will help us to inspect cluster solutions efficiently. It is not intended to be a substitute for detailed analysis—and it takes shortcuts such as treating categorical variables as numbers, which is inadvisable except for analysts who understand what they're doing—yet it provides a quick first check of whether there is something interesting (or uninteresting) occurring in a solution.

With a summary function of this kind we are easily able to answer the following questions related to the business value of a proposed solution:

- Are there obvious differences in group means?
- Does the differentiation point to some underlying story to tell?
- Do we see immediately odd results such as a mean equal to the value of one data level?

Why not just use a standard R function such as by() or aggregate()? There are several reasons. Writing our own function allows us to minimize typing by providing a short command. By providing a consistent and simple interface, it reduces risk of error. And it is extensible; as an analysis proceeds, we might decide to add to the function, expanding it to report variance metrics or to plot results, without needing to change how we invoke it.

11.3.2 Hierarchical Clustering: hclust() Basics

Hierarchical clustering is a popular method that groups observations according to their similarity. The hclust() method is one way to perform this analysis in R. hclust() is a distance-based algorithm that operates on a *dissimilarity* matrix, an N-by-N matrix that reports a metric for the *distance* between each pair of observations.

The hierarchical clustering method beings with each observation in its own cluster. It then successively joins neighboring observations or clusters one at a time according to their distances from one another, and continues this until all observations are linked. This process of repeatedly joining observations and groups is known as an *agglomerative* method. Because it is both very popular and exemplary of other methods, we present hierarchical clustering in more detail than the other clustering algorithms.

The primary information in hierarchical clustering is the *distance* between observations. There are many ways to compute distance, and we start by examining the best-known method, the *Euclidean distance*. For two observations (vectors) X and Y, the Euclidean distance d is:

$$d = \sqrt{\sum (X - Y)^2} \tag{11.1}$$

For single pairs of observations, such as $X = \{1, 2, 3\}$ and $Y = \{2, 3, 2\}$ we can compute the distance easily in R:

```
> c(1,2,3) - c(2,3,2)              # vector of differences
[1] -1 -1  1
> sum((c(1,2,3) - c(2,3,2))^2)     # the sum of squared differences
[1] 3
> sqrt(sum((c(1,2,3) - c(2,3,2))^2))  # root sum of squares
[1] 1.732051
```

When there are many pairs, this can be done with the dist() function. Let's check it first for the simple X, Y example, using rbind() to group these vectors as observations (rows):

```
> dist(rbind(c(1,2,3), c(2,3,2)))
         1
2 1.732051
```

The row and column labels tell us that dist() is returning a matrix for observation 1 (column) by observation 2 (row).

A limitation is that Euclidean distance is only defined when observations are numeric. In our data seg.df it is impossible to compute the distance between Male and Female (a fact many people suspect even before studying statistics). If we did not care about the factor variables, then we could compute Euclidean distance using only the numeric columns.

For example, we can select the three numeric columns in seg.df, calculate the distances, and then look at a matrix for just the first 5 observations as follows:

```
> d <- dist(seg.df[, c("age", "income", "kids")])
> as.matrix(d)[1:5, 1:5]
           1          2          3          4          5
1      0.000  13936.531   5313.626  31559.178  29870.205
2  13936.531      0.000   8622.906  45495.698  43806.727
3   5313.626   8622.906      0.000  36872.800  35183.828
4  31559.178  45495.698  36872.800      0.000   1688.977
5  29870.205  43806.727  35183.828   1688.977      0.000
```

As expected, the distance matrix is symmetric, and the distance of an observation from itself is 0.

For seg.df we cannot assume that factor variables are irrelevant to our cluster definitions; it is better to use *all* the data. The daisy() function in the cluster package [133] works with mixed data types by rescaling the values, so we use that instead of Euclidean distance:

```
> library(cluster)                       # daisy works with mixed data types
> seg.dist <- daisy(seg.df)
```

We inspect the distances computed by daisy() by coercing the resulting object to a matrix and selecting the first few rows and columns:

```
> as.matrix(seg.dist)[1:5, 1:5]
           1          2          3          4          5
1  0.0000000  0.2532815  0.2329028  0.2617250  0.4161338
2  0.2532815  0.0000000  0.0679978  0.4129493  0.3014468
3  0.2329028  0.0679978  0.0000000  0.4246012  0.2932957
4  0.2617250  0.4129493  0.4246012  0.0000000  0.2265436
5  0.4161338  0.3014468  0.2932957  0.2265436  0.0000000
```

The distances look reasonable (zeroes on the diagonal, symmetric, scaled [0, 1]) so we proceed to the hierarchical cluster method itself, invoking hclust() on the dissimilarity matrix:

```
> seg.hc <- hclust(seg.dist, method="complete")
```

We use the *complete* linkage method, which evaluates the distance between every member when combining observations and groups.

A simple call to plot() will draw the hclust object:

```
> plot(seg.hc)
```

The resulting tree for all N = 300 observations of seg.df is shown in Fig. 11.1. A hierarchical dendrogram is interpreted primarily by height and where observations are joined. The height represents the dissimilarity between elements that are joined. At the lowest level of the tree in Fig. 11.1 we see that elements are combined into small groups of 2–10 that are relatively similar, and then those groups are

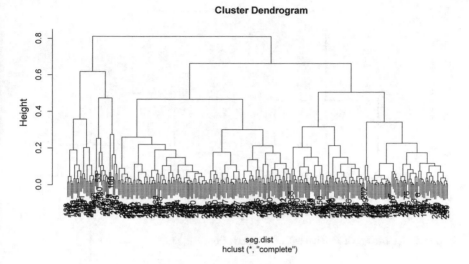

Fig. 11.1 Complete dendrogram for the segmentation data, using `hclust()`

successively combined with less similar groups moving up the tree. The horizontal ordering of branches is not important; branches could exchange places with no change in interpretation.

Figure 11.1 is difficult to read, so it is helpful to zoom in on one section of the chart. We can cut it at a specified location and plot just one branch as follows. We coerce it to a dendrogram object (`as.dendrogram(...)`), cut it at a certain height (`h=...`) and select the resulting branch that we want (`...$lower[[1]]`).

```
> plot(cut(as.dendrogram(seg.hc), h=0.5)$lower[[1]])
```

The result is shown in Fig. 11.2, where we are now able to read the observation labels (which defaults to the row names—usually the row numbers—of observations in the data frame). Each node at the bottom represents one customer, and the brackets show how each has been grouped progressively with other customers.

We can check the similarity of observations by selecting a few rows listed in Fig. 11.2. Observations 101 and 107 are represented as being quite similar because they are linked at a very low height, as are observations 278 and 294. On the other hand, observations 173 and 141 are only joined at the highest level of this branch and thus should be relatively dissimilar. We can check those directly:

```
> seg.df[c(101, 107), ]   # similar
        age gender    income kids ownHome subscribe
101 24.73796   Male 18457.85    1   ownNo    subYes
107 23.19013   Male 17510.28    1   ownNo    subYes
> seg.df[c(278, 294), ]   # similar
        age gender    income kids ownHome subscribe
278 36.23860 Female 46540.88    1   ownNo    subYes
294 35.79961 Female 52352.69    1   ownNo    subYes
```

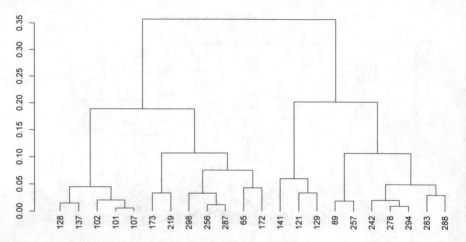

Fig. 11.2 A close up view of the left-most branch from Fig. 11.1

```
> seg.df[c(173, 141), ]   # less similar
         age gender   income kids ownHome subscribe
173 64.70641   Male 45517.15    0   ownNo    subYes
141 25.17703 Female 20125.80    2   ownNo    subYes
```

The first two sets—observations that are neighbors in the dendrogram—are similar
on all variables (age, gender, income, etc.). The third set—observations taken from
widely separated branches—differ substantially on the first four variables.

Finally, we might check one of the goodness-of-fit metrics for a hierarchical cluster solution. One method is the *cophenetic correlation* coefficient (CPCC), which
assesses how well a dendrogram (in this case seg.hc) matches the true distance
metric (seg.dist) [181]. We use cophenetic() to get the distances from the
dendrogram, and compare it to the dist() metrics with cor():

```
> cor(cophenetic(seg.hc), seg.dist)
[1] 0.7682436
```

CPCC is interpreted similarly to Pearson's r. In this case, CPCC > 0.7 indicates
a relatively strong fit, meaning that the hierarchical tree represents the distances
between customers well.

11.3.3 *Hierarchical Clustering Continued: Groups from* hclust()

How do we get specific segment assignments? A dendrogram can be cut into clusters at any height desired, resulting in different numbers of groups. For instance, if
Fig. 11.1 is cut at a height of 0.7 there are K=2 groups (draw a horizontal line at

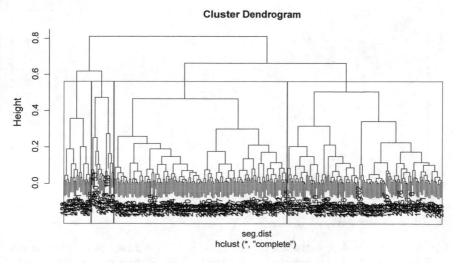

Fig. 11.3 The result of cutting Fig. 11.1 into K = 4 groups

0.7 and count how many branches it intersects; each cluster below is a group), while cutting at height of 0.4 defines K = 7 groups.

Because a dendrogram can be cut at any point, the analyst must specify the number of groups desired. We can see where the dendrogram would be cut by overlaying its `plot()` with `rect.hclust()`, specifying the number of groups we want (k=...):

```
> plot(seg.hc)
> rect.hclust(seg.hc, k=4, border="red")
```

The K = 4 solution is shown in Fig. 11.3.

We obtain the assignment vector for observations using `cutree()`:

```
> seg.hc.segment <- cutree(seg.hc, k=4)      # membership vector for 4 groups
> table(seg.hc.segment)
seg.hc.segment
  1    2    3    4
124  136   18   22
```

We see that groups 1 and 2 dominate the assignment. Note that the class labels (1, 2, 3, 4) are in arbitrary order and are not meaningful in themselves. `seg.hc.segment` is the vector of group assignments.

We use our custom summary function `seg.summ()`, defined above, to inspect the variables in `seg.df` with reference to the four clusters:

```
> seg.summ(seg.df, seg.hc.segment)
  Group.1      age   gender   income      kids  ownHome  subscribe
1       1 40.78456 2.000000 49454.08 1.314516 1.467742          1
2       2 42.03492 1.000000 53759.62 1.235294 1.477941          1
3       3 44.31194 1.388889 52628.42 1.388889 2.000000          2
4       4 35.82935 1.545455 40456.14 1.136364 1.000000          2
```

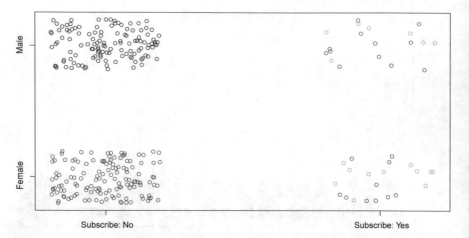

Fig. 11.4 Plotting the 4-segment solution from `hclust()` by gender and subscription status, with color representing segment membership. We see the uninteresting result that non-subscribers are simply divided into two segments purely on the basis of gender

We see that groups 1 and 2 are distinct from 3 and 4 due to subscription status. Among those who do not subscribe, group 1 is all male (`gender=2` as in `levels(seg.df$gender)`) while group 1 is all female. Subscribers are differentiated into those who own a home (group 3) or not (group 4).

Is this interesting from a business point of view? Probably not. Imagine describing the results to a set of executives: "Our advanced hierarchical analysis in R examined consumers who don't yet subscribe and found two segments to target! The segments are known as 'Men' and 'Women.'" Such insight is unlikely to win the analyst a promotion.

We confirm this with a quick plot of `gender` by `subscribe` with all of the observations colored by segment membership. To do this, we use a trick: we convert the factor variables to numeric, and call the `jitter()` function to add a bit of noise and prevent all the cases from being plotted at the same positions (namely at exactly four points: (1, 1), (1, 2), (2, 1), and (2, 2)). We color the points by segment with `col=seg.hc.segment`, and label the axes with more meaningful labels:

```
> plot(jitter(as.numeric(seg.df$gender)) ~
+       jitter(as.numeric(seg.df$subscribe)),
+       col=seg.hc.segment, yaxt="n", xaxt="n", ylab="", xlab="")
> axis(1, at=c(1, 2), labels=c("Subscribe: No", "Subscribe: Yes"))
> axis(2, at=c(1, 2), labels=levels(seg.df$gender))
```

The resulting plot is shown in Fig. 11.4, where we see clearly that the non-subscribers are broken into two segments (colored red and black) that are perfectly correlated with gender. We should point out that such a plot is a quick hack, which we suggest only for rapid inspection and debugging purposes.

Why did hclust() find a result that is so uninteresting? That may be answered in several ways. For one thing, machine learning techniques often take the path of least resistance and serve up obvious results. In this specific case, the scaling in daisy() rescales variables to [0, 1] and this will make two-category factors (gender, subscription status, home ownership) more influential. Overall, this demonstrates why you should expect to try several methods and iterate in order to find something useful.

11.3.4   Mean-Based Clustering: *kmeans ( )*

K-means clustering attempts to find groups that are most compact, in terms of the mean sum-of-squares deviation of each observation from the multivariate center (*centroid*) of its assigned group. Like hierarchical clustering, k-means is a very popular approach.

Because it explicitly computes a mean deviation, k-means clustering relies on Euclidean distance. Thus it is only appropriate for numeric data or data that can be reasonably coerced to numeric. In our seg.df data, we have a mix of numeric and binary factors. Unlike higher-order categorical variables, binary factors can be coerced to numeric with no alteration of meaning.

Although it is not optimal to cluster binary values with k-means, given that we have a mixture of binary and numeric data, we might attempt it. Our first step is to create a variant of seg.df that is recoded to numeric. We make a copy of seg.df and use ifelse() to recode the binary factors:

```
> seg.df.num <- seg.df
> seg.df.num$gender    <- ifelse(seg.df$gender=="Male", 0, 1)
> seg.df.num$ownHome   <- ifelse(seg.df$ownHome=="ownNo", 0, 1)
> seg.df.num$subscribe <- ifelse(seg.df$subscribe=="subNo", 0, 1)
> summary(seg.df.num)
      age               gender             income              kids
 Min.   :19.26    Min.    :0.0000    Min.    :  -5183    Min.    :0.00
 1st Qu.:33.01    1st Qu.:0.0000    1st Qu.: 39656    1st Qu.:0.00
 Median :39.49    Median :1.0000    Median : 52014    Median :1.00
 ...
```

There are several ways to recode data, but ifelse() is simple and explicit for binary data.

We now run the kmeans() algorithm, which specifically requires specifying the number of clusters to find. We ask for four clusters with centers=4:

```
> set.seed(96743)
> seg.k <- kmeans(seg.df.num, centers=4)
```

We use our custom function seg.summ() to do a quick check of the data by proposed group, where cluster assignments are found in the $cluster vector inside the seg.k model:

Fig. 11.5 Boxplot of
income by cluster as found
with kmeans()

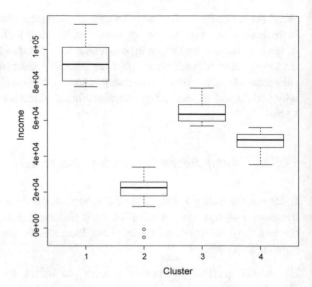

```
> seg.summ(seg.df, seg.k$cluster)
  Group.1      age    gender   income       kids  ownHome subscribe
1       1 56.37245 1.428571 92287.07 0.4285714 1.857143  1.142857
2       2 29.58704 1.571429 21631.79 1.0634921 1.301587  1.158730
3       3 44.42051 1.452632 64703.76 1.2947368 1.421053  1.073684
4       4 42.08381 1.454545 48208.86 1.5041322 1.528926  1.165289
```

Unlike with hclust() we now see some interesting differences; the groups appear
to vary by age, gender, kids, income, and home ownership. For example, we can
visually check the distribution of income according to segment (which kmeans()
stored in seg.k$cluster) using boxplot():

```
> boxplot(seg.df.num$income ~ seg.k$cluster, ylab="Income", xlab="Cluster")
```

The result is Fig. 11.5, which shows substantial differences in income by segment.
Note that in clustering models, the group labels are in arbitrary order, so don't worry
if your solution shows the same pattern with different labels.

We visualize the clusters by plotting them against a dimensional plot. clusplot()
will perform dimensional reduction with principal components or multidimensional
scaling as the data warrant, and then plot the observations with cluster membership
identified (see Chap. 8 to review principal component analysis and plotting). We
use clusplot from the cluster package with arguments to color the groups,
shade the ellipses for group membership, label only the groups (not the individual
points) with labels=4, and omit distance lines between groups (lines=0):

```
> library(cluster)
> clusplot(seg.df, seg.k$cluster, color=TRUE, shade=TRUE,
+          labels=4, lines=0, main="K-means cluster plot")
```

Fig. 11.6 Cluster plot
created with `clusplot()`
for the four group solution
from `kmeans()`. This
shows the observations on a
multidimensional scaling
plot with group membership
identified by the ellipses

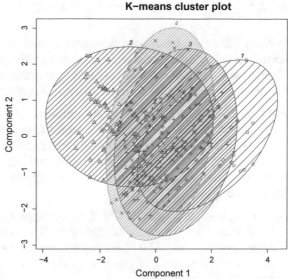

K−means cluster plot

Component 1

These two components explain 48.49 % of the point variability.

The code produces the plot in Fig. 11.6, which plots cluster assignment by color and ellipses against the first two principal components of the predictors (see Sect. 8.2.2). Groups 3 and 4 are largely overlapping (in this dimensional reduction) while group 1 and especially group 2 are modestly differentiated.

Overall, this is a far more interesting cluster solution for our segmentation data than the `hclust()` proposal. The groups here are clearly differentiated on key variables such as age and income. With this information, an analyst might cross-reference the group membership with key variables (as we did using our `seg.summ()` function) and then look at the relative differentiation of the groups (as in Fig. 11.6).

This may suggest a business strategy. In the present case, for instance, we see that group 1 is modestly well-differentiated, and has the highest average income. That may make it a good target for a potential campaign. Many other strategies are possible, too; the key point is that the analysis provides interesting options to consider.

A limitation of k-means analysis is that it requires specifying the number of clusters, and it can be difficult to determine whether one solution is better than another. If we were to use k-means for the present problem, we would repeat the analysis for k = 3, 4, 5 and so forth, and determine which solution gives the most useful result for our business goals.

One might wonder whether the algorithm itself can suggest how many clusters are in the data. Yes! To see that, we turn next to model-based clustering.

11.3.5 Model-Based Clustering: `Mclust()`

The key idea for model-based clustering is that observations come from groups
with different statistical distributions (such as different means and variances). The
algorithms try to find the best set of such underlying distributions to explain the
observed data. We use the `mclust` package [64, 178] to demonstrate this.

Such models are also known as "mixture models" because it is assumed that the data
reflect a mixture of observations drawn from different populations, although we don't
know which population each observation was drawn from. We are trying to estimate
the underlying population parameters and the mixture proportion. `mclust` models
such clusters as being drawn from a mixture of normal (also known as *Gaussian*)
distributions.

As you might guess, because `mclust` models data with normal distributions, it uses
only numeric data. We use the numeric data frame `seg.df.num` that we adapted
for `kmeans()` in Sect. 11.3.4; see that section for the code if needed. The model is
estimated with `Mclust()` (note the capital letter for the fitting function, as opposed
to the package name):

```
> library(mclust)
> seg.mc <- Mclust(seg.df.num)
> summary(seg.mc)
----------------------------------------------------
Gaussian finite mixture model fitted by EM algorithm
----------------------------------------------------

Mclust VEV (ellipsoidal, equal shape) model with 3 components:

 log.likelihood   n  df       BIC        ICL
      -5137.106 300  73 -10690.59 -10690.59

Clustering table:
  1    2    3
163   71   66
```

This tells us that the data are estimated to have 3 clusters (components) with the sizes
as shown in the table. `Mclust()` compared a variety of different mixture shapes
and concluded that an ellipsoidal model (modeling the data as multivariate ellipses)
fit best.

We also see log-likelihood information, which we can use to compare models. We
try a 4-cluster solution by telling `Mclust()` the number of clusters we want with
the `G=4` argument:

```
> seg.mc4 <- Mclust(seg.df.num, G=4)
> summary(seg.mc4)
...
Mclust VII (spherical, varying volume) model with 4 components:

 log.likelihood   n  df       BIC        ICL
     -16862.69 300  31 -33902.19 -33906.18

Clustering table:
  1    2    3    4
104   66   59   71
```

Forcing it to find 4 clusters resulted in quite a different model, with lower log-likelihood and a different multivariate pattern (spherical). Although we cannot be sure from the counts, they suggest that one of the groups in the 3-cluster solution may have been simply split into two.

11.3.6 Comparing Models with BIC()

We compare the 3-cluster and 4-cluster models using the Bayesian Information Criterion (BIC) [159] with BIC(model1, model2):

```
> BIC(seg.mc, seg.mc4)
            df        BIC
seg.mc    73  10690.59
seg.mc4   31  33902.11
```

The difference between the models is greater than 20,000. The key point to interpreting BIC is to remember this: the *lower* the value of BIC, on an infinite number line, the better. BIC of −1000 is better than BIC of −990; and BIC of 60 is better than BIC of 90. The three cluster model is highly preferred with these reformatted data.

There is one important note when interpreting BIC in R: some functions return the *negative* of BIC, which would then have to be interpreted in the opposite direction (i.e., higher is better). We see above that BIC() reports positive values while Mclust() output shows values in the negative direction. If you are ever unsure of the direction to interpret, use the BIC() function and interpret as noted (lower values are better). Alternatively, you could also check the log-likelihood values, where *higher* log-likelihood values are better (e.g., −1000 is better than −1100). Those are shown in the individual Mclust() model summaries (and we see, in this case that the 3-cluster solution with log-likelihood −5137 is preferable to the 4-cluster solution with log-likelihood −16862).

With that in mind, differences in BIC may be interpreted as shown in Table 11.1. Comparing the present models, we see that the Mclust() solution with 3 clusters (BIC = 10690) is a much stronger fit than the model with 4 clusters (BIC = 33902) because it is much lower. That doesn't mean that the 3-cluster model is *correct*; there's no absolute standard for such a statement. Rather, it means that between just these two models, as found by Mclust(), the 3-cluster solution has much stronger evidence based on the data.

You can also run a more exhaustive search to examine all possible solutions up to 9 clusters, across the various mixture models that Mclust() understands (which are beyond our scope to explain in detail here; see [178]). Use mclustBIC() to obtain that:

Table 11.1 Interpretation of the Bayesian Information Criterion (BIC) when comparing two models. Lower BIC is better, and the difference in BIC indicates the strength of evidence. Adapted from Raftery [159], p. 139

BIC difference	Odds of model superiority	Strength of the evidence
0–2	50–75%	Weak
2–6	75–95%	Positive
6–10	95–99%	Strong
>10	>99%	Very strong

```
> mclustBIC(seg.df.num)
fitting ...
  |=================================================================|
    100%
Bayesian Information Criterion (BIC):
          EII        VII        EEI        VEI        EVI        VVI        EEE
1  -37594.16  -37594.16  -11369.71  -11369.71  -11369.71  -11369.71  -11261.94
2  -36337.62  -36278.17  -11312.03  -11228.35         NA         NA  -11302.11
3  -35132.35  -34841.45         NA   10822.91         NA         NA         NA
4  -34321.30  -33902.19         NA         NA         NA         NA         NA
...
          EVE        VEE        VVE        EEV        VEV        EVV        VVV
1  -11261.94  -11261.94  -11261.94  -11261.94  -11261.94  -11261.94  -11261.94
2         NA         NA         NA  -11293.12  -11174.77         NA         NA
3         NA         NA         NA         NA  -10690.59         NA         NA
...
Top 3 models based on the BIC criterion:
     VEV,3      VEI,3      VEV,2
-10690.59  -10822.91  -11174.77
```

In these results, we see that the "VEV" method suggesting 3 clusters was the best fit to the data—among the solutions that could be found—with the highest-valued BIC (desirable because of the negative direction reported here) of −10690.59.

Will the 3-cluster solution provide useful insight for the business? We check the quick summary and plot the clusters:

```
> seg.summ(seg.df, seg.mc$class)
  Group.1      age   gender    income     kids  ownHome subscribe
1       1 44.68018 1.472393 52980.52 1.171779 1.865031  1.245399
2       2 38.02229 1.000000 51550.98 1.422535 1.000000  1.000000
3       3 36.02187 2.000000 45227.51 1.348485 1.000000  1.000000
> library(cluster)
> clusplot(seg.df, seg.mc$class, color=TRUE, shade=TRUE,
+          labels=4, lines=0, main="Model-based cluster plot")
```

The plot is shown in Fig. 11.7.

When we compare the `Mclust()` solution to the one found by `kmeans()`, there are arguments for and against each. The 4-cluster k-means solution had much crisper differentiation on demographics (Sect. 11.3.4). On the other hand, the most clearly differentiated segment (segment 2; cf. Fig. 11.6) had the lowest income and thus might be more difficult to sell to (or not—it depends on the product or service).

Looking closely at the `Mclust()` solution, we see that there is a great degree of overlap, with only one of the groups showing much differentiation (group 1).

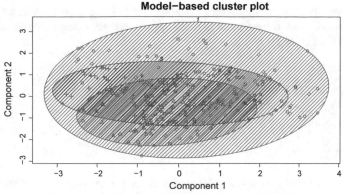

These two components explain 48.49 % of the point variability.

Fig. 11.7 A cluster plot using `clusplot()` for the 3-cluster model from `Mclust()`. The three groups show little differentiation on the first two multivariate dimensional components (*X* and *Y* axes)

They are almost concentric and nested. Also, the demographic differences reported in `seg.summ()` are not particularly interesting. Everyone in Groups 2 and 3 is a non-subscriber, Group 2 is all male, while Group 3 is all female, and there are no subscribers in Groups 2 or 3. The latter point could be useful; if the groups could be predicted (see Sect. 11.4 on classification below), then we might identify target groups to approach or avoid because of their low subscriber numbers. Alternatively, that may turn out to be a feature of the data that is identified by the clustering algorithm—there are subscribers and non-subscribers!—that turns out to be uninteresting. As always, the ultimate value depends on additional investigation, along with consideration of one'e strategy, business case, and modes available to target respondents, and the statistical solution in itself. The statistics provide information about how customers are similar and different, not a definitive answer.

11.3.7   Latent Class Analysis: *poLCA ( )*

Latent class analysis (LCA) is similar to mixture modeling in the assumption that differences are attributable to unobserved groups that one wishes to uncover. In this section we take a look at the `poLCA` package for *po*lytomous (i.e., categorical) LCA [130].

Whereas `mclust` and `kmeans()` work with numeric data, and `hclust()` depends on the distance measure, `poLCA` uses only categorical variables. To demonstrate it here, we adopt an opposite strategy from our procedure with k-means and `mclust` and convert our data `seg.df` to be all categorical data before analyzing it.

There are several approaches to convert numeric data to factors, but for purposes here we simply recode everything as binary with regards to a specified cutting point (for instance, to recode as 1 for income below some cutoff and 2 above that). In the

present case, we split each variable at the median() and recode using ifelse()
and factor() (we'll see a more general approach to recoding numeric values with
cut() in Sect. 12.4.1):

```
> seg.df.cut <- seg.df
> seg.df.cut$age      <- factor(ifelse(seg.df$age < median(seg.df$age), 1, 2))
> seg.df.cut$income <- factor(ifelse(seg.df$income < median(seg.df$income),
+                                       1, 2))
> seg.df.cut$kids     <- factor(ifelse(seg.df$kids < median(seg.df$kids), 1, 2))
> summary(seg.df.cut)
 age          gender        income   kids          ownHome          subscribe
 1:150    Female:157    1:150    1:121    ownNo  :159    subNo  :260
 2:150    Male  :143    2:150    2:179    ownYes:141    subYes:  40
```

With the data in place, we specify the model that we want to fit. poLCA can estimate
complex models with covariates, but for the present analysis we only wish to examine
the effect of cluster membership alone. Thus, we model the dependent variables (all
the observed columns) with respect to the model intercepts (i.e., the cluster positions).
We use with() to save typing, and ~1 to specify a formula with intercepts only:

```
> seg.f <- with(seg.df.cut,
+               cbind(age, gender, income, kids, ownHome, subscribe)~1)
```

Next we fit poLCA models for K = 3 and K = 4 clusters using poLCA(formula,
data, nclass=K):

```
> library(poLCA)
> set.seed(02807)
> seg.LCA3 <- poLCA(seg.f, data=seg.df.cut, nclass=3)
...
> seg.LCA4 <- poLCA(seg.f, data=seg.df.cut, nclass=4)
...
```

poLCA() displays voluminous information by default, which we have omitted.

Which model is better? We use str(seg.LCA3) to discover the bic value within
the object (as shown in the printed output from poLCA()). Comparing the two
models:

```
> seg.LCA4$bic
[1] 2330.043
> seg.LCA3$bic
[1] 2298.767
```

The 3-cluster model shows a lower BIC by 32 and thus a substantially stronger fit to
the data (see Table 11.1). As we've seen, that is not entirely conclusive as to business
utility, so we also examine some other indicators such as the quick summary function
and cluster plots:

```
> seg.summ(seg.df, seg.LCA3$predclass)
  Group.1       age    gender    income      kids  ownHome  subscribe
1       1  28.22385  1.685714  30075.32  1.1285714  1.285714  1.271429
2       2  54.44407  1.576923  60082.47  0.3846154  1.769231  1.105769
3       3  37.47652  1.277778  54977.08  2.0793651  1.325397  1.079365
> table(seg.LCA3$predclass)
```

```
   1   2   3
  70 104 126

> clusplot(seg.df, seg.LCA3$predclass, color=TRUE, shade=TRUE,
+          labels=4, lines=0, main="LCA plot (K=3)")

> seg.summ(seg.df, seg.LCA4$predclass)
  Group.1       age    gender    income        kids   ownHome  subscribe
1       1 36.62554  1.349593  52080.13  2.1951220  1.349593   1.113821
2       2 53.64073  1.535714  60534.17  0.5178571  1.785714   1.098214
3       3 30.22575  1.050000  41361.81  0.0000000  1.350000   1.000000
4       4 27.61506  1.866667  28178.70  1.1777778  1.066667   1.333333
> table(seg.LCA4$predclass)
   1   2   3   4
 123 112  20  45
> clusplot(seg.df, seg.LCA4$predclass, color=TRUE, shade=TRUE,
+          labels=4, lines=0, main="LCA plot (K=4)")
```

The resulting plots from `clusplot()` are shown in Fig. 11.8.

We interpret the LCA results by looking first at the cluster plots (Fig. 11.8). At a high level, it appears that "Group 2" is similar in both solutions. The primary difference is that "Group 3" buried inside the overlapping ellipses in the 4-cluster solution could be viewed as being largely carved out of two larger groups (Groups "2' and "3" as labeled in the 3-cluster solution). This is an approximate interpretation of the data visualization, not a perfect correspondence.

Does the additional group in the 4-cluster solution add anything to our interpretation? Turning to the quick summary from `seg.summ()` in the code block, we see good differentiation of groups in both models. One argument in favor of the 4-cluster solution is that Group 3 has no subscribers (as shown by the mean in the `seg.summ()` results) and is relatively well-identified (mostly younger women with no kids); that might make it an appealing group either for targeting or exclusion, depending on one's strategy. In either case, for these data the differentiation appears to be clearer

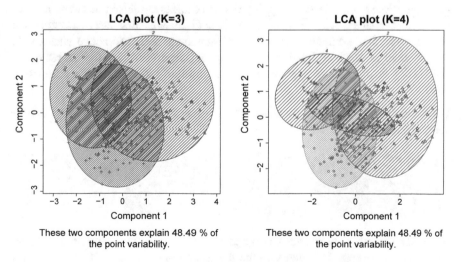

Fig. 11.8 3-cluster and 4-cluster latent class solutions for `seg.df` found by `poLCA()`

than the solutions we found above with Mclust; this demonstrates the value of trying multiple approaches.

As a final note on model-based clustering (and many other clustering methods such as kmeans()), the solutions are partially dependent on the random number seed. It can be useful to run the models with different random seeds and compare the results. This brings us to our next topic: comparing cluster solutions.

11.3.8 Comparing Cluster Solutions

One question we've avoided until now is this: given that we know the real group membership in seg.df, how does it compare to the clustering methods' results? The question is not as simple as counting agreement for two reasons. First, it is not obvious how to match one cluster solution to another because the order of group labels is arbitrary. "Group 1" in one solution might well be called "Group 2" or "Group C" in another solution.

Second, if we solve the matching problem we still need to adjust for chance agreement. Is an agreement rate of 90% good? It depends on the base rate. If you are attempting to predict the gender of each person in a random sample of Japanese citizens, then 90% accuracy is much better than chance (which would be roughly 51%, the proportion of women). On the other hand, if you are attempting to predict whether each respondent speaks Japanese, then 90% accuracy is terrible (just assigning everyone to "Yes" would achieve nearly perfect prediction, because the true rate is over 99%).

The mclust package provides tools to solve both issues. mapClass() solves the matching problem. It examines all permutations of how two sets of class assignments might be related and selects a mapping that maximizes agreement between the two assignment schemes. adjustedRandIndex() likewise matches two assignment schemes and then computes the degree of agreement over and above what might be attributed to "chance" by simply assigning all observations to the largest group [102, 161]. Its magnitude may be interpreted similarly to a standard r correlation coefficient.

We use table() to look at the cross-tabs between the LCA 3-cluster and 4-cluster solutions found above:

```
> table(seg.LCA3$predclass, seg.LCA4$predclass)

      1    2    3    4
  1   13    0   12   45
  2    0  104    0    0
  3  110    8    8    0
```

It would appear that observations assigned to "Group 1" in the 3-cluster solution are split between Groups 1, 3, and 4 in the 4-cluster solution, while "Group 3" maps closely to "Group 1" (in the 4 class solution) and "Group 2" is predominantly the same in both. However, matching groups manually is sometimes unclear and generally error-prone. Instead, we use mapClass(a, b) and adjustedRandIndex(a, b) to compare agreement between the two solutions:

```
> library(mclust)
> mapClass(seg.LCA3$predclass, seg.LCA4$predclass)
$aTOb
$aTOb$'1'
[1] 4
$aTOb$'2'
[1] 2
$aTOb$'3'
[1] 1
... # [similarly for mapping b to a, omitted]
> adjustedRandIndex(seg.LCA3$predclass, seg.LCA4$predclass)
[1] 0.7288822
```

This tells us that "1" in the LCA3 model (a) maps best to "4" in the LCA4 model (b), and so forth. The adjusted Rand index of 0.729 indicates that the match between the two assignment lists is much better than chance. From a business perspective, it also tells us that the 3-cluster and 4-cluster differ modestly from one another, which provides another perspective on choosing between them.

By comparison, R makes it easy to see what happens if we were to test a random assignment scheme:

```
> set.seed(11021)
> random.data <- sample(4, length(seg.LCA4$predclass), replace=TRUE)
> adjustedRandIndex(random.data, seg.LCA4$predclass)
[1] 0.002292031
```

In this case, the adjusted Rand index is near zero, because the match between the clusters is no better than random chance.

Finally we compare the LCA 4-cluster solution to the true segments in seg.raw:

```
> table(seg.raw$Segment, seg.LCA4$predclass)
              1   2   3   4
  Moving up  50   4   8   8
  Suburb mix 62  29   2   7
  Travelers   0  79   1   0
  Urban hip  11   0   9  30

> adjustedRandIndex(seg.raw$Segment, seg.LCA4$predclass)
[1] 0.3513031
```

With a Rand index of 0.35, the LCA solution matches the true segment assignments moderately better than chance alone. In many cases, of course, one would not have identified clusters for comparison; but when they are available from other projects or previous efforts, it is helpful to examine correspondence in this way.

11.3.9   Recap of Clustering

We've covered four statistical methods to identify potential groups of observations in a data set. In the next section we examine the problem of how to predict (classify) observations into groups after those groups have been defined. Before we move to that problem, there are two points that are crucial for success in segmentation projects:

- Different methods are likely to yield different solutions, and in general there is no absolute "right" answer. We recommend to try multiple clustering methods with different potential numbers of clusters.
- The results of segmentation are primarily about business value, and solutions should be evaluated in terms of both model fit (e.g., using BIC()) *and* business utility. Although model fit is an important criterion and should not be overlooked, it is ultimately necessary that an answer can be communicated to and used by stakeholders.

11.4   Classification

Whereas clustering is the process of *discovering* group membership, classification is the *prediction* of membership. In this section we look at two examples of classification: predicting segment membership, and predicting who is likely to subscribe to a service.

Classification uses observations whose status is *known* to derive predictors, and then applies those predictors to new observations. When working with a single data set it is typically split into a *training* set that is used to develop the classification model, and a *test* set that is used to determine performance. It is crucial not to assess performance on the same observations that were used to develop the model.

A classification project typically includes the following steps at a minimum:

- A data set is collected in which group membership for each observation is known or assigned (e.g., assigned by behavioral observation, expert rating, or clustering procedures).
- The data set is split into a training set and a test set. A common pattern is to select 50–80% of the observations for the training set (67% seems to be particularly common), and to assign the remaining observations to the test set.
- A prediction model is built, with a goal to predict membership in the training data as well as possible.
- The resulting model is then assessed for performance using the test data. Performance is assessed to see that it exceeds chance (base rate). Additionally one might assess whether the method performs better than a reasonable alternative (and simpler or better-known) model.

Classification is an even more complex area than clustering, with hundreds of methods and hundreds of R packages, thousands of academic papers each year, and enormous interest with technology and data analytics firms. Our goal is not to cover all of that but to demonstrate the common patterns in R using two of the best-known and most useful classification methods, the naive Bayes and random forest classifiers.

11.4.1 Naive Bayes Classification: `naiveBayes()`

A simple yet powerful classification method is the *Naive Bayes* (NB) classifier. Naive Bayes uses training data to learn the probability of class membership as a function of each predictor variable considered independently (hence "naive"). When applied to new data, class membership is assigned to the category considered to be most likely according to the joint probabilities assigned by the combination of predictors. Several R packages provide NB methods; we use the `e1071` package from the Vienna University of Technology (TU Wien) [139].

The first step in training a classifier is to split the data into *training* and *test* data, which will allow one to check whether the model works on the test data (or is instead overfitted to the training data). We select 65% of the data to use for training with the `sample()` function, and keep the unselected cases as holdout (test) data. Note that we select the training and test cases *not* from `seg.df`, which omitted the previously known segment assignments, but from the full `seg.raw` data frame. Classification requires known segment assignments in order to learn how to assign new values.

```
> set.seed(04625)
> train.prop  <- 0.65
> train.cases <- sample(nrow(seg.raw), nrow(seg.raw)*train.prop)
> seg.df.train <- seg.raw[train.cases, ]
> seg.df.test  <- seg.raw[-train.cases, ]
```

We then train a naive Bayes classifier to predict Segment membership from all other variables in the training data. This is a very simple command:

```
> library(e1071)
> (seg.nb <- naiveBayes(Segment ~ ., data=seg.df.train))
...
Y
 Moving up Suburb mix  Travelers  Urban hip
 0.2512821  0.3025641  0.2615385  0.1846154

Conditional probabilities:
...
            gender
Y                Female       Male
  Moving up   0.6530612  0.3469388
  Suburb mix  0.4576271  0.5423729
  Travelers   0.4705882  0.5294118
  Urban hip   0.3333333  0.6666667
...
```

Examining the summary of the model object seg.nb, we see how the NB model works. First, the a priori likelihood of segment membership—i.e., the estimated odds of membership before any other information is added—is 25.1% for the Moving up segment, 30.2% for the Suburb mix segment, and so forth. Next we see the probabilities conditional on each predictor. In the code above, we show the probabilities for gender conditional on segment. A member of the Moving up segment has a probability of being female of 65.3% in the training data.

The NB classifier starts with the observed probabilities of gender, age, etc., *conditional on segment* found in the training data. It then uses Bayes' Rules to compute the *probability of segment*, conditional on gender, age, etc. This can then be used to estimate segment membership in new observations such as the test data. You have likely seen a description of how Bayes' Rule works, and we will not repeat it here. For details, refer to a general text on Bayesian methods such as Kruschke [120].

Using the classifier model object seg.nb we can predict segment membership in the test data seg.df.test with predict():

```
> (seg.nb.class <- predict(seg.nb, seg.df.test))
  [1] Suburb mix Travelers   Suburb mix Suburb mix Suburb mix Suburb mix
  [7] Moving up  Suburb mix Suburb mix Suburb mix Travelers  Moving up
...
```

We examine the frequencies of predicted membership using table() and prop.table():

```
> prop.table(table(seg.nb.class))
seg.nb.class
 Moving up Suburb mix   Travelers  Urban hip
 0.2285714  0.3047619   0.3428571  0.1238095
```

A cluster plot of these segments against their principal components is created with the following code and shown in Fig. 11.9. In this case we remove the known segment assignments from the data using [, -7] because we are using the NB classifications:

```
> clusplot(seg.df.test[, -7], seg.nb.class, color=TRUE, shade=TRUE,
+          labels=4, lines=0,
+          main="Naive Bayes classification, holdout data")
```

How well did the model perform? We compare the predicted membership to the known segments for the 35% holdout (test) data. First we see the raw agreement rate, which is 80% agreement between predicted and actual segment membership:

```
> mean(seg.df.test$Segment==seg.nb.class)
[1] 0.8
```

As we saw in Sect. 11.3.8, instead of raw agreement, one should assess performance above chance. In this case, we see that NB was able to recover the segments in the test data imperfectly but substantially better than chance:

Fig. 11.9 A cluster plot for the naive Bayes classifier for segment membership predicted in holdout (test) data

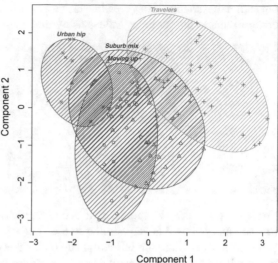

> These two components explain 45.71 % of the point variability.

```
> library(mclust)
> adjustedRandIndex(seg.nb.class, seg.df.test$Segment)
[1] 0.5626787
```

We compare performance for each category using `table()`. The resulting table is known in machine learning as a *confusion matrix*:

```
> table(seg.nb.class, seg.df.test$Segment)

seg.nb.class Moving up Suburb mix Travelers Urban hip
   Moving up        13        10         0         1
   Suburb mix        3        29         0         0
   Travelers         5         2        29         0
   Urban hip         0         0         0        13
```

The NB prediction (shown in the rows) was correct for a majority of observations in each segment, as shown in the diagonal. When we examine individual categories, we see that NB was correct for every proposed member of the Urban hip segment (13 correct out of 13 proposed), and for nearly 90% of the Suburb mix proposals (29 correct out of 32). However, it incorrectly classified 12 of the actual 41 Suburb mix respondents into other segments, and similarly failed to identify 1 of the true Urban hip segment.

This demonstrates the asymmetry of positive prediction (making a correct claim of *inclusion*) versus negative prediction (making a correct claim of *exclusion*). There is likely to be a different business gain for identifying true positives and true negatives, versus the costs of false positives and false negatives. If you have estimates of these costs, you can use the confusion matrix to compute a custom metric for evaluating your classification results.

As we did for clustering, we check the predicted segments' summary values using our summary function. However, because we now have labeled test data, we can also compare that to the summary values using the true membership:

```
> # summary data for proposed segments in the test data
> seg.summ(seg.df.test, seg.nb.class)
     Group.1     age   gender   income      kids  ownHome subscribe   Segment
1  Moving up 34.29258 1.125000 51369.52 2.2916667 1.416667  1.250000  1.541667
2  Suburb mix 41.24653 1.562500 58095.10 2.1875000 1.562500  1.000000  1.906250
3   Travelers 55.08669 1.444444 58634.10 0.0000000 1.666667  1.166667  2.666667
4   Urban hip 23.36047 1.461538 22039.69 0.8461538 1.307692  1.153846  4.000000

> seg.summ(seg.df.test, seg.df.test$Segment)
     Group.1     age   gender   income      kids  ownHome subscribe Segment
1  Moving up 36.88989 1.190476 53582.16 1.4761905 1.333333  1.190476       1
2  Suburb mix 39.61984 1.487805 56341.99 2.2439024 1.585366  1.048780       2
3   Travelers 58.57245 1.448276 59869.24 0.0000000 1.689655  1.206897       3
4   Urban hip 23.71537 1.428571 22700.06 0.9285714 1.357143  1.142857       4
```

Overall, we see that the summary of demographics for the proposed segments (the first summary above) is very similar to the values in the true segments (the second summary). Thus, although NB assigned some observations to the wrong segments, its overall model of the segment descriptive values—at least at the mean values—is similar for the proposed and true segments. By making such a comparison using the test data, we gain confidence that although assignment is not perfect on a case by case basis, the overall group definitions are quite similar.

For naive Bayes models, `predict()` can estimate not only the most likely segment but also the odds of membership in each segment, using the `type="raw"` argument:

```
> predict(seg.nb, seg.df.test, type="raw")
           Moving up   Suburb mix    Travelers    Urban hip
[1,] 4.070780e-01 5.928052e-01 4.848358e-05 6.832328e-05
[2,] 2.715183e-04 2.422066e-03 9.973064e-01 6.143554e-32
[3,] 2.671393e-01 7.326897e-01 1.710510e-04 2.844967e-40
[4,] 2.237216e-01 7.746457e-01 1.632613e-03 7.568258e-37
[5,] 2.255663e-01 7.740280e-01 4.057610e-04 9.030641e-11
...
```

This tells us that Respondent 1 is estimated to be about 59% likely to be a member of Suburb mix, yet 40% likely to be in Moving up. Respondent 2 is estimated nearly 100% likely to be in Travelers. This kind of individual-level detail can suggest which individuals to target according to the difficulty of targeting and the degree of certainty. For high-cost campaigns, we might target only those most certain to be in a segment; whereas for low-cost campaigns, we might target people for second-best segment membership in addition to primary segment assignment.

We conclude that the naive Bayes model works well for the data analyzed here, with performance much better than chance, overall 80% accuracy in segment assignment, and demographics that are similar between the proposed and actual segments. It also provides interpretable individual-level estimation of membership likelihood.

Of course there are times when naive Bayes may not perform well, and it's always a good idea to try multiple methods. For an alternative, we next examine random forest models.

11.4.2 Random Forest Classification: randomForest()

A random forest (RF) classifier does not attempt to fit a single model to data but instead builds an *ensemble* of models that jointly classify the data [21, 129]. RF does this by fitting a large number of classification trees. In order to find an assortment of models, each tree is optimized to fit only *some* of the observations (in our case, customers) using only *some* of the predictors. The ensemble of all trees is the *forest*.

When a new case is predicted, it is predicted by every tree and the final decision is awarded to the *consensus* value that receives the most votes. In this way, a random forest avoids dependencies on precise model specification while remaining resilient in the face of difficult data conditions, such as data that are collinear or wide (more columns than rows). Random forest models perform well across a wide variety of data sets and problems [58].

In R, a random forest may be created with code very similar to that for naive Bayes models. We use the same seg.df.train training data as in Sect. 11.4.1, and call randomForest() from the (surprise!) randomForest package to fit the classifier:

```
> library(randomForest)
> set.seed(98040)
> (seg.rf <- randomForest(Segment ~ ., data=seg.df.train, ntree=3000))
...
        OOB estimate of  error rate: 24.1%
Confusion matrix:
           Moving up Suburb mix Travelers Urban hip class.error
Moving up         29         19         0         1  0.40816327
Suburb mix        20         35         3         1  0.40677966
Travelers          0          3        48         0  0.05882353
Urban hip          0          0         0        36  0.00000000
```

There are two things to note about the call to randomForest(). First, random forests are random to some extent, as the name says. They select variables and subsets of data probabilistically. Thus, we use set.seed() before modeling. Second, we added an argument ntree=3000 to specify the number of trees to create in the forest. It is sometimes suggested to have 5–10 trees per observation for small data sets like the present one.

randomForest() returns a confusion matrix of its own based on the *training* data. How can it do that? Remember that RF fits many trees, where each tree is optimized for a portion of the data. It uses the remainder of the data—known as "out of bag" or OOB data—to assess the tree's performance more generally. In the confusion matrix, we see that the Travelers and Urban hip segments fit well, while the Moving up and Suburb mix segments had 40% error rates in the OOB data. This is an indicator that we may see similar patterns in our holdout data.

What does a random forest look like? Figure 11.10 shows two trees among those we fit above (using visualization code from Patrick Caldon [26]). The complete forest comprises 3000 such trees that differ in structure and the predictors used. When an observation is classified, it is assigned to the group that is predicted by the greatest number of trees within the ensemble.

A cluster plot of predicted segment membership is shown in Fig. 11.11, where we omit the known segment assignments in column 7 of `seg.df.test` because we want to see the differences on the baseline variables on the basis of segments identified in the RF model:

```
> seg.rf.class <- predict(seg.rf, seg.df.test) # predicted classes
> library(cluster)
> clusplot(seg.df.test[, -7], seg.rf.class, color=TRUE, shade=TRUE,
+         labels=4, lines=0, main="Random Forest classification, holdout data")
```

The RF clusters in Fig. 11.11 are quite similar in shape to those found by naive Bayes in Fig. 11.9, with respect to the principal components axes.

It is possible to inspect the distribution of predictions for individual cases. Add the `predict.all=TRUE` argument to the `predict()` call to get the estimate of every tree for every case in the test data. These are saved in the `$individual` element of the result object, where each row collects the predictions for one case, across all trees (on the columns). To see how this works, we `apply()` the `table()` function—wrapping `prop.table()` around it for proportions—to summarize the first five cases' predictions, as follows. Your proportions may differ slightly, depending on the random number seed:

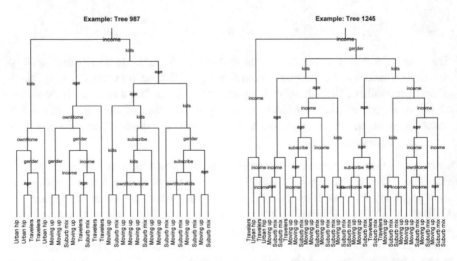

Fig. 11.10 Two examples among the 3000 trees in the ensemble found by `randomForest()` for segment prediction in `seg.df`. The trees differ substantially in structure and variable usage. No single tree is expected to be a particularly good predictor in itself, yet the ensemble of all trees may predict well in aggregate by voting on the assignment of observations to outcome groups

Fig. 11.11 A cluster plot for the random forest solution for segment membership predicted in holdout (test) data

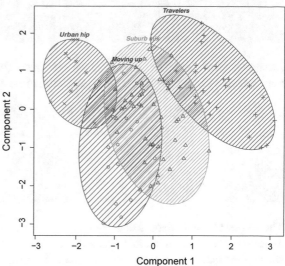

Random Forest classification, holdout data

These two components explain 45.71 % of the point variability.

```
> seg.rf.class.all <- predict(seg.rf, seg.df.test, predict.all=TRUE)
> apply(seg.rf.class.all$individual[1:5, ], 1,
+       function(x) prop.table(table(x)))
$`2`
x
 Moving up Suburb mix   Travelers   Urban hip
0.40766667 0.45533333  0.04166667  0.09533333
$`3`
x
   Moving up  Suburb mix    Travelers    Urban hip
0.081000000 0.492333333 0.424333333 0.002333333
...
```

Cases 2, 3, 4, and 6 are each assigned to the Suburb mix segment as the most likely class, although only cases 4 and 6 are assigned with an overall majority of the votes (proportion > 0.5). Case 7 is assigned to the Urban hip segment as the most likely, although with only an estimated 37% likelihood of that being its true class. This kind of probabilistic estimate is very valuable when you can multiply it by an estimated cost or value of targeting a group.

The proposed and actual segments are quite similar in the mean values of the variables in our summary function:

```
> seg.summ(seg.df.test, seg.rf.class)      # proposed segments
     Group.1      age   gender   income       kids  ownHome subscribe  Segment
1   Moving up 34.51905 1.142857 51794.56 2.57142857 1.476190 1.285714 1.666667
2 Suburb mix 40.57766 1.476190 57643.68 1.59523810 1.523810 1.000000 1.809524
3   Travelers 59.26118 1.464286 59812.04 0.03571429 1.714286 1.214286 2.892857
4   Urban hip 24.37450 1.500000 21842.73 1.00000000 1.285714 1.142857 3.857143

> seg.summ(seg.df.test, seg.df.test$Segment)  # actual segments
```

```
        Group.1       age    gender    income         kids  ownHome subscribe Segment
1   Moving up 36.88989 1.190476 53582.16 1.4761905 1.333333  1.190476       1
2   Suburb mix 39.61984 1.487805 56341.99 2.2439024 1.585366  1.048780       2
3   Travelers 58.57245 1.448276 59869.24 0.0000000 1.689655  1.206897       3
4   Urban hip 23.71537 1.428571 22700.06 0.9285714 1.357143  1.142857       4
```

As suggested by the OOB assessment we saw above for the training data, a confusion matrix reveals which segments were predicted more accurately:

```
> mean(seg.df.test$Segment==seg.rf.class)
[1] 0.7238095
> table(seg.df.test$Segment, seg.rf.class)
           seg.rf.class
            Moving up Suburb mix Travelers Urban hip
  Moving up         9         11         1         0
  Suburb mix       11         28         1         1
  Travelers         0          3        26         0
  Urban hip         1          0         0        13
```

The segment comparison using mean(.. == ..) calculates that RF correctly assigned 72% of cases to their segments, and the confusion matrix using table() shows that incorrect assignments were mostly in the Moving up and Suburb mix segments.

Finally, we note that the RF model performed substantially better than chance:

```
> library(mclust)
> adjustedRandIndex(seg.df.test$Segment, seg.rf.class)
[1] 0.4527604
```

11.4.3 Random Forest Variable Importance

Random forest models are particularly good for one common marketing problem: estimating the importance of classification variables. Because each tree uses only a subset of variables, RF models are able to handle very *wide* data where there are more—even many, many more—predictor variables than there are observations.

An RF model assesses the importance of a variable in a simple yet powerful way: for each variable, it randomly permutes (sorts) the variable's values, computes the model accuracy in OOB data using the permuted values, and compares that to the accuracy with the real data. If the variable is important, then its performance will degrade when its observed values are randomly permuted. If, however, the model remains just as accurate as it is with real data, then the variable in question is not very important [21].

To estimate importance, run randomForest() with the importance=TRUE argument. We reset the random seed and run RF again:

```
> set.seed(98040)
> (seg.rf <- randomForest(Segment ~ ., data=seg.df.train, ntree=3000,
                          importance=TRUE))
...
> importance(seg.rf)
          Moving up Suburb mix    Travelers Urban hip
age       59.926151  44.013275  122.6900323 86.496891
gender    13.161197  -3.690088   -3.6665717  9.174039
income    22.259442  17.992316   15.8721495 78.262846
kids      18.263661  14.264086   55.5604028  6.410428
ownHome    4.124127  -9.036638   22.6148866 19.842501
subscribe 18.588573   9.460176    0.4312472 -4.130187
          MeanDecreaseAccuracy MeanDecreaseGini
age                 129.354271        62.321942
gender                7.757333         3.356217
income               67.554326        36.212893
kids                 53.827310        20.634224
ownHome              15.964989         4.941645
subscribe            17.858784         3.010284
```

The upper block shows the variable importance by segment. We see for example that age is important for all segments, while gender is not very important. The lower block shows two overall measures of variable importance, the permutation measure of impact on accuracy (MeanDecreaseAccuracy), and an assessment of the variable's ability to assist classification better than chance labeling (MeanDecreaseGini, a measure of *Gini impurity* [21]).

The randomForest package includes varImpPlot() to plot variable importance:

```
> varImpPlot(seg.rf, main="Variable importance by segment")
```

The result is Fig. 11.12. The most important variables in this data set are age, income, and kids.

We plot the importance for variables by segment with information from importance(MODEL). The variable-by-segment data are in the first 4 columns of that object (as shown in the code output above). We transpose it to put segments on the rows and use heatmap.2() to plot the values with color:

```
> library(gplots)
> library(RColorBrewer)
> heatmap.2(t(importance(seg.rf)[ , 1:4]),
+           col=brewer.pal(9, "Blues"),
+           dend="none", trace="none", key=FALSE,
+           margins=c(10, 10),
+           main="Variable importance by segment"
+ )
```

The result is Fig. 11.13. We used the gplots package for heatmap.2(), and RColorBrewer to get a color palette. In the call to heatmap.2(), we specified col=brewer.pal(9, "Blues") to get 9 shades of blue, dend="none", trace="none", key=FALSE to turn off some plot options we didn't want (dendrograms and a legend), and margins=c(10, 10) to adjust the margins and make the axes more readable.

Variable importance by segment

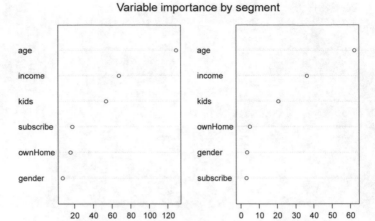

Fig. 11.12   Variable importance for segment classification from `randomForest()`

Fig. 11.13   A heatmap of
variable importance by
segment, produced with
`randomForest()` and
`heatmap.2()`. Darker
shades signify higher
importance for the variable
(column) in differentiating a
segment (row)

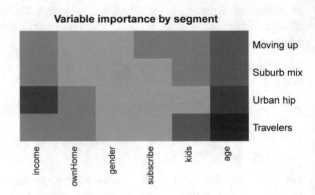

Variable importance by segment

Figure 11.13 highlights the importance of `age` in predicting all of the segments, the
importance of `income` to predict Urban hip, of `kids` to predict Travelers, and the
relatively low importance of the other predictors.

11.5   Prediction: Identifying Potential Customers*

We now turn to another use for classification: to predict potential customers. An
important business question—especially in high-churn categories such as mobile
subscriptions—is how to reach new customers. If we have data on past prospects
that includes potential predictors such as demographics, and an outcome such as
purchase, we can develop a model to identify customers for whom the outcome is

most likely among new prospects. In this section, we use a random forest model and attempt to predict subscription status from our data set `seg.df`.

As usual with classification problems, we split the data into a training sample and a test sample:

```
> set.seed(92118)
> train.prop   <- 0.65
> train.cases <- sample(nrow(seg.df), nrow(seg.df)*train.prop)
> sub.df.train <- seg.df[train.cases, ]
> sub.df.test   <- seg.df[-train.cases, ]
```

Next, we wonder how difficult it will be to identify potential subscribers. Are subscribers in the training set well-differentiated from non-subscribers? We use `clusplot()` to check the differentiation, removing `subscribe` from the data with `[, -6]` and using it instead as the cluster identifier:

```
> clusplot(sub.df.train[, -6], sub.df.train$subscribe, color=TRUE, shade=TRUE,
+          labels=4, lines=0, main="Subscriber clusters, training data")
```

The result in Fig. 11.14 shows that the subscribers and non-subscribers are not well differentiated when plotted against principal components (which reflect almost 56% of the variance in the data). This suggests that the problem will be difficult!

Fig. 11.14 Cluster plot for the subscribers and non-subscribers. The two groups show little differentiation on the principal components, which suggests that classifying respondents into the groups and predicting subscribers could be difficult

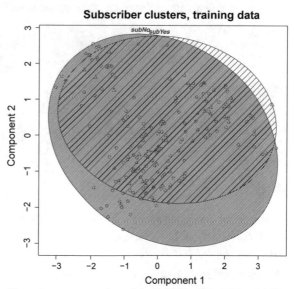

Subscriber clusters, training data

These two components explain 55.83 % of the point variability.

We fit an initial RF model to predict `subscribe`:

```
> library(randomForest)
> set.seed(11954)
> (sub.rf <- randomForest(subscribe ~ ., data=sub.df.train, ntree=3000))
...
        OOB estimate of  error rate: 14.87%
Confusion matrix:
         subNo subYes class.error
subNo      166      4  0.02352941
subYes      25      0  1.00000000
```

The results are not encouraging. Although the error rate might initially sound good at 14.9%, we have 100% error in predicting subscribers (`subYes`) with all 25 misclassified in the OOB data.

Why? This demonstrates the *class imbalance* problem in machine learning. When one category dominates the data, it is very difficult to learn to predict other groups. This frequently arises with small-proportion problems, such as predicting the comparatively rare individuals who will purchase a product, who have a medical condition, who are security threats, and so forth.

A general solution is to balance the classes by sampling more from the small group. In RF models, this can be accomplished by telling the classifier to use a balanced group when it samples data to fit each tree. We use `sampsize=c(25, 25)` to draw an equal number of subscribers and non-subscribers when fitting each tree (selecting $N = 25$ each because we have that many subscribers in the training data; these are sampled with replacement so trees are not all identical):

```
> set.seed(11954)
> (sub.rf <- randomForest(subscribe ~ ., data=sub.df.train, ntree=3000,
+                         sampsize=c(25, 25)) )

Call:
 randomForest(formula = subscribe ~ ., data = sub.df.train, ntree = 3000,
        sampsize = c(25, 25))
                  Type of random forest: classification
                        Number of trees: 3000
No. of variables tried at each split: 2

        OOB estimate of  error rate: 29.74%
Confusion matrix:
         subNo subYes class.error
subNo      128     42   0.2470588
subYes      16      9   0.6400000
```

Although our overall error rate is higher at 29.7%, we are successfully predicting 36% (i.e., 1-0.64) of the subscribers in the OOB data, which is greatly improved over zero.

We use `predict()` to apply the RF model to the holdout data and examine the confusion matrix:

```
> sub.rf.sub <- predict(sub.rf, sub.df.test)
> table(sub.rf.sub, sub.df.test$subscribe)
sub.rf.sub subNo subYes
     subNo    79      9
     subYes   11      6
```

The model correctly predicts 6 of the 15 subscribers in the holdout data, at a cost of incorrectly predicting 11 others as subscribers who are not. That may be an acceptable tradeoff if we are trying to identify prospects who are worth an effort to reach. For instance, in the present case, calling *all* prospects would result in 15/105 successes (14% success rate), while calling the suggested ones would result in 6/17 successes (35%). The ultimate value of each strategy—to call of them or not—depends on the cost of calling versus the value of successful conversion.

Another way to look at the result is this: those that the model said were non-subscribers were almost 90% correct (79 correct out of 88). If the cost to target customers is high, it may be very useful to predict those *not* to target with high accuracy.

Is the model predicting better than chance? We use `adjustedRandIndex()` to find that performance is modestly better than chance, and we confirm this with `cohen.kappa()` in the `psych` package, which provides confidence intervals:

```
> adjustedRandIndex(sub.rf.sub,  sub.df.test$subscribe)
[1]  0.1928668

> library(psych)
> cohen.kappa(cbind(sub.rf.sub,  sub.df.test$subscribe))
Call: cohen.kappa1(x = x, w = w, n.obs = n.obs, alpha = alpha)

Cohen Kappa and Weighted Kappa correlation coefficients and confidence
    boundaries
                     lower  estimate  upper
unweighted kappa  0.025      0.26     0.5
weighted kappa    0.025      0.26     0.5
```

With an adjusted Rand Index $= 0.19$ and Cohen's kappa $= 0.26$ (confidence interval 0.025–0.50), the model identifies subscribers in the test data modestly better than chance.

How could we further improve prediction? We would expect to improve predictive ability if we had more data: additional observations of the subscriber group and additional predictor variables. We have described prediction using a random forest model, but there are many other approaches such as logistic regression (Sect. 9.2) and other machine learning algorithms (see Sect. 11.7).

With a difficult problem—predicting a low incidence group, in data where the groups are not well-differentiated, and with a small sample—the random forest model performs modestly yet perhaps surprisingly well. There are no magic bullets in predictive modeling, but if you use the many tools available in R, avoid pitfalls such as class imbalance, and interpret results in terms of the business action, you will have good odds to achieve positive results.

11.6 Key Points

We addressed segmentation through the lenses of clustering and classification, each of which is a large area of statistics with active research. We examined several varieties of clustering methods and compared them. Once segments or groups are identified, classification methods can help to predict group membership status for new observations.

- The most crucial question in a segmentation project is the business aspect: will the results be useful for the purpose at hand? Will they inspire new strategies for marketing to customers? It is important to try multiple methods and evaluate the utility of their results (cf. Sect. 11.1.1).
- Distance-based clustering methods attempt to group similar observations. We examined hclust() for hierarchical clustering (Sect. 11.3.2) and kmeans() for k-means grouping (Sect. 11.3.4). Distance-based measures rely on having a way to express metric distance, which is a challenge for categorical data.
- Model-based clustering methods attempt to model an underlying distribution that the data express. We examined mclust for model-based clustering of data assumed to be a mix of normal distributions (Sect. 11.3.5), and poLCA for latent-class analysis with categorical data (Sect. 11.3.7).
- A feature of some model-based methods is that they propose the *number* of clusters, unlike distance-based measures in which the analyst must choose a number. We saw how to interpret the number of clusters for the mclust procedure (Sect. 11.3.5).
- The Bayesian Information Criterion (BIC) can identify models with the best statistical fit (Sect. 11.3.5). We recommend that the ultimate decision to use a model's solution be made on the grounds of both statistics (i.e., excellent fit) and the business applicability of the solution (i.e., actionable implications).
- With classification models, data should be split into training and test groups, and models validated on the test (holdout) data (Sect. 11.4).
- We examined naive Bayes models (naiveBayes(), Sect. 11.4.1) and random forest models (randomForest(), Sect. 11.4.2). These—and many other classification methods—have quite similar syntax, making it easy to try and compare models.
- A useful feature of random forest models is their ability to determine variable importance for prediction, even when there are a large number of variables (Sect. 11.4.3).
- A common problem in classification is class imbalance, where one group dominates the observations and makes it difficult to predict the other group. We saw how to correct this for random forest models with the sampsize argument, resulting in a more successful predictive model (Sect. 11.5).

11.7   Learning More*

We covered the basics of clustering and classification in this chapter. There are many places to learn more about those methods and related statistical models. A recommended introduction to the field of statistical learning is James et al., *An Introduction to Statistical Learning* (ISL) [107]. A more advanced treatment of the topics in ISL is Hastie et al., *The Elements of Statistical Learning* [95].

For cluster analysis, a readable text is Everitt et al., *Cluster Analysis* [54]. An introduction to latent class analysis is Collins and Lanza, *Latent Class and Latent Transition Analysis* [37]. If you often use random forests, the package randomForest Explainer can assist with understanding variable importance in greater depth [151].

R has support for a vast number of clustering algorithms that we cannot cover here, but a few are worth mentioning. Mixture modeling is an area with active and exciting work. In addition to mclust that we covered above, other packages of note are flexmix [84, 127], which fits more generalized models, and BoomMix [177], which finds mixtures using a variety of models (normal, Poisson, multinomial, Markov, and others). For very large datasets, the clara algorithm in the standard cluster package is a good starting point.

For classification and especially prediction, in addition to ISL noted above, an applied, practitioner-friendly text is Kuhn and Johnson's *Applied Predictive Modeling*. If you do classification in R, you owe it to yourself and your stakeholders to examine the caret package from Kuhn et al. [122]. caret provides a uniform interface to 149 machine learning and classification algorithms (as of writing time) along with tools to assess performance and streamline other common tasks.

A resource for data when practicing clustering and classification is the mlbench package [128]. mlbench provides data sets from a variety of applications in agriculture, forensics, politics, economics, genomics, engineering, and other areas (although not marketing).

Marketing segmentation has developed approaches and nuances that differ from the typical description in statistics texts. An excellent, modern introduction to concepts of marketing segmentation, with code in R, is Dolnicar, Grün, and Leisch, *Market Segmentation Analysis* [44]. Beyond routine segmentation, there are advanced models to consider. For instance, in addition to the static, cross-sectional models considered in this chapter (where segmentation examines data at just one point in time), one might wish to consider dynamic models that take into account customer lifestyle changes over time. An overview of diverse approaches in marketing is Wedel and Kamakura, *Market Segmentation: Conceptual and Methodological Foundations* [195].

There are various ways to model changes in class membership over time. One approach is latent transition analysis (LTA), described in Collins and Lanza [37]. At the time of writing, LTA was not supported by a specific package in R, but

Hwan Chung provided non-package R code at https://www.msu.edu/~chunghw/
Downloads/R/LTA_R.html. Another approach is a finite state model such as Markov
chain model (cf. Ross [165]). An alternative when change over time is metric (i.e.,
is conceptualized as change in a *dimension* rather than change between *groups*) is
to use longitudinal structural equation modeling or latent growth curve models. A
starting point is the growth() function in the lavaan package that we examined
in Chap. 10.

Finally, a generalized approach that is popular for clustering is cluster ensemble analysis. An ensemble method creates multiple solutions and determines group membership by likelihood or consensus among the solutions. Cluster ensembles are conceptually similar to random forest models for classification that we examined in this
chapter. A package for cluster ensemble analysis is clue [98].

11.8 Exercises

11.8.1 Music Subscription Data for Exercises

Besides the data we provide here, these exercises could be adapted to experiment with
many other data sets from this book, as well as various online sources of machine
learning data. At the time of writing, there were more than 450 data sets available
in the University of California, Irvine, repository at https://archive.ics.uci.edu/ml/
datasets.html.

As written, these exercises use a simulated CRM data set that comprises customer
information for an imagined music subscription service. Load the data as follows:

```
> seg.ex.raw <- read.csv("https://goo.gl/s1KEiF")    # original with segments
> seg.ex      <- seg.ex.raw                           # copy without segments
> seg.ex$Segment <- NULL
> summary(seg.ex.raw)
      age                sex          householdIncome      milesDrive        kidsAtHome
 Min.   :20.00    Male   :480    Min.   : 11042    Min.   :     0    Min.    :0.000
 1st Qu.:28.00    Female :415    1st Qu.: 34383    1st Qu.:10085    1st Qu.:0.000
 ...
   commuteCar        drivingEnthuse      musicEnthuse      subscribeToMusic
 Min.   :0.000    Min.   :1.000    Min.   :1.000    subNo :808
 1st Qu.:0.000    1st Qu.:3.000    1st Qu.:3.000    subYes: 87
 ...
          Segment
 CommuteNews  :170
 KidsAndTalk  :125
 LongDistance : 50
 MusicDriver  :260
 NonCar       :205
 Quiet        : 85
```

The variables comprise the following: age in years; sex as male or female;
householdIncome in US dollars; milesDrive, annual total miles driven in
a car; kidsAtHome, number of children under 18 years old living at home;
commuteCar, whether they regularly commute by car; drivingEnthuse,

reported enthusiasm for driving, according to a survey response, reported on a scale from 1–7 (highest); musicEnthuse, enthusiasm for music on the same 1–7 scale; subscribeToMusic, whether the respondent subscribes to our service; Segment, a known assignment to one of our six customer segments, based on prior research.

As we noted in the chapter, you must take care not to include known results when fitting a machine learning model. In the data assignments above, we keep the known segment assignments in the data frame seg.ex.raw, and create seg.ex as a copy without the known segment assignments. Take care to use the appropriate data in the exercises.

11.8.2 Exercises

Clustering

1. In the chapter, we suggested writing a small function to quickly examine group differences. Develop a summary function for the seg.ex data. Demonstrate its basic usage.
2. Using hierarchical clustering, cluster the seg.ex data. Cut it into a specific number of segments, and visualize those. How many segments did you choose and why?
3. Are the hclust() results in Exercise 2 interesting? Show a plot that demonstrates why or why not.
4. Using kmeans(), find a four group solution for the data. (You'll need to do some data conversion first.) Is the solution interesting? Plot two of the continuous variables by segment.
5. Plot the clusters from Exercise 4 by principal components of the data set. Interpret the plot.
6. Use Mclust() to fit a model-based cluster solution for the music subscription data. How many clusters does it suggest? Are they well-differentiated? How do they compare to the k-means solution from Exercise 4?
7. Mclust() can also fit a specified number of clusters (parameter "G"). Fit solutions for G=2 and G=4 clusters. When fit to the data, are they much worse than a G=3 solution?
8. Prepare the data for poLCA, recoding variables to binary factors, splitting as follows: age: less than 30, versus 30+. Household income: less than 55,000, versus greater. Kids at home: 0, versus more than 0. Music enthusiasm: a score of 5 or higher, versus less than that. We will not use miles driven or driving enthusiasm for this exercise.
9. Fit polytomous latent class models for 3-class and 4-class solutions to the data. Visualize them. How different are the two solutions in respondents' assignments? Which one is more useful? (Note: solutions depend in part on the random number sequence.)

Classification

10. Split the music subscription data set—with the segment assignments—into 65%/35% sets for classification model training and assessment. Compare the two sets. Are they suitably similar? (Note: be sure to set a random number seed for replicability.)

11. Fit a naive Bayes model to predict segment membership Segment from the other variables in the training data. Check its performance on the test data. Does it perform better than chance?

12. Fit a random forest model to predict segment membership. What is its out of bag error rate? Did you do anything to control class imbalance?

13. With the random forest model from Exercise 12, predict segments in the test data. Compare those to the actual segments. Does it predict segment membership better than chance?

14. In the random forest model, which variables are most important for predicting segment membership?

15. Predict subscription status subscribeToMusic in the data, using a random forest model. How well does the model predict the test data? Which variables are most important?

16. *(Stretch exercise.)* Use the hotel satisfaction data from the exercises in Chap. 7. Model something interesting in that data set, using either clustering or classification approaches (or both). How do you evaluate your model's performance? Fit a reasonable alternative model. Is your model preferable to the alternative?

Chapter 12
Association Rules for Market Basket Analysis

Many firms compile records of customer transactions. These data sets take diverse forms including products that are purchased together, services that are tracked over time in a customer relationship management (CRM) system, sequences of visits and actions on a Web site, and records of customer support calls. These records are very valuable to marketers and inform us about customers' purchasing patterns, ways in which we might optimize pricing or inventory given the purchase patterns, and relationships between the purchases and other customer information.

Such records may comprise an enormous number of data points yet with relatively little information in each observation. This means that simple analyses such as correlation and linear regression are not applicable because those methods assume complete or near-complete measurement for each case. For example, consider the number of products in a typical supermarket. Most items are not purchased with most other items in any transaction because there are so many possible combinations.

In this chapter we examine a strategy to extract insight from transactions and co-occurrence data: *association rule* mining. Association rule analysis attempts to find sets of informative patterns from large, sparse data sets. We demonstrate association rules using a real data set of more than 80,000 market basket transactions with 16,000 unique items [23]. We then examine how rule mining is potentially useful with non-transactional data and we use association rules to explore patterns in the subscription data from Chap. 5.

We develop the methods here from an *exploratory* point of view, to gain insight and form hypotheses about relationships in the data. Although it is out of scope for this chapter, if one is interested to demonstrate that the insights apply to new data or are stable over time, the same methods might be used with split samples and replication techniques (see Kuhn and Johnson [123] for an introduction to such approaches in general).

© Springer Nature Switzerland AG 2019
341
C. Chapman and E. M. Feit, *R For Marketing Research and Analytics*, Use R!,
https://doi.org/10.1007/978-3-030-14316-9_12

12.1   The Basics of Association Rules

The basic idea of association rule mining is this: when events occur together more often than one would expect from their individual rates of occurrence, such co-occurrence is an interesting pattern. For example, consider sales of sweet relish and hot dogs (summertime treats in the US). Imagine that hot dogs are sold in 5% of supermarket transactions during a summer month, while relish is sold in 3% of transactions. Are they related?

Suppose we just take the data for every sale that includes hot dogs, which is 5% of transactions. If the proportion of those hot dog sales that have relish is 3%, then there is no relationship because that is what we would expect for relish from the overall data, regardless of what else is sold. However, if relish is sold in 25% of the transactions that have hot dogs, that is quite different than the base rate and is evidence of an association.

There are some terms to understand for association rules. An *association* is simply the co-occurrence of two or more things. Hot dogs might be positively associated with relish, hot dog buns, soda, potato chips, and ketchup. An association is not necessarily strong. In a store such as Costco that sells everything from hot dogs to (sometimes) grand pianos, everything sold is associated with everything else but most of those associations are weak. A *set of items* is a group of one or more items, and might be written as {item1, item2, ...}. For instance, a set might be {relish} or {hot dogs, soda, potato chips}.

A *transaction* is a set of items that co-occur in an observation. In marketing, a common transaction is the *market basket*, the set of things that are purchased or considered for purchase at one time. Any data points that co-occur are considered to be a transaction, even if using the term "transaction" seems unusual in the context. For example, the set of web pages that a user visits during a session would be a transaction in this sense.

A *rule* expresses the incidence across transactions of one set of items as a *condition* of another set of items. The association of relish, conditional on hot dogs, is expressed in the rule {relish} $\Rightarrow$ {hot dogs}. Rules may express the relationship of multiple items; for instance, {relish, ketchup, mustard, potato chips} $\Rightarrow$ {hot dogs, hamburger patties, hot dog buns, soda, beer}. A condition in this sense does not imply a causal relationship, only an association of some strength, whether strong or weak.

Metrics. Association rules are expressed with a few common metrics that reflect the rules of conditional probability. The *support* for a set of items is the proportion of all transactions that contain the set. If {hot dogs, soda} appears in 10 out of 200 transactions, then $support(\{hotdogs, soda\}) = 0.05$. It does not matter if those 10 transactions contain other items; support is defined separately for every unique set of items.

Confidence is the support for the co-occurrence of all items in a rule, conditional on the support for the left hand set alone. Thus, $confidence(X \Rightarrow Y) =$

$support(X \cap Y)/support(X)$ (where "$\cap$" means "*and*"). How does that work? Consider the rule {relish} $\Rightarrow$ {hot dogs}. If {relish} occurs in 1% of transactions (in other words, $support(\{relish\}) = 0.01$) and {relish, hot dogs} appears in 0.5%, then $confidence(\{relish\} \Rightarrow \{hotdogs\}) = 0.005/0.1 = 0.5$. In other words, hot dogs appear alongside relish 50% of the time that relish appears.

Note that "confidence" in this context carries no implication about hypothesis testing, confidence intervals, or the like; it is only a measure of conditional association. Confidence is also not symmetric; unless $support(X) = support(Y)$, $confidence(X \Rightarrow Y) \neq confidence(Y \Rightarrow X)$.

Perhaps the most popular measure is *lift*, the support of a set conditional on the joint support of each element, or $lift(X \Rightarrow Y) = support(X \cap Y)/(support(X) \, support(Y))$. To continue the hot dog example, if $support(\{relish\}) = 0.01$, $support(\{hotdogs\}) = 0.01$, and $support(\{relish, hotdogs\}) = 0.005$, then $lift(\{relish \Rightarrow hotdogs\}) = 0.005/(0.01 * 0.01) = 50$. In other words, the combination {relish, hot dogs} occurs 50 times more often than we would expect if the two items were independent.

These three measures tell us different things. When we search for rules we wish to exceed a minimum threshold on each: to find item sets that occur relatively frequently in transactions (*support*), that show strong conditional relationships (*confidence*), and that are more common than chance (*lift*). As we will see, in practice an analyst sets the level of required support to a value such as 0.01, 0.10, 0.20 or so forth as is meaningful and useful for the business in consideration of the data characteristics (such as the size of the item set). Similarly, the level of required confidence might be high (such as 0.8) or low (such as 0.2) depending on the data and business. For lift, higher values are generally better and certainly should be above 1.0, although one must be mindful of outliers with huge lift.

We use the R package `arules` to illustrate association rules [88]. `arules` encapsulates many popular methods for mining associations and provides extensions for visualization [89]. Readers who are interested in the algorithms that generate association rules should review the references in the primary `arules` documentation [87, 88].

12.2 Retail Transaction Data: Market Baskets

The first two data sets we examine contain supermarket transaction data. We first examine a small data set that is included with the `arules` package. This data set is useful despite its small size because the items are labeled with category names, making them easier to read. Then we turn to a larger data set from a supermarket chain whose data is disguised but is more typical of large data sets.

12.2.1   Example Data: *Groceries*

We illustrate the general concepts of association rules with the Groceries data set in the arules package. This data set comprises lists of items purchased together (that is, market baskets), where the individual items have been recorded as category labels instead of product names. You should install the arules and arulesViz packages before proceeding.

We load the package and data, and then check the data as follows:

```
> library(arules)
> data("Groceries")
> summary(Groceries)
transactions as itemMatrix in sparse format with
 9835 rows (elements/itemsets/transactions) and
 169 columns (items) and a density of 0.02609146
...
> inspect(head(Groceries, 3))
  items
1 {citrus fruit, semi-finished bread, margarine, ready soups}
2 {tropical fruit, yogurt, coffee}
3 {whole milk}
```

The summary() shows us that the data comprise 9835 transactions with 169 unique items. Using inspect(head(Groceries)) we see a few examples from the baskets. For example, the second transaction includes fruit, yogurt, and coffee, while the third transaction is just a container of milk. In this output, notice that the item sets are structured with brackets, a visual clue that they reflect a new "transactions" data type that we examine in more detail below.

We now use apriori(data, parameters=...) to find association rules with the "apriori" algorithm [18, 88]. At a conceptual level, the apriori algorithm searches through the item sets that occur frequently in a list of transactions. For each item set, it evaluates the various possible rules that express associations among the items at or above a particular level of support, and then retains the rules that show confidence above some threshold value [17].

To control the extent that apriori() searches, we use the parameter=list() control to instruct the algorithm to search rules that have a minimum support of 0.01 (1% of transactions) and extract the ones that further demonstrate a minimum confidence of 0.3. The resulting rule set is assigned to the groc.rules object:

```
> groc.rules <- apriori(Groceries, parameter=list(supp=0.01, conf=0.3,
+                                            target="rules"))
Apriori

Parameter specification:
 confidence minval smax arem  aval originalSupport maxtime support
        0.3    0.1    1 none FALSE            TRUE       5    0.01
 minlen maxlen target   ext
      1     10  rules FALSE

Algorithmic control:
 filter tree heap memopt load sort verbose
    0.1 TRUE TRUE  FALSE TRUE    2    TRUE

Absolute minimum support count: 98

set item appearances ...[0 item(s)] done [0.00s].
set transactions ...[169 item(s), 9835 transaction(s)] done [0.00s].
```

```
sorting and recoding items ... [88 item(s)] done [0.00s].
creating transaction tree ... done [0.01s].
checking subsets of size 1 2 3 4 done [0.00s].
writing ... [125 rule(s)] done [0.00s].
creating S4 object ... done [0.00s].
```

The rules have been found and saved to an object that we shall inspect in a moment. Note that the values for the `support` and `confidence` parameters are found largely by experience (in other words, by trial and error) and should be expected to vary from industry to industry and data set to data set. We arrived at the values of `support=0.01` and `confidence=0.3` after finding that they resulted in a modest number of rules suitable for an example. In real cases, you would adapt those values to your data and business case (we will say more about this as we examine additional data sets).

To interpret the results of `apriori()` above, there are two key things to examine. First, check the number of *items* going into the rules, which is shown on the output line "`sorting and recoding items ...`" and in this case tells us that the rules found are using 88 of the total number of items. If this number is too small (only a tiny set of your items) or too large (almost all of them) then you might wish to adjust the support and confidence levels.

Next, check the number of rules found, as indicated on the "`writing ...`" line. In this case, the algorithm found 125 rules. Once again, if this number is too low it suggests the need to lower the support or confidence levels; if it is too high (such as many more rules than items) you might increase the support or confidence levels.

Once we have a rule set from `apriori()`, we use `inspect(rules)` to examine the association rules. The complete list of 125 from above is too long to examine here, so we select a `subset` of them with high lift, `lift > 3`. We find that five of the rules in our set have lift greater than 3.0:

```
> inspect(subset(groc.rules, lift > 3))
  lhs                      rhs                   support    confidence lift
1 {beef}             => {root vegetables}  0.01738688  0.3313953 3.040367
2 {citrus fruit,
   root vegetables}  => {other vegetables} 0.01037112  0.5862069 3.029608
3 {citrus fruit,
   other vegetables} => {root vegetables}  0.01037112  0.3591549 3.295045
4 {tropical fruit,
   root vegetables}  => {other vegetables} 0.01230300  0.5845411 3.020999
5 {tropical fruit,
   other vegetables} => {root vegetables}  0.01230300  0.3427762 3.144780
```

The first rule tells us that if a transaction contains {beef} then it is also relatively more likely to contain {root vegetables}—a category that we assume includes items such as potatoes and onions. That combination appears in 1.7% of baskets ("support"), and the lift tells us that combination is 3x more likely to occur together than one would expect from the individual rates of incidence alone.

A store might form several ideas on the basis of such information. For instance, the store might create a display for potatoes and onions near the beef counter to encourage shoppers who are examining beef to purchase those vegetables or consider recipes with them. It might also suggest putting coupons for beef in the root vegetable area, or featuring recipe cards somewhere in the store. We will see other ways to inspect such data and develop ideas later in this chapter.

12.2.2   Supermarket Data

We now investigate associations in a larger set of retail transaction data from a Belgian supermarket chain. This data set comprises market baskets of items purchased together, where each record includes arbitrarily numbered items numbers without item descriptions (to protect the chain's proprietary data). This data set is made publicly available by Brijs et al. [23].

First we use `readLines(url)` to get the data from the website where it is hosted:

```
> retail.raw <- readLines("http://fimi.ua.ac.be/data/retail.dat")
```

An alternative location on this book's website is the following (see Appendix E for more options):

```
> retail.raw <- readLines("http://goo.gl/FfjDAO")
```

As always, we check the `head`, `tail`, and `summary`:

```
> head(retail.raw)
[1] "0 1 2 3 4 5 6 7 8 9 10 11 12 13 14 15 16 17 18 19 20 21 22 23 24 25 ... "
[2] "30 31 32 "
...
> tail(retail.raw)
...
[5] "39 48 2528 "
[6] "32 39 205 242 1393 "
> summary(retail.raw)
   Length      Class       Mode
    88162  character  character
```

Each row in this object represents a single market basket of items purchased together. Within each row, the items have been assigned arbitrary numbers that simply start at 0 in the first transaction and add new item numbers as needed for all later transactions. The data comprise 88,162 transactions, where the first basket has 30 items (numbered 0–29, some truncated in the output here), the second has 3 items, and so forth. In the `tail()`, we see that the last market basket had 5 items, most of which—items 32, 39, 205, and 242—have low numbers reflecting that those particular items first appeared in transactions early in the data set.

In this text format, the data are not ready to mine; we must first split each of the transaction text lines into individual items. To do this, we use `strsplit(lines, " ")`. This command splits each line wherever there is a blank space character (`" "`) and saves the results to a list:

```
> retail.list <- strsplit(retail.raw, " ")
```

To label the individual transactions, we assign descriptive names using `names()` and `paste()`:

```
> names(retail.list) <- paste("Trans", 1:length(retail.list), sep="")
```

As usual, we check the data format again. Finally, we remove the `retail.raw` object that is no longer needed:

```
> str(retail.list)
List of 88162
 $ Trans1    : chr [1:30] "0" "1" "2" "3" ...
 $ Trans2    : chr [1:3] "30" "31" "32"
 ...
> library(car)
> some(retail.list)   # note: random sample; your results may vary
$Trans3742
[1] "488"   "1588" "2750" "2832" "4099"
 ...
> rm(retail.raw)
```

Using `str()` we confirm that the list has 88,162 entries and that individual entries look appropriate. `some()` samples a few transactions throughout the larger set for additional confirmation.

The transaction list could be used to find rules at this point, but we take an additional step to convert it to a formal *transactions* object, which enhances the ways we can work with the data and speeds up `arules` operations. To convert from a list to transactions, we cast the object using `as(..., "transactions")`:

```
> retail.trans <- as(retail.list, "transactions")   # takes a few seconds
> summary(retail.trans)
transactions as itemMatrix in sparse format with
 88162 rows (elements/itemsets/transactions) and
 16470 columns (items) and a density of 0.0006257289

most frequent items:
       39       48       38       32       41  (Other)
    50675    42135    15596    15167    14945   770058

element (itemset/transaction) length distribution:
sizes
    1    2    3    4    5    6    7    8    9   10   11   12   13   14   15
 3016 5516 6919 7210 6814 6163 5746 5143 4660 4086 3751 3285 2866 2620 2310
 ...
    Min. 1st Qu.  Median    Mean 3rd Qu.    Max.
    1.00    4.00    8.00   10.31   14.00   76.00
 ...
> rm(retail.list)   # no longer needed
```

Looking at the `summary()` of the resulting object, we see that the transaction-by-item matrix is 88162 rows by 16470 columns. Of those 1.4 billion intersections, only 0.06% have positive data (*density*) because most items are not purchased in most transactions. Item 39 appears the most frequently and occurs in 50675 baskets or more than half of all transactions. 3016 of the transactions contain only a single item ("sizes" = 1) and the median basket size is 8 items.

12.3 Finding and Visualizing Association Rules

With the data in transaction format, we are ready to find rules. As we have seen briefly already, the `apriori(data, parameters=...)` command finds association rules [18]. For the Belgian supermarket data, we specify `parameter=list(...)` with values of minimum `support = 0.001` and minimum `confidence = 0.4`. We assign the resulting rules to a new object:

```
> retail.rules <- apriori(retail.trans, parameter=list(supp=0.001, conf=0.4))
...
set transactions ...[16470 item(s), 88162 transaction(s)] done [0.36s].
sorting and recoding items ... [2117 item(s)] done [0.02s].
creating transaction tree ... done [0.06s].
checking subsets of size 1 2 3 4 5 6 done [0.15s].
writing ... [5944 rule(s)] done [0.01s].
creating S4 object  ... done [0.02s].
```

This finds a set of 5944 rules that exceed the required levels of support and confidence.

To get a sense of the rule distribution, we load the `arulesViz` package and then `plot()` the rule set, which charts the rules according to confidence (Y axis) by support (X axis) and scales the darkness of points to indicate lift. The commands are simply:

```
> library(arulesViz)
> plot(retail.rules)
```

The resulting chart is shown in Fig. 12.1. In that chart, we see that most rules involve item combinations that occur infrequently (that is, they have low support) while confidence is relatively smoothly distributed.

Simply showing points is not very useful, and a key feature with `arules` is *interactive plotting*. In Fig. 12.1 there are some rules in the upper left with high lift. We can use interactive plotting to inspect those rules. To do this, add `interactive=TRUE` to the `plot()` command:

```
> plot(retail.rules, interactive=TRUE)
```

In interactive mode, you can examine regions of rules. To do so, click once in the plot window at one corner of the area of interest, and then click again at the opposite corner. You can use `zoom in` to magnify that region, or `inspect` to list the rules in the region. When finished, click `end`.

Figure 12.2 shows an interactive plotting session in RStudio where we seek rules with high lift. To get Fig. 12.2 we previously selected the upper left region as was shown in Fig. 12.1 and zoomed in on that region. Then we selected a few rules from the zoomed-in area and clicked `inspect` to display them in the console. There were

Fig. 12.1 Plotting a large set of rules for confidence (Y axis) by support (X axis) and lift (shade). There are a few rules in the upper left with exceptionally high confidence and lift

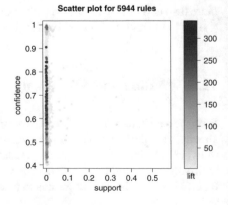

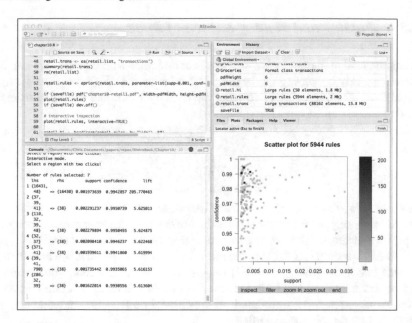

Fig. 12.2 Using `plot(..., interactive=TRUE)` to inspect rules of interest in interactive mode. In this screenshot from RStudio, we zoomed into a small region to `inspect()` a subgroup of the complete rule set. This reveals the selected rules in the console (lower left window)

7 rules in that subregion, as shown in the lower left console window. This revealed one exceptionally high lift rule:

```
    lhs              rhs           support confidence         lift
1 {16431,
     48}      => {16430} 0.001973639  0.9942857 205.770463
```

This rule tells us that the combination {16431, 48} occurs in about 0.2% of baskets (support = 0.00197), and when it occurs it almost always includes {16430} (confidence = 0.99). The combination occurs 200 times more often than we would expect from the individual incidence rates of {16431, 48} and {16430} considered separately (lift = 205).

Such information could be used in various ways. If we pair the transactions with customer information, we could use this for targeted mailings or email suggestions. For items often sold together, we could adjust the price and margins together; for instance, to put one item on sale while increasing the price on the other. Or perhaps—only somewhat facetiously—the cashiers might ask customers, "Would you like a 16430 with that?"

12.3.1 Finding and Plotting Subsets of Rules

A common goal in market basket analysis is to find rules with high lift. We can find
such rules easily by sorting the larger set of rules by lift. We extract the 50 rules
with highest lift using `sort()` to order the rules by `lift` and taking 50 from the
`head()`:

```
> inspect(retail.hi)
      lhs                    rhs      support       confidence lift      count
[1]   {696}              => {699}    0.001032191   0.5833333  338.3410   91
[2]   {699}              => {696}    0.001032191   0.5986842  338.3410   91
[3]   {1818,3311,795}    => {1819}   0.001088905   0.9056604  318.1069   96
[4]   {3402}             => {3535}   0.001417844   0.7062147  305.2024   125
...
```

The count tells us how exactly how many transactions include each association; this
is the *absolute support* for the rule. The values of the lift and the relative, proportional
support are identical for a set of items regardless of the items' order within a rule
(the left-hand or right-hand side of the rule). Thus the first two rules—which include
the same two items {696} and {699} on opposite sides of the conditional arrow—
are identical for support and lift. However, confidence reflects direction because it
computes occurrence the right-hand set conditional on the left-hand side set, and
differs slightly for the first two rules.

A *graph* display of rules may be useful to seek higher level themes and patterns. We
chart the top 50 rules by lift with `plot(..., method="graph")` and display
rules as the intersection of items by adding the graph option, `control=list
(type="item")`:

```
> plot(retail.hi, method="graph", control=list(type="items"))
```

The resulting chart is shown in Fig. 12.3. Each circle there represents a rule with
inbound arrows coming from items on the left-hand side of the rule and outbound
arrows going to the right-hand side. The size (area) of the circle represents the rule's
support, and shade represents lift (darker indicates higher lift). Positioning of rules
on the graph may differ for your system, but the rule clusters should be similar.

Figure 12.3 shows several patterns of interest. Items 696 and 699 form a tight set;
there are item clusters for {3402, 3535, 3537}, {309, 1080, 1269, 1378, 1379, 1380},
and so forth; and item 39 appears as a key item in two sets of items that otherwise
do not overlap. By exploring sets of rules with various levels of lift and support, and
with specific subsets of items (see the usage of %in% in `arules` help), an analyst
may be able to find patterns that suggest interesting hypotheses and trends. We will
see a further example of this for non-transactional data in Sect. 12.4 below.

12.3.2 Using Profit Margin Data with Transactions: An
Initial Start

An analyst will often wish to combine market basket transactions and rules with
other data; for instance, one might have information on item profitability (margin) or

Fig. 12.3 A graph using `arulesViz` of the top 50 association rules mined from the retail market basket data set. There are four distinct sets of rules (arrows and circular nodes), each relating a set of 2-6 items (the integer ID numbers). These rules have *lift* of 232x or more in the retail shopping data

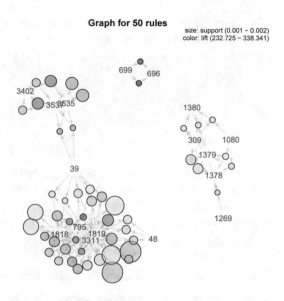

purchaser characteristics. In this section, we consider how to combine information on item cost and margin with transaction data.

How can we find the profit for a transaction? The answer may be complex and depend on the details of a firm and its transaction data. Because the Belgian supermarket data set does not include item price or cost, we simulate margin by items for illustration purposes. We assume that each item has a single margin value; if we had access to a firm's complete data it would be better to use information about costs and prices by date, along with discounts and other adjustments to estimate margin more accurately.

To simulate per-item margin data we first compile a list of the item names that we need. We do this by converting the complete transaction set to `list` format and then using `unlist()` to gather the individual items from the many transactions into a single vector. We take the `unique()` values to remove duplicates, and then `sort()` them:

```
> retail.itemnames <- sort(unique(unlist(as(retail.trans, "list"))))
> head(retail.itemnames); tail(retail.itemnames)
[1] "0"      "1"      "10"     "100"    "1000"   "10000"
[1] "9994" "9995" "9996" "9997" "9998" "9999"
```

Items are not in numeric order because the item labels are character data and `sort()` orders them alphabetically; this poses no problem here.

Next we generate the simulated margin data with one value for each item, using `rnorm()` with a mean and standard deviation of 0.30 currency units (such as € 0.30):

```
> set.seed(03870)
> retail.margin <- data.frame(margin=rnorm(length(retail.itemnames),
+                             mean=0.30, sd=0.30))
> quantile(retail.margin$margin)
        0%        25%        50%        75%       100%
-1.1090452  0.1045897  0.3026245  0.5050533  1.5542344
```

We make those values indexable by item name by adding the list of items from above as the `rownames()` for the random numbers:

```
> rownames(retail.margin) <- retail.itemnames
> head(retail.margin); tail(retail.margin)
          margin
0        0.88340359
1        0.52964087
...
9999   0.6850124
> library(car); some(retail.margin)
          margin
12336   0.18504274
...
```

In this format, we can look up the margin for an item—or set of items—using the relevant item names. For example, we find the item margins and then their sum for the basket {39, 48} as follows:

```
> retail.margin[c("39", "48"), ]
[1]    0.1217833 -0.2125105
> sum(retail.margin[c("39", "48"), ])
[1] -0.09072725
```

Item 39 has margin of 0.12, and the basket {39, 48} has total margin of −0.09.

To find the margin for a complete transaction—in this case, transaction #3 from the Belgian data—there is one more step. We have to convert the transaction to *list* form to find the items in it using `as(..., "list")`, at which point we can look up the margins for those items:

```
> (basket.items <- as(retail.trans[3], "list")[[1]])
[1] "33" "34" "35"
> retail.margin[basket.items, ]
[1] 0.3817115 0.6131403 0.1979879
> sum(retail.margin[basket.items, ])
[1] 1.19284
```

12.3.3   Language Brief: A Function for Margin Using an Object's `class`*

This optional section expands on the margin example by writing a more complex function. Along the way we will see one way to use objects' *classes* and how to write more error-resistant code. If you do not wish to dive deeply into programming, you may safely skip this section.

Motivation. Using a simple index to look up the margin for items as we did above is not very satisfactory because it depends on the exact format of the data, such as the fact that it is given in a `list` format. If we ever change the format or wish to explore margin for some other kind of data, it is necessary to find any code where data is treated as a list and alter it. That process would be tedious and likely to introduce errors.

A better solution is to write a function to look up margins. With a function, we can perform more complex logic such as date lookups and volume or customer discounts.

It also localizes all logic to a single place; if we call the function in each place that we need a margin lookup, we only need to change the procedure in one place.

In this section we create a initial working version of a more general lookup function. We also enhance the simple lookup capability in an important way: we make it work for transactions and rule sets as well as item names. A user may call the function with any of those data types and it will handle the data properly.

One way to make a function work for different kinds of input data is to use the R *class* system to determine the data type. (More advanced programmers may note that the approach here is a simple solution; a more complete solution—but well beyond the scope of this book—is to implement *S3* or *S4* methods for each data class that a function supports. For details on the various object-oriented programming paradigms in R, see [30, 74, 191, 197].)

Our function takes the form `retail.margsum(items, itemMargins)`, where `items` may be any of the following:

- A character vector of item names such as `c("39", "48")`, of class "character"
- One or more transactions such as `retail.trans` in our example above, of class "transactions"
- A set of rules such as `retail.hi` in our example above, of class "rules"

By checking the `class()`, our function is able to extract items appropriately from the data that a user provides, so the user will not have to extract item names from different kinds of objects.

Before inspecting the `retail.margsum()` code, we note that it has three key sections:

1. Convert the data we're given to a list of item name sets
2. Check that those item names are in our margin data (`itemMargins`)
3. Look up the margins and sum them

Here is the complete code:

```
retail.margsum <- function(items, itemMargins) {
  # Input: "items" == item names, rules or transactions in arules format
  #        "itemMargins", a data frame of profit margin indexed by name
  # Output: look up the item margins, and return the sum

  # check the class of "items" and coerce appropriately to an item list
  if (class(items) == "rules") {
    tmp.items <- as(items(items), "list")       # rules ==> item list
  } else if (class(items) == "transactions") {
    tmp.items <- as(items, "list")              # transactions ==> item list
  } else if (class(items) == "list") {
    tmp.items <- items                          # it's already an item list!
  } else if (class(items) == "character") {
    tmp.items <- list(items)                    # characters ==> item list
  } else {
    stop("Don't know how to handle margin for class ", class(items))
  }
  # make sure the items we found are all present in itemMargins
  good.items <- unlist(lapply(tmp.items, function (x)
                       all(unlist(x) %in% rownames(itemMargins))))
  if (!all(good.items)) {
```

```
    warning("Some items not found in rownames of itemMargins. ",
            "Lookup failed for element(s):\n",
            which(!good.items), "\nReturning only good values.")
    tmp.items <- tmp.items[good.items]
  }

  # and add them up
  return(unlist(lapply(tmp.items, function(x) sum(itemMargins[x, ]))))
}
```

We explain the code in detail below, but first let's see how it works. One way to use it is to find margin for an item set with simple item names:

```
> retail.margsum(c("39", "48"), retail.margin)
[1] -0.09072725
```

Another use is to find margin for each entry in a list with multiple, separate item sets:

```
> retail.margsum(list(t1=c("39", "45"), t2=c("31", "32")), retail.margin)
        t1        t2
0.9664982 0.2733963
```

It accepts one or more transaction objects:

```
> retail.margsum(retail.trans[101:103], retail.margin)
 Trans101  Trans102  Trans103
0.7171411 4.8989272 4.9470372
```

It also accepts sets of rules, such as our `retail.hi` set of the 50 highest list rules:

```
> retail.margsum(retail.hi, retail.margin)
 [1] 0.9609471 0.9609471 1.9327917 0.7084729 0.7084729 1.9327917
...
[45] 0.1624291 0.5067865 0.5067865 0.5442604 0.5442604 0.6285698
```

It also includes error detection. For instance, it gives an error in case of incorrect item names:

```
> retail.margsum(c("hello", "world"), retail.margin)  # error!
NULL
Warning message:
In retail.margsum(c("hello", "world"), retail.margin) :
  Some items not found in rownames of itemMargins. ...
```

In the above case, it returns a value of NULL as shown on the first line of the output because there was nothing valid to look up. However, if some of the data is bad while other parts are good, it finds whatever is possible:

```
> retail.margsum(list(a=c("39", "45"), b=c("hello", "world"), c=c("31", "32")),
+                retail.margin)      # only the first and third are OK
        a         c
0.9664982 0.2733963
Warning message:
...
```

In this case, the second element in the input is bad, so the function omits that and returns the sums for the other two item sets "a" and "c."

Now let's look at the function in detail to see how it works. In the first part of the code we convert the `items` input to proper types, by checking the `class()` and then applying an appropriate conversion:

```
# [ function excerpt, don't run on its own ]
  if (class(items) == "rules") {
    tmp.items <- as(items(items), "list")          # rules ==> item list
  } else if (class(items) == "transactions") {
    tmp.items <- as(items, "list")                 # transactions ==> item list
...
  } else {
    stop("Don't know how to handle margin for class ", class(items))
  }
```

In this part of the code, we use the `if ... else if ...` construct in R to check types successively. It ends with a final `else` clause in case the data is a type the function cannot handle. In that case, it calls `stop(message)` to issue an error message to the user and exit the function.

The second part of our code checks that the sets of items are present in the `itemMargins` data:

```
# [ function excerpt, don't run on its own ]
  good.items <- unlist(lapply(tmp.items, function (x)
                       all(unlist(x) %in% rownames(itemMargins))))

  if (!all(good.items)) {
    warning("Some items not found in rownames of itemMargins. ",
            "Lookup failed for element(s):\n",
            which(!good.items), "\nReturning only good values.")
    tmp.items <- tmp.items[good.items]
  }
```

This short code block has a few crucial elements. First it uses an anonymous function to check that items names are present in `itemMargins`. It uses `%in%` to look up each name from a single list element (with the names extracted by `unlist(x)`) and then uses `all()` to make sure that every one of the names is found successfully (that is, that `all` of the `%in%` matches are TRUE). The result of this is a flag whether a given element of `tmp.items` is good or not.

Then we use the `unlist()` function a second time to convert the individual results from `lapply()` to a master vector, which indicates whether each individual element of `tmp.items` is good or not. Finally, if any of the individual item sets has an item that was not found (and therefore, using ! for binary negation, `!all(good.items)` is TRUE) then we issue a `warning()` to the user, and retain only the good items for further processing. Unlike `stop()`, a function continues after a `warning()` to the user.

The third and final part of our code looks up the items and returns the sum of their margins:

```
# [ function excerpt, don't run on its own ]
  return(unlist(lapply(tmp.items, function(x) sum(itemMargins[x, ]))))
```

That line unpacks as follows, starting from the innermost part. An anonymous function looks up rows in `itemMargins`, and then sums them. Those rows x are determined by the surrounding `lapply()` that iterates over the individual sets of items that form the list `tmp.items`. Each member set of `tmp.items` has its items' margins summed. Finally, the line calls `unlist()` in order to convert the `lapply()` result—which is a list—to a more convenient vector.

But wait! That final, single line effectively delivers the whole purpose of the function. Why did we have to write so much else in the function? Isn't that needless complexity?

The answer depends on the circumstance, but this function exemplifies a common issue in programming: handling exceptions and doing error-checking is often the most complex part of a programming task. Just as getting data into shape is often the bulk of an analyst's work, much of a programmer's effort is to anticipate potential data problems when writing code. It is a good practice to include error-checking as we've done here. Don't assume your data will always be good; check it! You'll avoid many headaches for yourself and your colleagues.

Once the skeleton of a profit margin function is in place, an analyst will start to many uses for it. For example, one might use it on transactions to find the most valuable customers, to find potential loss-leading items that are associated with other, higher margin items, to find money-losing associations, and so forth. A simple function of the kind here would be a proof of concept; a next step might be to increase its precision by including time series data, discounts, and other important factors specific to a firm and category.

12.4   Rules in Non-transactional Data: Exploring Segments Again

There are many uses of association rules beyond retail transactions such as we considered above. The idea of a "transaction" broadly speaking is simply an observation of one or more data points that co-occur. For instance, when a user visits one or more web pages during a browsing session, the pages would constitute a transaction in this sense.

In the most general sense, one can consider any data points that occur together in a record—such as any variables observed for a customer, user, or survey respondent—to be a transaction. This means that association rules can be applied to other kinds of data such as general data frames (with some limitations that we'll discuss). In this section, we examine association rules as a way to explore consumer segmentation.

We use the simulated consumer segmentation data from Sect. 5.1.4. If you saved the data in that chapter (Sect. 5.1.4), reload it now. We suggested a file destination as `file="~ /segdf-Rintro-Ch5.RData"`. If you saved there, you can retrieve the data with:

```
> load("~/segdf-Rintro-Ch5.RData")
```

Alternatively, run the code in that chapter (Sects. 5.1.1–5.1.4) or download the file from this book's website:

```
> seg.df <- read.csv("http://goo.gl/qw303p")
```

After loading the data, check that it matches expectations:

```
> summary(seg.df)
      age                gender            income              kids            ownHome   ...
 Min.   :19.26     Female:157     Min.   :  -5183     Min.   :0.00     ownNo :159 ...
 1st Qu.:33.01     Male  :143     1st Qu.:  39656     1st Qu.:0.00     ownYes:141 ...
```

12.4.1   Language Brief: Slicing Continuous Data with `cut()`

Association rules work with *discrete* data yet `seg.df` includes three continuous (or quasi-continuous) variables: `age`, `income`, and `kids`. It's necessary to convert those to discrete factors to use with association rules in the `arules` package.

We could add factor variables as new columns appended to the original data frame. However, we use that data frame elsewhere in this book and thus prefer instead to make a copy and and alter it:

```
> seg.fac <- seg.df
```

Now we replace `age`, `income`, and `kids` with recoded factors (specifically, using the `ordered` factor class to code these data as ordinal values). `cut(data, breaks, labels)` transforms numeric data to a factor variable. `breaks=...` specifies either the number of bins or specific cut points, and `labels=...` specifies the text for a factor's category labels. We transform `age` as follows:

```
> seg.fac$age <- cut(seg.fac$age,
+                    breaks=c(0,25,35,55,65,100),
+                    labels=c("19-24", "25-34", "35-54", "55-64", "65+"),
+                    right=FALSE, ordered_result=TRUE)
```

This recodes `age` from an integer value into an ordered factor with 5 levels: 19–24, 25–34, and so forth. The argument `right=FALSE` ensures that continuous values have closed intervals on the left, giving us $[25-34)$ instead of $(25-34]$. We set `ordered_result=TRUE` to specify that the resulting factor is ordinal. We check the data and see that the recode was successful:

```
> summary(seg.fac$age)
19-24 25-34 35-54 55-64   65+
   38    58   152    38    14
```

Next we convert `income` and `kids` similarly:

```
> seg.fac$income <- cut(seg.fac$income,
+                       breaks=c(-100000, 40000, 70000, 1000000),
+                       labels=c("Low", "Medium", "High"),
+                       right=FALSE, ordered_result=TRUE)
> seg.fac$kids <- cut(seg.fac$kids,
+                     breaks=c(0, 1, 2, 3, 100),
+                     labels=c("No kids", "1 kid", "2 kids", "3+ kids"),
+                     right=FALSE, ordered_result=TRUE)
> summary(seg.fac)
     age              gender           income             kids             ownHome         subscribe
 19-24: 38     Female:157     Low    : 77     No kids:121     ownNo :159     subNo :260
 25-34: 58     Male  :143     Medium:183     1 kid  : 70     ownYes:141     subYes: 40
  ...
```

All variables are now coded as categorical factors and the `seg.fac` data frame is suitable for exploring associations.

Fig. 12.4 The distribution
of rules inferred from the
segmentation data set

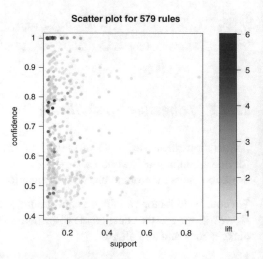

12.4.2   *Exploring Segment Associations*

A data frame in suitable discrete (factor) format can be converted to use in `arules`
by using `as(..., "transactions")` to code it as transaction data:

```
> library(arules)
> library(arulesViz)
> seg.trans <- as(seg.fac, "transactions")
> summary(seg.trans)
transactions as itemMatrix in sparse format with
 300 rows (elements/itemsets/transactions) and
 22 columns (items) and a density of 0.3181818
...
```

Rules are generated in the same way as for market basket data. We use `apriori()`
and specify `support=0.1` and `conf=0.4`. This finds 579 association rules:

```
> seg.rules <- apriori(seg.trans, parameter=list(support=0.1, conf=0.4,
+                                                 target="rules"))
...
> summary(seg.rules)
set of 579 rules ...
```

A default plot of the resulting `seg.rules` object is:

```
> plot(seg.rules)
```

This products Fig. 12.4, where we see a few rules with high confidence shown in
the upper left region. If we add the `interactive=TRUE` option for `plot()` (not
shown; see Sect. 12.3 for an explanation), we could explore those interactively to
find the following rules with both high confidence and high lift:

```
> plot(seg.rules, interactive=T)
...
  lhs                        rhs                      support confidence      lift
1 {age=19-24}            => {Segment=Urban hip} 0.1266667  1.0000000  6.000000
2 {age=19-24,
   income=Low}           => {Segment=Urban hip} 0.1266667  1.0000000  6.000000
3 {age=19-24,
   ownHome=ownNo}        => {Segment=Urban hip} 0.1000000  1.0000000  6.000000
```

```
4  {age=19-24,
     subscribe=subNo}      => {Segment=Urban hip} 0.1000000  1.0000000  6.000000
...
```

These show an association of `age` and other variables with membership in the Urban hip segment.

A graph plot visualizes clusters of rules to reveal higher-level patterns. We extract the top 35 highest-lift rules and visualize them as a `graph`:

```
> seg.hi <- head(sort(seg.rules, by="lift"), 35)
> inspect(seg.hi)
       lhs                     rhs                    support  confidence ...
[1]  {age=19-24}       => {Segment=Urban hip} 0.1266667  1.0000000 ...
...
> plot(seg.hi, method="graph", control=list(type="items")) # orientation varies
```

The resulting chart is shown in Fig. 12.5 (orientation of the chart may vary for you). There are two dominant clusters: a large cluster with many rules and relatively high lift that involve ages 19–24, no home ownership, lower income, and so forth; and a smaller cluster involving late middle-age consumers without kids in the travelers segment.

One might do further explorations by selecting additional sets of rules beyond the `head()` of the sorted rules. To do this, `sort()` the rules by lift (or other parameter as desired) and then index the rules you want. To examine the next 25 rules after the first 35 considered above:

```
> seg.next <- sort(seg.rules, by="lift")[36:60]
> plot(seg.next, method="graph", control=list(type="items")) # not shown
```

We omit the resulting chart in this case, which shows patterns involving factors such as the suburban mix segment and home ownership.

Fig. 12.5 Example of using a `graph` plot to explore rule clusters for the segmentation data set

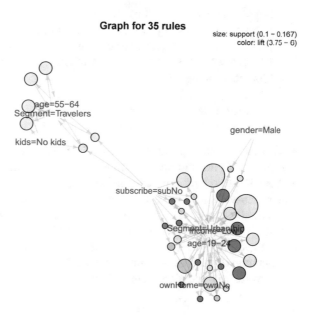

Graph for 35 rules

size: support (0.1 – 0.167)
color: lift (3.75 – 6)

The patterns demonstrate that association rules can be useful to seek patterns in such non-transactional data. A key point is that this is primarily an *exploratory* exercise. It is useful if it reveals interesting patterns for further investigation. One should confirm any such inferences before drawing final conclusions.

12.5   Key Points

Association rules are a powerful way to explore the relationships in a data set. The following points summarize some key suggestions from this chapter.

- Association rules are commonly used with sparse data sets that have many observations but little information per observation. In marketing, this is typical of market baskets and similar transaction data. (Sect. 12.1)
- The `arules` package is the standard R package for association rules. `arules` provides support for handling sparse data and finding rules and the `arulesViz` package provides visualization methods.
- Core metrics for evaluating association rules are *support* (frequency), *confidence* (co-occurrence), and *lift* (co-occurrence above the rate of association by pure chance). There is no absolute value required of them except that lift should be somewhat greater than 1.0 (or possibly very much less than 1.0, showing that the *non*-association is unexpected, as in fraud detection). Interpretation depends on experience with similar data and the usefulness for a particular business question (Sect. 12.1).
- A typical workflow for association rules (Sects. 12.2.1 and 12.2.2) is:
  - Import the raw data and use `as(data, "transactions")` to transform it to a transactions object for better performance.
  - Use `apriori(transactions, support= , confidence= , target="rules")` to find a set of association rules.
  - Plot the resulting rule with `plot(..., interactive=TRUE)` and inspect the rules (Sect. 12.3)
  - Look for patterns by selecting subsets of rules, such as those with highest lift, and use `plot(..., method="graph")` for visualization (Sect. 12.3.1)
- Data such as item profit margin may be used to extend analyses and look at the potential business impact of acting on particular rules (Sect. 12.3.2)
- Association rule mining can also be a useful exploratory technique for mining non-transactional data such as consumer segmentation data (Sect. 12.4).
- We used R functions `cut()` to slice continuous data (Sect. 12.4.1) and `class()` to determine an object's data type (Sect. 12.3.3)
- When you write a custom function, use `warning()` to report potential issues and violations of data assumptions (Sect. 12.3.3), and use `stop()` when a condition means that the function should not continue.

12.6 Learning More*

An approachable text for association rules is [185]. In that text, Chap. 6 discusses the fundamental concepts and algorithms of association rules, and Chap. 7 develops more advanced concepts and applications. Vipin Kuman, one of that text's authors, has published online materials related to the book and association rules, at http://www-users.cs.umn.edu/~kumar/dmbook/index.php.

The `arules` package is notable for its rich ecosystem of tools such as the `arulesViz` package that we used for charting. Other options include sequence mining and naive Bayes algorithms in addition to the standard apriori algorithm. For an overview of the `arules` ecosystem, see [87] and the vignettes that come with `arules`. The latest developments are available from the first author Michael Hahsler's site, http://michael.hahsler.net/.

Association rules have also been extended to the analysis of behavioral sequences, the topic of Chap. 14. We briefly discuss association sequences in Sect. 14.7 and provide an example in that chapter's code file.

12.7 Exercises

12.7.1 Retail Transactions Data for Exercises

For the exercises here, we use a data set of simulated transactions, plus another with item costs and margin, for a retail super center. This hypothetical store sells groceries along with other consumer and household goods, as well as some items more typical of home furnishing and big box stores, so the items range from very inexpensive ($0.09 USD) to quite expensive ($39009.00 USD).

We load the two data sets as follow, and additionally extract the item margins from the cost data frame to a simple vector, in order to match the approach taken in the chapter:

```
# load from website. 11MB, may be slow
retail.raw <- readLines ("https://goo.gl/wi8KHg")
retail.margin <- read.csv("https://goo.gl/Pidzpd")

# or load locally, if downloaded
# retail.raw     <- readLines("retail-baskets.csv")
# retail.margin <- read.csv("retail-margin.csv")
margin.short   <- data.frame(retail.margin$margin)
rownames(margin.short) <- retail.margin$item
```

As always, we suggest to explore and summarize the data before starting analyses.

12.7.2   Exercises

1. Convert the raw transaction lines, as read above, into a transactions object for `arules`. How many unique items are there? What are the five most popular items? What are the sizes of the smallest, largest, and median basket? (*Hint*: in case of trouble, check the format of the raw item lines.)
2. Find association rules in the retail data. Aim for somewhere between 100 and 1000 rules (consider tuning the rule length, support, and confidence parameters). Plot confidence versus support for the rules, and interpret that pattern.
3. Find the top 30 rules by lift and plot them. Which items are associated in the group with highest single-item support? Which items are in the largest group by total number of items?
4. In the chapter, we presented a function to calculate total margin for a set of rules. Among all the transactions, what are the top 10 baskets with the highest total margin?
5. Suppose we want to focus on the highest margin transactions. What proportion of baskets have a total margin of $200 or more? What are the most common items in those baskets? Plot the frequency of items that appear in 10% or more of those baskets. (*Hint*: there is an `arules` function called `itemFrequency()`.)
6. Add the item names to the plot axis for the previous exercise. (*Hint*: check Sect. 3.4.1, and also examine plotting parameters `cex.axis` and `las`.)
7. The retail.margin data frame, as loaded above, has both price and margin. Calculate the proportional margin for each item (margin divided by price). Plot those. If you transformed them, what would be an appropriate transformation? Plot that also.
8. (*Stretch programming exercise*). Write a function similar to `retail.margsum()` but that returns both the total margin and the total price for a basket. Find the top 10 baskets in terms of their margin to price ratio.

Chapter 13
Choice Modeling

Much of the data we observe in marketing describes customers purchasing products. For example, as we discussed in Chap. 12, retailers now regularly record the transactions of their customers. In that chapter, we discussed analyzing retail transaction records to determine which products tend to occur together in the same shopping basket. In this chapter we discuss how to analyze customers' product choices within a category to understand how features and price affect which product a customer will choose. For example, if a customer comes into the store and purchases a 30 oz. jar of Hellman's brand canola mayonnaise for $3.98, we can conceptualize this as the customer choosing that particular type of mayonnaise among all the other mayonnaise available at that store. This data on customers' choices can be analyzed to determine which features of a product (e.g., package size, brand, or flavor) are most attractive to customers and how they trade off desirable features against price.

On the surface, this may sound quite similar to what we discussed in Chap. 7, where we cover how to use linear models to identify drivers of outcomes. It is similar, except that product choice data doesn't fit well into the linear modeling framework, because the outcome we observe is not a number or a rating for each product. Instead, we observe that the customer makes a *choice* among several options, each of which has its own set of attributes. To accommodate this unique data structure, marketers have adopted choice models, which are well-suited to understanding the relationship between the attributes of products and customers' choices among sets of products. In this chapter, we focus on the *multinomial logit model*, the most frequently used choice model in marketing.

While choice models are often used to analyze retail purchase data, there are some settings where it is more difficult to collect data on customers' product choices. For example, when people shop for a car, they typically gather information from many sources over several months, so it is more difficult to reconstruct the set of products that they considered and the features and prices of those products. In these settings, marketers turn to choice-based *conjoint analysis*, which is a survey method where customers are asked to make choices among products with varying features and prices. We analyze these survey choices using the multinomial logit model just as we

© Springer Nature Switzerland AG 2019
C. Chapman and E. M. Feit, *R For Marketing Research and Analytics*, Use R!,
https://doi.org/10.1007/978-3-030-14316-9_13

might analyze real purchases. In this chapter, our example focuses on choice-based conjoint analysis, but the methods we describe could be applied to retail purchase data as well.

13.1   Choice-Based Conjoint Analysis Surveys

Suppose an automotive company such as Toyota or Ford is designing a new line of minivans and is trying to determine how large the minivan should be and what type of engine it should have. To inform this decision it would be helpful to understand how customers value those different features. Do customers like or dislike hybrid engines? If they like them, how much more would they be willing to pay for a hybrid engine? Are there segments of customers who like hybrid engines more than other customers?

Conjoint surveys give marketers information about how customers choose products by asking respondents to answer survey questions like the one shown in Fig. 13.1. In this question, respondents are asked to choose from three product profiles, each with a specific passenger capacity, cargo capacity, engine type, and price. The product options in the survey are called *alternatives* and the product features are called *attributes*. This conjoint analysis study has three alternatives in each question, described by four attributes. Each attribute occurs at some *level*. For example, the possible levels for cargo capacity in our example survey are 2 and 3 ft.

In a typical choice-based conjoint (CBC) survey, we ask respondents who are likely buyers of minivans to answer a number of questions similar to the one in Fig. 13.1. Each question has the same structure, but varies the levels of the attributes for the alternatives.

In the next section, we generate hypothetical data from a conjoint survey where each respondent answers 15 questions like the one in Fig. 13.1. Each question offers the respondent 3 alternatives to choose from, so each respondent sees a total of

Which of the following minivans would you buy?
Assume all three minivans are identical other than the features listed below.

	Option 1	Option 2	Option 3
	6 passengers	8 passengers	6 passengers
	2 ft. cargo area	3 ft. cargo area	3 ft. cargo area
	gas engine	hybrid engine	gas engine
	$35,000	$30,000	$30,000
I prefer (check one):	☐	☐	☑

Fig. 13.1 An example choice-based conjoint survey question

$15 \times 3 = 45$ product profiles. Conjoint surveys often include more attributes, more questions and more alternatives in each question; a typical study might have 5–10 attributes and include 10–20 questions for each respondent.

You may recall that we also discussed "conjoint analysis" in Chap. 9. In that chapter we asked respondents to rate single products instead of having them choose among sets of products. This is called "ratings-based conjoint" or "metric conjoint" and is analyzed with linear models as we did in Chap. 9. While asking respondents to give ratings allows us to use a linear model instead of a choice model, rating profiles is a more difficult task for the respondent. When was the last time you considered whether a product was a 7 or an 8 on a 10-point scale? Choosing products as in Fig. 13.1 is a natural task that consumers do every day. For this reason choice-based conjoint surveys have become a standard tool in the arsenal of marketing researchers. When marketers say "conjoint," they often mean choice-based conjoint analysis.

The key difference between choice-based conjoint and metric conjoint is the structure of the data you collect. In the minivan CBC survey, each observation is a choice among three alternatives with varying levels of the product attributes. The goal of our analysis is to relate the choice to the product attributes. To do this we use a choice model, which is tailored to this unusual data structure.

The next section, where we simulate CBC data, is written for readers who have some knowledge of choice models already. We encourage those of you who are new to choice modeling to download the data using the commands below and skip ahead to Sect. 13.3. Those who are familiar with choice modeling might wish to work through Sect. 13.2 to see how choice data is structured in R.

```
> cbc.df <- read.csv("http://goo.gl/5xQObB",
+                    colClasses = c(seat = "factor", price = "factor",
+                    choice="integer"))
> cbc.df$eng <- factor(cbc.df$eng, levels=c("gas", "hyb", "elec"))
> cbc.df$carpool <- factor(cbc.df$carpool, levels=c("yes", "no"))
> summary(cbc.df)
    resp.id          ques          alt       carpool       seat        cargo
 Min.   :  1.00   Min.   : 1   Min.   :1   yes:2655    6:3024   2ft:4501
 1st Qu.: 50.75   1st Qu.: 4   1st Qu.:1   no :6345    7:2993   3ft:4499
 Median :100.50   Median : 8   Median :2               8:2983
 Mean   :100.50   Mean   : 8   Mean   :2
 ...
```

13.2 Simulating Choice Data*

If you loaded the data above, you can skip this optional section and go to Sect. 13.3.

The first step in creating any conjoint survey is to decide on which product attributes to include in the survey. Since this study focuses on size and engine type, we include four attributes: number of seats in the minivan, the cargo capacity (measured by the depth of the cargo area), the engine type and the price. We create a list in R called attrib to store the attributes:

```
> attrib <- list(seat = c("6", "7", "8"),
+                cargo = c("2ft", "3ft"),
+                eng = c("gas", "hyb", "elec"),
+                price = c("30", "35", "40"))
```

Each element of this list is a character vector indicating levels of the attribute to include in the survey.

The next step is to generate *part worths* for the attributes. Part worths are conceived to be latent values a customer places on levels of an attribute when making choices. Each attribute in the choice model is treated like a factor in a linear model. As we discussed in Chap. 7, when we include a factor as a predictor in any model, that factor has to be coded. In this chapter, we use dummy coding, so that one level of the factor is considered the base level and the model includes coefficients that describe the part worth or value of that factor *over the base level*. If this is puzzling, you might review Sect. 7.4 on including factors as predictors in a linear model.

We designate the first level of each attribute to be the base level. We create names for the coefficients by looping over the attribute list, dropping the first level of the attribute, and then concatenating the name of the attribute and the level designation:

```
> coef.names <- NULL
> for (a in seq_along(attrib)) {
+   coef.names <- c(coef.names,
+                   paste(names(attrib)[a], attrib[[a]][-1], sep=""))
+ }
> coef.names
[1] "seat7"    "seat8"    "cargo3ft" "enghyb"   "engelec"  "price35"
[7] "price40"
```

Now we have a vector of 7 coefficient names.

To generate the simulated data we assume that the average part worths in the population are:

```
> mu <- c(-1, -1, 0.5, -1, -2, -1, -2)
> names(mu) <- coef.names
> mu
   seat7    seat8 cargo3ft   enghyb  engelec  price35  price40
    -1.0     -1.0      0.5     -1.0     -2.0     -1.0     -2.0
```

You can see that we've given names to the elements of the mu. While this isn't absolutely necessary, by keeping everything labeled using R's built in names, the output is easier to read.

We assume that each respondent has his or her own unique part worth coefficients and that these follow a multivariate normal distribution in the population with a covariance matrix Sigma:

```
> Sigma <- diag(c(0.3, 1, 0.1, 0.3, 1, 0.2, 0.3))
> dimnames(Sigma) <- list(coef.names, coef.names)
> Sigma["enghyb", "engelec"] <- Sigma["engelec", "enghyb"] <- 0.3
```

The last line above creates a correlation between the part worth for engelec (electric engine) and enghyb (hybrid engine), so respondents who have a stronger preference for engelec over enggas will also have a stronger preference for enghyb over enggas.

With `mu` and `Sigma` in hand, we generate each respondent's part worth coefficients using the `mvrnorm` function from the `MASS` package. We create a vector of respondent IDs for the 200 respondents (`resp.id`) and a factor variable indicating whether each respondent intends to use the minivan to carpool (`carpool`).

```
> set.seed(33040)
> resp.id <- 1:200 # respondent ids
> carpool <- sample(c("yes", "no"), size=length(resp.id), replace=TRUE,
+                   prob=c(0.3, 0.7))
> library(MASS)
> coefs <- mvrnorm(length(resp.id), mu=mu, Sigma=Sigma)
> colnames(coefs) <- coef.names
```

Finally, we adjust the part worths for respondents who use the minivan to carpool:

```
> coefs[carpool=="yes", "seat8"] <- coefs[carpool=="yes", "seat8"] + 2
> coefs[carpool=="yes", "seat7"] <- coefs[carpool=="yes", "seat7"] + 1.5
```

`coefs` is now a matrix where each row contains the part worths for each respondent. To get a better sense of what we have done, you could type `head(coefs)` or, better yet, `head(cbind(carpool, coefs))`. You can also use the `by()` command (Sect. 3.4.5) to compute mean part worths for those who do and do not carpool. Just keep in mind that these coefficients are parameters of the model we plan to *simulate* from, not the final *observed* data.

With `coefs` in hand, we are ready to generate our survey questions and the observed responses. Our survey includes 15 questions that each ask the respondent to choose from 3 alternative minivans. We set the number of questions and alternatives as variables (`nques` and `nalt`) so that we might easily change the size of the survey in the future:

```
> nques <- 15
> nalt <- 3
```

Next, we create a master list of all possible minivan profiles by passing the `attrib` list to `expand.grid()`, which we discuss below:

```
> profiles <- expand.grid(attrib)
> nrow(profiles)
[1] 54
> head(profiles)
  seat cargo eng price
1    6   2ft  gas    30
2    7   2ft  gas    30
3    8   2ft  gas    30
4    6   3ft  gas    30
5    7   3ft  gas    30
6    8   3ft  gas    30
```

As you can see, `profiles` has 54 rows, representing all possible combinations of 3 levels of seating capacity, 2 levels of cargo capacity, 3 levels of engine and 3 levels of price ($3 \times 2 \times 3 \times 3 = 54$). We can convert `profiles` to dummy coding using `model.matrix()`.

```
> profiles.coded <- model.matrix(~ seat + cargo + eng + price,
+                                data=profiles)[ , -1]
> head(profiles.coded)
  seat7 seat8 cargo3ft enghyb engelec price35 price40
1     0     0        0      0       0       0       0
2     1     0        0      0       0       0       0
3     0     1        0      0       0       0       0
4     0     0        1      0       0       0       0
5     1     0        1      0       0       0       0
6     0     1        1      0       0       0       0
```

`profiles.coded` now contains 54 rows, one for each possible combination of features, that are coded using the dummy coding scheme.

We haven't yet reviewed `expand.grid()` and `model.matrix()`; they are utility functions for handling factor variables. They are used under the hood in linear modeling routines such as `lm()` and `predict()` (Chap. 7). Because choice models are a variant of linear models, we can use these to generate our choice data. The only adjustment we need to make is to remove the intercept from the result of `model.matrix()` because choice models typically do not include intercepts.

Now that the respondent part worth coefficients are in `coefs` and the set of all possible minivan profiles is in `profiles.coded`, we are ready to generate our hypothetical survey questions and responses and store them in a data frame called `cbc.df`. For each of the 200 respondents, we choose `nques*nalt` (or $15 \times 3 = 45$) profiles at random from the list of all possible profiles in `profiles.coded`. The profiles indicated by the vector `profiles.i` are the profiles that we show respondent i in the survey: the first 3 profiles are the alternatives shown in choice 1, the next 3 profiles are the alternatives for choice 2, and so forth.

We compute each respondent's expected utility for each profile by multiplying the respondent's `coefs` by the coded product profile. (This happens in the line `utility <- profiles.coded[profiles.i, ]%*%coefs[i, ]` in the code below. We then compute choice probabilities for each alternative in the question according to the multinomial logit probabilities, computed as `probs <- exp(wide.util)/rowSums(exp(wide.util))`. We then take a random draw to determine which of the `nalt` products the customer chooses `choice <- apply(probs, 1, function(x) sample(1:nalt, size=1, prob=x))`. Finally, we append the choices and profiles to the `cbc.df` data frame. All of these steps are repeated for each respondent.

```
> cbc.df <- data.frame(NULL)
> for (i in seq_along(resp.id)) {
+    profiles.i <- sample(1:nrow(profiles), size=nques*nalt)
+    utility <- profiles.coded[profiles.i, ] %*% coefs[i, ]
+    wide.util <- matrix(data=utility, ncol=nalt, byrow=TRUE)
+    probs <- exp(wide.util) / rowSums(exp(wide.util))
+    choice <- apply(probs, 1, function(x) sample(1:nalt, size=1, prob=x))
+    choice <- rep(choice, each=nalt)==rep(1:nalt, nques)
+    conjoint.i <- data.frame(resp.id=rep(i, nques),
+                             ques = rep(1:nques, each=nalt),
+                             alt = rep(1:nalt, nques),
+                             carpool = rep(carpool[i], nques),
+                             profiles[profiles.i, ],
+                             choice = as.numeric(choice))
+    cbc.df <- rbind(cbc.df, conjoint.i)
+ }
> # Tidy up, keeping cbc.df and attrib
> rm(a, i, resp.id, carpool, mu, Sigma, coefs, coef.names,
+    conjoint.i, profiles, profiles.i, profiles.coded, utility,
+    wide.util, probs, choice, nalt, nques)
```

The code above leverages R's vector and matrix operations quite extensively. Going through it carefully and figuring out how each step works may take some time, but it will help you understand R's matrix computations and give you a clearer understanding of the assumptions of the multinomial logit model. At the core, this model is very similar to a linear model; the equation for `utility` is, in fact, a linear model. What makes a choice model distinct is that the utility is not observed directly; we only observe which product the respondent chooses. This why we haven't stored the utility in our synthetic data in cbc.df.

In the code above, we have generated data from a choice model called a *hierarchical multinomial logit model*. *Hierarchical* refers to the fact that there is a different set of coefficients for each respondent and that those coefficients follow an "upper level" model for the population. In our code, the parameters of the upper level model are mu, Sigma and the adjustments we made for people who use their minivan to carpool. At the "lower level," the choices of an individual consumer follow a multinomial logit. The *hierarchical multinomial logit model* has become the workhorse of choice-based conjoint and is incorporated into commercial software for conjoint analysis such as Sawtooth Software and JMP. In this chapter, we begin by analyzing the data using the simpler multinomial logit model in Sect. 13.3, and then estimate the *hierarchical* multinomial logit model in Sects. 13.4 and 13.5.

13.3 Fitting a Choice Model

The simulated choice-based conjoint data is in the cbc.df data frame.

```
> head(cbc.df)
   resp.id ques alt carpool seat cargo  eng price choice
19       1    1   1     yes    6  2ft   gas    35      0
12       1    1   2     yes    8  3ft   hyb    30      0
4        1    1   3     yes    6  3ft   gas    30      1
1        1    2   1     yes    6  2ft   gas    30      0
23       1    2   2     yes    7  3ft   gas    35      1
31       1    2   3     yes    6  2ft  elec    35      0
```

The first three rows in cbc.df describe the first question that was asked of respondent 1, which is the question shown in Fig. 13.1. The choice column shows that this respondent chose the third alternative, which was a 6-passenger gas engine minivan with 3ft of cargo capacity at a price of $30000 (represented in $1000s as "30"). resp.id indicates which respondent answered this question, ques indicates that these first three rows were the profiles in the first question and alt indicates that the first row was alternative 1, the second was alternative 2 and the third was alternative 3. (The row numbers all the way to the left in the output are not very meaningful. They indicate the profile number from our master list of 54 profiles that were used to generate the question; R carried this information over when we generated the data.) The variable choice indicates which alternative the respondent chose; it takes the value of 1 for the profile in each choice question that was indicated as the preferred alternative.

The cbc.df data frame organizes the data in what is sometimes called "long" format, where each profile is on its own line and there is a column that indicates which question the profile was displayed in. This is generally our preferred format for choice data, since it allows you to have a different number of profiles in each question by including additional rows. However, there are several other popular formats including a "wide" format, where each row corresponds to a different question and another format where the profiles are stored separately from the choices.

Because there is no standard format for choice data, when you work with different R packages or use data collected with other software systems, you need to pay close attention to how the package you are using expects the data to be formatted. Fortunately, there are R functions that can be helpful when reformatting data including base functions such as `reshape()`. You should never have to resort to tedious manual reformatting using a spreadsheet tool. Often someone else has written reliable R code to do the reformatting. For example, Rcbc [33] provides a helpful set of utilities for converting from the format used by Sawtooth Software into the format used by the `ChoiceModelR` package.

13.3.1 Inspecting Choice Data

Once you have your data properly formatted, it is tempting to estimate a complete choice model immediately. Popular choice modeling software packages make easy to fit a model without even doing basic descriptives on the data. Don't fall into this trap! As with any other modeling, it is important to first get an understanding of the data using basic descriptives. We start with `summary`:

```
> summary(cbc.df)
     resp.id              ques              alt         carpool        seat          cargo
 Min.   :   1.00    Min.   :  1     Min.   :1     yes:2655    6:3024    2ft:4501
 1st Qu.:  50.75    1st Qu.:  4     1st Qu.:1     no :6345    7:2993    3ft:4499
 Median :100.50     Median :  8     Median :2                8:2983
 Mean   :100.50     Mean   :  8     Mean   :2
 3rd Qu.:150.25     3rd Qu.: 12     3rd Qu.:3
 Max.   :200.00     Max.   : 15     Max.   :3
...
```

We see how many times each level of each attribute appeared in the questions (about 3000 times for three-level attributes and about 4500 times for two-level attributes). However, a more informative way to summarize choice data is to compute *choice counts*, which are cross tabs on the number of times respondents chose an alternative at each feature level. We can do this easily using `xtabs()`, covered in Chap. 5:

```
> xtabs(choice ~ price, data=cbc.df)
price
  30    35    40
1486   956   558
```

Respondents chose a minivan at the $30K price point much more often than they chose minivans priced at $35K or $40K. If we compute counts for the `cargo` attribute, we find that the choices were more balanced between the two options, suggesting that `cargo` was not as important to customers as `price`:

```
> xtabs(choice ~ cargo, data=cbc.df)
cargo
 2ft   3ft
1312  1688
```

We encourage you to compute choice counts for each attribute before estimating a choice model. If you find that your model's estimates or predicted shares are not consistent with the raw counts, consider whether there could be a mistake in the data formatting. Many times, a junior analyst has come to one of us saying, "The predictions from my choice model don't make sense to the client," and our first question is always, "Have you looked at the raw choice counts?"

Often this reveals a mistake, but when there is no mistake, it can be helpful to show the clients the raw choice counts to help them understand that your model predictions are based on how people responded in the survey. With that warning, we can now estimate our first choice model. By fitting a choice model, we can get a precise measurement of how much each attribute is associated with respondents' choices.

13.3.2 Fitting Choice Models with `mlogit()`

We use the `mlogit` package, which you may need to install with `install.packages()`. `mlogit` estimates the most basic and commonly-used choice model, the *multinomial logit* model. This model is also called the *conditional logit*. For faster computation with large models, you might consider the `mnlogit` package as an alternative.

`mlogit` requires the choice data to be in a special data format created using the `mlogit.data()` function. You pass your choice data to `mlogit.data`, along with a few parameters telling it how the data is organized. `mlogit.data` accepts data in either a "long" or a "wide" format and you tell it which you have using the `shape` parameter. The `choice`, `varying` and `id.var` parameters indicate which columns contain the response data, the attributes and the respondent ids, respectively.

```
> library(mlogit)
> cbc.mlogit <- mlogit.data(data=cbc.df, choice="choice", shape="long",
+                           varying=3:6, alt.levels=paste("pos",1:3),
+                           id.var="resp.id")
```

The resulting `cbc.mlogit` is an `mlogit.data` object that can be used to estimate a model with `mlogit()`. The syntax for `mlogit` uses formula notation similarly to other functions for regression models in R:

```
> m1 <- mlogit(choice ~ 0 + seat + cargo + eng + price, data = cbc.mlogit)
> summary(m1)
...
Frequencies of alternatives:
   pos 1    pos 2    pos 3
0.32700  0.33467  0.33833
...
Coefficients :
            Estimate Std. Error  t-value  Pr(>|t|)
seat7     -0.535280   0.062360  -8.5837  < 2.2e-16 ***
seat8     -0.305840   0.061129  -5.0032  5.638e-07 ***
cargo3ft   0.477449   0.050888   9.3824  < 2.2e-16 ***
enghyb    -0.811282   0.060130 -13.4921  < 2.2e-16 ***
engelec   -1.530762   0.067456 -22.6926  < 2.2e-16 ***
price35   -0.913656   0.060601 -15.0765  < 2.2e-16 ***
price40   -1.725851   0.069631 -24.7856  < 2.2e-16 ***
---
Signif. codes:  0 '***' 0.001 '**' 0.01 '*' 0.05 '.' 0.1 ' ? 1

Log-Likelihood: -2581.6
```

The output also looks quite similar to what we have seen for other models. At the bottom of the output is a table of the estimated part worth coefficients for the population. The `Estimate` lists the estimated parameter for each level; these must be interpreted relative to the base levels of each attribute. For example, the estimate for `seat7` measures the attractiveness of 7 passenger minivans *relative to 6 passenger minivans*. The negative sign tells us that, on average, our simulated customers preferred 6 seat minivans to 7 seat minivans. Estimates that are larger in magnitude indicate stronger preferences, so we can see that customers strongly disliked electric engines (relative to the base level, which is gas) and disliked the $40K price (relative to the base level price of $30). These parameter estimates are on the logit scale (Sect. 9.2.1) and typically range between -2 and 2.

The `Std. Error` column gives a sense of how precise the estimate is, given the data, along with a statistical test of whether the coefficient is different than zero. A non-significant test result indicates that there is no detectable difference in preference for that level relative to the base level. Just as with any statistical model, the more data you have in you conjoint study (for a given set of attributes), the smaller the standard errors will be. Similarly, if there are many attributes and levels in a study (for a fixed number of respondents answering a survey of a given length), the part worth estimates will be very imprecise. We'll discuss more what this means for an analysis in Sect. 13.6.

You may have wondered why we included `0 +` in the formula for `m1`, indicating that we did not want an intercept included in our model. We could estimate a model with an intercept:

```
> m2 <- mlogit(choice ~ seat + cargo + eng + price, data = cbc.mlogit)
> summary(m2)
...
Coefficients :
                   Estimate Std. Error  t-value   Pr(>|t|)
pos 2:(intercept)  0.028980   0.051277   0.5652     0.5720
pos 3:(intercept)  0.041271   0.051384   0.8032     0.4219
seat7             -0.535369   0.062369  -8.5840  < 2.2e-16 ***
seat8             -0.304369   0.061164  -4.9763  6.481e-07 ***
cargo3ft           0.477705   0.050899   9.3854  < 2.2e-16 ***
enghyb            -0.811494   0.060130 -13.4956  < 2.2e-16 ***
engelec           -1.529423   0.067471 -22.6677  < 2.2e-16 ***
price35           -0.913777   0.060608 -15.0769  < 2.2e-16 ***
price40           -1.726878   0.069654 -24.7922  < 2.2e-16 ***
...
Log-Likelihood: -2581.3
McFadden R^2:   0.21674
Likelihood ratio test : chisq = 1428.5 (p.value = < 2.22e-16)
```

When we include the intercept, `mlogit` adds two additional parameters that indicate preference for the different positions in the question (left, right or middle in Fig. 13.1): `pos2:(intercept)` indicates the relative preference of the second position in the question (versus the first) and `pos3:(intercept)` indicates the preference for the third position (versus the first.) These are sometimes called *alternative specific constants* or ASC's to differentiate them from the single intercept in a linear model.

In a typical conjoint analysis study, we don't expect that people will choose a minivan because it is on the left or the right in a survey question! For that reason, we would not expect the estimated alternative specific constants to differ from zero. If we found one of these parameters to be significant, that might indicate that some respondents are simply choosing the first or the last option without considering the question.

In this model, the intercept parameter estimates are non-significant and close to zero. This suggests that it was reasonable to leave them out of our first model, but we can test this formally using lrtest():

```
> lrtest(m1, m2)
Likelihood ratio test

Model 1: choice ~ 0 + seat + cargo + eng + price
Model 2: choice ~ seat + cargo + eng + price
  #Df  LogLik Df  Chisq Pr(>Chisq)
1   7 -2581.6
2   9 -2581.3  2 0.6789     0.7122
```

This function performs a statistical test called a likelihood ratio test, which can be used to compare two choice models where one model has a subset of the parameters of another model. Comparing m1 to m2, results in a p-value (Pr(>Chisq)) of 0.7122. Since the p-value is much greater than 0.05, we can conclude that m1 and m2 fit the data equally well. This suggests that we don't need the alternative specific constants to fit the present data.

There are a few occasions where alternative specific constants do make sense. In some conjoint studies, the respondent is presented with several "fixed" alternatives. Option 1 might be a salad, option 2 might be a sandwich and option 3 might be a soup. In each question, the attributes of those options vary, but the respondent is always asked to chose from one salad, one sandwich and one soup. Similarly, there might be a study of commuters' choice of transportation alternatives where alternative 1 is always a bus, alternative 2 is always a train and alternative 3 is always driving. In such cases, you should include the alternative specific constants, but in the majority of conjoint analysis surveys in marketing, alternative specific constants aren't used.

You don't have to treat every attribute in a conjoint study as a factor. As with linear models, some predictors may be factors while others are numeric. For example, we can include price as a numeric predictor with a simple change to the model formula. In the model formula, we convert price to character vector using as.character and then to a number using as.numeric. (If you use as.numeric without as.character first, price will be converted to the values 1, 2 and 3 due to the way R stores factors internally. Converting to a character first results in values of 30, 35 and 40.)

```
> m3 <- mlogit(choice ~ 0 + seat + cargo + eng
+                  + as.numeric(as.character(price)),
+          data = cbc.mlogit)
> summary(m3)
...
Coefficients :
                                  Estimate  Std. Error  t-value   Pr(>|t|)
seat7                            -0.5345392  0.0623518  -8.5730  < 2.2e-16 ***
seat8                            -0.3061074  0.0611184  -5.0084  5.488e-07 ***
cargo3ft                          0.4766936  0.0508632   9.3721  < 2.2e-16 ***
enghyb                           -0.8107339  0.0601149 -13.4864  < 2.2e-16 ***
engelec                          -1.5291247  0.0673982 -22.6879  < 2.2e-16 ***
as.numeric(as.character(price)) -0.1733053  0.0069398 -24.9726  < 2.2e-16 ***
---
Signif. codes:  0 '***' 0.001 '**' 0.01 '*' 0.05 '.' 0.1 ' ' 1

Log-Likelihood: -2582.1
```

The output now shows a single parameter for price. The estimate is negative indicating that people prefer lower prices to higher prices. A quick likelihood ratio test suggests that the model with a single price parameter fits just as well as our first model.

```
> lrtest(m1, m3)
Likelihood ratio test

Model 1: choice ~ 0 + seat + cargo + eng + price
Model 2: choice ~ 0 + seat + cargo + eng + as.numeric(as.character(price))
  #Df  LogLik Df  Chisq Pr(>Chisq)
1   7 -2581.6
2   6 -2582.1 -1 0.9054     0.3413
```

Given this finding, we choose m3 as our preferred model because it has fewer parameters.

13.3.3 Reporting Choice Model Findings

It is often difficult, even for those with training in choice models, to interpret choice model part worth estimates directly. The coefficients are on an unfamiliar scale and they measure relative preference for the levels, which can make them difficult to understand. So, instead of presenting the coefficients, most choice modelers prefer to focus on using the model to make *choice share predictions* or to compute *willingness-to-pay* for each attribute.

Willingness-to-Pay

In a model like m3 where we estimate a single parameter for price, we can compute the average willingness-to-pay for a particular level of an attribute by dividing the coefficient for that level by the price coefficient.

```
> coef(m3)["cargo3ft"]/(-coef(m3)["as.numeric(as.character(price))"]/1000)
cargo3ft
2750.601
```

The result is a number measured in dollars, $2,750.60 in this case. (We divide by 1000 because our prices were recorded in 1000's of dollars.) Willingness-to-pay is a bit of a misnomer; the proper interpretation of this number is that, on average, customers would be equally divided between a minivan with 2 ft of cargo space and a minivan with 3 ft of cargo space that costs $2,750.60 more. Another way to think of it is that $2,750.60 is the price at which customers become indifferent between the two cargo capacity options. This same willingness to pay value can be computed for every attribute in the study and reported to decision makers to help them understand how much customers value various features.

Simulating Choice Shares

While willingness-to-pay is more interpretable than attribute coefficients, it can still be difficult to understand. Many analysts prefer to focus exclusively on using the model to make share predictions. A share simulator allows you to define a number of different alternatives and then use the model to predict how customers would choose among those new alternatives. For example, you could use the model to predict choice share for the company's new minivan design against a set of key competitors. By varying the attributes of the planned minivan design, you can see how changes in the design affect the choice share.

Unfortunately, there isn't a handy `predict()` function for `mlogit` model objects, as there are for many other types of model objects. Luckily, it isn't too difficult to write our own:

```
> # Predicting shares
> predict.mnl <- function(model, data) {
+   # Function for predicting shares from a multinomial logit model
+   # model: mlogit object returned by mlogit()
+   # data: a data frame containing the set of designs for which you want to
+   #        predict shares.  Same format as the data used to estimate model.
+   data.model <- model.matrix(update(model$formula, 0 ~ .), data = data)[,-1]
+   utility <- data.model %*% model$coef
+   share <- exp(utility)/sum(exp(utility))
+   cbind(share, data)
+ }
```

In a moment, we'll walk through this code more carefully, but first let's see how it works. The comments tell us that the function takes two inputs: a model object returned from `mlogit()` and a data frame containing the set of designs for which you want to predict shares. We already have several model objects, so all we need to do is create new data. One way to do this is to create the full set of possible designs using `expand.grid()` and select the designs we want by row number:

```
> (new.data <- expand.grid(attrib)[c(8, 1, 3, 41, 49, 26), ])
   seat cargo  eng price
8     7   2ft  hyb    30
1     6   2ft  gas    30
3     8   2ft  gas    30
41    7   3ft  gas    40
49    6   2ft elec    40
26    7   2ft  hyb    35
```

We then pass these designs to `predict.mnl()` to determine what customers would choose if they had to pick among these 6 minivan alternatives:

```
> predict.mnl(m3, new.data)
       share seat cargo  eng price
8  0.11268892    7   2ft  hyb    30
1  0.43263922    6   2ft  gas    30
3  0.31855551    8   2ft  gas    30
41 0.07216867    7   3ft  gas    40
49 0.01657221    6   2ft elec    40
26 0.04737548    7   2ft  hyb    35
```

The model-predicted shares are shown in the column labeled `share` and we can see that among this set of products, we would expect respondents to choose the 7 seat hybrid engine minivan with 2 ft of cargo space at $30K a little more than 11% of the time. If a company was planning to launch a minivan like this, they could use the model to see how changing the attributes of this product would affect the choice shares. Note that these share predictions are always made relative to a particular set of competitors; the share for the first minivan would change if the competitive set were different.

For those who are new to choice models, we should caution against using share predictions based on survey data as a market share forecast. While these share predictions are typically a good representation of how respondents would behave if they were asked to choose among these 6 minivans in a new survey, that predicted survey response might not translate directly to sales in the marketplace. Customers might not be able to find the product in stores or they may react differently to the features when they see them in the showroom. We generally recommend that the analyst be careful to communicate this by labeling the predicted shares as "survey shares" or "preference shares" to alert others to this distinction. If you estimate a multinomial logit model using retail purchase data, as we discussed earlier, you would not need to make this caveat, as your predictions would be based on real-world purchases.

We could compute shares using model m1, which treated price as a factor rather than a continuous variable:

```
> predict.mnl(m1, new.data)
        share seat cargo  eng price
8  0.11273356    7   2ft  hyb    30
1  0.43336911    6   2ft  gas    30
3  0.31917819    8   2ft  gas    30
41 0.07281396    7   3ft  gas    40
49 0.01669280    6   2ft elec    40
26 0.04521237    7   2ft  hyb    35
```

We see that the predicted shares are almost identical, confirming our previous conclusion that m3 is very similar to m1. (Comparing predicted shares is not the best way to compare two models. For a formal comparison of models, we recommend lrtest().)

Now that we have seen how predict.mnl() works, let's take a closer look at the code for the function. Ignoring the comments, the code is just four lines. We repeat them here so that we can discuss each line, but you don't need to type them into the console again. On the first line, we convert the data, which is stored as factors, to a coded matrix:

```
data.model <- model.matrix(update(model$formula, 0 ~ .), data = data)[,-1]
```

We do this using two functions from base R for working with formulas. The function model.matrix, which we saw earlier in the chapter, converts the data from factors to coded effects. It requires the right-hand side of the formula from model, which we obtain using the update function for formulas. We also have to remove the first column of the result of model.matrix, because our choice model doesn't have an intercept. On the next line, we compute the utility for each product by multiplying the coded data by the model coefficients using matrix multiplication:

```
utility <- data.model %*% model$coef
```

The result is a utility value for each product in the set based on its attributes. Finally, we convert that to shares using the multinomial logit equation:

```
share <- exp(utility) / sum(exp(utility))
```

The function then returns the shares along with the product design data. (Experienced choice modelers will notice that we are slightly abusing terminology when we call this utility. More precisely this should be called the deterministic portion of the utility, since it doesn't include the error term. We do not include a stochastic

Fig. 13.2 Sensitivity plot showing how share for the planned design changes as we change each attribute, relative to a set of competing designs. The planned design is a 7-passenger hybrid minivan with 2 ft. of cargo space offered at $30000

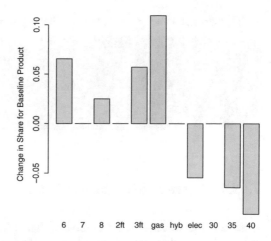

component in the share simulator, because we want to report the expected average shares across many choices.)

Sensitivity Plots

Often a product design team has a particular product design in mind and wants to know how share would change if they were to change their design. For example, suppose the minivan designers plan to build a 7-passenger hybrid minivan with 2 ft of cargo space and sell it at $30K. The model can be used to predict how share would change if different levels of the attributes were included (while keeping the competitive set fixed.) The plot in Fig. 13.2 shows how share would change if we changed each of the attributes of the design, one at a time. We see that changing the planned 7-seat design to a 6-seat design would increase share by just under 0.07. Increasing the price to $35K would decrease share by about 0.06. This gives the design team an at-a-glance picture of how changes in their design affect choice share.

Producing this plot using R is relatively simple: we just need loop through all the attribute levels, compute a share prediction and save the predicted share for the target design. Since this is an analysis we do regularly, we wrote a function to do it.

```
> sensitivity.mnl <- function(model, attrib, base.data, competitor.data) {
+    # Function for creating data for a share-sensitivity chart
+    # model: mlogit object returned by mlogit() function
+    # attrib: list of vectors with attribute levels to be used in sensitivity
+    # base.data: data frame containing baseline design of target product
+    # competitor.data: data frame containing design of competitive set
+    data <- rbind(base.data, competitor.data)
+    base.share <- predict.mnl(model, data)[1,1]
+    share <- NULL
+    for (a in seq_along(attrib)) {
+      for (i in attrib[[a]]) {
+        data[1,] <- base.data
+        data[1,a] <- i
+        share <- c(share, predict.mnl(model, data)[1,1])
+      }
+    }
+    data.frame(level=unlist(attrib), share=share, increase=share-base.share)
+ }
```

Using `sensitivity.mnl`, we create the plot in Fig. 13.2 with four commands:

```
> base.data <- expand.grid(attrib)[c(8), ]
> competitor.data <- expand.grid(attrib)[c(1, 3, 41, 49, 26), ]
> (tradeoff <- sensitivity.mnl(m1, attrib, base.data, competitor.data))
        level       share      increase
seat1       6 0.17831027   0.06557671
seat2       7 0.11273356   0.00000000
...
price3     40 0.02211862  -0.09061494
> barplot(tradeoff$increase, horiz=FALSE, names.arg=tradeoff$level,
+         ylab="Change in Share for Baseline Product")
```

13.3.4   Share Predictions for Identical Alternatives

Occasionally, you may want to predict shares for two designs that are identical in terms of the attributes that you've included in your conjoint study. For example, you might be planning to offer a design that is the same as a competitor. A naive analyst might include both designs in a set to estimate with `predict.mnl()` and there is nothing to stop one from doing that:

```
> new.data.2 <- expand.grid(attrib)[c(8, 8, 1, 3, 41, 49, 26), ]
> predict.mnl(m1, new.data.2)
         share seat cargo   eng price
8    0.10131227    7   2ft   hyb    30
8.1  0.10131227    7   2ft   hyb    30
1    0.38946350    6   2ft   gas    30
3    0.28684152    8   2ft   gas    30
41   0.06543701    7   3ft   gas    40
49   0.01500162    6   2ft  elec    40
26   0.04063181    7   2ft   hyb    35
```

However, these share predictions may be considered unrealistic. When we estimate shares from m1 with just one copy of design 8, we get a share of about 0.113. With two copies of the same design, each alternative is predicted to get a share of about 0.101 for a total of 0.202 between the two of them. It seems quite unreasonable that people would be more likely to choose a 7-passenger, 2 ft, hybrid at $30K just because there are two of them in the choice set. Beyond that, the relative shares of all the other vehicles have remained the same, including the higher-priced 7 passenger hybrid (design 26 in the last row). Why wouldn't design 8 steal more share from design 26 than from the other non-hybrid vehicles?

While this is confusing, multinomial logit models make predictions in this way. Much has been written about this property of the multinomial logit model and there are many arguments about whether it is desirable. In fact, the property has been given a name: the *independence of irrelevant alternatives* or IIA property. It is also sometimes called the "red bus/blue bus problem" based on an classic example that involves predicting share for two different color buses that have otherwise identical features. Predictions from the multinomial logit model for two identical alternatives or even two nearly-identical alternatives will exhibit this property.

More sophisticated hierarchical models, which we discuss in Sect. 13.5, relax this property somewhat, although they still may make predictions for similar or identical

alternatives that seem unreasonable [46]. There are a number of proposed methods to estimate choice models that do not have the IIA property including nested
logit, generalized logit, and multinomial probit. If you need to predict shares for
nearly-identical designs, we encourage you to review those alternatives. However,
the majority of marketers today use either the multinomial logit or the hierarchical
multinomial logit model, and—we hope—try to avoid including identical or nearly
identical designs when estimating shares.

13.3.5 Planning the Sample Size for a Conjoint Study

A crucial issue in planning a successful conjoint analysis study is to decide how
many respondents should complete the survey. To see how sample size affects the
model estimates and share predictions, let's estimate a model using just the data from
the first 25 respondents. We do this by creating small.conjoint, which is an
mlogit.data object with just the first $25 \times 15 \times 3 = 1125$ rows of our original
cbc.df data, corresponding to the survey responses for the first 25 respondents.

```
> small.cbc <- mlogit.data(data=cbc.df[1:(25*15*3),],
+                          choice="choice", shape="long",
+                          varying=3:6, alt.levels=paste("pos", 1:3),
+                          id.var="resp.id")
> m4 <- mlogit(choice ~ 0 + seat + cargo + eng + price, data = small.cbc)
```

If we take a look at the coefficient estimates for m4 and compare them to the coefficient estimates for m1 (above), we can see that the estimated coefficients for m4 are
similar, but the standard errors for the coefficients are more than three times as big,
reflecting the fact that with less data, our estimates of the model coefficients are less
precise.

```
> summary(m4)   # larger standard errors
...
          Estimate Std. Error t-value  Pr(>|t|)
seat7     -0.74326   0.17767  -4.1833 2.873e-05 ***
seat8     -0.15180   0.16859  -0.9004 0.3679142
cargo3ft   0.45613   0.14459   3.1546 0.0016071 **
enghyb    -0.59674   0.16838  -3.5440 0.0003941 ***
engelec   -1.62677   0.19764  -8.2311 2.220e-16 ***
price35   -0.81508   0.17304  -4.7105 2.471e-06 ***
price40   -1.71390   0.20304  -8.4410 < 2.2e-16 ***
...
```

The standard errors are also higher for the attribute-levels that are least often chosen,
including the engelec and price40 coefficients. In general, standard errors for
less-frequently chosen attributes will be higher. One method for planning sample
sizes focuses on reducing the standard errors of the estimates to acceptable levels.
We discuss this further when we discuss the design of conjoint surveys in Sect. 13.6.

We can also compare predictions between m1 and m4:

```
> cbind(predict.mnl(m4, new.data), predict.mnl(m1, new.data))
        share seat cargo  eng price       share seat cargo  eng price
8  0.10876219    7   2ft  hyb    30  0.11273356    7   2ft  hyb    30
1  0.41536666    6   2ft  gas    30  0.43336911    6   2ft  gas    30
3  0.35686673    8   2ft  gas    30  0.31917819    8   2ft  gas    30
41 0.05615650    7   3ft  gas    40  0.07281396    7   3ft  gas    40
```

```
49  0.01470947     6     2ft  elec     40  0.01669280     6     2ft  elec     40
26  0.04813846     7     2ft  hyb      35  0.04521237     7     2ft  hyb      35
```

Here we find that the two models make similar share predictions. This illustrates the fact that comparing share predictions is not the ideal way to compare two different conjoint survey designs. When we look at the standard errors for the coefficients, we see the difference between m1 and m4 more clearly.

If we looked at the standard errors of the share predictions, they would be more precise for m1, but we can't see that here because there are no standard errors reported for shares. While it is possible to compute standard errors for share predictions, it requires using the "delta method" or a bootstrapping strategy, both of which are difficult to do outside of a programming environment like R. So, among those who do not use R, it is uncommon to report standard errors or estimates of uncertainty for share predictions.

This is unfortunate; decision makers often see only the point estimates for share predictions and are not informed about the confidence intervals of those shares. An ambitious reader might write code to produce intervals for share predictions from the multinomial logit model, but we will hold off on estimating intervals for share predictions until we review choice models in a Bayesian framework in Sect. 13.5.

13.4   Adding Consumer Heterogeneity to Choice Models

Up to this point, we have focused on the multinomial logit model, which estimates a single set of part worth coefficients for a whole sample. In this section, we look at a model that allows for each respondent to have his or her own coefficients. Different people have different preferences, and models that estimate individual-level coefficients can fit data better and make more accurate predictions than sample-level models (see [168]). If you are not familiar with hierarchical models, you should review the basics in Sect. 9.3.

To estimate a model where each respondent has his or her own part worths, it is helpful to have multiple observations for each respondent. This is not a problem in a typical conjoint analysis study because each respondent answers multiple question. However, it can be a problem when estimating choice models using retail purchase data, because many people only make a single purchase. Most conjoint analysis practitioners routinely estimate heterogeneous choice models with conjoint survey data and it is easy to do this in R. In this section, we show how to estimate hierarchical choice models using mlogit, which uses frequentist methods. In Sect. 13.5, we show how to estimate heterogeneous choice models using Bayesian methods.

13.4.1 Estimating Mixed Logit Models with `mlogit()`

The statistical term for coefficients that vary across respondents (or customers) is *random coefficients* or random effects (see Sect. 9.3.1). To estimate a multinomial logit model with random coefficients using `mlogit`, we define a vector indicating which coefficients should vary across customers. `mlogit` requires a character vector the same length as the coefficient vector with a letter code indicating what distribution the random coefficients should follow across the respondents: 'n' for normal, 'l' for log-normal, 't' for truncated normal, and 'u' for uniform. For this analysis, we assume that all the coefficients are normally distributed across the population and call our vector `m1.rpar`.

```
> m1.rpar <- rep("n", length=length(m1$coef))
> names(m1.rpar) <- names(m1$coef)
> m1.rpar
   seat7      seat8  cargo3ft     enghyb   engelec   price35   price40
     "n"        "n"       "n"        "n"       "n"       "n"       "n"
```

We pass this vector to `mlogit` as the `rpar` parameter, which is short for "*random parameters*". In addition, we tell `mlogit` that we have multiple choice observations for each respondent (`panel=TRUE`) and whether we want to allow the random parameters to be correlated or independant. For this first run, we assume that we do not want random parameters to be correlated (`correlation=FALSE`), a setting we reconsider below.

```
> m1.hier <- mlogit(choice ~ 0 + seat + eng + cargo + price,
+                   data = cbc.mlogit,
+                   panel=TRUE, rpar = m1.rpar, correlation = FALSE)
```

The algorithm to estimate the heterogeneous logit model is computationally intensive, so it may take a few seconds to run. Once it finishes, you can look at the parameter estimates using `summary()`:

```
> summary(m1.hier)
...
Coefficients :
             Estimate Std. Error    t-value   Pr(>|t|)
seat7       -0.642241   0.070893    -9.0593  < 2.2e-16 ***
seat8       -0.390021   0.070460    -5.5353  3.106e-08 ***
enghyb      -0.926145   0.067456   -13.7296  < 2.2e-16 ***
engelec     -1.831864   0.083439   -21.9544  < 2.2e-16 ***
cargo3ft     0.550838   0.058459     9.4226  < 2.2e-16 ***
price35     -1.081310   0.070874   -15.2567  < 2.2e-16 ***
price40     -1.991787   0.085312   -23.3471  < 2.2e-16 ***
sd.seat7    -0.651807   0.101906    -6.3961  1.594e-10 ***
sd.seat8     0.995007   0.093397    10.6535  < 2.2e-16 ***
sd.enghyb    0.159495   0.137950     1.1562   0.247607
sd.engelec   0.973303   0.099850     9.7476  < 2.2e-16 ***
sd.cargo3ft  0.307194   0.131109     2.3430   0.019127 *
sd.price35  -0.260907   0.121369    -2.1497   0.031579 *
sd.price40   0.418148   0.128104     3.2641   0.001098 **
---
Signif. codes:  0 '***' 0.001 '**' 0.01 '*' 0.05 '.' 0.1 ' ' 1

Log-Likelihood: -2498.5

random coefficients
            Min.      1st Qu.      Median         Mean    3rd Qu.   Max.
seat7      -Inf   -1.0818780  -0.6422410   -0.6422410  -0.2026039    Inf
seat8      -Inf   -1.0611428  -0.3900209   -0.3900209   0.2811010    Inf
cargo3ft   -Inf    0.3436387   0.5508377    0.5508377   0.7580366    Inf
enghyb     -Inf   -1.0337226  -0.9261449   -0.9261449  -0.8185673    Inf
engelec    -Inf   -2.4883466  -1.8318636   -1.8318636  -1.1753805    Inf
```

```
price35   -Inf  -1.2572890  -1.0813097  -1.0813097  -0.9053304   Inf
price40   -Inf  -2.2738236  -1.9917870  -1.9917870  -1.7097505   Inf
```

The results show 14 estimated parameters, which is twice as many as we had in
m1. These parameters describe the average part worth coefficients across the population of respondents (labeled seat7, seat8, etc.) as well as how those parameters
vary across the population (reported as standard deviations and labeled sd.seat7,
sd.seat8, etc.)

The standard deviation parameter estimates indicate that there is a lot of heterogeneity
in preference for 7 or 8 seats over 6 seats. For example, the estimate of sd.seat8 is
about 0.995—larger than the mean estimate for the level of −0.39—which suggests
that some people prefer 6 seats to 8, while others prefer 8. Another way to see this
is in the output section labeled random coefficients, which shows the range
of respondent-level coefficients. For seat8, the first quartile is −1.06 (indicating
a preference for 6 seats) and the 3rd quartile is 0.281 (indicating a preference for
8 seats). Because we specified the random coefficients as normally distributed, the
model assumes that the majority of respondents are in the middle, slightly preferring
6 seats to 8. Given that there is a large fraction of respondents who prefer 8 seats,
it may make sense for the company to offer a minivan with 6 seats *and* a minivan
with 8 seats. To tell that for certain, you could make several share predictions and
compare the potential increase in market share to the costs of offering both options.

You might notice that some of the standard deviation estimates such as sd.seat7
are reported with *negative* values, which is impossible. This is an artifact of the
estimation routine, which occasionally reverses the sign. To check them, you may
use the stdev() function instead:

```
> stdev(m1.hier)
     seat7        seat8    cargo3ft      enghyb     engelec     price35     price40
0.6518068   0.9950068   0.3071936   0.1594949   0.9733032   0.2609073   0.4181480
```

There is one additional feature we can add to the random coefficients model using
mlogit(). Model m1 assumed that there were no correlations between the random coefficients, meaning that if one person prefers 8 seats over 6, we would not
expect that they also prefer 7 seats over 6. Including correlations in the random
coefficients allows us to determine, based on the data, whether people who like one
attribute also tend to like another attribute. This is easily done by including
correlations = TRUE as a parameter in the call to mlogit or by using the
update function provided by mlogit.

```
> m2.hier <- update(m1.hier, correlation = TRUE)
> summary(m2.hier)
...
Coefficients :
                 Estimate   Std. Error   t-value    Pr(>|t|)
seat7           -0.6571127   0.0730592    -8.9942   < 2.2e-16  ***
seat8           -0.4336405   0.0754669    -5.7461   9.132e-09  ***
enghyb          -0.9913358   0.0731532   -13.5515   < 2.2e-16  ***
engelec         -1.8613750   0.0855809   -21.7499   < 2.2e-16  ***
cargo3ft         0.6021314   0.0623728     9.6537   < 2.2e-16  ***
price35         -1.1819210   0.0770295   -15.3437   < 2.2e-16  ***
price40         -2.1749326   0.0960858   -22.6353   < 2.2e-16  ***
seat7.seat7      0.6830318   0.1046707     6.5255   6.776e-11  ***
seat7.seat8      1.0089934   0.1092730     9.2337   < 2.2e-16  ***
seat7.cargo3ft  -0.0624345   0.0962322    -0.6488   0.5164737
```

```
seat7.enghyb      -0.3517319   0.1146392   -3.0682  0.0021538  **
seat7.engelec     -0.1946944   0.0859581   -2.2650  0.0235131  *
seat7.price35      0.1318172   0.0973219    1.3544  0.1755947
...
```

The model m2.hier now includes many more parameters, so many that we have truncated the output. The additional parameters are the variance and covariance parameters between the random coefficients. seat7.seat7 is the variance of the seat7 random coefficient and seat7.seat8 is our estimate of the covariance between preference for 7 seats and preference for 8 seats. The estimate is significant and positive, indicating that people who prefer 7 seats also tend to prefer 8 seats. To get a better sense of the strength of this association, we can extract the covariance matrix using cov.mlogit and then convert it to a correlation matrix using cov2cor from base R.

```
> cov2cor(cov.mlogit(m2.hier))
              seat7        seat8     cargo3ft        enghyb      engelec  ...    price35
seat7     1.0000000   0.774540837  -0.1116303  -0.313095351  -0.4886197  ...  0.24366546
seat8     0.7745408   1.000000000   0.1364164  -0.001877182  -0.2351177  ... -0.07335863
cargo3ft -0.1116303   0.136416377   1.0000000   0.498038677  -0.6257625  ... -0.03750020
enghyb   -0.3130954  -0.001877182   0.4980387   1.000000000   0.1096523  ...  0.16249428
engelec  -0.4886197  -0.235117662  -0.6257625   0.109652292   1.0000000  ... -0.24671982
price35   0.2436655  -0.073358628  -0.0375002   0.162494277  -0.2467198  ...  1.00000000
price40   0.1318966  -0.034897989   0.3074710  -0.026541375  -0.4260211  ...  0.54721196
...
```

This matrix shows that the correlation between the part worth for 7 seats and the part worth for 8 seats is 0.77, a strong association. In real data, it is common to find correlations between levels of the same attribute; if an attribute is important to a respondent, then he or she will likely have parameters with larger absolute values for all the levels of that attribute. For this reason, we strongly recommend that you include correlations in all random coefficients choice models. When you review the estimates of those models, you should review both the mean part worth coefficients, which represent the *average* value that respondents place on each attribute, *and* the variance and covariances in preferences across the population.

We should emphasize that these model estimates are conditional on our assumption that decision makers' coefficients are normally distributed. Truncated normal distributions or uniform distributions should be considered in situations where the range of feasible values of the coefficients are bounded, e.g. when it should be assumed that everyone prefers a particular attribute. Recent research has investigated other specifications of heterogeneity, such as the generalized multinomial logit model [59] which is available in the gmnl package.

13.4.2   Share Prediction for Heterogeneous Choice Models

Reporting share predictions for heterogeneous choice models is largely the same as
for standard choice models. The key difference is in how those share predictions are
computed. The model assumes that there is a *population* of respondents, each with
different part worth coefficients. So, when we compute shares, we need to compute
the choice shares for many different respondents and then average over those to get
our overall share predictions. You can see how we do this by comparing our prediction
function for the hierarchical multinomial logit model to the prediction function we
had for the standard multinomial logit.

```
> predict.hier.mnl <- function(model, data, nresp=1000) {
+    # Function to predict shares of a hierarchical multinomial logit model
+    # model: mlogit object returned by mlogit()
+    # data: a data frame containing the set of designs for which you want to
+    #        predict shares.  Same format at the data used to estimate model.
+    # Note that this code assumes all model parameters are random
+    data.model <- model.matrix(update(model$formula, 0 ~ .), data = data)
+       [,-1]
+    coef.Sigma <- cov.mlogit(model)
+    coef.mu <- model$coef[1:dim(coef.Sigma)[1]]
+    draws <- mvrnorm(n=nresp, coef.mu, coet.Sigma)
+    shares <- matrix(NA, nrow=nresp, ncol=nrow(data))
+    for (i in 1:nresp) {
+       utility <- data.model%*%draws[i,]
+       share = exp(utility)/sum(exp(utility))
+       shares[i,] <- share
+    }
+    cbind(colMeans(shares), data)
+ }
```

The key difference is that we now compute the shares for each of `nresp=1000`
newly sampled, representative respondents. The part worths for these respondents
are drawn from a multivariate normal distribution with mean set at our estimated
value of `mu` and covariance equal to our estimated value of `Sigma` (`draws <-
mvrnorm(n=nresp, coef.mu, coef.Sigma)`). The computation for each
respondent is exactly the same as our computation in `predict.mnl`. Once we have
the shares for all of the representative respondents, we average across respondents
to get our overall share predictions.

We compute shares using `predict.hier.mnl` just as we did before with
`predict.mnl`. It may take a moment, because we are doing 1000 times more
computation.

```
> predict.hier.mnl(m2.hier, data=new.data)
    colMeans(shares) seat cargo   eng price
8        0.08959674    7   2ft   hyb    30
1        0.46390066    6   2ft   gas    30
3        0.34231092    8   2ft   gas    30
41       0.05370156    7   3ft   gas    40
49       0.01797406    6   2ft  elec    40
26       0.03251606    7   2ft   hyb    35
```

If you compare these share predictions to those we got with `predict.mnl(m1,
data=new.data)`, you will see that they are similar, but not quite the same. For
example, the electric minivan in the second-to-last row gets slightly more share with
the heterogeneous model. Models that account for heterogeneity often predict that
"niche" products attract a slightly larger share because the model accounts for the

fact that there are a small number of respondents who find those "niche" designs very attractive. These models do not strictly follow the IIA property (see Sect. 13.3.4); if two similar products appeal to the same subset of customers, they will compete more closely with each other than with other products.

The share predictions produced by `predict.hier.mnl` are still based on the *point* estimates of `coef.Sigma` and `coef.mu`. So, while we have accounted for consumer heterogeneity in these predictions, we still haven't accounted for our uncertainty in the parameter estimates. This makes it difficult to determine what would be a (statistically) meaningful difference in share for two alternative designs. While it is possible to estimate prediction intervals for these models in the frequentist framework, it is easier to do so in a Bayesian framework. We address prediction intervals for shares in the next section where we review Bayesian choice models.

13.5 Hierarchical Bayes Choice Models

In this section, we show how to estimate choice models with heterogeneity using Bayesian methods and point out advantages (and some disadvantages) of the Bayesian approach.

Moving into the Bayesian framework can be somewhat confusing, both because the Bayesian approach to estimation is different and because Bayesians often use different language to describe the same thing. Those who use the classical methods often refer to the model we estimated in the previous section as the "random-coefficients multinomial logit" or "mixed logit" model. Bayesians tend to refer to these same models (and some extensions of them) as hierarchical Bayes multinomial logit.

There are several available packages for estimating choice models using Bayesian methods. The `MCMCpack` package we used in Chap. 7 includes a function called `MCMCmnl` to estimate non-hierarchical multinomial choice models [134]. To estimate the hierarchical choice model here, we use the `ChoiceModelR` package [179], which builds on the `bayesm` package [167].

13.5.1 Estimating Hierarchical Bayes Choice Models with *ChoiceModelR*

Unfortunately, there isn't a universal standard for how choice data is stored and we have to reorganize our data slightly to use `ChoiceModelR`. `ChoiceModelR` requires the data to be stored in a "long" data frame where each row is an alternative (as we have already in `cbc.df`), but it requires the selected alternative to be stored as an integer number on the first row of each choice task, with zeros in the remaining rows. It turns out that it takes just a few lines of code to create the new choice data.

```
> choice <- rep(0, nrow(cbc.df))
> choice[cbc.df[,"alt"]==1] <- cbc.df[cbc.df[,"choice"]==1,"alt"]
> head(choice)
[1] 3 0 0 2 0 0
```

Since there are three alternatives in each question, the first element of choice indicates that the respondent chose the third alternative in the first choice task; the second and third elements for choice are left as zeros. Similarly, the fourth elements indicates that the respondent chose the second alternative in the second choice task, and the next two elements are zeros.

ChoiceModelR automatically codes factors but it uses a different scheme than mlogit. To be consistent with the models we've run before, we'll go ahead and code the factors manually ourselves using model.matrix.

```
> cbc.coded <- model.matrix(~ seat + eng + cargo + price, data = cbc.df)
> cbc.coded <- cbc.coded[, -1] # remove the intercept
```

Finally, we can create a new data frame that combines the coded attributes and the choice back together with the resp.id, ques and alt (which are the first three columns in cbc.df).

```
> choicemodelr.data <- cbind(cbc.df[,1:3], cbc.coded, choice)
> head(choicemodelr.data)
   resp.id ques alt seat8 enghyb engelec cargo3ft price35 price40 choice
19       1    1   1     0      0       0        0       1       0      3
12       1    1   2     1      1       0        1       0       0      0
4        1    1   3     0      0       0        1       0       0      0
1        1    2   1     0      0       0        0       0       0      2
23       1    2   2     0      0       0        1       1       0      0
31       1    2   3     0      0       1        0       1       0      0
```

The function we use to estimate the hierarchical Bayes choice model is choicemo delr(), which requires the data to be organized in exactly the format above: a number indicating which respondent answered the question, a number indicating which question the profile belongs to, and a number indicating which alternative this was, and then the attributes followed by the choice. The choice is stored as an integer number in the first row of each question.

A key advantage of the hierarchical Bayes framework is that it allows you relate a customer's part worths for the attributes to characteristics of the customer (sometimes called "demographics," although this is a very poor name as we discuss later.) In our data set, we happen to know whether each customer uses his or her car to carpool and it seems quite reasonable that people who carpool might have different part worths than people who don't carpool. To figure out whether this is true, we estimate a model where the part worths are a function of the respondent characteristics, following a linear model. Of course, this means we need to pass the data on the respondent characteristics to choicemodelr(), which expects this data to be formatted as a matrix with one row for each respondent and one column for each respondent characteristic.

```
> carpool <- cbc.df$carpool[cbc.df$ques==1 & cbc.df$alt==1]=="yes"
> carpool <- as.numeric(carpool)
> choicemodelr.demos <- as.matrix(carpool, nrow=length(carpool))
> str(choicemodelr.demos)
 num [1:200, 1] 1 0 0 0 1 0 0 1 0 0 ...
```

Note that each row in `choicemodelr.demos` represents a *respondent* and not a question or an alternative, and so we have 200 rows. A value of 1 indicates that the respondent does use their car to carpool and a value of 0 indicates that they don't.

With this bit of data re-organization done, we can call `choicemodelr()`:

```
> library(ChoiceModelR)
> hb.post <- choicemodelr(data=choicemodelr.data, xcoding=rep(1, 7),
+                         demos=choicemodelr.demos,
+                         mcmc=list(R=20000, use=10000),
+                         options=list(save=TRUE))
```

In addition to the `data` and the `demos`, there are a couple of additional parameters of `choicemodelr` that control the estimation routine. The `xcoding` parameter tells `choicemodelr` how you want the attributes coded; by setting this to a vector of 1s, we indicate that we've already done the coding. The `mcmc` and `options` parameters control several aspects of the algorithm, which we discuss below. You can always type `?choicemodelr` for more details, although the help files might be more helpful to experienced Bayesian modelers than to novices.

While we recommend `ChoiceModelR`, there are a few aspects that make it less "R-like" than some packages. For example, `choicemodelr()` does not use R's formula notation or the built-in functions for coding factors. It relies on the order of the columns in the data frame, rather than using column names. The package does not include common utility functions like `summary()` and `predict()`. Because R is open source, it is up to each package development team to decide how they want to structure their functions and how consistent the package is with other R functions. While it sometimes requires a bit of work to figure out how a particular package works, it is difficult to complain too much, since the package was donated by the developers. If there is some functionality you'd like to see in a package, you can always write it yourself and then suggest to the package developers that they include your extension in their next release. (The name and email address of every package's maintainer are available in the package listing on CRAN.)

If you ran the code above, you probably noticed that it took a long time to run and produced a lot of output about its process. We omitted that output here. In the graphics window, you might have noticed something similar to Fig. 13.3.

What is Fig. 13.3? The focus of Bayesian inference is on generating a posterior distribution for the parameters of a model. The posterior distribution samples the likely values of a model, given the observed data. Most Bayesian routines like `choicemodelr` produce a set of random draws from the posterior distribution. Figure 13.3 is called a trace plot and it shows the posterior draws that have been produced so far by the estimation routine.

Without getting into the details of how and why these algorithms work, it is important to know that they don't always start out producing posterior draws. There is typically a *burn-in* period, where the algorithm settles into the posterior distribution. Before we use draws from the distribution, we have to throw out these initial burn-in draws. The trace plot allows us to see where the burn-in period ends. Judging from Fig. 13.3

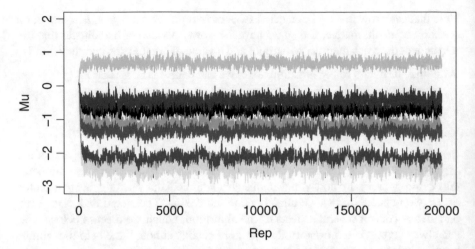

Fig. 13.3 Trace plot of posterior draws for a hierarchical Bayes choice model produced by `choicemodelr()`

the algorithm seems to have settled in after the first 1000 draws, because that is where the lines plotting the estimated values settle into a stable, horizontal pattern (apart from noise).

We used two other arguments with `choicemodelr()`. The `mcmc=list` `(R=20000, use=10000)` argument tells `choicemodelr` that we want to produce 20000 posterior draws and that we want to use only the last 10000 (giving us a wide margin on the burn-in). The `options=list(save=TRUE)` argument tells `choicemodelr()` to save those last 10000 posterior draws. By default, `choicemodelr()` saves every tenth draw, so it actually stores 1000 posterior draws.

When `choicemodelr()` finishes, the posterior draws are saved to the object we specified, `hb.post`, which becomes a list with four elements:

```
> names(hb.post)
[1] "betadraw"  "deltadraw" "compdraw"  "loglike"
```

The key parameters of the model are the average and the variance of the part worths across the population. We can access one posterior draw of these parameters by selecting an element of `hb.post$compdraw`. We arbitrarily look at draw 567.

```
> hb.post$compdraw[[567]]$mu
[1] -0.6565015 -0.4263809 -1.1496282 -1.8733265  0.5620929 -1.2089470
[7] -2.5772394
```

These are the average population part worths and you can compare them to the parameters we estimated with `mlogit()`. The parameters above come in the same order as the first 7 parameters estimated by `mlogit()`. For example, the average part worth for `seat7` was `-0.642` when we estimated it with `mlogit()` and for this posterior draw we get a value of `-0.657` from `choicemodelr()`.

There is one key difference between this model and the model we estimated with `mlogit()`. The parameters above represent the average part worth parameters among *respondents who do not use their car to carpool*. The hierarchical Bayes model also includes a set of "adjustments" for people who carpool; we can look at the 567th draw of these adjustment factors by looking at the appropriate row of `hb.post$deltadraw`.

```
> hb.post$deltadraw[567,]
[1]   1.63415698   1.78079508  -0.04400289  -0.12966126   0.02713614  -0.21926035
[7]  -0.19518696
```

You can see that there are huge adjustments in the part worths for the first two parameters: `seat7` and `seat8`. The average part worth for 7 seats (versus the base level of 6) for people who carpool is $-0.657 + 1.634 = 0.977$. This means that on average people who carpool actually *prefer* 7 over 6 seats while people who don't carpool prefer 6 seats on average. This is a potentially critical insight for product designers that we completely missed when we used the mixed logit model with `mlogit`. You may not see a major difference in share predictions between these two models, but the insight you get from reviewing the parameters can be quite valuable.

We caution readers that this potential insight comes at a cost. We had to estimate 7 additional parameters to describe the population. Adding a large number of additional parameters can make the burn-in period longer and it can add to uncertainty to the parameter estimates. We suggest you only include respondent characteristics that you believe should be related to the part worths. In this case, it seems reasonable that minivan preferences should be different for people who carpool. In general, covariates that are directly related to product usage are ideal. There are also potential issues with the scaling of these respondent characteristics; binary indicators tend to work well as they avoid these scaling issues. It is generally a bad idea to include general demographic variables like age, race or gender, just because you have them. Often demographic variables are not associated with product preferences [57]. For this reason, we avoid referring to covariates as "demographics."

We also have a set of parameters that describe the variance in part worths across the population. We can pull out the 567th draw from `hb.post`:

```
> hb.post$compdraw[[567]]$rooti
          [,1]         [,2]          [,3]         [,4]          [,5]          [,6]
[1,]  1.011972  -0.04367931  -0.045915749   0.1129225   0.005337426  -0.081773492
[2,]  0.000000   0.81711384   0.003180727   0.1535246   0.161135551  -0.192515134
[3,]  0.000000   0.00000000   1.011131267  -0.6173136   0.216005822  -0.011914137
[4,]  0.000000   0.00000000   0.000000000   0.8302175  -0.018093331  -0.002099283
[5,]  0.000000   0.00000000   0.000000000   0.0000000   1.146767704  -0.023986760
[6,]  0.000000   0.00000000   0.000000000   0.0000000   0.000000000   1.332875325
[7,]  0.000000   0.00000000   0.000000000   0.0000000   0.000000000   0.000000000
...
```

This set of parameters is actually stored as the Cholesky root of the covariance matrix. This is the matrix equivalent of a square root and we can recover the covariance matrix by "squaring" `rooti` with `crossprod()`:

```
> crossprod(hb.post$compdraw[[567]]$rooti)
            [,1]          [,2]          [,3]         [,4]          [,5]
[1,]   1.024087812  -0.044202250  -0.046465463   0.11427448   0.005401327
[2,]  -0.044202250   0.669582906   0.004604584   0.12051469   0.131432954
[3,]  -0.046465463   0.004604584   1.024504812  -0.62888172   0.218677697
```

```
[4,]    0.114274477    0.120514688   -0.628881721    1.10665848  -0.123023753
[5,]    0.005401327    0.131432954    0.218677697   -0.12302375   1.388055204
[6,]   -0.082752504   -0.153734971   -0.008904404   -0.03317798  -0.061500274
[7,]    0.014590162    0.073588053   -0.233576644    0.47484770   0.281647756
...
```

The diagonals of this matrix describe the variance across the population in the part worths and if you compare them to the estimates we got with `mlogit`, you will find that variation across the population is generally smaller, particularly for the first two parameters that describe preferences for number of seats. The reason for this is that the new model accounts for some of the differences between individuals who carpool versus not, so the remaining unexplained variation between respondents is smaller.

In addition to population level parameters, we look at posterior draws of the individual-level parameters:

```
> head(hb.post$betadraw[,,567])
           [,1]        [,2]        [,3]        [,4]        [,5]        [,6]  ...
[1,]  1.0112255   0.6282393  -0.2210578  -0.01774596   0.8777881  -0.8889406  ...
[2,] -2.1737290   1.2036846  -2.2063721  -3.21025972   0.3277637  -2.8757266  ...
[3,] -2.4349625  -1.5172192  -0.7548992  -0.76935985  -0.2273173  -1.2754315  ...
...
```

Each row of this output represents the part worths for each person, which you can see vary widely. For example, for this posterior draw the first respondent really likes 7 seats over 6 or 8, since 1.011 is larger than 0 or 0.628. The second respondent prefers 8 seats over 6 or 7. You could plot histograms of these part worth values to get a sense for how preferences vary across the population.

Up to this point, we've been talking about a single draw from the posterior (number 567). But if you look at hb.post$betadraw, you can see that there are 1000 posterior draws of the 7 part worths for each of 200 respondents.

```
> str(hb.post$betadraw)
 num [1:200, 1:7, 1:1000] 0.816 -1.083 -2.306 -0.91 2.043 ...
```

To fully characterize the posterior and our uncertainty about these parameters, we need summarize *all* of the posterior draws. Unfortunately, `choicemodelr` does not provide convenient summaries, but for the respondent-level `betadraws`, we can find the posterior means using `apply`.

```
> beta.post.mean <- apply(hb.post$betadraw, 1:2, mean)
> head(beta.post.mean)
           [,1]        [,2]        [,3]        [,4]        [,5]        [,6]
[1,]  0.6333957   0.26137739  -0.4483550  -1.426702   1.1568186  -0.4751817
[2,] -2.1134244   0.64602926  -1.0926311  -1.916450   0.9893599  -1.4853397
[3,] -1.9297260  -2.10100104  -0.9827285  -1.413800   0.4395638  -1.4189584
...
```

The values in beta.post.mean show our best estimate for each individual's part worths. While it is possible to obtain individual-level estimates using classical methods, it is much more common to for Bayesian choice modelers to focus on individual-level parameters.

It is also important to recognize that with just 15 choice questions for each respondent, there is still a great deal of uncertainty about those individual-level part worths. We can get a sense for how much uncertainty there is by looking at the posterior quantiles of the part worths for each respondent. We compute the 5th and 95th quantiles of the individual betadraws, then display the mean and quantiles for the first respondent:

```
> beta.post.q05 <- apply(hb.post$betadraw, 1:2, quantile, probs=c(0.05))
> beta.post.q95 <- apply(hb.post$betadraw, 1:2, quantile, probs=c(0.95))
> rbind(q05=beta.post.q05[1,], mean=beta.post.mean[1,], q95=beta.post.q95
    [1,])
            [,1]        [,2]        [,3]        [,4]        [,5]        [,6]
q05   -0.5380902 -1.1223590 -1.5063476 -2.876466010 0.05096963 -1.5266892
mean   0.6333957  0.2613774 -0.4483550 -1.426702290 1.15681862 -0.4751817
q95    1.8404189  1.5819603  0.6093953  0.001986669 2.36650000  0.6431527
...
```

These numbers represent how much uncertainty we have in our estimates of the first respondent's part worth estimates. Roughly, the range of likely values for respondent 1's preference for 7 seats over 6 (the first parameter) is about -0.538–1.840. In other words, given this data, we can say that our best guess is that respondent 1 prefers 7 seats (i.e., has a positive coefficient), but it is quite possible that the respondent prefers 6 (i.e., has a negative coefficient). This is a huge amount of uncertainty that we need to account for when making share predictions.

13.5.2   Share Prediction for Hierarchical Bayes Choice Models

The 1000 posterior draws in hb.post$betadraw give us a sense of the range of part worth values that each respondent might have and we can use these draws to figure out the likely range of shares that we might get for new vehicle designs. For each posterior draw, we can compute the shares for a new set of product designs based on the values of the part worth coefficients for that draw. Each time we do this, the shares we obtain represent a a posterior draw for the shares. (Being able to compute posterior draws for any function of the parameters in this way is one of the great advantages of Bayesian MCMC.) We can compute the shares for a number of different posterior draws (selected at random from the draws that we produced when we called choicemodelr) and then analyze the range of shares that we get.

We create a function for computing shares that loops over both the respondents and the posterior draws:

```
> predict.hb.mnl <- function(betadraws, data) {
+    # Function to predict shares from a hierarchical multinomial logit model
+    # model: mlogit object returned by mlogit()
+    # data: a data frame containing the set of designs for which you want to
+    #       predict shares.  Same format at the data used to estimate model.
+    data.model <- model.matrix(~ seat + eng + cargo + price, data = data)
+    data.model <- data.model[,-1] # remove the intercept
+    nresp <- dim(betadraws)[1]
+    ndraws <- dim(hb.post$betadraw)[3]
+    shares <- array(dim=c(nresp, nrow(data), ndraws))
+    for (d in 1:ndraws) {
+       for (i in 1:nresp) {
+          utility <- data.model%*%betadraws[i,,d]
+          shares[i,,d] = exp(utility)/sum(exp(utility))
+       }
+    }
```

```
+       shares.agg <- apply(shares, 2:3, mean)
+       cbind(share=apply(shares.agg, 1, mean),
+               pct=t(apply(shares.agg, 1, quantile, probs=c(0.05, 0.95))),
+               data)
+   }
```

The inner loop in this function for `i in 1:nresp` computes the shares for each respondent for a given posterior draw. The outer loop for `d in 1:ndraws` loops over the posterior draws. (If there were too many posterior draws, we could also use a random subset of them.) The function stores the share estimates for each user for each draw in `shares`. In the last few lines, the function averages the shares across respondents resulting in an estimate of the shares for each posterior draw. We then compute the mean as well as the quantiles of those posterior draws to get a sense for the likely range of shares.

When we compute the shares in this function, we use the estimated individual-level part worths for the respondents in our data, which is what most analysts do in practice. In contrast, when we computed share predictions in the previous section using the output from `mlogit()`, we sampled new representative respondents based on our estimates of the population mean and covariance. We should point out that it is possible to use the same approach with a Bayesian choice model, using the posterior draws of `mu`, `delta` and `rooti` and sampling a new set of respondents from the multivariate normal distribution. This would require a relatively small change to `predict.hb.mnl`.

When we apply `predict.hb.mnl` to the designs in `new.data`, we get both point estimates and ranges of potential shares for each design:

```
> predict.hb.mnl(hb.post$betadraw, new.data)
        share      pct.5%      pct.95% seat cargo  eng price
8  0.09920353 0.086505556 0.11352010    7   2ft   hyb    30
1  0.45300946 0.428510287 0.47765666    6   2ft   gas    30
3  0.32986260 0.305608282 0.35368987    8   2ft   gas    30
41 0.06947448 0.056391010 0.08434871    7   3ft   gas    40
49 0.01357954 0.009832746 0.01800444    6   2ft  elec    40
26 0.03487038 0.028179167 0.04215179    7   2ft   hyb    35
```

There is quite a bit of uncertainty in these share predictions. Our "best guess" estimate of the shares for the 6-passenger base engine minivan (number 1 in the second row) is 45.3%, but it could be as low as 42.9% or as high as 47.8%. Understanding the uncertainty in our model predictions helps in interpreting differences in share. For example, if we make a minor change such that 6-passenger gas minivan share increases to 46.0%, we would recognize that this change in share is well within the prediction error of our model, and we probably shouldn't make strong statements that one design will do better than the other in the marketplace. But if we change the seating to 7 passenger for that vehicle, the predicted share is 30.2% with a range of 28.2–32.1%. Because the prediction intervals do not overlap, we can say that the 7-passenger version of the design has significantly lower share, knowing that we are not over-interpreting the limited data that we have.

Given how easy it is to compute these share prediction ranges, we think it is surprising how rarely practitioners report prediction intervals of choice model shares. Many conjoint analysis studies unfortunately report only point estimates of share predictions. This leaves decision makers blind to the possibility that the share predictions they are relying on may not be very accurate. In extreme cases, when there are many attributes in the model and very few choice questions, one may find that the prediction intervals are extremely wide. This is an indication that there isn't sufficient data to make precise predictions and suggests that one might wish to collect more or different data. In the next section, we discuss the design of choice-based conjoint surveys.

13.6 Design of Choice-Based Conjoint Surveys*

Once you start looking at parameter estimates and share predictions for your choice models, you may start to wonder how you can make your parameter estimates and prediction intervals tighter. The easiest way to do this is to increase the amount of data you collect, either by increasing the number of respondents or increasing the number of questions that you ask each respondent. If you were to recreate data as we've used in this chapter with 1000 respondents instead of 200, you would see that the standard deviations for the parameter estimates and the prediction intervals would be smaller (as is true for any model).

A good way to assess sample sizes before fielding a conjoint analysis project is to simulate data from known parameters, estimate the model from the synthetic data, and examine the resulting prediction intervals. This would only require a few changes to the code presented in this chapter. Such analysis can help you determine how many respondents you need for a given number of attributes and levels, or, as is more often the case, how many attribute and levels you can afford given your available budget for collecting data.

Beyond getting more data, choosing the right questions to ask can also result in more precise parameter estimates and share predictions. The selection of questions to include in the conjoint survey is example of an *experimental design* problem.

If you review the code in Sect. 13.2, you will notice that when we generated the conjoint questions we selected a different set of minivan profiles *at random* to create the choice questions for each respondent. This approach works well and is robust, as long as you can give a different set of questions to each respondent. If your survey platform is limited so that every respondent must answer the same questions, a random design will not be very efficient. There are several other approaches you can use that can improve upon selecting questions randomly. The main design approaches are the following.

- **Random designs** use a randomly-selected set of profiles in each question.
- **Fractional factorial designs** are based on the assumption that there are no interactions between different attributes (e.g., there isn't some additional boost to having

8-seats *combined* with 3 ft of cargo space). Many of the advantages of fractional factorial designs, such as orthogonality, are only beneficial in the context of linear models and not choice models. However, fractional factorial designs are occasionally used in practice because they are readily available and were once the standard approach for conjoint analysis surveys. These designs are often constrained so that every respondent answers the same questions, or such that there are only a few survey versions.

- **Optimal designs** are created by selecting a set of questions that minimizes the standard error of the estimated parameters (called D-Optimal designs) or minimizes the standard error of share predictions (called G-Optimal designs). These designs are created by starting with an arbitrary design and then iteratively changing questions and assessing whether those changes make the sampling error or posterior intervals smaller. The routines may not always produce the true optimal design, but they can often improve substantially on the starting design. These designs may also be constrained so that every respondent answers the same question.
- There are a number of **heuristic conjoint design strategies** that aren't based a formal theory, but have produced good quality predictions in the past.
- **Adaptive designs** select successive choice questions based on the respondent's answers as he or she takes the survey. For instance, a survey might ask about preferred options and then focus on the features that a respondent identifies as important. One approach is called fast-polyhedral conjoint design [189]. Another method is Adaptive Choice-Based Conjoint (ACBC) from Sawtooth Software [174].

There is much debate in the conjoint analysis community about which of these methods is the best. While we can't answer that, we can say that each has worked well in at least some conditions. A common mistake when comparing these conjoint design methods is to look at whether different methods result in different point estimates of the share predictions (either in-sample or for holdout questions). Since many of these methods produce similar point estimates for shares, that is a poor way to compare different experimental design strategies. A better approach is to compare the prediction *range* between approaches. Better designs produce smaller prediction ranges, meaning that there will be less uncertainty in predictions.

Unfortunately, there aren't yet readily-available tools for the design of choice experiments in R. The `AlgDesign` package can produce fractional factorial and optimal designs, but it isn't customized for choice models and the package is no longer being maintained. For our own work, we tend to use random designs (which are easy to produce in R) or use other software to create designs. JMP includes routines for creating D-Optimal designs for choice models. Sawtooth Software offers a variety of heuristic and adaptive design strategies for choice models.

13.7 Key Points

- Choice models are used to understand how product attributes drive customers' choices. The most popular choice model in practice is the multinomial logit model. This model can be estimated using frequentist methods with `mlogit` or using Bayesian methods with `MCMCmnl` (Sect. 13.3).
- Choice data can be stored in "long" or "wide" formats and there is no universal standard for how the data should be organized. Before you use any choice modeling package, read the documentation carefully to understand how the package expects the data to be formatted (Sect. 13.3).
- Before analyzing any choice data, it is useful to compute raw choice counts for each attribute. This can be done very easily using `xtabs` (Sect. 13.3.1).
- Estimating a choice model is similar to estimating simpler linear models. The key output of the estimation is a set of parameters that describe how much each attribute is associated with the observed choices.
- Choice models can include both factors and numeric attributes in the choice alternatives. When you use a factor as a predictor, the factor has to be dummy coded, just as it would for a linear model. With dummy coding, the estimates are interpreted as the preference for a particular level of the attribute *relative* to the base level of the attribute (Sect. 13.3).
- Most choice models do not include intercepts. When a choice models does include intercepts, there is an intercept for each alternative in the choice questions; these are called alternative specific constants or ASCs (Sect. 13.3).
- When reporting choice models, it is best to focus on reporting *share predictions* from the model because parameter estimates are difficult for non-experts to interpret. If you model price as a numeric predictor, you can also report the willingness to pay for each attribute (Sect. 13.3.3).
- Heterogeneous choice models allow each respondent to have individually estimated part worths. This may result in share predictions that are slightly (and appropriately) higher for "niche" products (Sect. 13.4.2).
- Hierarchical choice models can be estimated using frequentist methods with `mlogit` and with Bayesian methods using `choicemodelr` (Sects. 13.4 and 13.5).
- Bayesian methods produce draws from the posterior distribution of the parameters. To understand the uncertainty in the parameters (given the data), examine the range of the posterior draws. To find the uncertainty in predicted shares, compute the share values for each posterior draw of the estimated parameters. The range of share estimates indicates the uncertainty in share predictions (Sect. 13.5).
- Bayesian methods allow you to incorporate an upper level model that relates respondent characteristics to attribute preferences. Good candidates for respondent characteristics are binary variables that describe product usage. (Sect. 13.5).
- In general, if you collect more data, your estimates of the parameters will be more precise and your prediction intervals will be smaller. Prediction intervals can also be made smaller by selecting better choice questions. There are several alternative approaches to choosing profiles to include in choice questions (Sect. 13.6).

13.8 Data Sources

Data for choice-based conjoint analysis is commonly collected through an online survey, authored using a survey platform that supports the specialized layout and randomization requirements for a CBC study. Large research suppliers often have proprietary systems for authoring CBC surveys. Several commercially available survey platforms, such as SurveyGizmo and Qualtrics, support CBC surveys. These tend to have various limitations with regards to experimental design, survey layout, and analyses. Sawtooth Software is a specialist provider for conjoint analysis survey tools that supports a large range of options (with corresponding platform complexity).

Unfortunately there is no common standard for formatting CBC data; many survey platforms have unique data file formats. As we'll see, different R packages also use slightly different formats. Depending on your choice of a survey platform and R package, you may need to reshape your data. Our examples in this chapter demonstrate proper formats for the relevant R packages (Sects. 13.3, 13.3.2, and 13.5.1).

13.9 Learning More*

In this chapter, we have given a brief overview of choice modeling in the context of conjoint analysis surveys, with examples of how to estimate choice models in R. For those who want to learn more about choice modeling, there are many additional resources, although no single text covers everything of importance.

For those who are interested strictly in conjoint surveys, Orme's *Getting Started with Conjoint Analysis* [149] offers an accessible introduction to how conjoint surveys are constructed and analyzed in practice while Louvier, Hensher, and Swait's *Stated Choice Methods* [131] provides a more extensive (but slightly dated) overview of the topic, including coverage of several variations on non-hierarchical multinomial logit models and how to create fractional factorial designs. Rossi, Allenby, McCulloch's *Bayesian Statistics and Marketing* provides technical coverage of the multinomial and hierarchical multinomial logit model from the Bayesian perspective and describes the `bayesm` package that `ChoiceModelR` uses heavily.

As we mentioned in the introduction, there are uses of choice models other than choice-based conjoint analysis surveys. One broad application area is the modeling of consumers' transportation choices. Kenneth Train (2009) offers an clear and concise overview of discrete choice methods [190] and their use in transportation economics, including coverage of both the mixed logit and hierarchical Bayes logit models; it is an ideal introduction for those using hierarchical choice models in nearly any context. Train also covers a number of alternative choice models including the nested logit model and the multinomial probit model. While there are advantages and disadvantages to each of these models, they are all based on the same premise that customers choose among a set of products based on part worths of the attributes of those products.

Another major application for choice models in marketing is to understand how consumers choose products in retail stores, such as grocery stores. Using data collected by grocery store scanners where customers are tracked over multiple visits (called *scanner panel* data), one can assemble observations that are nearly identical in structure to conjoint data [85]. Many marketing academics have used choice models with such data to assess the relationship between marketing actions such as price, promotion, and in-store display, and customers' product and brand choices. Much work has been published on extending these models to accommodate different types of consumer behavior such as stockpiling goods, learning about products, strategically trying new products, and changes in preferences over time.

13.10 Excercises

For the exercises in this chapter, we use a simulated conjoint data set where we observe respondents choices from among sets of sportscars. The attributes of sportscars in this data are number of *seats*, *convertible* top, *trans*mission type and *price*. The data also includes a *segment* variable that indicates which sportscar segment each respondent belongs to.

You can load the data by typing:

```
sportscar <- read.csv("https://goo.gl/8g7vtT")
```

1. Data inspection:
   - Use summary to identify the levels of each attribute in the data.
   - What was the price of the chosen alternative in the last question in the data frame?
   - Use xtabs() to determine the number of times a sportscar with automatic transmission was chosen. How does this compare to the number of times a sportscar with a manual transmission was chosen? What does that tell you about consumer preferences?

2. Fitting and interpreting a choice model:
   - (a) Fit a (non-hierarchical) choice model to predict choice as a function of all four attributes. Don't forget to convert the data to an mlogit.data object before passing it to mlogit. Also, be sure to remove the intercept in the model formula. Report the estimated coefficients and their standard errors.
   - (b) What is the ideal sportscar for the respondents based on this model. That is, what is most desirable level of each feature? You may have to look at both the model coefficients and the data summary to figure this out.
   - (c) Which coefficient is the most precisely estimated?

(d) Is it reasonable to charge $5000 for a convertable top? Hint: Compute the WTP for convertible top and compare it to $5000.

(e) Use the `predict.mnl()` function from the chapter to predict shares for the following set of sportscars:

```
newcars <- data.frame(seat=factor(c("2","4", "5")),
                trans=factor(c("manual", "automatic", "automatic")),
                convert=factor(c("no", "yes", "no")),
                price=c(40, 37, 35))
```

Note that it is very important that the factors in the `newcars` data frame have exactly the same levels as the factors in the data frame used to estimate the model.

(f) Use the `sensitivity.mnl()` function from the chapter to produce a sensitivity plot for the first sportscar in `newcars`. What suggestions would you make on changing the features of the product to get higher market share?

3. In the previous question, you fit a choice model using all the respondents and so your estimates represented the average preferences across the entire population of customers. Fit another choice model using just the customers from the racer segment and predict shares for `newcars`. Are your predictions different than what you found in the previous question?

4. Estimate a hierarchical multinomial logit model using the sportscar data, using the `rpar` input to the `mlogit()` function. Assume all the parameters are normally distributed. Which parameter has the greatest variation across respondents?

5. Estimate a hierarchical model using the Bayesian `ChoiceModelR` function. Don't forget you will have to re-format the data to be suitable for `ChoiceModelR` as described in Sect. 13.5.1. Use the segment variable for the demographics. Are the parameter estimates similar to those obtained with `mlogit()`?

Chapter 14
Behavior Sequences

Marketers often wish to understand sequences of customer behavior. If customers visit one web page, do they visit another? If they purchase one product, do they later purchase another? If they have some particular product experience, how does that change their subsequent product or market behavior? There is a vast array of analytical and statistical methods to address such questions, ranging from time series analysis to Markov models, from causal modeling to dynamic clustering.

In this chapter, we examine patterns in a public web server log. We explore web logs because they are a common source of behavioral sequence data. However, we approach the topic generically rather than using web analytics packages as such (see Sect. 14.7). In the first part of the chapter, we review functions to process an actual web log. Then we introduce Markov chains to model behavioral transitions (such as page-to-page navigation). These methods apply many kinds of marketing (and non-marketing) behavioral data.

As you will see, the analysis of a real data set may require a substantial amount of data cleaning. This is a reality that we have deemphasized in previous chapters. In this chapter, we focus on details of the original data and the structures needed for the analytic functions. This leads us to introduce important new programming topics—in particular, date and time functions and regular expressions—and to see additional applications for methods covered in earlier chapters.

14.1 Web Log Data

A web server log compiles all the requests from users' web browsers. These typically reflect loading a web page with text contents (such as HTML pages) and graphical elements (such as GIF and JPG images on a page), along with interactive elements such as shopping cart updates. The logs identify each request's Internet address

© Springer Nature Switzerland AG 2019
C. Chapman and E. M. Feit, *R For Marketing Research and Analytics*, Use R!,
https://doi.org/10.1007/978-3-030-14316-9_14

(IP address, often called the *host*) with a timestamp, along with the pages and graphics that are requested. This allows us to identify events for each user (host) and assemble them in order, yielding sequences.

Similar sequence data might come from many other data sources. These might include store transactions over time, eye tracking data, CRM (customer relationship management) system events, credit or loyalty card transactions, hotel or air reservations, or ticket sales. Such data may also arise from non-marketing situations, such as medical records (e.g., a sequence of diagnoses and/or treatments), gene expression data, email threads, and governmental data such as arrest records, border crossings, and voting records (we're not specifically advocating collecting or inspecting these kinds of data, just noting them).

14.1.1 EPA Web Data

Because web logs provide deep insight into a firm's business and its customers, there are few examples available for public usage. We will use a government web server log that has been made public, and that is otherwise substantively similar to a private web log. These data comprise requests to an HTTP (web) server for the US Environmental Protection Agency (EPA) and are available for redistribution [19]. We have decompressed the data, and corrected a few minor formatting issues with the text delimiters.

We recommend that you work through the data processing steps in the following section, because we introduce several new R topics, including functions to work with date and time data, regular expressions to match text strings, and sorting data.

However, if you prefer, you can download the final data from the book's website. The data structure is modestly complex, with a mix of character, numeric, factor, ordered factor, and time data. This would be complex to adapt from CSV data, so we use R's capability to read a formatted *RDS* (R data serialization) object with the readRDS() function. This loads an object with all of its attributes intact.

If you download the file from https://goo.gl/s5vjWz and save it somewhere (such as "/Downloads/"), you can read it with a simple readRDS() assignment:

```
> epa.df <- readRDS("~/Downloads/rintro-chapter14-epa.rds")
```

To download directly from the web, R needs to know additionally to read from a web address (url()) and to decompress the data (gzcon()):

```
> epa.df <- readRDS(gzcon(url("https://goo.gl/s5vjWz")))
```

In either case, check the data after it is loaded:

```
> summary(epa.df)
      host              timestamp           request                status
 host1986:  294    Length:47748      Length:47748       http200:36712   ...
 host1032:  292    Class :character   Class :character   http304:  5300  ...
```

```
      bytes                rawhost                 datetime
 Min.    :       0    Length:47748        Min.    :1995-08-29 23:53:25  ...
 1st Qu.:     231    Class :character     1st Qu.:1995-08-30 10:58:37   ...
 reqtype            pagetype             page
 GET :46014     gif  :22418     Length:47748          ...
 HEAD:   106    html : 8687     Class :character      ...
```

You might also wish to install two packages that we will use— clickstream and superheat—if you don't already have them:

```
> install.packages(c("clickstream", "superheat"))
Installing packages into ?/Users/chris/Library/R/3.5/library? ...
```

After this, skim the following data processing sections to understand what these variables represent and to review a few analyses and visualizations. Then continue with the session analytics in Sect. 14.3.2.

14.1.2   Processing the Raw Data

In this and the next few sections, we walk through the data cleaning process starting with raw server logs (as opposed to skipping ahead to the final, processed data as noted in the previous section). First, we load the raw log in text format and name the columns, as described by Bottomley [19]:

```
> epa.df.raw <- read.table("https://goo.gl/LPqmGb", sep=" ",
+                           header=FALSE, stringsAsFactors = FALSE)
> # name the columns
> names(epa.df.raw) <- c("host", "timestamp", "request", "status", "bytes")
> str(epa.df.raw)
'data.frame':      47748 obs. of   5 variables:
 $ host      : chr   "141.243.1.172" "query2.lycos.cs.cmu.edu" ...
 $ timestamp: chr   "[29:23:53:25]" "[29:23:53:36]" ...
 $ request   : chr   "GET /Software.html HTTP/1.0" ...
 $ status    : int   200 200 200 200 200 200 200 200 200 200 ...
 $ bytes     : chr   "1497" "1325" "1014" "4889" ...
```

As with many raw data sources, several steps are needed to make it more usable, and we perform those in the following sections. To some extent, the steps are unique to web server logs and this data set. However, they provide opportunity to introduce topics that are useful for handling date, time, and text data.

14.1.3   Cleaning the Data

We begin by making a copy of the raw data under the principle of never changing the original data (see Sect. 7.3.3). After that, we backup the host data—users' Internet (IP) addresses—as rawhost, and create a disguised alternative that simply numbers them. A simple way to do this is using factor(), which uses sequential integers to index the arbitrary labels for categorical data. Given those arbitrary integer values, we add the prefix "host" using paste0(), a variant of paste() (Sect. 3.4.4) that omits the default blank space separation character.

```
> epa.df$rawhost <- epa.df.raw$host
> epa.df$host     <- factor(paste0("host", as.numeric(factor(epa.df$rawhost))))
> head(epa.df$host)
[1] host195   host1888 host2120 host2273 host2273 host2273
2333 Levels: host1 host10 host100 host1000 host1001 host1002 ... host999
```

Why do we create host instead of just using the IP addresses? Because these addresses may be regarded as private identifiers that we don't need for routine analysis. It's good practice to disguise such data and not to use it during general analysis, reserving access of the original, private details only when they are actually needed. For example, we might use those to determine users' country location (as in Sect. 14.8, Exercise 7). If we didn't need the information, we could remove it from the data frame by reassigning the column a NULL value using the command epa.df$rawhost <- NULL, or simply overwrite host without creating rawhost.

14.1.4   Handling Dates and Times

Sequence data commonly includes dates and times, and these are among the most challenging data types in R. There are multiple, quite confusing systems for defining dates and times, and it can be difficult to convert them to a standardized format. One difficulty is that dates and times may be written in different ways, and we must tell R how to decode them. Looking at the timestamp column in the EPA data (see the results of str(epa.df.raw above), we see entries such as "[29:23:53:25]". Referring to the data source [19], this represents the day of the month in August 1995 (the 29th) and the time on that day (23:52:25).

One R command to convert times is the strptime() command, which takes three arguments: the data to convert, a format string defining the data layout, and the timezone of the observations. In this case, our data lack the year and month, so we first append those to the data using paste0("1995:08", ...). Using substr(..., start, end) we add the data from characters 2 to 12— the day of the month and time—omitting the initial and final "[   ]" characters. This gives a complete date and time string, such as "1995:08:29:23:52:25".

With the data in this fully specified format—year, month, day, and time—we define a conversion template for strptime() to extract the relevant pieces (year, month, day, etc.) Referring to ?strptime, we define the conversion using "%Y:%m:%d:%H:%M:%S", specifying the year, month, day of the month, hour, minute, and second, respectively. We add the timezone "America/New_York" for the data, based on the server's location in Raleigh, North Carolina [19].

Putting all of that together—removing the [ ] brackets with substr(), adding the year and month, converting with strptime(), and adding the time zone—we convert the times:

```
> epa.df$datetime <- strptime(paste0("1995:08:",
+                              substr(epa.df.raw$timestamp, 2, 12)),
+                       "%Y:%m:%d:%H:%M:%S", tz="America/New_York")
```

Next we use the `POSIXct` format, which internally represents the date as the number of seconds elapsed since the beginning of 1970 (which could be negative). This is a common data format, and makes the data compatible with plotting commands later:

```
> epa.df$datetime <- as.POSIXct(epa.df$datetime)
```

The times are now in a clean format with time zone information:

```
> head(epa.df$datetime)
[1] "1995-08-29 23:53:25 EDT" "1995-08-29 23:53:36 EDT" ...
```

14.1.5   Requests and Page Types

Examining the users' browser requests, we see a common structure. Each request consists of an action request (e.g., to "get" a page), the page or file requested, and the communication protocol ("HTTP/1.0"):

```
> head(epa.df$request)
[1] "GET /Software.html HTTP/1.0"
[2] "GET /Consumer.html HTTP/1.0" ...
```

We will extract the pages and actions from this. First, we eliminate the communication protocol because it never varies. The function `sub(pattern, replacement)` replaces a search string in character data; we replace each occurrence of "HTTP/1.0" with an empty string:

```
> epa.df$request <- sub(" HTTP/1.0", "", epa.df.raw$request)
> head(epa.df$request)
[1] "GET /Software.html"              "GET /Consumer.html"   ...
```

Next we determine the browser action. This is most commonly a GET request (retrieve content from the server), but also may be a POST (send data) or HEAD (get information about a page's content—such as its length—without loading the page itself). To do this, we first create a new column `reqtype` to code the request type for each line. Then we search each request for the relevant commands, using `grepl()` (which searches for the presence of a particular text string) and update `reqtype` accordingly:

```
> epa.df$reqtype <- NA
> epa.df$reqtype[grepl("POST ", epa.df.raw$request)] <- "POST"
> epa.df$reqtype[grepl("GET ", epa.df.raw$request)]  <- "GET"
> epa.df$reqtype[grepl("HEAD ", epa.df.raw$request)] <- "HEAD"
> epa.df$reqtype <- factor(epa.df$reqtype)
> table(epa.df$reqtype)
  GET  HEAD  POST
46014   106  1622
```

Because we started by specifying `reqtype` as NA, we can easily determine whether our recoding covered all of the data. In this case, we see no entry NA in the `table()`, confirming that the data were all coded appropriately. As expected, most of the requests were GET requests for content that users clicked on.

Similarly, it is helpful to examine the content (technically, the *file*) that a user requested. Consider the typical structure of a traditional web page: it has content (generally in an HTML file) along with images (typically GIF and JPG files) and documents (such as PDF files). To understand users' behavior we will be interested primarily in their patterns of accessing the HTML files, which provide the primary content and link to one another. Image files may be downloaded with those, but are less interesting for understanding the sequence of behavior. In order to filter that data, we code each request for the type of file that was requested:

```
> epa.df$pagetype <- "other"
> epa.df$pagetype[grepl("\\.gif",  epa.df.raw$request,
+                        ignore.case=TRUE)] <- "gif"
> epa.df$pagetype[grepl("\\.html", epa.df.raw$request,
+                        ignore.case=TRUE)] <- "html"
> epa.df$pagetype[grepl("\\.pdf",  epa.df.raw$request,
+                        ignore.case=TRUE)] <- "pdf"
> epa.df$pagetype <- factor(epa.df$pagetype)
>
> table(epa.df$pagetype)
  gif   html  other    pdf
22418   8687  16536    107
```

Note here that we are using a very simple *regular expression* with grepl() to find the file type of interest. A regular expression (also known as a *regex*) is a structured way to find strings that follow a specific pattern—such as being all numbers or having the structure of a standard file name. A complete explanation of regexes is beyond our scope here, and in fact is the subject of several books, such as [80]. In R, see ?regex for a starting point.

In the present data, by searching for "\\.gif", we are asking grepl() to determine whether ".gif" appears inside each request. The backslashes are used to note that the period character "." should not be interpreted as a *special character*. By default, a period is used in a regex to match *any* character, but in this case, we want to match an actual period. We add the argument ignore.case=TRUE in order to match upper or lower case, such as "gif" or "GIF".

What were the "other" page types? We use some() from the car package to sample them (your results will vary; try the command a few times):

```
> some(epa.df$request[epa.df$pagetype=="other"])
 [1] "GET /OWPubs/"
 [2] "GET /"
 [3] "POST /cgi-bin/waisgate/134.67.99.11=earth1=210=/usr1 ...
 [4] "GET /OSWRCRA/non-hw/indust/"
 [5] "GET /waisicons/eye2.xbm" ...
```

We see that many of the "other" types are unspecified directories, while some are links to other types of servers (e.g., the antiquated Gopher protocol), and other file types (e.g., XBM graphics). Deeper investigation might reveal that some of these are actually page requests, and, if so, could be categorized as HTML requests. For our purposes here, we simply leave them uncategorized.

Now we find the actual page or file that the user requested. We do this by copying the request to a new column page, and using sub(..., " ") to remove "GET", "POST", or "HEAD":

```
> epa.df$page <- epa.df$request
> epa.df$page <- sub("GET ",  "", epa.df$page)
> epa.df$page <- sub("HEAD ", "", epa.df$page)
> epa.df$page <- sub("POST ", "", epa.df$page)
```

```
> head(epa.df$page)
[1]  "/Software.html"                    "/Consumer.html"
[3]  "/News.html"                        "/"
[5]  "/icons/circle_logo_small.gif" "/logos/small_gopher.gif"
```

14.1.6   Additional HTTP Data

Finally, web logs include data about whether a request was successful, such as the well-known "404 Not Found" error for a missing page, and the size of the data sent. We add these as the request status and number of bytes transmitted. We add the HTTP status as an `ordered` factor variable, where the sequential, alphabetical order has meaning and is not simply a nominal label. The order has meaning because status values of 400 or higher indicate errors.

```
> epa.df$status <- ordered(paste0("http", epa.df.raw$status))
> epa.df$bytes <- as.numeric(epa.df.raw$bytes)
Warning message:
NAs introduced by coercion
> summary(epa.df)
      host          timestamp              request              status
 host1986:  294  Length:47748       Length:47748        http200:36712
 host1032:  292  Class :character   Class :character    http304:  5300
 host2247:  266  Mode  :character   Mode  :character    http302:  4506
 host1439:  263                                         http404:   611
 ...
      bytes                rawhost              datetime
 Min.   :       0   Length:47748       Min.    :1995-08-29 23:53:25
 1st Qu.:     231   Class :character   1st Qu.:1995-08-30 10:58:37
 Median :    1260   Mode  :character   Median  :1995-08-30 13:57:46
 ...
  reqtype           pagetype               page
 GET :46014    gif   :22418    Length:47748
 HEAD:  106    html  : 8687    Class :character
 POST: 1622    other :16536    Mode  :character
 NA's:    6    pdf   :  107
```

We already see some interesting results, such as hundreds of "404 page not found" errors in the `status` column. Next we investigate the frequencies of events in the data set.

14.2   Basic Event Statistics

Many behavioral questions involve frequencies of events: which actions are most common? How do they change over time? What errors occur? Which customers are most active? We examine each of these in our web log data.

14.2.1   Events

Which behaviors—in this case, page requests—are most common? We count the events using `table()`, then `sort()` them by frequency, and display the top 10

results using `head()`. To specify the direction for sorting, we add `decreasing=`
`TRUE` to the `sort()` command.

```
> head(sort(table(epa.df$page), decreasing = TRUE), 10)
/icons/circle_logo_small.gif  3203
/                             2381
/logos/small_gopher.gif       1851
/logos/us-flag.gif            1817  ...
```

The most common requests are for .gif files, such as logos that might be used on
many pages. However, to understand customers' interests, it is more informative to
understand *page* interaction, so we repeat the table, filtering for HTML requests:

```
> head(sort(table(epa.df$page[epa.df$pagetype=="html"]),
+             decreasing = TRUE), 10)

   /Rules.html          /Software.html         /docs/WhatsNew.html
          312                   169                         159
    /Info.html          /Offices.html          /docs/Internet.html  ...
          151                   139                         137  ...
```

The most commonly requested pages involve EPA rules, software, and "what's new."

14.2.2　Events by Time

When are our users most active? Because we took care in Sect. 14.1.4 to code the
times, we can easily plot frequency of events versus time. The `ggplot2` package
understands standard date and time data as coordinates.

```
> library(ggplot2)
> p <- ggplot(epa.df, aes(x=datetime)) +
+ geom_density()
> p
```

The `geom_density()` function draws a smoothed histogram for the frequency.
The resulting figure is simple and usable, but it may be improved:

```
> library(scales)          # install if needed
> p <- ggplot(epa.df, aes(x=datetime, fill=I("lightblue"))) + # color
+     geom_density(alpha=0.5, bw = "SJ-dpi", adjust=2.0) +       # granular
+     scale_x_datetime(breaks = date_breaks("2 hours"),
+                date_labels = "%b %d %H:%M") +                  # axis labels
+     theme(axis.text.x =                                        # rotate
+              element_text(angle = 45, vjust = 1, hjust = 1)) +
+     ylab("HTTP Requests (proportion)") +                       # label axes
+     xlab("Date / Time")
> p
```

The result is shown in Fig. 14.1. If you look closely, you will see that the core of
this command is the same as the previous, very short code block, with several additional features. First, we fill the shape with "lightblue" color. We adjust the density
smoothing using a different smoothing estimation method, "SJ-dpi" and increase
the level of smoothing with `adjust=2.0` (higher values produce more smoothing).
Instead of a solid fill, we request a semi-transparent fill with `alpha=0.5`.

Next, we format the chart information to be more readable. We request X axis labels
at 2 h increments and format their appearance using `scale_x_datetime()` (see

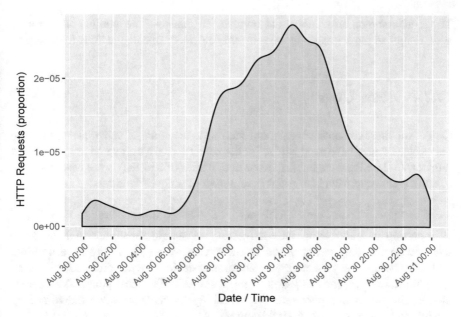

Fig. 14.1 Web requests by time in the EPA data

help for details on the format string). We rotate the X axis labels to 45° with the
`element_text(angle=...)` option. Finally we add `xlab()` and `ylab()`
axis labels.

Not surprisingly, we see that the server is busiest during daytime hours, and there is an
additional peak around midnight. We might use such data to inform decisions about
when to staff a call center, update files, or set shipping times. Also, it suggests patterns
that might be explored in qualitative research such as interviews or observation.

14.2.3 Errors

All of us have experienced web pages that cannot be found. An important task for
website developers is to track errors so that they can be identified and eliminated.
How do we find those errors in the EPA data?

First, we flag the requests that resulted in an error, which is easily identified by
an HTTP status of 400 or higher. Then we count the occurrences with `table()`
and `sort()` them as above:

```
> err.page <- epa.df$page[epa.df$status >= "http400"]
> head(sort(table(err.page), decreasing = TRUE))
err.page
      /waisicons/unknown.gif      /Region5/images/left.gif
                         206                            83
       /Region5/images/up.gif /Region5/images/epalogo.gif ...
                          83                            82 ...
```

The most common errors appear to involve GIF images. The administrators might need to upload those images to the relevant folders, or update the links from pages.

14.2.4 Active Users

One of the most common engagement metrics is the count of active users. In some data sets, you may have an identifier for the user, such as a user name or loyalty card number. In the EPA data, the disguised host name (IP address) is the best available identifier. One approach is to count the number of unique identifiers:

```
> length(unique(epa.df$host))
[1] 2333
```

In reporting or interpreting such a metric, we should remember that the user-to-identifier mapping is imprecise. In these data, some users may have multiple addresses because they use multiple networks or devices. Also, some addresses may have multiple users, such as people using a single WiFi access point. More generally, log in user names, phone numbers, and loyalty cards are often shared among household (and even non-household) members.

Who are the most active users? `table()` will count them. Then we can plot the counts and find the top 10 users:

```
> host.tab <- sort(table(epa.df$host), decreasing = TRUE)
> plot(host.tab)
> head(host.tab, 10)
host1986 host1032 host2247 host1439 host1028 host1656 host1511   host924 ...
     294      292      266      263      248      176      174       172 ...
```

The resulting plot is shown in Fig. 14.2. As is typical in such data, the pattern is roughly anti-logarithmic; a small proportion of users account for most transactions. (Try plotting the `log()` of the table to see a more linear relationship.)

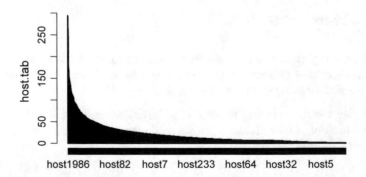

Fig. 14.2 Total page requests by user. A small number of users request many pages

14.3   Identifying Sequences (Sessions)

When working with any sequence data, an important decision must be made: among sequential actions, what counts as a *sequence*? For example, suppose you are interested in retail shopping behavior. Do you want to model what someone purchased in a single visit? Or all visits in a week? A month? A year? In their lifetime?

In the case of online behavior, it is common to assume that a sequence of interest, called a *session*, comprises all behaviors within a single period of time that is demarcated by a *gap* of inactivity from other sessions. For example, we might assume that if a user is active in two periods of time, with a gap between the periods of more than 15 or 30 or 60 min, then those are two distinct sets of behaviors.

In the EPA data, we need to identify those sessions. We'll look at the time gap between successive behaviors, assessing activity on a scale of minutes. For other data, you might use day, months, or years. For example, a model of engagement in an amusement park might logically use a scale of days (e.g., if we had data on in-park activities for our customers in Sect. 7.1). A model of personal banking and finance might be on the scale of years, while applications to personal health behavior (such as identifying the connection between behavior X and outcome Y) might use lifetime data.

Our discussion here is lengthy and may seem somewhat tedious. However, we discuss the process in detail for several reasons. First, there are important new functions, including `order()` to sort data, `cumsum()` for cumulative (running) totals, and `rle()` to count repetitions of values. Second, it demonstrates the importance of paying attention to small details such as offsetting indices when comparing sets of rows. Finally, it provides a structure that could be easily modified for other data, where you might care about sequence boundaries that are determined by other variables or by different gaps in time.

14.3.1   Extracting Sessions

We find sessions in `epa.df` in the following way: sort the behaviors in order of the user (`host`) as the primary sort key, and the timestamp (`datetime`) as the secondary key, and then split the data by time gaps. In R, sorting is commonly accomplished as a two step process. First, use `order()` to determine the appropriate order of elements according to the sort criteria, and then use indexing to put the object into that order. Note that—unlike sorting in a spreadsheet or other applications— `order()` does not *change* the order of your data. It just tells you what the ordering is.

Here's a simple example. We create a vector x of unordered numbers. `order(x)` tells us the position of each element that would put them into order (increasing order, by default):

```
> x <- c(22, 46, 66, 11, 33, 55)
> order(x)
[1] 4 1 5 2 6 3
> x[order(x)]
[1] 11 22 33 46 55 66
```

The command order(x) reports that the first element of the *ordered* version would be element 4 of x, followed by element 1, and so forth. This is what we need to create an index of x that will put it into the correct order, x[order(x)]. To order by more than dimension, list them separated by commas.

For the EPA data, we order by host and then datetime and save the result as a new data frame. It is not strictly required to save the result, but it simplifies the syntax for repeatedly using it later. (An alternative would be to index epa.df each time we need it in sorted order.)

```
> epa.ordered <- epa.df[order(epa.df$host, epa.df$datetime), ]
```

You should inspect head(epa.ordered, 50) or tail() to confirm the order. Next we find time gaps between successive rows:

```
> epa.ordered$time.diff <-
+    c(NA,
+      as.numeric(
+        epa.ordered$datetime[2:nrow(epa.ordered)] -
+        epa.ordered$datetime[1:(nrow(epa.ordered)-1)],
+        units="mins")
+      )
```

This is a long single line of code, but it is not complex if we break it down. First of all, it has the structure of comparing each row to the previous row, which it accomplishes by comparing rows 2:nrow(...) to rows 1:(nrow(...)-1). For data coded as timestamps (see Sect. 14.1.4), R can calculate differences. In this case, we calculate the difference in units of minutes, and find that by subtracting rows 1:(nrow(...)-1) from rows 2:nrow(). Next we assign those as a new column time.diff, but first add a difference of NA at the beginning. Why? Because our calculation applies starting from the *second* row, and the first row has no time difference from anything else.

Finally, we need to inspect the gaps between rows and identify which of them denote new sessions. There are three cases that could indicate a new session: (1) the first row of data, which is a new session by definition; (2) a different user (host) than the previous row; (3) the same user as the previous row, but with a time gap that exceeds a specific cutoff value.

For these data, we will define the cutoff time as 15 min between behaviors, assuming that if someone is inactive for that long and then return, they are likely to be doing a new task. This should be set according to your business question. Apart from assuming a cutoff interval, the choice might be informed by qualitative research and observation, or by quantitative analysis, such as the empirical distribution of gaps or the degree to which models using various assumptions about the gaps are effective at predicting behavior.

We set our assumed gap interval in minutes, and add a column newsession to track whether each row is part of a new session versus the previous row:

```
> session.time                    <- 15   # exceed (mins) ==> new session
> epa.ordered$newsession          <- NA   # is this row a new session?
> epa.ordered$newsession[1] <- TRUE  # row 1 is always a new session
```

We determine for each row whether it has either a new user host or a time gap greater than session.time:

```
> epa.ordered$newsession[2:nrow(epa.ordered)]  <-
+    ifelse(epa.ordered$host[2:nrow(epa.ordered)] !=
+               epa.ordered$host[1:(nrow(epa.ordered)-1)],    # hosts differ
+           TRUE,                                              # so diff session
+           epa.ordered$time.diff[2:nrow(epa.ordered)] >=
+               session.time )                                # else base on time
```

As with our time calculation above, this is a long line of code comparing rows 2:nrow() to previous rows 1:(nrow()-1). The core is an ifelse(test, yes, no) statement that assigns a value of TRUE in the case of a new session, or FALSE otherwise (ifelse() is discussed in Sect. 2.7.1). In pseudocode, it says this:

```
> newsession[currentrow] <-
+    if(host[currentrow] != host[previousrow],
+       then: newsession <- TRUE
+       else: newsession <- time.diff >= session.time
```

We take advantage of the fact that a boolean test in R returns TRUE and FALSE values for us; the ifelse() "no" (i.e., "else") clause simply assigns the direct value of comparing time.diff to session.time.

At this point we have a flag that identifies whether each row is part of a new session:

```
> epa.ordered[1:20, c("host", "datetime", "newsession")]
         host            datetime newsession
33393   host1 1995-08-30 16:03:45       TRUE
12383  host10 1995-08-30 11:07:35       TRUE
12388  host10 1995-08-30 11:07:50      FALSE
...
12462  host10 1995-08-30 11:09:01      FALSE
13891  host10 1995-08-30 11:32:21       TRUE
13895  host10 1995-08-30 11:32:27      FALSE
...
```

We see, for example, that "host10" was active from 11:07 to 11:09, and then had a break for 23 min. The next row at 11:32 is identified as starting a new session.

R treats TRUE as a value of 1, and FALSE as a value of 0, so we can count and number the sessions by taking a running total of newsession. The function cumsum() gives a running total:

```
> epa.ordered$session <- cumsum(epa.ordered$newsession)
```

Note that time.diff would have incorrect values wherever the log changes from one user to another; there is no in-session time difference from what another user did. We clean those up by assigning NA values for the time difference at the start of every session.

```
> epa.ordered$time.diff[epa.ordered$newsession==1] <- NA   # new sessions
```

Finally, we inspect the data using summary() (omitted here) and sample some of the rows:

```
> epa.ordered[1:100, c(1,  7,  11:13)]
              host            datetime  time.diff newsession session
33393       host1 1995-08-30 16:03:45         NA       TRUE       1
12383      host10 1995-08-30 11:07:35         NA       TRUE       2
12388      host10 1995-08-30 11:07:50 0.25000000      FALSE       2
...
12462      host10 1995-08-30 11:09:01 0.03333333      FALSE       2
13891      host10 1995-08-30 11:32:21         NA       TRUE       3
13895      host10 1995-08-30 11:32:27 0.10000000      FALSE       3
...
```

14.3.2   Session Statistics

If you have skimmed the chapter so far, it's time to load the data (Sect. 14.1.1). We will review a few basic descriptive statistics for sessions.

We saw in Sect. 14.2.4 that there are 2333 unique users in the EPA data. How many unique sessions are there? There are several equivalent ways to determine that:

```
> sum(epa.ordered$newsession)
[1] 3314
> sum(is.na(epa.ordered$time.diff))
[1] 3314
> max(epa.ordered$session)
[1] 3314
```

This reveals some redundancy in the data frame, which is often a good thing because it helps us check that our code is correct.

How many requests are there per session? A naive answer would simply divide the requests by sessions:

```
> nrow(epa.ordered) / sum(epa.ordered$newsession)
[1] 14.40797
```

However, as analysts we should always wonder about the *distribution* of such data. Remember that we have the counter `session` that is unique for each session (Sect. 14.3.1), and the data are ordered by that. To find the number of requests that occur within each session, we need to count them. The `rle(x)` function does this; it counts the number of times that a particular value is repeated in a row. We use this to count the number of times that a particular session identifier is observed sequentially.

```
> session.length <- rle(epa.ordered$session)$lengths
> table(session.length)
session.length
    1    2    3    4    5    6    7    8    9   10   11   12   13   14   15   16   17   18   19 ...
  357  251  129  114  103  115  460  147  126  106   77  101   92   84   64   52   53   54   54 ...
> plot(table(session.length))
```

The resulting plot is shown in Fig. 14.3.

As usual, we are also interested in the summary of the distribution:

```
> summary(session.length)
   Min. 1st Qu.  Median    Mean 3rd Qu.    Max.
   1.00    4.00    8.00   14.41   18.75  228.00
```

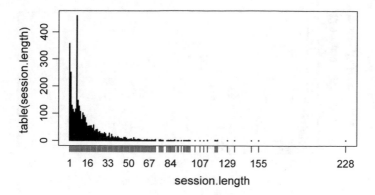

Fig. 14.3 Frequency of session length (in number of requests per session) for the complete EPA data. There is a spike for sessions with length 7

We see in the `summary()` that the median session length is 8 requests, but Fig. 14.3 shows a spike at the most common value of 7 requests. Why is that? Let's examine a few sessions of length 7. To do that, we need a way to select the rows that are part of sessions of length 7. We've already seen that `rle()` tells us the lengths of sessions. However, for a session of a given length, it simply reports that length—i.e., for a session with 10 requests, `rle()` just reports "10". It would be more convenient if it repeated that 10 times, because then it would align with the requests themselves. We can obtain that by using `rep()` with `session.length`: create a vector where each length is repeated exactly its own number of times:

```
> (sesslen  <- rep(session.length, session.length))
   [1]    1   13   13   13   13   13   13   13   13   13   13   13   13   13   13   13   13   13
  [19]   13   13   13   13   13   13   13   13   13   48   48   48   48   48   48   48   48 ...
```

That vector is now the same length as the rows in the data frame. For each row in the data frame, it answers the question, "what is the length of the session that includes this row?"

Given that, we are able to sample a few sessions with length 7, and examine the requests. We use the `%in%` operator to find sessions that match a random sample of desired sessions (`sesssamp`):

```
> set.seed(98245)
> sesssamp <- sample(unique(epa.ordered$session[sesslen==7]), 10)
> epa.ordered[epa.ordered$session %in% sesssamp, c("session", "page")]
        session                       page
17495       124                          /
17499       124      /logos/small_gopher.gif
17500       124  /icons/circle_logo_small.gif
17501       124         /logos/small_ftp.gif
17503       124             /icons/book.gif
17504       124            /icons/ok2-0.gif
17505       124          /logos/us-flag.gif
39953       604                          /
39969       604  /icons/circle_logo_small.gif
39971       604      /logos/small_gopher.gif
...
```

Ah! So many sessions have length 7 because the root page ("/") had 6 GIFs and each one of them was loaded by the browser as a separate request. That is not very

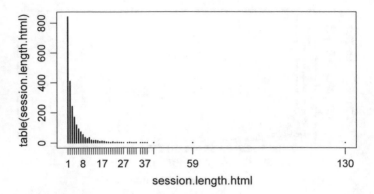

Fig. 14.4 Frequency of session lengths after filtering for only HTML requests. The spike at length 7 in Fig. 14.3 is no longer observed

interesting because it is so repetitive. We filter for just the HTML requests and inspect the session lengths again:

```
> session.length.html <-
+    rle(epa.ordered$session[epa.ordered$pagetype=="html"])$lengths
> plot(table(session.length.html))
```

The result is shown in Fig. 14.4 and makes more sense. It is a nearly perfect power-law relationship (Sect. 4.5.4), with a session length of just 1 page request as the most common observation.

14.4 Markov Chains for Behavior Transitions

We are now ready to explore sequences of user behavior. As we noted in the chapter introduction, there are many approaches to modeling such data. In this section, we introduce Markov chains (MCs) to model transitions between behavioral states. In our view, Markov chains have an unwarranted reputation for complexity. We believe their practical application can be straightforward. At the same time, MC methods and literature offer many options for more complex analyses when needed.

You might recall the term "Markov chain" from our discussion of Bayesian estimation methods (Sect. 6.6.2). In this chapter, forget about that! Although there is a deep connection—Markov chains are often used as part of a computational apparatus to determine parameters in Bayesian estimation—for purposes of this chapter, we recommend to keep the concepts separate. A Markov chain (MC) may be regarded as an interpretable behavioral state transition mechanism, whereas a Markov chain Monte Carlo (MCMC) procedure is a computational process used for other purposes (for more, see [73]). In short, this chapter is about MC, not MCMC.

14.4.1 Key Concepts and Demonstration

A Markov chain (MC) has two essential elements: a set of *states*, and a matrix of *transition probabilities* that define the odds of moving between states. For example, consider marriage. There are several possible states: {unmarried}, {married}, {divorced}, and {widowed}. Each of those has some probability, i.e., the proportion of the population who is in that state. We might also define or estimate a *transition matrix* for moving among those states. For example, the probability of moving from {married} to {divorced} in one year might be p=0.02 (for opposite-sex couples in the United States), while the probability of transitioning from {unmarried} to {divorced} is p=0, because one must first go through the state of being {married}. We may use an MC estimation method to infer such transition probabilities from observed data.

Let's consider such states in the context of web pages. Suppose we have 3 web pages on a site, and observe that 70% of users start on Page 1, 20% on Page 2, and 10% on Page 3. We represent that in R as a vector of starting probabilities:

```
> p.start <- c(0.7, 0.2, 0.1)
```

That establishes the first necessity of an MC, the *states*. Next we define the *transition probabilities* among the pages. Usually we would determine or estimate these from observations, but for this example we predefine them in order to see how the process works:

```
> p.trans <- matrix(c(0.1, 0.5, 0.2,
+                     0.6, 0.4, 0.8,
+                     0.3, 0.1, 0.0), nrow=3, byrow=TRUE)
```

If someone is at Page 1 (first column) then the odds for their next page after clicking are p=0.1 to remain at Page 1 (matrix position [1, 1]), p=0.6 to move to Page 2 (position [2, 1]) and p=0.3 for Page 3 (position [3, 1]).

Note on the Transition Matrix Layout (especially for experienced Markov chain users). Compared to many common expositions of Markov chains, we use a transposed matrix here for the transition probabilities, where the states transition from the *column* to the *row*. We present it this way in order to match the order used in the `clickstream` package later in this chapter. In general, one should carefully check whether a transition matrix should be read as representing row-to-column transition order (the most common case in MC literature) or column-to-row transition.

We compute the probabilities for page locations after one user step by (matrix-) multiplying the transitional probabilities p.trans by the initial state odds p.start:

```
> p.trans %*% p.start            # one click from start
        [,1]
[1,]  0.19
[2,]  0.58
[3,]  0.23
>
```

After 1 click among our pages, 19% of users would be at Page 1, 58% at Page 2, and 23% at Page 3. It may help to check one of the results manually. We can compute the Page 1 proportion after one click as follows: 70% start on Page 1 and remain on Page 1 with p=0.1; another 20% start on Page 2 and transition to Page 1, p=0.5; and 10% start on Page 3 and move to Page 1, p=0.2. In R:

```
> 0.7*0.1 + 0.2*0.5 + 0.1*0.2          # manual calc, transition to page 1
[1] 0.19
```

That is the same as we see for the first element in the matrix multiplication above. To obtain the state probabilities after a second click, we multiply by the transition matrix again:

```
> p.trans %*% p.trans %*% p.start          # two clicks from start
      [,1]
[1,]  0.355
[2,]  0.530
[3,]  0.115
```

An interesting property of some Markov chains—known as *regular* chains—is that their long-range predictions become stable after multiple steps and are independent of the starting position. To determine this, we may examine exponential powers of the transition matrix, multiplying it by itself many times to see whether the results are stable. We can exponentiate a transition matrix T to some high power, such as T^{100} using the expm package [78]:

```
> library(expm)                        # matrix exponentiate, install if needed
> p.trans %^% 100                      # 100 steps
      [,1]   [,2]   [,3]
[1,]  0.325  0.325  0.325
[2,]  0.525  0.525  0.525
[3,]  0.150  0.150  0.150
```

We find that, regardless of the originating page (the column, in this layout), 32.5% of users will end up on Page 1, 52.5% on Page 2, and 15% on Page 3 (the rows) after 100 steps. We can check that by estimating the state from quite different starting points:

```
> p.trans %^% 100 %*% c(1,0,0)             # starting from all page 1
      [,1]
[1,]  0.325
[2,]  0.525
[3,]  0.150
> p.trans %^% 100 %*% c(0.333, 0.334, 0.333) # starting equal 3 pages
      [,1]
[1,]  0.325
[2,]  0.525
[3,]  0.150
```

14.4.2 Formatting the EPA Data for clickstream Analysis

In this section, we use the clickstream package [175] to find transition probabilities in the EPA data. As usual, the first step is to format the data as expected by the package. The clickstream package expects data to be formatted such that all events for onesequence appear on a single line, such as "user1, page2, page2, page1, page3". We start by loading the package:

```
> library(clickstream)        # install first, if needed
```

One choice is whether to model *all* data or not. In the case of the EPA data, there are 6565 unique pages (`length(unique(epa.df$page))`). A matrix with 6565 columns transitioning to 6565 rows would be both computationally difficult as well as nearly impossible to interpret. We limit ourselves to analysis of the 20 most common pages. We find those page names and filter the data to HTML pages that are in the top 20:

```
> # .. for simplicity here, restrict to top 20 most frequent pages
> top.pages <- names(head(sort(table(epa.df$page[epa.df$pagetype=="html"]),
+                         decreasing = TRUE), 20))
> epa.html     <- subset(epa.ordered, pagetype=="html" & page %in% top.pages)
```

At this point, we have events in multiple rows per session. We `split()` the data by `session` and then remove any sessions of length 1 (this is not strictly required, but there is little point modeling transition probabilities in sessions with no transition):

```
> # split the sessions
> epa.session <- split(epa.html, epa.html$session)
> # .. optional, remove any of length 1
> epa.stream.len <- lapply(epa.session, nrow)
> epa.session <- epa.session[epa.stream.len > 1]
```

We check the data to see that the sessions are correctly split, and find $N = 521$ sessions:

```
> str(head(epa.session))
List of 6
 $ 13:'data.frame': 3 obs. of  13 variables:
  ..$ host      : Factor w/ 2333 levels "host1","host10",..: 10 10 10
  ..$ timestamp : chr [1:3] "[30:15:55:42]" "[30:16:10:08]" "[30:16:10:16]"
  ..$ request   : chr [1:3] "GET /docs/WhatsNew.html" "GET /Offices.html" "GET
    /Offices.html"
...
> length(epa.session)
[1] 521
```

One decision we have to make with sequence data is whether and how to identify end states. With web data, a session eventually ends; in an e-commerce application, users make a purchase or not; in medical applications, a patient may manifest a symptom or disease. If the end state is of specific interest for the analytical question, you may need to append the outcome to the sequence. In the present case, we will assume that it is of interest—for example, to gain insight into user retention—and add an "END" state to each sequence, denoting where their session ended.

Now we are able to compile the events onto individual lines for each session. To do this, we iterate over the sessions, and for each one we aggregate a line comprising the user identifier (`host`), the sequence of events (multiple `page` entries), and a final end state:

```
> epa.stream <- unlist(lapply(epa.session,
+                       function(x)
+                         paste0(unique(x$host), ",",
+                                paste0(unlist(x$page), collapse=","),
+                                ",END")))
```

Reviewing that command, it breaks down as follows. First of all, we use `lapply()` with an anonymous function (Sect. 2.7.2) to process each of the sessions in `epa.session`. That function has two parts. In the inner part, we `unlist()` all the individual pages and combine them into a single character string, using the collapse option of paste0() (which is a variation of paste() with no extra spaces; see Sect. 3.4.4). Then we use paste0() again to add the host identifier in front of the set of pages, and "END" at the end. After doing that for every session, we finally unlist() all of them. This gives a vector with individual lines for each session:

```
> head(epa.stream)
13   "host1006,/docs/WhatsNew.html,/Offices.html,/Offices.html,END"
17   "host101,/Info.html,/Research.html,END" ...
```

As it happens, clickstream removes all characters from page names other than letters and numbers. However, this can make the directory structure difficult to read. We avail ourselves of regex capability (Sect. 14.1.5) to replace all of the "/" and "." characters with unique combinations. The gsub(find, replace, x) function will replace all matching text in a character vector. We replace "/" with "ii" and ".html" with nothing (""); it is redundant because every page is HTML. Before altering the data, we use grepl() to make sure that "ii" is unique and not already part of any page names:

```
> any(grepl("ii", epa.stream))          # before gsub, does ii appear?
[1] FALSE
```

We are safe to use "ii", so we use gsub() to make the replacement:

```
> epa.stream <- gsub("/", "ii", epa.stream)
> epa.stream <- gsub(".html", "", epa.stream, fixed=TRUE)
```

Because "." is a special regex pattern that matches any single character, we need to tell gsub() to match the actual period in ".html". The option fixed=TRUE is one way to accomplish this, as it matches an exact string. The converted data still have a readable structure (with some squinting):

```
> head(epa.stream)
13   "host1006,iidocsiiWhatsNew,iiOffices,iiOffices,END"
17   "host101,iiInfo,iiResearch,END" ...
```

Finally, we import the data into a clickstream object. To do that, we write the data to a temporary file (created with the tempfile() function) and read it from there with readClickstreams():

```
> click.tempfile <- tempfile()
> writeLines(epa.stream, click.tempfile)
> epa.trans <- readClickstreams(click.tempfile, header = TRUE)
```

As always, we check the first few and last few results to see whether something went wrong:

```
> head(epa.stream)
13   "host1006,iidocsiiWhatsNew,iiOffices,iiOffices,END"
17   "host101,iiInfo,iiResearch,END"
...
> head(epa.trans)
$host1006
[1] "iidocsiiWhatsNew" "iiOffices"         "iiOffices"         "END"
$host101
[1] "iiInfo"        "iiResearch" "END"
...
> tail(epa.stream)
...
3298 "host987,iidocsiiWelcomeiiEPA,iiPIC,END"
3310 "host996,iiRules,iiInitiatives,END"
> tail(epa.trans)
```

```
...
$host987
[1] "iidocsiiWelcomeiiEPA" "iiPIC"                    "END"
$host996
[1] "iiRules"            "iiInitiatives" "END"
```

At this point, the `epa.trans` object is ready for `clickstream` analysis.

14.4.3 Estimating the Markov Chain

With the data formatted, estimating the Markov chain is straightforward. The main choice is the *order*—the number of states considered in the transition matrix—that we wish to consider. In general, we recommend to start analysis with an order of 1, where the next state (i.e., page) depends only on the current state. That is computationally simple and easy to interpret. After that, consider higher order models (Sect. 14.4.5). We fit the MC model with order 1 using `fitMarkovChain()`:

```
> epa.mc <- fitMarkovChain(epa.trans, order=1)
```

The observed transition matrix is in the `@transitions` slot of the `epa.mc` object:

```
> epa.mc@transitions
$`1`
                END       iiInfo iiInitiatives       iiNews    iiOffices
END               0   0.24358974    0.19696970   0.36923077   0.39743590
iiInfo            0   0.11538462    0.03030303   0.07692308   0.01282051
iiInitiatives     0   0.02564103    0.07575758   0.04615385   0.03846154
iiNews            0   0.10256410    0.01515152   0.03076923   0.02564103
iiOffices         0   0.07692308    0.03030303   0.04615385   0.10256410
...
```

We read column-to-row (per `clickstream` order) and find that users transition {Info → Info} with p=0.115, {Info → News} with p=0.102, {News → Info} with p=0.0769, {Offices → END} with p=0.397, and so forth.

One thing we can immediately read from the transition matrix is which pages are most associated with leaving the site—the pages with high values for transition to "END." If we have a goal of user retention, these would be pages to examine for user frustration, errors, or other design problems.

Are you surprised that this step was so easy? A winemaker acquaintance of Chris's once told him that winemaking is 95% janitation (cleaning crushing equipment, tanks, barrels, bottles, etc). The same is true for much data analysis: 95% of the effort is cleaning the data. Fitting the model is often a simple step.

14.4.4 Visualizing the MC Results

A transition matrix is easy to inspect and interpret as a heat map. We suggest the `superheat` package to visualize it [6] (`heatmap.2()` would also work;

see Sect. 8.1.2). We first extract the transition matrix to a separate object in order to use gsub() to fix the "/" structure that we disguised earlier. We transpose the transition matrix using t() because row-to-column is easier to read on a heat map:

```
> epa.mc.mat <- t(epa.mc@transitions[[1]])        # t() because easier to read
> dimnames(epa.mc.mat)[[1]] <- gsub("ii", "/", dimnames(epa.mc.mat)[[1]])
> dimnames(epa.mc.mat)[[2]] <- gsub("ii", "/", dimnames(epa.mc.mat)[[2]])
```

We use superheat() with options to resize and rotate the labels, a red color scheme (higher red saturation for larger transition probabilities), and clustering the results into pages with similar transition patterns. We set a random number seed because the layout is partially determined at random:

```
> library(superheat)                              # install if needed
> set.seed(70510)
> superheat(epa.mc.mat[-1, ],                     # remove transitions from "END"
+           bottom.label.size = 0.4,
+           bottom.label.text.size = 3.5,
+           bottom.label.text.angle = 270,
+           left.label.size = 0.3,
+           left.label.text.size = 4,
+           heat.col.scheme = "red",
+           n.clusters.rows = 5, n.clusters.cols = 5,
+           left.label = "variable", bottom.label = "variable",
+           title="Transitions, in sequences of top 20 pages (Row-to-Col)")
```

Note that we remove the first row of the transition matrix epa.mc.mat[-1,] because "END" never transitions to any other page. The result is shown in Fig. 14.5, and reveals several patterns, such as the close relationship between the "WhatsHot" and "Internet" pages, a strong association of "efhome" (the unitary page in the next-to-last column cluster) as a destination from "docs/major" and "Software", and a few clusters of similar pages.

Another useful way to view MC transitions is with a graph layout. The clickstream package provides a plot() method to do this, given a fitted MC object. For a cleaner graph, we request transitions with a minimum probability of 0.25:

```
> set.seed(59911)
> plot(epa.mc, minProbability=0.25)          # layout varies; partially random
```

This gives Fig. 14.6, which reveals associated pages and common paths to "END."

14.4.5 Higher Order Chains and Prediction

What if we want to model transitions from multiple pages? We fit a Markov chain with a higher order parameter. This requires filtering the data to relevant sessions that have a sufficient number of events. For example, to model transitions after two pages, the sessions must have length 3 or greater. In a higher-order model, transition matrices cannot be directly *observed* from the data but are *estimated* from the observations using a linear optimization method (see ?fitMarkovChain). In this case, we take a subset of epa.trans, selecting sessions with 3 pages or more using lapply(..., length) >= 4 (using 4 instead of 3 because of the END state), and fit a second order model by setting order=2:

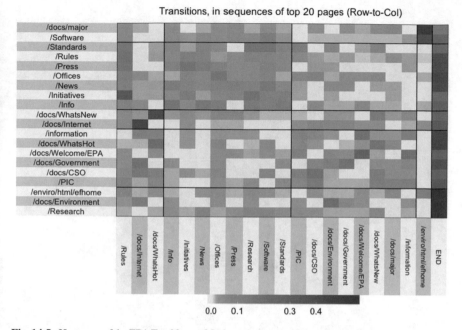

Fig. 14.5 Heat map of the EPA Top 20 page Markov chain transitions using `superheat`, clustering the rows and columns. Note that the transition matrix here is read as transitioning from the *row* to the *column*, as is traditional for Markov chains

```
> epa.trans.ge3 <- epa.trans[lapply(epa.trans, length) >= 4]
> epa.mc2       <- fitMarkovChain(epa.trans.ge3, order=2)
```

This yields two @`transition` matrices, in which a state's likelihood is proportional to the summed product of the respective transition odds for the two previous states (see ?`predict,MarkovChain-method`). The proportionality is relative to potential *absorbing states*, a more complex topic than space allows here; cf. Grinstead and Snell, Sect. 11.2 [81].

Apart from inspecting the transition matrices, we use them to predict states that might follow a particular sequence. Consider sequence 160 in our data, which happens to have length of 10 page views. First we review the sequence and, for convenience, copy it to a new `clickstream` sequence object:

```
> epa.trans[160]
$host1632
 [1] "iiRules"              "iidocsiimajor"       "iidocsiiInternet"
 [4] "iidocsiiGovernment"   "iiinformation"       "iidocsiiWelcomeiiEPA"
 [7] "iiPIC"                "iiRules"             "iiRules"
[10] "iiInitiatives"        "END"
> epa.ex <- new("Pattern", sequence=head(unlist(epa.trans[160]), -1))
```

Notice a new use of indexing: we selected `head(..., -1)` to get all of the sequence *except* the final observation (because that is "END" and doesn't lead to any other states).

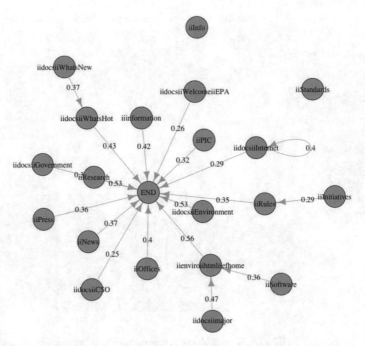

Fig. 14.6 Graph of the EPA Top 20 page transitions in the Markov chain model, for transition probabilities ≥ 0.25, using the default `plot()` method from `clickstream`

We use `predict()` to predict the next page (" `dist=1`" means a distance of one page):

```
> predict(epa.mc2, epa.ex, dist=1)
Sequence: iiRules
Probability: 0.2858429 ...
```

The next page is most likely to be "Rules", with probability 0.286. We could predict additional pages after that, if we wished, such as the next 4 likely pages:

```
> predict(epa.mc2, epa.ex, dist=4)        # most just end up with "END"
Sequence: iiRules END
Probability: 0.0730788 ...
```

After one or two pages, sequences are likely to arrive at the end state. This is consistent with the paths shown for the first order model in Fig. 14.6. End states may dominate the model for a simple reason: there may be only one or a few end states, but many other states lead to them. Thus, transitions to the relatively small number of end states will have higher probabilities. If you are interested in transitions among the other states (pages), it may be helpful to do a parallel analysis without the end states.

14.5 Discussion and Questions

What kinds of actions might we take with this kind of information? As always, it depends on the business goals, but as a starting point, we would ask questions such as these:

1. Are there pages missing that we would expect to see? If so, they may be insufficiently exposed in the site design, and might benefit from promotion (or, possibly fixing broken links).
2. Are there links that are surprising? For instance, does it make sense for our intended site experience that "Initiatives" leads most strongly to "Rules" (Fig. 14.5), and similarly for other links? Do those patterns suggest a need to clarify or reorganize the site, or to share common design elements among them?
3. When pages cluster in a common origination or destination group (Fig. 14.5), should they have a common navigation structure (such as site menu)? Is that actually the case in the page design?
4. Are the observed clusters desirable—in which case we might, for example, wish to ensure consistency of the navigation experience—or are the groupings undesirable, suggesting that we should change the navigation paths, menus, or other elements to differentiate them?
5. Do the clusters suggest *state transitions* where pages may indicate user flow into different tasks with related pages? (See both Figs. 14.5 and 14.6.) Is there any logical progress or grouping? For example, in Fig. 14.6 there seem to be groups related to general overviews of information (WhatsNew, WhatsHot) and to specific programs and detailed information (Press, Offices, Initiatives, etc). These suggest high-level areas for site design in consideration of user tasks.
6. After we identify transitions of interest, are they present less often or more often than we wish, in the overall user data? How should we change the site in view of our goals?
7. If we model end states—such as a purchase or leaving the site—which pages lead to those states? Do those suggest errors or problems with the design? Do they suggest interventions for promotion or retention?

We use this kind of information along with qualitative observation, such as usability lab tests, to examine and better understand users' needs. This is quite valuable to determine where the site contents and structure might be improved, where pages should be promoted, and where we need to reconcile or differentiate pages and designs.

14.6   Key Points

- In this chapter, we examined sequential patterns of movement across discrete states. This kind of analysis may be applied to web site behavior, yet it is also applicable to many kinds of sequence data, such as historical purchasing patterns, life events, biomedical data, and others.
- This chapter demonstrates the most complex data cleaning process in this text. Real-world data needs careful, stepwise processing with careful consideration and inspection along the way. Throughout the chapter, we limited analyses to relevant data such as "GET" events and HTML page requests (Sects. 14.1.5 and 14.4.2).
- When text data represents dates or times, it requires careful translation to a native R data format. The relatively simple but rigid `strptime()` command (Sect. 14.1.4) can do this for user-defined patterns. Other packages provide more comprehensive and flexible options (see Sect. 14.7).
- Regular expressions (regexes) provide very powerful processing for text data with identifiable structure. We decoded a regex that parses HTTP requests and identifies the specific page names (Sect. 14.1.5) and used another one for text substitutions (Sect. 14.4.2).
- Log data often needs to be divided into sessions, where events represent actions taken by one user in a specific block of time. It can be difficult and somewhat arbitrary to determine the boundaries of sessions—how much inactivity is long enough? The `rle()` function is especially useful to find repeating values (e.g., recurrent identifiers) that help to identify sessions. We found session boundaries with a combination of users' identifiers along with time gaps between actions (Sect. 14.3.1).
- Markov chains are a good initial choice for a method to analyze transitions among different behavior states (Sect. 14.4). A Markov chain proposes a transition matrix that defines the odds of moving from one state to another. We used the `clicksteam` package to estimate a transition matrix for the Top 20 pages in the EPA data. Because a web site may have hundreds, thousands, or millions of pages, one may need to reduce the state space before modeling (Sect. 14.4.2).
- One decision is whether to model end states, such as leaving the site or purchasing an item. These are often of high interest because they reveal where a site may be working poorly (or well) relative to our goals (Sect. 14.4.2). However, end states may also be dominant and lead to uninteresting predictive modeling (Sect. 14.4.5).
- Heatmaps are useful to visualize transition matrices. They are even more useful when the rows and columns are clustered to reveal groupings of items whose transition patterns are similar. The clustering options in `superheat` can reveal common patterns of page transitions (Sect. 14.4.4).
- Higher order Markov chains may be used to predict states from a series of multiple previous states (Sect. 14.4.5). To fit them, you may need to filter the data to a subset with sequences of sufficient length.
- In the `clickstream` package, `predict(object, startPattern)` may be used to predict the next state, or multiple successive states, for a given pattern (Sect. 14.4.5).

14.7 Learning More*

As mentioned in the chapter introduction, we purposely avoided packages that are specific to web log analysis in order to learn several new techniques and to develop general methods that apply to other kinds of sequences. However, if you do much work with web logs, you may wish to use dedicated tools. If your server uses Google Analytics, you will wish to check the RGoogleAnalytics package [152] among others. Mark Edmondson, author of googleAnalyticsR [50], describes several options to use Google Analytics with R at https://goo.gl/njr723.

If your platform uses Adobe Analytics, review the RSiteCatalyst package [150] maintained by Randy Zwitch. RSiteCatalyst includes tools to access data from your Adobe Analytics account including data on visitors, sites, and segments, and to perform reporting.

We briefly examined date and time data, as well as regular expressions. If you often use data with times or dates, you will want to examine the lubridate package [82]. When working with text data, regular expressions (regexes) are extremely powerful. If you often handle text, you'll wish to develop modest fluency with regexes. They can be complex to debug, and their implementation in R differs in several ways from other platforms. To be effective, you will wish to use a combination of R documentation, texts such as Goyvaerts and Levithan [80], and sites that allow you to test and debug the expressions, such as https://regex101.com [42].

We used Markov chains to examine page-to-page transitions. There is a large literature on Markov processes that one might consider for further analyses. Gagniuc (2017) provides a readable and code-oriented introduction to Markov models [68]. Another excellent introduction is Chap. 11 of Grinstead and Snell [81], which is offered both freely online and in print [81]. One might also consider whether there are groups with different patterns; sequence data may reflect underlying unobserved *hidden states* (such as customer segments or types) with differing transition matrices. *Hidden Markov models* (HMMs) may be used to models such groups and their sequence patterns. Netzer, Lattin, and Srinivasan (2008) describe the application of HMMs to customer relationship data [146]. Another approach is to cluster the user sequences; clickstream provides clusterClickstreams() for K-means clustering of sequences [175], and the ClickClust package offers a model-based clustering approach [138].

An alternative to Markov chain analysis is association sequence mining. That approach does not use transition matrices but attempts to find sequences that occur more often than random chance, similar to the association rule mining approach we discussed in Chap. 12. The R package arulesSequences implements sequential rule mining [24]. In the healthcare domain, Reps et al. (2012) used association sequence analysis to examine longitudinal relationships among illnesses, treatments, and outcomes in UK medical records [162]. If you find association rules appealing, the online code for this chapter has an example analysis of the EPA data with arulesSequences.

If you are primarily analyzing life stage changes—which in marketing might involve changes in behavior due to lifestyle events such as graduation, marriage, relocation, parenting, group affiliations, or prior product experience—the `TraMineR` package [67] provides useful visualization tools. We find it especially helpful when examining changes in group composition over time.

Finally, if you do a lot of work with sequence data, you may wish to investigate a parallel and vast ecosystem of additional R resources for bioinformatics, where sequence analysis is used for genomic and other biomedical analyses. `Bioconductor` is a set of more than 1000 R packages to work with genomic data [13]. The tools to understand gene expression (i.e., genetic event sequences) may be particularly useful. Note, however, that translation to other domains can be challenging with those packages; much of the jargon and many specifics of the tools and data sets refer to bioinformatic tasks. Jones and Pevzner [109] is an approachable and interesting introductory text in this area (although not specific to R or Bioconductor).

14.8 Exercises

In these exercises, we try to expand your horizons in the final two questions, which propose larger-scale projects.

1. Plot the number of *bytes* requested by user in the EPA data. Should the values be transformed? Why or why not? If so, plot them with and without the transformation, and discuss the differing interpretation.
2. There is one value for "total number of bytes downloaded" that is especially frequent in the EPA data. For example, in the previous exercise it appears as a spike in the plot. What value is it? Why it is frequent?
3. Omit the end states from the sequences and repeat the Markov chain analysis. Are there differences in your interpretation of the result?
4. Now model the sequences using the top 40 pages instead of top 20 (and without end states). How do you need to change the visualizations to be more useful?
5. *(Thought exercise without code.)* Suppose the EPA asked you to consult on their web site. They give you the present data as background, and suggest that you will be able to collect the same kind of data again, and that you also might be able to collect additional variables. Assume that you can collect up to 10 additional variables. Based on the analyses in this chapter and other chapters in this book, what other data would you wish to have, and why?
6. *(This is a more extensive, full project with a different data set.)* Additional web log data sets are available, as of publication date, at http://ita.ee.lbl.gov/html/traces.html. Choose one of the data sets there and repeat the analyses in this chapter. For modest size, we suggest the San Diego Supercomputer Center (SDSC) data set [154], although you might also wish to try one of the larger data sets. (Note: the SDSC data set is also available at https://goo.gl/jpWMVh.) If you use the SDSC

data, note that the host address has two parts: "N+H", where "N" is a particular network and "H" is a machine (host) within that network. It is a unique identifier.

7. *(Stretch exercise: the longest one in the book, which requires detailed programming and determining on your own how to use two new packages.)* Using the IP addresses in the EPA data, find the geographic location of the requesting machines and plot them on a choropleth map (Sect. 3.4.6). Because online services to look up data can be slow, cache lookup results locally, such that if you run the procedure again, it loads a local file instead of looking up results. (Hint: check out the packages `iptools` and `rgeolocate`, and the function `file.exists()`.)

Conclusion

We covered many topics in this book, from basic programming to Bayesian methods. As a final note, we would like to summarize key suggestions and lessons that apply to everything we discussed.

1. Summarize, explore, and visualize data before starting to build models. It is easy to overlook bad data points ...especially if you don't even look (Sects. 3.3.3, 3.5, 9.2.7).
2. Model building is an interactive process. Start with a simple model and build on it progressively, assessing at each stage whether a more complex model is an improvement (Sects. 6.5.3, 7.3, and 7.5.3).
3. Human behavior and marketing data often yield observations that are correlated, yet high correlation may make a statistical model unstable. Consider reducing data to key dimensions before modeling, and assess models for collinearity (Sects. 8.2 and 9.1).
4. It is important to understand and to report the uncertainty in any statistic that you estimate from sampled data. Report confidence intervals whenever possible. This can often be done with a minimum of statistical jargon by using graphics (Sects. 6.5.2, 6.6.4, and 7.3).
5. Statistical significance is a necessary condition for a model to be interesting, yet it does not imply that a model is appropriate, useful, or even the best-fitting. When possible, compare alternative models and evaluate a model in terms of its usefulness to answer important questions (Sects. 9.2.7, 11.3.1, 11.3.6).
6. Hierarchical models that estimate differences by individual, sample, or group are often very useful in marketing, and are not as complex as they might seem at first. Once you know how to estimate basic linear models in R, it is relatively easy to start considering hierarchical models. These may be fit with either traditional maximum likelihood or Bayesian methods (Sects. 9.3, 9.4, and 13.4).
7. Don't simply assume that a data set, especially from a consumer survey, reflects underlying concepts as expected. Methods such as factor analysis and structural equation modeling make it possible to assess latent variables and determine whether a model fits your data (Sects. 8.3 and 10.1).

© Springer Nature Switzerland AG 2019
C. Chapman and E. M. Feit, *R For Marketing Research and Analytics*, Use R!,
https://doi.org/10.1007/978-3-030-14316-9

Perhaps our most important point is this: R is a dynamic ecosystem and there is always more to learn. As you work with R over the years, consider how you might contribute. Whether you teach a colleague, contribute code, share data sets externally, or simply ask great questions, you can give back to the R community. If we each do that, we all benefit from more useful and powerful tools. And that means we will do better, more satisfying work for our organizations, firms, colleagues, and customers.

Appendix A
R Versions and Related Software

R is available in several versions. Just as R packages are contributed by authors who like to share their innovations, others have adapted R itself for commercial purposes and to work with other programming tools.

Our recommended installation depends on your background:

- For new or casual Windows programmers: R base + RStudio.
- For Mac users: R base, and optionally RStudio or one of the editors below.
- For new or casual Linux users: R base + RStudio.
- For experienced Windows programmers: R base + your favorite editor, RStudio, or Microsoft Open R.
- For Emacs users: R base + Emacs Speaks Statistics.
- For Java, C, or C++ programmers: R base + your favorite editor, or Eclipse + StatET.
- For instructors and students: any of the above, or R Commander, Deducer, or Rattle.

These notes are current as of the time of writing (2018) although the R landscape is rich and evolving.

A.1   R Base

R base is generic R. In Windows, it runs as a graphical user interface (GUI) program like other applications, with relatively limited capability for code editing and plots. R users on Windows will want to supplement R base with a programming editor such as RStudio or another choice noted below.

For Mac users, the GUI version is more sophisticated than on Windows and features syntax highlighting, plot exporting, and other features. Figure A.1 shows R on a Mac OS X system with highlighted syntax, direct execution of code from the editor in

© Springer Nature Switzerland AG 2019

C. Chapman and E. M. Feit, *R For Marketing Research and Analytics*, Use R!,
https://doi.org/10.1007/978-3-030-14316-9

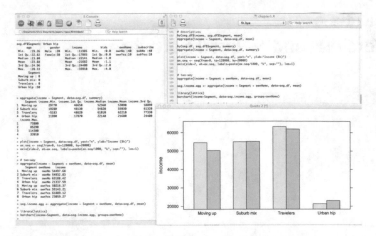

Fig. A.1 R base GUI on Mac OS X, showing syntax-aware editing, plot window, and the console

the R console, and integrated plotting. Mac users may be satisfied with the default R GUI for simple and moderate-sized projects.

On Linux, R runs as a terminal (command line) program. Much R development occurs first on Linux, and Linux is a great system to run R. However, you will also want RStudio or another code editing option, as R base has no GUI support on Linux.

R is available at the Comprehensive R Archive Network (CRAN): http://cran.r-project.org. R has also been widely ported to other operating systems. You can find many versions as well as source code at CRAN.

A.2   RStudio

RStudio is a separate application that works with R to provide an integrated development environment (IDE), similar to other language platforms such as Eclipse and Microsoft Visual Studio. Unlike Eclipse and Visual Studio, RStudio is tailored to R and is less complex for new and casual programmers.

Some of the appealing features of RStudio are the syntax-aware editor that shows code elements with highlighting, an object inspector that allows you to look at memory contents, an integrated debugger, plot exporting, and an easily navigable layout for help content, files, package installation, and multiple code windows. RStudio exports plots to the clipboard and resizes them nicely, which is very helpful when copying plots into office software such as Microsoft Office and Google Docs.

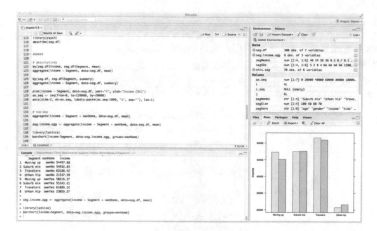

Fig. A.2 RStudio showing the syntax-aware editor, the console, object inspector, and plot window

An exceptional feature of RStudio is its integration of tools for code management, documentation, and reproducible research. RStudio integrates Sweave to create documents that mix LATEX with R code, results, and graphics, along with the flexible and easy to use knitr system [70, 206]. These markup tools allow an analyst to create reports and documentation that combine readable text with actual R commands used to perform the analysis. RStudio supports code *projects* with version control using Git and Subversion [70]. See Appendix B for a quick introduction to reproducibility in RStudio.

To use RStudio, you first install R base as above (Sect. A.1) and then install the RStudio application from http://www.rstudio.com. Figure A.2 shows the RStudio interface on a Mac laptop.

A.3 ESS: Emacs Speaks Statistics

Emacs Speaks Statistics (ESS) [169] is a set of extensions to the Emacs text editor [183] to interface with R and other statistics programs. Emacs is a powerful editing platform that includes a Lisp-based programming language. ESS extends that interface to R with syntax coloring, plot display, and other IDE functions.

ESS is available for Windows, Mac, and Linux from http://ess.r-project.org/. There are several software prerequisites such as Emacs and an X Window system, depending on your operating system. Installing those is straightforward on Mac OS X and Linux,

Fig. A.3 ESS with the code
editor above and R console
below. Plots open in a
separate window

but rather more complex in Windows as they require adding the Linux-like Cygwin
system to Windows. Figure A.3 presents a screenshot of ESS on Mac OS X [77].

If you know Emacs already, ESS may be your environment of choice. On the other
hand, if you do not know Emacs, it may be frustrating; Emacs has its own set of
keystrokes for many commands functions and although those are elegant and efficient, they may seem antiquated and non-obvious (the reference card at http://ess.r-
project.org/refcard.pdf provides a sample of those).

A.4 Eclipse + StatET

If you have professional programming experience in Java or C++, you may be familiar
with Eclipse. The StatET plug-in for Eclipse adds functionality for R, including
integration of the R console into Eclipse, browsing R memory objects, plots, and
interface between R and the Eclipse debugger. It is similar to RStudio in its feature
set for R, although the overall Eclipse environment is more complex.

Eclipse + StatET is available by installing Eclipse from http://www.eclipse.org and
then adding the StatET plug-in from http://www.walware.de/goto/statet. Figure A.4
shows Eclipse "Kepler" + StatET 3.3 running on OS X. *Warning*: setting up StatET
is modestly complex with several steps in strictly dependent order; we recommend
to search online for the latest instructions for your platform.

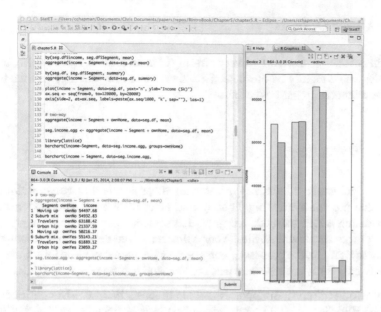

Fig. A.4 Eclipse + StatET, showing the code editor, R console, and integrated plot display

Eclipse provides powerful code editing capability needed by professional programmers and integrates with other coding tools such as Git. However, some users find StatET integration to be finicky and less performant than RStudio. We recommend Eclipse + StatET if you are a programmer looking for more code editing power than RStudio, or if you already use Eclipse.

A.5   Microsoft R

Microsoft acquired Revolution Analytics in 2015 and began offering both open source and licensed versions of R. Microsoft Open R is an open source, freely available version of R with enhancements to support higher performance computation as well as replicable computing with package versioning. It is available for Windows, Mac OS X, and Linux systems. Microsoft also offers hosted, licensed versions of R known as Microsoft Machine Learning Server. At the time of writing, Machine Learning Server supported both Python and R languages and libraries. The Microsoft Visual Studio development environment and the free Visual Studio Code editor also support R.

A.6   Other Options

We will not attempt to compile every offering of interest in the R ecosystem, and any such list would rapidly be obsolete. Still, there are a few offerings that we believe deserve attention for various readers.

A.6.1   Text Editors

Many programming editors support R with either standard or user-provided templates that provide syntax highlighting and other features. If you have a favorite programming editor, the odds are good that someone has written a language definition for it to work with .R files. Your editor may even be able to send commands directly to R; if not, the process of copy + switch window + paste into R console is typically only 3 keystrokes—and was our standard solution for many years.

Multiplatform editors that support R include Bluefish, Eclipse + StatET (Sect. A.4), Emacs + ESS (Sect. A.3), Komodo Edit + SciViews-K, RStudio (Sect. A.2), Sublime Text, UltraEdit, Vim, and Visual Studio Code. The supported platforms vary and usually include include Windows, Mac OS X, and popular Linux distributions.

For Windows, other editors with R support include Crimson Editor, TextPad, Tinn-R (built especially for R), Visual Studio, and WinEdt using the RWinEdt R package (an editor especially appealing to LATEX users).

For Mac, in addition to the multiplatform editors above, the popular TextMate editor has an R definition, as does the Kate editor.

For Linux, the lightweight gedit editor has a plugin for R (Rgedit) with console integration, and the Kate editor has R syntax support.

A.6.2   R Commander

R Commander [60] provides a GUI for R with menus and other enhancements for basic statistics. It is often used in introductory courses with undergraduates and provides easy access to functions such as loading data, running descriptive statistics, doing basic inferential statistics such as t-tests and ANOVA, fitting common models such as linear regression and factor analysis, and plotting.

R Commander is designed explicitly to be a tool to help GUI users—general computer users and analysts who use other software such as SPSS—make the transition to R. It shows the commands that it runs and resists going much beyond the basics, due to its goal to assist users to transition to full command-line and script usage. More details are available at http://socserv.mcmaster.ca/jfox/Misc/Rcmdr/.

A.6.3 Rattle

Rattle is a GUI for R that is intended to help newcomers to R perform data mining tasks easily and quickly [203]. Rattle is menu-driven and includes commands for loading and handling data, transforming data, descriptive statistics, and a variety of data mining tasks such as visualization (using `ggplot2`), clustering, supervised and unsupervised machine learning, and decision trees.

Rattle is available for Windows, Mac OS X, and Linux systems at http://rattle. togaware.com/, and is detailed in Williams [202]. Rattle may be particularly appealing to analysts who work in teams with members who vary in R skills, yet wish to share analyses and common data sets.

A.6.4 Deducer

Deducer is a GUI for R that features general data handling and basic analytic tasks (similar to R Commander, Sect. A.6.2) with a spreadsheet-like interface for inspecting and manipulating data. In addition to general functionality designed for newcomers to R, Deducer offers extensions for regression analysis, factor analysis, clustering, and other multivariate procedures that are intended to enhance productivity for more experienced R users. Deducer uses JGR, the Java GUI for R, and runs on Windows, Mac OS X, and Linux. It is available at http://www.deducer.org/.

Appendix B
An Introduction to Reproducible Results with R Notebooks

When an analysis includes more than a few simple steps, it becomes difficult to remember what you've done and even more difficult for others to understand it. In the worst case, you might perform analyses with undocumented console commands or out-of-sequence commands run from a code file. In that case, the code file doesn't reflect the true sequence, and the results may be non-reproducible. If you run the code again, you may get a different answer because the steps are in a different order. This has reached the level of scandal among academic researchers in many disciplines (cf. [76]).

We recommend that you start early in your R career to ensure that your analyses are completely reproducible. Luckily, the R community has demonstrated leadership in addressing these issues and provided many powerful tools that can help. We cannot detail all of them here, but some of the available options are:

- **.R code files**. As noted in Sect. 2.3, we recommend as part of minimal R hygiene to regularly save the exact commands that you use in a .R file, and periodically run them from the top with a clean workspace.
- **Sweave**. Sweave provides integration between R and LATEX mathematical authoring and typesetting tools [126]. Sweave allows authoring of a LATEX document with embedded R code, whose results are included (often said to be *"knitted"*) into the resulting PDF document. Although LATEX is extremely powerful (for example, this book is written and typeset with LATEX), it is also complex for beginners. If you need an extremely professional and meticulously typeset document, especially for repeated reports or journal articles, Sweave may appeal to you.
- **R Markdown**. R Markdown is similar to Sweave in offering integrated R code, output, and formatted text, but uses a substantially simpler set of formatting commands (with correspondingly less control over output). Instead of learning LATEX, you can format text with simple codes such as ``**[text]**``, where the asterisks denote bolded output: **[text]**. R Markdown can be used to create everything from simple web pages with R results to entire books [70, 207].

© Springer Nature Switzerland AG 2019
C. Chapman and E. M. Feit, *R For Marketing Research and Analytics*, Use R!,
https://doi.org/10.1007/978-3-030-14316-9

- **R Notebooks**. Offered in RStudio, R Notebooks provide R Markdown live inside the RStudio environment. With an R Notebook, you can write R code and explanatory text, and see it integrated in realtime with output results and graphics in RStudio. In the following section, we will demonstrate some of the basic features of R Notebooks. Although we focus here on RStudio notebooks, similar capabilities are found in other coding tools such as Jupyter Notebooks [117]. For classroom usage, we provide a simple R Notebook for homework exercises on the book's website (see also Sect. 2.11).

If you decide to use an R editor other than RStudio (see Appendix A), this Appendix should still encourage you, as many of these options noted below will be available using R Markdown and *knit* capabilities (perhaps with less integration than RStudio). Check the documentation for your preferred R environment, with attention to options for "markdown" and "knit".

For the remainder of this Appendix, we discuss R Notebooks. For further discussion of the other options above, see Sect. C.5.

B.1   R Notebooks

An R Notebook allows you to include all of the following in a single, integrated document:

- *R code*, organized into delineated "chunks" with a shaded background
- *R text output*, as would be shown in the R console, placed below the corresponding code chunk
- *R graphics*, putting the plots
- *Text with formatting*. This text can be whatever you would like. You might document what you've done, or—very powerfully—use it to write the deliverable report for your analysis.
- *Other code and output*. R Notebooks understand several other programming languages besides R, such as C++, SQL, and the Stan statistical modeling language. These details are out of scope for this appendix, but we would note one feature in particular: if you set up a SQL database connection, you can use RStudio to write and see the results of SQL queries. See [171] for more.

R Notebooks offer several options to save your results, in addition to showing the integrated code and results in RStudio. A formatted notebook with your text, code, and graphics can be saved to a PDF document, an HTML web page, or a Microsoft Word document. This is a great way to share your exact work with colleagues or professors!

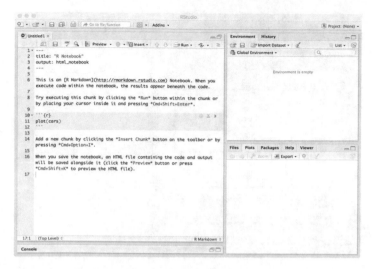

Fig. B.1 The default template for an R Notebook in RStudio (as of Version 1.0.153)

B.1.1 A Basic R Notebook

To create an R Notebook, launch RStudio and select *File—New File—R Notebook*. The default R Notebook template will appear as an untitled document, as shown in Fig. B.1.

In Fig. B.1, we note a few features of notebooks. At the top is a section with document settings, demarcated with three dashes, specifying the title ("R Notebook", which you may edit) and the targeted output format (HTML). Below that, there are two paragraphs of text, followed by an R *code chunk* with a gray background.

The R code chunk may contain any R commands, and they will be executed when the green "Run" (triangular) icon is clicked (or choose *Code—Run Region—Run Current Chunk* from the menu or shortcut keys). When we run the chunk in the default notebook, it plots the `cars` data set and shows the result inline in RStudio, as shown in Fig. B.2.

B.1.2 Saving and Sharing

When you wish to share an analysis, there are several options. With colleagues or a professor, you might wish to share the notebook code itself. To do so, save the file (*File—Save*) and then share the resulting `.Rmd` file. As long as your colleague has

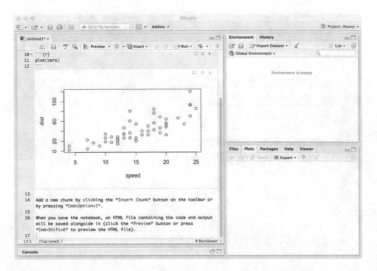

Fig. B.2 Inline plot shown in the notebook by clicking the green "Run current chunk" icon

access to any data files you may be using, she will be able to recreate your exact results in the notebook.

You might also wish to share the results formatted as a deliverable. For instance, you might write a complete report in text blocks in your notebook, with interspersed R results and charts. The *Preview* button at the top of the Notebook window allows output to various formats. Note that the *Preview* button may change its name to *Knit* at times, for reasons we will not detail.

Click *Preview* and save the file (take care about the target directory, as it may default to an undesired high-level folder). RStudio will format the notebook in HTML and display the result, as shown in Fig. B.3. You may share this document by looking in the folder where you saved the notebook, and find the file with extension .nb.html. You could place that file on a web server or send to a colleague to view in a web browser.

In professional settings, you might wish to create a document that is compatible with Microsoft Office. An R Notebook can create a Microsoft Word style .docx file, with R results, graphics, and formatting. In RStudio, look to the right of the *Publish* (or *Knit*) button at the top of the editor window, and click on the drop-down icon (downward-pointing triangle). Select *Knit to Word*.

This will create a document in your target folder with the name of the notebook and a .docx extension (and might also open Word or another .docx viewer).The

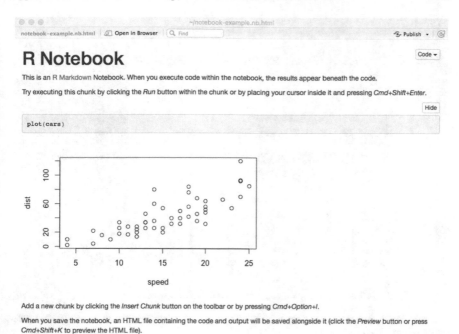

Fig. B.3 HTML file created by the "Preview" command; it automatically includes the written text, R code chunks, R output, and charts

default notebook in .docx format is shown in LibreOffice (an open source office suite) in Fig. B.4. You may edit these documents just like any other office document. Just be careful not to overwrite any edits if you update the notebook in the future; we recommend to do editing in the R Notebook so everything is in sync and reproducible.

For classroom usage, we suggest sharing your notebook in PDF format. This can be done by selecting *Knit to PDF* from the *Knit* or *Preview* button at the top of the RStudio editing window. An example of the output is shown in Fig. B.5.

Note that all of the options for reproducible formats—notebooks, HTML, Word format, and PDF—may require installation of additional packages the first time you create such documents. RStudio should install the packages automatically. If your output does not appear the first time, try knitting the output again after package installation.

B.1.3   Brief Formatting Options

The default document shown in Fig. B.2 demonstrates a few features of R Markdown: the title (line 2), square brackets ([and]) that specify text linked to a URL (line

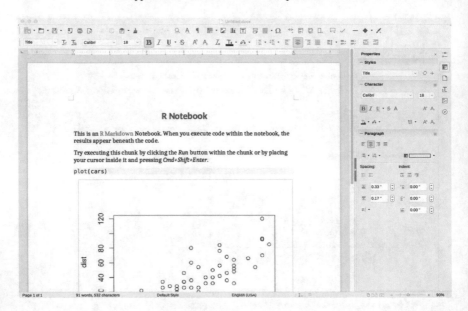

Fig. B.4 The default notebook shown in office suite format (.docx output), as viewed in Libre-Office version 5.3.4.2

6) and asterisks (* . . . *) to italicize text (lines 8, 14, and 16). We see the results of those in the HTML document in Fig. B.3 and the Word document in Fig. B.4.

Additional features of R Markdown include bolded text (bounded by double asterisks, ** . . . **), section and subsection headers, bulleted and numbered lists, inclusion of image files, and equations written in LATEX syntax, among other options. For an overview, see the quick reference in RStudio (*Help | Markdown Quick Reference*). For more details on the power of R Markdown see Gandrud [70], and Xie [207].

Finally, you may *Publish* a document directly from RStudio to various online hosting services. Discussion of those options is beyond our scope here. As a minor caution, we would note that, depending on the setup, and published documents may be publicly visible, so review these processes with care if that is a concern.

B.2 Final Note on Reproducibility

It is difficult to overstate the advantages of working with R Notebooks (or another variety of reproducible research noted above). They allow you to document your analysis as you work on it, making it easier to debug or to understand in the future. It is easy to run an entire notebook from the top to ensure that the steps are correct and in order. You can share a notebook with colleagues to collaborate or demonstrate your work. And finally, they make it easy to publish results to the web or as drafts of deliverable Word documents.

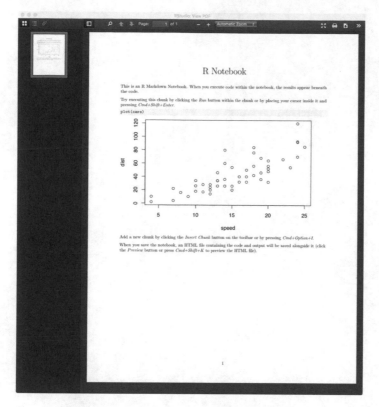

Fig. B.5 The default notebook shown in PDF format. This appears in the RStudio PDF viewer after selecting *Knit to PDF*, and saves in PDF format to your working directory

As a basic level, this kind of workflow minimizes the risk of copy and paste errors, as well as accidental execution of commands out of order. As you become more proficient, it may allow easy automation of reporting. For example, if you have a standard monthly report, you might write it once as an R Notebook, and then just change the data file source for each month with no need to rewrite any of the subsequent analysis.

Appendix C
Scaling Up

As you develop R skills, you will wish to take on larger projects that stretch R in various ways. You might wish to work with diverse data sources, larger data, greater computational power, or automated reporting. In this appendix we provide brief introductions to R packages and other resources that may be of assistance.

The resources outlined here are especially subject to change as these are dynamic areas of development in the R community. Thus, we provide general guidance here rather than detailed exposition. R code in this appendix is provided for illustration only, not as complete working code.

C.1 Handling Data

C.1.1 Data Wrangling

Two of the most useful packages for data handling are data.table [47] and dplyr [201]. Each of them is so useful that we considered using it for data handling throughout this book. We ultimately decided that it was preferable to handle data using the standard approaches of base R, because that approach is most stable over time, and is universally available and understood within the R community (Sect. 1.5). Still, we recommend that you consider the advantages of data.table and dplyr as your R fluency develops.

data.table [47] supplies an alternative to data frames with higher performance, more efficient memory usage, faster read-write capability, enhanced indexing capability, and the ability to query data with more complex logic. If you use large data sets in memory, or find that data manipulation is slow, consider moving your data to data.table (see also Sects. C.2 and C.3 below). Transitioning code from data.frame to data.table is often quite smooth, as the data.table syntax is very similar to data.frame.

© Springer Nature Switzerland AG 2019
C. Chapman and E. M. Feit, *R For Marketing Research and Analytics*, Use R!,
https://doi.org/10.1007/978-3-030-14316-9

dplyr [201] attempts to be a complete data handling solution that implements a more consistent, efficient, and higher order grammar for data operations. dplyr provides standard methods for selecting, filtering, recoding, and performing common aggregation tasks on data, and works with both in-memory and database sources (see Sect. C.1.4).

C.1.2 Microsoft Excel: `readxl`

The readxl package[199] provides the capability to read data from Microsoft Excel spreadsheets using syntax based on the familiar read.csv() command. For example, consider data on US corporate financials that is provided in XLS format by Aswath Damodaran at New York University [41], hosted at http://pages.stern. nyu.edu/~adamodar/New_Home_Page/datacurrent.html. If we download the file for "Price and Value to Sales Ratios and Margins by Industry Sector" to the local Downloads folder, then we can read it using the read_excel() function as follows:

```
> library(readxl)
> psdata <- as.data.frame(read_excel(
+   path="~/Downloads/psdata.xls",
+   sheet=1, skip=7))
> head(psdata)
      Industry Name Number of firms Price/Sales Net Margin EV/Sales
1        Advertising              40   1.0158827 0.05447810 1.663870
2 Aerospace/Defense              87   1.8427984 0.07218634 2.088553
3      Air Transport              17   0.9361391 0.07027801 1.558021
...
```

When importing Excel data, check carefully that you are importing variables in the correct format; columns with special formatting might need to be converted manually.

The gdata package provides an alternative way to read Excel files [194]. Another option to import data from Excel files is to use ODBC functionality (as described below for connecting to SQL databases, Sect. C.1.4).

C.1.3 SAS, SPSS, and Other Statistics Packages: `foreign`

The foreign package [155] provides the capability to read data in a variety of other formats including those used by Minitab, Octave, SAS, SPSS, Stata, and other systems. Because commercial software may change data formats between versions, it may not work with all data files. Users of SPSS and Stata could also review the memisc package [51], which supports a broader set of SPSS and Stata files.

Following is sample code that uses foreign and read.spss() to load the "tenure" data set provided in SPSS format with Singer and Willet, *Applied Longitudinal Data Analysis* [180]. In this case, we load the data from a local file; a download is available from links at http://gseacademic.harvard.edu/alda/.

```
> library(foreign)
> tenure.df <- read.spss("~/Downloads/aldaspss/tenure_orig.sav",
+                        to.data.frame=TRUE)
> summary(tenure.df)
      ID              TIME            CENSOR
 Min.   :  111   Min.   :1.000   Min.   :0.0000
 1st Qu.: 9989   1st Qu.:4.000   1st Qu.:0.0000
 Median :19067   Median :6.000   Median :0.0000
 Mean   :20433   Mean   :5.669   Mean   :0.3615
 3rd Qu.:30135   3rd Qu.:7.000   3rd Qu.:1.0000
 Max.   :50310   Max.   :9.000   Max.   :1.0000
```

If you are familiar with SAS or SPSS, you may appreciate the detailed task comparisons and guidance in Muenchen's book, *R for SAS and SPSS Users* [143]. For Stata users, check Muenchen and Hilbe, *R for Stata Users* [144]. The `R.matlab` package works with MATLAB files.

As always, a general option is to export data from another system to a CSV file or to a database (see Sect. C.1.4) and import that into R.

C.1.4 SQL: `RSQLite`, `sqldf` and `RODBC`

Many analysts are familiar with the Structured Query Language (SQL) for data processing, and R provides capabilities for SQL. We differentiate two aspects of SQL: the SQL *language*, and SQL *data sources*.

SQL language. A full SQL instance (using SQLite, http://www.sqlite.org/) may be run inside R through the `RSQlite` package [106]. This allows access to nearly all the features of a complete SQL database.

A particularly easy way to access the SQL `SELECT` statement for R data frames is with the `sqldf` package [83]. For instance, referring to the corporate finance data loaded in Sect. C.1.2 above, we can select firms in the data set with a forward price-earnings ratio greater than 100 using a `SELECT` statement:

```
> sqldf("SELECT *
+        FROM psdata
+        WHERE `Net Margin` > 0.25")
                            Industry Name Number of firms Price/Sales
1                      Bank (Money Center)              11   3.647450...
2 Financial Svcs. (Non-bank & Insurance)             264   2.821212 ...
3                                  Tobacco              24   5.838507 ...
```

Note that the SQL language understands a period (".") very differently than R—in R, a period is a symbol that is generally used like any letter or number in an object name, but in SQL it signifies a database to table relationship. The backtick character (`) may be used inside the quoted SQL statement to delimit column names that contain periods, spaces, or other problematic characters (such as the spaces in this data set). If you use `sqldf` often, you might wish to change such column names (Sect. 3.3.3).

SQL data sources. Remote SQL databases and tables can be accessed directly from R using either the `odbc` package [97] or `RODBC` package [164]. ODBC (open database connectivity) protocol allows access to many different database systems using a standard interface. There are several steps to setting up an ODBC connection. First, you configure ODBC access permission on the data system that will serve the data (such as a MySQL, Oracle, or Microsoft SQL system). Second, you configure a *data source name* (DSN) in your operating system to connect to the ODBC remote system. Finally, you tell R to connect to the DSN and pull data from it.

The process of setting up an external database with a DSN lies outside the scope of this book; you could seek assistance from a database administrator for those steps. For purposes here, we will illustrate with RODBC using a previously-established local DSN called "mydata". We can connect to it and get data in R using an SQL query passed to the external database:

```
> library(RODBC)
> sqlconn <-odbcConnect("mydata", uid="username", pwd="*****")
> mysqldata <- sqlQuery(sqlconn, "select * from MyTable")
> close(sqlconn)
```

There is extensive support for querying the database for table information, and for sending SQL commands to perform complex queries. For more details, see the extensive RODBC vignette at http://cran.r-project.org/web/packages/RODBC/vignettes/RODBC.pdf [164].

For databases that are too large to fit into memory, the biglm package noted in Sect. C.2 provides the capability to fit regression models from multiple smaller chunks. As we noted in Sect. C.1.1, the dplyr package provides access to data in databases along with other performance and syntax enhancements.

C.2   Handling Large Data Sets

By default, R holds data objects in system random access memory (RAM). However, you might need to work with a data set too large to fit in memory. There are a few strategies to handle these situations:

- **Observation sampling**. This is often the best choice to handle large data; for many purposes it is not necessary to fit a model to all observations. For instance, a linear model fit to 100,000 rows appropriately sampled from a data set of 100 million rows will give a model very close to that of the full sample model (if other general assumptions about model suitability and sampling are met). One way to do this in R is to use readlines() or scan() to read a smaller block of lines from a CSV file, keep some of those observations according to a uniform probability distribution (runif()), and iterate until the entire file has been sampled. If the data are in a database, sampling might instead be done in SQL, with the caution that some SQL systems have poor implementations of pseudorandom number generators; check your SQL implementation documentation.

- **Compact storage**. This is a feasible option when a data set does not dramatically exceed RAM and especially when it is sparse (i.e., when a relatively small number of cells in a matrix are non-zero). The `Matrix` package [7] implements sparse matrices, and some packages such as `glmnet` [65] can fit models to sparse objects. See the `glmnet` vignette (http://www.stanford.edu/~hastie/glmnet/glmnet_alpha.html#spa) for an example.
- **Disk-augmented memory**. The `bigmemory` package [115] implements compact storage with the option to manage large objects transparently by keeping portions of them outside RAM in one or more disk files; it will swap portions of objects into memory as needed. Related packages such as `biganalytics` [52] implement models that work with these `bigmemory` objects.
- **Database storage**. If the data are stored in a database, then you may be able to use observations directly from there with an RODBC or similar database connection (see Sect. C.1.4). The `biglm` package [132] works with data sets that exceed memory size by estimating regression models progressively using blocks of data.

The choice among these methods depends on the problem at hand. We highly recommend first to consider sampling observations such that the data will fit in memory; this is fastest and allows the full range of options in R for model fitting and estimation. Sampling also allows bootstrap estimation of stability and easily affords cross-validation samples. It is crucial to ensure that a random sample of the data is taken appropriately. Two issues to consider in particular are whether the random number generation approach scales appropriately and whether there is order bias, as would be produced, for instance, by sampling from the top until some number of rows has been collected.

When it is more suitable to work with as large a sample as possible, we look to database and memory augmentation options according to the precise model support that is needed.

C.3 Speeding Up Computation

Some analyses take a very long time to complete. One of Chris's projects, for instance, involved repeatedly running code that took several days per iteration on a typical workstation. However, R does not have to be slow. At Google, for example, R is deployed in applications that use Google data centers to reduce the runtime in some cases by more than 99% (Stokely, Rohani, and Tassone, 2011 [184]). The key to performance is to optimize code and to use more powerful server infrastructure when needed.

We outline here a few strategies in order of progressive complexity to handle slow code (and see also the following Sect. C.3.2 on enhancing the R engine).

C.3.1   Efficient Coding and Data Storage

A good place to begin when code is slow is to use `Rprof()` to profile one's code and see which parts use the most time to execute, and then optimize those. There are four common bottlenecks for R code:

- **Reinventing the wheel** is when a programmer writes code for something that already exists. Examples include writing code for tasks such as search and replace (try `gsub()`), vector-to-matrix expansion (`expand.grid()`), or finding the maximum column by row (`max.col()`). If you have code that seems like it *should* occur commonly enough to have a common solution, the odds are that an efficient alternative exists; the trick is to find that solution. We recommend to consult with other R users about ways to optimize the code. For instance, the R language forums at Stack Overflow are a good source.
- **for loops** can be problematic on several fronts. If you have slow code and it involves a `for` loop, think hard about whether it could be vectorized with `apply()` and anonymous functions or has parts that could be speeded up with common code as noted above. Matloff's *The Art of R Programming* is a good starting point to learn about more efficient R coding [135]. Wickham's *Advanced R* focuses on the advantages and practice of functional programming that helps with efficient and effective programming [197]. `for` loops are also good candidates for parallel computation; see Sect. C.3.2 below.
- **Data frames** are another source of slow R execution, especially for large data structures. There are many non-obvious occasions that cause R to create a copy of a data frame, which can take a long time in itself and force time-consuming memory cleanup by the system. If you work with large data sets, consider using `data.table` or `dplyr` objects instead of data frames (see Sect. C.1.1).
- **Compiled code** can be faster than interpreted R code. Starting with version 2.13, R provides the `compiler` package (which comes with R, not downloaded separately) that can do partial compilation of code, which is sometimes faster in R. It is easy to try for slow code. A more comprehensive but complex solution is to rewrite parts of your code in C++ or another language, compile it, and call the compiled code from R. See Eddellbuettel, 2013, *Seamless R and C++ Integration with Rcpp* for instructions on how to do this with the `Rcpp` package [49].

C.3.2   Enhancing the R Engine

Another way to increase computation power and speed is to enhance or replace your R engine. We describe a few options for both local (workstation) and server-based solutions.

One approach is to make R more powerful on your workstation by increasing its mathematics performance, and to use parallel computation where possible:

- **BLAS**. Like all statistical computing packages, R uses linear algebra heavily. Your operations may be speeded up significantly—sometimes by a factor of 5 or more—by using a basic linear algebra subprograms (BLAS) system that is optimized for your computer's processor and operating system. This area is evolving rapidly so we suggest doing a web search for "BLAS for R" and reading recent articles for your system (Windows, Linux, Mac).
- **Parallelization**. `parallel`, `foreach`. If you have already optimized code as noted above (Sect. C.3.1) and still seek a modest amount of additional speed—say, 2x-10x improvement in speed—then parallel processing may help. There are two general options here: using multiple processor cores on a single machine using multicore processors, and using multiple machines with networked communication. The `parallel` package (which comes with R) provides options for both, using multicore versions of `apply()`, such as `mclapply()` to use multiple cores and `makeCluster()` to network multiple machines for parallel processing (which can be complex, especially in secure computing environments). The `foreach` package [25] provides a relatively simple way to parallelize computation inside a `for()` loop across multiple processors or machines. Two important things to consider are whether your code can run in independent, parallel blocks, and whether you need special handling of independent random number streams. See the CRAN High-Performance and Parallel Computing task page (http://cran.r-project.org/web/views/HighPerformanceComputing.html) for the latest information and list of packages that support parallel computing.
- **Microsoft R** offers open source and commercial versions of R with enhancements for larger data and higher performance computing. See Sect. A.5 for more information.

The ultimate computational power in R comes from multi-machine, server-based, and cloud-hosted solutions:

- **Multi-machine parallelism**. See the discussion above of workstation-based parallelization for options to deploy simple network-based combinations of workstations.
- **Microsoft Machine Learning Server** is a licensed platform that supports R and Python, to be deployed with on-premises servers. See Sect. A.5 for more information.
- **Cloud computing**. For maximum computing power, Amazon Web Services, Google Cloud Platform, and Microsoft Azure offer cloud-based hosting for R, where you can choose to run an R model on dozens, hundreds, or thousands of high-powered servers simultaneously. RStudio Cloud is an offering whose interface is similar to the RStudio desktop IDE. If you are interested in cloud solutions for performance (as opposed to convenience), a general strategy is to design your code for parallel computing, as described in the *Parallelization* notes above, and then port it to a cloud system. Because this is a rapidly changing area, the best bet to learn more is a web search for recent documentation and tutorials, such as "R on Google Cloud" or "RStudio Cloud."

One thing to remember is that runtime speed is not the best measure of R performance; you also need to account for development and maintenance time. If it takes 3 h to develop and deploy a cloud solution for a process that would run in 2 h on a workstation, the cloud solution is a net loss in performance.

C.4   Time Series Analysis, Repeated Measures, and Longitudinal Analysis

We have not covered time series analysis in this book due to space, yet it is strongly supported in R. The array of available options is, like most things in R, diverse and somewhat confusing. Here are a few pointers to get started.

A first thing to know is that the default time series objects in R (created with `ts()`) assume *equal spacing of observations*. They work well for regular intervals such as daily measurements or quarterly financials, but do not handle irregularly spaced observations such as transactions or typical longitudinal behavior or survey waves. For such observations, we recommend to start with the `zoo` package [208], which handles irregularly (and regularly) spaced data, and adds many features for time series analysis.

A text that covers the basics of time series with a progressive, hands-on approach and approachable mathematics is Cowpertwait and Metcalfe (2009), *Introductory Time Series with R* [38].

The literature on time series analysis is, not surprisingly, especially large in the areas of finance and econometrics. For mathematically oriented readers, those areas' textbooks and R packages provide a rich set of resources. Less complex time series models are often used in the biological and related physical sciences such as marine biology and environmental science, and these may be useful to marketers with a bit of imaginative translation. For example, a model of the change in fish population after a habitat cleanup might use R code that is almost identical to a model of unit sales in response to a promotion. Pointers to resources in all of these areas are on CRAN in the Time Series view, http://cran.r-project.org/web/views/TimeSeries.html.

Longitudinal analysis is the study of outcomes with repeated observations over time. At a conceptual level, this differs from time series analysis in that there is relatively less emphasis on the time component itself as a predictor or covariate, and more emphasis on understanding the individual (customer, respondent, system, etc.) that is being measured. Longitudinal models are an example of *repeated measures* models. In R, many of the basic linear modeling packages include options for repeated measures and other forms of longitudinal measures. One place to start is with mixed effects models (Sect. 9.3.1) where it it possible to specify effects for time or observation block.

A special case of longitudinal analysis common in marketing is the family of so-called "buy 'til you die" models (BTYD) for customer transactions [56]. Several implementations of BTYD for non-contractual purchase models are implemented in the BTYD package [48].

C.5   Automated and Interactive Reporting

An especially attractive benefit of R is the ability to automate work, and there are tools available to automate not only analyses but also reporting. In the R and statistics community, such solutions are commonly described as "reproducible research" where the data, code, and written output are bundled together. For example, some statistics journals require that articles be written with all analytic code embedded in the article, including code that creates charts and tables, such that a typeset article is produced directly from the code with no human copy-and-paste or inclusion of independently created tables or graphics. In marketing, we think of this more as "automated reporting," yet the concepts and tools are identical.

We discuss *R Notebooks*—an RStudio feature for combined code editing and reproducible results—in Appendix B. This section discusses more general options for reporting. Because R is a general purpose programming language, in principle you could write any automated output system you might want. However, we suggest a few tools to consider first:

- **Markdown and `knitr`.** The RStudio environment provides a simple way to combine the output of R code and graphics with arbitrary text to create an HTML document, using the `knitr` package [206] and integrated RStudio publishing tools. Using the example `grocery` data that we saw in Chap. 12, the following code snippet loads the `arules` package and data, and uses R commands to describe the data and display a chart:

```
```{r setup, echo=FALSE, results="hide", message=FALSE}
require(arules)
data(Groceries)
```

Our data from the __supeRmarket__ chain comprises `r nrow(Groceries)` cash
register transactions covering `r ncol(Groceries)` categories of items.We
see the top 20 best selling items in the following chart:

```{r plot example, echo=FALSE}
itemFrequencyPlot(Groceries, topN=20)
```

Whole milk is the most popular single category in our data, although less
popular than the combination of soda and bottled water.
```

In this code, the sections between ``` marks are executed as R code with the results either shown (as for the `itemFrequencyPlot`) or not. Other text is arbitrary but may be interspersed with the output of R commands using the ` marker and

Our data from the **supeRmarket** chain comprises 9835 cash register transactions covering 169 categories of items. We see the top 20 best selling items in the following chart:

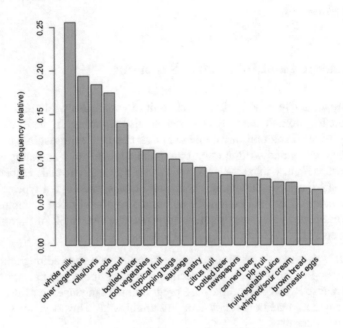

Whole milk is the most popular single category in our data, although less popular than the combination of soda and bottled water.

Fig. C.1 An example of HTML output using `knitr` to combine R output and graphics with explanatory text

marked up with font styles using codes such as ___ (bold). The resulting HTML output from this code snippet is shown in Fig. C.1.

Markdown can also produce documents in PDF or Microsoft Word formats. When creating a new file in RStudio, simply choose the appropriate template (menu sequence: *File | New File | R Markdown ...*), or select "Knit to PDF" or "Knit to Word" from a markdown document's Knit menu.

- **LATEX output with `Sweave()`**. R provides rich tools for those who are familiar with LATEX, including the `Sweave()` command [126] that can produce a PDF document from a single file that mixes R code and LATEX markup. The markup language with LATEX is substantially more complex than that used by `knitr` but it has more powerful options and capabilities (for instance, this book is written in LATEX).

- **odfWeave**. Another option to create documents that are compatible with Microsoft Word and Open Office Writer is the `odfWeave` package [121]. `odfWeave` uses markup styles based on `Sweave` but produces an open document format (ODF) file

Iris k-means clustering

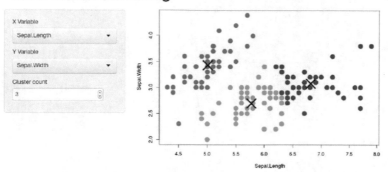

Fig. C.2 An interactive web application using R and Shiny, reproduced from http://shiny.rstudio. com/gallery/kmeans-example.html. This example shows the result of k-means clustering of the `iris` data set. The model is run in response to a user's selection in the control boxes and the chart is updated automatically

instead of a PDF file. ODF files can be read by most office software packages. Word document output is also available from Markdown (see above) and R Notebooks (Appendix B.1.2).

- **officer**. The `officer` package offers a more programmatic route to create Microsoft Word or PowerPoint documents [75]. In `officer`, R commands are used to add elements to documents. This is overly complex for ad hoc document creation, yet can be very valuable for automated production of repetitive reports using code.
- **Interactive applications: Shiny**. For interactive web-based applications, such as reporting dashboards, consider Shiny from RStudio. Shiny uses a web server (hosted locally on your network or as a cloud service from RStudio) to host R code and produce interactive graphics. For details, a tutorial, and examples, see http:// shiny.rstudio.com. An example of an interactive cluster analysis session is shown in Fig. C.2.

Appendix D
Packages Used

We have used many packages in this book and provide a reference to them here with brief notes. Following are tables that arrange the packages by general topic (statistics models, graphics, and so forth). For each package, we note the name, a comment on its purpose or use as we see it, and a reference to one or more places where we mention it. The comments on usage are admittedly brief for some packages that are complex and defy summarization. In some cases, we only mentioned a package briefly in the text, yet we reference it here because it is helpful to augment and contrast the other tools presented.

Packages that we particularly recommend or use often are in bold font, such as **cluster**. In a few instances, we list a package in more than one category. The list is far from complete for R overall because there are thousands of packages available.

Most of the packages in this list can be installed from CRAN with the typical package installation routine (`install.packages("NAME")`), although a few are included in the standard R system (`cluster`, `compiler`, `foreign`, `lattice`, `MASS`, `Matrix`, `parallel`) and may be accessed with `library()` with no additional installation required. Details of package availability change often; check CRAN (http://cran.r-project.org) for the latest information.

The lists here reflect the contents of this book and its aim to provide an introduction to R. Thus, although we recommend the packages here, the topic areas are not meant to be comprehensive guides to the R packages available in their areas. CRAN task views http://cran.r-project.org/web/views/) provide more systematic guidance to the packages for specific topics and applications.

D.1 Core and Classical Statistics

The following packages add statistical estimation routines for a variety of models ranging from assessment of binomial variables (`binom`) to complex hierarchical models(`lme4`).

© Springer Nature Switzerland AG 2019
C. Chapman and E. M. Feit, *R For Marketing Research and Analytics*, Use R!,
https://doi.org/10.1007/978-3-030-14316-9

Package	Brief summary	Section
binom [45]	Additional options for binomial models, tests, and confidence intervals	6.3.2
car [62]	Tools for interpreting and visualizing regression models, plus other utilities; source of some() and scatterplotMatrix()	3.1.2, 10.2.1
e1071 [139]	Assorted econometrics and machine learning extensions; we use it for naive Bayes classification with naiveBayes()	11.4.1
expm [78]	Exponential functions for matrices	14.4.1
lme4 [8]	Estimating linear mixed-effects models for nested effects	7.8, 9.3
MASS [192]	A diverse collection of utility, machine learning, and statistics functions and data sets to accompany Venables and Ripley [192]	7.8
multcomp [100]	Multiple comparisons for linear models	6.5.2
psych [163]	Methods for psychometrics and survey analysis, especially for factor analytic and item response models; we scratch the surface with the describe() command	3.3, 4.6.2
zoo [208]	Methods and classes for irregularly and regularly spaced time series	C.4

D.2   Graphics

We used the following packages to produce the graphics in the book. The list includes packages that make particular tasks easy (such as rworldmap), that handle specific families of models (arulesViz, semPlot), and that are powerful and broad (lattice, ggplot2).

Package	Brief summary	Section
arulesViz [89]	Visualization for association rules of transactional data and market baskets; works with the arules package	12.3
beanplot [114]	Violin plots which are an attractive alternative to boxplots	3.4.2
coefplot [125]	Plot confidence intervals for coefficients from linear models	7.3
corrplot [196]	Enhanced graphics for correlation matrices	4.5.2
ggplot2 [198]	Grammar of graphics implementation for sophisticated plotting	6.6.4
gplots [193]	Assorted plotting routines, including enhanced heatmaps (heatmap.2()) and color interpolation (colorpanel())	8.1.2, 4.5
lattice [173]	Trellis-based plots that build on core plotting capabilities	5.2.3
RColorBrewer [148]	Optimized color palettes for continuous and categorical data	3.4.6, 8.1.2
rworldmap [182]	Straightforward choropleth maps for the whole world or regions	3.4.6
semPlot [53]	Draw structural diagrams for exploratory and confirmatory factor analysis and structural equation models	8.3.3, 10.2.2
superheat [6]	Heat maps for matrices, with many options to style, cluster, and smooth results	14.4.4
TraMineR [67]	Mining and visualizing discrete sequence data	14.7
vcd [140]	Visualize categorical data, such as mosaic and doubledecker plots	9.2.7

D.3 Bayesian Methods

A general, nearly all-purpose Bayesian estimation engine in R is `MCMCpack`. Other packages in this table add utilities (e.g., `BayesFactor`), models (e.g., `e1071`), and marketing applications (`bayesm`).

Package	Brief summary	Section
BayesFactor [142]	Easy to use functions to estimate and compare Bayesian linear models	6.6.2
bayesm [167]	Hierarchical Bayesian models for marketing applications; a companion to Rossi, Allenby, and McCulloch [168]	
binom [45]	Additional options for binomial models, tests, and confidence intervals	6.3.2
BoomMix [177]	Bayesian methods for mixture model analysis	11.7
MCMCpack [134]	A core estimation engine for Bayesian models using Markov chain Monte Carlo method; very fast posterior sampling implemented in C++	6.6.2, 7.5.4

D.4 Advanced Statistics

These packages focus on specific statistical problems such as working with sparse or very large data sets (e.g., `biglm`), add capabilities to base models (e.g., `GPArotation`), or add specific models such as structural equation model estimation (e.g., `lavaan`, `semPLS`).

Package	Brief summary	Section
biganalytics [52]	Basic statistics and handling for `bigmemory` objects (very large datasets)	C.2
biglm [132]	Fit linear models to data that is too large for memory, either from databases or `bigmemory` objects	C.2
ClickClust [138]	Model-based clustering for clickstream data	14.7
clickstream [175]	Markov chain analysis for clickstream data	14.4.2
forecast [103]	Models and extensions for forecasting, especially with time series data. We use `BoxCox()` to perform data transformation	9.1
glmnet [65]	Regularization and lasso fitting for generalized linear models; also works with sparse data (very large matrices)	C.2
gmnl [94]	Estimation of hierarchical multinomial logit models including the generalized multinomial logit model [59]	13.3.2
GPArotation [11]	Additional rotation methods for factor analysis, with multiple variants of both oblique and orthogonal rotations	8.3.3
lavaan [166]	Estimate structural equation (SEM) and confirmatory factor analysis (CFA) models	10.2.1, 10.2.2
mlogit [39]	Estimate multinomial logit models by maximum likelihood including hierarchical models	13.3.2, 13.3.2
mnlogit [93]	Estimate multinomial logit models using faster algorithms than `mlogit`	13.3.2
nFactors [160]	Find the number of factors for factor analysis	8.3.2
OpenMx [14]	Another powerful engine to estimate structural equation and confirmatory factor models; an alternative to `lavaan`	10.6
sem [63]	Basic structural equation models (SEM); an alternative to `lavaan`	10.6
semPLS [141]	Estimate structural equation models using partial least squares (PLS)	10.4.1
semTools [112]	Compare structural equation models	10.2.3

D.5   Machine Learning

There are hundreds of packages for R that relate to machine learning. The following are ones that we use to illustrate various applications of machine learning and to estimate specific models. Moving from breadth to specificity of application, the packages cluster, randomForest, and arules are especially helpful to be familiar with. The caret package provides a structured way to use and evaluate a large array of machine learning procedures.

Package	Brief summary	Section
arules [88]	Association rules for transaction and market basket analysis	12.2
arulesSequences [24]	Association rules for sequence data such as web logs	14.7
caret [122]	Provides a systematic interface to access, use, and evaluate hundreds of machine learning models and their fit for your problem	11.7
cluster [133]	Basic functions for clustering data, representing multiple approaches	11.3
clue [98]	Cluster ensemble analysis for clustering	11.7
e1071 [139]	Assorted econometrics and machine learning extensions; we use it for naive Bayes classification with naiveBayes()	11.4.1
flexmix [84, 127]	Flexible mixture modeling for latent classes	11.7
mclust [64, 178]	Model-based clustering for finite mixture models	11.3.5
mlbench [128]	Benchmark data sets for machine learning	11.7
poLCA [130]	Latent class analysis and clustering for data with categorical observations	11.3.7
randomForest [129]	Random forest classification and variable importance	11.4.2

D.6   Data Handling

In Appendix C we described options to work with databases and data from other software programs, and to increase R performance with large data sets. The following table summarizes those packages.

Package	Brief summary	Section
biglm [132]	Fit linear models to data that is too large for memory	C.2
bigmemory [115]	Tools to work with very large data sets that exceed memory size	C.2
data.table [47]	A powerful alternative to standard data frames; higher performance plus advanced query and indexing options including keys	C.2, C.1.1
dplyr [201]	A higher-order approach to common data handling tasks, including querying, recoding, and accessing data in databases	C.1.1
foreign [155]	Read data from SAS, SPSS, and other systems	C.1.3
gdata [194]	Import data, especially Microsoft Excel files, and manipulate data format	C.1.2
glmnet [65]	Regularization and lasso fitting for general linear models; also works with sparse data (very large matrices)	C.2
googleAnalyticsR [50]	Access Google Analytics data in R	14.7
lubridate [82]	Easier handling of date and time data	14.7
Matrix [7]	Handling for sparse and dense matrices to reduce memory, increase performance, and access linear algebra optimizations	C.2
memisc [51]	Work with survey data, handle common survey metadata such as variable labels and codebooks, import data from SPSS and Stata, and simulate data	C.1.3
odbc [97]	Connect and query databases that support ODBC	C.1.4
R.matlab [10]	Work with MATLAB files	C.1.3
RGoogleAnalytics [152]	Functional wrappers for Google Analytics API	14.7
RODBC [164]	Another way to connect and query databases that support ODBC	C.1.4
RSiteCatalyst [150]	Access Adobe Analytics data in R	14.7
RSQLite [106]	Host a complete SQL database instance within R	C.1.4
sqldf [83]	Run SQL queries on data frames	C.1.4

D.7 Other Packages

These packages provide access to higher performance and automated reporting, along with various other capabilities.

Package	Brief summary	Section
Bioconductor [13]	A separately maintained collection of more than 1000 packages for working—mostly, but not exclusively—with bioinformatics data	14.7
compiler [156]	Compile functions for (sometimes) more efficient processing	C.3.1
datasets [156]	A diverse collection of interesting and illustrative datasets	9.2.7
knitr [206]	Produce reports in HTML and other formats that combine text with output from R, such as computations and graphics. RStudio [172] provides direct knitr integration.	C.5
odfWeave [121]	Creates open document format (ODF) files such as word processing documents that include results, graphics, and tables from R	C.5
officer [75]	Create and manipulate Microsoft Word and PowerPoint documents with R code	C.5
parallel [156]	Run R processes such as apply() in parallel across multiple processor cores or workstations	C.3.2
randomForest Explainer [151]	Assess and visualize variable importance in random forest models	11.7
Rcpp [49]	Use C++ with R for faster processing and data exchange	C.3.1
Sweave() [126]	Produces LaTeX documents and PDFs with inline results and charts from R (and is not technically a package on its own, but is built into R in the standard utils package)	C.5
vcdExtra [66]	Additional tools to assist with visualizing categorical data; use use expand.dft() to convert a table to a complete data frame	9.2.5

Appendix E
Online Materials and Data Files

The dedicated website for this book is http://r-marketing.r-forge.r-project.org. All data files and .R code files are available there and it is the source for news and updates for the book.

At the website, code files are available in the /code directory, specifically: http://r-marketing.r-forge.r-project.org/code.

Data files are available in the /data folder: http://r-marketing.r-forge.r-project.org/data. These may be downloaded directly to your local system individually or all at once in a .ZIP file, and also may be downloaded programmatically using the code in each chapter.

All data sets made available for download are simulated, not real data, except for the supermarket transaction records provided by Brijs et al. [23] and EPA web logs from Bottomley [19]. See Sect. 1.6.2 for discussion of why we use simulated data.

E.1 Data File Structure

The data files are organized as follows:

- File names ending with ".csv" are comma-separated value (CSV) text files, and may be read with the read.csv() function (Sect. 2.6.2).
- The supermarket transaction file name ends with ".dat" and is a text file delimited with spaces. This may be read with readLines() (Sect. 12.2.2).
- "..." in Tables E.1 and E.2 below refers to the data folder http://r-marketing.r-forge.r-project.org/data, which should be used as a prefix to the file names.

Typical examples of reading the data files are as follows. First, if you have downloaded a file to a local directory, you can read it using its local path:

```
> satData <- read.csv("~/Downloads/rintro-chapter2.csv")
```

© Springer Nature Switzerland AG 2019

C. Chapman and E. M. Feit, *R For Marketing Research and Analytics*, Use R!,
https://doi.org/10.1007/978-3-030-14316-9

To read from the website, you could use the goo.gl short version, starting with "https://":

```
> satData <- read.csv("https://goo.gl/UDv12g")
```

Alternatively, use the full URL as shown in Table E.1:

```
> satData <- read.csv(
         "http://r-marketing.r-forge.r-project.org/data/rintro-chapter2.csv")
```

E.2   Data File URL Cross-Reference

In the R code listings in the book chapters, we provide short goo.gl URLs in order to save typing. Table E.1 lists the data sets used in each chapter and the corresponding R code files, and cross-references the short names with the corresponding complete, long, direct URL addresses. Table E.2 does the same for data sets used exclusively in chapter exercises. For the long URLs, replace "..." with "http://r-marketing.r-forge.r-project.org/data/".

Update on Data Locations

Although we use R Forge for the book's website, which has been stable over time, all sites are liable to change. If you suspect the site no longer functions, send mail to cnchapman+bookupdate@gmail.com for an automated message with news, or do a web search for the authors.

Table E.1 Data used in text

Data	Short URL	Long URL (replace "..." as above)	Sections
Short satisfaction survey	goo.gl/UDv12g	.../rintro-chapter2.csv	2.2
Weekly store data	goo.gl/QPDdM1	.../rintro-chapter3.csv	3.1
Customer transaction data	goo.gl/PmPkaG	.../rintro-chapter4.csv	4.1, 9.1
Consumer segmentation survey	goo.gl/qw303p	.../rintro-chapter5.csv	5.1, 6.1, 11.2, 12.4
Amusement park satisfaction survey	goo.gl/HKn174	.../rintro-chapter7.csv	7.1
Brand perception ratings	goo.gl/IQ18nc	.../rintro-chapter8.csv	8.1
Amusement park season ticket sales	goo.gl/J8MH6A	.../rintro-chapter9.csv	9.2.2
Ratings-based (metric) conjoint analysis	goo.gl/G8knGV	.../rintro-chapter9conjoint.csv	9.3.2
Product involvement survey	goo.gl/yT0XwJ	.../rintro-chapter10pies.csv	10.2
Satisfaction and repurchase survey	goo.gl/MhghRq	.../rintro-chapter10sat.csv	10.3
Supermarket transaction data [23]	goo.gl/O495RV	fimi.ua.ac.be/data/retail.dat	12.2.2
Alternative for supermarket data, with permission [22]	goo.gl/FfjDAO	.../retail.dat	12.2.2
Choice-based conjoint analysis	goo.gl/5xQObB	.../rintro-chapter13conjoint.csv	13.2
EPA web server log [19]	goo.gl/LPqmGb	.../epa-http-copy.txt	14.1.1

Data files and download URLs for primary analyses in the text and accompanying code files

Table E.2 Data used in exercises

Data	Short URL	Long URL (replace "..." as above)	Sections
E-commerce transactions	goo.gl/hzRyFd	.../ecommerce-data.csv	3.8, 4.10, 5.6, 6.9
Hotel satisfaction ratings	goo.gl/hzRyFd	.../ecommerce-data.csv	7.9
Electronic device brands (sample 1)	goo.gl/z5P8ce	.../chapter8-brands1.csv	8.8, 10.7
Online visits and sales	goo.gl/4Akgkt	.../chapter9-sales.csv	9.9
Handbag conjoint analysis	goo.gl/gEKSQt	.../chapter9-bag.csv	9.9
Electronic device brands (sample 2)	goo.gl/BTxyFB	.../chapter10-cfa.csv	10.7
Purchase intent	goo.gl/6U5aYr	.../chapter10-sem.csv	10.7
Music subscription segments	goo.gl/s1KEiF	.../music-sub.csv	11.8
Retail transactions	goo.gl/wi8KHg	.../retail-baskets.csv	12.7
Retail item margins	goo.gl/Pidzpd	.../retail-margin.csv	12.7
Sports car conjoint analysis	goo.gl/8g7vtT	.../sportscar_choice_long.csv	13.10
EPA web server log (same as above, reused in exercises) [19]	goo.gl/LPqmGb	.../epa-http-copy.txt	14.8

File names and download URLs for data sets used in chapter exercises

References

1. Agresti, A. (2012). *Categorical data analysis* (3rd ed.). New Jersey: Wiley.
2. Agresti, A., & Coull, B. A. (1998). Approximate is better than "exact" for interval estimation of binomial proportions. *The American Statistician, 52*(2), 119–126.
3. Akaike, H. (1974). A new look at the statistical model identification. *IEEE Transactions on Automatic Control, 19*(6), 716–723.
4. Albert, J., & Rizzo, M. L. (2012). *R by example*. Berlin: Springer.
5. Association for Computing Machinery, (1999). ACM honors Dr. John M. Chambers of Bell Labs with the 1998 ACM software system award for creating "S System" software. http://www.acm.org/announcements/ss99.html.
6. Barter, R., & Yu, B. (2017). *superheat: A graphical tool for exploring complex datasets using heatmaps*. https://CRAN.R-project.org/package=superheat, R package version 0.1.0.
7. Bates, D., & Maechler, M. (2018). *Matrix: Sparse and dense matrix classes and methods*. http://CRAN.R-project.org/package=Matrix, R package version 1.2-14.
8. Bates, D., Maechler, M., Bolker, B., & Walker, S. (2018). *lme4: Linear mixed-effects models using Eigen and S4*. http://CRAN.R-project.org/package=lme4, R package version 1.1-17.
9. Beaujean, A. A. (2014). *Latent variable modeling using R: A step-by-step guide*. Abingdon: Routledge.
10. Bengtsson, H. (2016). *R.matlab: Read and write MAT files together with R-to-MATLAB connectivity*. http://CRAN.R-project.org/package=R.matlab, R package version 3.6.1.
11. Bernaards, C. A., & Jennrich, R. I. (2005). Gradient projection algorithms and software for arbitrary rotation criteria in factor analysis. *Educational and Psychological Measurement, 65*, 676–696.
12. Bickel, P., Hammel, E., & O'Connell, J. (1975). Sex bias in graduate admissions: Data from Berkeley. *Science, 187*(4175), 398–404.
13. Bioconductor, (2018). *Bioconductor: Open source software for bioinformatics*. https://www.bioconductor.org/.
14. Boker, S., Neale, M., Maes, H., Wilde, M., Spiegel, M., Brick, T., et al. (2011). OpenMx: an open source extended structural equation modeling framework. *Psychometrika, 76*(2), 306–317.
15. Borg, I., & Groenen, P. J. (2005). *Modern multidimensional scaling: Theory and applications*. Berlin: Springer.
16. Borg, I., Groenen, P. J., & Mair, P. (2018). *Applied multidimensional scaling and unfolding* (2nd ed.). Berlin: Springer.
17. Borgelt, C. (2002). The apriori algorithm for finding association rules. http://www.borgelt.net/docs/apriori.pdf, last retrieved October 11, 2014.
18. Borgelt, C., Kruse, R., & (2002). Induction of association rules: apriori implementation. Compstat,. (2002). *Proceedings in Computational Statistics* (pp. 395–400). Heidelberg: Physica Verlag.
19. Bottomley, L, (1995). Epa-http. http://ita.ee.lbl.gov/html/contrib/EPA-HTTP.html.

© Springer Nature Switzerland AG 2019

C. Chapman and E. M. Feit, *R For Marketing Research and Analytics*, Use R!,
https://doi.org/10.1007/978-3-030-14316-9

20. Bowman, D., & Gatignon, H. (2010). *Market response and marketing mix models. Foundations and trends in marketing*. The Netherlands: Now Publishers Inc.
21. Breiman, L. (2001). Random forests. *Machine Learning, 45*(1), 5–32.
22. Brijs, T. (2014). Retail transaction data. *Personal Communication*, September 17, 2014.
23. Brijs, T., Swinnen, G., Vanhoof, K., & Wets, G. (1999). Using association rules for product assortment decisions: A case study. In *Proceedings of the Fifth ACM SIGKDD International Conference on Knowledge Discovery and Data Mining, Association for Computing Machinery* (pp. 254–260).
24. Buchta, C., Hahsler, M., & with contributions from Diaz, D. (2018). *arulesSequences: Mining frequent sequences*. https://CRAN.R-project.org/package=arulesSequences, R package version 0.2-20.
25. Calaway, R., Microsoft., & Weston, S. (2017). *foreach: Foreach looping construct for R*. http://CRAN.R-project.org/package=foreach, R package version 1.4.4.
26. Caldon, P. (2013). *to.dendrogram*. http://stats.stackexchange.com/a/45161.
27. Callegaro, M., Baker, R. P., Bethlehem, J., Göritz, A. S., Krosnick, J. A., & Lavrakas, P. J. (2014). *Online panel research: A data quality perspective*. New Jersey: Wiley.
28. Callegaro, M., Manfreda, K. L., & Vehovar, V. (2015). *Web survey methodology*. Thousand Oaks: Sage.
29. Chambers, J. (2008). *Software for data analysis: Programming with R*. Berlin: Springer.
30. Chambers, J. M. (2004). *Programming with data: A guide to the S language (corrected* (edition ed.). Berlin: Springer.
31. Chang, W. (2018). *R graphics cookbook* (2nd ed.). Massachusetts: O'Reilly Media.
32. Chapman, C. N., Love, E., Staton, M., & Lahav, M. (2014). The development of a hierarchical and universal scale for product involvement: The product involvement and engagement scale ("PIES"), available from first author.
33. Chapman, C. N., Bahna, E., Alford, J. L., & Ellis, S. (2018). *Rcbc: Marketing research tools for choice-based conjoint analysis*. http://r-marketing.r-forge.r-project.org/code/Rcbc. R, version 0.30.
34. Cohen, J. (1988). *Statistical power analysis for the behavioral sciences* (2nd ed.). New Jersey: Lawrence Erlbaum Associates.
35. Cohen, J. (1994). The earth is round (p < .05). *American Psychologist, 49*(12), 997.
36. Cohen, J., Cohen, P., West, S. G., & Aiken, L. S. (2003). *Applied multiple regression/correlation analysis for the behavioral sciences* (3rd ed.). New Jersey: Lawrence Erlbaum.
37. Collins, L. M., & Lanza, S. T. (2010). *Latent class and latent transition analysis: With applications in the social, behavioral, and health sciences*. New Jersey: Wiley.
38. Cowpertwait, P. S., & Metcalfe, A. V. (2009). *Introductory time series with R*. Berlin: Springer.
39. Croissant, Y. (2018). *mlogit: Multinomial logit models*. https://CRAN.R-project.org/package=mlogit, R package version 0.3-0.
40. Dalgaard, P. (2008). *Introductory statistics with R*. Berlin: Springer.
41. Damodaran, A. (2018). *Damodaran online*. http://pages.stern.nyu.edu/~adamodar/.
42. Dib, F. (2018). *Regular expressions 101*. https://regex101.com.
43. Dobson, A. J., & Barnett, A. G. (2018). *An introduction to generalized linear models* (4th ed.). United Kingdom: Chapman & Hall.
44. Dolnicar, S., Grün, B., & Leisch, F. (2018). *Market segmentation analysis: Understanding it, doing it, and making it useful*. Berlin: Springer.
45. Dorai-Raj, S. (2014). *binom: Binomial confidence intervals for several parameterizations*. http://CRAN.R-project.org/package=binom, R package version 1.1-1.
46. Dotson, J. P., Howell, J. R., Brazell, J. D., Otter, T., Lenk, P. J., MacEachern, S., et al. (2018). A probit model with structured covariance for similarity effects and source of volume calculations. *Journal of Marketing Research, 55*(1), 35–47.
47. Dowle, M., Short, T., Lianoglou, S., & Srinivasan, A. (2018). *data.table: Extension of data.frame*. http://CRAN.R-project.org/package=data.table, W with contributions from R. Saporta & E. Antonyan. R package version 1.9.2.

48. Dziurzynski, L., Wadsworth, E., Fader, P., Feit, E. M., McCarthy, D., Hardie, B., et al. (2014). BTYD: Implementing buy'til you die models. *R Package Version, 2*, 3.
49. Eddelbuettel, D. (2013). *Seamless R and C++ integration with Rcpp*. Berlin: Springer.
50. Edmondson, M. (2018). *googleAnalyticsR*. https://cran.r-project.org/web/packages/googleAnalyticsR/vignettes/googleAnalyticsR.html.
51. Elff, M. (2017). *memisc: Tools for management of survey data, graphics, programming, statistics, and simulation*. http://CRAN.R-project.org/package=memisc, R package version 0.99.14.9.
52. Emerson, J. W., & Kane, M. J. (2016). *biganalytics: A library of utilities for big.matrix objects of package bigmemory*. http://CRAN.R-project.org/package=biganalytics, R package version 1.1.14.
53. Epskamp, S. (2017). *semPlot: Path diagrams and visual analysis of various SEM packages' output*. http://CRAN.R-project.org/package=semPlot, R package version 1.1.
54. Everitt, B. S., Landau, S., Leese, M., & Stahl, D. (2011). *Cluster analysis* (5th ed.). Wiley series in probability and statistics. New Jersey: Wiley.
55. Fabrigar, L. R., & Wegener, D. T. (2011). *Exploratory factor analysis*. Oxford: Oxford University.
56. Fader, P. S., & Hardie, B. G. (2009). Probability models for customer-base analysis. *Journal of Interactive Marketing, 23*(1), 61–69.
57. Fennell, G., Allenby, G. M., Yang, S., & Edwards, Y. (2003). The effectiveness of demographic and psychographic variables for explaining brand and product category use. *Quantitative Marketing and Economics, 1*(2), 223–244.
58. Fernández-Delgado, M., Cernadas, E., Barro, S., & Amorim, D. (2014). Do we need hundreds of classifiers to solve real world classification problems? *Journal of Machine Learning Research, 15*, 3133–3181.
59. Fiebig, D. G., Keane, M. P., Louviere, J., & Wasi, N. (2010). The generalized multinomial logit model: Accounting for scale and coefficient heterogeneity. *Marketing Science, 29*(3), 393–421.
60. Fox, J. (2005). Getting started with the R commander: A basic-statistics graphical user interface to R. *Journal of Statistical Software, 14*(9), 1–42.
61. Fox, J. (2006). Teacher's corner: structural equation modeling with the sem package in R. *Structural Equation Modeling, 13*(3), 465–486.
62. Fox, J., & Weisberg, S. (2011) *An R companion to applied regression* (2nd edn.). Thousand Oaks: Sage. http://socserv.socsci.mcmaster.ca/jfox/Books/Companion.
63. Fox, J., Nie, Z., & Byrnes, J. (2017). *sem: Structural equation models*. http://CRAN.R-project.org/package=sem, R package version 3.1-9.
64. Fraley, C., & Raftery, A. E. (2002). Model-based clustering, discriminant analysis, and density estimation. *Journal of the American Statistical Association, 97*(458), 611–631.
65. Friedman, J., Hastie, T., & Tibshirani, R. (2010). Regularization paths for generalized linear models via coordinate descent. *Journal of Statistical Software, 33*.
66. Friendly, M. (2017). *vcdExtra: vcd extensions and additions*. http://CRAN.R-project.org/package=vcdExtra, R package version 0.7-1.
67. Gabadinho, A., Ritschard, G., Studer, M., & Müller, N. S. (2009). Mining sequence data in R with the TraMineR package: A users guide for version 1.2.
68. Gagniuc, P. A. (2017). *Markov chains: From theory to implementation and experimentation*. New Jersey: Wiley.
69. Gałecki, A., & Burzykowski, T. (2013). *Linear mixed-effects models using R: A step-by-step approach*. Berlin: Springer.
70. Gandrud, C. (2015). *Reproducible research with R and RStudio* (2nd ed.). United Kingdom: Chapman & Hall/CRC.
71. Gansner, E. R., & North, S. C. (2000). An open graph visualization system and its applications to software engineering. *Software: Practice and Experience, 30*(11), 1203–1233.
72. Gelman, A., & Hill, J. (2006). *Data analysis using regression and multilevel/hierarchical models*. Cambridge: Cambridge University Press.

73. Gelman, A., Carlin, J. B., Stern, H. S., Dunson, D. B., Vehtari, A., & Rubin, D. B. (2013). *Bayesian data analysis* (3rd ed.). United Kingdom: Chapman & Hall.
74. Genolini, C. (2008). A (not so) short introduction to S4. Technical report.
75. Gohel, D. (2018). *officer: Manipulation of microsoft word and powerpoint documents*. https://CRAN.R-project.org/package=officer, R package version 0.3.2.
76. Goodman, S. N., Fanelli, D., & Ioannidis, J. P. (2016). What does research reproducibility mean? *Science Translational Medicine, 8*(341), 341ps12–341ps12.
77. Goulet, V. (2018). *Emacs modified for macOS*. https://vigou3.github.io/emacs-modified-macos/.
78. Goulet, V., Dutang, C., Maechler, M., Firth, D., Shapira, M., & Stadelmann, M. (2017). *expm: Matrix exponential, log, etc*. https://CRAN.R-project.org/package=expm, R package version 0.999-2.
79. Gower, J., Groenen, P. J., Van de Velden, M., & Vines, K. (2010). Perceptual maps: The good, the bad and the ugly. Technical Report. ERIM Report Series Reference No. ERS-2010-011-MKT, Erasmus Research Institute of Management.
80. Goyvaerts, J., & Levithan, S. (2012). *Regular expressions cookbook: Detailed solutions in eight programming languages*. Massachusetts: O'Reilly Media.
81. Grinstead, C. M., & Snell, J. L. (1997). *Introduction to probability*. Providence: American Mathematical Society.
82. Grolemund, G., & Wickham, H. (2011). Dates and times made easy with lubridate. *Journal of Statistical Software, 40*(3):1–25. http://www.jstatsoft.org/v40/i03/.
83. Grothendieck, G. (2017). *sqldf: Perform SQL selects on R data frames*. http://CRAN.R-project.org/package=sqldf, R package version 0.4-11.
84. Grün, B., & Leisch, F. (2008). FlexMix version 2: Finite mixtures with concomitant variables and varying and constant parameters. *Journal of Statistical Software, 28*(4), 1–35. http://www.jstatsoft.org/v28/i04/.
85. Guadagni, P. M., & Little, J. D. (1983). A logit model of brand choice calibrated on scanner data. *Marketing Science, 2*(3), 203–238.
86. Hadfield, J. D. (2010). MCMC methods for multi-response generalized linear mixed models: The MCMCglmm R package. *Journal of Statistical Software, 33*(2), 1–22. http://www.jstatsoft.org/v33/i02/.
87. Hahsler, M., Grün, B., & Hornik, K. (2005) arules: A computational environment for mining association rules and frequent item sets. *Journal of Statistical Software, 14*.
88. Hahsler, M., Buchta, C., Grün, B., Hornik, K., Johnson, I., & Borgelt, C. (2018a). *arules: Mining association rules and frequent itemsets*. http://CRAN.R-project.org/package=arules, R package version 1.6-1.
89. Hahsler, M., Tyler, G., & Chelluboina, S. (2018b). *arulesViz: Visualizing association rules and frequent itemsets*. http://CRAN.R-project.org/package=arulesViz, R package version 1.3-1.
90. Hair, J. F., Sarstedt, M., Ringle, C. M., & Mena, J. A. (2012). An assessment of the use of partial least squares structural equation modeling in marketing research. *Journal of the Academy of Marketing Science, 40*(3), 414–433.
91. Hair, J. F, Jr., Hult, G. T. M., Ringle, C., & Sarstedt, M. (2016). *A Primer on Partial Least Squares Structural Equation Modeling (PLS-SEM)* (2nd ed.). Thousand Oaks: Sage.
92. Harrell, F. E. (2015). *Regression modeling strategies: With applications to linear models, logistic and ordinal regression, and survival analysis* (2nd ed.). Berlin: Springer.
93. Hasan, A., Zhiyu, W., & Mahani, A. S. (2016). *mnlogit: Multinomial logit model*. https://CRAN.R-project.org/package=mnlogit, R package version 1.2.5.
94. Hasan, A., Zhiyu, W., & Mahani, A. S. (2018). *gmnl: Multinomial logit models with random parameters*. https://CRAN.R-project.org/package=gmnl, R package version 1.1-3.1.
95. Hastie, T., Tibshirani, R., & Friedman, J. (2016). *The elements of statistical learning: Data mining, inference, and prediction* (2nd ed.). Berlin: Springer.
96. Henseler, J., Ringle, C., & Sinkovics, R. (2009). The use of partial least squares path modeling in international marketing. *Advances in International Marketing (AIM), 20*, 277–320.

97. Hester, J., & Wickham, H. (2018). *odbc: Connect to ODBC compatible databases (using the DBI interface)*. https://CRAN.R-project.org/package=odbc, R package version 1.1.6.
98. Hornik, K. (2005). A CLUE for CLUster ensembles. *Journal of Statistical Software, 14*(12),
99. Hosmer, D. W, Jr., Lemeshow, S., & Sturdivant, R. X. (2013). *Applied logistic regression* (3rd ed.). New Jersey: Wiley.
100. Hothorn, T., Bretz, F., & Westfall, P. (2008). Simultaneous inference in general parametric models. *Biometrical Journal, 50*(3), 346–363.
101. Hubbard, R., & Armstrong, J. S. (2006). Why we don't really know what statistical significance means: Implications for educators. *Journal of Marketing Education, 28*(2), 114–120.
102. Hubert, L., & Arabie, P. (1985). Comparing partitions. *Journal of Classification, 2*(1), 193–218.
103. Hyndman, R. J. (2018). *forecast: Forecasting functions for time series and linear models*. http://CRAN.R-project.org/package=forecast, with contributions from G. Athanasopoulos, S. Razbash, D. Schmidt, Z. Zhou, Y. Khan, C. Bergmeir, E. Wang, F. Yasmeen, R. Core Team, R. Ihaka, D. Reid, Y. Tang, & Z. Zhou. R package version 8.4.
104. Iacobucci, D. (2009). Everything you always wanted to know about SEM (structural equations modeling) but were afraid to ask. *Journal of Consumer Psychology, 19*(4), 673–680.
105. Iacobucci, D. (2010). Structural equations modeling: Fit indices, sample size, and advanced topics. *Journal of Consumer Psychology, 20*(1), 90–98.
106. James, D. A., Wickham, H., James, D. A., Falcon, S., the authors of SQLite, (2018). *RSQLite: SQLite interface for R*. http://CRAN.R-project.org/package=RSQLite, R package version 2.1.1.
107. James, G., Witten, D., Hastie, T., & Tibshirani, R. (2013). *An introduction to statistical learning: With applications in R*. Berlin: Springer.
108. Jolliffe, I. T. (2002). *Principal component analysis* (2nd ed.). Berlin: Springer.
109. Jones, N. C., & Pevzner, P. (2004). *An Introduction to bioinformatics algorithms*. Cambridge: MIT Press.
110. Jöreskog, K. G. (1973). Analysis of covariance structures. In P. R. Krishnaiah (Ed.), *Multivariate analysis* (Vol. 3, pp. 263–285). New York: Academic.
111. Jöreskog, K. G., & Sörbom, D. (1996). LISREL 8: User's reference guide. *Scientific Software,*. International.
112. Jorgensen, T. D., Pornprasertmanit, S., Miller, P., Schoemann, A., & Rosseel, Y. (2018). *semTools: Useful tools for structural equation modeling*. http://CRAN.R-project.org/package=semTools, R package version 0.5-0.
113. Kahle, D., & Wickham, H. (2016). *ggmap: A package for spatial visualization with Google Maps and OpenStreetMap*. http://CRAN.R-project.org/package=ggmap, R package version 2.6.1.
114. Kampstra, P. (2014). *beanplot: Visualization via Beanplots (like Boxplot/Stripchart/Violin Plot)*. https://CRAN.R-project.org/package=beanplot, R package version 1.2.
115. Kane, M. J., Emerson, J., & Weston, S. (2013). Scalable strategies for computing with massive data. *Journal of Statistical Software, 55*(14), 1–19. http://www.jstatsoft.org/v55/i14/.
116. Kline, R. B. (2015). *Principles and practice of structural equation modeling* (4th ed.). New York: Guilford Press.
117. Kluyver, T., Ragan-Kelley, B., Pérez, F., Granger, B. E., Bussonnier, M., Frederic, J. et al. (2016). Jupyter notebooks-a publishing format for reproducible computational workflows. In *Proceedings of the international conference on electronic publishing (ELPUB)*.
118. Knuth, D. (1997). *The art of computer programming*, Vol 2: Seminumerical algorithms (3rd edn.). Boston: Addison-Wesley.
119. Kruschke, J. K. (2010). What to believe: Bayesian methods for data analysis. *Trends in Cognitive Sciences, 14*(7), 293–300.
120. Kruschke, J. K. (2015). *Doing bayesian data analysis: A tutorial with R, JAGS, and Stan* (2nd ed.). Cambridge: Academic.
121. Kuhn, M. (2014). *odfWeave: Sweave processing of Open Document Format (ODF) files*. http://CRAN.R-project.org/package=odfWeave, R package version 0.8.4. With contributions from S. Weston, N. Coulter, P. Lenon, Z. Otles, & the R. Core Team.

122. Kuhn, M. (2018). *caret: Classification and regression training*. http://CRAN.R-project.org/package=caret, R package version 6.0-80.
123. Kuhn, M., & Johnson, K. (2013). *Applied predictive modeling*. Berlin: Springer.
124. Lander, J. P. (2017). *R for everyone: Advanced analytics and graphics* (2nd ed.). Boston: Addison-Wesley.
125. Lander, J. P. (2018). *coefplot: Plots coefficients from fitted models*. http://CRAN.R-project.org/package=coefplot, R package version 1.2.6.
126. Leisch, F. (2002). Sweave: Dynamic generation of statistical reports using literate data analysis. In W. Härdle & B. Rönz (Eds.), *Compstat 2002: Proceedings in computational statistics* (pp. 575–580). Heidelberg: Physica Verlag.
127. Leisch, F. (2004). FlexMix: A general framework for finite mixture models and latent class regression in R. *Journal of Statistical Software, 11*(8), 1–18. http://www.jstatsoft.org/v11/i08/.
128. Leisch, F., & Dimitriadou, E. (2010). *mlbench: Machine learning benchmark problems*. R package version 2.1-1.
129. Liaw, A., & Wiener, M. (2002). Classification and regression by randomforest. *R News, 2*(3), 18–22, http://CRAN.R-project.org/doc/Rnews/.
130. Linzer, D. A., & Lewis, J. B. (2011). poLCA: An R package for polytomous variable latent class analysis. *Journal of Statistical Software, 42*(10), 1–29. http://www.jstatsoft.org/v42/i10/.
131. Louviere, J. J., Hensher, D. A., & Swait, J. D. (2000). *Stated choice methods: Analysis and applications*. Cambridge: Cambridge University Press.
132. Lumley, T. (2016). *biglm: Bounded memory linear and generalized linear models*. http://CRAN.R-project.org/package=biglm, R package version 0.9-1.
133. Maechler, M., Rousseeuw, P., Struyf, A., Hubert, M., & Hornik, K. (2018). *Cluster: Cluster analysis basics and extensions*, R package version 2.0.7-1.
134. Martin, A. D., Quinn, K. M., & Park, J. H. (2011). MCMCpack: Markov chain monte carlo in R. *Journal of Statistical Software, 42*(9), 22. http://www.jstatsoft.org/v42/i09/.
135. Matloff, N. S. (2011). *The art of R programming: A tour of statistical software design*. San Francisco: No Starch Press.
136. McElreath, R. (2016). *Statistical rethinking: A bayesian course with examples in R and Stan* (Vol. 122). Boca Raton: CRC Press.
137. Meehl, P. E. (1990). Why summaries of research on psychological theories are often uninterpretable. *Psychological Reports, 66*(1), 195–244.
138. Melnykov, V. (2016). ClickClust: An R package for model-based clustering of categorical sequences. *Journal of Statistical Software, 74*(9), 1–34. https://doi.org/10.18637/jss.v074.i09.
139. Meyer, D., Dimitriadou, E., Hornik, K., Weingessel, A., Leisch, F., Chang, C. C. et al. (2017a). *e1071: Misc functions of the department of statistics (e1071), TU Wien*. http://CRAN.R-project.org/package=e1071, R package version 1.6-8.
140. Meyer, D., Zeileis, A., & Hornik, K. (2017b). *vcd: Visualizing categorical data*. R package version 1.4-4.
141. Monecke, A., & Leisch, F. (2012). semPLS: Structural equation modeling using partial least squares. *Journal of Statistical Software, 48*(3), 1–32. http://www.jstatsoft.org/v48/i03/.
142. Morey, R. D., & Rouder, J. N. (2018). *BayesFactor: Computation of Bayes factors for common designs*. http://CRAN.R-project.org/package=BayesFactor, R package version 0.9.12-4.2.
143. Muenchen, R. A. (2011). *R for SAS and SPSS users* (2nd ed.). Berlin: Springer.
144. Muenchen, R. A., & Hilbe, J. M. (2010). *R for stata users*. Berlin: Springer.
145. Mulaik, S. A. (2009). *Foundations of factor analysis* (2nd edn.). Statistics in the Social and Behavioral Sciences. United Kingdom: Chapman & Hall/CRC.
146. Netzer, O., Lattin, J. M., & Srinivasan, V. (2008). A hidden Markov model of customer relationship dynamics. *Marketing Science, 27*(2), 185–204.
147. Netzer, O., Feldman, R., Goldenberg, J., & Fresko, M. (2012). Mine your own business: Market-structure surveillance through text mining. *Marketing Science, 31*(3), 521–543.

148. Neuwirth, E. (2014). *RColorBrewer: ColorBrewer palettes*. http://CRAN.R-project.org/package=RColorBrewer, R package version 1.1-2.
149. Orme, B. K. (2014). *Getting started with conjoint analysis: Strategies for product design and pricing research* (3rd ed.). Research Publishers.
150. Paling, W., Zwitch, R., & Joseph, J. (2018). *RSiteCatalyst: R client for adobe analytics API*. https://cran.r-project.org/web/packages/RSiteCatalyst/index.html.
151. Paluszynska, A., & Biecek, P. (2017). *randomForestExplainer: Explaining and visualizing random forests in terms of variable importance*. https://CRAN.R-project.org/package=randomForestExplainer, R package version 0.9.
152. Pearmain, M., Mihailowski, N., Prajapati, V., Shah, K., & Remy, N. (2014). *RGoogleAnalytics: R wrapper for the Google analytics API*. https://developers.google.com/analytics/solutions/r-google-analytics.
153. Pinheiro, J. C., & Bates, D. M. (2000). *Mixed-effects models in S and S-PLUS*. Berlin: Springer.
154. Polterock, J., Braun, H. W., & Claffy, K. (1995). *SDSC-HTTP*. San Diego Supercomputer Center, http://ita.ee.lbl.gov/html/contrib/SDSC-HTTP.html.
155. R Core Team, (2018a). *foreign: Read data stored by Minitab, S, SAS, SPSS, Stata, Systat, Weka, dBase, ...* http://CRAN.R-project.org/package=foreign, R package version 0.8-70.
156. R Core Team, (2018b). *R: A language and environment for statistical computing*. R foundation for statistical computing, Vienna, Austria. http://www.R-project.org/.
157. R Core Team, (2018c). R data import/export (version 3.5.0). Technical report, R Core Team. http://cran.r-project.org/doc/manuals/r-release/R-data.html.
158. R Core Team, (2018d). R language definition (version 3.5.0). Technical report, R Core Team.
159. Raftery, A. E. (1995). Bayesian model selection in social research. *Sociological Methodology, 25*, 111–164.
160. Raiche, G. (2010). *An R package for parallel analysis and non graphical solutions to the Cattell scree test*. http://CRAN.R-project.org/package=nFactors, R package version 2.3.3.
161. Rand, W. M. (1971). Objective criteria for the evaluation of clustering methods. *Journal of the American Statistical Association, 66*(336), 846–850.
162. Reps, J., Garibaldi, J. M., Aickelin, U., Soria, D., Gibson, J. E., & Hubbard, R. B. (2012). Discovering sequential patterns in a UK general practice database. *Proceedings of 2012 IEEE-EMBS International Conference on Biomedical and Health Informatics* (pp. 960–963).
163. Revelle, W. (2018). *psych: Procedures for psychological, psychometric, and personality research*. Evanston: Northwestern University. http://CRAN.R-project.org/package=psych, R package version 1.8.4.
164. Ripley, B., & Lapsley, M. (2017). *RODBC: ODBC database access*. R package version 1.3-15.
165. Ross, S. M. (2014). *Introduction to probability models* (11th ed.). Cambridge: Academic.
166. Rosseel, Y. (2012). lavaan: An R package for structural equation modeling. *Journal of Statistical Software* 48(2):1–36, http://www.jstatsoft.org/v48/i02/.
167. Rossi, P. (2017). *bayesm: Bayesian inference for marketing/micro-econometrics*. http://CRAN.R-project.org/package=bayesm, R package version 3.1-0.1.
168. Rossi, P. E., Allenby, G. M., & McCulloch, R. E. (2005). *Bayesian statistics and marketing*. New Jersey: Wiley.
169. Rossini, A., Heiberger, R., Hornik, K., Maechler, M., Sparapani, R., Eglen, S. et al. (2017). *ESS – Emacs speaks statistics*. The ESS developers (17th ed.).
170. Rouder, J. N., Morey, R. D., Speckman, P. L., & Province, J. M. (2012). Default Bayes factors for ANOVA designs. *Journal of Mathematical Psychology*.
171. RStudio, (2018a). knitr language engines. Technical report. Boston: RStudio. http://rmarkdown.rstudio.com/authoring_knitr_engines.html.
172. RStudio, (2018b). *RStudio: Integrated development environment for R*. Boston: RStudio. http://www.rstudio.org/, version 1.1.447.
173. Sarkar, D. (2008). *Lattice: Multivariate data visualization with R*. Berlin: Springer.
174. Sawtooth Software, (2014). *Adaptive choice-based conjoint technical paper*. http://www.sawtoothsoftware.com/downloadPDF.php?file=acbctech2014.pdf.

175. Scholz, M. (2016). R package clickstream: Analyzing clickstream data with Markov chains. *Journal of Statistical Software*, *74*(4), 1–17. https://doi.org/10.18637/jss.v074.i04.

176. Schwarz, J., Chapman, C., Feit, E. M. (Forthcoming). *Python for marketing research and analytics*. New York: Springer.

177. Scott, S. L. (2014). *BoomMix*. https://sites.google.com/site/stevethebayesian/googlepageforstevenlscott/boom.

178. Scrucca, L., Fop, M., Murphy, T. B., & Raftery, A. E. (2017). mclust 5: Clustering, classification and density estimation using Gaussian finite mixture models. *The R Journal*, *8*(1), 205–233. https://journal.r-project.org/archive/2017/RJ-2017-008/RJ-2017-008.pdf.

179. Sermas, R. (2012). *ChoiceModelR: Choice modeling in R*. http://CRAN.R-project.org/package=ChoiceModelR, R package version 1.2.

180. Singer, J. D., & Willett, J. B. (2003). *Applied longitudinal data analysis: Modeling change and event occurrence*. Oxford: Oxford University Press.

181. Sokal, R. R., & Rohlf, F. J. (1962). The comparison of dendrograms by objective methods. *Taxon*, *11*(2), 33–40.

182. South, A. (2011). rworldmap: A new R package for mapping global data. *The R Journal*, *3*(1), 35–43. http://journal.r-project.org/archive/2011-1/RJournal_2011-1_South.pdf.

183. Stallman, R. M. (1981). EMACS: The extensible, customizable self-documenting display editor. In *Proceedings of the ACM Conference on Text Processing, Association for Computing Machinery* (Vol. 16).

184. Stokely, M., Rohani, F., & Tassone, E. (2011). Large-scale parallel statistical forecasting computations in R. In *JSM (Joint Statistical Meetings) Proceedings, Section on Physical and Engineering Sciences*, Alexandria.

185. Tan, P. N., Steinbach, M., Karpatne, A., & Kumar, V. (2018). *Introduction to data mining* (2nd ed.). London: Pearson.

186. Teetor, P. (2011). *R Cookbook*. Massachusetts: O'Reilly Media.

187. Thompson, B. (2004). *Exploratory and confirmatory factor analysis: Understanding concepts and applications*. Massachusetts: American Psychological Association.

188. Tibshirani, R. (1996). Regression shrinkage and selection via the lasso. *Journal of the Royal Statistical Society Series B (Methodological)*, 267–288.

189. Toubia, O., Simester, D. I., Hauser, J. R., & Dahan, E. (2003). Fast polyhedral adaptive conjoint estimation. *Marketing Science*, *22*(3), 273–303.

190. Train, K. E. (2009). *Discrete choice methods with simulation*. Cambridge: Cambridge University Press.

191. Venables, W., & Ripley, B. D. (2000). *S programming*. Berlin: Springer.

192. Venables, W. N., & Ripley, B. D. (2002). *Modern applied statistics with S* (4th ed.). New York: Springer.

193. Warnes, G. R., Bolker, B., Bonebakker, L., Gentleman, R., Liaw, W. H. A., Lumley, T. et al. (2016). *gplots: Various R programming tools for plotting data*. http://CRAN.R-project.org/package=gplots, R package version 3.0.1.

194. Warnes, G. R., Bolker, B., Gorjanc, G., Grothendieck, G., Korosec, A., Lumley, T. et al. (2017) *gdata: Various R programming tools for data manipulation*. http://CRAN.R-project.org/package=gdata, R package version 2.18.0.

195. Wedel, M., & Kamakura, W. A. (2000). *Market segmentation: Conceptual and methodological foundations* (2nd edn.). International series in quantitative marketing. Dordrecht: Kluwer Academic.

196. Wei, T. (2017). *corrplot: Visualization of a correlation matrix*. http://CRAN.R-project.org/package=corrplot, R package version 0.84.

197. Wickham, H. (2014). *Advanced R*. United Kingdom: Chapman & Hall/CRC.

198. Wickham, H. (2016). *ggplot2: Elegant graphics for data analysis* (2nd ed.). Berlin: Springer.

199. Wickham, H., & Bryan, J. (2018). *readxl: Read excel files*. https://CRAN.R-project.org/package=readxl, R package version 1.1.0.

200. Wickham, H., & Grolemund, G. (2016). *R for data science: Import, tidy, transform, visualize, and model data*. Massachusetts: O'Reilly Media.

201. Wickham, H., Francois, R., Henry, L., Müller, K., & RStudio. (2018). *dplyr: A grammar of data manipulation*. http://CRAN.R-project.org/package=dplyr, R package version 0.7.6.
202. Williams, G. (2011). *Data mining with rattle and R: The art of excavating data for knowledge discovery*. Berlin: Springer.
203. Williams, G. J. (2009). Rattle: A data mining GUI for R. *The R Journal, 1*(2), 45–55.
204. Wolpert, D. H., & Macready, W. G. (1997). No free lunch theorems for optimization. *IEEE Transactions on Evolutionary Computation, 1*(1), 67–82.
205. Wong, D. M. (2013). *The wall street journal guide to information graphics: The dos and don'ts of presenting data, facts, and figures*. New York: WW Norton & Company.
206. Xie, Y. (2015). *Dynamic documents with R and knitr* (2nd ed.). United Kingdom: Chapman & Hall/CRC.
207. Xie, Y. (2016). *Bookdown: Authoring books and technical documents with R Markdown*. Boca Raton: CRC Press.
208. Zeileis, A., & Grothendieck, G. (2005). zoo: S3 infrastructure for regular and irregular time series. *Journal of Statistical Software, 14*(6), 1–27. http://www.jstatsoft.org/v14/i06/.
209. Zuur, A. F., Ieno, E. N., & Meesters, E. H. (2009). *A beginner's guide to R*. Berlin: Springer.
210. Zwitch, R., Feit, E. M., & Chapman, C. (Forthcoming) *Julia for marketing research and analytics*. New York: Springer.

Index

© Springer Nature Switzerland AG 2019
C. Chapman and E. M. Feit, *R For Marketing Research and Analytics*, Use R!,
https://doi.org/10.1007/978-3-030-14316-9